World Military Guide
United Kingdom

Compiled by
Eldon Mcmillian

Scribbles

Year of Publication 2018

ISBN : 9789352979066

Book Published by

Scribbles

(An Imprint of Alpha Editions)

email - alphaedis@gmail.com

Produced by: PediaPress GmbH
Limburg an der Lahn
Germany
http://pediapress.com/

The content within this book was generated collaboratively by volunteers. Please be advised that nothing found here has necessarily been reviewed by people with the expertise required to provide you with complete, accurate or reliable information. Some information in this book may be misleading or simply wrong. Alpha Editions and PediaPress does not guarantee the validity of the information found here. If you need specific advice (for example, medical, legal, financial, or risk management) please seek a professional who is licensed or knowledgeable in that area.

Sources, licenses and contributors of the articles and images are listed in the section entitled "References". Parts of the books may be licensed under the GNU Free Documentation License. A copy of this license is included in the section entitled "GNU Free Documentation License"

The views and characters expressed in the book are those of the contributors and his/her imagination and do not represent the views of the Publisher.

Contents

Articles   1

Introduction   1
   British Armed Forces 1

History   21
   History of the Royal Navy 21
   History of the British Army 58
   History of the Royal Air Force 89

Structure   105
   Structure of the British Armed Forces in 1989 105

Nuclear Weapons   113
   Nuclear weapons and the United Kingdom 113

Overseas Bases   153
   Overseas military bases of the United Kingdom 153

Royal Navy Today — 157

- Royal Navy 157
- List of active Royal Navy ships 210
- Royal Navy Surface Fleet 227
- Fleet Air Arm 237
- Royal Marines 257
- Standing Royal Navy deployments 290
- List of Royal Navy shore establishments 301
- Customs and traditions of the Royal Navy 317

British Army — 321

- British Army 321
- List of equipment of the British Army 363
- Structure of the British Army 386
- Recruitment in the British Army 404
- List of British Army installations 424
- Selection and Training in the British Army 437

Royal Air Force — 445

- Royal Air Force 445
- List of Royal Air Force groups 482
- List of Royal Air Force stations 494
- List of Royal Air Force aircraft squadrons 509
- List of Royal Air Force schools 543
- List of active United Kingdom military aircraft 560
- AirTanker Services 566
- Future of the Royal Air Force 569

Ministry of Defence — 583

- Ministry of Defence (United Kingdom) 583

Appendix 599

References 599

Article Sources and Contributors 631

Image Sources, Licenses and Contributors 634

Article Licenses 641

Index 643

Introduction

British Armed Forces

British Armed Forces	
Service branches	• ⚓ Naval Service 　• Royal Navy 　• 🪖 Royal Marines • 🎖 British Army • ✈ Royal Air Force
Headquarters	Ministry of Defence, London
Leadership	
Commander-in-Chief	Queen Elizabeth II[1]
Defence Secretary	Gavin Williamson
Chief of the Defence Staff	General Sir Nick Carter
Manpower	
Military age	16
Conscription	No
Active personnel	153,770[2]
Reserve personnel	81,850[3]

Expenditures	
Budget	£49 billion; FY 2018–19[4] (≈$69.2 billion)[5]
Percent of GDP	2.0%; FY 2018–19
Industry	
Domestic suppliers	BAE Systems Rolls-Royce Holdings
Related articles	
History	Military history of the United Kingdom Conflicts involving the UK
Ranks	• Army officer ranks • Army other ranks • Navy officer ranks • Navy ratings • Air Force officer ranks • Air Force other ranks

The **British Armed Forces**,[6] also known as **Her Majesty's Armed Forces**, are the military services responsible for the defence of the United Kingdom, its overseas territories and the Crown dependencies. They also promote Britain's wider interests, support international peacekeeping efforts and provide humanitarian aid.[7]

Since the formation of a Kingdom of Great Britain in 1707 (later succeeded by the United Kingdom), the armed forces have seen action in a number of major wars involving the world's great powers, including the Seven Years' War, the Napoleonic Wars, the Crimean War, the First World War, and the Second World War. Repeatedly emerging victorious from conflicts has allowed Britain to establish itself as one of the world's leading military and economic powers.

Today, the British Armed Forces consist of: the Royal Navy, a blue-water navy with a fleet of 77 commissioned ships; the Royal Marines, a highly specialised amphibious light infantry force; the British Army, the UK's principal land warfare branch; and the Royal Air Force, a technologically sophisticated air force with a diverse operational fleet consisting of both fixed-wing and rotary aircraft. The British Armed Forces include standing forces, Regular Reserve, Volunteer Reserves and Sponsored Reserves. The Commander-in-chief of the British Armed Forces is the British monarch, Queen Elizabeth II, to whom members of the forces swear allegiance.

The UK Parliament approves the continued existence of the British Army by passing an Armed Forces Act at least once every five years, as required by the Bill of Rights 1689. The Royal Navy, Royal Air Force and Royal Marines among with all other forces do not require this act. The armed forces are

Figure 1: *A modern reproduction of an 1805 poster commemorating the Battle of Trafalgar.*

managed by the Defence Council of the Ministry of Defence, headed by the Secretary of State for Defence.

The United Kingdom is one of five recognised nuclear powers, is a permanent member on the United Nations Security Council, is a founding and leading member of the NATO military alliance, and is party to the Five Power Defence Arrangements. Overseas garrisons and facilities are maintained at Ascension Island, Bahrain, Belize, Bermuda, British Indian Ocean Territory, Brunei, Canada, Cyprus, the Falkland Islands, Germany, Gibraltar, Kenya, Montserrat, Nepal, Qatar, Singapore and the United States.

History

Empire and World Wars

With the Acts of Union 1707, the armed forces of England and Scotland were merged into the armed forces of the Kingdom of Great Britain.[8]

During the later half of the seventeenth century, and in particular, throughout the eighteenth century, British foreign policy sought to contain the expansion of rival European powers through military, diplomatic and commercial means – especially of its chief competitors; Spain, the Netherlands and

France. This saw Britain engage in a number of intense conflicts over colonial possessions and world trade, including a long string of Anglo-Spanish and Anglo-Dutch wars, as well as a series of "world wars" with France, such as; the Seven Years' War (1756–1763), the French Revolutionary Wars (1792–1802) and the Napoleonic Wars (1803–1815). During the Napoleonic wars, the Royal Navy victory at Trafalgar (1805) under the command of Horatio Nelson (aboard HMS *Victory*) marked the culmination of British maritime supremacy, and left the Navy in a position of uncontested hegemony at sea.[9] By 1815 and the conclusion of the Napoleonic Wars, Britain had risen to become the world's dominant great power and the British Empire subsequently presided over a period of relative peace, known as Pax Britannica.[10]

With Britain's old rivals no-longer a threat, the nineteenth century saw the emergence of a new rival, the Russian Empire, and a strategic competition in what became known as The Great Game for supremacy in Central Asia. Britain feared that Russian expansionism in the region would eventually threaten the Empire in India. In response, Britain undertook a number of pre-emptive actions against perceived Russian ambitions, including the First Anglo-Afghan War (1839–1842), the Second Anglo-Afghan War (1878–1880) and the British expedition to Tibet (1903–1904). During this period, Britain also sought to maintain the balance of power in Europe, particularly against Russian expansionism, who at the expense of the waning Ottoman Empire had ambitions to "carve up the European part of Turkey". This ultimately led to British involvement in the Crimean War (1854–1856) against the Russian Empire.

The beginning of the twentieth century served to reduce tensions between Britain and the Russian Empire, partly due to the emergence of a unified German Empire. The era brought about an Anglo-German naval arms race which encouraged significant advancements in maritime technology (e.g. Dreadnoughts, torpedoes and submarines), and in 1906, Britain had determined that its only likely naval enemy was Germany.[11] The accumulated tensions in European relations finally broke out into the hostilities of the First World War (1914–1918), in what is recognised today, as the most devastating war in British military history, with nearly 800,000 men killed and over 2 million wounded. Allied victory resulted in the defeat of the Central Powers, the end of the German Empire, the Treaty of Versailles and the establishment of the League of Nations.

Although Germany had been defeated during the First World War, by 1933 fascism had given rise to Nazi Germany, which under the leadership of Adolf Hitler re-militarised in defiance of the Treaty of Versailles. Once again tensions accumulated in European relations, and following Germany's invasion of Poland in September 1939, the Second World War began (1939–1945). The

Figure 2: *Soldiers from the Royal Irish Rifles in the Battle of the Somme's trenches 1916.*

conflict was the most widespread in British history, with British Empire and Commonwealth troops fighting in campaigns from Europe and North Africa, to the Middle East and the Far East. Approximately 390,000 British Empire and Commonwealth troops lost their lives. Allied victory resulted in the defeat of the Axis powers and the establishment of the United Nations (replacing the League of nations).

The Cold War and War on Terror

Post–Second World War economic and political decline, as well as changing attitudes in British society and government, were reflected by the armed forces' contracting global role,[12,13] and later epitomised by its political defeat during the Suez Crisis (1956).[14] Reflecting Britain's new role in the world and the escalation of the Cold War (1947–1991), the country became a founding member of the NATO military alliance in 1949. Defence Reviews, such as those in 1957 and 1966, announced significant reductions in conventional forces,[15] the pursuement of a doctrine based on nuclear deterrence,[16,17] and a permanent military withdrawal East of Suez.[18,19] By the mid-1970s, the armed forces had reconfigured to focus on the responsibilities allocated to them by NATO.[20,21] The British Army of the Rhine and RAF Germany consequently represented the largest and most important overseas commitments that the armed forces

Figure 3: *The Vulcan Bomber was the mainstay of Britain's airborne nuclear capability for much of the Cold War.*

had during this period,[22] while the Royal Navy developed an anti-submarine warfare specialisation, with a particular focus on countering Soviet submarines in the Eastern Atlantic and North Sea.

While NATO obligations took increased prominence, Britain nonetheless found itself engaged in a number of low-intensity conflicts, including a spate of insurgencies against colonial occupation.[23] However the Dhofar Rebellion (1962–1976) and The Troubles (1969–1998) emerged as the primary operational concerns of the armed forces. Perhaps the most important conflict during the Cold War, at least in the context of British defence policy, was the Falklands War (1982).

Since the end of the Cold War, an increasingly international role for the armed forces has been pursued, with re-structuring to deliver a greater focus on expeditionary warfare and power projection. This entailed the armed forces often constituting a major component in peacekeeping and humanitarian missions under the auspices of the United Nations, NATO, and other multinational operations,[24] including: peacekeeping responsibilities in the Balkans and Cyprus, the 2000 intervention in Sierra Leone and participation in the UN-mandated no-fly zone over Libya (2011). Post-September 11, the armed forces have been heavily committed to the War on Terror (2001–present), with lengthy campaigns in Afghanistan (2001–Present) and Iraq (2003–2009), and more recently as part of the Military intervention against ISIL (2014–present).

Figure 4: *The Ministry of Defence building at Whitehall, Westminster, London*

Britain's military intervention against Islamic State was expanded following a parliamentary vote to launch a bombing campaign over Syria; an extension of the bombing campaign requested by the Iraqi government against the same group. In addition to the aerial campaign, the British Army has trained and supplied allies on the ground and the Special Air Service (British special forces) has carried out various missions on the ground in both Syria and Iraq.

Figures released by the Ministry of Defence on 31 March 2016 show that 7,185 British Armed Forces personnel have lost their lives in medal earning theatres since the end of the Second World War.[25]

Today

Command organisation

As Sovereign and head of state, Queen Elizabeth II is Head of the Armed Forces[26] and their Commander-in-Chief. Long-standing constitutional convention, however, has vested *de facto* executive authority, by the exercise of Royal Prerogative powers, in the Prime Minister and the Secretary of State for Defence, and the Prime Minister (acting with the support of the Cabinet) makes the key decisions on the use of the armed forces. The Queen, however, remains the ultimate authority of the military, with officers and personnel swearing allegiance to the monarch. It has been claimed that this includes the power to prevent unconstitutional use of the armed forces, including its nuclear weapons.

The Ministry of Defence[27] is the Government department and highest level of military headquarters charged with formulating and executing defence policy for the armed forces; it currently employs 56,860 civilian staff as of 1 October 2015.[28] The department is controlled by the Secretary of State for Defence and contains three deputy appointments: Minister of State for the Armed Forces, Minister for Defence Procurement, and Minister for Veterans' Affairs. Responsibility for the management of the forces is delegated to a number of committees: the Defence Council, Chiefs of Staff Committee, Defence Management Board and three single-service boards. The Defence Council, composed of senior representatives of the services and the Ministry of Defence, provides the "formal legal basis for the conduct of defence". The three constituent single-service committees (Admiralty Board, Army Board and Air Force Board) are chaired by the Secretary of State for Defence.

The Chief of the Defence Staff is the professional head of the armed forces and is an appointment that can be held by an Admiral, Air Chief Marshal or General. Before the practice was discontinued in the 1990s, those who were appointed to the position of CDS had been elevated to the most senior rank in their respective service (a 5-star rank).[29] The CDS, along with the Permanent Under Secretary, are the principal advisers to the departmental minister. The three services have their own respective professional chiefs: the First Sea Lord, the Chief of the General Staff and the Chief of the Air Staff.

Personnel

The British Armed Forces are a professional force with a strength of 153,470 UK Regulars and Gurkhas, 35,200 Volunteer Reserves and 8,160 "Other Personnel"[30] as of 1 May 2016[31].[32] This gives a total strength of 196,840 "UK Service Personnel".[33] As a percentage breakdown of UK Service Personnel, 78.0% are UK Regulars and Gurkhas, 17.9% are Volunteer Reserves and 4.1% are composed of Other Personnel. In addition, all ex-Regular personnel retain a "statutory liability for service" and are liable to be recalled (under Section 52 of the Reserve Forces Act (RFA) 1996) for duty during wartime, which is known as the Regular Reserve. MoD publications since April 2013 no longer report the entire strength of the Regular Reserve, instead they only give a figure for Regular Reserves who serve under a fixed-term reserve contract. These contracts are similar in nature to those of the Volunteer Reserve.[34] As of 1 April 2015[31], Regular Reserves serving under a fixed-term contract numbered 44,600 personnel.[35]

As of 1 April 2016[31], there were a total of 16,040 Regular service personnel stationed outside of the United Kingdom, 5,540 of those were located in

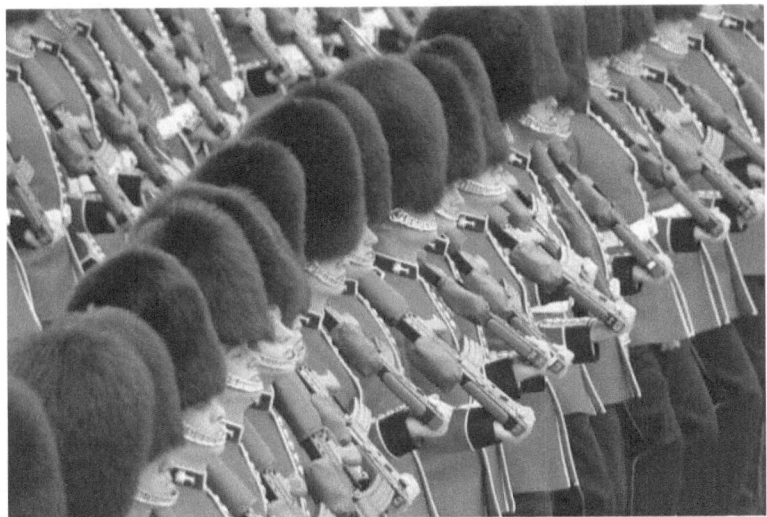

Figure 5: *Welsh Guards Trooping the Colour.*

Germany. 140,450 Regular service personnel were stationed in the United Kingdom, the majority located in the South East and South West of England with 38,860 and 36,340 Regular service personnel, respectively.[36]

Defence expenditure

According to the International Institute for Strategic Studies and the Stockholm International Peace Research Institute, the United Kingdom has the fifth-largest defence budget in the world. For comparisons sake, this sees Britain spending more in absolute terms than France, Germany, India or Japan, a similar amount to that of Russia, but less than China, Saudi Arabia or the United States. In September 2011, according to Professor Malcolm Chalmers of the Royal United Services Institute, current "planned levels of defence spending should be enough for the United Kingdom to maintain its position as one of the world's top military powers, as well as being one of NATO-Europe's top military powers. Its edge – not least its qualitative edge – in relation to rising Asian powers seems set to erode, but will remain significant well into the 2020s, and possibly beyond."[37] The Strategic Defence and Security Review 2015 committed to spending 2% of GDP on defence and announced a £178 billion investment over ten years in new equipment and capabilities.

Figure 6: *A Trident II SLBM being launched from a Vanguard-class submarine*

Nuclear weapons

The United Kingdom is one of five recognised nuclear weapon states under the Non-Proliferation Treaty and maintains an independent nuclear deterrent, currently consisting of four *Vanguard*-class ballistic missile submarines, UGM-133 Trident II submarine-launched ballistic missiles, and 160 operational thermonuclear warheads. This is known as Trident in both public and political discourse (with nomenclature taken after the UGM-133 Trident II ballistic missile). Trident is operated by the Royal Navy Submarine Service, charged with delivering a 'Continuous At-Sea Deterrent' (CASD) capability, whereby one of the *Vanguard*-class strategic submarines is always on patrol.[38] According to the British Government, since the introduction of Polaris (Tridents predecessor) in the 1960s, from April 1969 "the Royal Navy's ballistic missile boats have not missed a single day on patrol", giving what the Defence Council described in 1980 as a deterrent "effectively invulnerable to pre-emptive attack". As of 2015, it has been British Government policy for the *Vanguard*-class strategic submarines to carry no more than 40 nuclear warheads, delivered by eight UGM-133 Trident II ballistic missiles.[39] In contrast with the other recognised nuclear weapon states, the United Kingdom operates only a submarine-based delivery system, having decommissioned its tactical WE.177 free-fall bombs in 1998.

Figure 7:
Overseas military installations of the United Kingdom, and locally raised units of British Overseas Territories. Military interventions since 2000: Palliser (Sierra Leone); Herrick (Afghanistan); Enduring Freedom (Horn of Africa); Telic (Iraq); Ellamy (Libya); and Shader (Islamic State of Iraq and the Levant).

The House of Commons voted on 18 July 2016 in favour of replacing the *Vanguard*-class submarines with a new generation of *Dreadnought*-class submarines. The programme will also contribute to extending the life of the UGM-133 Trident II ballistic missiles and modernise the infrastructure associated with the CASD.

Former weapons of mass destruction possessed by the United Kingdom include both biological and chemical weapons. These were renounced in 1956 and subsequently destroyed.

Overseas military installations

The British Armed Forces maintain a number of overseas garrisons and military facilities which enable the country to conduct operations worldwide. All of Britain's permanent military installations are located on British Overseas Territories (BOTs) or former colonies which retain close diplomatic ties with the United Kingdom, and located in areas of strategic importance. The most significant of these are the "Permanent Joint Operating Bases" (PJOBs), located on the four overseas territories of Cyprus (British Forces Cyprus), Gibraltar (British Forces Gibraltar), the Falkland Islands (British Forces South Atlantic Islands) and Diego Garcia (British Forces British Indian Ocean Territories).[40] While not a PJOB, Ascension Island (another BOT) is home to the airbase RAF Ascension Island, notable for use as a staging post during the 1982 Falklands War, the territory is also the site of a joint UK-US signals intelligence facility.

Qatar is home to RAF Al Udeid, a Royal Air Force outpost at Al Udeid Air Base which serves as the operational headquarters for No. 83 Expeditionary Air Group and its operations across the Middle East. A large Royal Navy Naval Support Facility (NSF) is located in Bahrain, established in 2016 it marks the British return East of Suez. In support of the Five Power Defence Arrangements (FPDA), the United Kingdom retains a naval repair and logistics support facility at Sembawang wharf, Singapore.[41] Other overseas military installations include; British Forces Brunei, British Forces Germany, the British Army Training Unit Kenya, British Army Training Unit Suffield in Canada, British Army Training and Support Unit Belize, and British Gurkhas Nepal.

Some British Overseas Territories also maintain locally raised units and regiments; The Royal Bermuda Regiment, the Falkland Islands Defence Force, the Royal Gibraltar Regiment and the Royal Montserrat Defence Force. Though their primary mission is "home defence", individuals have volunteered for operational duties. The Royal Gibraltar Regiment mobilised section-sized units for attachment to British regiments deployed during the Iraq War.[42,43] The Isle of Man, a Crown dependency hosts a multi-capability recruiting and training unit of the British Army Reserve.

Expeditionary forces

The British Armed Forces place significant importance in the ability to conduct expeditionary warfare.[44] While the armed forces are expeditionary in nature, it maintains a core of "high readiness" forces trained and equipped to deploy at very short notice, these include; the Joint Expeditionary Force (Maritime) (Royal Navy), 3 Commando Brigade (Royal Marines), 16 Air Assault Brigade (British Army) and No. 83 Expeditionary Air Group (Royal Air Force). Oftentimes, these will act in conjunction with a larger tri-service effort, such as the UK Joint Rapid Reaction Force, or along with like-minded allies under the UK Joint Expeditionary Force. Similarly, under the auspices of NATO, such expeditionary forces are designed to meet Britain's obligations to the Allied Rapid Reaction Corps and other NATO operations.

In 2010, the governments of the United Kingdom and France signed the Lancaster House Treaties which committed both governments to the creation of a Franco-British Combined Joint Expeditionary Force. It is envisaged as a deployable joint force, for use in a wide range of crisis scenarios, up to and including high intensity combat operations. As a joint force it involves all three armed Services: a land component composed of formations at national brigade level, maritime and air components with their associated Headquarters, together with logistics and support functions.

Figure 8: *HMS Queen Elizabeth, a Queen Elizabeth-class supercarrier on sea trials in June 2017.*

The Armed Forces

Royal Navy

The Royal Navy is a technologically sophisticated naval force, and as of April 2015 consists of 77 commissioned ships. Command of deployable assets is exercised by the Fleet Commander of the Naval Service.[45] Personnel matters are the responsibility of the Second Sea Lord/Commander-in-Chief Naval Home Command, an appointment usually held by a vice-admiral.

The Surface Fleet consists of amphibious warfare ships, destroyers, frigates, patrol vessels, mine-countermeasure vessels, and other miscellaneous vessels. The Surface Fleet has been structured around a single fleet since the abolition of the Eastern and Western fleets in 1971.[46] The recently built Type 45 destroyers are technologically advanced air-defence destroyers. The Royal Navy is building two *Queen Elizabeth*-class aircraft carriers, embarking an air-group including the advanced fifth-generation multi-role fighter, the F-35B.

A submarine service has existed within the Royal Navy for more than 100 years. The Submarine Service's four *Vanguard*-class nuclear-powered submarines carry Lockheed Martin's Trident II ballistic missiles, forming the United Kingdom's nuclear deterrent. Seven *Astute*-class nuclear-powered attack submarines have been ordered, with three completed and four under construction. The *Astute* class are the most advanced and largest fleet submarines

Figure 9: *The Challenger 2 main battle tank*

ever built for the Royal Navy, and will maintain Britain's nuclear-powered submarine fleet capabilities for decades to come.

Royal Marines

The Royal Marines are the Royal Navy's amphibious troops. Consisting of a single manoeuvre brigade (3 Commando) and various independent units, the Royal Marines specialise in amphibious, arctic, and mountain warfare.[47] Contained within 3 Commando Brigade are three attached army units; 383 Commando Petroleum Troop RLC, 29 Commando Regiment Royal Artillery, a field artillery regiment based in Plymouth, and 24 Commando Regiment Royal Engineers.[48] The Commando Logistic Regiment consists of personnel from the Army, Royal Marines, and Royal Navy.[49]

British Army

The British Army is made up of the Regular Army and the Army Reserve. The army has a single command structure based at Andover and known as "Army Headquarters".[50,51] Deployable combat formations consist of two divisions (1st Armoured and 3rd Mechanised) and eight brigades.[52,53] Within the United Kingdom, operational and non-deployable units are administered by two divisions, Force Troops Command, and London District.

The Army has 50 battalions (36 regular and 14 reserve) of regular and reserve infantry, organised into 17 regiments.[54] The majority of infantry regiments contains multiple regular and reserve battalions. Modern infantry have diverse capabilities and this is reflected in the varied roles assigned to them. There are four operational roles that infantry battalions can fulfil: air assault, armoured infantry, mechanised infantry, and light role infantry. Regiments and battalions e.g.: the Parachute Regiment, exist within every corps of the Army, functioning as administrative or tactical formations.

Armoured regiments are equivalent to an infantry battalion. There are 14 armoured regiments within the army, ten regular and four yeomanry (armoured reserve), of which four are designated as "Armoured", three as "Armoured Cavalry", and six as "Light Cavalry". Army 2020 Refine has seen developments which will further modify the Royal Armoured Corps. with two existing regiments forming the core of two new STRIKE Brigades. These two regiments, along with the Armoured Cavalry will be equipped with the "Ajax" armoured fighting vehicle, a new £3.5 billion procurement programme. The Ajax will be employed in the task organisation and roles of both Armoured Cavalry and Medium Armour. With a slight exception of the Household Cavalry, which maintains quasi-autonomy within the Household Division, armoured regiments and their yeomanry counterparts collectively form the Royal Armoured Corps.

Arms and support units are also formed into similar collectives organised around specific purposes, such as the Corps of Royal Engineers, Army Air Corps and Royal Army Medical Corps.[55]

Royal Air Force

The Royal Air Force has a large operational fleet that fulfils various roles, consisting of both fixed-wing and rotary aircraft. Frontline aircraft are controlled by Air Command, which is organised into three groups defined by function: 1 Group (Air Combat), 2 Group (Air Support)[56] and 22 Group (training aircraft and ground facilities). In addition 83 Expeditionary Air Group directs formations in the Middle East and the 38 Group combines the expeditionary combat support and combat service support units of the RAF. Deployable formations consist of Expeditionary Air Wings and squadrons—the basic unit of the Air Force.[57,58] Independent flights are deployed to facilities in Afghanistan, the Falkland Islands, Iraq, and the United States.[59]

The Royal Air Forces operates multi-role and single-role fighters, reconnaissance and patrol aircraft, tankers, transports, helicopters, unmanned aerial vehicles, and various types of training aircraft.[60] Ground units are also maintained by the Royal Air Force, most prominently the RAF Police and the Royal Air Force Regiment (RAF Regt). The Royal Air Force Regiment essentially functions as the ground defence force of the RAF, optimised for the specialist role of fighting on and around forward airfields, which are densely packed

Figure 10: *The Eurofighter Typhoon multirole combat aircraft*

with operationally vital aircraft, equipment, infrastructure and personnel.[61] The Regiment contains nine regular squadrons, supported by five squadrons of the Royal Auxiliary Air Force Regiment. In addition, it provides the UK's specialist Chemical, Biological, Radiological and Nuclear capability. It also provides half of the UK's Forward Air Controllers and the RAF's contribution to the Special Forces Support Group. By March 2008, the three remaining Ground Based Air Defence squadrons (equipped with Rapier Field Standard C) had disbanded or re-roled and their responsibilities transferred to the British Army's Royal Artillery.[62]

Ministry of Defence

The Ministry of Defence maintains a number civilian agencies in support of the British Armed Forces. Although they are civilian, they play a vital role in supporting Armed Forces operations, and in certain circumstances are under military discipline:

- The **Royal Fleet Auxiliary** (RFA) operates 12 ships which primarily serve to replenish Royal Navy warships at sea, and also augment the Royal Navy's amphibious warfare capabilities through its three Bay-class landing ship dock vessels. It is manned by 1,850 civilian personnel and is funded and run by the Ministry of Defence.

Figure 11: *RFA Argus (left), the fleet's aviation training and hospital ship*

- The **Ministry of Defence Police** (MDP) has an established strength of 2,700 police officers which provide armed security, counter terrorism, uniformed policing and investigative services to Ministry of Defence property, personnel, and installations throughout the United Kingdom.
- The **Defence Equipment and Support** (DE&S) is the merged procurement and support organisation within the UK Ministry of Defence (United Kingdom). It came into being on 2 April 2007, bringing together the MoD's Defence Procurement Agency and the Defence Logistics Organisation under the leadership of General Sir Kevin O'Donoghue as the first Chief of Defence Materiel. As of 2012[31] it has a civilian and military workforce of approx. 20,000 personnel. DE&S is overseen by the Minister for Defence Equipment, Support and Technology.
- The **UK Hydrographic Office** (UKHO) is an organisation within the UK government responsible for providing navigational and other hydrographic information for national, civil and defence requirements. The UKHO is located in Taunton, Somerset on Admiralty Way and has a workforce of approximately 1,000 staff.

Figure 12: *One of the most recognisable recruiting posters of the British Army; from World War I featuring Kitchener.*

Recruitment

All three services of the British Armed Forces recruit primarily from within the United Kingdom, although citizens from the Commonwealth of Nations and the Republic of Ireland are equally eligible to join.[63] The minimum recruitment age is 16 years (although personnel may not serve on armed operations below 18 years, and if under 18 must also have parental consent to join); the maximum recruitment age depends whether the application is for a regular or reserve role; there are further variations in age limit for different corps/regiments. The normal term of engagement is 22 years; however, the minimum service required before resignation is 4 years, plus, in the case of the Army, any service person below the age of 18.[64] At present, the yearly intake into the armed forces is 11,880 (per the 12 months to 31 March 2014).[65]

Excluding the Brigade of Gurkhas and the Royal Irish Regiment, as of 1 April 2014 there are approximately 11,200 Black and Minority Ethnic (BME) persons serving as Regulars across the three service branches; of those, 6,610 were recruited from outside the United Kingdom. In total, Black and Minority Ethnic persons represent 7.1% of all service personnel, an increase from 6.6% in 2010.

Since the year 2000, sexual orientation has not been a factor considered in recruitment, and homosexuals can serve openly in the armed forces. All branches of the forces have actively recruited at Gay Pride events. The forces keep no formal figures concerning the number of gay and lesbian serving soldiers, saying that the sexual orientation of personnel is considered irrelevant and not monitored.

Role of women

Women have been integrated into the British Armed Forces since the early 1990s, including flying fast jets and commanding warships or artillery batteries. However, they remain excluded from primarily close combat units in the Army (Royal Armoured Corps and Infantry), Royal Marines, and Royal Air Force Regiment.[66] As of 1 April 2014, there are approximately 15,840 women serving in the armed forces, representing 9.9% of all service personnel. The first female military pilot was Flight Lieutenant Julie Ann Gibson while Flight Lieutenant Jo Salter was the first fast-jet pilot, the former flying a Tornado GR1 on missions patrolling the then Northern Iraqi No-Fly Zone. Flight Lieutenant Juliette Fleming and Squadron Leader Nikki Thomas recently were the first Tornado GR4 crew.[67] While enforcing the Libyan No-Fly Zone, Flight Lieutenant Helen Seymour was identified as the first female Eurofighter Typhoon pilot. In August 2011, it was announced that a female Lieutenant Commander, Sarah West, was to command the frigate HMS Portland. In July 2016, it was announced that women would be allowed to serve in close combat, starting with the Royal Armoured Corps. In July 2017, the Secretary of Defence announced that women will be allowed to enlist in the RAF Regiment from September 2017, a year ahead of schedule. As of 2019, women will be able to serve as a soldier in the British Army's Infantry.

External links

 Wikimedia Commons has media related to *Military of the United Kingdom*.

> Look up *Appendix:Glossary of British military slang and expressions* in Wiktionary, the free dictionary.

- British Ministry of Defence[68] (gov.uk)
- Defence Academy of the United Kingdom[69] (.da.mod.uk)
- Royal Navy official website[70] (royalnavy.mod.uk)
- Royal Marines official webpage[71] (royalnavy.mod.uk)
- British Army official website[72] (army.mod.uk)
- Royal Air Force official website[73] (raf.mod.uk)

History

History of the Royal Navy

Her Majesty's Naval Service of the British Armed Forces
Components
- **Royal Navy** - Surface Fleet - Fleet Air Arm - Submarine Service - Royal Naval Reserve - Royal Navy Medical Service - Nursing Service (QARNNS) - Chaplaincy - Royal Navy Police - **Royal Marines** - Royal Marines Reserve - Special Boat Service - **Naval Careers Service**
History and future
- History of the Royal Navy / Royal Marines - Customs and traditions - Future
Ships
- Current fleet - Current deployments - Historic ships
Personnel
- The Admiralty - Senior officers - Uniforms - Officer / ratings rank insignia

Auxiliary services
• Royal Fleet Auxiliary • Marine Services
• v • t • e[74]

The official **history of the Royal Navy** began with the formal establishment of the Royal Navy as the national naval force of the Kingdom of England in 1660, following the Restoration of King Charles II to the throne. However, for more than a thousand years before that there had been English naval forces varying in type and organization. In 1707 it became the naval force of the Kingdom of Great Britain after the Union between England and Scotland which merged the English navy with the much smaller Royal Scots Navy, although the two had begun operating together from the time of the Union of the Crowns in 1603.

Before the creation of the Royal Navy, the English navy had no defined moment of formation; it started out as a motley assortment of "King's ships" during the Middle Ages assembled only as needed and then dispersed, began to take shape as a standing navy during the 16th century, and became a regular establishment during the tumults of the 17th century. The Navy grew considerably during the global struggle with France that started in 1690 and culminated in the Napoleonic Wars, a time when the practice of fighting under sail was developed to its highest point.

The ensuing century of general peace saw considerable technological development, with sail yielding to steam and cannon supplanted by large shell-firing guns, and ending with the race to construct bigger and better battleships. That race, however, was ultimately a dead end, as aircraft carriers and submarines came to the fore and, after the successes of World War II, the Royal Navy yielded its formerly preeminent place to the United States Navy. The Royal Navy has remained one of the world's most capable navies, however, and currently operates a fleet of modern ships.

England and Scotland before 1603

England

The early English kingdoms

Some evidence of English ship construction in the Anglo-Saxon period is available from the boat burials at Snape (about 550) and Sutton Hoo (about 625), though warships would probably have been larger than the vessels interred there. There is little evidence of the naval activities of the English kingdoms before the mid-9th century, but King Edwin of Northumbria (616/7-633/4) conquered the Isle of Man and Anglesey, and another King of Northumbria, Ecgfrith, sent a military expedition to Ireland in 684.[75]

The threat from Vikings increased significantly in the early part of the 9th Century and invasions became a serious menace from about 835.[76] In 851 an unprecedently large force of Danes invaded southern England, carried on about 350 ships. Campaigning inland, this force was decisively defeated by King Æthelwulf of Wessex at the Battle of Aclea, but a naval action was also won by Æthelwulf's son Æthelstan and Ealdorman Ealhere at Sandwich, Kent, capturing nine ships.[77]

The Danish "Great Army" which conquered about half of England during its campaigns in 865-79 operated largely by land, and no naval operations against it by the English kingdoms are recorded. However, in the following years a number of clashes are recorded between Viking raiders and the forces of Alfred the Great, the last remaining English king. These included a victory over four ships by a squadron led by the king himself in 882, and operations against the Danes of East Anglia in 884, which saw an entire Danish squadron of sixteen ships captured by an English force, which was then itself defeated on its way home by another fleet.[78] In 896 Alfred had a number of new ships built to his own design, "nearly twice as long as the others, some having 60 oars, some even more", to counter raids along the south coast.[79] A clash in the Solent later that year saw nine of his new ships defeat six Danish ships.

United England

Naval operations are glimpsed again in 934, when King Æthelstan, now ruler of all England, invaded Scotland with a combined sea and land force.[80] Under King Edgar (959-975) the kings of Scotland, Cumbria and of four other kingdoms would regularly swear to be King Edgar's faithful allies by land and sea.[81]

The renewal of serious Viking attacks in the reign of Æthelred the Unready led to a general muster of ships at London in 992 against the fleet of Olaf Tryggvason, but amid confusion and alleged treachery the English fleet suffered heavy losses. In 1008, Æthelred ordered a new programme of naval construction, under which one warship was to be provided for every 310 hides of land in the kingdom. In 1009 the king took the new fleet out to Sandwich, Kent to guard against the threat of invasion (this port, near the junction of the North Sea and the English Channel and lying within the sheltered offshore anchorage of the Downs, appears frequently in the sources for this period as a position where fleets were stationed on guard). However, this deployment ended in disaster due to internal dissension. Accusations against the great Sussex thegn Wulfnoth (probably the father of Godwin, later Earl of Wessex) led to his flight from the fleet with 20 ships manned by his supporters. A force of 80 ships sent after him was wrecked by a storm and the beached ships burnt by Wulfnoth, after which the remainder of the fleet dispersed in confusion.[82]

English naval forces were supplemented by Scandinavian mercenaries. Directly after the fiasco of 1009 a new invasion force led by the Danish warlord Thorkell the Tall began a devastating campaign in England. When the attackers were finally bought off and dispersed in 1012, Thorkell entered Æthelred's service with 45 ships. When the King of Denmark Swein Forkbeard conquered England in 1013, the fleet remained loyal to Æthelred after the rest of the kingdom had submitted to the invader. Swein's death in 1014 led to Æthelred's brief return to power, but in 1015-16 England was again conquered by Swein's son Cnut, whose invasion force had been joined by 40 ship-loads of Danish mercenaries who defected from Æthelred's service. Having secured the throne, Cnut dismissed the bulk of his fleet, but maintained a standing force of 40 ships, funded by national taxation. In 1025 Cnut led an Anglo-Danish fleet to campaign against his enemies in Scandinavia, and in 1028 he conquered Norway with a force including 50 English ships. The standing fleet was in time reduced to 16 ships, but increased again after Cnut's son Harthacnut brought a fleet from Denmark to claim the throne in 1040.[83]

The early years of Edward the Confessor's reign saw a series of large naval operations under the king's own command, including in 1045 the deployment at Sandwich of a particularly big fleet to guard against an expected invasion from Norway, and a blockade of Flanders in 1049, in support of a land campaign by the German Emperor Henry III. In 1050 Edward reduced the standing force, then numbering 14 ships, to five. After a political crisis in 1051 saw Earl Godwin and his sons driven into exile, Edward sent out a force of 40 ships to Sandwich to guard against their return. However Godwin, returning with ships from Flanders, eluded them, and he and his son Harold, coming from Ireland, gathered a powerful fleet from the "butsecarles" (literally "boatmen") of the Earldom of Wessex. With this fleet and an army also gathered from Wessex, Godwin came to London and confronted the king, who was supported by an army and a fleet of 50 ships. The crisis ended with the negotiated reinstatement of Godwin and his sons to their former possessions and power.[84]

In 1063 Earl Harold Godwinson led a fleet to Wales against Gruffydd ap Llywelyn of Gwynedd, while his brother Tostig invaded by land. Harold put Gruffydd to flight and destroyed his fleet and his residence at Rhuddlan, defeats which led to Gruffydd's murder by his own people in order to end the war. King Edward installed Gruffydd's half-brothers in his place, and they swore to serve him "on water and on land", suggesting that England's native naval forces could be supplemented by tributary contingents from neighbouring dependent territories as well as by foreign mercenaries.[85]

In 1066, following Edward's death and his own election as king, Harold assembled a powerful army and fleet in the Solent to guard against the invasion being prepared by William of Normandy. However, having waited all summer without the Normans appearing, their provisions were exhausted and Harold was forced to dismiss them; many of the ships were wrecked on the way back to London. William was then able to cross unopposed.[86]

After the Norman Conquest

William the Conqueror sent a fleet to Scotland in 1072 but by the early 12th century the fleet had almost disappeared. Yet in 1141 Henry II invaded Ireland while a fleet of 167 ships sailed from Dartmouth on a crusade to capture Lisbon from the Moors. A further fleet was raised for the Third Crusade in 1190. The Norman kings had a regular need for cross-Channel transport and raised a naval force in 1155, with the Cinque Ports required to provide a total of 57 ships crewed by 21 sailors apiece. However, with the loss of Normandy by King John (who even so had a fleet of 500 sail in an attempt to regain it), this had to become a force capable of preventing invasion (e.g. the 1215–1217 French invasion of England) and protecting traffic to and from Gascony. In the first years of the 13th century William de Wrotham appears in the records as the clerk of a force of galleys to be used against Philip Augustus of France. In 1206 King John ordered 54 royal galleys to be constructed and between 1207 and 1211 £5000 was spent on the royal fleet. The fleet also started to have an offensive capability, as in 1213 when ships commanded by the Earl of Salisbury raided Damme in Flanders, where they burned many ships of the French fleet.

An infrastructure was also developing—by 1212 a base existed at Portsmouth, supporting at least ten ships. Later in the 13th century ships begin to be mentioned regularly as support for various campaigns under Edward I, most notably in Luke de Tany's capture of Anglesey in 1282. Edward II of England attempted to blockade Scotland, but ineffectively. Naval expenses were considerable, with twenty 120-oared galleys being ordered in 1294 because of a fear of French invasion. In 1224 the first *Admiral of England* is recorded in charters with Henry III granting the title to Sir Richard de Lucy. Four other men were granted the same title but styled differently, they were in 1263 Sir Thomas de Moleton as *Captain and Guardian of the English Seas* and in 1286 Sir William de Leybourne, as *Admiral of the English Seas* both of these offices were granted by King Edward I. In 1321 Sir Richard de Leyburn is granted the title *Admiral of England, Wales and Ireland*, by Edward II and Sir John de Beauchamp, 1st Baron Beauchamp de Warwick, as *High Admiral of England* the office granted by Edward III in 1360. Although each holding the title of *Admiralis Angliae* the civil jurisdiction of their offices was never used nor did they officially receive letters patent from the monarch.

In 1321 Sir John de Beauchamp, 1st Baron Beauchamp de Warwick is also appointed Admiral of the South, North and West effectively the English Navy's first Admiral of the Fleet. The first Admiral to be granted a patent by the monarch was Richard FitzAlan, 10th Earl of Arundel as *High Admiral of England, Ireland and Aquitaine* given by King Richard III in 1385 . In the early 13th century English Admirals tended to be knights or barons and their role was essentially administrative not operational. In 1294 Edward I divided the English Navy into three geographical 'admiralties' each assigned a fleet and each of them administered by an admiral, they were the Admiral of the Northern Fleet, Admiral of the Western Fleet and Admiral of the Southern Fleet, each was responsible for managing and enforcing admiralty jurisdiction in their respective areas and raising and administering the ships. It also allowed Edward I to mount expeditions to Brittany, Flanders or Scotland with greater ease.

The Hundred Years' War (1337–1453) included frequent cross-Channel raids, frequently unopposed due to the lack of effective communications and the limitations of naval organisation. The navy was used for reconnaissance as well as attacks on merchantmen and warships. Prize ships and cargos were shared out. The Battle of Sluys in 1340 was a significant English victory, with Edward III of England's 160 ships (mostly hired merchant vessels) assaulting a French force in the Zwyn estuary and capturing 180 French ships in hand-to-hand combat. Les Espagnols sur Mer, fought in the Channel off Winchelsea in 1350, is possibly the first major battle in the open sea in English history; the English captured 14 Spanish ships. The 14th century also saw the creation of the post of Clerk of the King's Ships, who appears from 1344 on as in charge of some 34 royal vessels. At one point in the mid-fourteenth century Edward III's navy overall had some 700 ships in service.[87] In 1364 the Northern and Western admiralities and fleets are combined commanded by the Admiral of the North and West, and remain so on an adhoc basis until 1414.

English fortunes declined in the 1370s, with merchants objecting to the continual borrowing of their ships. There was objection to the taxation to man the king's ships, and by the end of the reign of Richard II of England only four were left, and by 1409 only two. Henry V of England revived the navy, building a number of balingers and "great ships", increasing the fleet from six in 1413 to 39 in 1417/8. This included the 1,400-ton *Grace Dieu* (which still exists, buried in the Hamble estuary), and won victories in the Channel, reaching a high point in 1417 when the French fleet was destroyed. An invasion of France took place in 1415 which led to the capture of Harfleur and the victory at Agincourt. A second invasion, beginning in 1419, led to the conquest of the Channel coast of France, almost eliminating any seaborne threat to England and enabling the running-down of Henry's naval forces.[88]

Dealing with the matter of naval administration during the 15th century the most significant development was the establishment of the first Admiralty of England this was brought about in 1412 when the remaining geographic 'admiralties' the Northern Admiralty and Western Admiralty were abolished and their functions were unified under a single administrative and operational command the Admiralty Office later called the Admiralty and Marine Affairs Office.

Significant new construction did not occur until the 1480s, by which time ships mounted guns regularly; the *Regent* of 1487 had 225 *serpentines*, an early type of cannon. Henry VII deserves a large share of credit in the establishment of a standing navy. Although there is no evidence for a conscious change of policy, Henry soon embarked on a program of building ships larger than heretofore. He also invested in dockyards, and commissioned the oldest surviving dry dock in 1495 at Portsmouth.[89]

The beginnings of an organized English navy, 1485–1603

Henry VIII ordered a major expansion of the fleet, which increased from five ships in 1509 to thirty in 1514 including the *Henri Grâce a Dieu* ("*Great Harry*") of 1500 tons and *Mary Rose* of 600 tons. Most of the fleet was laid up after 1525 but, because of the break with the Catholic Church, 27 new ships were built with money from the sale of the monasteries as well as forts and blockhouses. In 1544 Boulogne was captured. The French navy raided the Isle of Wight and was then fought off in the Battle of the Solent in 1545, prior to which *Mary Rose* sank.

A detailed and largely accurate contemporary document, The Anthony Roll, was written in 1540. It gave a nearly complete account of the English navy, which contained roughly 50 ships, including carracks, galleys, galleasses and pinnaces. The carracks included famous vessels such as the *Mary Rose*, the *Peter Pomegranate* and the *Henry Grace à Dieu*.

In 1580 Spanish and Portuguese troops were sent to Ireland but were defeated by an English army and naval force.

In the 1550s English gentlemen opposed to the Catholicism of Philip and Mary took refuge in France and were active in the English Channel as privateers under letters of marque from the French king. Six of their vessels were captured off Plymouth in July 1556.[90]

In the late 16th century the Spanish Empire, at the time Europe's superpower and the leading naval power of the 16th century, threatened England with invasion to restore Catholicism in England. Francis Drake attacked Cadiz and A

Coruña to delay the attack. The Spanish Armada finally set sail in 1588 to enforce Spain's dominance over the English Channel and transport troops from the Spanish Netherlands to England. The Spanish plan failed due to maladministration, logistical errors, blocking actions by the Dutch, bad weather, and the significant defeat by the English at the naval Battle of Gravelines. However, the bungled Drake-Norris Expedition of 1589 and the more successful raid by Lord Howard in 1596 prevented further invasion plans from occurring. A blockade of the Spanish coast was undertaken by John Hawkins and Martin Frobisher in 1590. Under the reign of Elizabeth I England raided Spain's ports and attacked Spanish ships crossing the Atlantic Ocean, capturing much treasure.[91]

While Henry VIII had launched the Royal Navy, his successors King Edward VI and Queen Mary I had ignored it and it was little more than a system of coastal defence. Elizabeth made naval strength a high priority.[92] She risked war with Spain by supporting the "Sea Dogs", such as John Hawkins and Francis Drake, who preyed on the Spanish merchant ships carrying gold and silver from the New World. The Navy yards were leaders in technical innovation, and the captains devised new tactics. Parker (1996) argues that the full-rigged ship was one of the greatest technological advances of the century and permanently transformed naval warfare. In 1573 English shipwrights introduced designs, first demonstrated in the "Dreadnaught", that allowed the ships to sail faster and maneuver better and permitted heavier guns.[93] Whereas before warships had tried to grapple with each other so that soldiers could board the enemy ship, now they stood off and fired broadsides that would sink the enemy vessel. When Spain finally decided to invade and conquer England it was a fiasco. Superior English ships and seamanship foiled the invasion and led to the destruction of the Spanish Armada in 1588, marking the high point of Elizabeth's reign. Technically, the Armada failed because Spain's over-complex strategy required coordination between the invasion fleet and the Spanish army on shore. But the poor design of the Spanish cannons meant they were much slower in reloading in a close-range battle, allowing England to take control. Spain and France still had stronger fleets, but England was catching up.[94,95]

Scotland

The Royal Scots Navy (or Old Scots Navy) was the navy of the Kingdom of Scotland until its merger with the Kingdom of England's Royal Navy in 1707 as a consequence of the Treaty of Union and the Acts of Union that ratified it. From 1603 until 1707, the Royal Scots Navy and England's Royal Navy were organised as one force, though not technically merged, as a consequence of

Figure 13: *The Scottish Red Ensign, flown by ships of the Royal Scots Navy*

the Union of the Crowns when James VI of Scotland became King of England also, as James I.[96]

Though the Lord of the Isles had a large fleet of galleys in the 13th and 14th centuries, there appears little or no trace of a Scots navy during the Wars of Scottish Independence. With Scottish independence established, Robert the Bruce turned his attention to the upbuilding of Scots shipping and of a Scots navy. In his later days he visited the Western Isles, which was part of the domain of the powerful Lords of the Isles who owed only a loose allegiance to him, and established a royal castle at East Loch Tarbert in Argyll to overawe the semi-independent Islemen. The Exchequer Rolls of 1326 record the feudal services of certain of his vassals on the western coast in aiding him with their vessels and crews. This process probably began in the thirteenth century, but would be intensified under Robert.[97]

15th century expansion

In the 15th century, James I gave close attention to the shipping interests of his country, establishing a shipbuilding yard, a house for marine stores, and a workshop at Leith. In 1429 James went to the Western Isles with one of his ships to curb his vassals there. In the same year Parliament enacted a law that each four merk land on the north and west coasts of Scotland within six miles of the sea was, in feudal service to the king, to furnish one oar. This was the nearest approach ever made in Scotland to the ship money of England. His successor, James II, developed the use of gunpowder and artillery. James III and James IV continued to build up the navy, with James III having 38 ships built for the fleet and founding two new dockyards. In addition, the Scots Parliaments passed legislation in 1493 and 1503 requiring all seaboard burghs to keep "busches" of 20 tons to be manned by idle able-bodied men.

James IV succeeded in building up a navy that was truly royal. Dissatisfied with sandbanks at Leith, James himself sited a new harbour at Newhaven in May 1504, and two years later ordered the construction of a dockyard at the Pools of Airth. The upper reaches of the Forth were protected by new fortifications on Inchgarvie.[98] His greatest achievement was the construction of *Great Michael*, the largest ship up to that time launched in Scotland, the building of which cost £30,000. Work on the ship commenced in 1506, first launched on 11 October 1511 at Newhaven, she sailed up the Forth to Airth for further fitting. The *Michael* weighed 1,000 tons, was 240 feet (73 m) in length, was manned by 1,000 seamen and 120 gunners and was then the largest ship in Europe (according to the chronicler Lindsay of Pitscottie). In 1514 the *Great Michael* was sold to France for 40,000 francs tournais.[99]

Neglect and eventual merger

The Scottish Reformation in 1560 established a government that was friendly to England and this resulted in less military necessity to maintain a fleet of great ships. With the Union of the Crowns in 1603, the incentive to rebuild a separate royal fleet for Scotland diminished further since James VI now controlled the powerful English Royal Navy, which could send ships north to defend Scottish interests, and which now opened its ranks to Scottish officers.[100]

From 1603 until union with England in 1707, Scotland and England continued to have separate navies, though they operated as one force. Thomas Gordon became the last commander of the Royal Scots Navy, taking charge of HMS *Royal Mary* on the North Sea patrol, moving to *Royal William* when she entered service in 1705, and being promoted to commodore in 1706. With the Act of Union in 1707, the Royal Scottish Navy was merged with the English Royal Navy, but there were already much larger English ships called *Royal William* and *Mary*, so the Scottish frigates were renamed HMS *Edinburgh* and HMS *Glasgow*, while only HMS *Dumbarton Castle* retained its name.

The development of the single British navy

After 1603 the English and Scottish fleets were organized together under James I but the efficiency of the Navy declined gradually, while corruption grew until brought under control in an inquiry of 1618. James concluded a peace with Spain and privateering was outlawed. Notable construction in the early 17th century included the 1,200-ton HMS *Prince Royal*, the first three-decker, and *HMS Sovereign of the Seas* in 1637, designed by Phineas Pett. Operations under James I did not go well, with expeditions against Algerian pirates in 1620/1, Cadiz in 1625, and La Rochelle in 1627/8 being expensive failures.[101]

Expansion of the fighting force, 1642–1689

Charles I levied "ship money" from 1634 and this unpopular tax was one of the main causes of the first English Civil War from 1642–45. At the beginning of the war the navy, then consisting of 35 vessels, sided with Parliament. During the war the royalist side used a number of small ships to blockade ports and for supplying their own armies. These were afterwards combined into a single force. Charles had surrendered to the Scots and conspired with them to invade England during the second English Civil War of 1648–51. In 1648 part of the Parliamentary fleet mutinied and joined the Royalist side. However, the Royalist fleet was driven to Spain and destroyed during the Commonwealth period by Robert Blake. The execution of Charles I forced the rapid expansion of the navy, by multiplying England's actual and potential enemies, and many vessels were constructed from the 1650s onward. This reformation of the navy was also carried out by Blake.

The Navigation Act 1651 cut out Dutch shippers from English trade. Operations of the late 17th century were dominated by the three Anglo-Dutch Wars, which stretched from 1652 to 1674. Forty new ships were built between 1650 and 1654. Triggered by seemingly trivial incidents, but motivated by economic competition, they were notable as purely naval wars fought in the English Channel and the North Sea. In February 1653 the English Channel was closed to Dutch ships which were then forced back to their home ports.

The Interregnum saw a considerable expansion in the strength of the navy, both in number of ships and in internal importance within English policy. The Restoration Monarchy inherited this large navy and continued the same policy of expansion of the navy, focusing on making a strong navy full of large ships in order to provide a strong defence under Charles II. At the start of the Restoration, Parliament listed forty ships of the Royal Navy (not of the Summer's Guard) with a complement of 3,695 sailors.

Figure 14: *The Battle of Scheveningen, 10 August 1653*

The administration of the navy was greatly improved by Sir William Coventry and Samuel Pepys, both of whom began their service in 1660 with the Restoration. While it was Pepys' diary that made him the most famous of all naval bureaucrats, his nearly thirty years of administration were crucial in replacing the *ad hoc* processes of years past with regular programmes of supply, construction, pay, and so forth. He was responsible for introduction of the "Navy List" which fixed the order of promotion. In 1683 the "Victualling Board" was set up which fixed the ration scales. In 1655 Blake routed the Barbary pirates and started a campaign against the Spanish in the Caribbean, capturing Jamaica.[102]

In 1664 the English captured New Amsterdam (later New York City) resulting in the Second Dutch War (1665–1667). In 1666 the Four Days Battle was a defeat for the English but the Dutch fleet was crushed a month later off Orfordness. In 1667 the Dutch mounted the Raid on the Medway, breaking into Chatham Dockyard and capturing or burning many of the Navy's largest ships at their moorings,[103] which resulted in the most humiliating defeat in the Royal Navy's history.[104] The English were also defeated at Solebay in 1672. The experience of large-scale battle was instructive to the Navy; the Articles of War regularizing the conduct of officers and seaman, and the "Fighting Instructions" establishing the line of battle, both date from this period.[105] The influence and reforms of Samuel Pepys, the Chief Secretary to the Admiralty under both King Charles II and subsequently King James II, were important in the early professionalisation of the Royal Navy.[106]

Wars with France, Spain and America, 1690–1793

The Glorious Revolution of 1688 rearranged the political map of Europe, and led to a series of wars with France that lasted well over a century. This was the classic age of sail; while the ships themselves evolved in only minor ways, technique and tactics were honed to a high degree, and the battles of the Napoleonic Wars entailed feats that would have been impossible for the fleets of the 17th century. Because of parliamentary opposition, James II fled the country. The landing of William III and the Glorious Revolution itself was a gigantic effort involving 100 warships and 400 transports carrying 11,000 infantry and 4,000 horses. It was not opposed by the English or Scottish fleets. Louis XIV declared war just days later, a conflict which became known as the War of the Grand Alliance. The English defeat at the Battle of Beachy Head of 1690 led to an improved version of the Fighting Instructions, and subsequent operations against French ports proved more successful, leading to decisive victory at La Hougue in 1692.[107]

Naval operations in the War of the Spanish Succession (1702–13) were with the Dutch against the Spanish and French. They were at first focused on the acquisition of a Mediterranean base, culminating in an alliance with Portugal and the capture of Gibraltar (1704) and Port Mahon in Minorca (1708). In addition Newfoundland and Nova Scotia were obtained. Even so, freedom of action in the Mediterranean did not decide the war, although it gave the new Kingdom of Great Britain (created by the Union of England and Scotland in 1707) an advantage when negotiating the Peace of Utrecht, and made Britain a recognized great power. Spanish treasure fleets were sunk in 1704 and 1708, and the Spanish Empire was opened up to British slaving voyages. The British fleet ended Spanish occupation of Sicily in 1718 and in 1727 blockaded Panama.[108]

The subsequent quarter-century of peace saw a few naval actions. The navy was used against Russia and Sweden in the Baltic from 1715 to 1727 to protect supplies of naval stores. It was used at the Cape Passaro in 1718, during the Great Northern War, and in the West Indies (1726). There was a war against Spain in 1739 over the slave trade. In 1745 the navy contributed to collapse of the Jacobite rising.[109]

The War of Jenkins' Ear (1739–48) saw various naval operations in the Caribbean under admirals Vernon and Anson against Spanish trade and possessions, before the war subsequently merged into the wider War of the Austrian Succession (1740–1748). This, in turn, brought a new round of naval operations against France, including a blockade of Toulon. In 1747 the navy twice defeated the French off Finisterre.

The Seven Years' War (1756–63) began somewhat inauspiciously for the Navy, with a French siege of Minorca and the failure of Admiral John Byng to relieve it; he was executed on his own quarterdeck. Voltaire famously wrote, in reference to Byng's execution, that "in this country it is wise to kill an admiral from time to time to encourage the others" (admirals). (Today the French phrase *"pour encourager les autres"* used in English euphemistically connotes a threat by example.) Minorca was lost but subsequent operations went more successfully (due more to government support and better strategic thinking, rather than admirals "encouraged" by Byng's example), and the British fleet won several victories. The French tried to invade Britain in 1759 but their force was defeated at Quiberon Bay off the coast of Brittany. Spain entered the war against Britain in 1762 but lost Havana and Manila, though the latter was given back in exchange for Florida. The Treaty of Paris ended the war.

At the beginning of the American Revolutionary War (1775–83), the Royal Navy dealt with the fledgling Continental Navy handily, destroying or capturing many of its vessels. However, France soon took the American side, and in 1778 a French fleet sailed for America, where it attempted to land at Rhode Island and nearly engaged with the British fleet before a storm intervened, while back home another fought the British in the First Battle of Ushant. Spain and the Dutch Republic entered the war in 1780. Action shifted to the Caribbean, where there were a number of battles with varying results. A Spanish fleet was defeated at the battle of Cape Saint Vincent in 1780 while a Franco-Spanish fleet was defeated in the West Indies in 1782. The most important operation came in 1781 when, in the Battle of the Chesapeake, the British failed to lift the French blockade of Lord Cornwallis, resulting in a British surrender in the Battle of Yorktown. Although combat was over in North America, it continued in the Caribbean (Battle of the Saintes) and India, where the British experienced both successes and failures. Though Minorca had been recaptured, it was returned to the Spanish.

French Revolutionary and Napoleonic Wars (1793–1815)

The French Revolutionary Wars of 1793–1802 and the Napoleonic Wars of 1803–15 saw the Royal Navy reach a peak of efficiency, dominating the navies of all Britain's adversaries. Initially Britain did not involve itself in the French Revolution, but in 1793 France declared war, leading to the Glorious First of June battle in the following year off Brest, followed by the capture of French colonies in the Caribbean. The Dutch Republic declared war in 1795 and Spain in 1796, on the side of France. Further action came in 1797 and 1798, with the Battle of Cape St Vincent and the Battle of the Nile (also known as the Battle of Aboukir Bay), which brought Admiral Horatio Nelson to the public's attention. The latter engagement cut off Napoleon's expedition to Egypt, though French forces remained in control of that country for three more years. In 1800 Russia, Sweden and Denmark agreed to resist British warships searching neutral shipping for French goods and in 1801 the Danes closed their ports to British shipping. This caused Britain to attack ships and the fort at the Battle of Copenhagen.

The Peace of Amiens in 1802 proved to be but a brief interruption in the years of warfare, and the Navy was soon blockading Napoleon's France. In 1805 French invasion forces were massed on the French coast with 2,300 vessels. The French fleet at Toulon went to the West Indies where it was intended to meet the Spanish one but it was chased by the British fleet and returned without meeting up. After fighting an action off Finisterre the French fleet withdrew to Cadiz where it met up with the Spanish one. The height of the Navy's achievements came on 21 October 1805 at the Battle of Trafalgar where a numerically smaller but more experienced British fleet under the command of Admiral Lord Nelson decisively defeated the combined French and Spanish fleet. The victory at Trafalgar consolidated the United Kingdom's advantage over other European maritime powers, but Nelson was killed during the battle.

By concentrating its military resources in the navy, Britain could both defend itself and project its power across the oceans as well as threaten rivals' ocean trading routes. Britain therefore needed to maintain only a relatively small, highly mobile, professional army that sailed to where it was needed, and was supported by the navy with bombardment, movement, supplies and reinforcement. The Navy could cut off enemies' sea-borne supplies, as with Napoleon's army in Egypt.

Theoretically, the highest commands of the Royal Navy were open to all within its ranks showing talent. In practice, family connections, political or professional patronage were very important for promotion to ranks higher than Commander. British captains were responsible for recruiting their ship's crew from a combination of volunteers, impressment and the requisitioning of existing crew members from ships in ordinary. From 1795 a Quota System was also applied, where each British county was required to supply a certain number of volunteers. Many nationalities served on British ships, with foreigners comprising fifteen per cent of crews by the end of the Napoleonic Wars. Americans were the most common foreign nationality in naval service, followed by Dutch, Scandinavian and Italian.[110] While most foreigners in the Navy were obtained through impressment or from prison ships, around 200 captured French sailors were also persuaded to join after their fleet was defeated at the Battle of the Nile.

The conditions of service for ordinary seamen, while poor by modern standards, were better than many other kinds of work at the time. However, inflation during the late 18th century eroded the real value of seamen's pay while, at the same time, the war caused an increase in pay for merchant ships. Naval pay also often ran years in arrears, and shore leave decreased as ships needed to spend less time in port with better provisioning and health care, and copper bottoms (which delayed fouling). Discontent over these issues eventually resulted in serious mutinies in 1797 when the crews of the Spithead and Nore fleets refused to obey their officers and some captains were sent ashore. This resulted in the short-lived *"Floating Republic"* which at Spithead was quelled by promising improvements in conditions, but at the Nore resulted in the hanging of 29 mutineers. It is worth noting that neither of the mutinies included flogging or impressment in their list of grievances and, in fact, the mutineers themselves continued the practice of flogging to preserve discipline.

Napoleon acted to counter Britain's maritime supremacy and economic power, closing European ports to British trade. He also authorised many privateers, operating from French territories in the West Indies, placing great pressure on British mercantile shipping in the western hemisphere. The Royal Navy was too hard-pressed in European waters to release significant forces to combat the privateers, and its large ships of the line were not very effective at seeking out and running down fast and manoeuvrable privateers which operated as widely spread single ships or small groups. The Royal Navy reacted by commissioning small warships of traditional Bermuda design. The first three ordered from Bermudian builders—HMS *Dasher*, HMS *Driver* and HMS *Hunter*—were sloops of 200 tons, armed with twelve 24-pounder guns. A great many more ships of this type were ordered, or bought from trade, primarily for use as couriers. The most notable was HMS *Pickle*, the former Bermudian merchantman that carried news of victory back from Trafalgar.[111]

Although brief in retrospect, the years of the Napoleonic wars came to be remembered as the apotheosis of "fighting sail", and stories of the Royal Navy at this period have been told and retold regularly since then, most famously in the Horatio Hornblower series of C. S. Forrester.

War of 1812

In the years following the battle of Trafalgar there was increasing tension at sea between Britain and the United States. American traders took advantage of their country's neutrality to trade with both the French-controlled parts of Europe, and Britain. Both France and Britain tried to prevent each other's trade, but only the Royal Navy was in a position to enforce a blockade. Another irritant was the suspected presence of British deserters aboard US merchant and naval vessels. Royal Navy ships often attempted to recover these deserters. In one notorious instance in 1807, otherwise known as the Chesapeake–Leopard Affair, HMS *Leopard* fired on USS *Chesapeake* causing significant casualties before boarding and seizing suspected British deserters.

In 1812, while the Napoleonic wars continued, the United States declared war on the United Kingdom of Great Britain and Ireland and invaded Canada. Occupied by its struggle with France, British policy was to commit only sufficient forces to the American War of 1812 to prevent American victory. On land, this meant a great reliance on militia and Native American allies. On the water, the Royal Navy kept its large men-of-war in Europe, relying on smaller vessels to counter the weak United States Navy. Some of the action consisted of small-scale engagements on the Great Lakes.

A key element of the war was the battle for control of the Great Lakes. Without the support of ships to move soldiers, equipment and supplies, either side would be at a great disadvantage, especially against an enemy who was able to make full use of the lakes. All of the Royal Naval vessels on Lake Erie were captured at the decisive Battle of Lake Erie on 10 September 1813. The British Army, along with militia and Indian units, was now cut off from supplies and retreated eastward. They were caught and defeated at the Battle of the Thames on 5 October 1813, which gave Americans the control over western Ontario, and destroyed the Indian alliance the British Army had depended upon. In 1814 the British Army, bringing in veteran units from the Peninsular War, launched a major invasion of New York State under General Sir George Prévost. However, the supporting Royal Navy vessels on Lake Champlain were sunk by the American fleet at the Battle of Plattsburgh on 11 September 1814, forcing Prévost to retreat back to Canada despite his much larger army.[112]

At sea, the War of 1812 was characterised by single-ship actions between small ships, and disruption of merchant shipping. The Royal Navy struggled to build as many ships as it could, generally sacrificing on the size and armament of vessels, and struggled harder to find adequate personnel, trained or barely trained, to crew them. Royal Naval vessels were often under-manned, without sufficient men to fire a full broadside. Many of the men crewing Royal Naval vessels were rated only as *landsmen*, and many of those rated as *seamen* were impressed (conscripted), with resultingly poor morale. The US Navy could not begin to equal the Royal Navy in number of vessels, and had concentrated in building a handful of better-designed frigates. These were larger, heavier and better-armed (both in terms of number of guns, and in the range to which the guns could fire) than their British counterparts, and were handled well by larger volunteer crews (where the Royal Navy was hindered by a relative shortage of trained seamen, the US Navy was not large enough to make full use of the large number of American merchant seamen put out of work, even before the war, by the Embargo Act). As a result, a significant number of British ships were defeated and, midway through the war, the Admiralty issued the order not to engage American frigates individually.

There were also significant losses of merchant shipping to American privateers, a total of 1,300 vessels;[113] however, the Royal Navy, operating from its new base and dockyard, off the US Atlantic Seaboard in Bermuda, gradually reinforced the blockade of the American coast, virtually halting all trade by sea, capturing many merchant ships, and forcing the US navy frigates to stay in harbour or risk being captured. Despite successful American claims for damage having been pressed in British courts against British privateers several years before, the War was probably the last occasion on which the Royal Navy made considerable reliance on privateers to boost Britain's maritime power. In Bermuda, privateering had thrived until the build-up of the regular Royal Naval establishment, which began in 1795, reduced the Admiralty's reliance on privateers in the Western Atlantic. During the American War of 1812, however, Bermudian privateers alone captured 298 enemy ships (the total captures by all British naval and privateering vessels between the Great Lakes and the West Indies was 1,593 vessels.)[114]

By this time, the Royal Navy was building a naval base and dockyard in Bermuda. It had begun buying land, mostly at the West End of Bermuda, notably Ireland Island, following American independence, permanently establishing itself in the colony in 1795. The development of the intended site was delayed by a dozen years as a suitable passage through the surrounding reefline needed to be located. Until then, the Royal Navy operated from the old capital in the East End, St. George's. Bermuda replaced Newfoundland initially as the winter base of the North America and West Indies Squadron, and then as its year-round headquarters, naval station, and dockyard, with its Admiralty House at Mount Wyndham, in Bailey's Bay, and then at Spanish Point, opposite Ireland Island on the mouth of Great Sound.

Located 1,030 kilometres (640 mi) off Cape Hatteras, North Carolina, 1,239 kilometres (770 mi) South of Cape Sable Island, Nova Scotia, and 1,770 kilometres (1,100 mi) North-East of Miami, Bermuda replaced the continental bases between Canada and the West Indies that the Royal Navy had been deprived of by American independence. During the War of 1812 the Royal Navy's blockade of the US Atlantic ports was coordinated from Bermuda and Halifax, Nova Scotia.

The blockade kept most of the American navy trapped in port. The Royal Navy also occupied coastal islands, encouraging American slaves to defect. Military-aged males were enlisted into a Corps of Colonial Marines while their families were sent to the dockyard in Bermuda for the duration of the war, employed by the Royal Navy. These marines fought for the Crown on the Atlantic Seaboard, and in the attack on Washington, D.C. and the Chesapeake.

After British victory in the Peninsular War, part of Wellington's Light Division was released for service in North America. This 2,500-man force, composed of detachments from the 4, 21, 44, and 85 Regiments with some elements of artillery and sappers and commanded by Major-General Ross, arrived in Bermuda in 1814 aboard a fleet composed of the 74-gun HMS *Royal Oak*, three frigates, three sloops and ten other vessels. The combined force was to launch raids on the coastlines of Maryland and Virginia, with the aim of drawing US forces away from the Canada–US border. In response to American actions at Lake Erie (the Burning of York), however, Sir George Prevost requested a punitive expedition which would "deter the enemy from a repetition of such outrages". The British force arrived at the Patuxent on 17 August and landed the soldiers within 36 miles of Washington, D.C.. Led by Rear Admiral Sir George Cockburn, the British force drove the US government out of Washington, D.C.. Ross shied from the idea of burning the city, but Cockburn and others set it alight. Buildings burned included the US Capitol and the US President's Mansion.

Pax Britannica, 1815–1895

After 1827 there were no major battles until 1914. The navy was used against shore installations, such as those in the Baltic and Black Sea in 1854 and 1855, to fight pirates; to hunt down slave ships; and to assist the army when sailors and marines were landed as naval brigades, as on many occasions between the siege of Sebastopol and the 1900 Boxer Rebellion. With a fleet larger than any two rivals combined, the British nation could take security for granted, but at all times the national leaders and public opinion supported a powerful navy, and service was of high prestige.[115]

Operations

The first action of the period was the bombardment of Algiers under Lord Exmouth, conducted in 1816. This was to force the freeing of Christian slaves. During the Greek War of Independence, at the Battle of Navarino in 1827, the Turkish fleet was destroyed by the combined fleets of Britain, France and Russia. This was the last major action between fleets of sailing ships. Ottoman involvement continued, with the bombardment of Acre in 1840, and additional Mediterranean crises during the rest of the decade.[116]

To try to prevent Russia gaining access to a warm water port, the Crimean War was fought in the 1850s. Britain (in concert with the Turks and French) sent 150 transports and 13 warships and the Russian Black Sea fleet was destroyed. The Crimean War became known as a testing ground for the new technologies of steam and shell. It was shown that explosive shells ripped wooden hulls to pieces, which led to the development of the "iron clad" ship. It also showed the need for a permanent pool of trained seamen. There were two Anglo-French campaigns against Russia. In the Black Sea, success at Sevastopol was paralleled by successful operations in the Baltic including the bombardments of Bomarsund and Sveaborg.

The Chinese government placed unilateral restraints on British trade with China. In 1839 a Chinese official impounded opium from India, but the British insisted on the British Empire being allowed to export to China and instituted a blockade of Canton, beginning the First Opium War. There was a Second Opium War from 1856 to 1860. In 1857 the British captured Canton and threatened Beijing, thrown back by the Chinese in 1859 but succeeding the following year. As a result of these actions Britain gained a base at Hong Kong in 1839 and a base in Canton in 1857.

In 1864 the bombardment of Kagoshima forced Japan to accept foreign traders.[117] During the Russo-Turkish War the British sent a fleet of battleships under Admiral Geoffrey Hornby to intimidate Russia from entering Constantinople.[118] Over the next thirty years, only a bombardment of Alexandria in 1882 brought the fleet into action, carried out to ensure control of the Suez Canal.[119]

Technology

Steam power was of interest to the Royal Navy from the beginning of the 19th century, since it neatly solved the difficult and dangerous sailing problems encountered in estuaries and other inshore areas. It was first adopted in the HMS *Comet* of 1821, and in 1824 HMS *Lightning* accompanied the expedition to Algiers. Steam vessels appeared in greater numbers through the 1830s and 1840s, all using side-mounted paddlewheels; screw propellers were introduced in the 1830s and, after some reluctance, were adopted in the mid-1840s (the famous tug-of-war between the screw-propelled HMS Rattler and the paddlewheeled *Alecto* (1839) was entertaining, but records show the Admiralty had already decided on and ordered screw ships). The first major steam warship was HMS *Agamemnon*. In the 1850s Naval Arms Race screw battleships and frigates, both conversions and new constructions, were built in large numbers. These ships retained a full capacity for sail as steam engines were not yet efficient enough to permit long ocean voyages under power. Steam power was intended only for use during battle and to allow ships to go to sea at will instead of being held in port by adverse winds. A triple expansion steam engine was introduced in 1881 which was more efficient than earlier ones.[120]

Iron in ship construction was first used for diagonal-cross-bracing in major warships. The adoption of iron hulls for ocean-going ships had to wait until after Admiralty experiments had solved the problem of an iron-hull's effect on compass deviation. Because iron hulls were much thinner than wooden hulls, they appeared to be more vulnerable to damage when ships ran aground. Although Brunel had adopted iron in the *Great Britain*, the Admiralty was also concerned about the vulnerability of iron in combat, and experiments with iron in the 1840s seemed to indicate that iron would shatter under impact.[121]

In 1858 France built the first seagoing ironclad, *Gloire*, and Britain responded with *Warrior* of 1860, the first of the 1860s Naval Arms Race—an intensive programme of construction that eclipsed French efforts by 1870. She was called a "Black Snake" by Napoleon III, but was soon superseded.

When armoured ships were first introduced, in-service guns had very little ability to penetrate their armour. However, starting in 1867, guns started to be introduced into service capable of penetrating the armour of the first generation iron-clads, albeit at favourable angles and at short range. This had already been anticipated, and armour thicknesses grew, resulting in turn in a gun *calibre-race* as larger guns gave better penetration. The explosive shell was introduced in 1820.[122]

In parallel with this there was a debate over how guns should be mounted on ship. Captain Cowper Coles had developed a turret design in the late-1850s as a result of experience in the Crimean War. Initial designs, published in *Blackwood's Magazine* in 1859 were for a ship with far more than 10 turrets. Consequently, a range of coastal-service turret-ships were built in parallel with the seagoing iron-clads. Because of agitation from Captain Coles and his supporters, the issue of turret-ships became deeply political, and resulted in the ordering of *Captain* (1869) an unsatisfactory private design by Lairds and Captain Coles. The rival Admiralty design, *Monarch* (1868), had a long and successful career. However the need to combine high-free-board at the bow with sails meant that both these ships had very poor end-on fire. The Admiralty's next seagoing mastless turret-ship design *Devastation* (1871) solved these problems by having very large coal bunkers, and put the 35-ton guns in turrets on a breastwork.

Tank testing of hull models was introduced and mechanical calculators as range finders. The torpedo came in during the 1870s and the first ship to fire one in battle was HMS *Shah*. This led to the development of torpedo boats and torpedo boat destroyers (later called just destroyers).[123]

> "
> Being unchallenged and unchallengable, Britain was able to exercise her maritime imperium of the *Pax Britanica* at remarkably modest expense. The British defence burden fell progressively to a minimum of 2 percent (of GDP) in 1870. Britain's dominance flowed not so much from the size of her active fleets as from the vast potential strength implicit in the reserve fleet and, behind that, the unrivalled capacity of her industry.[124]
> "

At this time, 80% of merchant steamships were built in British shipyards. The rate of French construction was low, and construction times were stretched out. For instance, the last of the three French *1872-programme* battleships was not completed until October 1886.[125] Many of these long-delayed ships were completed in the second half of the 1880s, and this was misrepresented as the French having more new battleships than the Royal Navy in various publications including the famous 1884 articles in the Liberal magazine *Pall Mall Gazette*, which alarmed the public just before the General Election, and helped create an increased market for books on naval matters such as the *Naval Annual*, which was first published in 1887.[126]

Two-power standard

The age of naval dominance at low cost was ended by increased naval competition from old rivals, such as France, and new ones such as Imperial Germany and Japan. These challenges were reflected by the Naval Defence Act 1889, which received the Royal Assent on 31 May 1889, to increase the United Kingdom's naval strength and formally adopt the country's "two-power standard". The standard called for the Royal Navy to be as strong as the world's next two largest navies combined (at that point, France and Russia) by maintaining a number of battleships at least equal to their combined strength.[127]

That led to a new ship building programme, which authorised ten new battleships, 38 cruisers, and additional vessels. Alfred Thayer Mahan's books and his visit to Europe in the 1890s heightened interest even more.[128] When Prime Minister William Ewart Gladstone held out against another large programme of naval construction in 1894, he found himself alone, and so resigned.[129]

Age of the battleship, 1895-1919

Both naval construction and naval strategizing became intense, prompted by the development of torpedoes and submarines (from 1901), which challenged traditional ideas about the power of battleships. At the same time the *Dreadnought* committed to the "big gun only" concept and caused a shift in thinking around the world, giving Britain the undisputed lead. This ship had ten 12-inch guns with a top speed of 21.5 knots. The British were aided in this development by having Naval Observers aboard the Japanese fleet at the battle of Tsushima straits in 1904 where the Japanese decisively defeated the Russian fleet.[130]

Another innovative (though ultimately unsuccessful) concept was the battlecruiser, fast and light but still hard-hitting. However, to achieve this the ship's armour was sacrificed. The result was a potentially fatal weakness.

The Royal Navy began developing submarines beginning on 4 February 1901. These submarines were ordered in late 1900 and were built by Vickers under a licensing agreement with the American Electric Boat Company.[131] The first British Holland No. 1 (Type 7) submarine (assembled by Vickers) was 63 feet 4 inches long.

Major reforms of the British fleet were undertaken, particularly by Admiral Jackie Fisher as First Sea Lord from 1904 to 1909. During this period, 154 obsolete ships, including 17 battleships, were scrapped to make way for newer vessels. Reforms in training and gunnery were introduced to make good perceived deficiencies, which in part Tirpitz had counted upon to provide his ships with a margin of superiority. Changes in British foreign policy, such as The Great Rapprochement with the United States, the Anglo-Japanese Alliance, and the Entente Cordiale with France allowed the fleet to be concentrated in home waters. By 1906 the Royal Navy's only likely opponent was the Imperial German Navy.[132]

Also, around this time, an important new development was under way. It was the steam turbine, invented by Charles Parsons, demonstrated by the Turbinia in 1899.

In 1910, the NID was shorn of its responsibility for war planning and strategy when the outgoing Fisher created the Navy War Council as a stop-gap remedy to criticisms emanating from the Beresford Inquiry that the Navy needed a naval staff—a role the NID had been in fact fulfilling since at least 1900, if not earlier. After this reorganisation, war planning and strategic matters were transferred to the newly created Naval Mobilisation Department and the NID reverted to the position it held prior to 1887—an intelligence collection and collation organisation.

Some countries from within the British Empire started developing their own navies. In 1911 the Royal Australian Navy and the Royal Canadian Navy came into being. In 1941 the New Zealand Division became the Royal New Zealand Navy.

All these reforms and innovations of course required a large increase in funding. Between 1900 and 1913 the Naval Estimates nearly doubled to total £44,000,000.[133] This was over half the total defence budget of £74,000,000 (£6.68 billion in 2018).[134]

World Wars, 1914–1945

First World War

The accumulated tensions in international relations finally broke out into the hostilities of World War I. From the naval point of view, it was time for the massed fleets to prove themselves, but caution and manoeuvring resulted in only a few minor engagements at sea. During the First World War the majority of the Royal Navy's strength was deployed at home in the Grand Fleet in an effort to blockade Germany and to draw the Hochseeflotte (the German "High Seas Fleet") into an engagement where a decisive victory could be gained. Although there was no decisive battle, the Royal Navy and the Kaiserliche Marine fought many engagements: the Battle of Heligoland Bight, the Battle of Coronel, the Battle of the Falkland Islands, the Battle of Dogger Bank and the Battle of Jutland. The British numerical advantage proved insurmountable, leading the High Seas Fleet to abandon any attempt to challenge British dominance.

At the start of the war the German Empire had armed cruisers scattered across the globe. Some of them were used to attack Allied merchant shipping. The Royal Navy systematically hunted them down, though not without some embarrassment from its inability to protect friendly shipping. Most of the German East Asia Squadron was defeated at the Battle of the Falkland Islands in December 1914.

Soon after the outbreak of hostilities the British initiated a Naval Blockade of Germany, preventing supplies from reaching its ports. International waters were mined to prevent any ships from entering entire sections of sea. Since there was limited response to this tactic, Germany expected a similar response to its tactic of unrestricted submarine warfare. This attempted to cut supply lines to Britain.

The Royal Naval Air Service was formed in 1914 but was mainly limited to reconnaissance. Converted ships were initially used to launch aircraft with landings in the sea. The first purpose-built aircraft carrier was HMS *Argus*, launched in 1918.

The Royal Navy was also heavily committed in the Dardanelles Campaign against the Ottoman Empire. During the war, the Navy contributed the Royal Naval Division to the land forces of the New Army. The Royal Marines took part in many operations including the raid on Zeebrugge.

Energy was a critical factor for the British war effort. Most of the energy supplies came from coal mines in Britain. Critical however was the flow of oil for ships, lorries and industrial use. There were no oil wells in Britain so everything was imported. In 1917, total British consumption was 827 million barrels, of which 85% was supplied by the United States, and 6% by Mexico.[135] Fuel oil for the Royal Navy was the highest priority. In 1917, the Royal Navy consumed 12,500 tons a month, but had a supply of 30,000 tons a month from the Anglo-Persian Oil Company, using their oil wells in Persia.

Inter-war period

In the inter-war period the Royal Navy was stripped of much of its power. The Washington Naval Treaty of 1922 imposed limits on individual ship tonnage and gun calibre, as well as total tonnage of the navy. The treaty, together with the deplorable financial conditions during the immediate post-war period and the Great Depression, forced the Admiralty to scrap all capital ships from the Great War with a gun calibre under 13.5 inches and to cancel plans for new construction. The *G3*-class of 16-inch battlecruisers and the *N3*-class battleship of 18-inch battleships were cancelled. Three of the *Admiral*-class battlecruisers had already been cancelled. Also under the treaty, three "large light cruisers"—*Glorious*, *Courageous* and *Furious*—were converted to aircraft carriers. New additions to the fleet were therefore minimal during the 1920s, the only major new vessels being two *Nelson*-class battleships and fifteen *County*-class cruisers and *York*-class heavy cruisers.[136]

The London Naval Treaty of 1930 deferred new capital ship construction until 1937 and reiterated construction limits on cruisers, destroyers and submarines. As international tensions increased in the mid-1930s the Second London Naval Treaty of 1935 failed to halt the development of a naval arms race and by 1938 treaty limits were effectively ignored. The Navy made a show of force against Mussolini's war in Abyssinia, and operated in China to evacuate British citizens from cities under Japanese attack. The re-armament of the Royal Navy was well under way by this point however, with the King George V-class battleship of 1936, limited to 35,000 tons and 14-inch armament, the aircraft carrier *Ark Royal*, and the *Illustrious*-class aircraft carrier, the *Town*-class and *Crown Colony*-class classes of light cruiser and the *Tribal*-class destroyers.

During this period the Royal Navy was used for evacuation and gunboat diplomacy. There were significant pay cuts in the 1920s, culminating in the Invergordon Mutiny of 1931. The crews of various warships refused to sail on exercises, which caused great shock. This led to changes and the pay rates were restored in 1934.

Second World War

At the start of World War II, Britain's global commitments were reflected in the Navy's deployment. Its first task remained the protection of trade, since Britain was heavily dependent upon imports of food and raw materials, and the global empire was also interdependent. The navy's assets were allocated between various Fleets and Stations[137]

Fleet / Station	Area of Responsibility
Home Fleet	Home waters, i.e., north-east Atlantic, North Sea, English Channel (sub-divided into commands and sub-commands)
Mediterranean Fleet	Mediterranean
South Atlantic Station	South Atlantic region
America and West Indies Station	Western north Atlantic, Caribbean, eastern Pacific
East Indies Station / Eastern Fleet	Indian Ocean (excluding South Atlantic and Africa Station, Australian waters and waters adjacent to Dutch East Indies)
China Station /- Eastern Fleet	North-west Pacific and waters around Dutch East Indies

The Royal Navy suffered heavy losses in the first two years of the war, including the carriers HMS *Courageous*, *Glorious* and *Ark Royal*, the battleships *Royal Oak* and *Barham* and the battlecruiser *Hood* in the European Theatre, and the carrier *Hermes*, the battleship *Prince of Wales*, the battlecruiser *Repulse* and the heavy cruisers *Exeter*, *Dorsetshire* and *Cornwall* in the Asian Theatre. Of the 1,418 men on the *Hood*, only three survived its sinking.[138] Over 3,000 people were lost when the converted troopship RMS *Lancastria* was sunk in June 1940, the greatest maritime disaster in Britain's history. There were however also successes against enemy surface ships, as in the battles of the River Plate in 1939, Narvik in 1940 and Cape Matapan in 1941, and the sinking of the German capital ships *Bismarck* in 1941 and *Scharnhorst* in 1943.

The Royal Navy was vital in interdicting Axis supplies to North Africa and in the resupply of its base in Malta. The losses in Operation Pedestal were high but the convoy got through. The Royal Navy was also vital in guarding the sea lanes that enabled British forces to fight in remote parts of the world

Figure 15: *British Battlecruiser HMS Hood*

such as North Africa, the Mediterranean and the Far East. Convoys were used from the start of the war and anti-submarine hunting patrols used. From 1942, responsibility for the protection of Atlantic convoys was divided between the various allied navies: the Royal Navy being responsible for much of the North Atlantic and Arctic oceans.

The defence of the ports and harbours and keeping sea-lanes around the coast open was the responsibility of Coastal Forces and the Royal Naval Patrol Service. Naval supremacy was vital to the amphibious operations carried out, such as the invasions of Northwest Africa, Sicily, Italy, and Normandy. The use of the Mulberry harbours allowed the invasion forces to be kept resupplied.

The successful invasion of Europe reduced the European role of the navy to escorting convoys and providing fire support for troops near the coast as at Walcheren, during the battle of the Scheldt.

The British Eastern Fleet had been withdrawn to East Africa because of Japanese incursions into the Indian Ocean. Despite opposition from the U.S. naval chief, Admiral Ernest King, the Royal Navy sent a large task force to the Pacific (British Pacific Fleet). This required the use of wholly different techniques, requiring a substantial fleet support train, resupply at sea and an emphasis on naval air power and defence. Their largest attack was on the oil refineries in Sumatra to deny Japanese access to supplies.

The Navy from 1945

Post-War period, 1945–1956

After the Second World War, the decline of the British Empire and the economic hardships in Britain forced the reduction in the size and capability of the Royal Navy. All of the pre-war ships (except for the Town-class light cruisers) were quickly retired and most sold for scrapping over the years 1945–48, and only the best condition ships (the four surviving KG-V class battleships, carriers, cruisers, and some destroyers) were retained and refitted for service. The increasingly powerful United States Navy took on the former role of the Royal Navy as global naval power and police force of the sea. The combination of the threat of the Soviet Union, and Britain's commitments throughout the world, created a new role for the Navy. Governments since the Second World War have had to balance commitments with increasing budgetary pressures, partly due to the increasing cost of weapons systems, what historian Paul Kennedy called the Upward Spiral.[139]

Cold War, 1956–1990

A modest new construction programme was initiated with some new carriers (*Majestic*- and *Centaur*-class light carriers, and *Audacious*-class large carriers being completed between 1948 through 1958), along with three *Tiger*-class cruisers (completed 1959–61), the *Daring*-class destroyers in the 1950s, and finally the County-class guided missile destroyers completed in the 1960s.

Lord Mountbatten of Burma continued with development, and by 1962 a new *Dreadnought* became Britain's first nuclear-powered submarine and in 1968 the first ballistic missile submarine *Resolution* was commissioned, armed with the Polaris missile. The Royal Navy later became wholly responsible for the maintenance of the UK's nuclear deterrent. Even so, the Labour government announced in 1966 that Britain would not mount major operations without the help of allies, and that the existing carrier force would be maintained into the 1970s; Christopher Mayhew and Sir David Luce resigned in protest, but to no avail. Britain withdrew from the east of Suez, cancelling its planned CVA-01 large carrier, and other than Polaris focused on its NATO responsibilities of anti-submarine warfare, defending US Navy carrier groups in the GIUK gap.

In the North Atlantic, the United Kingdom became engaged in a protracted dispute with Iceland over fishing rights. The Royal Navy, supported by tugs from the MAFF and British civilian trawlers, was involved in three major confrontations with the Icelandic Coast Guard from 1958 to 1976. These largely bloodless incidents became known as the Cod Wars, and ended with the recognition by Britain of Iceland's exclusive 200 nautical miles fishery zone.

Chatham Naval Base was used for refitting nuclear submarines from 1963 but it closed in 1984.

Falklands War, 1982

The most important operation conducted predominantly by the Royal Navy after the Second World War was the defeat in 1982 of Argentina in the Falkland Islands War. Only four days after the invasion on 2 April, a Task Force sailed for the South Atlantic, with other warships and support ships following. On 25 April the navy retook South Georgia, crippling an Argentine submarine called the Santa Fé. Despite losing four naval ships and other civilian and RFA ships the Royal Navy proved it was still able to fight a battle 8,345 miles (12,800 km) from Great Britain. HMS *Conqueror* is the only nuclear-powered submarine to have engaged an enemy ship with torpedoes, sinking the Argentine cruiser ARA *General Belgrano*.

Operations after 1982

In the latter stages of the Cold War, the Royal Navy was reconfigured with three anti-submarine warfare (ASW) aircraft carriers and a force of frigates and destroyers. Its purpose was to search for and destroy Soviet submarines in the North Atlantic. There were also mine countermeasures and submarine forces as well as support ships. As the Cold War ended, the Royal Navy fought in the Gulf War against Iraq, with Sea Skua anti-ship missiles sinking a large proportion of the Iraqi Navy. The WRNS was amalgamated with the RN in 1993.

The Strategic Defence Review of 1998 and the follow-on Delivering Security in a Changing World White Paper of 2004 promised a somewhat brighter long-term future for the Navy, putting in place the largest naval procurement programme since the end of the Second World War in order to enhance and rebuild the fleet, with a view to bringing the Navy's capabilities into the 21st century, and restructuring the fleet from a North Atlantic-based, large Anti-Submarine force into a true blue water navy once more. Whilst several smaller vessels were to be withdrawn from service, it was confirmed that two new large aircraft carriers would be constructed.

Vessel class	SDR Requirement	2007 levels
Carriers	3 Invincible class or 2 CVF	3 Invincible class
Amphibious warfare	8	5 (inc RFA vessels)
Attack submarines	10	9
Destroyers and frigates	32	25
Mine warfare	22	16

The Navy took part in the 2003 Iraq War which saw RN warships bombard positions in support of the Al Faw Peninsula landings by Royal Marines.[140] Also during that war, HMS *Splendid* and *Turbulent* (S87) launched a number of Tomahawk cruise missiles at targets in Iraq.

In 2004, Iranian armed forces took Royal Navy personnel prisoner, including Royal Marines, on the Shatt al-Arab (Arvand Rud in Persian) river, between Iran and Iraq. They were released three days later following diplomatic discussions between the UK and Iran. In August 2005 the Royal Navy rescued seven Russians stranded in a submarine off the Kamchatka peninsula. Using its Scorpio 45, a remote-controlled mini-sub, the submarine was freed from the fishing nets and cables that had held the Russian submarine for three days.

In 2007, Iranian armed forces also took prisoner Royal Navy personnel, including Royal Marines, when a boarding party from HMS *Cornwall* was seized in the waters between Iran and Iraq, in the Persian Gulf. They were released thirteen days later. The Royal Navy was also involved in an incident involving Somali pirates in November 2008, after the pirates tried to capture a civilian vessel.

Trends in ship strength

In numeric terms the Royal Navy has significantly reduced in size since the 1960s, reflecting the reducing requirement of the state. This raw figure does not take into account the increase in technological capability of the Navy's ships, but it does show the general reduction of capacity. The following table is a breakdown of the fleet numbers since 1960. The separate types of ship and how their numbers have changed are shown.[141]

History of the Royal Navy

Year	Submarines				Carriers			Assault ships	Surface combatants				Mine counter-measure vessels	Patrol ships and craft	Total
	Total	SSBN	SSN	SS & SSK	Total	CV	CV(L)		Total	Cruisers	Destroyers	Frigates			
1960	48	0	0	48	9	6	3	0	145	6	55	84	?	?	202
1965	47	0	1	46	6	4	2	0	117	5	36	76	?	?	170
1970	42	4	3	35	5	3	2	2	97	4	19	74	?	?	146
1975	32	4	8	20	3	1	2	2	72	2	10	60	43	14	166
1980	32	4	11	17	3	0	3	2	67	1	13	53	36	22	162
1985	33	4	14	15	4	0	4	2	56	0	15	41	45	32	172
1990	31	4	17	10	3	0	3	2	49	0	14	35	41	34	160
1995	16	4	12	0	3	0	3	2	35	0	12	23	18	32	106
2000	16	4	12	0	3	0	3	3	32	0	11	21	21	23	98
2005	15	4	11	0	3	0	3	2	28	0	9	19	16	26	90
2010	12	4	8	0	3	0	3	3	24	0	7	17	16	23	78
2015	10	4	6	0	0	0	0	3	19	0	6	13	15	23	70

- One icebreaker patrol ship in service, counted under "patrol ships and craft".
- A third Astute class submarine HMS *Artful* has been launched, and will start sea trials in late 2015. The submarine will replace the recently decommissioned HMS *Tireless* of the Trafalgar class submarine.
- Current figures exclude the main 13 auxiliary support vessels currently used by the Royal Fleet Auxiliary that provide at sea replenishment, as sea maintenance if required, some patrol tasks acting as "mothership" and also form as a main logistics transport fleet, utilizing vessels such as the Bay-class landing ship and others.

English navy/Royal Navy timeline and battles

- 1213 Battle of Damme
- 1338 Battle of Arnemuiden
- 1340 Battle of Sluys
- 1350 Battle of Winchelsea
- 1372 Battle of La Rochelle
- 1512 Battle of Saint-Mathieu
- 1545 Battle of the Solent
- 1585–1604 Anglo–Spanish War (1585)
- 1625 Cádiz Expedition (1625)
- 1627–1629 Anglo-French War (1627–1629)
- 1652–1654 First Anglo–Dutch War
- 1654–1660 Anglo-Spanish War (1654)
- 1665–1667 Second Anglo-Dutch War
- 1672–1674 Third Anglo-Dutch War
- 1688–1697 Nine Years' War
- 1701–1713 War of the Spanish Succession
- 1718–1720 War of the Quadruple Alliance
- 1740–1748 War of the Austrian Succession
- 1754–1763 Seven Years' War
- 1778–1783 American War of Independence
- 1793–1802 French Revolutionary Wars
- 1803–1815 Napoleonic Wars
- 1812–1814 War of 1812
- 1821 First paddle steamer for auxiliary use
- 1827 Battle of Navarino is the last fleet action between wooden sailing ships.
- 1839–1842 Opium War
- 1840 First screw-driven warship, *Rattler*
- 1853–1856 Crimean War

- 1856–1860 Second Opium War
- 1860 First iron-hulled armoured battleship, *Warrior*
- 1902 First British submarine, HMS *Holland 1*
- 1905 First steam turbine-powered "all big-gun" battleship, *Dreadnought*
- 1914–1918 First World War
- 1918 First true aircraft carrier, HMS *Argus*
- 1918–1920 Russian Civil War
- 1931 Invergordon Mutiny
- 1939–1945 Battle of the Atlantic
- 1940 Norwegian Campaign
- 1940 Dunkirk evacuation
- 1940–1944 Battle of the Mediterranean
- 1941–1945 Arctic Convoys
- 1941–1945 South-East Asian Theatre
- 1944 Normandy Landings
- 1944–1945 British Pacific Fleet
- 1946 Corfu Channel Incident
- 1949 *Amethyst* incident on the Yangtze River
- 1950–1953 Korean War
- 1956 Suez Crisis
- 1958–1976 Cod Wars
- 1959 The last battleship, *Vanguard*, is decommissioned.
- 1962–1966 Indonesia–Malaysia confrontation
- 1963 First British nuclear submarine, *Dreadnought*
- 1966–1975 Beira Patrol against Rhodesia
- 1977 Operation Journeyman to guard the Falkland Islands
- 1980–2002 Armilla patrol in the Persian Gulf
- 1982 Falklands War
- 1991 First Gulf War
- 1999 Operation Allied Force – Kosovo conflict
- 2000 Operation Palliser – Sierra Leone
- 2001–2014 Operation Herrick – Afghanistan Campaign
- 2002–present Combined Maritime Forces in the Indian Ocean
- 2003–2009 Operation Telic – Invasion of Iraq
- 2011 Operation Ellamy – Libyan Civil War
- 2014–present Operation Shader – Military intervention against the Islamic State of Iraq and the Levant

Sources

- Ballantyne, Iain (2004). *Strike From the Sea*. US Naval Institute Press. ISBN 978-1591148449.
- Barrow, Geoffrey Wallis Steuart (2005). *Robert Bruce and the Community of the Realm of Scotland*. Edinburgh: Edinburgh University Press. ISBN 0-7486-2022-2.
- Brooks, David (2000). *Gladstone Centenary Essays: Gladstone's Fourth Administration, 1892–1894, David Bebbington and Roger Swift (eds.)*. Liverpool University Press. ISBN 978-0853239352.
- Coward, Barry (2002). *The Cromwellian Protectorate*. Manchester University Press. ISBN 978-0-7190-4317-8.
- Day, Lance; McNeil, Ian (2013). *Biographical Dictionary of the History of Technology*[142]. Routledge. ISBN 0-203-02829-5.
- Durston, Gregory (2017). *The Admiralty Sessions, 1536-1834: Maritime Crime and the Silver Oar*[143]. Cambridge Scholars Publishing. ISBN 9781443873611.
- Fissel, Mark Charles (1991). *War and government in Britain, 1598-1650*[144]. Manchester University Press. ISBN 0-7190-2887-6.
- Gardiner, Robert; Gray, Randal; Budzbon, Przemyslaw (1984). *Conway's All the World's Fighting Ships: 1906–1922*. Annapolis: Naval Institute Press. ISBN 0-87021-907-3.
- Gardiner, Robert (2004). *The Line of Battle: The Sailing Warship 1650-1840*. Conway Maritime Press. ISBN 978-0851779546.
- Grantham, John (2012). *Iron, as a material for ship-building; being a communication to the Polytechnic society of Liverpool*. Rare Books. ISBN 978-1130800548.
- Harbottle, Thomas Benfield; Bruce, George (1979). *Harbottle's Dictionary of Battles* (second ed.). Granada. ISBN 0-246-11103-8.
- Heathcote, Tony (2002). *The British Admirals of the Fleet 1734 – 1995*. Pen & Sword Ltd. ISBN 0-85052-835-6.
- Herwig, Holger H. (1980). *Luxury Fleet, The Imperial German Navy 1888–1918*. London: The Ashfield Press. ISBN 0-948660-03-1.
- Kennedy, Paul (1989). *The Rise and Fall of Great Powers*. London: Fontana. ISBN 978-0049090194.
- Lyon, David (1996). *The First Destroyers*. Chatham Publishing. ISBN 1-55750-271-4.
- Marley, David (1998). *Wars of the Americas, a Chronology of Armed Conflict in the New World, 1492 to the Present*. ABC-CLIO. ISBN 9780874368376.
- Marriott, Leo (2005). *Treaty Cruisers: The first international warship building competition*. Pen & Sword Maritime, Barnsley. ISBN 1-84415-

188-3.
- Massie, Robert (1992). *Dreadnought*. Ballantine Books. ISBN 0-345-37556-4.
- Ollard, Richard Lawrence (1984). *Pepys: A biography*. Atheneum. ISBN 978-0689706790.
- Pemsel, Helmut (1977). *Atlas of Naval Warfare*. Arms and Armour Press. ISBN 978-0853683513.
- Reid, Stuart (2002). *Culloden Moor 1746: The Death of the Jacobite Cause*. Campaign series. **106**. Osprey Publishing. ISBN 1-84176-412-4.
- Rodger, Nicholas (2004). *The Command of the Ocean: A Naval History of Britain, 1649–1815*. Allen Lane. p. 1000. ISBN 978-0141026909.
- Royle, Charles (1900). *The Egyptian Campaigns (1882–1885)*[145]. London: Hurst and Blackett.
- Savage, Anne (1996). *Anglo-Saxon Chronicles*. Tiger Books. ISBN 978-1855016866.
- Sondhaus, Lawrence (2001). *Naval Warfare, 1815-1914*. New York: Routledge. ISBN 978-0415214780.
- Swanton, Michael (2000). *Anglo-Saxon Chronicles*. Phoenix Press. ISBN 1-842120034.
- Wagner, John (2006). *Encyclopedia of the Hundred Years War*. Greenwood Publishing Group. ISBN 978-0-313-32736-0.
- Wills, Rebecca (2002). *The Jacobites and Russia, 1715-1750*. Dundurn. ISBN 1862321426.
- Winfield, Rif (2009). *British Warships in the Age of Sail 1603-1714: Design, Construction, Careers and Fates*. Seaforth. ISBN 978-1848320406.

Further reading

- Ashworth, William J. (2014). *Expertise and authority in the Royal Navy, 1800–1945*. Journal for Maritime Research. pp. 103–116.
- Bell, Christopher M. (2012). *Churchill and Sea Power*. Oxford University Press. ISBN 978-0199693573.
- Davey, James (2016). *In Nelson's Wake: The Navy and the Napoleonic Wars*. Yale University Press. ISBN 978-0300200652.
- Farquharson-Roberts, Mike (2014). *A History of the Royal Navy: World War I*. B Tauris. ISBN 978-1780768380.
- Friel, Ian (2003). *The British Museum Maritime History of Britain and Ireland: C.400 – 2001*. British Museum Press. ISBN 978-0-7141-2718-7.
- Grimes, Shawn T. (2012). *Strategy and War Planning in the British Navy*. Boydell. ISBN 978-1843836988.

- Hamilton, Charles I. (2011). *The making of the modern Admiralty: British naval policy-making, 1805–1927*. Cambridge University Press. ISBN 9780521765183.
- Herman, Artur (2004). *To Rule the Waves: How the British Navy Shaped the Modern World*. Harper Perennial. ISBN 978-0060534257.
- Hill, J.R. (1995). *The Oxford Illustrated History of the Royal Navy*. Oxford University Press. ISBN 978-0198605270.
- Kennedy, Paul (1976). *The Rise and Fall of British Naval Mastery*. Scribner's. ISBN 978-0141011554.
- Loades, David (2009). *The Making of the Elizabethan Navy 1540–1590: From the Solent to the Armada*. Boydell and Brewer. ISBN 978-1843834922.
- Marder, Arthur (1961). *From the Dreadnought to Scapa Flow: the Royal Navy in the Fisher era, 1904-1919*. Oxford University Press. ISBN 978-0192151223.
- Lavery, Brian (2012). *Nelson's Navy: The Ships, Men and Organisation, 1793-1815*. Naval Institute Press. ISBN 978-1591146124.
- Lavery, Brian (2009). *Empire of the Seas*. Conway Publishing. ISBN 978-1844861323.
- Rodger, Nicholas (1997). *The Safeguard of the Sea: A Naval History of Britain 660–1649*. **1**. HarperCollins. ISBN 978-0140297249.
- Parkinson, Roger (2008). *The Late Victorian Navy: The Pre-Dreadnought Era and the Origins of the First World War*. Boydell Press. ISBN 978-1843833727.
- Preston, Anthony (1985). *History of the Royal Navy*. W.H.Smith. ISBN 978-0-86124-121-7.
- Redford, Duncan; Grove, Philip D. (2014). *The Royal Navy: A History since 1900*. London, I. B. Tauris. ISBN 978-1780767826.
- Redford, Duncan (2014). *A History of the Royal Navy: World War II*. London, I. B. Tauris. ISBN 978-1780765464.
- Robson, Martin (2014). *A History of the Royal Navy: The Napoleonic Wars*. I. B. Tauris. ISBN 978-1780765440.
- Willis, Sam (2013). *In the Hour of Victory: The Royal Navy at War in the Age of Nelson*. Atlantic Books. ISBN 978-0857895707.
- Wilson, Ben (2013). *Empire of the Deep: The Rise and Fall of the British Navy*. W&N. ISBN 978-0297864080.

Historiography

- Harding, Richard. *Review of History of the Royal Navy"*, Reviews in History[146]. doi: 10.14296/RiH/2014/1706[147].
- Higham, John (2015). *A Guide to the Sources of British Military History*[148]. Routledge.

- Rasor, Eugene L. (2004). *English/British Naval History to 1815: A Guide to the Literature*. Westport, Connecticut: Praeger. ISBN 978-0313305474.
- Rasor, Eugene L. (1990). *British Naval History after 1815: A Guide to the Literature*. New York: Garland.
- Seligmann, Matthew S. (2013). *The Renaissance of Pre-First World War Naval History*. Journal of Strategic Studies. pp. 454–479.

External links

- Royal Navy History[149], extensive source for Royal Navy History with photos and documents.
- Royal Navy - Royal Navy History[150]
- A Naval History of Great Britain[151]
- Download service records of officers who joined the Royal Navy between 1756–1917 from The National Archives[152]
- Download wills made by seamen of the Royal Navy between 1786- 1882 from The National Archives.[153]
- The service registers of Royal Naval Seamen 1873 – 1923[154]
- Royal Navy in World War 1, Campaigns, Battles, Warship losses[155]
- Naval-History.Net[156], Naval History of the 20th Century, World Wars 1, 2, post-war and Falklands War – navies, ships, ship losses, casualties
- American Vessels captured by the British During the American Revolution and the War of 1812[157]

History of the British Army

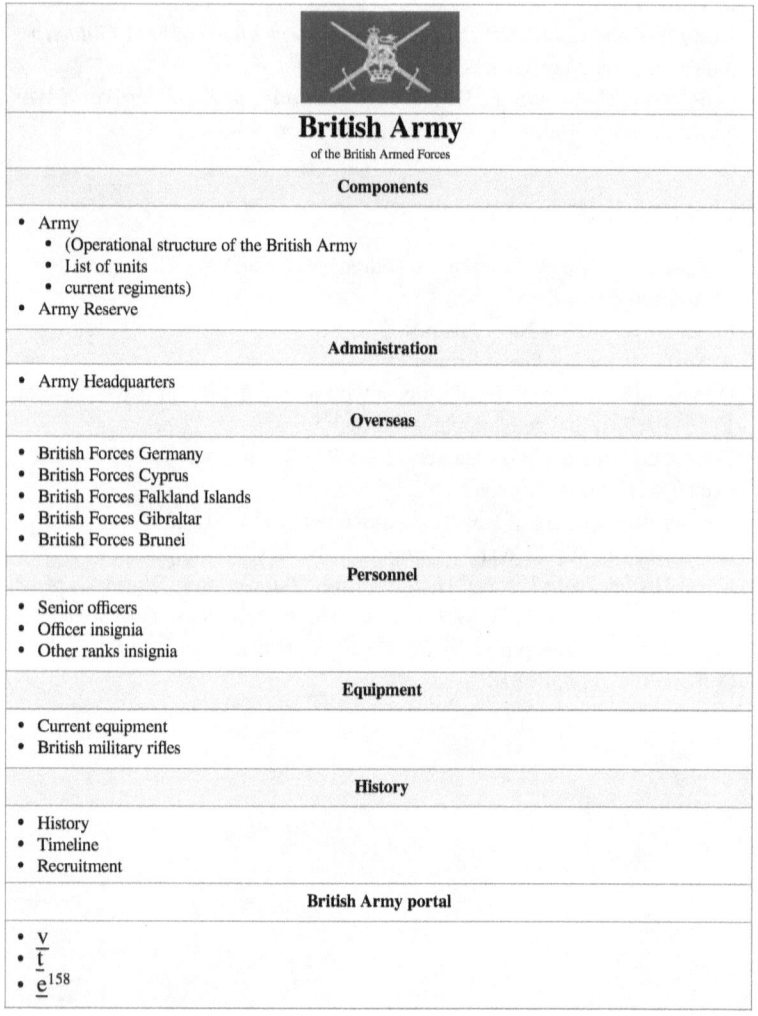

The **history of the British Army** spans over three and a half centuries since its founding in 1660 and involves numerous European wars, colonial wars and world wars. From the late 17th century until the mid-20th century, the United Kingdom was the greatest economic and imperial power in the world, and although this dominance was principally achieved through the strength of the Royal Navy (RN), the British Army played a significant role.

As of 2015[159], there were 92,000 professionals in the regular army (including 2,700 Gurkhas) and 20,480 Volunteer Reserves. Britain has generally maintained only a small regular army during peacetime, expanding this as required in time of war, due to Britain's traditional role as a sea power. Since the suppression of Jacobitism in 1745, the British Army has played little role in British domestic politics (except for the Curragh incident), and, apart from Ireland, has seldom been deployed against internal threats to authority (one notorious exception being the Peterloo Massacre).

The British Army has been involved in many international conflicts, including the Napoleonic Wars, the Crimean War and both World War I and World War II. Historically, it contributed to the expansion and retention of the British Empire.

The British Army has long been at the forefront of new military developments. It was the first in the world to develop and deploy the tank, and what is now the Royal Air Force (RAF) had its origins within the British Army as the Royal Flying Corps (RFC). At the same time the British Army emphasises the continuity and longevity of several of its institutions and military tradition.

Origins

The English Army was first established as a standing military force in 1660.[160] In 1707 many regiments of the English and Scottish armies were already combined under one operational command and stationed in the Netherlands fighting in the War of Spanish Succession. Consequently, although the regiments were now part of the new British military establishment, they remained under the same operational command, and so not only were the regiments of the old armies transferred *in situ* to the new army so too was the institutional ethos, customs, and traditions, of the old standing armies that had been created shortly after the restoration of the monarchy 47 years earlier.

Stuart Asquith argues for roots before 1660:[161]

> Many authorities quote the Restoration of 1660 as the birth date of our modern British Army. While this may be true as far as continuity of unit identity is concerned, it is untrue in a far more fundamental sense. The evidence of history shows that the creation of an efficient military machine [, The New Model Army,] and its proving on the battlefield, predates the Restoration by 15 years. It was on the fields of Naseby, Dunbar and Dunes that the foundations of the British professional army were laid.

The New Model Army was the first full-time professional army raised within the three kingdoms of England, Ireland and Scotland.[162] It was created in 1645 by the English Long Parliament and it proved supreme in field. At the end of

Figure 16: *Oliver Cromwell (1656) by Samuel Cooper.*

the First Civil War the New Model Army survived attempts by Parliament to disband it. Winston Churchill described its prowess thus:[163]

> *The Story of the Second English Civil War is short and simple. King, Lords and Commons, landlords, merchants, the City and the countryside, bishops and presbyters, the Scottish army, the Welsh people, and the English Fleet, all now turned against the New Model Army. The Army beat the lot!*

Having survived Parliament's attempts to disband it, the New Model Army prospered as an institution during the Interregnum. It was disbanded in 1660 with the restoration of the monarchy under Charles II.

At his restoration Charles II sought to create a small standing army made up of some former Royalist and New Model Army regiments. On 26 January 1661, Charles II issued the Royal Warrant that created the first regiments of what would become the *British Army*,[164] although Scotland and England maintained separate military establishments until the Acts of Union 1707.[165]

King Charles put into these regiments those cavaliers who had attached themselves to him during his exile on the European continent and had fought for him at the Battle of the Dunes against the Roundheads of the Protectorate and their French allies. For political expediency he also included some elements of the New Model Army. The whole force consisted of two corps of horse and five or

Figure 17: *Charles II (c. 1680–1685) by John Riley.*

six of infantry. It is, however, on this narrow and solid basis that the structure of the English army was gradually erected. The horse consisted of two regiments the Life Guards (formed from exiled cavaliers) ; and The Blues (or The Oxford Blues), formed by Lord Oxford, out of some of the best New Model Army horse regiments. The foot regiments were Grenadier Guards (initially two regiments Lord Wentworth's Regiment and John Russell's Regiment of Guards which amalgamated in 1665), the Coldstream Guards (the New Model Army regiment of General Monck), the Royal Scots (formed from the Scotch guard in France), and the Second Queen's Royals.[166]

Many of Charles' subjects were uneasy at his creation of this small army. Pamphleteers wrote tracts voicing the fear of a people who within living memory had experienced the Rule of the Major-Generals and had liked neither the imposition of military rule, or the costs of keeping an army in being when the country was not at war with itself or others. People also remembered the "Eleven Years' Tyranny" of Charles I and feared that a standing army under royal command would allow monarchs in the future to ignore the wishes of Parliament.[167]

The English were not fully reconciled to the need for a standing army until the reign of William III when the near perpetual wars with other European states made a modest standing army a necessity to defend England and to maintain

Figure 18: *An English grenadier with a captured French colour at the Battle of Blenheim.*

her prestige in the world. But public opinion, always anxious of the bad old days, was resolved to allow itself no rest until it had defined the prerogatives of the crown on this delicate point. Parliament finally succeeded in acquiring a control over the army, and under a general bill, commonly called the Mutiny Act, laid down the restrictions which, whilst respecting the rights of the sovereign, were likewise to shield the liberty of the people. It did this by making the standing army conditional on an annually renewed act of parliament.[168] To this day, annual continuation notices are required for the British Army to remain legal. On paper, this also guarantees representative government, as Parliament must meet at least once a year to ratify the Order in Council renewing the Army Act (1955) for a further year.[169] As another measure to avoid a dangerous concentration of power in the hands of any one person, responsibility for the various branches of the army and its administration were deliberately assigned to different high officials.

Creation of British Army

The order of seniority for the most senior line regiments in the British Army is based on the order of seniority in the English army. Scottish and Irish regiments were only allowed to take a rank in the English army from the date of their arrival in England or the date when they were first placed on the English establishment. For example, in 1694 a board of general officers was convened to decide upon rank of English, Irish and Scots regiments serving in the Netherlands, the regiment that became known as the Scots Greys were designated as the 4th dragoons because there were three English regiments raised prior to 1688 when the Scot Greys were first placed on the English establishment. In 1713 when a new board of general officers was convened to decide upon rank of several regiments, the seniority of the Scots Greys was reassessed and based on their entry into England in June 1685. At that time there was only one English regiment of dragoons and so after some delay the Scots Greys obtained the rank of 2nd dragoons in the British Army.[170]

Eighteenth century

Organisation

By the middle of the century, the army's administration had developed the form which it would retain for more than a hundred years. Ultimately, the main bodies responsible for the army were:

- The War Office was responsible for day-to-day administration of the army, and for the cavalry and infantry;[171]
- The Board of Ordnance was responsible for the supply of weapons and ammunition, and administered the Royal Artillery and Royal Engineers;[172]
- The Commissariat was responsible for the supply of rations and transport. It occasionally raised its own fighting units, such as "battoemen" (armed watermen and pioneers in North America).[173]

None of these bodies were usually represented in the Cabinet, nor were they responsible for overall strategy, which was in the hands of the Secretary of State for War (an office later merged into the Secretary of State for War and the Colonies). The resulting tangled lines of control often greatly hampered efficient operation through and beyond the Napoleonic Wars.

In the field, a commander's staff consisted of an Adjutant General (who handled finance, troop returns and legal matters), and a Quartermaster General (who was responsible for billeting and organising movements).[174] There were separate commanders of the Artillery, and Commissary Officers who handled the supplies. The commander of an Army might also have a Military Secretary, responsible for appointments, courts martial and official correspondence. In the field as in peacetime, the conflicting lines of responsibility often caused problems.

Figure 19: *The Battle of Ramillies, the 16th Foot charging the French infantry.*

Infantry and cavalry units had originally been known by the names of their colonels, such as "Sir John Mordaunt's Regiment of Foot". This could be confusing if Colonels succeeded each other rapidly; and two regiments (the Buffs and the Green Howards) had to be distinguished by their facing colour in official correspondence because for several years, both had Colonels named Howard. In time, these became the official names of the regiments. In 1751 a numeral system was adopted,[175] with each regiment gaining a number according to their rank in the order of precedence, so John Mordaunt's Regiment became the 47th Regiment of Foot.[176]

The later Jacobite risings were centred in the Scottish Highlands. From the late 17th century, the Government had organised Independent Highland Companies in the area, from clans which supported the Hanoverian monarchs or the Whig governments, to maintain order or influence in the Highlands. In 1739 the first full regiment, the 42nd Regiment of Foot, was formed in the region.[177] More were subsequently raised. For many years, highland regiments were to be the most colourful and distinctive units in the British Army, retaining much of the traditional highland dress such as the kilt.

Towards the end of the 18th century, the battalion became the major tactical unit of the army. On the continent of Europe, where large field formations were usual, a regiment was a formation of two or more battalions, under a colonel who was a field commander. The British Army, increasingly compelled to disperse units in far-flung colonial outposts, made the battalion the basic unit, under a lieutenant colonel. The function of the Regiment became administrative rather than tactical. The Colonel of a regiment remained an influential figure but rarely commanded any of its battalions in the field. Many regiments consisted of one battalion only, plus a depot and recruiting parties in Britain or Ireland if the unit was serving overseas. Where more troops were required for a war or garrison duties, second, third and even subsequent battalions of a regiment were raised, but it was rare for more than one battalion of a regiment to serve in the same brigade or division.[178]

Strategy and role

From the late 17th century onwards, the British army was to be deployed in three main areas of conflict (America, Europe and Scotland), one of which (Scotland) was effectively ended at the Battle of Culloden in 1746.[179] The major theatre was often the continent of Europe. Not only did Britain's monarchs have dynastic ties with Holland or Hanover, but Britain's foreign policy often required intervention to maintain a balance of power in Europe (usually at the expense of France).

Within England and especially Scotland, there were repeated attempts by the deposed House of Stewart to regain the throne, leading to severe uprisings. These were often related to European conflict, as the Stuart Pretenders were aided and encouraged by Britain's continental enemies for their own ends. After the Battle of Culloden in 1746, these rebellions were crushed.

Finally, as the British empire expanded, the army was increasingly involved in service in the West Indies, North America and India.[180] Troops were often recruited locally, to lessen the burden on the Army. Sometimes these were part of the British army, for example the 60th (Royal American) Regiment of Foot.[181] On other occasions (as in the case of troops raised by the British East India Company), the local forces were administered separately from the British Army, but cooperated with it.

Troops sent to serve overseas could expect to serve there for years, in an unhealthy climate far removed from the comforts of British society. This led to the army being recruited from the elements of society with the least stake in it; the very poorest or worst-behaved. The red-coated soldier, "Thomas Lobster", was a much-derided figure.[182]

Seven Years' War

The Seven Years' War, which took place from 1755 to 1763, has sometimes been described as the first true world war, in that conflict took place in almost every continent and on almost all the oceans. Although there were early setbacks, British troops eventually were victorious in every theatre.[183]

Figure 20: *The death of General Wolfe after the Battle of the Plains of Abraham, in which Britain defeated the French to take Canada*

Britain's main enemy was France, as was usual. The war can be said to have started in North America, where it was known as the French and Indian War. The early years saw several British defeats.[184] The British units first despatched to the Continent were untrained in the bush warfare they met. To provide light infantry, several corps such as Rogers' Rangers were raised from the colonists. (A light infantry regiment, the 80th Regiment of Light-Armed Foot, was raised by Colonel Thomas Gage, but subsequently disbanded). During the war, General James Wolfe amalgamated companies from several regiments into an ad hoc unit, the Louisbourg Grenadiers.[185]

There were also disagreements between high-ranking British officers and the North American colonists. It was laid down that even the most senior Provincial officers were subordinate to comparatively junior officers in the British Army. The first concern of the colonists' representatives was the protection of the settlers from raids by Indian war parties, while the British generals often had different strategic priorities. Partly through the naval superiority gained by the Royal Navy, Britain was eventually able to deploy superior strength in North America, winning a decisive battle at Quebec.[186]

Similarly, in India, the French armies and those of the most powerful Indian rulers were defeated after a prolonged struggle, allowing the steady expansion of British-controlled territory.[187]

In Europe, although Britain's allies (chiefly Prussia) carried the main burden of the struggle, British troops eventually played an important role at the decisive Battle of Minden.

Aftermath

The result of this war was to leave Britain as the dominant imperial power in North America, and the only European power east of the Mississippi (although it would return southern Florida to Spain). There was increasing tension between the British government and the American colonists, especially when it was decided to maintain a standing army in North America after the war. For the first time, the British Army would be garrisoned in North America in significant numbers in a time of peace.[188]

With the defeat of France, the British government no longer sought actively to curry the favour of Native Americans. Urged by his superiors to cut costs, Commander in Chief General Jeffery Amherst initiated policy changes that helped prompt Pontiac's War in 1763, an uprising against the British military occupation of the former New France.[189] Amherst was recalled during the war and replaced as commander in chief by Thomas Gage.[190]

American War of Independence

For the British Army, the American War of Independence had its origins in the military occupation of Boston in 1768. Tensions between the army and local civilians helped contribute to the Boston Massacre of 1770, but outright warfare did not begin until 1775, when an army detachment was sent to seize colonial munitions at Lexington and Concord.

Reinforcements were sent to America to put down what was initially expected to be a short-lived rebellion. Because the British army was understrength at the outset of the war, the British government hired the armed forces of several German states, referred to generically as "Hessians", to fight in North America. As the war dragged on, the ministry also sought to recruit Loyalist soldiers. Five American units (known as the *American Establishment*, formed in 1779) were placed on the regular army roster, though there were many other Loyalist units.[191]

When the war ended in 1783 with defeat and the independence of the United States, many of the Loyalists fled north to Canada, where many subsequently served with the British Army. The Army itself had established many British units during the war to serve in North America or provide replacements for garrisons. All but three (the 23rd Regiment of (Light) Dragoons and two Highland infantry regiments, the 71st and 78th Foot) were disbanded immediately after the war.[192]

The Army was forced to adapt its tactics to the poor communications and forested terrain of North America. Large numbers of light infantry (detached from line units) were organised, and the formerly rigid drills of the line infantry were modified to a style known as "loose files and an American scramble". While the British defeated the colonists in most of the set-piece battles of the war, none of these had any decisive result, whereas the British defeats at the Battle of Saratoga and Siege of Yorktown adversely affected British morale, prestige and manpower.[193]

Napoleonic Wars

The British Army during the Napoleonic Wars experienced a time of rapid change. At the beginning of the French Revolutionary Wars in 1793, the army was a small, awkwardly administered force of barely 40,000 men.[194] By the end of the period, the army had been through a series of structural, recruitment, tactical and training reforms and its manpower had vastly increased. At its peak, in 1813, the regular army contained over 250,000 men.[195] The British infantry was "the only military force not to suffer a major reverse at the hands of Napoleonic France."[196]

The later nineteenth century

During the long reign of Queen Victoria, British society underwent great changes such as industrialisation and the enactment of liberal reforms within Britain. The period was also marked by the steady expansion and consolidation of the British Empire. The role of the military was to defend the Empire and, for the Army, to control the natives.[197]

The Crimean War (1854–56) had so many blunders and failures—most famously the ill-advised "Charge of the Light Brigade"—that it became an iconic symbol of logistical, medical and tactical failures and mismanagement. Public opinion in Britain was outraged at the failures of traditional methods in the face of modernization everywhere else in British society; the newspapers demanded drastic reforms, and parliamentary investigations exposed a multiplicity of grave problems. However, the reform campaign was not well organized. This allowed the traditional aristocratic leadership of the Army to pull itself together and block all serious reforms. No one was punished. The outbreak of the Indian Rebellion of 1857 shifted attention to the heroic defense of British interests by the Army, and further talk of reform went nowhere.[198] The demand for professionalization was, however, achieved by Florence Nightingale, who gained worldwide attention for pioneering and publicizing modern nursing while treating the wounded.[199]

Figure 21: *The bad conditions of the sick and injured in the Crimean War were widely publicized*

These two wars demonstrated that reforms were urgently needed to guarantee that the Army could protect both the home nation and the Empire. Nevertheless, reform did not take place until much later when Liberal governments enacted wide-ranging reforms (the Cardwell Reforms and Childers Reforms) from 1870 to 1881. These gave the army the form it would take at the outbreak of the First World War.

The Industrial Revolution had changed the Army's weapons, transport and equipment, and social changes such as better education had prompted changes to the terms of service and outlook of many soldiers. Nevertheless, it retained many features inherited from the Duke of Wellington's army, and since its prime function was to maintain the expanding British Empire, it differed in many ways from the conscripted armies of continental Europe. For example, it did not undertake large-scale manoeuvres. Indeed, the Chobham Manoeuvres of 1853 involving 7,000 troops were the first such manoeuvres since the Napoleonic Wars.[200]

First World War (1914–18)

The British Army during World War I could trace its origins to the increasing demands of imperial expansion together with inefficiencies highlighted during the Crimean War, which led to the Cardwell and Childers Reforms of the late 19th century. These gave the British Army its modern shape, and defined its regimental system. The Esher Report in 1904, recommended radical reform of the British Army, such as the creation of an Army Council, a General Staff and the abolition of the office of Commander in Chief of the Forces and the creation of a Chief of the General Staff.[201] The Haldane Reforms in 1907, created an expeditionary force of seven divisions, it also reorganized the volunteers into a new Territorial Force of fourteen cavalry brigades and fourteen infantry divisions, and changed the old militia into the special reserve to reinforce the expeditionary force.[202]

The British Army was different from the French and German Armies at the beginning of the conflict in that it was made up from volunteers not conscripts.[203] It was also considerably smaller than its French and German counterparts.[204] The outbreak of the First World War in August 1914 saw the bulk of the changes in the Haldane reforms put to the test. The British Expeditionary Force (BEF) of six divisions was quickly sent to the Continent, while the Territorial Forces fourteen divisions and Reserves were mobilised as planned to provide a second line.[205]

During the war there were three distinct British Armies. The 'first' army was the small volunteer force of about 400,000 soldiers (comprising the Regular Army of 247,000[206] and Territorial Force of 145,000), over half of which were posted overseas to garrison the British Empire. This total included the Regular Army and reservists in the Territorial Force. Together they formed the BEF, for service in France and became known as the Old Contemptibles. The 'second' army was Kitchener's Army, formed from the volunteers in 1914–1915, which was destined to go into action at the Battle of the Somme.[207] The 'third' was formed after the introduction of conscription in January 1916 and by the end of 1918 the British Army had reached its peak of strength of four million men and could field over seventy divisions.

The war also saw the introduction of new weapons and equipment. The Maxim machine gun was replaced by the improved and lighter Vickers and Lewis machine guns, the Brodie helmet was supplied for better personnel protection against shrapnel and the Mark I tank was invented to try to end the stalemate of trench warfare.[208]

The vast majority of the British Army fought in France and Belgium on the Western Front but some units were engaged in the Mediterranean, the Middle East, Africa and Mesopotamia, mainly against the Ottoman Empire. One battalion also fought in China during the Siege of Tsingtao.[209]

Figure 22: *Image taken during the Battle of Broodseinde, showing a group of British soldiers of the 8th (Service) Battalion, East Yorkshire Regiment, part of the 62nd Brigade of the 21st Division, moving up to the front, silhouetted against the skyline. Photo taken by Ernest Brooks.*

Inter-war period (1919–1939)

Organisation

In the immediate aftermath of the First World War, Britain faced serious economic woes. Heavy defence cuts were consequently imposed by the British Government in the early 1920s as part of a reduction in public expenditure known as the "Geddes Axe" after Sir Eric Geddes.[210] The Government introduced the Ten Year Rule, stating its belief that Britain would not be involved in another major war for 10 years from the date of review. This ten-year rule was continually extended until it was abandoned in 1932. The Royal Tank Corps (which later became the Royal Tank Regiment) was the only corps formed in World War I that survived the cuts. Corps such as the Machine Gun Corps were disbanded, their functions being taken by specialists within infantry units.[211] One new corps was the Royal Signals, formed in 1920 from within the Royal Engineers to take over the role of providing communications.[212]

Within the cavalry, sixteen regiments were amalgamated into eight, producing the "Fraction Cavalry"; units with unwieldy titles combining two regimental numbers. There was a substantial reduction in the number of infantry battalions and the size of the Territorial Force, which was renamed the Territorial Army. On 31 July 1922, the Army also lost six Irish regiments (5 infantry and 1 cavalry) on the creation of the Irish Free State.[213] Many Irishmen from the south nevertheless continued to join the British Army.

Until the early 1930s, the Army was effectively reduced to the role of imperial policeman, concentrated on responding to the small imperial conflicts that rose up across the Empire. It was unfortunate that certain of the officers who rose to high rank and positions of influence within the army during the 1930s were comparatively backward-looking.[214] This meant that trials such as the Experimental Mechanized Force of 1927–28 did not go as far as they might have.[215]

Operations

One of the first post-war campaigns that the Army took part in was the Allied intervention in Russia in 1919 to assist the "White Army" against the Communist Bolsheviks during their Civil War.[216] The British Army was also maintaining occupation forces in the defeated powers of World War I. In Germany, a British Army of the Rhine (BAOR) was established.[217] The BAOR would remain in existence until 1929 when British forces were withdrawn.[218] Another British occupation force was based in Constantinople in Turkey, and a number of British units fought against Turkish rebels during the Turkish War of Independence. A small British Military Mission was also advising the Polish Army during the Polish–Soviet War (1919–1921).[219]

The Army, throughout the inter-war period, also had to deal with quelling paramilitary organisations seeking the removal of the British. In British Somaliland, Sayyid Mohammed Abdullah Hassan (known to the British Army as 'The Mad Mullah', although he was neither mad nor a mullah) resumed his campaign against the British, a campaign he had first begun in 1900.[220] The operations against him were prominent due to the newly formed RAF being instrumental in his defeat. The Army also took part in operations in Ireland against the IRA during the Anglo-Irish War. Both sides committed atrocities, some units becoming infamous, such as the paramilitary Black and Tans where many recruits were veterans of the First World War.[221] The British Army was also supporting Indian Army operations in the North-West Frontier of British India against numerous tribes, known collectively as the Pathans, hostile to the British. The Army had been operating in the volatile North-West Frontier area since the mid-19th century. The last major uprising that the Army had to deal with before the start of the Second World War, was the uprising in Palestine that began in 1936.[222]

Rearmament and development

By the mid-1930s, Germany was controlled by Hitler's Nazi Party and was becoming increasingly aggressive and expansionist. Another war with Germany appeared certain. The Army was not properly prepared for such a war, lagging behind the technologically advanced and potentially much larger Heer of the German Wehrmacht. With each armed service vying for a share of the defence budget, the Army came last behind the Royal Navy and Royal Air Force in allocation of funds.[223]

During the years after the First World War, the Army's strategic concepts had stagnated. Whereas Germany, when it began rearming following Hitler's rise to power, eagerly embraced concepts of mechanised warfare as advocated by individuals such as Heinz Guderian, many high-ranking officers in Britain had little enthusiasm for armoured warfare, and the ideas of Basil Liddell Hart and J. F. C. Fuller were largely ignored.[224]

One step to which the Army was committed was the mechanisation of the cavalry, which had begun in 1929. This first proceeded at a slow pace, having little priority. By the mid-1930s, mechanisation in the British Army was gaining momentum and on 4 April 1939, with the mechanisation process nearing completion, the Royal Armoured Corps was formed to administer the cavalry regiments and Royal Tank Regiment (except for the Household Cavalry). The mechanisation process was finally completed in 1941 when the Royal Scots Greys abandoned their horses.[225]

After the Munich Crisis in 1938, a serious effort was undertaken to expand the Army, including the doubling in size of the Territorial Army, helped by the reintroduction of conscription in April 1939.[226] By mid-1939 the Army consisted of 230,000 Regulars and 453,000 Territorials and Reservists.[227] Most Territorial formations were understrength and badly equipped. Even this army was dwarfed, yet again, by its continental counterparts. Just before the war broke out, a new British Expeditionary Force was formed.[228] By the end of the year, over 1 million had been conscripted into the Army. Conscription was administered on a better planned basis than in the First World War. People in certain reserved occupations, such as dockers and miners, were exempt from being called up as their skills and labour were necessary for the war effort.[229]

Between 1938 and 1939, following a substantial expansion in the Army, a number of new organisations were formed, including the Auxiliary Territorial Service for women in September 1938; its duties were vast, and helped release men for front-line service.

Figure 23: *25 pounders firing in support of the Guards Armoured Division during Operation Market Garden, September 1944.*

Second World War (1939–45)

The British Army in 1939 was a volunteer army that introduced conscription shortly before the declaration of war with Germany. During the early years of the Second World War, the army suffered defeat in almost every theatre it deployed, due to a variety of reasons, mainly because of decisions made before the war and politicians and senior commanders being unclear on what the army's role was. With mass conscription the expansion of the army was reflected in the creation of more divisions, army corps, armies and army groups. From 1943, the British Army's fortunes turned and it hardly suffered a strategic defeat.[230]

The pre-war British Army was trained and equipped to garrison and police the British Empire and, as became evident during the war, was woefully unprepared and ill-equipped to conduct a war against multiple enemies on multiple fronts. At the start of the war the army was small in comparison to its enemies', and remained an all-volunteer force until 1939. By the end of the war the British Army had grown to number over 3.5 million.[231]

The British Army fought around the world, with campaigns in Norway, Belgium and France in 1940 and, after the collapse of both the latter countries, in Africa, the Mediterranean and Middle East and the Far East. After a series of

Figure 24: *The flag of the UN*

setbacks, retreats and evacuations the British Army and its Allies eventually gained the upper hand. This started with victory over the Italian and German forces in the Tunisia Campaign.[232] Italy was then forced to surrender after the invasion of Sicily and mainland Italy.[233] Then in the last years of the war, the British Army, with its allies, returned to France, driving the German Army back into Germany and in the Far East forced the Japanese back from the Indian border into Burma.[234] Both the Germans and Japanese were defeated by 1945, and surrendered within months of each other.[235]

With the expansion of the British Army to fight a world war, new armies had to be formed, and eventually army groups were created to control even larger formations. In command of these new armies, eight men would be promoted to the rank of field marshal. The army commanders not only had to manage the new armies, but also a new type of soldier in formations that had been created for special service, which included the Special Air Service, Army Commandos and the Parachute Regiment.[236]

End of the Empire and Cold War (1945–1990)

Organisation

The United Nations (UN) was formed on 24 October 1945, with Britain one of five permanent members of the UN Security Council.[237] The British Empire at the time was considered a global power, despite its military having been surpassed by the two new superpowers—the USA and Soviet Union. Another global organisation, known as the North Atlantic Treaty Organisation (NATO), was established on 4 April 1949 with Britain one of its founding members.[238] The creation of NATO signified the beginning of the "Cold War" between the ideologically divided "Western Allies" and the Eastern Communist powers, controlled by the Soviet Union; they created their own NATO equivalent in 1955, known as the Warsaw Pact.[239] An integral part of NATO's defences in the now divided Europe was the British Army of the Rhine (BAOR) in West Germany, the British Army's new overseas 'home' that replaced independent India. The British Army, just as in the aftermath of World War I, had established BAOR in the immediate aftermath of the war which was centred on I Corps (upon its re-establishment in 1951),[240] at its peak reaching about 80,000 troops. At home, there were five regional commands: Eastern, Western, Northern, Scottish, and Southern Command, which all eventually merged to become HQ UK Land Forces or UKLF in 1972.[241]

The Army was beginning to draw down its forces, beginning demobilisation shortly after the end of the war. The Territorial units were placed in 'suspended animation', being reconstituted upon the reformation of the TA in 1947. On 1 January 1948, National Service, the new name for conscription, formally came into effect.[242] The Army was, however, being reduced in size upon the end of British rule in India, including the second battalions of every Line Infantry regiment either amalgamating with the 1st Battalions to maintain the 2nd Battalion's history and traditions, or simply disband, thus ending the two-battalion policy implemented by Childers in 1881. This proved too severe a decision for the overstretched Army, and a number of regiments reformed their second battalion in the 1950s. The year 1948 also saw the Army receive four Gurkha regiments (eight battalions in total) transferred to them from the Indian Army and were formed into the Brigade of Gurkhas, initially based in Malaya.[243]

More reforms of the armed forces took place with the 1957 Defence White Paper, which saw further reductions implemented; the Government realised after the debacle of the Suez War that Britain was no longer a global superpower and decided to withdraw from most of its commitments in the world, limiting the armed forces to concentrating on NATO, with an increased reliance upon nuclear weapons. The White Paper announced that the Army would be reduced in size from about 330,000 to 165,000, with National Service ending by 1963 (it officially ended on 31 December 1960, with the last conscript being discharged in May 1963) with the intention of making the Army into an entirely professional force. This enormous reduction in manpower led to, between 1958 and 1962, eight cavalry and thirty infantry regiments being amalgamated, the latter amalgamations producing fifteen single-battalion regiments. Brigade cap badges superseded the regimental cap badge in 1959.[244]

Many of the regiments created during the 1957 White Paper would have only a brief existence, most being amalgamated into new 'large' regiments – The Queen's, Royal Fusiliers, Royal Anglian, Light Infantry, Royal Irish Rangers, and the Royal Green Jackets—all of whose 'junior' battalions were disbanded by the mid-1970s. Two regiments – The Cameronians (Scottish Rifles) and The York and Lancaster Regiment—opted to be disbanded rather than amalgamated. The fourteen administrative brigades (created in 1948) were replaced by six administrative divisions in 1968,[245] with regimental cap badges being re-introduced the following year. The Conservative Government came to power in 1970, one of its pledges included the saving of the Argyll and Sutherland Highlanders after a popular campaign to save it had been provoked by the announcement of its intended demise. The Government also decided to stop the planned amalgamation of The Gloucestershire Regiment with The Royal Hampshire Regiment. Further cavalry and infantry regiments were, however, amalgamated between 1969 and 1971, with six cavalry (into three)[246,247] and six infantry (also into three) regiments doing so.[248,249]

For the structure of the Army during this period, see List of British Army regiments (1962). HQ UK Land Forces was formed in 1972, and the previous home commands were effectively downgraded to districts.[250]

Post-World War II operations outside Great Britain

Far East

In the immediate aftermath of the war in the Far East, the Army was tasked with reoccupying former British territories such as Malaya, Singapore, and Hong Kong. The British Army also played an active part, if only briefly, in the military actions by other European nations in their attempts to restore their pre–World War II governance, occupation, and control of South-Eastern Asian countries.

For example, British and Indian Army forces were sent to the island of Java in the Dutch East Indies in September 1945 to disarm and help repatriate the Japanese occupation forces. It was a month after the local nationalists—who had been provided with arms by the Japanese—had declared an independent Indonesia. The situation in Java was quite chaotic with much violence taking place. The British and Indian forces experienced fierce resistance from the nationalists; the former Japanese occupation force was also employed by the British to help maintain order, and fought alongside the British and Indian forces. Dutch forces gradually arrived in number and the British and Indians left by November 1946.[251]

A similar situation existed in French Indochina after Vietnamese leader Ho Chi Minh declared the independence of Vietnam on 2 September 1945. British and Indian troops, commanded by Major-General Douglas Gracey, were deployed to occupy the south of the country shortly afterwards, while Nationalist Chinese attempted to occupy the northern areas of Vietnam. Vietnam was at this time in chaos and the population did not want French rule restored. The British military decided to rearm numerous French POWs—who then went on a rampage—and British forces also re-armed Japanese troops to help maintain order. The British and Indians departed by February 1946 and the First Indochina War began shortly afterwards. War in Vietnam would continue for more than twenty years.

British de-colonialisation and the British Army

The latter part of the 1940s saw the British start to begin to withdraw from the Empire, the Army playing a prominent role in its dismantlement. The first colony the British withdrew from was India, the largest British possession as measured by population, though not the largest by geographical area.

In 1947 the British government announced India would become independent on 15 August, after being separated into two countries, one mostly Muslim (Pakistan) and the other mostly Hindu (India). The last British Army unit to leave active service in the Indian subcontinent was the 1st Battalion, The Somerset Light Infantry (Prince Albert's) on 28 February 1948.[252]

In Palestine, there was a surge in attacks against the British mandate and occupation by Zionist organisations such as Irgun and the Stern Gang after the British attempted to limit Jewish immigration into Palestine. British military and other forces eventually withdrew in 1948 and the State of Israel was established on 14 May.[253]

Elsewhere, within British territories, Communist guerrillas launched an uprising in Malaya, starting the Malayan Emergency.[254]

In the early 1950s, trouble began in Cyprus, and in Kenya—the Mau Mau uprising.[255] In Cyprus, an organisation known as EOKA sought unity with Greece, the situation being stabilised just before Cyprus was given independence in 1960. Kenya was one of many deployments for the Army in Africa during the 1950s, most of the others being former Italian colonies placed in the temporary control of Britain and the British Army.

Korea

The British Army also participated in the 1st Commonwealth Division during the Korean War (1950–53), fighting in battles such as Imjin River which included Gloster Hill.

Figure 25: *British soldiers driving through South Belfast in 1981*

More British de-colonialisation

Elsewhere, the Army withdrew from the Suez Canal Zone in Egypt in 1955. The following year, along with France and Israel, the British invaded Egypt in a conflict known as the Suez War, after the Egyptian leader, President Nasser nationalised the Suez Canal which privately owned businesses in Britain and France owned shares in. The British Army contributed forces to the amphibious assault on Suez and British paratroopers took part in the airborne assault. This brief war was a military success. However, international pressure, especially from the US government, soon forced the British government to withdraw all their military forces soon afterwards. British military forces were replaced by UN peacekeeping troops.[256]

In the 1960s two conflicts featured heavily with the Army, the Aden Emergency and the Indonesia–Malaysia confrontation in Borneo.

Operations within the United Kingdom

Northern Ireland

In 1969 a surge of sectarian violence and attacks in Northern Ireland against Catholics by Protestants, loyalists and the RUC in which seven people were killed, hundreds more wounded and thousands of Catholic families were driven from their homes led to British troops being sent into Northern Ireland to try to stop the violence. This became Operation Banner.[257] Among those killed in the attacks by the RUC was Trooper Hugh McCabe, the first British soldier to die in the conflict.[258] The troops were initially welcomed by the Catholic community as they believed the troops would protect them; however, this developed into opposition as the troops began to support the RUC, and the Provisional Irish Republican Army (PIRA), a militant break-away from the IRA which had been quiet since the 1962 cessation of the Border Campaign, began to target British troops. The British Army's operations in the early phase of its deployment had it placed in a policing role, for which, in many cases, it was ill-suited. This involved seeking to prevent confrontations between the Catholics and Protestants, as well as putting down riots and stopping Republican and Loyalist paramilitary groups from committing terrorist attacks.[259]

However, as the Provisional IRA campaign 1969–1997 grew in ferocity in the early 1970s, the Army was increasingly caught in a situation where its actions were directed against the IRA and the Catholic Irish nationalist community which harboured it. In the early period of the conflict, British troops mounted several major field operations. The first of these was the Falls Curfew of 1971, when over 3,000 troops imposed a 3-day curfew on the Falls Road area of Belfast and fought a sustained gun battle with local IRA men. In Operation Demetrius in June 1971, 300 paramilitary suspects were interned without trial, an action which provoked a major upsurge in violence.[260] The largest single British operation of the period was Operation Motorman in 1972, when about 21,000 troops were used to restore state control over areas of Belfast and Derry, which were then controlled by republican paramilitaries.[261] The British Army's reputation suffered further from an incident in Derry on 30 January 1972, Bloody Sunday in which 13 Catholic civilians were murdered by The Parachute Regiment. The biggest single loss of life for British troops in the conflict came at Narrow Water, where eighteen British soldiers were killed in a PIRA bomb attack on 27 August 1979, on the same day Lord Mountbatten of Burma was assassinated by the PIRA in a separate attack.[262] In all almost 500 British troops died in Northern Ireland between 1969 and 1997. Most of these deaths however occurred in the early 1970s, when British troops were placed at the forefront of the conflict and had little experience in dealing with a low intensity conflict in a predominantly urban, heavily populated area.

By the late 1970s, the British Army was replaced to some degree as "frontline" security service, in preference for the local Royal Ulster Constabulary and the Ulster Defence Regiment (raised 1970) as part of the Ulsterisation policy. By the 1980s and early 1990s, British Army casualties in the conflict had dropped. Moreover, British Special Forces had some successes against the PIRA – see Operation Flavius and the Loughgall Ambush. Nevertheless, the conflict tied up over 12,000 British troops on a continuous basis until the late 1990s and was ended with the Good Friday Agreement which detailed a path to a political solution to the conflict.[263]

Operation Banner came to an end in 2007 making it the longest continuous operation in the British Army's history, lasting over thirty-eight years. Troop numbers where reduced to 5,000.[264]

England

In 1980, the Special Air Service emerged from its secretive world when its most high-profile operation, the ending of the Iranian Embassy Siege in London, was broadcast live on television.[265] By the 1980s, even though the Army was being increasingly deployed abroad, most of its permanent overseas garrisons were gone, with the largest remaining being the BAOR in Germany, while others included Belize, Brunei, Gibraltar, and Hong Kong.

Falklands War

One remaining garrison provided by the Royal Marines was the Falkland Islands in the South Atlantic, 6,000 to 8,000 miles (13,000 km) (11,000 to 15,000 km) from Britain. The Argentinians invaded the Falklands in April 1982. The British quickly responded and the Army had an active involvement in the campaign to liberate the Falklands upon the landings at San Carlos, taking part in a series of battles that led to them reaching the outskirts of the capital, Stanley. The Falklands War ending with the formal surrender of the Argentinian forces on 14 June.[266]

1990–present

Organisation

The collapse of the Soviet Union, ending the Cold War, saw a new defence white paper, Options for Change produced.[267] This saw inevitable reductions in the British armed forces. The Army experienced a substantial cut in its manpower (reduced to about 120,000), which included yet more regimental amalgamations, including two of the large regiments of the 1960s—the Queen's Regiment and Royal Irish Rangers—and the third battalions of the remaining large regiments being cut. The British Army in Germany was also affected, with the British Army of the Rhine replaced by British Forces Germany and personnel numbers being reduced from about 55,000 to 25,000; the replacement of German-based I Corps by the British-led Allied Rapid Reaction Corps also took place.[268] Nine of the Army's administrative corps were amalgamated to form the Royal Logistic Corps and the Adjutant General's Corps. One major development was the disbandment of the Women's Royal Army Corps (though the largest elements were absorbed by the AGC) and their integration into services that had previously been restricted to men; however, women were still prohibited from joining armoured and infantry units. The four Gurkha regiments were amalgamated to form the three-battalion Royal Gurkha Rifles, reduced to two in 1996 just before the handover of Hong Kong to the People's Republic of China in 1997.[269]

The Labour Party became the country's new government and after their election victory in 1997 a new defence white paper was prepared, known as the Strategic Defence Review (1998).[270] Some of the Army's reforms included the creation of two deployable divisions – 1st (UK) Armoured Division and 3rd Mechanised Division, with the 1st Division being based in Germany—and three 'regenerative' divisions – 2nd, 4th, and 5th Divisions. The 16 Air Assault Brigade was formed from 24 Airmobile Brigade and elements of 5 Airborne Brigade to provide the Army with increased mobility, and would include the Westland WAH-64 Apache attack helicopter. Other attempts to make the Army more mobile was the creation of the Joint Rapid Reaction Force, intended to provide a corps-sized force capable of reacting quickly to situations similar to Bosnia. The Army Air Corps's helicopters also helped form the multi-service Joint Helicopter Command.[271]

For the structure of the British Army during this period, see List of British Army regiments (1994).

Another defence review was published in 2004, known as Delivering Security in a Changing World. The defence white paper stated that the Army's manpower would be reduced by 1,000, with four infantry battalions being cut and the manpower being redistributed elsewhere. One of the most radical aspects of the reforms was the announcement that most single-battalion regiments would amalgamate into large regiments, with most of the battalions retaining their previous regimental titles in their battalion names. The TA would also be further integrated into the Army, with battalions being numbered into the regiment's structure. These are reminiscent, in some respects, to the Cardwell-Childers reforms and the 1960s reforms.[272]

The elite units of the Army are also playing an increasingly prominent role in the Army's operations and the SAS was allocated further funds in the 2004 defence paper, conveying the SAS's increasing importance in the War on Terror. Another élite unit became operational in 2005, the Special Reconnaissance Regiment. The 1st Battalion of the Parachute Regiment became the core of a tri-service Special Forces Support Group formed in 2006 to support the SAS and the Navy's SBS, being described as the Army's equivalent to the U.S. Army Rangers.

Figure 26: *C Company, 1st Battalion, The Staffordshire Regiment, 1 (UK) Armoured Division*

Operations

The end of the Cold War did not provide the British Army with any respite, and the political vacuum left by the Soviet Union has seen a surge of instability in the world. Saddam Hussein's Iraq invaded Kuwait, one of its neighbours, in 1990, provoking condemnation from the United Nations, primarily led by the United States. The Gulf War and the British contribution, known as Operation Granby, was large, with the Army providing about 28,000 troops and 13,000 vehicles, mostly centred on 1 (UK) Armoured Division. After air operations ended, the land campaign against Iraq began on 24 February. 1st Armoured Division took part in the left-hook attack that helped destroy many Iraqi units. The ground campaign had lasted just 100-hours, Kuwait being officially liberated on 27 February.[273]

The British Army has also played an increasingly prominent role in peacekeeping operations, gaining much respect for its comparative expertise in the area. In 1992, during the wars in the Balkans provoked by the gradual disintegration of Yugoslavia, UN forces intervened in Croatia and later Bosnia. British forces contributed as part of UNPROFOR (United Nations Protection Force).[274] The force was a peacekeeping one, but with no peace to keep, it proved ineffective and was replaced by the NATO IFOR though this was in turn replaced the following year by SFOR.[275] As of 2005, Britain's contribution numbers about 3,000 troops. In 1999 the UK took a lead role in the NATO war against Slobodan Milošević's forces in Kosovo.[276] After the air war ended, the Parachute Regiment and Royal Gurkha Rifles provided the spearhead for ground forces entering Kosovo. In 2000, British forces, as part of Operation Palliser, intervened in a civil war ravaging Sierra Leone, with the intention of evacuating British, Commonwealth and EU citizens. The SAS also played a prominent role when they, along with the Paras, launched the successful Operation Barras to rescue 6 soldiers of the Royal Irish Regiment being held by the rebels. The British force remained and provided the catalyst for the stabilisation of the country.[277]

The early 21st century saw the world descend into a new war after the 9/11 terrorist attacks on the World Trade Center in New York City by Al Qaida: the War on Terrorism.[278] A US-led invasion of Taliban-ruled Afghanistan followed, with the British contribution led by the RN and RAF; the most important Army element being the SAS. The British later took part in the invasion of Iraq in 2003, Britain's contribution being known as Operation Telic, The Army played a more significant role in Iraq than Afghanistan, deploying a substantial force, centred on 1 (UK) Armoured Division with, again, around 28,000 troops.[279] The war began in March and the British fought in the southern area of Iraq, eventually capturing the second largest city, Basra, in April. The Army remained in Iraq upon the end of the war and subsequently led the Multi-National Division (South East), with the Army presence in Iraq numbering about 5,000 soldiers.[280]

Official rifle of the Army 1722–present

See British military rifles

The British Army has mixed extreme conservatism, 'penny-pinching', and extraordinarily exacting standards in its rifles. For example, the move to percussion-caps was not made until 1842, while an 1866 trial examined 104 weapons and declined to award a first prize, or that the specifications for an SLR in the 1930s were so stiff "it is doubtful if any... rifle of the present day could meet it in its entirety."

Changes were usually forced on the Army as a result of conflict or the actions of other armies. Note the rapid pace of change in the period 1850–1895 as the Crimean War forced changes and then the foreign demonstrations of the needle-gun, the Chassepot, and the Mannlicher–Mauser designs frightened the Army.

In the 19th century the change-overs were not instant, many colonial units soldiered on with older weapons – some units missing two cycles of change –

while some weapons (italicized in the list below) were only issued to specialist rifle brigades or in very limited numbers.

As happens, the Army's men often had the weapons to fight the *last* war by the time of the following conflict. Most of the 19th century weapons were technologically obsolete at their introduction or within five years, and despite the apparently exhaustive testing many inadequate weapons were issued.

- Brown Bess 1722–1838
  - Long Land Pattern 1722–1802
  - Short Land Pattern 1777–1802
  - New Land Pattern Musket 1802–1842
- *Baker rifle 1800–1835*
- *Pattern 1836 Brunswick rifle 1836–1851*
- *Pattern 1851 Minié rifle 1851–1855*
- Enfield
  - Pattern 1853 1855–1860
  - Pattern 1860 1860–1864
- Snider–Enfield (or Converted Enfield) 1864–1871
- Martini–Henry 1871–1888
  - Martini–Enfield 1884–1888
- Lee–Metford 1888–1895
- Lee–Enfield 1895–1956
  - SMLE 1903–1956
- L1A1 SLR 1957–1985
- L85 1985-

Sources

- Anderson, Fred (2001). *Crucible of War: The Seven Years' War and the Fate of Empire in British North America, 1754-1766*. Faber and Faber. ISBN 978-0-375-70636-3.
- Asquith, Stuart (1981). *New Model Army 1645-60* (illustrated ed.). Osprey. p. 3[281]. ISBN 0-85045-385-2.
- Bamford, Andrew. *Sickness, Suffering, and the Sword: The British Regiment on Campaign, 1808–1815* (2013). excerpt[282]
- Beckett, Ian F. W., and Keith Simpson. *A Nation in Arms: A Social Study of the British Army in the First World War* (1990)
- Bond, Brian, et al., *Look To Your Front: Studies in the First World War* (1999) 11 chapters by experts on noncombat aspects of First World War army.
- Bowman, Timothy, and Mark L. Connelly. *The Edwardian Army: Recruiting, Training, and Deploying the British Army, 1902–1914* (Oxford UP, 2012). DOI:10.1093/acprof:oso/9780199542789.001.0001 online

- Carver, Michael. *Seven Ages of the British Army* (1984) Covers 1900 to 1918
- Cassidy, Robert M (2006). *Counterinsurgency and the Global War on Terror: Military Culture and Irregular War.* Greenwood Publishing Group. ISBN 0-275-98990-9.
- Chandler, David, ed. *The Oxford History of the British Army* (1996) online[283]
- Chappell, Mike (2003). *The British Army in World War I: The Western Front 1914-16.* Osprey Publishing. ISBN 1-84176-399-3.
- Chartrand, René (2008). *American Loyalist Troops 1775-84.* Osprey Publishing. ISBN 978-1-84603-314-8.
- Curtis, Edward E. *The Organization of the British Army in the American Revolution* (Yale U.P. 1926) online[284]
- Ensor, (Sir) Robert (1936). *England: 1870–1914. (The Oxford History of England, Volume XIV)* (Revised, 1980 ed.). Oxford: Oxford University Press. ISBN 0-19-821705-6.
- Ferguson, Niall (2004). *Colossus: The Price of America's Empire.* Penguin. ISBN 1-59420-013-0.
- Glover, Richard (1973). *Britain at Bay: Defence Against Bonaparte, 1803–14.* Historical problems: Studies and documents. No.20. George Allen and Unwin Ltd. ISBN 978-0-04-940044-3.
- Grant, Charles; Youens, Michael (1972). *Royal Scots Greys.* Osprey Publishing. ISBN 978-0-85045-059-0.
- Jones, Spencer (2013). *From Boer War to World War: Tactical Reform of the British Army, 1902-1914.* University of Oklahoma Press. ISBN 978-0806142890.
- Le Mesurier, Havilland (1801). *The British Commissary: in two parts. A system for the British Commissariat on Foreign Service.* C Roworth.
- Mallinson, Allan (2009). *The Making of the British Army.* Bantam Press. ISBN 978-0-593-05108-5.
- Nester, William R. *Titan: The Art of British Power in the Age of Revolution and Napoleon* (2016)
- O'Brien, Brendan (1995). *The Long War: The IRA and Sinn Féin, 1985 to today.* Syracuse University Press. ISBN 978-0-8156-0319-1.
- Parker, John (2005). *The Gurkhas: The Inside Story of the World's Most Feared Soldiers.* Headline Book Publishing Publishing. ISBN 978-0-7553-1415-7.
- Reid, Stuart (2002). *Culloden Moor 1746: The Death of the Jacobite Cause.* Campaign series. **106**. Osprey Publishing. ISBN 1-84176-412-4.
- Royal Scots Greys (1840). *Historical record of the Royal regiment of Scots dragoons: now the Second, or Royal North British dragoons, commonly called the Scots greys, to 1839.* p. 56[285]-57.

- Simkins, Peter. *Kitchener's Army: The Are raising of New Armies, 1914–16* (1988)
- Taylor, AJP (1976). *The Second World War: An Illustrated History*. Penguin books. ISBN 0-14-004135-4.
- Taylor, Peter (1997). *Provos The IRA & Sinn Féin*. Bloomsbury Publishing. ISBN 0-7475-3818-2.
- Tucker, Spencer; Roberts, Priscilla Mary (2005). *World War I: encyclopedia*. ABC-CLIO. ISBN 1-85109-420-2.
- Watson, Graham; Renaldi, Richard (2005). *The British Army in Germany: An Organizational History 1947-2004*. Tiger Lily. ISBN 978-0-9720296-9-8.
- Willmott, H P; Kindersley, Dorling (2008). *First World War*. Dorling Kindersley. ISBN 1-4053-2986-6.
- Winter, Denis. *Death's Men: Soldiers of the Great War* (1978)

Primary sources

- This article incorporates text from a publication now in the public domain: Colburn, H. (December 1860), "French view of our military institutions: The English Army", *The United Service Magazine*, Part 3 (385): 566[286]–567

Further reading

- Barnett, Correlli. *Britain and Her Army, 1509–1970: A Military, Political and Social Survey* (1970), a standard scholarly history; 525pp
- Chandler, David, and Ian Beckett, eds. *The Oxford History of the British Army* (2003). excerpt[287]; Illustrated edition published as *The Illustrated Oxford History of the British Army*
- Firth, C.H. *Cromwell's Army* (1902) online[288]
- Fortescue, John William. *History of the British Army from the Norman Conquest to the First World War* (1899–1930), in 13 volumes with six separate map volumes. Available online for downloading[289]; online volumes[290]; The standard highly detailed full coverage of operations.
- French, David. *Army, Empire, and Cold War: The British Army and Military Policy, 1945–1971* (2012).
- French, David. *Military Identities: The Regimental System, the British Army, and the British People c.1870–2000* (2008).
- French, David. *Raising Churchill's Army: The British Army and the War against Germany 1919–1945* (2001).
- Haswell, Jock, and John Lewis-Stempel. *A Brief History of the British Army* (2017).

- Higham, John, ed. *A Guide to the Sources of British Military History* (1972) 654 pages excerpt[291]
- Holmes, Richard. *Redcoat: The British Soldier in the Age of Horse and Musket* (HarperCollins ISBN 0-00-653152-0)
- Holmes, Richard. *Tommy: The British Soldier on the Western Front* (Perennial ISBN 0-00-713752-4)
- James, Lawrence. *Warrior Race: A History of the British at War* (2004) online edition[292]
- Noakes, Lucy. *Women in the British Army: War and the Gentle Sex, 1907–1948* (2006) excerpt[293]
- Reece, Henry. *The Army in Cromwellian England: 1649–1660* (Oxford University Press, 2013). xv, 267 pp.
- White, Arthur S. *Bibliography of Regimental Histories of the British Army* (Naval and Military Press ISBN 1-84342-155-0)
- *The British Army Handbook: The Definitive Guide by the MoD* (Brassey's Ltd ISBN 1-85753-393-3)

External links

- The National Archives of Scotland: Doing research. Guides. Military records[294].
- The Age of George III: Ireland in the American War (1776-83). Mentions Anglo-Irish militarism, & enlistment of Catholics[295].
- History In Focus:The British Isles and the War of American Independence[296]
- Britain's Small Wars[297]
- National Army Museum[298]
- The Long, Long Trail[299]
- Royal Engineers Museum[300] – Royal Engineers History
- Anne S. K. Brown Military Collection, Brown University Library[301] Military history and graphics
- SaBRE[302]

 Wikimedia Commons has media related to *History of the British Army*.

History of the Royal Air Force

The **history of the Royal Air Force**, the air force of the United Kingdom, spans a century of British military aviation.

The RAF was founded on 1 April 1918, towards the end of the First World War by merging the Royal Flying Corps and the Royal Naval Air Service. After the war, the RAF was greatly reduced in size and during the inter-war years was used to "police" the British Empire. The RAF underwent rapid expansion prior to and during the Second World War. During the war it was responsible for the aerial defence of Great Britain, the strategic bombing campaign against Germany and tactical support to the British Army around the world.

During the Cold War, the main role of the RAF was the defence of the continent of Europe against potential attack by the Soviet Union, including holding the British nuclear deterrent for a number of years. After the end of the Cold War, the RAF took part in several large scale operations, including the Gulf War, the Kosovo War, the War in Afghanistan, and the Iraq War.

Formation and the inter-war years

Formation

While the British were not the first to make use of heavier-than-air military aircraft, the RAF is the world's oldest independent air force: that is, the first air force to become independent of army or navy control.[303] The RAF was founded on 1 April 1918 by the amalgamation of the Royal Flying Corps and the Royal Naval Air Service and was controlled by the British Government Air Ministry which had been established three months earlier. The Royal Flying Corps had been born out of the Air Battalion of the Royal Engineers and was under the control of the British Army. The Royal Naval Air Service was its naval equivalent and was controlled by the Admiralty. The decision to merge the two services and create an independent air force was a response to the events of World War I, the first war in which air power made a significant impact. The creation of the new force was based on the Smuts Report prepared by Field Marshal Jan Smuts for the Imperial War Cabinet on which he served.

To emphasize the merger of both military and naval aviation in the new service, many of the titles of officers were deliberately chosen to be of a naval character, such as flight lieutenant, wing commander, group captain, and air commodore.

The newly created RAF was the most powerful air force in the world on its creation, with over 20,000 aircraft and over 300,000 personnel (including the Women's Royal Air Force). The squadrons of the RFC kept their numerals while those of the RNAS were renumbered from 201 onwards. At the time of

Figure 27: *Airco DH.9A*

the merger, the Navy's air service had 55,066 officers and men, 2,949 aircraft, 103 airships and 126 coastal stations. The remaining personnel and aircraft came from the RFC. A memorial to the RAF was commissioned after the war in central London. The RAF's last known surviving founder member was the World War I veteran Henry Allingham who died in 2009 aged 113.

Following the end of World War I and the accompanying British defence cuts, the newly independent (and still temporary) RAF waited nine months to see if it would be retained by the Cabinet. 6,500 officers, all holding temporary commissions or seconded from the Army and Navy, applied for permanent commissions. The Cabinet sanctioned a maximum of 1,500 and the Air Ministry offered 1,065 to the applicants, publishing the first list on 1 August 1919, 75% of them short-term (two to five years). The service as a whole had been reduced in strength to 35,500.[304]

Policing the Empire

The RAF took up the task of policing the British Empire from the air. It was argued that the use of air power would prove to be a more cost-effective way of controlling large areas than by using conventional land forces. Sir Hugh Trenchard, the Chief of the Air Staff, had formulated ideas about the use of aircraft in colonial policing and these were first put into practice in 1920 when

Figure 28: *An RAF aircraft in Somaliland*

the RAF and imperial ground units defeated rebel Somaliland dervishes. The following year, in 1921, the RAF was given responsibility for all British forces in Iraq with the task of 'policing' the tribal unrest. The RAF also saw service in Afghanistan in 1925, where they were employed independently for the first time in their history, then again in 1928, when following the outbreak of civil war, the British Legation and some European diplomatic staff based in Kabul were cut off.

Activities in Great Britain

It was during the inter-war years that the RAF had to fight for its survival[305,306] - some questioned the need for a separate air force, especially in peacetime. To prevent itself being disbanded and its duties returned to the Army and the Navy, the RAF spent considerable energies keeping itself in the public eye by such things as the annual Hendon Air Show, supporting a team for the Schneider Trophy air racing competition, and by producing documentary films. In 1936, a reorganisation of RAF command saw the creation of Fighter Command, Bomber Command and Coastal Command.[307]

Naval aviation

The creation of the RAF removed all aircraft and flying personnel from the Navy, although the Admiralty remained in control of aircraft carriers. On 1 April 1924, the Fleet Air Arm of the Royal Air Force was formed under

Air Ministry control. It consisted of those RAF units that were normally embarked on aircraft carriers and fighting ships.[308] The Chief of the Air Staff, Lord Trenchard, his air staff and his successors argued that "air is one and indivisible" and hence that naval aviation was properly the responsibility of the RAF. The Admiralty took the opposite view and, during the first half of the 1920s, pressed hard for the return of naval aviation to their control. It has been argued that the British defence arrangements in the inter-war years had a serious impact upon the doctrinal development of British naval air power as the Navy lacked experienced naval aviators.[309]

During the 1920s and first half of the 1930s, Government spending on the RAF was limited and the air staff put a higher priority on strategic bombing than on naval aviation. The result of this was that by the late 1930s the Fleet Air Arm was equipped with outdated aircraft — like the Fairey Swordfish three-man biplane torpedo bomber, among others — in limited numbers, as the rival Imperial Japanese Naval Air Service began using the Nakajima B5N all-metal low-winged monoplane torpedo bomber from the IJN's aircraft carriers by 1938 as one example of how the Fleet Air Arm's aviation technology was literally "being left behind" by one of its future foes. By 1936, the Admiralty were once again campaigning for the return of naval aviation to their control. This time they were successful and on 30 July 1937, the Admiralty took over responsibility for the administration of the Fleet Air Arm. Under two years later, on 24 May 1939, the Fleet Air Arm was returned to full Admiralty control under the *Inskip Award* and renamed the Air Branch of the Royal Navy.

Strategic bombing

The RAF developed its doctrine of strategic bombing which led to the construction of long-range bombers and became the basic philosophy in the Second World War.[310]

World War II (1939–1945)

The RAF underwent rapid expansion following the outbreak of war against Germany in 1939. This included the training of British aircrews in British Commonwealth countries under the British Commonwealth Air Training Plan, and the secondment of many whole squadrons, and tens of thousands of individual personnel, from Commonwealth air forces. For example, by the end of the war, Royal Canadian Air Force personnel had contributed more than 30

Figure 29: *RAF Darrell's Island, Bermuda, during WWII.*

squadrons to service with RAF formations; almost a quarter of Bomber Command's personnel were Canadian.[311] Similarly, about nine percent of the personnel who served with the RAF in Europe and the Mediterranean were seconded from the Royal Australian Air Force. To these and other British Commonwealth personnel were later added thousands of men from other countries, including many who had fled from German-occupied Europe.

A defining period of the RAF's existence came during the Battle of Britain. Over the summer of 1940, the RAF held off the *Luftwaffe* in perhaps the most prolonged and complicated air campaign in history. This arguably contributed immensely to the delay and cancellation of German plans for an invasion of the United Kingdom (Operation Sea Lion). Of these few hundred RAF fighter pilots, Prime Minister Winston Churchill famously said in the House of Commons on 20 August, "Never in the field of human conflict was so much owed by so many to so few". Although, he first spoke these words upon exiting the Battle of Britain Bunker at RAF Uxbridge on 16 August. However, in recent years some military historians have controversially suggested that the RAF's actions would not have prevented an invasion and that the key deterrent was the Royal Navy's command of the sea.[312]

The main RAF effort during the war was the strategic bombing campaign against Germany. From 31 May 1942 RAF Bomber Command was able to mount large-scale night raids, sometimes involving up to 1,000 aircraft. From mid-1942 increasing numbers of these aircraft were heavy four-engined

Figure 30: *Residential area of Hamburg after the 1943 RAF attack (Operation Gomorrah)*

bombers such as the Handley-Page Halifax and the Avro Lancaster. Noteworthy raids include Operation Millennium against Cologne, the first 1000-bomber raid; Operation Chastise, the 'Dambusters' raids on targets in the Ruhr Valley; Operation Gomorrah, the destruction of Hamburg; and the 'Battle of Berlin'. The lighter, fast two-engine de Havilland Mosquito fighter-bomber was used for tactical raids like Operation Carthage, a raid on the Gestapo headquarters in Copenhagen, as well as a night-fighter.

There exists considerable historical controversy about the ethics of large-scale firebombing attacks against German cities during the last few months of the war, such as the bombing of Dresden, the bombing of Pforzheim, the bombing of Heilbronn, and other German cities.[313]

1948 Arab–Israeli War

Following the end of the British Mandate of Palestine, the State of Israel was founded on 14 May 1948. Egyptian forces crossed into Israeli territory as part of a wider Arab League military coalition, with the Royal Egyptian Air Force providing light bombers as well as Spitfires. On 22 May, the Egyptians attacked RAF Ramat David, believing the base had already been taken over by Israeli forces. Two Royal Egyptian Air Force Spitfire LF.IXs strafed RAF

Figure 31: *The Avro Vulcan was a strategic bomber used during the Cold War to carry conventional and nuclear bombs.*

Spitfire FR.XVIIIs of No. 32 Squadron and No. 208 Squadron on the ground. Flying Officers Geoff Cooper and Roy Bowie of 208 Squadron. then took off in their Spitfire FR.XVIIIs to mount a standing patrol. Three Egyptian Spitfire LF.IXs launched a second attack, two of which were shot down by Cooper and Bowie. Flying Officers McElhaw and Hully, also of 32 Squadron, took over the standing patrol before the third wave of Egyptian Spitfires arrived. Flying Officer McElhaw shot both of these down.

Due to the confused circumstances of the 1948 Middle East conflict, the RAF found itself fighting the Jewish militias, and later, the nascent Israeli Air Force. Royal Air Force bases in the region were attacked by both sides and reconnaissance aircraft were shot down. Among others, on January 7, 1949, Flying Officer McElhaw, who participated in the action against Egyptians described above, and two other pilots, were shot down by Israeli Spitfires while reconnoitering the aftermath of air attack on an Israeli column by Egyptian aircraft.

Cold War (1947–1990)

After victory in World War II, the RAF was to be further re-organized, as technological advances in air warfare saw the arrival of jet fighters and bombers. The first significant Cold War action of the RAF was its support to the Berlin Airlift in 1948 and 1949 which was originally designated Operation Knicker and Operation Carter-Paterson and later titled Operation Plainfare.

Although the United Kingdom did not base any RAF squadrons in Korea during the Korean War, the *Independent* reported that 41 RAF officers seconded to serve with the United States Air Force, several RAF pilots saw action while on exchange with the USAF, mainly flying F-86 Sabres, they were credited with seven kills. At least one pilot was killed when his F-84E Thunderjet was shot down by anti-aircraft fire on 2 January 1952 as he attempted to strafe a column of trucks near Sunsan, a village north of Pyongyang.[314] Other RAF pilots flew Meteors in Royal Australian Air Force squadrons on ground support attacks. Two flights of Army Cooperation aircraft flew in support of artillery spotting and reconnaissance. In addition, three RAF squadrons of flying boats based in Singapore detached one squadron at a time on a monthly rotational basis to Japan and flew maritime and meteorological reconnaissance missions in the Yellow sea and Tushima Straits.

To complement the UK nuclear weapons which were difficult to manufacture quickly, in 1958 the RAF and other NATO nations were provided with American nuclear weapons under Project E as a stopgap measure. The UK had manufactured less than 50 of the 200 atomic and hydrogen bombs it required at that stage. The RAF V bomber squadrons took sole responsibility for carrying the UK's nuclear deterrent until the development of the Royal Navy's Polaris submarines. Following the introduction of Polaris in 1968 the RAF's strategic nuclear role was reduced to a tactical one, using the WE.177 gravity bombs. This tactical role was continued by the V bombers into the 1980s and until 1998 by Tornado GR1s.[315,316]

The primary role of the RAF in the Cold War years was the defence of Western Europe against potential attack by the Soviet Union, with many squadrons based in West Germany. With the decline of the British Empire, global operations were scaled back, and RAF Far East Air Force was disbanded on 31 October 1971.[317]

Despite this, the RAF fought in many battles in the Cold War period. In June 1948 the RAF commenced Operation Firedog against Malayan terrorists during the Malayan Emergency. Operations continued for the next 12 years until 1960 with aircraft flying out of RAF Tengah and RAF Butterworth. The RAF played a minor role in the Korean War, with flying boats taking part. From 1953 to 1956 the RAF Avro Lincoln squadrons carried out anti-Mau Mau operations in Kenya using its base at RAF Eastleigh. The Suez Crisis in 1956 saw a large RAF role, with aircraft operating from RAF Akrotiri and RAF Nicosia on Cyprus and RAF Luqa and RAF Hal Far on Malta as part of Operation Musketeer. The Konfrontasi against Indonesia in the early 1960s did see use of RAF aircraft, but due to a combination of deft diplomacy and selective ignoring of certain events by both sides, it never developed into a full-scale war.

Belize (1975–1994)

Belize (the former British Honduras) had been threatened for a number of years by Guatemala which claimed rights to the territory. In 1975 following the breakdown in negotiations between the United Kingdom and Guatemala, Guatemalan troops were active close to the border, and in October 1975 three Westland Puma helicopters were flown out to Belize Airport as the British garrison was reinforced to a 1,000 troops. In November six Hawker Siddeley Harriers of 1 Squadron were flown to Belize to provide some defence of the border and support the troops. By April 1976 the threat had reduced the Harriers were flown back to the United Kingdom. Further negotiations failed to come to an agreement and in June 1977 the garrison was again reinforced with six Harriers returning in July. Although Belize was not invaded the Pumas and Harriers were kept in Belize, the three Pumas as 1563 Flight (manned in rotation from 33 and 230 Squadrons, and 1417 Flight with four Harriers (manned in rotation from 1, 3 and 4 Squadrons). The airfield was defended by the RAF Regiment with Rapier and Bofors L40/70 detachments. While there was a civil war in Guatemala in the 1970s and 1980s, the British forces provided a deterrent as well as using the country for jungle warfare training. In 1991 Guatemala recognised Belize and the Harriers left in July 1993 and the Pumas in 1994.[318]

Falklands War

The Falklands War in 1982 was mainly fought by the Navy and Army due to the distance of the battlefield from friendly airfields. However RAF aircraft were deployed in the mid-Atlantic at RAF Ascension Island and on board the Navy's aircraft carriers alongside aircraft of the Fleet Air Arm. A detachment from No. 1 Squadron was deployed to the British Fleet during the War, operating from HMS *Hermes* and flying ground attack missions against Argentine forces.[319,320] RAF pilots also flew Royal Navy Sea Harriers in the air-to-air combat role and four RAF pilots shot down five Argentine aircraft.

The most high-profile RAF missions in this conflict were the famous Black Buck raids using Avro Vulcans flying from Ascension Island. However, the Service did many other things during the conflict, with its helicopters in the Falklands themselves, its Harrier GR3s flying from HMS *Hermes*, its fighter aircraft protecting Ascension, Nimrod MR2 maritime patrol aircraft scanning the South Atlantic, and tanker and transport fleet helping in the enormous logistical effort required for the war.

After the war the RAF remained in the South Atlantic to provide air defence to the Falkland Islands. The mid-Atlantic base on Ascension Island continued to be used as a staging post for the air bridge between the Great Britain and the

Figure 32: *Vulcan over Ascension Island on 18 May 1982*

Falkland Islands. In 1984 RAF Mount Pleasant was built to provide a fighter and transport facility on the islands thereby strengthening the defence capacity of the British Forces. Various radar sites were established and a detachment of the RAF Regiment provided anti-aircraft support until that role was transferred to the Royal Artillery. In 2009 the air defence F3s were replaced by four Typhoons which are based at RAF Mount Pleasant.

1990–2000

Gulf War

During the build-up to the Gulf War, RAF fighters were based in Saudi Arabia and Kuwait. On 17 January 1991, the main air campaign began and over 100 RAF aircraft took part in virtually every conceivable role. It marked an important turning point in the RAF's history as it was the first time the service had used precision-guided munitions in significant amounts. In the years following the end of the war, the RAF were involved in operations to enforce the no-fly zones over Iraq and the Service took part in the Bombing of Iraq in 1998.

Figure 33: *RAF GR4 Tornado fighter on a combat missson over Iraq during Operation Telic.*

Balkans

In 1993, RAF Tornado F3s and AWACS aircraft contributed to Operation Deny Flight, NATO's operation to restrict airspace movements over Bosnia and Herzegovina. The operation continued until late 1995.

The Kosovo War in 1999 saw the RAF fight over Europe for the first time since World War II. During the bombing of Yugoslavia, the RAF operated the Harrier GR7 and Tornado ground attack jets as well as an array of support aircraft.

2001–present

War on Terror

As part of the British contribution (codenamed Operation Veritas) to the 2001 invasion of Afghanistan at the start of the War in Afghanistan, the RAF provided support to the United States by operating air-to-air refuelling tankers and reconnaissance aircraft as well as proving the use of its bases. Chinook helicopters have provided airlift support to coalition forces. In late 2004, as part of Operation Herrick, RAF Harriers were based at Kandahar Airfield in Afghanistan, operating in the close air support role against the Taliban. The

Harriers were replaced by an equivalent force of Tornados GR4 in spring 2009.[321]

The 2003 invasion of Iraq saw a large RAF deployment to the Gulf, including RAF strike aircraft. The RAF also staged the base for the 4 US B-52 Bombers which attacked Iraq almost every night. The only RAF losses were a friendly fire incident when an RAF Tornado jet was shot down by a US Patriot missile killing both pilot and Weapons Systems Operator due to the Patriot missile mistakenly recognising the Tornado as a Mig, and a Hercules transport plane shot down by ground fire killing the ten personnel on board just after take off from the US controlled airfield. Following the invasion occupation of southern Iraq by British Forces, the RAF was deployed at Basra. As part of Operation Telic, Merlin, Puma and Chinook helicopters operated from Basra, protected by the RAF Regiment, forming 903 Expeditionary Air Wing.

In January 2013, the *BBC* reported that the RAF supported Operation Serval- the French-led operation against Islamist militants in Mali. The UK's contribution was codenamed Operation Newcombe, C-17 Globemasters from No. 99 Squadron transported French armored vehicles from French Évreux Air Base to Bamako. The *BBC* also reported that the RAF deployed a Sentinel R1 aircraft at the request of the French for surveillance support.

The *Guardian* reported that the RAF conducted Operation Turus in response the Chibok schoolgirls kidnapping by Boko Haram in Nigeria in April 2014. A source involved with the Operation told the *Observer* that "The girls were located in the first few weeks of the RAF mission," and that "We [RAF] offered to rescue them, but the Nigerian government declined," this was because it viewed any action to be taken as a "national issue," and for it to be resolved by Nigerian intelligence and security services, the source added that the girls were then tracked by the aircraft as they were dispersed into progressively smaller groups over the following months. As of 4 March 2017, 195 out of the 276 of the girls kidnapped are still missing.

The RAF is currently participating in the Military intervention against the Islamic State of Iraq and the Levant, the British participation is codenamed Operation Shader. Flying out of RAF bases in Cyprus, they have been known to have destroyed multiple ISIL targets and deliver humanitarian aid in Iraq (2014–present) as well as carry out surveillance missions in Syria.

Libyan civil war

In 2011 the RAF played a significant role in the NATO intervention in Libya. The British participation was codenamed Operation Ellamy and the RAF contribution involved the deployment of Typhoon multirole fighters, Tornado GR4

Figure 34: *Tail of Tornado GR4 ZG750, marking 25 years of Tornado GR operations, at the 2016 Farnborough Airshow.*

interdictor/strike aircraft, Sentry AEW.1 AWACS aircraft, a Nimrod R1 signals intelligence aircraft,[322] a Sentinel R1 airborne standoff radar aircraft, VC10 air-to-air refuelling tankers and TriStar air-to-air refuelling tankers.

Other operations and activities

In 2004, four RAF Panavia Tornado F.3s deployed to the Baltic States for three months to provide the British contribution to the NATO-led Baltic Air Policing operation and in 2005 support and transport aircraft were dispatched to South East Asia following the 2004 Indian Ocean earthquake disaster in order to provide aid relief support.

The RAF's 90th anniversary was commemorated on 1 April 2008 by a flypast of 9 Red Arrows and 4 Typhoons along the Thames, in a straight line from just south of London City Airport Tower Bridge, the London Eye, the RAF Memorial and (at 13.00) the Ministry of Defence building.

In September 2016, it was reported that four RAF Typhoon fighter jets from No. 2 Squadron (with supporting Voyager aircraft from No. 10 and 101 Squadrons, as well as C-17 Globemaster transport aircraft) were deployed to South Korea to take part in Exercise Invincible Shield: which marked the first time that South Korea hosted a major air exercise with an air force other than the United States. The Exercise's goal was to enhance interoperability between the RAF, Korean Air Force and USAF, whilst deepening the UK and

Republic of Korea's partnership in security and defence. In October 2016, it was reported that they were also deployed to Japan as part of Invincible Shield where they took part in their first-ever joint exercise drills with the Japanese air self-defence force, South Korean and USAF air assets also took part in the exercises. The Japan's defence ministry said to the *Guardian* that "The purpose of this exercise is to enhance tactical skills of Japan air self-defence force unit and strengthen Japan-UK defence cooperation. We have no specific country or region in our mind," South Korean and US officials said the drill would improve the allies' ability to strike key targets in North Korea, including military facilities and those linked to the regime's leader, Kim Jong-un; the drill in Japan was also known as Exercise Guardian North 16 and it ended in early November. The exercises in South Korea included the first UK-Republic of Korea Fighter exercise, that took place from 4 to 11 November.

The RAF celebrated its 100th anniversary on 1 April 2018 and to commemorate the achievement, a range of special events and celebrations will take place throughout the year.

Number of personnel

Following the end of World War I, the RAF was greatly reduced in size and only rebuilt in significant number in the years immediately pre-ceding World War II. At its peak during World War II, there were over one million RAF servicemen. Following the demobilization after World War II, the RAF has steadily declined in numbers.

Year	1918	1951[323]	1975[324]	1985	1993	1997	2005/2006[325,326]	2009	2011[327]	2012	2015[328]
Regular	316,170[329]	148,900	95,000	93,400	80,900	56,900	48,700	43,800	40,090	38,930[330]	31,830
National Service	N/A	88,900	N/A	N/A	N/A	N/A	N/A	N/A	N/A	N/A	N/A
Regular Reserve	N/A	N/K	N/K	29,800	46,100	45,400	35,000	35,160	6,900[331,332]	6,660	2,220
Voluntter Reserve	N/A	18,100	N/K	1,200	1,800	1,400	1,400	1,480	1,360[333]	1,360	

Sources

- Bowyer, Chaz (1988). *RAF Operations 1918–1938*. London: William Kimber. ISBN 0-7183-0671-6.
- Finn, C. J. et al. (2004). *Air Publication 3003 - A Brief History of the Royal Air Force*. HMSO
- Flintham, Vic (2009). *High Stakes - Britain's Air Arms in Action 1945-1990* Pen and Sword ISBN 978 1 84415 815 7
- Chant, Christopher (1993). *The History of the RAF*. Regency House Publishing. ISBN 1-85361-126-3
- Ferté, Philiip Joubert de la. *The Birds and the Fishes: The Story of Coastal Command*. Hutchinson. 1960. (No ISBN) OCLC 223965469[334].
- Halpenny, Bruce, *To Shatter the Sky: Bomber Airfield at War* (ISBN 978-0-85059-678-6)
- Halpenny, Bruce *Fight for the Sky: Stories of Wartime Fighter Pilots* (ISBN 978-0-85059-749-3)
- Norwood, Stephen H. (2013). *Antisemitism and the American Far Left*. Cambridge University Press. ISBN 9781107036017.
- Orange, Vincent (1990). *Coningham: A Biography of Air Marshal Sir Arthur Coningham* Methuen Publishing (ISBN 978-0413145802)
- Robinson, Derek (2005). *Invasion 1940: The truth about the Battle of Britain and what stopped Hitler* Constable ISBN 1845291514
- Till, Geoffey (1979). *Air Power and the Royal Navy, 1914–1945: An historical survey* Macdonald's and Janes ISBN 0354012045

External links

- Royal Engineers Museum[335] Royal Engineers and Aeronautics
- Royal Engineers Museum[336] Origins of the Royal Flying Corps/Royal Air Force
- Royal Engineers Museum[337] Early British Military Ballooning (1863)
- Royal Air Force History[338] RAF History pages portal

Structure

Structure of the British Armed Forces in 1989

At the end of the Cold War in 1989 the British Armed Forces structure was as follows:

- Ministry of Defence, Westminster, London
  - Defence Council of the United Kingdom
    - Army Board
    - Admiralty Board
    - Air Force Board
  - Minister for Defence Procurement
    - Ministry of Defence Procurement Executive
      - Atomic Weapons Establishment, RAF Aldermaston
        - ROF Burghfield
        - ROF Cardiff
      - Admiralty Research Establishment, Portsdown
      - Aeroplane and Armament Experimental Establishment, RAF Boscombe Down
      - Chemical Defence Establishment, Porton Down
      - Microbiological Research Establishment, Porton Down
      - Royal Armament Research and Development Establishment, Fort Halstead
      - Royal Aircraft Establishment, RAE Farnborough & RAE Bedford
      - Royal Signals and Radar Establishment, Malvern
  - Ministry of Defence Police
  - Judge Advocate General of the Armed Forces
  - Defence Nuclear, Biological and Chemical School, Winterbourne Gunner
  - Defence Intelligence Staff

Figure 35: *The Ministry of Defence building at Whitehall, Westminster, London*

- Welbeck College, Worksop
- Defence Test and Evaluation Organisation Portland Bill
- Chief Scientific Adviser to the Ministry of Defence
- Defence Munitions munitions depots at Crombie, Glen Douglas and Gosport

In 1989 the British Armed Forces had a peacetime strength of 311,600 men and defense expenditures were 4.09% of GDP.

Royal Navy

- Strength 65,500

British Army

- British Army: 152,800
- **Brunei** (Seria, Brunei)
    - HQ British Forces Brunei & Brunei Signal Troop, Queen's Gurkha Signals
    - 1st Btn, 10th Princess Mary's Own Gurkha Rifles
    - C Flight, 660 Squadron AAC, Anduki Airfield, (Scout AH.1)
    - Brunei Troop, Gurkha Transport Regiment

Royal Air Force

- Royal Air Force: 93,300

Director Special Forces

- **Director Special Forces**, commands United Kingdom Special Forces
  - **Special Air Service**, Stirling Lines, Hereford
    - HQ Special Air Service & 264 (SAS) Signal Squadron, Hereford
    - 22nd Special Air Service Regiment, Stirling Lines, Hereford
    - 8 Flight AAC, (4x A109A Hirundo), Stirling Lines, Hereford
  - **Special Air Service Group**, (Stay-behind Observation Posts and Long Range Reconnaissance Patrols for I British Corps)
    - 63 (SAS) Signal Squadron (V), Thorney Island
    - 21 Special Air Service Regiment (Artists) (V), Chelsea
    - Special Air Service Regiment (V), Birmingham
  - Special Boat Service, Royal Marines, Poole
  - 14 Intelligence Company, British Army, RAF Aldergrove

Joint Establishments

Joint establishments were tri-service units providing services to all three branches of the British Armed Forces/

- Joint Service Defence College, Greenwich
- Joint Forward Air Controller Training and Standards Unit, RAF Leeming
- Joint Air Transport Establishment, RAF Brize Norton

Defence Operations Executive

The Defence Operations Executive, led by the Deputy Chief of the Defence Staff (Commitments) and including the Assistant Chiefs of the Naval, General, and Air Staffs, supervised the Joint Operations Centre which in turn passed orders to the forces in Cyprus, Belize, the Falklands, and Hong Kong. These commands consisted of units of all three services and were commanded by one or 2-star rank flag officers.[339] CBF Cyprus was a rotational post between the Army and RAF, at two-star level; CBF Belize was an Army brigadier; CBF Falklands was a rotational post between all three services at two-star level; and CBF Hong Kong was an Army major general.

British Forces Belize

The Commander British Forces Belize was a British Army Brigadier.

- **British Forces Belize**, Belize City, Belize
  - **British Army**, Price Barracks, Ladyville
    - 1st Btn, Welsh Guards, six month roulement from April to October 1989
    - 1x Armoured Reconnaissance Troop, six month roulement
    - 1x Field Battery, Royal Artillery, six month roulement
    - 1x Field Squadron, Royal Engineers, six month roulement
    - 24th Squadron, Royal Corps of Transport
    - 78th Ordnance Company, Royal Army Ordnance Corps
    - 25 Flight AAC, Belize Airport, Ladyville, (Gazelle AH.1)
  - **Royal Air Force**, Belize Airport, Ladyville
    - No. 1417 Flight RAF, (Harrier GR.3)
    - No. 1563 Flight RAF, (Puma HC.1)
    - 1x Air Defence Troop, RAF Regiment, six month roulement, (2× Rapier launch stations)
  - **Royal Navy**
    - West Indies Guard Ship, as needed.Wikipedia:Citation needed

British Forces Cyprus

The post of Commander British Forces Cyprus rotated between British Army and Royal Navy 2-star rank flag officers (Major General and Rear admiral).

- **British Forces Cyprus**, Episkopi, Cyprus
  - HQ, British Forces Cyprus, Episkopi
  - **British Army**:
    - 2nd Btn, Coldstream Guards, Episkopi, two-year deployment: February 1988 to February 1990
    - 9th Signal Regiment (Radio), Royal Signals, at Ayios Nikolaos Signals Intelligence station
    - 30th Transport Regiment, Royal Corps of Transport, Episkopi
    - B Squadron, 17th/21st Lancers, Episkopi, six month roulement
    - 62nd Cyprus Support Squadron, Royal Engineers, Dhekelia
    - 259th Signal Squadron, Episkopi
    - 262nd Signal Squadron, Dhekelia
    - 16 Flight AAC, Kingsfield Airfield in Dhekelia, (Gazelle AH.1)
    - UNFICYP Flight AAC, Nicosia Airport, (Gazelle AH.1, supported the United Nations Peacekeeping Force in Cyprus)
  - **Royal Air Force**:
    - No. 84 Squadron RAF, RAF Akrotiri (Wessex HC.2)

- No. 34 Squadron RAF Regiment, RAF Akrotiri, (Light Armour, 15× Spartan, 6× Scorpion)
- No. 13 Signals Unit, RAF Episkopi
- No. 33 Signals Unit, Ayios Nikolaos, (Signals intelligence)
- No. 280 Signals Unit, RAF Troodos, (Signals intelligence)

British Forces Falkland Islands

The post of Commander British Forces Falkland Islands rotated between British Army, Royal Navy and Royal Air Force 2-star rank flag officers (Major General, Rear admiral and Air vice-marshal).

- **British Forces Falkland Islands**, RAF Mount Pleasant, Falkland Islands
  - HQ British Forces Falkland Islands & Joint Communications Unit Falklands Islands,
  - Joint Force Workshop, RAF Mount Pleasant
  - Falkland Islands Defence Force, Stanley
    - **British Army**, RAF Mount Pleasant
      - Infantry company from 1st Btn, Cheshire Regiment, six month roulement April to October 1989; replaced by infantry company from 1st Btn, Green Howards
      - 1x Artillery Battery, Royal Artillery, six month roulement (6x L118 Light Guns)
      - 1x Field Squadron, Royal Engineers, six month roulement
      - 1x Air Defence Troop, Royal Artillery, six month roulement, (12x Javelin)
      - 67th Port Squadron, Royal Corps of Transport
      - 73rd Squadron, Royal Corps of Transport
      - 77th Ordnance Company, Royal Army Ordnance Corps
    - **Royal Air Force**, RAF Mount Pleasant
      - No. 78 Squadron RAF, (Air assault CH-47 Chinook HC.1, Search & Rescue Sea King HAR.3)
      - No. 1435 Flight RAF, (Phantom FGR.2)
      - No. 1312 Flight RAF, (Aerial refueling Hercules C.1K)
      - No. 7 Signals Unit
      - No. 303 Signals Unit
      - No. 751 Signals Unit
      - 1x Air Defence Troop, RAF Regiment, six month roulement, (2× Rapier launch stations)
    - **Royal Navy**, Stanley
      - Castle-class patrol vessel: HMS Leeds Castle (crew on a six-month roulement)

Figure 36: *A Royal Hong Kong Auxiliary Air Force Aerospatiale Dauphin helicopter leaving its hangar during a Search and Rescue exercise in 1982.*

British Forces Hong Kong

The Commander British Forces Hong Kong was a British Army Major General.

- **Commander British Forces Hong Kong**, Hong Kong
    - HQ British Forces Hong Kong & 248th Gurkha Signal Squadron, Headquarters House
    - **British Army**, Prince of Wales Building
        - **48th Gurkha Infantry Brigade**
            - HQ 48th Gurkha Infantry Brigade & 246th Gurkha Signal Squadron
            - 1st Btn, Duke of Edinburgh's Royal Regiment, Stanley Fort
            - 1st Btn, 6th Queen Elizabeth's Own Gurkha Rifles
            - 1st Btn, 7th Duke of Edinburgh's Own Gurkha Rifles
            - 2nd Btn, 2nd King Edward VII's Own Gurkha Rifles, Gallipoli Lines
        - Queen's Gurkha Signals
            - 247th Gurkha Signal Squadron
        - Queen's Gurkha Engineers
            - 67th Gurkha Field Squadron
            - 68th Gurkha Field Squadron
            - 70th Support Squadron

- Gurkha Transport Regiment
  - 28th Gurkha Transport Squadron
  - 29th Transport Squadron
  - 31st Gurkha Transport Squadron
- 660 Squadron AAC, RAF Sek Kong, (Scout AH.1, C Flight detached to British Forces Brunei)
- 50th Command Workshop, Royal Electrical and Mechanical Engineers
- Hong Kong Provost Company & Hong Kong Dog Company, Royal Military Police
- 415th Maritime Troop, Royal Corps of Transport
- British Military Hospital, Hong Kong
- Hong Kong Military Service Corps
  - Defence Animal Support Unit, Royal Army Veterinary Corps
- **Commander Royal Air Force**, RAF Sek Kong
  - No. 28 Squadron RAF, (8x Wessex HC.2)
- **Captain-in-Charge Royal Navy**, HMS Tamar
  - **Hong Kong Patrol Squadron**, HMS Tamar with:
    - Peacock-class corvettes: HMS Peacock, HMS Plover, HMS Starling
  - Hong Kong Royal Naval Volunteer Reserve

The two local auxiliary defence forces were administered by the Hong Kong Government, but when called out would have come under the command of Commander British Forces:

- Royal Hong Kong Regiment (The Volunteers) (V)
- Royal Hong Kong Auxiliary Air Force, Kai Tak Airport, (4x T-67M-200 Firefly, 2x B200C King Air, 3x SA-365-C Dauphin 2, 1x BN-2 Islander)

Nuclear Weapons

Nuclear weapons and the United Kingdom

United Kingdom	
Nuclear program start date	10 April 1940
First nuclear weapon test	3 October 1952
First fusion weapon test	15 May 1957
Last nuclear test	26 November 1991
Largest yield test	3 Mt (13 PJ) (28 April 1958)
Total tests	45 detonations
Peak stockpile	520 warheads (1970s)
Current stockpile (usable and not)	215 warheads (2016)
Current strategic arsenal	120 warheads (2016)
Maximum missile range	12,000 kilometres (7,500 mi)) (UGM-133 Trident II)
NPT party	Yes (1968, one of five recognised powers)

Nuclear weapons
Background

- History
- Warfare
- Design
- Testing
- Delivery
- Yield
- Effects and estimated megadeaths of explosions
- Winter

- Workers
- Ethics
- Arsenals
- Arms race
- Espionage
- Proliferation
- Disarmament
- Terrorism
- Opposition

Nuclear-armed states
NPT recognized   United States   Russia   United Kingdom   France   China
Others   India   Israel (undeclared)   Pakistan   North Korea
Former   South Africa   Belarus   Kazakhstan   Ukraine

- v
- t
- e^{340}

In October 1952, the United Kingdom became the third country to independently develop and test nuclear weapons. It is one of the five nuclear-weapon states under the Treaty on the Non-Proliferation of Nuclear Weapons. Since the 1958 US–UK Mutual Defence Agreement, the United States and the UK have cooperated extensively on nuclear security matters. The nuclear Special Relationship between the two countries has involved the exchange of classified scientific data and fissile materials such as uranium-235 and plutonium.

The UK has not had a programme to develop an independent delivery system since the cancellation of the Blue Streak in 1960. Instead, it has purchased US delivery systems for UK use, fitting them with warheads designed and manufactured by the UK's Atomic Weapons Establishment (AWE) and its predecessor. In 1974, a US proliferation report discussing British nuclear and missile development noted that "In many cases, it is based on technology received from the US and could not legitimately be passed on without US permission."

Since 1998, when the UK decommissioned its tactical WE.177 bombs, the Trident has been the only operational nuclear weapons system in British service. The delivery system consists of four *Vanguard*-class submarine based at

HMNB Clyde in Scotland. Each submarine is armed with up to sixteen Trident II missiles, each carrying warheads in up to eight Multiple independently targetable reentry vehicles (MIRVs). With at least one submarine always on patrol, the *Vanguards* perform a strategic deterrence role and are also have a sub-strategic capability.

History

Tube Alloys

The neutron was discovered by James Chadwick at the Cavendish Laboratory at the University of Cambridge in February 1932,[341] and in April 1932, his Cavendish colleagues John Cockcroft and Ernest Walton split lithium atoms with accelerated protons.[342] In December 1938, Otto Hahn and Fritz Strassmann at Hahn's laboratory in Berlin-Dahlem bombarded uranium with slow neutrons,[343] and discovered that barium had been produced, and therefore that the uranium nucleus had been split.[344] Hahn wrote to his colleague Lise Meitner, who, with her nephew Otto Frisch, developed a theoretical justification for the process based on Niels Bohr's liquid drop model of the nucleus, which they published in *Nature* in 1939.[345] By analogy with the division of biological cells, they named the process "fission".[346]

The discovery of fission raised the possibility that an extremely powerful atomic bomb could be created.[347] The term was already familiar to the British public through the writings of H. G. Wells, with a continuously-exploding bomb in his 1913 novel *The World Set Free*.[348] George Paget Thomson, at Imperial College London, and Mark Oliphant, an Australian physicist at the University of Birmingham, were tasked with carrying out a series of experiments on uranium.[349] Oliphant delegated the task to two German refugee scientists, Rudolf Peierls and Frisch, who ironically could not work on the university's secret projects like radar because they were enemy aliens and therefore lacked the necessary security clearance.[350] They calculated the critical mass of a metallic sphere of pure uranium-235, and found that instead of tons, as everyone had assumed, as little as 1 to 10 kilograms (2.2 to 22.0 lb) would suffice, which would explode with the power of thousands of tons of dynamite.[351,352]

Oliphant took the Frisch–Peierls memorandum to Sir Henry Tizard, the chairman of the Tizard Committee,[353] and the MAUD Committee was established to investigate further.[354] It directed an intensive research effort, and in July 1941, produced two comprehensive reports that reached the conclusion that an atomic bomb was not only technically feasible, but could be produced before the war ended, perhaps in as little as two years. The Committee unanimously recommended pursuing the development of an atomic bomb as a matter of urgency, although it recognised that the resources required might be beyond those available to Britain.[355,356] A new directorate known as Tube Alloys was created to coordinate this effort. Sir John Anderson, the Lord President of the Council, became the minister responsible, and Wallace Akers from Imperial Chemical Industries (ICI) was appointed the director of Tube Alloys.[357]

Manhattan Project

In July 1940, Britain had offered to give the United States access to its scientific research,[358] and the Tizard Mission's John Cockcroft briefed American scientists on British developments.[359] He discovered that the American S-1 Project (later renamed the Manhattan Project) was smaller than the British, and not as far advanced.[355] The British and American projects exchanged information, but did not initially combine their efforts. British officials did not reply to an August 1941 American offer to create a combined project.[360] In November 1941, Frederick L. Hovde, the head of the London liaison office of the American Office of Scientific Research and Development (OSRD), raised the issue of cooperation and exchange of information with Anderson and Lord Cherwell, who demurred, ostensibly over concerns about American security. Ironically, it was the British project that had already been penetrated by atomic spies for the Soviet Union.[361]

The United Kingdom did not have the manpower or resources of the United States, and despite its early and promising start, Tube Alloys fell behind its American counterpart and was dwarfed by it.[362] On 30 July 1942, Anderson advised the Prime Minister, Winston Churchill, that: "We must face the fact that ... [our] pioneering work ... is a dwindling asset and that, unless we capitalise it quickly, we shall be outstripped. We now have a real contribution to make to a 'merger.' Soon we shall have little or none."[363]

The British considered producing an atomic bomb without American help, but it would require overwhelming priority, disruption to other wartime projects was inevitable, and it was unlikely to be ready in time to affect the outcome of the war in Europe. The unanimous response was that before embarking on this, another effort should be made to secure American cooperation.[364] At the Quebec Conference in August 1943, Churchill and the President of the United States, Franklin Roosevelt, signed the Quebec Agreement, which merged the two national projects.[365] The Quebec Agreement established the Combined Policy Committee and the Combined Development Trust to coordinate their efforts, and that the weapons could only be used if both the USA and UK governments agreed.[366] The 19 September 1944 Hyde Park Agreement extended both commercial and military cooperation into the post-war period.[367]

A British mission led by Akers assisted in the development of gaseous diffusion technology at the SAM Laboratories in New York.[368] Another, led by Oliphant, who acted as deputy director at the Berkeley Radiation Laboratory, assisted with the electromagnetic separation process.[369] Cockcroft became the director of the Anglo-Canadian Montreal Laboratory.[370] The British mission to the Los Alamos Laboratory was led by James Chadwick, and later Peierls. It included distinguished scientists such as Geoffrey Taylor, James Tuck, Niels Bohr, William Penney, Frisch, Ernest Titterton and Klaus Fuchs, who was later revealed to be a Soviet spy.[371,372] As overall head of the British Mission, Chadwick forged a close and successful partnership with Brigadier General Leslie R. Groves, the director of the Manhattan Project.[373] He ensured that British participation was complete and wholehearted.[374]

Penney worked on means to assess the effects of a nuclear explosion, and wrote a paper on what height the bombs should be detonated at for maximum effect in attacks on Germany and Japan. He served as a member of the target committee established by Groves to select Japanese cities for atomic bombing,[375] and on Tinian with Project Alberta as a special consultant. Along with Group Captain Leonard Cheshire, sent by Wilson as a British representative, he watched the bombing of Nagasaki from the observation plane *Big Stink*. He also formed part of the Manhattan Project's post-war scientific mission to Hiroshima and Nagasaki that assessed the extent of the damage caused by the bombs.[376]

End of American cooperation

With the end of the war, the Special Relationship between Britain and the United States "became very much less special".[377] The British government had trusted that America would share nuclear technology, which it considered a joint discovery.[378] On 8 August 1945 the Prime Minister, Clement Attlee, sent a message to President Harry Truman in which he referred to themselves as "heads of the Governments which have control of this great force".[378] But Roosevelt had died on 12 April 1945, and the Hyde Park Agreement was not binding on subsequent administrations.[379] In fact, it was physically lost. When Wilson raised the matter in a Combined Policy Committee meeting in June, the American copy could not be found.[380]

On 9 November 1945, Attlee and the Prime Minister of Canada, Mackenzie King, went to Washington, D.C., to confer with Truman about future cooperation in nuclear weapons and nuclear power.[381,382] A Memorandum of Intention they signed replaced the Quebec Agreement. It made Canada a full partner, continued the Combined Policy Committee and Combined Development Trust, and reduced the obligation to obtain consent for the use of nuclear weapons to merely requiring consultation.[383] The three leaders agreed that there would be full and effective cooperation on atomic energy, but British hopes were soon disappointed;[384] the Americans restricted cooperation to basic scientific research.[385]

The next meeting of the Combined Policy Committee on 15 April 1946 produced no accord on collaboration, and resulted in an exchange of cables between Truman and Attlee. Truman cabled on 20 April that he did not see the communiqué he had signed as obligating the United States to assist Britain in designing, constructing and operating an atomic energy plant.[386] The passing of the Atomic Energy Act of 1946 (McMahon Act) in August 1946, which was signed by Truman on 1 August 1946, and went into effect at midnight on 1 January 1947,[387] ended technical cooperation. Its control of "restricted data" prevented the United States' allies from receiving any information.[388]

This partly resulted from the arrest for espionage of British physicist Alan Nunn May, who had worked in the Montreal Laboratory, in February 1946, while the legislation was being debated.[389] It was but the first of a series of spy scandals. The arrest of Klaus Fuchs in January 1950,[390] and the June 1951 defection of Donald Maclean, who had served as a British member of the Combined Policy Committee from January 1947 to August 1948, left Americans with a distrust of British security arrangements.[391] The remaining British scientists working in the United States were denied access to papers that they had written just days before.[392]

Resumption of independent UK efforts

Attlee set up a cabinet sub-committee, the Gen 75 Committee (known informally by Attlee as the "Atomic Bomb Committee"),[393] on 10 August 1945 to examine the feasibility of an independent British nuclear weapons programme.[394] The Chiefs of Staff Committee considered the issue of nuclear weapons in July 1946, and recommended that Britain acquire them.[395] The Chief of the Air Staff, Marshal of the Royal Air Force Lord Tedder, officially requested an atomic bomb in 9 August 1946.[396,397] The Chiefs of Staff estimated that 200 bombs would be required by 1957.[398] A nuclear reactor and plutonium-processing facility was approved by the Gen 75 committee on 18 December 1945 "with the highest urgency and importance".[399]

The Tube Alloys Directorate was transferred from the Department of Scientific and Industrial Research to the Ministry of Supply effective 1 November 1945.[400] To coordinate the atomic energy effort, Marshal of the Royal Air

Force Lord Portal, the wartime Chief of the Air Staff, was appointed the Controller of Production, Atomic Energy (CPAE) in March 1946.[401] The Gen 75 Committee considered the proposal in October 1946.[402] In October 1946, Attlee called a meeting to discuss building a gaseous diffusion plant for uranium enrichment. Michael Perrin, who was present, later recalled that:

> The meeting was about to decide against it on grounds of cost, when [Ernest] Bevin arrived late and said "We've got to have this thing. I don't mind it for myself, but I don't want any other Foreign Secretary of this country to be talked at or to by the Secretary of State of the United States as I have just been in my discussion with Mr Byrnes. We've got to have this thing over here, whatever it costs ... We've got to have the bloody Union Jack flying on top of it."[394,403]

The decision to proceed was formally made on 8 January 1947 at a meeting of Gen 163, a subcommittee of the Gen 75 Committee consisting of six Cabinet members, including Attlee,[404] and was publicly announced in the House of Commons on 12 May 1948. D notice No. 25 prohibited the publication of details on the design, construction or location of atomic weapons.[405,406] The project was given the cover name "High Explosive Research".[407] As Chief Superintendent Armament Research (CSAR, pronounced "Caesar"), Penney directed bomb design from Fort Halstead.[408] In 1951 his design group moved to a new site at Aldermaston in Berkshire.[409]

Production facilities were constructed under the direction of Christopher Hinton, who established his headquarters in a former Royal Ordnance Factory at Risley in Lancashire.[410] These included a uranium metal plant at Springfields,[411] nuclear reactors and a plutonium processing plant at Windscale,[412] and a gaseous diffusion uranium enrichment facility at Capenhurst, near Chester.[413] The two Windscale reactors became operational in October 1950 and June 1951.[414] The gaseous diffusion plant at Capenhurst began producing highly enriched uranium in 1954.

Uranium ore was stockpiled at Springfields. As the American nuclear programme expanded, its requirements became greater than the production of the existing mines. To gain access to the stockpile, they reopened negotiations in 1947. This resulted in the 1948 *Modus Vivendi*,[415] which allowed for consultation on the use of nuclear weapons, and limited sharing of technical information between the United States, Britain and Canada.[416,417] In the meantime, nuclear deterrence was provided by the United States Strategic Air Command,[418] which had begun operating from British bases in 1949.[419]

Unsuccessful attempt to renew American partnership

By 1949, international control of atomic weapons seemed almost impossible to achieve, and Truman proposed to the Joint Committee on Atomic Energy in July a "full partnership" with Britain in exchange for uranium; negotiations between the two countries began that month. While the first Soviet atomic bomb test in August 1949 was embarrassing to the British (who had not expected a Soviet atomic weapon until 1954) for having been beaten, it was for the Americans another reason for cooperation. Although they would soon have their own nuclear capability, the British proposed that instead of building their own uranium-enrichment plant they would send most of their scientists to work in the US, and swap plutonium from Windscale for enriched uranium from the US. While Britain would not formally give up building or researching its own weapons, the US would manufacture all the bombs and allocate some to Britain.[420,421]

By agreeing to subsume its own weapons program within the Americans', the plan would have given Britain nuclear weapons much sooner than its own target date of late 1952. Although a majority of Americans including Truman supported the proposal, several key officials, including the United States Atomic Energy Commission's Lewis Strauss and Senator Arthur Vandenberg, did not. Their opposition, along with security concerns raised by the arrest of Fuchs, who was working at Harwell, ended the negotiations in January 1950.[422] After Britain developed nuclear weapons through its own efforts, the engineer Sir Leonard Owen stated that "the McMahon Act was probably one of the best things that happened ... as it made us work and think for ourselves along independent lines."[423]

First test and early systems

Churchill, now again prime minister, announced on 17 February 1952 that the first British weapon test would occur before the end of the year. Operation Hurricane was detonated in the frigate HMS *Plym* anchored in the Monte Bello Islands, Western Australia on 3 October 1952.[423] Britain thereby became the third country to develop and test nuclear weapons.[424]

This led to the development of the first deployed weapon, the Blue Danube free-fall bomb. It had a 60-inch (1,500 mm) diameter, 32 explosive lens implosion system with a levitated pit suspended within a natural uranium tamper.[425] The warhead was contained within a bomb casing measuring 62 inches (1,600 mm) diameter and 24 feet (7.3 m) long, and it weighed approximately

4.5 tonnes (4.4 long tons), of which about 2.5 tonnes (2.5 long tons) was high explosive.[426] The first Blue Danube bombs were delivered to the Royal Air Force (RAF) Bomber Command in November 1953,[427] although the bombers to deliver them did not become available until 1955.[428,429]

About fifty-eight Blue Danube bombs were produced.[430] The first bombs had plutonium cores, but all service models were modified to use a composite core which used both uranium-235 and plutonium. The bomb had a yield of 10 to 12 kilotonnes of TNT (42 to 50 TJ). The cores were stored separately from the high explosive components in concrete "igloos" at RAF Barnham in Suffolk and RAF Faldingworth in Lincolnshire. Some casings were stored elsewhere in the UK and in Cyprus for "second strike" use.[431] It remained in service until 1962, and was replaced by Red Beard, a smaller tactical boosted fission weapon. The Blue Danube cores were recycled, and the plutonium used in other nuclear weapons.[430]

Being so big and heavy, Blue Danube could only be carried by the V bombers, so-called because they all had names starting with a "V".[432] The three strategic bombers, known collectively as the V class, comprised the United Kingdom's strategic nuclear strike force during the 1950s and 1960s, which was known as V force of the Main Force.[433,434] The three V bombers were the Vickers Valiant, which entered service in February 1955;[435] the Avro Vulcan, which entered service in May 1956; and the Handley Page Victor, which entered service in November 1957. The V Bomber force reached its peak in June 1964, when 50 Valiants, 70 Vulcans and 39 Victors were in service.

Thermonuclear weaponry

A month after Britain's first atomic weapons test, America tested the first thermonuclear (hydrogen) bomb. The Soviets responded with Joe 4, a boosted fission weapon, in 1953. Penney believed that Britain could not afford to develop a hydrogen bomb.[436] Henry Tizard believed that the nation should focus on conventional forces instead of duplicating the nuclear capabilities of the American Strategic Air Command, which already defended Britain and Europe:[437] "We are a great nation, but if we continue to behave like a Great Power we shall soon cease to be a great nation. Let us take warning from the fate of the Great Powers of the past and not burst ourselves with pride."[437]

The First Sea Lord, Admiral Lord Mountbatten, and Chief of the Imperial General Staff, General Sir Gerald Templer supported the development of a hydrogen bomb, but preferred more support for conventional forces. They believed that the large American and Soviet nuclear forces acted as mutual deterrents for nuclear war, making conventional war more likely.[438] Others proposed that, instead of repeated unsuccessful attempts to increase cooperation with the Americans, Britain work with Australia, Canada, and other Commonwealth countries. Britain could not disclose atomic information to Australia despite testing weapons there because of agreements with the United States.[439]

The Chiefs of Staff Committee and the Churchill ministry, however, believed that

> *If we did not develop megaton weapons we would sacrifice immediately and in perpetuity our position as a first-class power. We would have to rely on the whim of the United States for the effectiveness of the whole basis of our strategy.*[440]

The government decided on 27 July 1954 to begin development of a thermonuclear bomb, and announced its plans in February 1955.[441] British knowledge of thermonuclear weapons was based on the work done at the Los Alamos Laboratory during the war. Two British scientists, Egon Bretscher and Klaus Fuchs, had attended the conference there on the Super (as it was then called) in April 1946, and Chadwick had written a secret report on it in May 1946,[442] but the design was found to be unworkable.[443] Some intelligence about Joe 4 was derived from its debris, which was provided to Britain under the 1948 *Modus Vivendi*.[444] Penney established three megaton bomb projects at Aldermaston: Orange Herald, a large boosted fission weapon; Green Bamboo, an interim thermonuclear design similar to the Soviet Layer Cake used in Joe 4 and the American Alarm Clock; and Green Granite, a true thermonuclear design.[445]

The Green Granite prototype, known as Short Granite, was tested in the first of the Operation Grapple test series, Grapple 1. The bomb was dropped from a height of 45,000 feet (14,000 m) by a Vickers Valiant piloted by Wing Commander Kenneth Hubbard, off the shore of Malden Island in the Pacific on 15 May 1957. It was Britain's second airdrop of a nuclear bomb after the Operation Buffalo test at Maralinga on 11 October 1956, and the first of a thermonuclear weapon.[446] The United States had not attempted an airdrop of a hydrogen bomb until the Operation Redwing Cherokee test on 21 May 1956.[447] Short Granite's yield was estimated at 300 kilotonnes of TNT (1,300 TJ), far below its designed capability.[448] Despite its failure, the test was hailed as a successful thermonuclear explosion, and the government did not confirm or deny reports that the UK had become a third thermonuclear power. When documents on the series began to be declassified in the 1990s, they were denounced as a hoax. The reports were unlikely to have fooled the American observers.[449]

The next test was Grapple 2, of Orange Herald,[450] the first British weapon to incorporate an external neutron initiator.[451] It was dropped on 31 May,[450] and exploded with a force of 720 to 800 kilotonnes of TNT (3,000 to 3,300 TJ). The yield was the largest ever achieved by a single stage device,[452] which made it technically a megaton weapon.[453] The bomb was hailed as a hydrogen bomb, and the truth that it was actually a large fission bomb was kept secret by the British government until the end of the Cold War.[454,455] Penney cancelled the planned Green Granite test, and substituted Purple Granite, a Short Granite with some minor modifications.[448] Its yield was a very disappointing 300 kilotonnes of TNT (1,300 TJ), even less than Short Granite; the changes had not worked.[453]

An Operational Requirement (OR1142) was issued in 1955 for a thermonuclear warhead for a medium-range ballistic missile, which became Blue Streak. This was revised in November 1955, with "megaton" replacing "thermonuclear". Orange Herald could then meet the requirement.[456] Codenamed Green Grass, the unsuccessful fusion boosting was omitted, and it used Green Bamboo's 72-lens implosion system instead of Orange Herald's 32. This allowed the amount of highly enriched uranium to be reduced from 120 to 75 kg. Its yield was estimated at 0.5 megatonnes of TNT (2.1 PJ).[452] It was placed in a Blue Danube casing, and became known as Violet Club. Road transport of the weapon was hazardous. As a safety measure 120,000 steel ball bearings were used to fill a cavity inside the core and keep the fissile components apart. In an accident, the steel bung was removed and the ball bearings spilled on the floor of an aircraft hanger, leaving the bomb armed and dangerous.[457] About ten were delivered.[458]

The scientists at Aldermaston had not yet mastered the design of thermonuclear weapons. They produced a new design, called Round A.[459,460] Another trial was scheduled, known as Grapple X.[459,461] Round A was dropped on 8 November 1957.[462,463] To save time and money,[459] the target was off the southern tip of Christmas Island rather than off Malden Island, just 20 nautical miles (37 km; 23 mi) from the airfield where 3,000 men were based.[461] This time the yield of 1.8 megatonnes of TNT (7.5 PJ) exceeded expectations. Round A was a true hydrogen bomb, but it used a relatively large quantity of expensive highly enriched uranium.[464]

Aldermaston had plenty of ideas about how to follow up Grapple X. A new design used lithium deuteride that was less enriched in lithium-6 (and therefore had more lithium-7), but more of it, thereby reducing the amount of uranium-235 in the core. Because of the possibility of an international moratorium on atmospheric testing, plans for the trial, codenamed Grapple Y, were given verbal approval by the Prime Minister, and known only to a handful of officials.[465] The bomb was dropped off Christmas on 28 April 1958.[466,467] It had an explosive yield of about 3 megatonnes of TNT (13 PJ), and remains the largest British nuclear weapon ever tested.[467] The design of Grapple Y was notably successful because much of its yield came from its thermonuclear reaction instead of fission of a uranium-238 tamper, making it a true hydrogen bomb, and because its yield had been correctly predicted—indicating that its designers understood what they were doing.[460,468]

On 22 August 1958, US President Dwight D. Eisenhower announced a moratorium on nuclear testing. This did not mean an immediate end to testing; on the contrary, the United States, the Soviet Union and the United Kingdom all rushed to perform as much testing as possible before the deadline.[469] A new British test series, known as Grapple Z, commenced on 22 August. It explored new technologies such as the use of external neutron initiators, which had first been tried out with Orange Herald. Core boosting using tritium and external boosting with layers of lithium deuteride were successfully tested, allowing a smaller, lighter two-stage devices.[470] The international moratorium commenced on 31 October 1958, and Britain ceased atmospheric testing for good.[471]

An independent deterrent

Believing that the United Kingdom was extremely vulnerable to a nuclear attack to which defence was impossible, the Chiefs of Staff and the RAF first advocated a British nuclear deterrence—not just nuclear weapons—in 1945: "It is our opinion that our only chance of securing a quick decision is by launching a devastating attack upon [enemy cities] with absolute weapons." In 1947 the Chiefs of Staff stated that even with American help the United Kingdom could not prevent the "vastly superior" Soviet forces from overrunning Western Europe, from which Russia could destroy Britain with missiles without using atomic weapons. Only "the threat of large-scale damage from similar weapons" could prevent the Soviet Union from using atomic weapons in a war.[472]

Air Chief Marshal Sir John Slessor, who became Chief of the Air Staff in 1950, wrote that year that the Soviet superiority in European forces was so great that even "an ultimatum by Russia within the next two to three years" might cause Western Europe to surrender without a war. He feared that the United Kingdom might also do so "unless we can make ourselves far less defenceless than we are now." By 1952 the Air Ministry had abandoned the concept of a conventional defence of Western Europe.[473] The hydrogen bomb increased the threat to Britain. In 1957, a government study stated that although RAF fighters would "unquestionably be able to take a heavy toll of enemy bombers, a proportion would inevitably get through. Even if it were only a dozen, they could with megaton bombs inflict widespread devastation." Although disarmament remained a British goal, "the only existing safeguard against major aggression is the power to threaten retaliation with nuclear weapons."[474]

Churchill stated in a 1955 speech that deterrence would be "the parents of disarmament" and that, unless Britain contributed to Western deterrence with its own weapons, during a war the targets that threatened it the most might not be prioritised. The Prime Minister, Harold Macmillan, advanced the position that nuclear weapons would give Britain influence over targeting and American policy, and would affect strategy in the Middle East and Far East. His Minister of Defence, Duncan Sandys, considered that nuclear weapons reduced Britain's dependence on the United States.[475] The 1956 Suez Crisis demonstrated that Britain was longer a great power,[476] but increased the value to Britain of an independent nuclear deterrent that would give it greater influence with the US and USSR.[477] While the military target of British nuclear weapons was the Soviet Union, the political target was the United States.[478]

Independent targeting was vital. The Chiefs of Staff believed that—contrary to Tizard's view—once the Soviet Union became able to attack the United States itself with nuclear weapons in the late 1950s, America might not risk its own cities to defend Europe, or not emphasise targets that endangered the United Kingdom more than the United States:[479,480]

> *When New York is vulnerable to attack the United States will not use her strategic weapon in defence of London. The United Kingdom must, therefore, have its own retaliatory defence. Similarly, however, we will not be prepared to sacrifice the United Kingdom in the defence of say Darwin, and eventually each political unit must have its own means of retaliation.*[481,482]

Britain thus needed the ability to convince the USSR that attacking Europe would be too costly regardless of American participation. Part of the perceived effectiveness of an independent deterrent was the willingness to target enemy cities. Slessor saw atomic weapons as a way to avoid a third devastating world war given that the two previous ones had begun without them. While he sought to de-emphasise city targeting in British plans as Air Chief,[483] Slessor wrote in 1954 after retirement:

> *And if [war] is forced upon us, we must be able to instantly deliver a crushing counter-attack upon aggression at its source—not merely at its airfields, its launching sites and submarine bases, at its armies in the field but at the heart of the aggressor country. There will be the battlefield if battlefield there must be.*[484]

When Air Marshal Sir George Mills became head of RAF Bomber Command in 1955 he similarly insisted on targeting Soviet cities, writing "Whoever would be afraid of launching a sudden attack if he thought the greater part of our retaliation would come back to his airfields?"[485] The belief in the importance of retaining an independent capability has continued over several decades and changes in government. As the Defence Council stated in 1980:

> our force has to be visibly capable of making a massive strike on its own ... We need to convince Soviet leaders that even if they thought ... the US would hold back, the British force could still inflict a blow so destructive that the penalty for aggression would have proved too high.

When France developed its own nuclear weapons, British politicians contended that Europe required a independent deterrent other than that of France.[486]

Renewed American partnership

The Soviet Union's launch of Sputnik 1, the world's first artificial satellite, on 4 October 1957, came as a tremendous shock to the American public, who had trusted that American technological superiority ensured their invulnerability. Now, suddenly, there was incontrovertible proof that, in some areas at least, the Soviet Union was actually ahead. In the widespread calls for action in response to the Sputnik crisis, officials in the United States and Britain seized an opportunity to mend the relationship with Britain that had been damaged by the Suez Crisis.[487] Macmillan wrote to Eisenhower on 10 October urging that the two countries pool their resources to meet the challenge.[488]

British information security, or the lack thereof, no longer seemed so important now that the Soviet Union was apparently ahead, and British scientists had demonstrated that they understood how to build a hydrogen bomb with a different form of the Teller-Ulam design to the Americans. The opposition that had derailed previous attempts was now absent.[489] The McMahon Act was amended,[490] paving the way for the 1958 US–UK Mutual Defence Agreement (MDA).[491] Macmillan called this "the Great Prize".[492]

Under the MDA, 5.37 tonnes of UK-produced plutonium was sent to the US in exchange for 6.7 kg of tritium and 7.5 tonnes of HEU between 1960 and 1979. A further 470 kg of plutonium was swapped between the US and the UK for reasons that remain classified. Much of the HEU supplied by the US was used not for weapons, but as fuel for the growing fleet of UK nuclear submarines. Under the MDA, the US supplied the UK with not just nuclear submarine propulsion technology, but a complete S5W pressurised water reactor of the kind used to power the US *Skipjack*-class submarines. This was used in the Royal Navy's first nuclear-powered submarine, HMS *Dreadnought*, which was launched in 1960 and commissioned in 1963. The S5W had a Nuclear reactor core that used uranium enriched to between 93 and 97 per cent uranium-235.[493] Reactor technology was transferred from Westinghouse to Rolls Royce,[494] which used it as the basis for its PWR1 reactor used in the UK's nuclear submarines.[495]

The MDA has been renewed or amended many times. Most amendments merely extended the treaty for another five or ten years; others added definitions and made minor changes. As of 2018[496], the most recent renewal was on 22 July 2014, extending the treaty to 31 December 2024. A 1974 US proliferation report discussing British nuclear and missile development noted that "In many cases, it is based on technology received from the US and could not legitimately be passed on without US permission."

US nuclear weapons

Production of British nuclear weapons was slow and Britain had only ten atomic bombs on hand in 1955 and just fourteen in 1956.[497] At the three-power Bermuda Conference with Eisenhower in December 1953, Churchill, suggested that the United States allow Britain to have access to American nuclear weapons to make up the shortfall.[498] The provision on American weapons was called Project E.[499] The agreement was confirmed by Eisenhower and Macmillan, who was now the Prime Minister, during their March 1957 meeting in Bermuda,[500,501] and a formal Memorandum of Understanding (MOU) was signed on 21 May 1957.[502,503]

Four squadrons of English Electric Canberra bombers based in Germany were equipped with US Mark 7 nuclear bombs stored at RAF Germany bases. There were also four squadrons of nuclear-armed Canberras based in the UK, which were capable of using either the Mark 7 or the British Red Beard. They too were assigned to the SACEUR in October 1960.[504] The planned V-bomber force was reduced to 144 aircraft, and it was intended to equip half of them with Project E weapons,[505] so 72 Mark 5 nuclear bombs were supplied for the V-bombers.[506,507] When the MDA came into force, the US agreed to supply the V-bombers with megaton weapons in place of the Mark 5,[508] in the form of Mark 15 and Mark 39 nuclear bombs.[506]

Under the Project E MOU, US personnel had custody of the weapons. This meant they performed all the tasks related to their storage, maintenance and readiness. The bombs were stored in Secure Storage Areas (SSAs) on the same bases as the bombers which British staff were not permitted to enter. It was therefore impossible to store British and Americans bombs together in the same SSA.[509] US custody also created operational problems. The procedure for handing over the bombs added an extra ten minutes to the bombers' reaction time,[510] and the requirement that US personnel had guardianship of the weapons at all times meant that neither they nor the bombers could be relocated to dispersal airfields as the RAF desired.[511] The operational restrictions imposed by Project E "effectively handed the US government a veto over the use of half of Britain's nuclear deterrent".[512]

The Air Council decided on 7 July 1960 that Project E weapons would be phased out by December 1962, by which time it was anticipated that there would be sufficient British megaton weapons to equip the entire strategic bomber force.[513] Project E weapons were replaced by British Yellow Sun bombs.[514] Problems encountered in the development Red Beard bomb meant that the replacement of kiloton weapons took longer.[515] The Air Ministry decided to replace the Canberras with Valiants as the long-range Avro Vulcan and Handley Page Victor V-bombers became available. A Valiant squadron at RAF Marham was assigned to SACEUR on 1 January 1961, followed by two more in July. The UK-based Canberra squadrons were then disbanded. Each of the 24 Valiants was equipped with two Project E Mark 28 nuclear bombs.[504] These were replaced by the newer Mark 43 nuclear bombs in early 1963.[504] The Valiants were withdrawn from service in 1965.[516]

Project E nuclear warheads were also used on the sixty Thor Intermediate Range Ballistic Missiles (IRBMs) that were operated by the RAF from 1959 to 1963 under Project Emily.[517] During the Cuban Missile Crisis, the RAF's bombers and Thor missiles targeted 16 cities, 44 airfields, 10 air defence control centres and 20 IRBM sites.[518] The RAF high command never warmed to missiles, and always ranked them secondary to the V bomber force. The missile bases were separate from the rest of the RAF and its personnel considered outside the mainstream. Project Emily gave the RAF considerable experience in missile operations, but the 1960 cancellation Blue Streak in favour of the American Skybolt, an air-launched ballistic missile, rendered this expertise of dubious value.[519] An Air Council meeting on 31 May 1962 decided that Project Emily should be terminated by the end of 1963,[520] and the last Thor squadrons were inactivated on 23 August 1963.[521]

The availability of US weapons and designs under the MDA led to the cancellation of several research projects. Indigo Hammer and the smaller Pixie were warheads intended for use with the Red Duster and Seaslug surface-to-air missiles; a British version of the US W44 was chosen instead.[522] Blue Peacock, a 16,000-pound (7,300 kg) atomic demolition munition (ADMs) based on Blue Danube, was cancelled in 1958 in favour of the lighter Violet Mist, based on Red Beard. The development of the even smaller and lighter US ADMs led to its cancellation as well in 1961.[523,524] The US Medium Atomic Demolition

Munition with the W45 was acquired instead.[525] Yellow Anvil was a British artillery warhead. It was cancelled in 1958, and the US supplied the British Army of the Rhine (BAOR) with 36 W33 nuclear warheads that equipped four batteries of eight-inch M115 howitzers. These were later replaced by M110 howitzers.[526,524]

The British Army purchased 113 Corporal missiles from the United States in 1954. It was intended that they would be equipped with British warheads under a project codenamed Violet Vision, but Project E offered a quicker, simpler and cheaper alternative.[527] The US supplied 100 W7 warheads, which had to be drawn from US Army storage sites in southern Germany until arrangements were made for local storage in August 1959.[528,526] A British missile, Blue Water, with an Indigo Hammer warhead, was developed to replace Corporal. The US offered the Honest John missile as an interim replacement. The offer was accepted, and 120 Honest John missiles with W31 warheads were supplied in 1960, enough to equip three artillery regiments.[526,524] Blue Water was cancelled in July 1962,[529] and Honest John remained in service until 1977, when it was replaced by the Lance missile.[526] The British Army deployed more US nuclear weapons than the RAF and Royal Navy combined, peaking at 327 out of 392 in 1976–1978.[525]

A maritime version of Project E, known as Project N supplied US Navy weapons. Providing American atomic bombs for Royal Navy ships would have involved similar dual key arrangements and detachments of US Marines on board Royal Navy ships, which was deemed impractical even for ships and weapons dedicated to use in European waters. However, RAF Coastal Command acquired Mk 101 Lulu nuclear depth bombs (with the W34 nuclear warhead) for its Avro Shackleton and Hawker Siddeley Nimrod maritime patrol aircraft from 1965 to 1971 under Project N.[530,531] These were later replaced by the more capable Mark 57, which was stockpiled at RAF St Mawgan and RAF Machrihanish. When the Cold War ended in 1991, the BAOR still had about 85 Lance missiles, and more than 70 W33 eight-inch and W48 155 mm nuclear artillery shells. The last Project E warheads, including the Mark 57 nuclear depth bombs and those used by the BAOR, were withdrawn in July 1992.[532]

British nuclear weapons

The MDA made fully developed and tested American designs available quickly and cheaply. The first of these was the B28 nuclear bomb, which was "Anglicised" and manufactured in the UK as Red Snow. Exact copies of American designs were not pursued; the high explosive used in American warheads were more sensitive that British high explosive, and had caused fatal accidents in the US. Its use was not contemplated in the UK after an accident at Aldermaston on 28 February 1959 when two men were killed after a piece of British high explosive fell from a lorry. British high explosive was also bulkier, so a redesign was required.[533]

Red Snow was far more economical in its use of fissile material than the Green Grass warhead in the Yellow Sun Mk.1 bomb, Britain's first production hydrogen bomb. A Yellow Sun Mk.2 with Red Snow, therefore, cost £500,000 compared to £1.2 million for the Mk.1. RAF Bomber Command wanted Violet Club replaced as soon as possible, so 37 Yellow Sun Mk.1s were delivered by the end of 1959. Deliveries of the Yellow Sun Mk.2 commenced in January 1961, and 43 were delivered by the end of the year. In November 1958, Red Snow also replaced Green Grass as the warhead in the Blue Steel stand-off missile.[534] A kiloton nuclear weapon, Red Beard, was developed for use by the Canberras and the Royal Navy's Fleet Air Arm. Technical problems delayed its introduction into service,[535] but over 100 were delivered by the end of 1961.[536]

In 1960 the government decided to cancel the Blue Streak missile based on the Chiefs of Staff's conclusion that it was too vulnerable to attack and thus was only useful for a first strike, and decided to purchase the American air-launched Skybolt missile instead.[537] Macmillan met with Eisenhower in March 1960, and secured permission to buy Skybolt without strings attached. In return, the Americans were given permission to base the US Navy's Polaris-equipped ballistic missile submarines at Holy Loch in Scotland.[538]

The Americans initially intended to pair Skybolt with the W47 warhead, an innovative light-weight design from the Lawrence Radiation Laboratory developed for Polaris. The British wanted to use Red Snow, partly for safety reasons and partly because it was not certain that the advanced M47 design would be made available without strings attached. The technical problem was that Red Snow was 1,000 pounds (450 kg) heavier, and therefore the range of the Skybolt would be reduced from 1,000 to 650 miles (1,610 to 1,050 km). A megaton design known as RE.179 based on the W49 warhead used in American ICBMs was developed for Skybolt.[539]

At the same time, work was in progress on a Red Beard replacement for use with the RAF's BAC TSR-2 and the Royal Navy's Blackburn Buccaneer. Ultimately, a warhead was produced in two variants: the high-yield (300 to 450 kilotonnes of TNT (1,300 to 1,900 TJ)) WE.177B and the low-yield (0.5 or 10 kilotonnes of TNT (2.1 or 41.8 TJ)) WE.177A as a Red Beard replacement, and for use in depth charges and anti-submarine missiles. WE.177 was later adapted for use with Polaris, and would become the longest-serving British nuclear weapon.[540]

The deployment of ships carrying nuclear weapons caused embarrassment during the Falklands War, and in the aftermath it was decided to stockpile them ashore in peacetime. When the US withdrew its theatre nuclear weapons from Europe, the British government followed suit.[541] The nuclear depth bombs were withdrawn from service in 1992, followed by the WE.177 free-fall bombs on 31 March 1998, and all were dismantled by the end of August.

Polaris

The Kennedy administration cancelled Skybolt in December 1962 because the United States Secretary of Defense, Robert McNamara, determined that other delivery systems were progressing better than expected, and a further expensive system was surplus to US requirements.[542] In London, over one hundred Conservative members of Parliament, nearly one third of the parliamentary party, signed a motion urging Macmillan to ensure that Britain remained an independent nuclear power.[543]

Macmillan met with President John F. Kennedy and brokered the Nassau Agreement. Macmillan rejected offers of other systems, and insisted that the UK needed to purchase Polaris. nuclear-capable Polaris submarine-launched ballistic missiles. These represented more advanced technology than Skybolt, and the US was not inclined to provide them except as part of a Multilateral Force within the North Atlantic Treaty Organisation (NATO).[544] In the end, Kennedy did not wish to see Macmillan's government collapse,[545] which would imperil Britain's entry into the European Economic Community (EEC),[546] so a face-saving compromise was reached: the US agreed to provide the UK with Polaris missile, which would be assigned to NATO,[547] and could be used independently only when "supreme national interests" intervened.

The Polaris Sales Agreement was signed on 6 April 1963.[548] The UK retained its deterrent force, although its control passed from the RAF to the Royal Navy.[549] The Polaris missiles were equipped with British warheads.[550,551] A base was developed for the Polaris submarines at Faslane on the Firth of Clyde, not far from the US Navy's base at Holy Loch.[552] It was served by a weapons store at nearby Coulport.[553] The first of four Polaris submarines, HMS *Resolution* was launched in September 1966, and commenced its first deterrent patrol in June 1968.[554] The annual running costs of the Polaris boats came to around two per cent of the defence budget, and they came to be seen as a credible deterrent that enhanced Britain's international status.[555] British politicians did not like to talk about "dependence" on the United States, preferring to describe the Special Relationship as one of "interdependence".[556]

Polaris had not been designed to penetrate ABM defences, but the Royal Navy had to ensure that its small Polaris force operating alone, and often with only one submarine on patrol, could penetrate the ABM screen around Moscow.[557] The Wilson government publicly ruled out the purchase of Poseidon missiles in June 1967, and without such a commitment, the Americans were unwilling to share information about warhead vulnerability.[558] The result was Chevaline, an Improved Front End (IFE) that replaced one of the three warheads with multiple decoys and other defensive countermeasures. in what was known as a Penetration Aid Carrier (PAC).[559] It was the most technically complex defence project ever undertaken in the United Kingdom.[560] Chevaline's existence, along with its formerly secret codename, was revealed by the Secretary of State for Defence, Francis Pym, during a debate in the House of Commons on 24 January 1980.[561] By this time the project had gone on for a decade.[562] The final cost reached £1,025 million.[563]

Trident

In 1982, the Thatcher government announced its decision to purchase 65 American Trident II D-5 missiles. These operated as part of a shared pool of weapons based at Naval Submarine Base Kings Bay in the United States. The US would maintain and support the missiles, while the UK would manufacture its own submarines and warheads. The warheads and missiles would be mated in the UK.[564] Four *Vanguard*-class submarine were designed and built,[565]

Each submarine could carry up to 16 missiles, each of which can each carry up to 8 warheads. However, when the decision to purchase Trident II was announced, it was stressed that British Trident boats would carry no more than 128 warheads—the same number as Polaris. In November 1993, the Secretary of State for Defence, Malcolm Rifkind, announced that each boat would deploy no more than 96 warheads.[566] In 2010 this was reduced to a maximum of 40 warheads, split between eight missiles. The missiles have a range of 12,000 kilometres (7,500 mi).

The first Trident boat, HMS *Vanguard*, collected a full load of 16 missiles in 1994, but the second, HMS *Victorious* drew only 12 in 1995, and the third, HMS *Vigilant*, 14 in 1997, leaving the remaining missile tubes empty.[567] Although the UK designed, manufactured and owns the warheads, there is evidence that the warhead design is similar to, or even based on, the US W76 warhead fitted in some US Navy Trident missiles, with design data being supplied by the United States through the MDA.

Since 1969 the United Kingdom has always had at least one ballistic-missile submarine on patrol, giving it a nuclear deterrent that is, what the Defence Council described in 1980 as, "effectively invulnerable to pre-emptive attack". In the Strategic Defence Review published in July 1998, the government stated that once the *Vanguard* submarines became fully operational (the fourth and final one, HMS *Vengeance*, entered service on 27 November 1999), it would "maintain a stockpile of fewer than 200 operationally available warheads".[568] As of 2016[496], the UK had a stockpile of 215 warheads, of which 120 were operational.

The current Trident system cost £12.6 billion to build (at 1996 prices) and £280m a year to maintain. Options for replacing Trident range from £5 billion for the missiles alone to £20–30 billion for missiles, submarines and research facilities. At minimum, for the system to continue after around 2020, the missiles will need to be replaced. The price of replacement of submarine has risen to £31 billion and it is estimated by Ministry of Defence that the cost of Trident replacement program for 30 years to be at £167 billion. The Campaign for Nuclear Disarmament estimated that the cost could be as high as £205 billion.

Trident renewal

Now that the tactical nuclear weapons had been withdrawn from service, Trident was the UK's only remaining nuclear weapons system. Not renewing Trident meant that Britain would become an non-nuclear power. It would spell the end of the Special Relationship with the United States,[569] and strike at Britain's self-image as a great power.[570] A decision on the renewal of Trident was made on 4 December 2006. Prime Minister Tony Blair told MPs it would be "unwise and dangerous" for the UK to give up its nuclear weapons. He outlined plans to spend up to £20bn on a new generation of ballistic missile submarines. The new boars would continue to carry the Trident II D-5 missiles, but submarine numbers might be cut from four to three, and the number of nuclear warheads would be cut by 20% to 160. He said although the Cold War had ended, the UK needed nuclear weapons, as no-one could be sure another nuclear threat would not emerge in the future.

The 2010 coalition government agreed "that the renewal of Trident should be scrutinised to ensure value for money. Liberal Democrats will continue to make the case for alternatives." Research and development work continued, but the final decision to proceed with building a replacement was scheduled for 2016, after the next election. There was already some urgency to move

Figure 37: *Faslane Naval Base, home of the Vanguard-class submarines which carry the UK's nuclear arsenal.*

ahead because some experts predicted it could take 17 years to develop the replacement for the *Vanguard*-class submarines. The vote in the House of Commons on whether to replace the existing four *Vanguard*-class submarines was held on 18 July 2016. The Trident renewal programme motion passed with a significant majority with 472 MPs voting in favour and 117 against. The Leader of the Opposition, Jeremy Corbyn, and 47 other Labour MPs had voted against it; 41 did not vote but 140 Labour votes were cast in favour of the motion. The four new *Dreadnought*-class submarines were expected to come into operation in the early 2030s, with the programme lasting until at least the 2060s.

Nuclear tests

The UK's first nuclear test, codenamed Operation Hurricane, occurred on 3 October 1952, in a shallow bay in the Montebello Islands of Western Australia.[423] They were followed by the first nuclear tests on the Australian mainland, which were were conducted at Emu Field in the Great Victoria Desert in South Australia as part of Operation Totem on 14 and 26 October 1953. Two further tests were held on the Montebello Islands as part of Operation Mosaic on 6 May and 19 June 1956. In the 1980s there emerged a claim that the second Mosaic test was of a significantly higher explosive yield than suggested by available figures—98 kilotonnes of TNT (410 TJ) as compared to the official figure of 60 kilotonnes of TNT (250 TJ)—but this claim does not stand up to scrutiny.[571]

The British government formally requested a permanent test facility on 30 October 1953. Due to concerns about nuclear fallout from the previous tests at Emu Field and the site's inadequate infrastructure and water supply, the recently surveyed site at Maralinga in South Australia was selected for this purpose.[572] The new site was announced in May 1955.[573] It was developed as a joint, co-funded facility between the British and Australian governments. Seven British nuclear tests at Maralinga were conducted between 27 September 1956 and 9 October 1957.

In addition to the major tests involving explosions, many subcritical minor trials were also carried out between June 1955 and April 1963. While the major tests had been carried out with some publicity, the minor tests were carried out in absolute secrecy. The "Kitten" tests tested bomb components, while "Tims" and "Rats" were early subcritical hydronuclear tests. The "Vixen" tests involved safety testing of nuclear weapons—assuring that the core would not accidentally undergo criticality in the event of a fire or crash.[574] These minor tests left a legacy of radioactive contamination at Maralinga.

The Australian government prohibited hydrogen bomb tests in Australia, so Britain had to look for another test site for it hydrogen bombs. The first British hydrogen bombs were tested during Operation Grapple at Malden Island and Christmas Island in the Central Pacific Ocean.[575] Nine tests were conducted there in 1957, 1958 and 1959,[576] ultimately demonstrating that the UK had developed expertise in thermonuclear weapons.[577]

Beginning in December 1962, the UK conducted 24 tests at the Nevada Test Site in the United States. The final test being the Julin Bristol shot which took place on 26 November 1991. British nuclear testing was abruptly halted by President George H. W. Bush in October 1992.[578,579] Because Britain did not test as often as the United States for financial and political reasons, and did not have the Americans' state-of-the-art computer facilities, British weapons design depended more on theoretical understanding, with potential for both greater advances and greater risks between tests.[436]

The United Kingdom, along with the United States and the Soviet Union, signed the Partial Test Ban Treaty, which restricted it to underground nuclear tests by outlawing testing in the atmosphere, underwater, or in outer space, on 5 August 1963. The UK signed the Comprehensive Test Ban Treaty, ending all nuclear testing, on 24 September 1996,[580] and ratified it on 6 April 1998,[581] having passed the necessary legislation on 18 March 1998 as the Nuclear Explosions (Prohibition and Inspections) Act 1998. Subcritical nuclear tests continued to occur, most notably the Etna test in February 2002, and the Krakatau test in February 2006.[582]

US nuclear weapons in the UK

In the early years of the Cold War, the US Strategic Air Command (SAC) the majority of the bomber force was made of of Boeing B-29 Superfortress bombers, and later its successors, the Boeing B-50 Superfortress and the Boeing B-47 Stratojet, all of which lacked the necessary range to reach targets in the Soviet Union from bases in the continental United States. Even small number of Convair B-36 Peacemaker bombers could not make it there and back. Overseas bases were therefore required, and the need for bases in the UK was a feature of American war planning for over a decade.[583]

Obtaining British permission was easy thanks to the wartime comradeship between the RAF and the United States Army Air Forces (USAAF). Bypassing the politicians, General Carl Spaatz, the commander of the USAAF, came to an agreement with the Chief Of the Air Staff, Marshal of the Royal Air Force Lord Tedder, in June and July 1946. Work began on extended and strengtheners runways at RAF airbases in East Anglia to receive the B-29s. In June 1947, nine B-29s of the 97th Bombardment Group deployed to RAF Marham, where they were greeted by Tedder.[584] This was merely a test; the bombers were not nuclear-capable. Only the Silverplate B-29s of the 509th Bombardment Group could do so.[585] Their first deployment was in April 1949.[586] Ninety sets of bomb assemblies—atomic bombs without the fissile cores—were stored in the UK by July 1950, and authority to deploy the cores as well was given in April 1954.[587]

The 3d Air Division was formed in 1949 to control the deployments of B-29s to the UK. It was soon upgraded to the status of a major command, and became the Third Air Force in May 1951 as part of the United States Air Forces in Europe. SAC then formed the 7th Air Division to control the nuclear bomber deployments.[588] In fulfilment of NATO's plans to halt a Soviet invasion of Western Europe using tactical nuclear weapons, the 3rd Air Force received its own nuclear weapons when the 20th Fighter Wing deployed to RAF Wethersfield in Essex on 1 June 1952, with Republic F-84F Thunderstreak fighters and Mark 7 nuclear bombs. It reequipped with the North American F-100 Super Sabre in 1957, and then the General Dynamics F-111 in 1970.[589] The US

Navy's Polaris ballistic missile submarines arrived at Holy Loch in Scotland in March 1961.

With the introduction to service of long-range bombers and intercontinental ballistic missiles, the need for a SAC presence in the UK diminished, On 3 April 1964, the last SAC aircraft, a B-47 from the 380th Bombardment Wing, left RAF Brize Norton, ending nearly 12 years' of continual B-47 deployments, and the 7th Air Division on 30 June 1964.[590] The tactical nuclear weapons remained. In the 1970s, up to 60 F-111s based in the UK were on quick reaction alert, each carrying multiple B61 nuclear bombs.[589]

During the 1980s nuclear armed USAF Ground Launched Cruise Missiles (GLCMs) were deployed at RAF Greenham Common and RAF Molesworth,[591] as a consequence of the 1979 NATO Double-Track Decision, under which NATO countries agreed to modernise the alliance's nuclear weapons.[592] Under the terms of the 1987 Intermediate-Range Nuclear Forces Treaty with the Soviet Union, the United States withdrew its surface naval nuclear weapons and short-range nuclear forces. The GLCMs were withdrawn from the UK in 1991,[532] and the Polaris submarine base at Holy Loch was closed in 1992.[566] The US continued to store tactical nuclear weapons in the UK until about 2006, when approximately 110 tactical B61s stored at RAF Lakenheath for deployment by USAF F-15E Strike Eagle aircraft were removed.[532]

Nuclear defence

Warning systems

The UK has relied on the Ballistic Missile Early Warning System (BMEWS) and, in later years, Defense Support Program (DSP) satellites for warning of a nuclear attack. Both of these systems are owned and controlled by the United States, although the UK has joint control over UK-based systems. One of the four component radars for the BMEWS is based at RAF Fylingdales in North Yorkshire.[593]

In 2003 the UK government stated that it would consent to a request from the US to upgrade the radar at Fylingdales for use in the US National Missile Defense system,[593] but missile defence was not a significant political issue within the UK. The ballistic missile threat was perceived to be less severe, and consequently less of a priority, than other threats to its security. Fylingdales was enhanced to an Upgraded Early Warning Radar (UEWR) in 2008, and became part of the United States national missile defense system in 2011.

Figure 38: *This solid-state phased array radar at RAF Fylingdales in North Yorkshire is a UK-controlled early warning station and part of the American-controlled Ballistic Missile Early Warning System.*

Attack scenarios

During the Cold War, a significant effort by government and academia was made to assess the effects of a nuclear attack on the UK. There were four major exercises:

- **Exercise *Inside Right*** took place in 1975.[594]
- **Exercise *Scrum Half*** was conducted in 1978.[594]
- **Exercise *Square Leg*** was conducted in 1980.[594] The scenario involved around 130 warheads with a total yield of 205 megatons (69 ground burst, 62 air burst) with an average of 1.5 megatons per bomb. The exercise was criticised as unrealistic as an actual exchange would be much larger, and did not include targets in Inner London such as Whitehall.[595] Even so, the effect of the limited attack in Square Leg was estimated to be 29 million dead (53 per cent of the population) and 6.4 million seriously injured.[596]
- **Exercise *Hard Rock*** was a combined communications and civil defence exercise planned for September and October 1982. It assumed a conventional war in Europe lasting two to three days, during which the UK would be attacked with conventional weapons, then a limited nuclear exchange, with 54 nuclear warheads used against military targets in the UK. 250,000 people protested against the exercise and 24 councils refused to participate. The limited scenario still assumed casualties of 7.9 million dead

and 5 million injured.[596] The scenario was ridiculed by the Campaign for Nuclear Disarmament and the exercise was postponed indefinitely.[597] The *New Statesman* later claimed the Ministry of Defence insisted on having a veto over proposed targets in the exercise and several were removed to make them politically more acceptable; for example, the nuclear submarine base at Faslane was removed from the target list.

Civil defence

Succesive governments developed civil defence programmes aimed to prepare civilian and local government infrastructure for a nuclear strike on the UK. A series of seven Civil Defence Bulletin films were produced in 1964,[598] and in the 1980s the most famous such programme was probably the series of booklets and public information films entitled *Protect and Survive*.

> *If the country was ever faced with an immediate threat of nuclear threat or complete annihilation, a copy of this booklet would be distributed to every household as part of a public information campaign which would include announcements on television and radio and in the press. The booklet has been designed for free and general distribution in that event. It is being placed on sale now for those who wish to know what they would be advised to do at such a time.*

The booklet contained information on building a nuclear refuge within a so-called "fall-out room" at home, sanitation, limiting fire hazards, and descriptions of the audio signals for attack warning, fall-out warning and all clear. It was anticipated that families might need to stay in their fall-out room for up to 14 days after an attack almost without leaving it at all. The government also prepared a recorded announcement which was to have been broadcast by the BBC if a nuclear attack ever did occur. Sirens left over from the London Blitz during World War II were also to be used to warn the public. The system was mostly dismantled in 1992.

Research and production facilities

The Atomic Weapons Establishment (AWE), Aldermaston, formerly the Atomic Weapons Research Establishment (AWRE), is situated on a 750-acre (300 ha) near Reading in Berkshire. It was built on the site of the former RAF Aldermaston, which was converted to nuclear weapons research, design and development establishment, and opened on 1 April 1950. In 1954 the AWRE took control of the nearby 225-acre (91 ha) Royal Ordnance Factory (ROF) at ROF Burghfield, where warheads were assembled, and the test ranges at Foulness and Orford Ness. Components for nuclear weapons were also produced at the former ROF Cardiff site.

The Atomic Weapons Research Establishment became part of the United Kingdom Atomic Energy Authority on 1 January 1955. The last trials at Orford Ness were conducted on 9 June 1971, and the site was closed on 1 October 1971. Cardiff closed in 1997, and Foulness by the end of that year.[599] In 1989, the government announced its intention to find a private company to run AWE, with the government retaining ownership of the site and control of AWE though a golden share arrangement. In 1993, the contract was awarded to a consortium of Hunting Engineering, Brown and Root and AEA Technology. In 1999, the contract was transferred to a consortium of BNFL, Lockheed Martin and Serco. In 2008, the British government sold the BNFL share to Jacobs Engineering Group.

Nuclear warheads from the Trident missiles are transported by road convoy several times a year from Coulport to Burghfield for refurbishment. Between 2000 and 2016 there were 180 accidents involving the vehicles, ranging from minor traffic accidents to a sudden total loss of power in one of the 44-tonne lorries that halted a convoy and caused a double lane closure and a tailback on the M6 motorway. The accidents have been more frequent in recent years.

Anti-nuclear movement

The anti-nuclear movement in the United Kingdom consists of groups who oppose nuclear technologies such as nuclear power and nuclear weapons. Many different groups and individuals have been involved in anti-nuclear demonstrations and protests over the years. One of the most prominent anti-nuclear groups in the UK is the Campaign for Nuclear Disarmament (CND). This national movement was founded in the late 1950s, initially in opposition to nuclear testing. It reached its peak around 1960, by which time it had evolved into a broader movement calling for Britain to unilaterally give up nuclear weapons, withdraw from NATO, and end the basing of US bombers armed with nuclear weapons in the UK.[600]

The end of atmospheric nuclear testing, internal squabbles, and activists focusing their energies on other causes led to a rapid decline, but it revived in the early 1980s in the wake of the Thatcher government's December 1979 decision to deploy GLCMs in the UK under the NATO Double-Track Decision, and the announcement of the decision to purchase Trident in July 1980. Membership leapt from 3,000 in 1980 to 50,000 a year later, and rallies for unilateral nuclear disarmament in London in October 1981 and June 1982 attracted 250,000 marchers, the largest ever mass demonstrations in the UK up to that time.[600]

End of cross-party support

There was little dissent in the House of Commons; nuclear weapons had almost bipartisan support until 1960, with only the Liberals dissenting in 1958. Despite opposition from its left wing the Labour party supported British nuclear weapons but opposed tests, and Labour Opposition Leader Hugh Gaitskell and shadow foreign secretary Aneurin Bevan agreed with Sandys on the importance of reducing dependence on the American deterrent. The Bevan told his colleagues that their demand for unilateral nuclear disarmament would send a future Labour government "naked into the conference chamber" during international negotiations.[601]

The *Manchester Guardian* and other newspapers critical of the Conservative government supported the British deterrent, although the *Guardian* did criticise the government for relying on developing bombers rather than missiles to carry the weapons.[602] In 1962 it stated that the forthcoming Chinese nuclear weapon was a reason for having more than one Western nuclear nation. From 1955 the government chose to emphasize the nuclear deterrent and de-emphasize conventional forces.[603] *The Economist*, the *New Statesman*, and many left-wing newspapers supported the reliance on nuclear deterrence and nuclear weapons, but in their view considered that of the United States would suffice, and that of the costs of the "nuclear umbrella" was best left to be borne by the United States alone.[604]

Gaitskell's Labour party ceased supporting an independent deterrent in 1960 via its new "Policy for Peace", after the cancellation of Blue Streak made nuclear independence less likely. Labour also adopted a resolution favoring unilateral disarmament. Although Gaitskell opposed the resolution and it was reversed in 1961 in favor of continuing support of a general Western nuclear deterrent, the party's opposition to a British deterrent remained and became more prominent. This became a campaign issue during the 1964 general election. Alec Douglas-Home's incumbent Conservatives stated that the British deterrent was both necessary for independence from the Americans and maintaining British world influence, and was "working for peace" in such cases as the passage of the Nuclear Test Ban Treaty. Led by Gaitskell's successor Harold Wilson, Labour emphasized domestic economic issues but called deterrence the "Tory Nuclear Pretense" which would be neither independent nor effective. The populace's greater interest in domestic over foreign policy likely contributed to Labour's victory.[605]

The 1982 Labour Party Conference adopted a platform calling for the removal of the GLCMs, the scrapping of Polaris and the cancellation of Trident. This was reaffirmed by the 1986 conference. While the party was given little chance of winning the 1983 election in the aftermath of the Falklands War, polls had shown Labour ahead of the Conservatives in 1986 and 1987. In the wake of Labour's unsuccessful performance in the 1987 election, the Labour Party leader, Neil Kinnock, despite his own unilateralist convictions, moved to drop the party's disarmament policy, which he saw as a contributing factor in its defeat.[606] The party formally voted to do so in October 1989.[607]

Pro-independence Scottish political parties—the Scottish National Party (SNP), Scottish Green Party, Scottish Socialist Party (SSP) and Solidarity—are opposed to the basing of the Trident system close to Glasgow, Scotland's largest city.[608] Some members and ex-members of those parties, such as Tommy Sheridan and Lloyd Quinan, have taken part in blockades of the base. In the House of Commons vote in 2007, the majority of Scottish members of parliament (MPs) voted against upgrading the system, while a substantial majority of English, Welsh and Northern Irish MPs voted in favour.

Nuclear posture

The UK has relaxed its nuclear posture since the collapse of the Soviet Union. The Labour government's 1998 Strategic Defence Review made reductions from the plans announced by the previous Conservative government:

- The stockpile of "operationally available warheads" was reduced from 300 to "less than 200"
- The final batch of missile bodies would not be purchased, limiting the fleet to 58.
- A submarine's load of warheads were reduced from 96 to 48. This reduced the explosive power of the warheads on a Vanguard class Trident submarine to "one third less than a Polaris submarine armed with Chevaline." However, 48 warheads per Trident submarine represents a 50% increase on the 32 warheads per submarine of Chevaline. Total explosive power has been in decline for decades as the accuracy of missiles has improved, therefore requiring less power to destroy each target. Trident can destroy 48 targets per submarine, as opposed to 32 targets that could be destroyed by Chevaline.
- Submarines' missiles would not be targeted, but rather at several days "notice to fire".
- Although one submarine would always be on patrol it will operate on a "reduced day-to-day alert state". A major factor in maintaining a constant patrol is to avoid "misunderstanding or escalation if a Trident submarine were to sail during a period of crisis."

Current UK posture is as it has been for many years; Trident SLBMs still provide the long-range strategic element. Until 1998 the aircraft-delivered, free-fall WE.177A, WE.177B and WE.177C bombs provided a sub-strategic option in addition to their designed function of tactical battlefield weapons. With the retirement of WE.177, a sub-strategic warhead is to be used with some (but not all) deployed Trident missiles. The 2010 Strategic Defence and Security Review further pledged to reduce its requirement for operationally available warheads from fewer than 160 to no more than 120. In a January 2015 written statement, Defence Secretary Michael Fallon reported that " All Vanguard Class SSBNs on continuous at-sea deterrent patrol now carry 40 nuclear warheads and no more than eight operational missiles". In April 2017 Defence Secretary Michael Fallon confirmed that the UK would use nuclear weapons in a "pre-emptive strike" in "the most extreme circumstances".

Nuclear weapons control

The precise details of how a British Prime Minister would authorise a nuclear strike remain secret, although the principles of the Trident missile control system is believed to be based on the plan set up for Polaris in 1968, which has now been declassified. A closed-circuit television system was set up between 10 Downing Street and the SSBN Control Officer at the Northwood Headquarters of the Royal Navy. Both the Prime Minister and the SSBN Control Officer would be able to see each other on their monitors when the command was given. If the link failed – for instance during a nuclear attack or when the PM was away from Downing Street – the Prime Minister would send an authentication code which could be verified at Northwood. The PM would then broadcast a firing order to the SSBN submarines via the Very Low Frequency radio station at Rugby. The UK has not deployed control equipment requiring codes to be sent before weapons can be used, such as the U.S. Permissive Action Link, which if installed would preclude the possibility that military officers could launch British nuclear weapons without authorisation.

Until 1998, when it was withdrawn from service, the WE.177 bomb was armed with a standard tubular pin tumbler lock (as used on bicycle locks) and a standard allen key was used to set yield and burst height. Currently, British Trident missile commanders are able to launch their missiles without authorisation, whereas their American counterparts cannot. At the end of the Cold War the U.S. Fail Safe Commission recommended installing devices to prevent rogue commanders persuading their crews to launch unauthorised nuclear attacks. This was endorsed by the Nuclear Posture Review and Trident missile Coded Control Devices were fitted to all U.S. SSBNs by 1997. These devices prevented an attack until a launch code had been sent by the Chiefs of Staff on behalf of the President. The UK took a decision not to install Trident CCDs or their equivalent on the grounds that an aggressor might be able to wipe out the British chain of command before a launch order had been sent.

In December 2008 BBC Radio 4 made a programme titled *The Human Button*, providing new information on the manner in which the United Kingdom could launch its nuclear weapons, particularly relating to safeguards against a rogue launch. The former Chief of the Defence Staff and Chief of the General Staff, General Lord Guthrie of Craigiebank, explained that the highest level of safeguard was against a prime minister ordering a launch without due cause. The constitutional structure of the United Kingdom provided some protection against such an occurrence, as while the Prime Minister is the chief executive and so practically commands the armed services, the formal commander-in-chief is the monarch, to whom the chief of the defence staff could appeal: "the chief of the defence staff, if he really did think the prime minister had gone mad, would make quite sure that that order was not obeyed... You have to remember that actually prime ministers give direction, they tell the chief of the defence staff what they want, but it's not prime ministers who actually tell a sailor to press a button in the middle of the Atlantic. The armed forces are loyal, and we live in a democracy, but actually their ultimate authority is the Queen."

The same interview pointed out that while the Prime Minister would have the constitutional authority to fire the Chief of the Defence Staff, he could not appoint a replacement as the position is appointed by the monarch. The programme also addressed the workings of the system; detailing that two persons are required to authenticate each stage of the process before launching, with the submarine captain only able to access the firing trigger after two safes have been opened with keys held by the ship's executive and weapons engineering officers. It was explained that all Prime Ministers issue hand-written orders, termed the letters of last resort, seen by their eyes only, sealed and stored within the safes of each of the four Royal Navy Vanguard class submarines. These notes instruct the submarine commander of what action to take in the event of the United Kingdom being attacked with nuclear weapons that destroy Her Majesty's Government in the United Kingdom and/or the chain of command.

Although the final orders of the Prime Minister are at his or her discretion, and no fixed options exist, there were four known options: retaliating with nuclear weapons, not retaliating with nuclear weapons, the submarine commander uses his own judgement, or the submarine commander places himself under United States or Australian command if possible. This system of issuing notes containing orders in the event of the head of government's death is said to be unique to the United Kingdom (although the concept of written last orders, particularly of a ship's captain, is a naval tradition), with other nuclear powers using different procedures. The letters are destroyed unopened whenever a Prime Minister leaves office.

All former prime ministers have supported an "independent nuclear deterrent", including David Cameron and Theresa May. Only one, Lord Callaghan, has given any insight on his orders; Callaghan stated that, although in a situation where nuclear weapon use was required – and thus the whole purpose and value of the weapon as a deterrent had failed – he would have ordered use of nuclear weapons, if needed: "...if we had got to that point, where it was, I felt it was necessary to do it, then I would have done it (used the weapon)...but if I had lived after pressing that button, I could have never forgiven myself." Lord Healey, Secretary of State for Defence and "alternate decision-taker" under Prime Minister Harold Wilson, said that in the event of Soviet nuclear weapons attacking the United Kingdom and the Prime Minister had been killed or incapacitated, he would not have ordered a retaliation.

Legality

After the government announced its plans to refurbish its Trident missiles and build new submarines to carry them, it published a white paper on *The Future of the United Kingdom's Nuclear Deterrent*, in which it stated that the renewal is fully compatible with the United Kingdom's treaty commitments and international law. At the start of the House of Commons debate to authorise the replacement of Trident, Margaret Beckett, the Secretary of State for Foreign and Commonwealth Affairs, stated:

> *Article VI of the NPT imposes an obligation on all states: "to pursue negotiations in good faith on effective measures relating to cessation of the nuclear arms race at an early date and to nuclear disarmament, and on a Treaty on general and complete disarmament". The NPT Review Conference held in 2000 agreed, by consensus, 13 practical steps towards nuclear disarmament. The UK remains committed to these steps and is making progress on them. We have been disarming. Since the Cold War ended, we have withdrawn and dismantled our tactical maritime and airborne nuclear capabilities. We have terminated our nuclear capable Lance missiles and artillery. We have the smallest nuclear capability of any recognised nuclear weapon state accounting for less than one per cent of the global inventory. And we are the only nuclear weapon state that relies on a single nuclear system.*

The subsequent vote was won overwhelmingly, including unanimous support from the opposition Conservative Party. The Government's position remained that it was abiding by the NPT in renewing Trident, and Britain has the right to possess nuclear weapons, a position reiterated by Tony Blair on 21 February 2007. Only the United Kingdom has expressed its opposition to the establishment of a new legally binding treaty to prevent the threat or use of nuclear weapons against non-nuclear states, through its vote in the United Nations General Assembly in 1998.

References

<templatestyles src="Template:Refbegin/styles.css" />

- Aldrich, Richard J. (July 1998). "British Intelligence and the Anglo-American 'Special Relationship' during the Cold War". *Review of International Studies*. **24** (3): 331–351. doi: 10.1017/s0260210598003313[609]. JSTOR 20097530[610].
- Arnold, Lorna; Pyne, Katherine (2001). *Britain and the H-bomb*. Basingstoke, Hampshire: Palgrave. ISBN 978-0-230-59977-2. OCLC 753874620[611].
- Arnold, Lorna; Smith, Mark (2006). *Britain, Australia and the Bomb: The Nuclear Tests and Their Aftermath*. Basingstoke: Palgrave Macmillan. ISBN 978-1-4039-2102-4. OCLC 70673342[612].
- Aylen, Jonathan (January 2015). "First Waltz: Development and Deployment of Blue Danube, Britain's Post-War Atomic Bomb". *The International Journal for the History of Engineering & Technology*. **85** (1): 31–59. doi: 10.1179/1758120614Z.00000000054[613]. ISSN 1758-1206[614].
- Ball, S. J. (1995). *The Bomber in British Strategy: Britain's World Role, 1945–1960*. Boulder, Colorado: Westview Press. ISBN 0-8133-8934-8. OCLC 231678791[615].
- Baylis, John (Summer 1994). *The Development of Britain's Thermonuclear Capability 1954–61: Myth or Reality?*. Contemporary Record. **8**. pp. 159–164. doi: 10.1080/13619469408581287[616]. ISSN 1361-9462[617].
- Baylis, John (1995). *Ambiguity and Deterrence: British Nuclear Strategy 1945–1964*. Oxford: Clarendon Press. ISBN 0-19-828012-2.
- Baylis, John; Stoddart, Kristan (December 2003). "Britain and the Chevaline Project: The Hidden Nuclear Programme, 1967–82". *The Journal of Strategic Studies*. **26** (4): 124–155. doi: 10.1080/0141-2390312331279718[618]. ISSN 0140-2390[619].
- Baylis, John (June 2008). "The 1958 Anglo-American Mutual Defence Agreement: The Search for Nuclear Interdependence". *The Journal of Strategic Studies*. **31** (3): 425–466. doi: 10.1080/01402390002024726[620]. ISSN 0140-2390[619].

- Baylis, John; Stoddart, Kristan (2015). *The British Nuclear Experience: The Roles of Beliefs, Culture and Identity*. Oxford: Oxford University Press. ISBN 978-0-19-870202-3. OCLC 900506637[621].
- Bernstein, Barton J. (June 1976). "The Uneasy Alliance: Roosevelt, Churchill, and the Atomic Bomb, 1940–1945". *The Western Political Quarterly*. University of Utah. **29** (2): 202–230. doi: 10.2307/448105[622]. JSTOR 448105[623].
- Bernstein, Jeremy (March 2010). "John von Neumann and Klaus Fuchs: An Unlikely Collaboration". *Physics in Perspective*. **12** (1): 36–50. Bibcode: 2010PhP....12...36B[624]. doi: 10.1007/s00016-009-0001-1[625]. ISSN 1422-6944[626].
- Bernstein, Jeremy (2011). "A Memorandum that Changed the World"[627] (PDF). *American Journal of Physics*. **79** (5): 440–446. Bibcode: 2011AmJPh..79..440B[628]. doi: 10.1119/1.3533426[629]. ISSN 0002-9505[630].
- Botti, Timothy J. (1987). *The Long Wait: the Forging of the Anglo-American Nuclear Alliance, 1945–58*. Contributions in Military Studies. New York: Greenwood Press. ISBN 978-0-313-25902-9. OCLC 464084495[631].
- Bowie, Christopher J.; Platt, Alan (1984). *British Nuclear Policymaking*[632]. Santa Monica, California: Rand Corporation. ISBN 0-8330-0534-0. OCLC 29212035[633]. Retrieved 10 July 2018.
- Bronk, Justin (2014). "Britain's 'Independent' V-Bomber Force and US Nuclear Weapons, 1957–1962". *Journal of Strategic Studies*. **37** (6–7): 974–997. doi: 10.1080/01402390.2013.770736[634]. ISSN 1743-937X[635].
- Brookes, Andrew (1982). *V Force: The History of Britain's Airborne Deterrent*. London: Jane's Publishing Company Ltd. ISBN 0-7106-0238-3.
- Butler, Nicola; Bromley, Mark (November 2001). "Secrecy and Dependence: The UK Trident System in the 21st Century"[636] (PDF). British American Information Council. ISBN 978-1-874533-44-3. OCLC 78965689[637]. BASIC Research Report, Number 2001.3. Retrieved 13 July 2018.
- Campbell, Duncan (1982). *War Plan UK*. London: Burnett Books. ISBN 0-586-08479-7. OCLC 1027281129[638].
- Cathcart, Brian (1995). *Test of Greatness: Britain's Struggle for the Atom Bomb*. London: John Murray. ISBN 0-7195-5225-7. OCLC 31241690[639].
- Chalmers, Malcolm (1 March 1999). "Bombs Away? Britain and Nuclear Weapons under New Labour". *Security Dialogue*. **30** (1): 61–74. doi: 10.1177/0967010699030001005[640]. ISSN 0967-0106[641].
- Clark, Ronald W. (1961). *The Birth of the Bomb: Britain's Part in the Weapon that Changed the World*. London: Phoenix House. OCLC

824335[642].
- Cocroft, Wayne D.; Newsome, Sarah (2009). Atomic Weapons Research Establishment Foulness, Essex – Survey Report[643] (Report). Research Department Report Series 13-2009. Eastney, Portsmouth: English Heritage. ISSN 1478-7008[644]. Retrieved 2 August 2018.
- Dawson, R.; Rosecrance, R. (1966). "Theory and Reality in the Anglo-American Alliance". *World Politics*. **19** (1): 21–51. doi: 10.2307/2009841[645]. JSTOR 2009841[646].
- Dombey, N.; Grove, E. (1992). "Britain's Thermonuclear Bluff"[647]. *London Review of Books*. **14** (20): 8–9. Retrieved 15 May 2017.
- Dumbrell, John (2006). *A Special Relationship: Anglo-American Relations from the Cold War to Iraq*. Basingstoke, Hampshire: Palgrave Macmillan. ISBN 9781403987747. OCLC 433341082[648].
- Epstein, L. D. (1966). "The Nuclear Deterrent and the British Election of 1964". *Journal of British Studies*. **5** (2): 139–163. doi: 10.1086/385523[649]. ISSN 0021-9371[650]. JSTOR 175321[651].
- Farmelo, Graham (2013). *Churchill's Bomb: How the United States Overtook Britain in the First Nuclear Arms Race*. New York: Basic Books. ISBN 978-0-465-02195-6.
- Goldberg, Alfred (July 1964). "The Atomic Origins of the British Nuclear Deterrent". *International Affairs*. **40** (3): 409–429. doi: 10.2307/2610825[652]. JSTOR 2610825[653].
- Gott, Richard (April 1963). "The Evolution of the Independent British Deterrent". *International Affairs*. **39** (2): 238–252. doi: 10.2307/2611300[654]. JSTOR 2611300[655].
- Gowing, Margaret (1964). *Britain and Atomic Energy 1939–1945*. London: Macmillan. OCLC 3195209[656].
- Gowing, Margaret; Arnold, Lorna (1974a). *Independence and Deterrence: Britain and Atomic Energy, 1945–1952, Volume 1, Policy Making*. London: Macmillan. ISBN 0-333-15781-8. OCLC 611555258[657].
- Gowing, Margaret; Arnold, Lorna (1974b). *Independence and Deterrence: Britain and Atomic Energy, 1945–1952, Volume 2, Policy and Execution*. London: Palgrave Macmillan. ISBN 0-333-16695-7. OCLC 946341039[658].
- Grant, Rebecca (March 2011). "Victor Alert"[659] (PDF). *Air Force Magazine*. pp. 58–62. Retrieved 31 July 2018.
- Groom, A. J. R. (1974). *British Thinking About Nuclear Weapons*. London: Frances Pinter. ISBN 978-0-903804-01-1. OCLC 462212978[660].
- Grove, Eric J. (1987). *Vanguard to Trident; British Naval Policy since World War II*. Annapolis, Maryland: United States Naval Institute. ISBN 0-87021-552-3. OCLC 15081825[661].

- Harrison, Kevin (1982). "From Independence to Dependence: , Skybolt, Nassau and Polaris". *The RUSI Journal*. **127** (4): 25–31. doi: 10.1080/03071848208523423[662]. ISSN 0307-1847[663].
- Hawkings, David (Summer 2002). "Blue Peacock: the British Army's Forgotten Weapon"[664] (PDF). *Discovery*. pp. 42–43. Archived from the original[665] (PDF) on 5 October 2007.
- Hewlett, Richard G.; Anderson, Oscar E. (1962). *The New World, 1939–1946*[666] (PDF). University Park, Pennsylvania: Pennsylvania State University Press. ISBN 0-520-07186-7. OCLC 637004643[667]. Retrieved 26 March 2013.
- Hewlett, Richard G.; Duncan, Francis (1969). *Atomic Shield, 1947–1952*[668] (PDF). A History of the United States Atomic Energy Commission. University Park, Pennsylvania: Pennsylvania State University Press. ISBN 0-520-07187-5. OCLC 3717478[669]. Retrieved 7 March 2015.
- Hewlett, Richard G.; Holl, Jack M. (1989). *Atoms for Peace and War, Volume III, 1953–1961 Eisenhower and the Atomic Energy Commission*[670] (PDF). A History of the United States Atomic Energy Commission. University Park, Pennsylvania: Pennsylvania State University Press. ISBN 0-520-06018-0. OCLC 82275622[671].
- Hubbard, Kenneth; Simmons, Michael (2008). *Dropping Britain's first H-bomb: The Story of Operation Grapple 1957/58*. Barnsley, South Yorkshire: Pen & Sword Aviation. ISBN 978-1-84415-747-1. OCLC 436867016[672].
- Jones, Jeffrey (2017). *Volume I: From the V-Bomber Era to the Arrival of Polaris, 1945–1964*. The Official History of the UK Strategic Nuclear Deterrent. Milton Park, Abingdon, Oxfordshire: Routledge. ISBN 978-1-138-67493-6. OCLC 1005663721[673].
- Jones, Vincent (1985). *Manhattan: The Army and the Atomic Bomb*[674] (PDF). Washington, DC: United States Army Center of Military History. OCLC 10913875[675]. Retrieved June 8, 2013.
- Leonard, Zeb (22 May 2014). "Tampering with history: varied understanding of Operation Mosaic". *Journal of Australian Studies*. **38** (2): 205–219. doi: 10.1080/14443058.2014.895956[676].
- Ludlam, Steve (2008). "The Role of Nuclear Submarine Propulsion". In Mackby, Jenifer; Cornish, Paul. *US-UK Nuclear Cooperation After 50 Years*. Washington, DC: Center for Strategic and International Studies Press. pp. 247–258. ISBN 978-0-89206-530-1. OCLC 845346116[677].
- MacDonald, Fraser (March 2006). "Geopolitics and 'The Vision Thing': Regarding Britain and America's First Nuclear Missile". *Transactions of the Institute of British Geographers*. **31** (1): 53–71. doi: 10.1111/j.1475-5661.2006.00196.x[678]. ISSN 0020-2754[679]. JSTOR 3804419[680].

- Macmillan, Harold (1971). *Riding the Storm: 1956–1959*. London: Macmillan. ISBN 9780333103104. OCLC 198741[681].
- McIntyre, Donald (2006). *The Development of Britain's Megaton Warheads*[682] (PDF) (MA). University of Chester. Retrieved 29 May 2017.
- Middeke, Michael (Spring 2000). "Anglo-American Nuclear Weapons Cooperation After Nassau"[683]. *Journal of Cold War Studies*. **2** (2): 69–96. ISSN 1520-3972[684]. Retrieved 5 November 2011.
- Moore, Richard (2010). *Nuclear Illusion, Nuclear Reality: Britain, the United States and Nuclear Weapons, 1958–64*. Basingstoke: Palgrave Macmillan. ISBN 978-0-230-23067-5. OCLC 428030700[685].
- Nailor, Peter (1988). *The Nassau Connection: The Organisation and Management of the British Polaris Project*. HMSO. ISBN 0-11-772526-9. OCLC 231046793[686].
- Norris, Robert S.; Kristensen, Hans M. (2013). "The British nuclear stockpile, 1953-2013". *Bulletin of the Atomic Scientists*. **69** (4): 69–75. doi: 10.1177/0096340213493260[687]. ISSN 0096-3402[688].
- Openshaw, Stan; Steadman, Philip; Greene, Owen (1983). *Doomsday, Britain after Nuclear Attack*. Oxford: Basil Blackwell. ISBN 0-631-13394-1. OCLC 470911157[689].
- Paul, Septimus H. (2000). *Nuclear Rivals: Anglo-American Atomic Relations, 1941–1952*. Columbus, Ohio: Ohio State University Press. ISBN 978-0-8142-0852-6. OCLC 43615254[690].
- Phelps, Stephen (2010). *The Tizard Mission: The Top-Secret Operation that Changed the Course of World War II*. Yardley, Pennsylvania: Westholme. ISBN 978-1-59416-116-2. OCLC 642846903[691].
- Ritchie, Nick (2008). "Trident and British Identity: Letting Go of Nuclear Weapons"[692]. Bradford, West Yorkshire: University of Bradford. OCLC 682883281[693]. Retrieved 14 July 2018.
- Ritchie, Nick (2014). *Nuclear Weapons-Free World?: Britain, Trident and the Challenges Ahead*. Basingstoke, Hampshire: Palgrave Macmillan. ISBN 978-1-349-33185-7. OCLC 951512317[694].
- Ritchie, Nick (2016). "Nuclear identities and Scottish independence". *The Nonproliferation Review*. **23** (5–6): 653–675. doi: 10.1080/10736700.2017.1345517[695]. ISSN 1073-6700[696].
- Ritchie, Nick (February 2015). "The UK Naval Nuclear Propulsion Programme and Highly Enriched Uranium"[697] (PDF). Washington, DC: Federation of American Scientists. Retrieved 12 September 2017.
- Scott, Len (March 2012). "Selling or Selling Out Nuclear Disarmament? Labour, the Bomb, and the 1987 General Election". *The International History Review*. **34** (1): 115–137. doi: 10.1080/07075332.2012.620242[698]. ISSN 0707-5332[699].

- Spinardi, Graham (August 1997). "Aldermaston and British Nuclear Weapons Development: Testing the 'Zuckerman Thesis'". *Social Studies of Science*. **27** (4): 547–582. doi: 10.1177/030631297027004001[700]. ISSN 0306-3127[701]. JSTOR 285558[702].
- Stocker, Jeremy (July 2004). *Britain's Role in US Missile Defense*[703] (PDF). Carlisle, Pennsylvania: US Army War College. ISBN 1-58487-163-6. OCLC 56021256[704]. Retrieved 29 July 2018.
- Stoddart, Kristan (2012). *Losing an Empire and Finding a Role: Britain, the USA, NATO and Nuclear Weapons, 1964–70*. Basingstoke, Hampshire: Palgrave Macmillan. ISBN 978-1-349-33656-2. OCLC 951512907[705].
- Stoddart, Kristan (2014a). *The Sword and the Shield: Britain, America, NATO and Nuclear Weapons, 1970–1976*. Basingstoke, Hampshire: Palgrave Macmillan. ISBN 978-0-230-30093-4. OCLC 870285634[706].
- Stoddart, Kristan (2014b). *Facing Down the Soviet Union: Britain, the USA, NATO and Nuclear Weapons, 1976–83*. Basingstoke, Hampshire: Palgrave Macmillan. ISBN 978-1-137-44031-0. OCLC 900698250[707].
- Szasz, Ferenc Morton (1992). *British Scientists and the Manhattan Project: The Los Alamos Years*. New York: St. Martin's Press. ISBN 978-0-312-06167-8. OCLC 23901666[708].
- Wade, Troy E. II (2008). "Nuclear Testing: A US Perspective". In Mackby, Jenifer; Cornish, Paul. *US-UK Nuclear Cooperation After 50 Years*. Washington, DC: Center for Strategic and International Studies Press. pp. 200–211. ISBN 978-0-89206-530-1. OCLC 845346116[677].
- Wheeler, N. J. (Winter 1985–1986). "British Nuclear Weapons and Anglo-American Relations 1945–54". *International Affairs*. **62** (1): 71–86. JSTOR 2618068[709].
- Wittner, Lawrence S. (2003). *Toward Nuclear Abolition: A History of the World Nuclear Disarmament Movement, 1971–Present*. Stanford, California: Stanford University Press. ISBN 0-8047-4862-4. OCLC 249977055[710].
- Wynn, Humphrey (1997). *RAF Strategic Nuclear Deterrent Forces, Their Origins, Roles and Deployment, 1946–1969. A Documentary History*. London: The Stationery Office. ISBN 0-11-772833-0. OCLC 39225127[711].
- Young, Ken (January 2007). "US 'Atomic Capability' and the British Forward Bases in the Early Cold War". *Journal of Contemporary History*. **42** (1): 117–136. JSTOR 30036432[712].
- Young, Ken (Spring 2007). "A Most Special Relationship: The Origins of Anglo-American Nuclear Strike Planning". *Journal of Cold War Studies*. **9** (2): 5–31. doi: 10.1162/jcws.2007.9.2.5[713]. ISSN 1520-3972[684].

- Young, Ken (2016). *The American Bomb in Britain: US Air Forces' Strategic Presence 1946–64*. Manchester: Manchester University Press. ISBN 978-0-7190-8675-5. OCLC 942707047[714].
- Zimmerman, David (1995). "The Tizard Mission and the Development of the Atomic Bomb". *War in History*. **2** (3): 259–273. doi:10.1177/096834459500200302[715].

External links

- British Nuclear Weapons Stockpile, 1953–2013[716] at History in Pieces[717]
- Video archive of the UK's Nuclear Testing[718] at sonicbomb.com[719]
- British Nuclear Policy[720], BASIC
- Table of UK Nuclear Weapons models[721]
- *The Real Meaning of the Words: a Pedantic Glossary of British Nuclear Weapons*[722] (PDF)

Overseas Bases

Overseas military bases of the United Kingdom

Overseas military bases of the United Kingdom enable the British Armed Forces to conduct expeditionary warfare. Bases tend to be located in or near areas of strategic or diplomatic importance, often used for the build-up or re-supply of military forces, as was seen during the 1982 Falklands War and the use of RAF Ascension Island as a staging post. Most of the bases are located on British Overseas Territories or former colonies which retain close diplomatic ties with the UK.

In total, the UK has 16 overseas military bases, second only to the United States. They often have been used by its allies, predominantly the US. A number of military operations would not have been possible without the strategic island of Diego Garcia in British Indian Ocean Territory. It was used for major operations during the War on Terror, Operation Granby (1991), Operation Herrick (2001–14; NATO), Operation Tellic (2003–11), Operation Shader (2014–present), Operation Desert Storm (1991), Operation Desert Fox (1998), Operation Enduring Freedom (2001–14), Operation Iraqi Freedom (2003–11), and Operation Inherit Resolve (2014–present; NATO).Wikipedia:Citation needed

Overseas military installations

The British Armed Forces maintain a number of garrisons and military facilities around the world:

Location	Details	Note
Ascension Island	RAF Ascension: The RAF maintains an airbase on Ascension Island; notable for use as a staging post during the 1982 Falklands War, the territory is also the site of a joint UK-US signals intelligence facility.	
Bahrain	HMS *Jufair*: Britain's return East of Suez was marked with the establishment of a large Naval Support Facility. officially opened in 2018, at the Bahraini port of Mina Salman. The base can support vessels up-to the size of aircraft carriers. Bahrain is also home to the UK Maritime Component Command, which supports Royal Navy mine countermeasures vessels deployed in the Middle East.	
Belize	British Army Training and Support Unit Belize (BATSUB): Used primarily for jungle warfare training, with access to 5,000 square miles (13,000 km^2) of jungle terrain. Although British facilities were mothballed in the Strategic Defence and Security Review 2010, BATSUB is still seeing increased usage.	
British Indian Ocean Territory	British Forces British Indian Ocean Territories: A Permanent Joint Operating Base. Although the Naval Support Facility Diego Garcia and airbase facilities on Diego Garcia are leased to the United States, the UK retains ownership and continual access. The small but permanent British garrison, known as Naval Party 1002, forms the civil administration on this British Overseas Territory.	723
Brunei	British Forces Brunei: A garrison made up of one battalion from the Royal Gurkha Rifles and No. 7 Flight AAC. Established in 1959, it also hosts routine jungle warfare courses for the British Army and Royal Marines.	
Canada	British Army Training Unit Suffield: Home to a large contingent of in-service British Army vehicles, such as the Challenger 2 and Warrior IFV. It is the British Army's largest armoured warfare training facility, training up-to 5 battlegroups, each consisting of 1,400 personnel, every year.	
Cyprus	British Forces Cyprus: A Permanent Joint Operating Base with significant garrisons in Akrotiri and Dhekelia, including RAF Akrotiri, the joint signals intelligence stations RAF Troodos and Ayios Nikolaos, and facilities to support two resident infantry battalions and supporting British Army units.	
Falkland Islands	British Forces South Atlantic Islands: A Permanent Joint Operating Base. The British garrison is centred around RAF Mount Pleasant (the Mount Pleasant Complex) and includes commitments from all branches of the Armed Forces, most notably; No. 1435 Flight RAF (4 x Typhoons), No. 1312 Flight RAF (one Voyager and one Hercules), a Type 45 destroyer or Type 23 frigate, HMS *Clyde*, and 1,000 British Army personnel. There are also early-warning and airspace-control radar stations at critical locations, and East Cove Military Port, a deep-water port operated by Naval Party 2010.	
Germany	British Forces Germany (BFG): Home of the 20th Armoured Infantry Brigade and supporting elements. BFG will be rebased inside the UK by 2019.	
Gibraltar	British Forces Gibraltar: A Permanent Joint Operating Base. Britain has maintained a military presence in Gibraltar since its capture (1704) and the subsequent Treaty of Utrecht (1713). Facilities include (but are not limited too) the airbase RAF Gibraltar and the Port of Gibraltar.	

Kenya	British Army Training Unit Kenya: Used primarily for the training of British infantry battalions in the arid and rugged terrain of the Great Rift Valley. Routine Royal Engineers and Royal Army Medical Corps exercises also carry out civil engineering projects and health care assistance to the local communities.
Nepal	British Gurkhas Nepal: The British Army maintains a small outpost in Nepal for recruitment purposes to the Brigade of Gurkhas.
Oman	UK Joint Logistics Support Base: A military logistics centre and training facility under construction in Duqm that will have a dry dock and be able to accommodate submarines and Queen Elizabeth-class aircraft carriers. It could be linked to other Persian Gulf countries by the Gulf Railway.
Qatar	RAF Al Udeid: An outpost at Al Udeid Air Base serving as the headquarters for No. 83 Expeditionary Air Group and its operations across the Middle East.
Singapore	Naval Party 1022: A Royal Navy repair and logistics support facility at Sembawang wharf in support of the Five Power Defence Arrangements.[724]

Locally raised units of British Overseas Territories

Four British Overseas Territories also maintain their own locally raised units for home defence and security:

Location	Details	Official website
Bermuda	The Royal Bermuda Regiment : Formed in 1965.	www.bermudaregiment.bm[725]
Falkland Islands	Falkland Islands Defence Force: Traces its origins back to 1847. The force consists of one light infantry company and trains once per week. It is manned entirely by the local population, following British Army doctrine, training and operations.	www.fig.gov.fk/fidf[726]
Gibraltar	Royal Gibraltar Regiment: Raised in 1943. The regiment consists of one infantry battalion (1 x HQ company and 3 x infantry companies) and is regarded as a colonial force within the structure of the British Army.	royalgibraltarregiment.gi[727]
Montserrat	Royal Montserrat Defence Force: Raised in 1899.	

External links

- Overseas Military Bases of the United Kingdom[728] (www.youtube.com)

Royal Navy Today

Royal Navy

<indicator name="pp-default"> 🔒 </indicator>

	Royal Navy
Founded	1546
Country	United Kingdom[729]
Branch	Her Majesty's Naval Service
Type	Navy
Role	Naval warfare
Size	33,280 Regular 3,040 Maritime Reserve 7,960 Royal Fleet Reserve[730] 75 commissioned ships[731] 174 aircraft[732]
Part of	Ministry of Defence
Naval Staff Offices	Whitehall, London, England, UK
Nickname(s)	Senior Service

Motto(s)	"Si vis pacem, para bellum" (Latin) *"If you wish for peace, prepare for war"*
Colours	Red and white
March	"Heart of Oak" 🔊 Play Wikipedia:Media helpFile:Heart of Oak.ogg
Fleet	1 ship of the line 1 aircraft carrier 10 submarines 2 amphibious transport docks 6 destroyers 13 frigates 4 offshore patrol vessels 13 mine countermeasures vessels 18 fast patrol boats 4 survey ships 1 ice patrol ship 1 static ship
Website	royalnavy<wbr/>.mod<wbr/>.uk[733]
Commanders	
Lord High Admiral	Prince Philip, Duke of Edinburgh
First Sea Lord	Admiral Sir Philip Jones KCB
Fleet Commander	Vice Admiral Ben Key CBE
Second Sea Lord	Vice Admiral Tony Radakin
Insignia	
White Ensign[734]	
Naval Jack[735]	
Pennant	
Aircraft flown	
Attack	Wildcat, F-35B Lightning II
Fighter	F-35B Lightning II
Patrol	Wildcat, Merlin, Sea King
Reconnaissance	Wildcat, Merlin, ScanEagle
Trainer	Tutor, Hawk

| Transport | Merlin, Dauphin |

Her Majesty's Naval Service
of the British Armed Forces

Components

- **Royal Navy**
- Surface Fleet
- Fleet Air Arm
- Submarine Service
- Royal Naval Reserve
- Royal Navy Medical Service
- Nursing Service (QARNNS)
- Chaplaincy
- Royal Navy Police
- **Royal Marines**
- Royal Marines Reserve
- Special Boat Service
- **Naval Careers Service**

History and future

- History of the Royal Navy / Royal Marines
- Customs and traditions
- Future

Ships

- Current fleet
- Current deployments
- Historic ships

Personnel

- The Admiralty
- Senior officers
- Uniforms
- Officer / ratings rank insignia

Auxiliary services

- Royal Fleet Auxiliary
- Marine Services

- v
- t
- e[736]

The **Royal Navy** (**RN**) is the United Kingdom's naval warfare force. Although warships were used by the English kings from the early medieval period, the first major maritime engagements were fought in the Hundred Years War against the Kingdom of France. The modern Royal Navy traces its origins to the early 16th century; the oldest of the UK's armed services, it is known as the **Senior Service**.

From the middle decades of the 17th century, and through the 18th century, the Royal Navy vied with the Dutch Navy and later with the French Navy for maritime supremacy. From the mid 18th century, it was the world's most powerful navy until surpassed by the United States Navy during the Second World War. The Royal Navy played a key part in establishing the British Empire as the unmatched world power during the 19th and first part of the 20th centuries. Due to this historical prominence, it is common, even among non-Britons, to refer to it as "the Royal Navy" without qualification.

Following World War I, the Royal Navy was significantly reduced in size,[737] although at the onset of World War II it was still the world's largest. By the end of the war, however, the United States Navy had emerged as the world's largest. During the Cold War, the Royal Navy transformed into a primarily anti-submarine force, hunting for Soviet submarines and mostly active in the GIUK gap. Following the collapse of the Soviet Union, its focus has returned to expeditionary operations around the world and remains one of the world's foremost blue-water navies.[738] However, twenty-first century reductions in naval spending have led to a personnel shortage and a reduction in the number of warships.[739,740]

The Royal Navy maintains a fleet of technologically sophisticated ships and submarines[741] including an aircraft carrier, two amphibious transport docks, four ballistic missile submarines (which maintain the UK's nuclear deterrent), six nuclear fleet submarines, six guided missile destroyers, 13 frigates, 13 mine-countermeasure vessels and 22 patrol vessels. As of April 2018, there are 73 commissioned ships (including submarines) in the Royal Navy, plus 10 ships of the Royal Fleet Auxiliary (RFA); there are also five Merchant Navy ships available to the RFA under a private finance initiative. The RFA replenishes Royal Navy warships at sea, and augments the Royal Navy's amphibious warfare capabilities through its three Bay-class landing ship vessels. It also works as a force multiplier for the Royal Navy, often doing patrols that frigates used to do. The total displacement of the Royal Navy is approximately 407,000 tonnes (603,000 tonnes including the Royal Fleet Auxiliary and Royal Marines).

The Royal Navy is part of Her Majesty's Naval Service, which also includes the Royal Marines. The professional head of the Naval Service is the First Sea Lord who is an admiral and member of the Defence Council of the United Kingdom. The Defence Council delegates management of the Naval Service to the Admiralty Board, chaired by the Secretary of State for Defence. The Royal Navy operates three bases in the United Kingdom where commissioned ships are based; Portsmouth, Clyde and Devonport, the last being the largest operational naval base in Western Europe.

Role

As the seaborne branch of HM Armed Forces, the RN has various roles. As it stands today, the RN has stated its 6 major roles as detailed below in umbrella terms.

- Preventing Conflict – On a global and regional level
- Providing Security At Sea – To ensure the stability of international trade at sea
- International Partnerships – To help cement the relationship with the United Kingdom's allies (such as NATO)
- Maintaining a Readiness To Fight – To protect the United Kingdom's interests across the globe
- Protecting the Economy – To safe guard vital trade routes to guarantee the United Kingdom's and its allies' economic prosperity at sea
- Providing Humanitarian Aid – To deliver a fast and effective response to global catastrophes

History

Development of navies in England and Scotland

Middle Ages

The strength of the fleet of the Kingdom of England was an important element in the kingdom's power in the 10th century.[742] At one point Aethelred II had an especially large fleet built by a national levy of one ship for every 310 hides of land, but it is uncertain whether this was a standard or exceptional model for raising fleets.[743] During the period of Danish rule in the 11th century, the authorities maintained a standing fleet by taxation, and this continued for a time under the restored English regime of Edward the Confessor (reigned 1042–1066), who frequently commanded fleets in person.[744]

English naval power seemingly declined as a result of the Norman conquest.[745] Medieval fleets, in England as elsewhere, were almost entirely composed of merchant ships enlisted into naval service in time of war. From time to time a few "king's ships" owned by the monarch were built for specifically warlike purposes; but, unlike some European states, England did not maintain a small permanent core of warships in peacetime. England's naval organisation was haphazard and the mobilisation of fleets when war broke out was slow.[746]

Figure 39: *The Battle of Sluys as depicted in Froissart's Chronicles; late 14th century*

With the Viking era at an end, and conflict with France largely confined to the French lands of the English monarchy, England faced little threat from the sea during the 12th and 13th centuries, but in the 14th century the outbreak of the Hundred Years War dramatically increased the French menace. Early in the war French plans for an invasion of England failed when Edward III of England destroyed the French fleet in the Battle of Sluys in 1340.[747] Major fighting was thereafter confined to French soil and England's naval capabilities sufficed to transport armies and supplies safely to their continental destinations. However, while subsequent French invasion schemes came to nothing, England's naval forces could not prevent frequent raids on the south-coast ports by the French and their Genoese and Castilian allies. Such raids halted finally only with the occupation of northern France by Henry V.[748]

Henry VII deserves a large share of credit in fostering sea power. He embarked on a program of building merchant ships larger than heretofore. He also invested in dockyards, and commissioned the oldest surviving dry dock in 1495 at Portsmouth.[749]

There are mentions in medieval records of fleets commanded by Scottish kings including William the Lion[750] and Alexander II. The latter took personal command of a large naval force which sailed from the Firth of Clyde and anchored off the island of Kerrera in 1249, intended to transport his army in a campaign against the Kingdom of the Isles, but he died before the campaign could begin.[751,752] Viking naval power was disrupted by conflicts between the Scandinavian kingdoms, but entered a period of resurgence in the 13th century when Norwegian kings began to build some of the largest ships seen in Northern European waters. These included king Hakon Hakonsson's *Kristsúðin*, built at Bergen from 1262–63, which was 260 feet (79 m) long, of 37 rooms.[753] In 1263 Hakon responded to Alexander III's designs on the Hebrides by personally leading a major fleet of forty vessels, including the *Kristsúðin*, to the islands, where they were boosted by local allies to as many as 200 ships.[754] Records indicate that Alexander had several large oared ships built at Ayr, but he avoided a sea battle. Defeat on land at the Battle of Largs and winter storms forced the Norwegian fleet to return home, leaving the Scottish crown as the major power in the region and leading to the ceding of the Western Isles to Alexander in 1266.[755]

English naval power was vital to King Edward I's successful campaigns in Scotland from 1296, using largely merchant ships from England, Ireland and his allies in the Islands to transport and supply his armies.[756] Part of the reason for Robert I's success was his ability to call on naval forces from the Islands. As a result of the expulsion of the Flemings from England in 1303, he gained the support of a major naval power in the North Sea. The development of naval power allowed Robert to successfully defeat English attempts to capture him in the Highlands and Islands and to blockade major English controlled fortresses at Perth and Stirling, the last forcing King Edward II to attempt the relief that resulted at English defeat at Bannockburn in 1314. Scottish naval forces allowed invasions of the Isle of Man in 1313 and 1317 and Ireland in 1315. They were also crucial in the blockade of Berwick, which led to its fall in 1318.

After the establishment of Scottish independence, King Robert I turned his attention to building up a Scottish naval capacity. This was largely focused on the west coast, with the Exchequer Rolls of 1326 recording the feudal duties of his vassals in that region to aid him with their vessels and crews. Towards the end of his reign he supervised the building of at least one royal man-of-war near his palace at Cardross on the River Clyde. In the late 14th century naval warfare with England was conducted largely by hired Scots, Flemish and French merchantmen and privateers.[757] King James I of Scotland (1394–1437, reigned 1406–1437), took a greater interest in naval power. After his return to Scotland in 1424, he established a shipbuilding yard at Leith, a house for marine stores, and a workshop. King's ships were built and equipped there to be used for trade as well as war, one of which accompanied him on his expedition to the Islands in 1429. The office of Lord High Admiral was probably founded

Figure 40: *A late 16th-century painting of the Spanish Armada in battle with English warships*

in this period. It would soon become a hereditary office, in the control of the Earls of Bothwell in the 15th and 16th centuries and the Earls of Lennox in the 17th century.[758]

King James II (1430–1460, reigned 1437–1460) is known to have purchased a caravel by 1449.[759] Around 1476 the Scottish merchant John Barton received letters of marque that allowed him to gain compensation for the capture of his vessels by the Portuguese by capturing ships under their colours. These letters would be repeated to his three sons John, Andrew and Robert, who would play a major part in the Scottish naval effort into the 16th century.[760] In his struggles with his nobles in 1488 James III (r. 1451–88) received assistance from his two warships the *Flower* and the *King's Carvel* also known as the *Yellow Carvel*, commanded by Andrew Wood of Largo. After the king's death Wood served his son James IV (r. 1488–1513), defeating an English incursion into the Forth by five English ships in 1489 and three more heavily armed English ships off the mouth of the River Tay the next year.[761]

1500–1707

A standing "Navy Royal", with its own secretariat, dockyards and a permanent core of purpose-built warships, emerged during the reign of Henry VIII.[762] Under Elizabeth I England became involved in a war with Spain, which saw

Figure 41: *The Battle of Scheveningen in 1653*

privately owned vessels combining with the Queen's ships in highly profitable raids against Spanish commerce and colonies.[763] In 1588, Philip II of Spain sent the Spanish Armada against England to end English support for Dutch rebels, to stop English corsair activity and to depose the Protestant Elizabeth I and restore Catholicism to England. The Spaniards sailed from Lisbon, planning to escort an invasion force from the Spanish Netherlands but the scheme failed due to poor planning, English harrying, blocking action by the Dutch, and severe storms.[764] A major English expedition the following year was intended by Elizabeth to destroy the survivors of the Spanish fleet, but instead dissipated its efforts in unsuccessful schemes to intercept a Spanish treasure convoy or foment revolt against Spanish rule in Portugal.[765]

During the early 17th century, England's relative naval power deteriorated, and there were increasing raids by Barbary corsairs on ships and English coastal communities to capture people as slaves, which the Navy had little success in countering.[766] Charles I undertook a major programme of warship building, creating a small force of powerful ships, but his methods of fundraising to finance the fleet contributed to the outbreak of the English Civil War.[767] In the wake of this conflict and the abolition of the monarchy, the new Commonwealth of England, isolated and threatened from all sides, dramatically expanded the Navy, which became the most powerful in the world.[768]

The new regime's introduction of Navigation Acts, providing that all merchant shipping to and from England or her colonies should be carried out by English ships, led to war with the Dutch Republic.[769] In the early stages of this First

Anglo-Dutch War (1652–1654), the superiority of the large, heavily armed English ships was offset by superior Dutch tactical organisation and the fighting was inconclusive.[770] English tactical improvements resulted in a series of crushing victories in 1653 at Portland, the Gabbard and Scheveningen, bringing peace on favourable terms.[771] This was the first war fought largely, on the English side, by purpose-built, state-owned warships. It was followed by a war with Spain, which saw the English conquest of Jamaica in 1655 and successful attacks on Spanish treasure fleets in 1656 and 1657, but also the devastation of English merchant shipping by the privateers of Dunkirk, until their home port was captured by Anglo-French forces in 1658.[772]

The English monarchy was restored in May 1660, and Charles II assumed the throne. One of his first acts was to re-establish the Navy, but from this point on, it ceased to be the personal possession of the reigning monarch, and instead became a national institution—with the title of "The Royal Navy".

As a result of their defeat in the First Anglo-Dutch War, the Dutch transformed their navy, largely abandoning the use of militarised merchantmen and establishing a fleet composed mainly of heavily armed, purpose-built warships, as the English had done previously. Consequently, the Second Anglo-Dutch War (1665–1667) was a closely fought struggle between evenly matched opponents, with English victory at Lowestoft (1665) countered by Dutch triumph in the epic Four Days Battle (1666).[773] The deadlock was broken not by combat but by the superiority of Dutch public finance, as in 1667 Charles II was forced to lay up the fleet in port for lack of money to keep it at sea, while negotiating for peace. Disaster followed, as the Dutch fleet mounted the Raid on the Medway, breaking into Chatham Dockyard and capturing or burning many of the Navy's largest ships at their moorings.[774] In the Third Anglo-Dutch War (1672–1674), Charles II allied with Louis XIV of France against the Dutch, but the combined Anglo-French fleet was fought to a standstill in a series of inconclusive battles, while the French invasion by land was warded off.[775]

During the 1670s and 1680s, the English Royal Navy succeeded in permanently ending the threat to English shipping from the Barbary corsairs, inflicting defeats which induced the Barbary states to conclude long-lasting peace treaties.[776] Following the Glorious Revolution of 1688, England joined the European coalition against Louis XIV in the War of the Grand Alliance (1688–1697). Louis' recent shipbuilding programme had given France the largest navy in Europe. A combined Anglo-Dutch fleet was defeated at Beachy Head (1690), but victory at Barfleur-La Hogue (1692) was a turning-point, marking the end of France's brief pre-eminence at sea and the beginning of an enduring English, later British, supremacy.[777]

In the course of the 17th century, the English Royal Navy completed the transition from a semi-amateur Navy Royal fighting in conjunction with private

Figure 42: *The Dutch Raid on the Medway in 1667 during the Second Anglo–Dutch War*

vessels into a fully professional institution. Its financial provisions were gradually regularised, it came to rely on dedicated warships only, and it developed a professional officer corps with a defined career structure, superseding an earlier mix of "gentlemen" (upper-class soldiers) and "tarpaulins" (professional seamen, who generally served on merchant or fishing vessels in peacetime).[778]

James IV put the Royal Scots Navy on a new footing, founding a harbour at Newhaven in May 1504, and two years later ordering the construction of a dockyard at the Pools of Airth. The upper reaches of the Forth were protected by new fortifications on Inchgarvie.[779] Scottish ships had some success against privateers, accompanied the king in his expeditions in the islands and intervened in conflicts in Scandinavia and the Baltic Sea.[780] Expeditions to the Highlands to Islands to curb the power of the MacDonald Lord of the Isles were largely ineffective until in 1504 the king accompanied a squadron under Wood heavily armed with artillery, which battered the MacDonald strongholds into submission. Since some of these island fortresses could only be attacked from seaward, naval historian N. A. M. Rodger has suggested this may have marked the end of medieval naval warfare in the British Isles, ushering in a new tradition of artillery warfare. The king acquired a total of 38 ships for the Royal Scottish Navy, including the *Margaret*, and the carrack *Michael* or *Great Michael*, the largest warship of its time (1511).[781] The latter, built at great expense at Newhaven and launched in 1511, was 240 feet (73 m) in length, weighed 1,000 tons, had 24 cannon, and was, at that time, the largest ship in

Figure 43: *An English ship battles with a Barbary ship and two galleys in Tripoli in 1676*

Europe.[782] It marked a shift in designed as it was designed specifically to carry a main armament of heavy artillery.

During the Rough Wooing, the attempt to force a marriage between James V's heir Mary, Queen of Scots and Henry VIII's son, the future Edward VI, in 1542, the *Mary Willoughby*, the *Lion*, and the *Salamander* under the command of John Barton, son of Robert Barton, attacked merchants and fishermen off Whitby. They later blockaded a London merchant ship called the *Antony of Bruges* in a creek on the coast of Brittany.[783] In 1544, Edinburgh was attacked by an English marine force and burnt. The *Salamander* and the Scottish-built *Unicorn* were captured at Leith. The Scots still had two royal naval vessels and numerous smaller private vessels.[784]

When, as a result of the series of international treaties, Charles V declared war upon Scotland in 1544, the Scots were able to engage in a highly profitable campaign of privateering that lasted six years and the gains of which probably outweighed the losses in trade with the Low Countries.[785]

The Scots operated in the West Indies from the 1540s, joining the French in the capture of Burburuta in 1567.[786] English and Scottish naval warfare and privateering broke out sporadically in the 1550s.[787] When Anglo-Scottish relations deteriorated again in 1557 as part of a wider war between Spain and France, small ships called 'shallops' were noted between Leith and France, passing as fishermen, but bringing munitions and money. Private merchant ships were rigged at Leith, Aberdeen and Dundee as men-of-war, and the regent Mary of Guise claimed English prizes, one over 200 tons, for her fleet.[788] The re-fitted

Figure 44: *The Battle of Barfleur in 1692*

Mary Willoughby sailed with 11 other ships against Scotland in August 1557, landing troops and six field guns on Orkney to attack the Kirkwall Castle, St Magnus Cathedral and the Bishop's Palace. The English were repulsed by a Scottish force numbering 3000, and the English vice-admiral Sir John Clere of Ormesby was killed, but none of the English ships were lost.[789]

After the Union of Crowns in 1603 conflict between Scotland and England ended, but Scotland found itself involved in England's foreign policy, opening up Scottish shipping to attack. In the 1620s, Scotland found herself fighting a naval war as England's ally, first against Spain and then also against France, while simultaneously embroiled in undeclared North Sea commitments in the Danish intervention in the Thirty Years' War. In 1626 a squadron of three ships was bought and equipped, at a cost of least £5,200 sterling, to guard against privateers operating out of Spanish-controlled Dunkirk and other ships were armed in preparation for potential action. The acting High Admiral John Gordon of Lochinvar organised as many as three marque fleets of privateers.[790] It was probably one of Lochinvar's marque fleets that was sent to support the English Royal Navy in defending Irish waters in 1626.[791] In 1627, the Royal Scots Navy and accompanying contingents of burgh privateers participated in the major expedition to Biscay.[792] The Scots also returned to the West Indies, with Lochinvar taking French prizes and founding the colony of Charles Island. In 1629, two squadrons of privateers led by Lochinvar and William Lord Alexander, sailed for Canada, taking part in the campaign that resulted

Figure 45: *HMS Victory, Nelson's flagship at Trafalgar, is still a commissioned Royal Navy ship, although she is now permanently kept in dry-dock*

in the capture of Quebec from the French, which was handed back after the subsequent peace.[793]

By 1697 the English Royal Navy had 323 warships, while Scotland was still dependent on merchantman and privateers. In the 1690s, two separate schemes for larger naval forces were put in motion. As usual, the larger part was played by the merchant community rather than the government. The first was the Darien Scheme to found a Scottish colony in Spanish controlled America. It was undertaken by the Company of Scotland, who created a fleet of five ships, including the *Caledonia* and the *St. Andrew*, all built or chartered in Holland and Hamburg. It sailed to the Isthmus of Darien in 1698, but the venture failed and only one ship returned to Scotland.[794] In the same period it was decided to establish a professional navy for the protection of commerce in home waters during the Nine Years' War (1688–97) with France, with three purpose-built warships bought from English shipbuilders in 1696. These were the *Royal William*, a 32-gun fifth rate and two smaller ships, the *Royal Mary* and the *Dumbarton Castle*, each of 24 guns, generally described as frigates.

Development of Britain's navy

1707–1815

The Acts of Union, which created the Kingdom of Great Britain in 1707, established the Royal Navy of the newly united kingdom. The Scots office of Lord High Admiral was subsumed within the office of the Admiral of Great Britain. The three vessels of the small Royal Scottish Navy were transferred to the Royal Navy.[795]

Throughout the 18th and 19th centuries, the Royal Navy was the largest maritime force in the world, but until 1805 combinations of enemies repeatedly matched or exceeded its forces in numbers.[796] Despite this, it was able to maintain an almost uninterrupted ascendancy over its rivals through superiority in financing, tactics, training, organisation, social cohesion, hygiene, dockyard facilities, logistical support and (from the middle of the 18th century) warship design and construction.[797]

During the War of the Spanish Succession (1702–1714), the Navy operated in conjunction with the Dutch against the navies of France and Spain, in support of the efforts of Britain's Austrian Habsburg allies to seize control of Spain and its Mediterranean dependencies from the Bourbons. Amphibious operations by the Anglo-Dutch fleet brought about the capture of Sardinia, the Balearic Islands and a number of Spanish mainland ports, most importantly Barcelona. While most of these gains were turned over to the Habsburgs, Britain held on to Gibraltar and Menorca, which were retained in the peace settlement, providing the Navy with Mediterranean bases. Early in the war French naval squadrons had done considerable damage to English and Dutch commercial convoys. However, a major victory over France and Spain at Vigo Bay (1702), further successes in battle, and the scuttling of the entire French Mediterranean fleet at Toulon in 1707 virtually cleared the Navy's opponents from the seas for the latter part of the war. Naval operations also enabled the conquest of the French colonies in Nova Scotia and Newfoundland.[798] Further conflict with Spain followed in the War of the Quadruple Alliance (1718–1720), in which the Navy helped thwart a Spanish attempt to regain Sicily and Sardinia from Austria and Savoy, defeating a Spanish fleet at Cape Passaro (1718), and in an undeclared war in the 1720s, in which Spain tried to retake Gibraltar and Menorca.[799]

After a period of relative peace, the Navy became engaged in the War of Jenkins' Ear (1739–1748) against Spain, which was dominated by a series of costly and mostly unsuccessful attacks on Spanish ports in the Caribbean, primarily a huge expedition against Cartagena de Indias in 1741. These led to heavy loss of life from tropical diseases.[800,801,802] In 1742 the Kingdom of the Two Sicilies was driven to withdraw from the war in the space of half an hour by the threat

Figure 46: *The British expedition against Cuba in 1762*

of a bombardment of its capital Naples by a small British squadron. The war became subsumed in the wider War of the Austrian Succession (1744–1748), once again pitting Britain against France. Naval fighting in this war, which for the first time included major operations in the Indian Ocean, was largely inconclusive, the most significant event being the failure of an attempted French invasion of England in 1744.[803]

The subsequent Seven Years' War (1756–1763) saw the Navy conduct amphibious campaigns leading to the conquest of New France, of French colonies in the Caribbean and West Africa, and of small islands off the French coast, while operations in the Indian Ocean contributed to the destruction of French power in India.[804] A new French attempt to invade Britain was thwarted by the defeat of their escort fleet in the extraordinary Battle of Quiberon Bay in 1759, fought in a gale on a dangerous lee shore. Once again the British fleet effectively eliminated the French Navy from the war, leading France to abandon major operations.[805] In 1762 the resumption of hostilities with Spain led to the British capture of Manila and of Havana, along with a Spanish fleet sheltering there.[806]

In the American War of Independence (1775–1783) the Royal Navy readily obliterated the small Continental Navy of frigates fielded by the rebel colonists, but the entry of France, Spain and the Netherlands into the war against Britain

Figure 47: *The Battle of the Saintes (1782). On the right, the French flagship, the Ville de Paris, in action against HMS Barfleur.*

produced a combination of opposing forces which deprived the Navy of its position of superiority for the first time since the 1690s, briefly but decisively. The war saw a series of inconclusive battles in the Atlantic and Caribbean, in which the Navy failed to achieve the decisive victories needed to secure the supply lines of British forces in North America and to cut off the colonial rebels from outside support.[807] The most important operation of the war came in 1781 when, in the Battle of the Chesapeake, the British fleet failed to lift the French blockade of Lord Cornwallis's army, resulting in Cornwallis's surrender at Yorktown.[808] Although this disaster effectively concluded the fighting in North America, hostilities continued in the Indian Ocean, where the French were prevented from re-establishing a meaningful foothold in India, and in the Caribbean. British victory in the Caribbean in the Battle of the Saintes in 1782 and the relief of Gibraltar later the same year symbolised the restoration of British naval ascendancy, but this came too late to prevent the independence of the rebellious Thirteen Colonies.[809]

The eradication of scurvy from the Royal Navy in the 1790s came about due to the efforts of Gilbert Blane, chairman of the Navy's Sick and Hurt Board, which ordered fresh lemon juice to be given to sailors on ships. Other navies soon adopted this successful solution.[810]

The French Revolutionary Wars (1793–1801) and Napoleonic Wars (1803–1814 and 1815) saw the Royal Navy reach a peak of efficiency, dominating the navies of all Britain's adversaries, which spent most of the war

Figure 48: *The Bombardment of Algiers in 1816 to support the ultimatum to release European slaves*

blockaded in port. The Navy achieved an emphatic early victory at the Glorious First of June (1794), and gained a number of smaller victories while supporting abortive French Royalist efforts to regain control of France. In the course of one such operation, the majority of the French Mediterranean fleet was captured or destroyed during a short-lived occupation of Toulon in 1793.[811] The military successes of the French Revolutionary régime brought the Spanish and Dutch navies into the war on the French side, but the losses inflicted on the Dutch at the Battle of Camperdown in 1797 and the surrender of their surviving fleet to a landing force at Den Helder in 1799 effectively eliminated the Dutch navy from the war.[812] The Spithead and Nore mutinies in 1797 incapacitated the Channel and North Sea fleets, leaving Britain potentially exposed to invasion, but were rapidly resolved.[813] The British Mediterranean fleet under Horatio Nelson failed to intercept Napoleon Bonaparte's 1798 expedition to invade Egypt, but annihilated the French fleet at the Battle of the Nile, leaving Bonaparte's army isolated.[814] The emergence of a Baltic coalition opposed to Britain led to an attack on Denmark, which lost much of its fleet in the Battle of Copenhagen (1801) and came to terms with Britain.[815]

During these years, the Navy also conducted amphibious operations that captured most of the French Caribbean islands and the Dutch colonies at the Cape of Good Hope and Ceylon. Though successful in their outcome, the

Figure 49: *The Battle of Trafalgar, depicted here in its opening phase*

expeditions to the Caribbean, conducted on a grand scale, led to devastating losses from disease. Except for Ceylon and Trinidad, these gains were returned following the Peace of Amiens in 1802, which briefly halted the fighting.[816] Menorca, which had been repeatedly lost and regained during the 18th century, was restored to Spain, its place as the Navy's main base in the Mediterranean being taken by the new acquisition of Malta. War resumed in 1803 and Napoleon attempted to assemble a large enough fleet from the French and Spanish squadrons blockaded in various ports to cover an invasion of England. The Navy frustrated these efforts, and following the abandonment of the invasion plan, Nelson defeated the combined Franco-Spanish fleet at Trafalgar (1805).[817]

After Trafalgar, large-scale fighting at sea remained limited to the destruction of small, fugitive French squadrons, and amphibious operations which again captured the colonies which had been restored at Amiens, along with France's Indian Ocean base at Mauritius and parts of the Dutch East Indies, including Java and the Moluccas.[818] In 1807, French plans to seize the Danish fleet led to a pre-emptive British attack on Copenhagen, resulting in the surrender of the entire Danish navy.[819] The impressment of British and American sailors from American ships contributed to the outbreak of the War of 1812 (1812–1814) against the United States, in which the naval fighting was largely confined to commerce raiding and single-ship actions.[820] The brief renewal of war after Napoleon's return to power in 1815 did not bring a resumption of naval combat.[821]

Figure 50: *HMS Warrior, the first iron-hulled, armour-plated warship*

1815–1914

Between 1815 and 1914, the Navy saw little serious action, owing to the absence of any opponent strong enough to challenge its dominance. During this period, naval warfare underwent a comprehensive transformation, brought about by steam propulsion, metal ship construction, and explosive munitions. Despite having to completely replace its war fleet, the Navy managed to maintain its overwhelming advantage over all potential rivals. Due to British leadership in the Industrial Revolution, the country enjoyed unparalleled shipbuilding capacity and financial resources, which ensured that no rival could take advantage of these revolutionary changes to negate the British advantage in ship numbers.

In 1859, the fleet was estimated to number about 1000 in all, including both combat and non-combat vessels. In 1889, Parliament passed the Naval Defence Act, which formally adopted the 'two-power standard', which stipulated that the Royal Navy should maintain a number of battleships at least equal to the combined strength of the next two largest navies.[822]

The first major action that the Royal Navy saw during this period was the Bombardment of Algiers in 1816 by a joint Anglo-Dutch fleet under Lord Exmouth, to force the Barbary state of Algiers to free Christian slaves and to halt the practice of enslaving Europeans. During the Greek War of Independence, the combined navies of Britain, France and Russia defeated an Ottoman

Figure 51: *The British assault on Canton during the First Opium War in 1841*

fleet at the Battle of Navarino in 1827, the last major action between sailing ships. During the same period, the Royal Navy took anti-piracy actions in the South China Sea. Between 1807 and 1865, it maintained a Blockade of Africa to counter the illegal slave trade. It also participated in the Crimean War of 1854–56, as well as numerous military actions throughout Asia and Africa, notably the First and Second Opium Wars with Qing dynasty China. On 27 August 1896, the Royal Navy took part in the Anglo-Zanzibar War, which was the shortest war in history.

The end of the 19th century saw structural changes brought about by the First Sea Lord Jackie Fisher, who retired, scrapped or placed into reserve many of the older vessels, making funds and manpower available for newer ships. He also oversaw the development of HMS *Dreadnought*, launched in 1906. Its speed and firepower rendered all existing battleships obsolete. The industrial and economic development of Germany had by this time overtaken Britain, enabling the Imperial German Navy to attempt to outpace British construction of dreadnoughts. In the ensuing arms race, Britain succeeded in maintaining a substantial numerical advantage over Germany, but for the first time since 1805 another navy now existed with the capacity to challenge the Royal Navy in battle.[823]

Reforms were also gradually introduced in the conditions for enlisted men with the abolition of military flogging in 1879, amongst others.

Figure 52: *HMS Dreadnought*

1914–1939

During the First World War, most of the Royal Navy's strength was mostly deployed at home in the Grand Fleet, confronting the German High Seas Fleet across the North Sea. Several inconclusive clashes took place between them, chiefly the Battle of Jutland in 1916. The British numerical advantage proved insurmountable, leading the High Seas Fleet to abandon any attempt to challenge British dominance.

Elsewhere in the world, the Navy hunted down the handful of German surface raiders at large. During the Dardanelles Campaign against the Ottoman Empire in 1915, it suffered heavy losses during a failed attempt to break through the system of minefields and shore batteries defending the straits.

Upon entering the war, the Navy had immediately established a blockade of Germany. The Navy's Northern Patrol closed off access to the North Sea, while the Dover Patrol closed off access to the English Channel. The Navy also mined the North Sea. As well as closing off the Imperial German Navy's access to the Atlantic, the blockade largely blocked neutral merchant shipping heading to or from Germany. The blockade was maintained during the eight months after the armistice was agreed to force Germany to end the war and sign the Treaty of Versailles.[824]

Figure 53: *HMS Ark Royal*

The most serious menace faced by the Navy came from the attacks on merchant shipping mounted by German U-boats. For much of the war this submarine campaign was restricted by prize rules requiring merchant ships to be warned and evacuated before sinking. In 1915, the Germans renounced these restrictions and began to sink merchant ships on sight, but later returned to the previous rules of engagement to placate neutral opinion. A resumption of unrestricted submarine warfare in 1917 raised the prospect of Britain and its allies being starved into submission. The Navy's response to this new form of warfare had proved inadequate due to its refusal to adopt a convoy system for merchant shipping, despite the demonstrated effectiveness of the technique in protecting troop ships. The belated introduction of convoys sharply reduced losses and brought the U-boat threat under control.

In the inter-war period, the Royal Navy was stripped of much of its power. The Washington and London Naval Treaties imposed the scrapping of some capital ships and limitations on new construction. In 1932, the Invergordon Mutiny took place over a proposed 25% pay cut, which was eventually reduced to 10%. International tensions increased in the mid-1930s and the Second London Naval Treaty of 1935 failed to halt the development of a naval arms race. By 1938, treaty limits were effectively being ignored. The re-armament of the Royal Navy was well under way by this point; the Royal Navy had begun construction of the still treaty-affected and undergunned new battleships and its first full-sized purpose-built aircraft carriers. In addition to new construction, several existing old battleships (whose gun power offset to a significant extent the weakly armed new battleships), battlecruisers and heavy cruisers were reconstructed, and anti-aircraft weaponry reinforced, while new technologies, such as ASDIC, Huff-Duff and hydrophones, were developed. The Navy had lost control of naval aviation when the Royal Naval Air Service was merged with the Royal Flying Corps to form the Royal Air Force in 1918, but regained control of ship-board aircraft with the return of the Fleet Air Arm to Naval control in 1937.

1939–1945

At the start of World War II in 1939, the Royal Navy was the largest in the world, with over 1,400 vessels, including:

- 7 aircraft carriers – with 5 more under construction
- 15 battleships and battlecruisers – with 5 more under construction
- 66 cruisers – with 23 more under construction
- 184 destroyers – with 52 under construction
- 45 escort and patrol vessels – with 9 under construction and one on order
- 60 submarines – with 9 under construction

During one of the earliest phases of the War the Royal Navy provided critical cover during Operation Dynamo, the British evacuations from Dunkirk. At Taranto, Admiral Cunningham commanded a fleet that launched the first all-aircraft naval attack in history. Cunningham was determined that the Navy be perceived as the United Kingdom's most daring military force: when warned of risks to his vessels during the Allied evacuation after the Battle of Crete he said, "It takes the Navy three years to build a new ship. It will take three hundred years to build a new tradition. The evacuation will continue."[825]

The Royal Navy suffered heavy losses in the first two years of the war, including the carriers *Courageous*, *Glorious* and *Ark Royal*, the battleships *Royal Oak* and *Barham* and the battlecruiser *Hood* in the European Theatre, and the carrier *Hermes*, the battleship *Prince of Wales*, the battlecruiser *Repulse* and the heavy cruisers *Exeter*, *Dorsetshire* and *Cornwall* in the Asian Theatre. Of the 1,418 men aboard *Hood*, only three survived its sinking.[826] Over 3,000 people were lost when the converted troopship *Lancastria* was sunk in June 1940, the greatest maritime disaster in Britain's history. There were however also successes against enemy surface ships, as in the battles of the River Plate in 1939, Narvik in 1940 and Cape Matapan in 1941, and the sinking of the German capital ships *Bismarck* in 1941 and *Scharnhorst* in 1943.

The Navy's most critical struggle was the Battle of the Atlantic defending Britain's vital commercial supply lines against U-boat attack. A traditional

Figure 54: *British battlecruiser HMS Hood*

convoy system was instituted from the start of the war, but German submarine tactics, based on group attacks by "wolf-packs", were much more effective than in the previous war, and the threat remained serious for well over three years. Defences were strengthened by deployment of purpose-built escorts, of escort carriers, of long-range patrol aircraft, improved anti-submarine weapons and sensors, and by the deciphering of German signals by the code-breakers of Bletchley Park. The threat was at last effectively broken by devastating losses inflicted on the U-boats in the spring of 1943. Intense convoy battles of a different sort, against combined air, surface and submarine threats, were fought off enemy-controlled coasts in the Arctic, where Britain ran supply convoys through to Russia, and in the Mediterranean, where the struggle focused on Convoys to Malta.

The Navy was also vital in guarding the sea lanes that enabled British forces to fight in North Africa, the Mediterranean and the Far East. Naval supremacy was essential to amphibious operations such as the invasions of Northwest Africa, Sicily, Italy, and Normandy. By the end of the war the Royal Navy comprised over 4,800 ships, and was the second largest fleet in the world.

Postwar period and early 21st century

After the Second World War, the decline of the British Empire and the economic hardships in Britain forced the reduction in the size and capability of the Royal Navy. All of the pre-war ships (except for the Town-class light cruisers) were quickly retired and most sold for scrapping over the years 1945–48, and

Figure 55: *HMS Vanguard of the current Vanguard-class ballistic missile submarines*

only the best condition ships (the four surviving KG-V class battleships, carriers, cruisers, and some destroyers) were retained and refitted for service. The increasingly powerful United States Navy took on the former role of the Royal Navy as global naval power and police force of the sea. The combination of the threat of the Soviet Union, and Britain's commitments throughout the world, created a new role for the Navy. Governments since the Second World War have had to balance commitments with increasing budgetary pressures, partly due to the increasing cost of weapons systems, what historian Paul Kennedy called the Upward Spiral.[827]

These pressures were exacerbated by bitter inter-service rivalry. A modest new construction programme was initiated with some new carriers (*Majestic*- and *Centaur*-class light carriers, and *Audacious*-class large carriers, such as HMS *Ark Royal*, being completed between 1948 through 1958), along with three *Tiger*-class cruisers (completed 1959–61), the *Daring*-class destroyers in the 1950s, and finally the County-class guided missile destroyers completed in the 1960s.

HMS *Dreadnought*, the Royal Navy's first nuclear submarine, was launched in the 1960s. The navy also received its first nuclear weapons with the introduction of the first of the *Resolution*-class submarines armed with the Polaris

Figure 56: *HMS Illustrious, an Invincible-class aircraft carrier*

missile. The introduction of Polaris followed the cancellation of the GAM-87 Skybolt missile which had been proposed for use by the Air Force's V bomber force. By the 1990s, the navy became responsible for the maintenance of the UK's entire nuclear arsenal. The financial costs attached to nuclear deterrence became an increasingly significant issue for the navy.

The Navy began plans to replace its fleet of aircraft carriers in the mid-1960s. A plan was drawn up for three large aircraft carriers, each displacing about 60,000 tons; the plan was designated CVA-01. These carriers would be able to operate the latest aircraft coming into service and keep the Royal Navy's place as a major naval power. The new Labour government that came to power in 1964 was determined to cut defence expenditure as a means to reduce public spending, and in the 1966 Defence White Paper the project was cancelled.[828] The existing carriers (all built during, or just after World War II) were refitted, two (*Bulwark* and *Albion*) becoming *commando* carriers, and four (*Victorious*, *Eagle*, *Hermes*, and *Ark Royal*) being completed or rebuilt. Starting in 1965 with *Centaur*, one by one these carriers were decommissioned without replacement, culminating with the 1979 retirement of *Ark Royal*. By the early 1980s, only *Hermes* survived and received a refit (just in time for the Falklands War), to operate Sea Harriers. She operated along with three much smaller *Invincible*-class aircraft carriers, and the fleet was now centred around antisubmarine warfare in the north Atlantic as opposed to its former position with

Figure 57: *HMS Albion, an Albion-class landing platform dock on exercise with the Netherlands Marine Corps in 2008*

worldwide strike capability. Along with the war era carriers, all of the war built cruisers and destroyers, along with the post-war built *Tiger*-class cruisers and large County-class guided missile destroyers were either retired or sold by 1984.

One of the most important operations conducted predominantly by the Royal Navy after the Second World War was the 1982 defeat of Argentina in the Falkland Islands War. Despite losing four naval ships and other civilian and RFA ships, the Royal Navy fought and won a war over 8,000 miles (12,000 km) from Great Britain. HMS *Conqueror* is the only nuclear-powered submarine to have engaged an enemy ship with torpedoes, sinking the cruiser ARA *General Belgrano*.

Before the Falklands War, Defence Secretary John Nott had advocated and initiated a series of cutbacks to the Navy. The Falklands War though, provided a reprieve in Nott-proposed cutbacks, and proved a need for the Royal Navy to regain an expeditionary and littoral capability which, with its resources and structure at the time, would prove difficult. At the beginning of the 1980s, the Royal Navy was a force focused on blue-water anti-submarine warfare. Its purpose was to search for and destroy Soviet submarines in the North Atlantic, and to operate the nuclear deterrent submarine force. For a time *Hermes* was retained, along with all three of the *Invincible*-class light aircraft carriers. More Sea Harriers were ordered; not just to replace losses, but to also increase the size of the Fleet Air Arm. New and more capable ships were built; notably the *Sheffield*-class destroyers, the Type 21, Type 22, and Type 23 frigates, new LPDs of the *Albion* class, and HMS *Ocean*, but never in the numbers of the ships that they replaced. As a result, the Royal Navy surface fleet continues to reduce in size. A 2013 report found that the current RN was already too small, and that Britain would have to depend on her allies if her territories were attacked.

The Royal Navy also took part in the Gulf War, the Kosovo conflict, the Afghanistan Campaign, and the 2003 Iraq War, the last of which saw RN warships bombard positions in support of the Al Faw Peninsula landings by Royal Marines. In August 2005, the Royal Navy rescued seven Russians stranded in a submarine off the Kamchatka peninsula. The Navy's Scorpio 45 remote-controlled mini-sub freed the Russian submarine from the fishing nets and cables that had held it for three days. The Royal Navy was also involved in an incident involving Somali pirates in November 2008, after the pirates tried to capture a civilian vessel.

The global economic recession of 2008 had a significant impact on the Royal Navy resulting in the **Strategic Defence & Security Review 2010** which made sweeping cuts to the Navy's budget. The *Harrier* aircraft were retired with some being presented to museums and the rest being sold to the United States for spare parts to keep their aircraft flying. The carrier *Ark Royal* and the remaining Type-22 frigates were all removed from service and sold for scrap. *HMS Illustrious* however, was retained through to 2014 in the LPH role, until *HMS Ocean* completed her refit. Plans were made to allow *Illustrious* to be retained as a floating museum, but by summer of 2016 she too was sold for scrap. The future of *Albion* and *Bulwark* is uncertain as funds may not be available to allow them to remain in service. The Royal Navy was to receive 12 Type 45 destroyers as a replacement for the older Type 42 class that was completely retired by 2013. The number was later reduced to 6 vessels, all in service by 2012.[829]

In 2015, the Royal Navy was deployed to the Mediterranean in the mission to rescue migrants crossing the Mediterranean from Libya to Italy.[830] By spring 2018, the Royal Navy had decommissioned HMS *Ocean*, as well as started the replacement of the River class Offshore Patrol Vessels. The first of the new *Queen Elizabeth*-class carriers was undergoing tests and workups before her first fixed-wing aircraft arrive later in the year, and design work was underway for the new generation of nuclear deterrent submarines. By July 2017 the first of 8 new frigates was laid down, the Type 26 frigate.[831] There is also plans to build up to 10 Global Combat Ships to replace some of the older frigates in the fleet.[832]

Figure 58: *Britannia Royal Naval College*

Royal Navy today

Personnel

HMS *Raleigh* at Torpoint, Cornwall, is the basic training facility for newly enlisted personnel. Britannia Royal Naval College is the initial officer training establishment for the navy, located at Dartmouth, Devon. Personnel are divided into a general duties branch, which includes those seamen officers eligible for command, and other branches including the Royal Naval Engineers, medical, and Logistics Officers, the renamed Supply Officer branch. Present day officers and ratings have several different Royal Navy uniforms; some are blue, others are white. Women began to join the Royal Navy in 1917 with the formation of the Women's Royal Naval Service (WRNS), which was disbanded after the end of the First World War in 1919. It was revived in 1939, and the WRNS continued until disbandment in 1993, as a result of the decision to fully integrate women into the structures of the Royal Navy. Women now serve in all sections of the Royal Navy including the Royal Marines.

By January 2015, the Naval Service (Royal Navy and Royal Marines) numbered some 32,880 Regular[833] and 3,040 Maritime Reserve personnel (Royal Naval Reserve and Royal Marines Reserve),[834] giving a combined component strength of 35,920 personnel. In addition to the active elements of the Naval

Figure 59: *HMS Queen Elizabeth*, a Queen Elizabeth-class supercarrier on sea trials in June 2017.

Service (Regular and Maritime Reserve), all ex-Regular personnel remain liable to be recalled for duty in a time of need, this is known as the Regular Reserve. In 2002, there were 26,520 Regular Reserves of the Naval Service, of which 13,720 served in the Royal Fleet Reserve.[835] Publications since April 2013 no-longer report the entire strength of the Regular Reserve, instead they only give a figure for Regular Reserves who serve in the Royal Fleet Reserve.[836] They had a strength of 7,960 personnel in 2013.[837]

Surface fleet

Large fleet units – amphibious and carriers

The large fleet units in the Royal Navy consisted of amphibious warfare ships and aircraft carriers, until August 2014, when the last Invincible-class aircraft carrier was decommissioned. Amphibious warfare ships in current service include two landing platform docks (HMS *Albion* and HMS *Bulwark*). While their primary role is to conduct amphibious warfare, they have also been deployed for humanitarian aid missions.

HMS *Illustrious* was the sole remaining aircraft carrier in service with the Royal Navy. Following the retirement of the Harrier GR9 aircraft in 2010, *Illustrious* had been serving as an amphibious assault ship while *Ocean* was in refit. *Illustrious* was decommissioned on 28 August 2014, after *Ocean* had returned to active duty.[838] However, two much larger *Queen Elizabeth*-class aircraft carriers are under construction. These carriers are expected to cost £6 billion (double the original estimate), displace 70,600 tonnes and commence flight trials in 2018. Both are intended to operate the STOVL variant of the F-35 Lightning II. The first, HMS *Queen Elizabeth* began sea trials in June 2017 and will enter service in 2020, while the second, HMS *Prince of Wales* will enter service in 2023.

The Navy's large fleet units are supported by the Royal Fleet Auxiliary which possesses three amphibious transport docks within its operational craft. These are known as the *Bay*-class landing ships, of which four were introduced in 2006–2007, but one was sold to the Royal Australian Navy in 2011. In November 2006, the First Sea Lord Admiral Sir Jonathon Band described the Royal Fleet Auxiliary vessels as "a major uplift in the Royal Navy's war fighting capability."

Major surface combatants – destroyers and frigates

The escort fleet, in the form of guided missile destroyers and frigates, is the traditional workhorse of the Navy. As of January 2018[839] there are six Type 45 destroyers and 13 Type 23 frigates in active service. Among their primary roles is to provide escort for the larger capital ships—protecting them from air, surface and subsurface threats. Other duties include undertaking the Royal Navy's standing deployments across the globe, which often consists of: counter-narcotics, anti-piracy missions and providing humanitarian aid.

All six Type 45 destroyers have been built and are in commission, with HMS *Duncan* being the last and final Type 45 entering service in September 2013.[840] The new Type 45 destroyers replaced the older Type 42 destroyers. The Type 45 is primarily designed for anti-aircraft and anti-missile warfare and the Royal Navy describe the destroyers mission as "to shield the Fleet from air attack".[841] They are equipped with the PAAMS (also known as Sea Viper) integrated anti-aircraft warfare system which incorporates the sophisticated SAMPSON and S1850M long range radars and the Aster 15 and 30 missiles.

Initially, 16 Type 23 frigates were delivered to the Royal Navy, with the final vessel, HMS *St Albans*, commissioned in June 2002. However, the 2004 review of defence spending (Delivering Security in a Changing World) announced that three frigates of the fleet of sixteen would be paid off as part of a continuous cost-cutting strategy, and these were subsequently sold to the Chilean Navy.[842] The 2010 Strategic Defence and Security Review announced that the remaining 13 Type 23 frigates would eventually be replaced by the Global Combat Ship.

Figure 60: *HMS Duncan, the Type 45 guided missile destroyer*

Patrol and survey vessels

At the beginning of the 1990s, the Royal Navy had two classes of offshore patrol vessel, the *Island*-class, and the larger *Castle*-class. However, in 1997, a decision was taken to replace them; this decision came in the form of three much larger offshore patrol vessels, the *River*-class. Unusually, the three River-class ships were owned by Vosper Thorneycroft, and leased to the Royal Navy until 2013. This relationship was defined by a ground-breaking contractor logistic support contract which contracts the ships' availability to the RN, including technical and stores support. A modified River-class vessel, HMS *Clyde*, was commissioned in July 2007 and became the Falkland Islands guard-ship. In November 2013, it was announced that in order to sustain shipbuilding capabilities on the Clyde, five new ocean-going patrol vessels with Merlin-capable flightdecks would be ordered for delivery from 2017. These ships will replace the four existing River Class ships. In October 2014, the Ministry of Defence announced the names of the first three ships as HMS *Forth*, HMS *Medway* and HMS *Trent*. The fourth and fifth ships were ordered in December 2016, these will be named HMS *Spey* and HMS *Tamar* respectively.

The Royal Navy's largest patrol ship is HMS *Protector*. *Protector* is a dedicated Antarctic patrol ship that fulfils the nations mandate to provide support to the British Antarctic Survey (BAS).

Figure 61: *HMS Protector, a Royal Navy Antarctic patrol ship*

Mine countermeasure

Mine countermeasure vessels in service with the Royal Navy include: seven *Sandown*-class minehunters and six Hunt-class mine countermeasure vessels. The Hunt-class vessels combine the separate roles of the traditional minesweeper and the active minehunter in one hull. If required, the *Sandown* and Hunt-class vessels can take on the role of offshore patrol vessels. HMS *Scott* is an ocean survey vessel and at 13,500 tonnes is one of the largest ships in the Navy. The other survey vessels of the Royal Navy are the two multi-role ships of the *Echo*-class, which came into service in 2002 and 2003.

Submarine Service

The Submarine Service is the submarine based element of the Royal Navy. It is sometimes referred to as the "*Silent Service*", as the submarines are generally required to operate undetected. The service was founded in 1901. The service made history in 1982 when, during the Falklands War, HMS *Conqueror* became the first nuclear-powered submarine to sink a surface ship, the ARA *General Belgrano*. Today, the Submarine Service consists of ballistic missile submarines (SSBN) and fleet submarines (SSN). All of the Royal Navy's submarines are nuclear-powered.

Of ballistic missile submarines, the Royal Navy operates the four *Vanguard*-class, each displacing nearly 16,000 tonnes and equipped with Trident II missiles (armed with nuclear weapons) and heavyweight Spearfish torpedoes, with

Figure 62: *HMS Astute, the first Astute-class nuclear submarine*

the purpose to carry out Operation Relentless, the United Kingdom's Continuous At Sea Deterrent (Abbreviated to CASD). In December 2006, the Government published recommendations for a new class of four ballistic missile submarines to replace the current *Vanguard*-class, starting 2024. These new *Dreadnought*-class submarines will mean that the United Kingdom will maintain a nuclear ballistic missile submarine fleet and the ability to launch nuclear weapons.

Six fleet submarines are presently in service, with three *Trafalgar*-class and three *Astute*-class (with the remainder in construction) making up the total. The *Trafalgar*-class displace little over 5,300 tonnes when submerged and are armed with Tomahawk land-attack missiles and Spearfish torpedoes. The *Astute*-class at 7,400 tonnes are much larger and carry a larger number of Tomahawk missiles and Spearfish torpedoes. Four more *Astute*-class fleet submarines are expected to be commissioned and will eventually replace the remaining *Trafalgar*-class boats. HMS *Artful* was the latest *Astute*-class boat to be commissioned.

In the 2010 Strategic Defence and Security Review, the UK Government reaffirmed its intention to procure seven *Astute*-class submarines.[843]

Figure 63: *The F-35B will be operated from the Queen Elizabeth-class aircraft carriers*

Fleet Air Arm

The Fleet Air Arm (FAA) is the branch of the Royal Navy responsible for the operation of naval aircraft, it can trace its roots back to 1912 and the formation of the Royal Flying Corps. The Fleet Air Arm currently operates helicopters: the AgustaWestland Merlin, the AgustaWestland Wildcat, and the Westland Sea King. Pilots designated for rotary wing service train at the Defence Helicopter Flying School at RAF Shawbury.

With the retirement of the Joint Force Harrier and the Harrier GR7/GR9 strike aircraft in 2010, the FAA has no fixed-wing aircraft in front-line operations. There is an intention to operate the Lockheed Martin F-35 Lightning II B version with the Royal Air Force. 809 NAS is hoped to be the first FAA Squadron to operate that aircraft. The F-35B will be operated from the Navy's new *Queen Elizabeth*-class aircraft carriers starting 2018 for initial flight training.

Royal Marines

The Royal Marines are an amphibious, specialised light infantry force of commandos, capable of deploying at short notice in support of Her Majesty's Government's military and diplomatic objectives overseas.[844] The Royal Marines are organised into a highly mobile light infantry brigade (3 Commando Brigade) and a number of separate units, including 1 Assault Group Royal Marines, 43 Commando Fleet Protection Group Royal Marines and a

Figure 64: *Royal Marines in Sangin, 2010*

company strength commitment to the Special Forces Support Group. The Corps operates in all environments and climates, though particular expertise and training is spent on amphibious warfare, Arctic warfare, mountain warfare, expeditionary warfare and commitment to the UK's Rapid Reaction Force. The Royal Marines are also the primary source of personnel for the Special Boat Service (SBS), the Royal Navy's contribution to the United Kingdom Special Forces.

The Royal Marines have seen action in a number of wars, often fighting beside the British Army; including in the Seven Years' War, the Napoleonic Wars, the Crimean War, World War I and World War II. In recent times, the Corps has been deployed in expeditionary warfare roles, such as the Falklands War, the Gulf War, the Bosnian War, the Kosovo War, the Sierra Leone Civil War, the Iraq War and the War in Afghanistan. The Royal Marines have international ties with allied marine forces, particularly the United States Marine Corps and the Netherlands Marine Corps/Korps Mariniers.

Naval bases

The Royal Navy currently uses three major naval bases in the UK, each housing its own flotilla of ships and boats ready for service:

- HMNB Devonport (HMS Drake) – Currently the largest operational naval base in Western Europe, Devonport's flotilla consists of the RN's two

Figure 65: *HMS Albion during the HMNB Devonport Navy days 2006*

amphibious assault vessels (HM Ships *Albion* and *Bulwark*), and half the fleet of Type 23 frigates. Also, Devonport homes some of the RN's Submarines service, including the fleet of Trafalgar Class Submarines.
- HMNB Portsmouth (HMS Nelson) – Home to the future Queen Elizabeth Class supercarriers, Portsmouth is also the home to the Daring Class Stealth Destroyers (commonly known as Type 45) as well as mine-clearance vessels, and a moderate fleet of Type 23 frigates as well as Fishery Protection Squadrons.
- HMNB Clyde (HMS Neptune Or Simply 'Faslane') – Situated in Central Scotland along the Clyde River, Faslane is known as the home of the UK's nuclear deterrent, as it maintains the fleet of Vanguard Class Ballistic Missile Submarines, as well as the fleet of Astute Class Fleet (Hunter-Killer) submarines. By 2020, Faslane will become the home to all Royal Navy submarines, and thus the RN Submarine Service. As a result, 43 Commando (Fleet Protection Group) are stationed in Faslane alongside to guard the base as well as The Royal Naval Armaments Depot at Coulport. Moreover, Faslane also operates a medium-sized fleet of patrol vessels.

The current role of the Royal Navy is to protect British interests at home and abroad, executing the foreign and defence policies of Her Majesty's Government through the exercise of military effect, diplomatic activities and other

Figure 66: *HMS Vigilant alongside Faslane Naval Base*

Figure 67: *Royal Navy EH-101 Merlin at RIAT 2009*

activities in support of these objectives. The Royal Navy is also a key element of the British contribution to NATO, with a number of assets allocated to NATO tasks at any time. These objectives are delivered via a number of core capabilities:

- Maintenance of the UK Nuclear Deterrent through a policy of *Continuous at Sea Deterrence*.
- Provision of two medium scale maritime task groups with the Fleet Air Arm.
- Delivery of the UK Commando force.
- Contribution of assets to the Joint Helicopter Command.
- Maintenance of standing patrol commitments.
- Provision of mine counter measures capability to United Kingdom and allied commitments.
- Provision of hydrographic and meteorological services deployable worldwide.
- Protection of Britain and EU's Exclusive Economic Zone.

Current deployments

The Royal Navy is currently deployed in different areas of the world, including some standing Royal Navy deployments. These include several home tasks as well as overseas deployments. The Navy is deployed in the Mediterranean as part of standing NATO deployments including mine countermeasures and NATO Maritime Group 2. In both the North and South Atlantic RN vessels are patrolling. There is always a Falkland Islands patrol vessel on deployment, currently HMS *Clyde*.

The Royal Navy operates a Response Force Task Group (a product of the 2010 Strategic Defence and Security Review), which is poised to respond globally to short-notice tasking across a range of defence activities, such as non-combatant evacuation operations, disaster relief, humanitarian aid or amphibious operations. In 2011, the first deployment of the task group occurred under the name 'COUGAR 11' which saw them transit through the Mediterranean where they took part in multinational amphibious exercises before moving further east through the Suez Canal for further exercises in the Indian Ocean.[845,846]

In the Persian Gulf, the RN sustains commitments in support of both national and coalition efforts to stabilise the region. The Armilla Patrol, which started in 1980, is the navy's primary commitment the Gulf region. The Royal Navy also contributes to the combined maritime forces in the Gulf in support of coalition operations.[847] The UK Maritime Component Commander, overseer of all of Her Majesty's warships in the Persian Gulf and surrounding waters, is also deputy commander of the Combined Maritime Forces.[848] The Royal

Figure 68: *The RN presence in the Persian Gulf typically consists of a Type 45 destroyer and a squadron of minehunters supported by an RFA Bay-class "mothership"*

Navy has been responsible for training the fledgling Iraqi Navy and securing Iraq's oil terminals following the cessation of hostilities in the country. The Iraqi Training and Advisory Mission (Navy) (Umm Qasr), headed by a Royal Navy captain, has been responsible for the former duty whilst Commander Task Force Iraqi Maritime, a Royal Navy commodore, has been responsible for the latter.[849,850]

The Royal Navy contributes to standing NATO formations and maintains forces as part of the NATO Response Force. The RN also has a long-standing commitment to supporting the Five Powers Defence Arrangements countries and occasionally deploys to the Far East as a result.[851] This deployment typically consists of a frigate and a survey vessel, operating separately. Operation Atalanta, the European Union's anti-piracy operation in the Indian Ocean, is permanently commanded by a senior Royal Navy or Royal Marines officer at Northwood Headquarters and the navy contributes ships to the operation.[852]

Command, control and organisation

The titular head of the Royal Navy is the Lord High Admiral, a position which has been held by the Duke of Edinburgh since 2011. The position had been held by Queen Elizabeth II from 1964 to 2011; the Sovereign is the Commander-in-chief of the British Armed Forces.[853] The professional head of the Naval Service is the First Sea Lord, an admiral and member of the Defence Council of the United Kingdom. The Defence Council delegates management of the Naval Service to the Admiralty Board, chaired by the Secretary of State for Defence, which directs the Navy Board, a sub-committee of the Admiralty Board comprising only naval officers and Ministry of Defence (MOD) civil servants. These are all based in MOD Main Building in London, where the First Sea Lord, also known as the Chief of the Naval Staff, is supported by the Naval Staff Department.[854]

Organisation

The Fleet Commander has responsibility for the provision of ships, submarines and aircraft ready for any operations that the Government requires. Fleet Commander exercises his authority through the Navy Command Headquarters, based at HMS *Excellent* in Portsmouth. An operational headquarters, the Northwood Headquarters, at Northwood, London, is co-located with the Permanent Joint Headquarters of the United Kingdom's armed forces, and a NATO Regional Command, Allied Maritime Command.

The Royal Navy was the first of the three armed forces to combine the personnel and training command, under the Principal Personnel Officer, with the operational and policy command, combining the Headquarters of the Commander-in-Chief, Fleet and Naval Home Command into a single organisation, Fleet Command, in 2005 and becoming Navy Command in 2008. Within the combined command, the Second Sea Lord continues to act as the Principal Personnel Officer.

The Naval Command senior appointments are:

Rank and pre-nominal	Name	post-nominal(s)	Position
Professional Head of the Royal Navy			
Admiral	Sir Philip Jones	KCB	First Sea Lord and Chief of Naval Staff (1SL/CNS)
Fleet Commander			
Vice admiral	Ben Key	CBE	Fleet Commander
Navy Command Headquarters			
Rear admiral	Nicholas Hine	CB	Assistant Chief of Naval Staff (Policy)
Major general	Robert Magowan	CB, CBE, RM	Assistant Chief of Naval Staff (Capability)/-Chief of Staff Naval HQ
Rear admiral	Paul Halton	OBE	Commander Operations
Rear admiral	Paul Bennett	CB, OBE	Commander UK Maritime Forces

Major general	Charles Stickland	OBE, RM	Commander UK Amphibious Forces
Rear admiral	John Wheale	OBE	Flag Officer Scotland and Northern Ireland & also Rear Admiral Submarines
Second Sea Lord, Chief of Naval Personnel & Training and Deputy Chief of Naval Staff			
Vice admiral	Tony Radakin	CB	Second Sea Lord & Deputy Chief of Naval Staff
Rear admiral	Simon Williams	CB CVO	Chief of Staff (Personnel)/Naval Secretary
Rear admiral	William Warrender	CBE	Flag Officer Sea Training
The Venerable	Ian Wheatley	QHC	Chaplain of the Fleet

Intelligence support to fleet operations is provided by intelligence sections at the various headquarters and from MOD Defence Intelligence, renamed from the Defence Intelligence Staff in early 2010.

Locations

The Royal Navy currently operates from three bases in the United Kingdom where commissioned ships are based; Portsmouth, Clyde and Devonport, Plymouth—Devonport is the largest operational naval base in the UK and Western Europe. Each base hosts a flotilla command under a commodore, or, in the case of Clyde, a captain, responsible for the provision of operational capability using the ships and submarines within the flotilla. 3 Commando Brigade Royal Marines is similarly commanded by a brigadier and based in Plymouth. Historically, the Royal Navy maintained Royal Navy Dockyards around the world. Dockyards of the Royal Navy are harbours where ships are overhauled and refitted. Only four are operating today; at Devonport, Faslane, Rosyth and at Portsmouth. A Naval Base Review was undertaken in 2006 and early 2007, the outcome being announced by Secretary of State for Defence, Des Browne, confirming that all would remain however some reductions in manpower were anticipated.

The academy where initial training for future Royal Navy officers takes place is Britannia Royal Naval College, located on a hill overlooking Dartmouth, Devon. Basic training for future ratings takes place at HMS *Raleigh* at Torpoint, Cornwall, close to HMNB Devonport.

Significant numbers of naval personnel are employed within the Ministry of Defence, Defence Equipment and Support and on exchange with the Army and Royal Air Force. Small numbers are also on exchange within other government departments and with allied fleets, such as the United States Navy. The navy also posts personnel in small units around the world to support ongoing operations and maintain standing commitments. Nineteen personnel are

Figure 69: *Portsmouth dockyard during the Trafalgar 200 International Fleet Review. Seen here are commissioned ships from; the United Kingdom, the Netherlands, Greece, Pakistan and Nigeria.*

Figure 70: *HMNB Clyde, Faslane, home of the Vanguard-class submarines*

Figure 71: *Type 23 frigates or "Duke class" are named after British dukes*

stationed in Gibraltar to support the small Gibraltar Squadron, the RN's only permanent overseas squadron. A number of personnel are also based at East Cove Military Port and RAF Mount Pleasant in the Falkland Islands to support APT(S). Small numbers of personnel are based in Diego Garcia (Naval Party 1002), Miami (NP 1011 – AUTEC), Singapore (NP 1022), Dubai (NP 1023) and elsewhere.[855]

On 6 December 2014, the Foreign and Commonwealth Office announced it would expand the UK's naval facilities in Bahrain to support larger Royal Navy ships deployed to the Persian Gulf. Once complete, it will be the UK's first permanent military base located East of Suez since it withdrew from the region in 1971. The base will reportedly be large enough to accommodate Type 45 destroyers and *Queen Elizabeth*-class aircraft carriers.

Titles and naming

Of the Navy

The navy of the United Kingdom is commonly referred to as the "Royal Navy" both in the United Kingdom and other countries. Navies of other Commonwealth countries where the British monarch is also head of state include their national name, e.g. Royal Australian Navy. Some navies of other monarchies, such as the *Koninklijke Marine* (Royal Netherlands Navy) and *Kungliga Flottan* (Royal Swedish Navy), are also called "Royal Navy" in their own language. The Danish Navy stands out with the term Royal incorporated in its official name (Royal Danish Navy), but only using the term "Flåden" (Navy) in everyday speech.[856] The French Navy, despite France being a republic since 1870, is often nicknamed *"La Royale"* (literally: The Royal).

Of ships

Royal Navy ships in commission are prefixed since 1789 with Her Majesty's Ship (His Majesty's Ship), abbreviated to "HMS"; for example, HMS *Beagle*. Submarines are styled HM Submarine, also abbreviated "HMS". Names are allocated to ships and submarines by a naming committee within the MOD and given by class, with the names of ships within a class often being thematic (for example, the Type 23s are named after British dukes) or traditional (for example, the *Invincible*-class aircraft carriers all carry the names of famous historic ships). Names are frequently re-used, offering a new ship the rich heritage, battle honours and traditions of her predecessors. Often, a particular vessel class will be named after the first ship of that type to be built. As well as a name, each ship and submarine of the Royal Navy and the Royal Fleet Auxiliary is given a pennant number which in part denotes its role. For example, the destroyer HMS *Daring* displays the pennant number 'D32'.

Ranks, rates, and Insignia

The Royal Navy ranks, rates and insignia form part of the uniform of the Royal Navy. The Royal Navy uniform is the pattern on which many of the uniforms of the other national navies of the world are based (e.g. Ranks and insignia of NATO navies officers, Uniforms of the United States Navy, Uniforms of the Royal Canadian Navy, French Naval Uniforms).

For officers (see also Royal Navy officer rank insignia):

Royal Navy

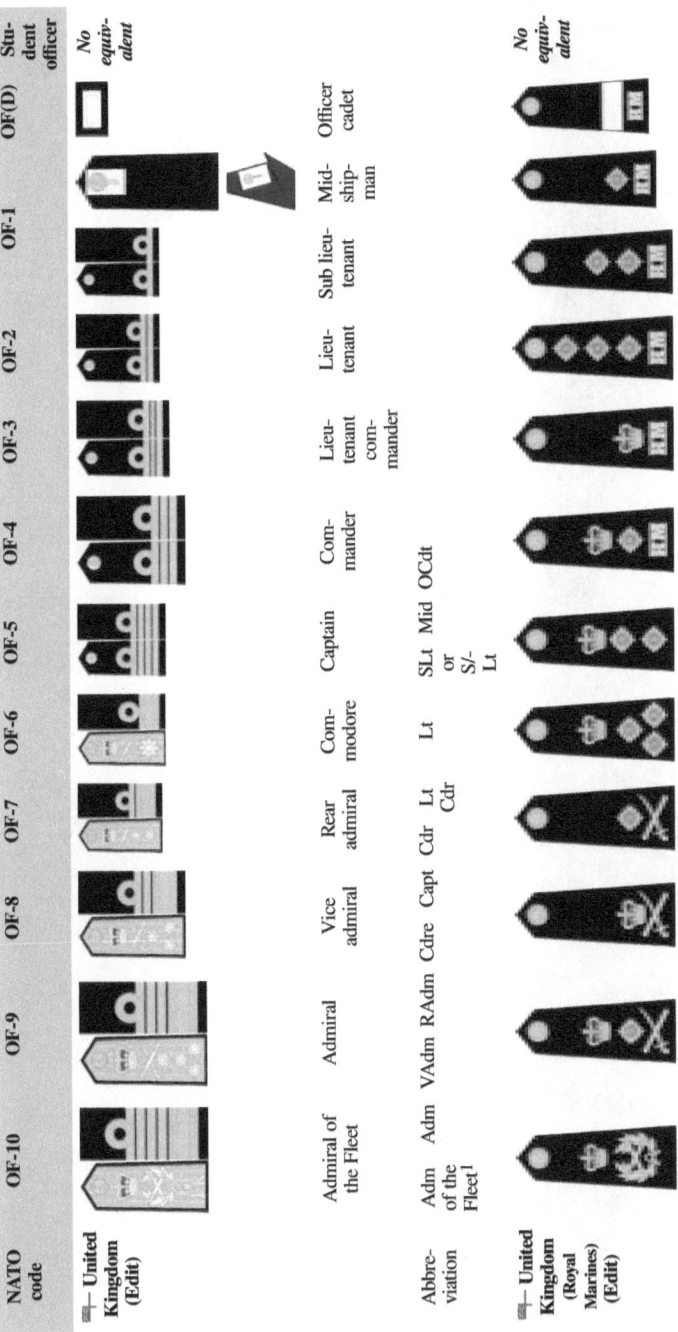

Rank	Abbreviation	NATO code
Captain General Royal Marines	Gen	OF-10
General	Lt Gen	OF-9
Lieutenant-General	Maj Gen	OF-8
Major-General	Brig	OF-7
Brigadier	Col	OF-6
Colonel	Lt Col	OF-5
Lieutenant-Colonel	Maj	OF-4
Major	Capt	OF-3
Captain	Lt	OF-2
Lieutenant	2Lt	OF-1
Second Lieutenant	OCdt	
Officer Cadet		OF(D)
Student officer		

Royal Navy

[1] Rank in abeyance – routine appointments no longer made to this rank, though honorary awards of this rank are occasionally made to senior members of the Royal family and prominent former First Sea Lords.

For Enlisted rates (see also Royal Navy ratings rank insignia):

NATO Code	OR-9	OR-8	OR-7	OR-6	OR-5	OR-4	OR-3	OR-2	OR-1
United Kingdom (Edit)		No equivalent			No equivalent		No equivalent		No equivalent
	Warrant officer		Chief petty officer	Petty officer		Leading rate		Able rate	
Abbreviation	WO1		CPO	PO	LH	AB1			
United Kingdom (Royal Marines) (Edit)					No equivalent			No equivalent	No insignia
	Warrant officer class 1	Warrant officer class 2	Colour sergeant	Sergeant		Corporal	Lance corporal		Marine
Abbreviation	WO1	WO2	CSgt	Sgt	Cpl	L/- Cpl			Mne
NATO Code	OR-9	OR-8	OR-7	OR-6	OR-5	OR-4	OR-3	OR-2	OR-1

The Royal Navy has the following branch of service badges:

Link to image

Badge of Royal Naval Pilot of the Fleet Air Arm wings.

Badge of fully qualified submariner.

Custom and tradition

The Royal Navy has several formal customs and traditions including the use of ensigns and ships badges. Royal Navy ships have several ensigns used when under way and when in port. Commissioned ships and submarines wear the White Ensign at the stern whilst alongside during daylight hours and at the main-mast whilst under way. When alongside, the *Union Jack* is flown from the jackstaff at the bow, and can only be flown under way either to signal a court-martial is in progress or to indicate the presence of an admiral of the fleet on-board (including the Lord High Admiral or the monarch).

The Fleet Review is an irregular tradition of assembling the fleet before the monarch. The first review on record was held in 1400, and the most recent review as of 2009[839] was held on 28 June 2005 to mark the bi-centenary of the Battle of Trafalgar; 167 ships from many different nations attended with the Royal Navy supplying 67.

There are several less formal traditions including service nicknames and Naval slang. The nicknames include "The Andrew" (of uncertain origin, possibly after a zealous press ganger) and "The Senior Service". The RN has evolved a rich volume of slang, known as "Jack-speak". Nowadays the British sailor is usually "Jack" (or "Jenny") rather than the more historical "Jack Tar". Royal Marines are fondly known as "Bootnecks" or often just as "Royals". A compendium of Naval slang was brought together by Commander A. Covey-Crump and his name has in itself become the subject of Naval slang; Covey Crump. A game traditionally played by the Navy is the four-player board game "Uckers". This is similar to Ludo and it is regarded as easy to learn, but difficult to play well.

Navy Cadets

The Royal Navy sponsors or supports four youth organisations:

- Volunteer Cadet Corps – consisting of Royal Naval Cadets and Royal Marines Cadets, the VCC was the first youth organisation officially supported or sponsored by the Admiralty in 1901.
- Combined Cadet Force – consisting of Naval cadets although now under the operational command of the British Army.
- Sea Cadets – supporting teenagers who are interested in naval matters.

Figure 72: *The Queen and Admiral Sir Alan West during a Fleet Review*

The above organisations are the responsibility of the CUY branch of Commander Core Training and Recruiting (COMCORE) who reports to Flag Officer Sea Training (FOST).

In popular culture

The Royal Navy of the 18th century is depicted in many novels and several films dramatising the voyage and mutiny on the Bounty. The Royal Navy's Napoleonic campaigns of the early 19th century are also a popular subject of historical novels. Some of the best-known are Patrick O'Brian's Aubrey-Maturin series and C. S. Forester's Horatio Hornblower chronicles.

The Navy can also be seen in numerous films. The fictional spy James Bond is "officially" a commander in the Royal Navy. The Royal Navy is featured in *The Spy Who Loved Me*, when a nuclear ballistic-missile submarine is stolen, and in *Tomorrow Never Dies* when a media baron sinks a Royal Navy warship in an attempt to trigger a war between the UK and People's Republic of China. *Master and Commander: The Far Side of the World* was based on Patrick O'Brian's Aubrey-Maturin series. The *Pirates of the Caribbean* series of films also includes the Navy as the force pursuing the eponymous pirates. Noël Coward directed and starred in his own film *In Which We Serve*, which tells the story of the crew of the fictional HMS *Torrin* during the Second World

War. It was intended as a propaganda film and was released in 1942. Coward starred as the ship's captain, with supporting roles from John Mills and Richard Attenborough.

C. S. Forester's Hornblower novels have been adapted for television. The Royal Navy was the subject of an acclaimed 1970s BBC television drama series, *Warship*, and of a five-part documentary, *Shipmates*, that followed the workings of the Royal Navy day to day.

Television documentaries about the Royal Navy include: *Empire of the Seas: How the Navy Forged the Modern World*, a four-part documentary depicting Britain's rise as a naval superpower, up until the First World War; *Sailor*, about life on the aircraft carrier HMS *Ark Royal*; and *Submarine*, about the submarine captains' training course, 'The Perisher'. There have also been Channel 5 documentaries such as *Royal Navy Submarine Mission*, following a nuclear-powered fleet submarine.

The popular BBC radio comedy series *The Navy Lark* featured a fictitious warship ("HMS *Troutbridge*") and ran from 1959 to 1977.

Bibliography

- Beatson, Robert (1790). *Naval and Military Memoirs of Great Britain, from 1727 to 1783. 3*. Strachan. OCLC 937652092[858].
- Brown, D. K.; Moore, George (2012). *Rebuilding the Royal Navy: Warship Design Since 1945*. Seaforth. ISBN 9781848321502.
- Browning, Reed (1993). *The War of the Austrian Succession*. St. Martin's Press. ISBN 9780312094836.
- Grimes, Shawn T. (2012). *Strategy and War Planning in the British Navy, 1887–1918*. Boydell. ISBN 9781846158179.
- Harding, Richard (2005). *The Royal Navy 1930–2000: Innovation and Defence*. Frank Cass. ISBN 9780203337684.
- Howard, David Armine (2003). *British Sea Power: How Britain Became Sovereign of the Seas*. Carroll & Graf. ISBN 9780786712496.
- Hyde-Price, Adrian (2007). *European Security in the Twenty-First Century: The Challenge of Multipolarity*. London: Routledge. ISBN 1134164408.
- Kennedy, Paul (1989). *The Rise and Fall of Great Powers*. London: Fontana. ISBN 978-0049090194.
- Nelson, Arthur (2001). *The Tudor navy: the ships, men and organisation, 1485–1603*. Conway Maritime Press. ISBN 9780851777856.
- Potter, E. B. (1984). *Sea Power: A Naval History*. Naval Institute press. ISBN 9780870216077.

- Rodger, N.A.M. (1997). *The Safeguard of the Sea: A Naval History of Britain, 660–1649*. **1**. Harper Collins. ISBN 978-0006388401.
- Rodger, N.A.M. (2004). *The Command of the Ocean: A Naval History of Britain, 1649–1815*. **2**. Penguin. ISBN 978-0141026909.
- Rose, Lisle A. (2006). *Power at Sea: The Breaking Storm, 1919–1945*. **2**. University of Missouri Press. ISBN 9780826216946.
- Simms, Brendan (2008). *Three Victories and a Defeat: The Rise and Fall of the First British Empire*. Penguin Books. ISBN 978-0465013326.
- Sondhaus, Lawrence (2001). *Naval Warfare, 1815–1914*. New York: Routledge. ISBN 978-0415214780.
- Willmott, H. P. (2009). *The Last Century of Sea Power, Volume 1: From Port Arthur to Chanak, 1894–1922*. Indiana University Press. ISBN 9780253352149.
- Willmott, H. P. (2010). *The Last Century of Sea Power, Volume 2: From Washington to Tokyo, 1922–1945*. Indiana University Press. ISBN 9780253353597.
- Wilson, Ben (2013). *Empire of the Deep: the rise and fall of the British Navy*. Weidenfeld & Nicolson. ISBN 9780297864080.
- Winfield, Rif (2007). *British Warships of the Age of Sail 1714–1792: Design, Construction, Careers and Fates*. Seaforth. ISBN 9781844157006.

External links

Wikimedia Commons has media related to *Royal Navy*.

Wikisourcehas original text related to this article:
Royal Navy

- Official Website of the Royal Navy[859]
- History of the Royal Navy[860]
- The history of the Royal Naval Patrol Service[861]
- 3-Decks Naval History Website[862]
- Sea Your History[863] Website from the Royal Naval Museum – Discover detailed information about the Royal Navy in the 20th century.
- Royal Marines Museum[864]
- List of sunken ships of the Royal Navy on the wrecksite[865]
- Navy News – Royal Navy Newspaper[866]
- Royal Navy Community Friends[867]

Video clips

- Royal Navy's channel[868] on YouTube
- TwoSix Royal Navy Communication's channel[869] on YouTube

List of active Royal Navy ships

Her Majesty's Naval Service of the British Armed Forces
Components
• **Royal Navy** • Surface Fleet • Fleet Air Arm • Submarine Service • Royal Naval Reserve • Royal Navy Medical Service • Nursing Service (QARNNS) • Chaplaincy • Royal Navy Police • **Royal Marines** • Royal Marines Reserve • Special Boat Service • **Naval Careers Service**
History and future
• History of the Royal Navy / Royal Marines • Customs and traditions • Future
Ships
• Current fleet • Current deployments • Historic ships
Personnel
• The Admiralty • Senior officers • Uniforms • Officer / ratings rank insignia
Auxiliary services
• Royal Fleet Auxiliary • Marine Services
• v • t • e[870]

List of active Royal Navy ships

The Royal Navy is the principal naval warfare service branch of the British Armed Forces. As of August 2018, there are 75 commissioned ships in the Royal Navy. 20 of the commissioned vessels are major surface combatants (six guided missile destroyers, 13 frigates and one aircraft carrier), and 10 are nuclear-powered submarines (four ballistic missile submarines and six fleet submarines). In addition the Navy possesses two amphibious transport docks, 13 mine countermeasures vessels, 22 patrol vessels, five survey vessels, one icebreaker and two historic warships (*Victory* and *Bristol*).

The Royal Navy currently operates three bases where commissioned ships are based; HMNB Portsmouth, HMNB Devonport and HMNB Clyde. In addition, a number of commissioned vessels belonging to the University Royal Naval Units (URNU) are stationed at various locations around the United Kingdom. The total displacement of the Royal Navy is approximately 407,000 tonnes (641,000 tonnes including the Royal Fleet Auxiliary and Royal Marines).

Besides the Royal Navy, the Royal Fleet Auxiliary and the Royal Marines operate their own flotillas of naval vessels which complement the assets of the Royal Navy, however they are not included in this list or the above figures. In addition, the naval training vessels *Brecon* and *Cromer* can be found based at the Royal Navy shore establishment HMS *Raleigh* and the Britannia Royal Naval College, respectively, along with a number of P1000's and Motor Whalers. As a supporting contingent of Her Majesty's Naval Service, the civilian Marine Services operate a large number of auxiliary ships (including coastal logistics, tugs and research vessels) in support of Royal Navy and Royal Fleet Auxiliary operations.[871]

All ships and submarines currently in commission with the Royal Navy were built in the United Kingdom, with the exception of icebreaker *Protector* which was built in Norway. All vessels of the Royal Navy bear the ship prefix "HMS", for Her Majesty's Ship.

Flagship of the First Sea Lord

Classic first-rate

Class	Ship	Pennant No.	Commissioned	Displacement	Type	Homeport	Note
Ship of the Line	HMS *Victory*	—	1778[872]	3,556 tonnes	First-rate ship of the line	Portsmouth	

Figure 73: *Victory*

Submarine Service

Strategic

Class	Boat	Pennant No.	Commissioned	Displacement	Type[873]	Homeport	Note
Vanguard class	HMS *Vanguard*	S28	1993	15,900 tonnes	Ballistic missile submarine	Clyde	
	HMS *Victorious*	S29	1995	15,900 tonnes	Ballistic missile submarine	Clyde	
	HMS *Vigilant*	S30	1996	15,900 tonnes	Ballistic missile submarine	Clyde	
	HMS *Vengeance*	S31	1999	15,900 tonnes	Ballistic missile submarine	Clyde	

List of active Royal Navy ships

Figure 74: *Vanguard (Vanguard class)*

Attack

Class	Boat	Pennant No.	Commis-sioned	Displace-ment	Type[874]	Home-port	Note
Astute class	HMS *Astute*	S119	2010	7,400 tonnes	Fleet sub-marine	Clyde	
	HMS *Ambush*	S120	2013	7,400 tonnes	Fleet sub-marine	Clyde	
	HMS *Artful*	S121	2016	7,400 tonnes	Fleet sub-marine	Clyde	
Trafalgar class	HMS *Trenchant*	S91	1989	5,300 tonnes	Fleet sub-marine	Devon-port	
	HMS *Talent*	S92	1990	5,300 tonnes	Fleet sub-marine	Devon-port	
	HMS *Triumph*	S93	1991	5,300 tonnes	Fleet sub-marine	Devon-port	

Figure 75: *Ambush (Astute class)*

Figure 76: *Trenchant (Trafalgar class)*

Surface Fleet

Aircraft carriers

Class	Ship	Pennant No.	Commissioned	Displacement	Type	Homeport	Note
Queen Elizabeth class	HMS *Queen Elizabeth*	R08	2017	70,400 tonnes	Aircraft carrier	Portsmouth	875

Figure 77: *Queen Elizabeth* (Queen Elizabeth class)

Amphibious warfare

Class	Ship	Pennant No.	Commissioned	Displacement	Type	Homeport	Note
Albion class	HMS *Albion*	L14	2003	19,560 tonnes	Amphibious transport dock	Devonport	
	HMS *Bulwark*	L15	2004	19,560 tonnes	Amphibious transport dock	Devonport	876

In addition, the Royal Fleet Auxiliary possess three 16,160 tonne Bay-class dock landing ships (LSD).

Figure 78: *Albion (Albion class)*

Major surface combatants

Class	Ship	Pennant No.	Commissioned	Displacement	Type	Homeport	Note
Type 45 or *Daring* class	HMS *Daring*	D32	2009	8,500 tonnes	Guided missile destroyer	Portsmouth	877
	HMS *Dauntless*	D33	2010	8,500 tonnes	Guided missile destroyer	Portsmouth	
	HMS *Diamond*	D34	2011	8,500 tonnes	Guided missile destroyer	Portsmouth	
	HMS *Dragon*	D35	2012	8,500 tonnes	Guided missile destroyer	Portsmouth	
	HMS *Defender*	D36	2013	8,500 tonnes	Guided missile destroyer	Portsmouth	
	HMS *Duncan*	D37	2013	8,500 tonnes	Guided missile destroyer	Portsmouth	
Type 23 or **Duke** class	HMS *Argyll*	F231	1991	4,900 tonnes	Frigate	Devonport	
	HMS *Lancaster*	F229	1992	4,900 tonnes	Frigate	Portsmouth	878

List of active Royal Navy ships

HMS *Iron Duke*	F234	1993	4,900 tonnes	Frigate	Portsmouth
HMS *Monmouth*	F235	1993	4,900 tonnes	Frigate	Devonport
HMS *Montrose*	F236	1994	4,900 tonnes	Frigate	Devonport
HMS *Westminster*	F237	1994	4,900 tonnes	Frigate	Portsmouth
HMS *Northumberland*	F238	1994	4,900 tonnes	Frigate	Devonport
HMS *Richmond*	F239	1995	4,900 tonnes	Frigate	Portsmouth
HMS *Somerset*	F82	1996	4,900 tonnes	Frigate	Devonport
HMS *Sutherland*	F81	1997	4,900 tonnes	Frigate	Devonport
HMS *Kent*	F78	2000	4,900 tonnes	Frigate	Portsmouth
HMS *Portland*	F79	2001	4,900 tonnes	Frigate	Devonport
HMS *St Albans*	F83	2002	4,900 tonnes	Frigate	Portsmouth

Figure 79: *Daring (T45 Daring class)*

Figure 80: *Northumberland (T23 Duke class)*

Offshore patrol

Class	Ship	Pennant No.	Commissioned	Displacement	Type	Homeport	Note
River class	HMS *Tyne*	P281	2003	1,700 tonnes	Offshore patrol vessel	Portsmouth	
	HMS *Mersey*	P283	2003	1,700 tonnes	Offshore patrol vessel	Portsmouth	
	HMS *Clyde*	P257	2007	2,000 tonnes	Offshore patrol vessel	Portsmouth	879
	HMS *Forth*	P222	2018	2,000 tonnes	Offshore patrol vessel	Portsmouth	

In addition to the above vessels, the Border Force possess five cutters.

List of active Royal Navy ships

Figure 81: *Clyde (River class)*

Mine countermeasures

Class	Ship	Pennant No.	Commissioned	Displacement	Type	Homeport	Note
Hunt class	HMS *Ledbury*	M30	1981	750 tonnes	Minehunter	Portsmouth	
	HMS *Cattistock*	M31	1982	750 tonnes	Minehunter	Portsmouth	
	HMS *Brocklesby*	M33	1983	750 tonnes	Minehunter	Portsmouth	
	HMS *Middleton*	M34	1984	750 tonnes	Minehunter	Portsmouth	
	HMS *Chiddingfold*	M37	1984	750 tonnes	Minehunter	Portsmouth	
	HMS *Hurworth*	M39	1985	750 tonnes	Minehunter	Portsmouth	
Sandown class	HMS *Penzance*	M106	1998	600 tonnes	Minehunter	Clyde	
	HMS *Pembroke*	M107	1998	600 tonnes	Minehunter	Clyde	
	HMS *Grimsby*	M108	1999	600 tonnes	Minehunter	Clyde	
	HMS *Bangor*	M109	2000	600 tonnes	Minehunter	Clyde	

	HMS *Ramsey*	M110	2000	600 tonnes	Mine-hunter	Clyde	
	HMS *Blyth*	M111	2001	600 tonnes	Mine-hunter	Clyde	
	HMS *Shoreham*	M112	2001	600 tonnes	Mine-hunter	Clyde	

Figure 82: *Hurworth (Hunt class)*

Figure 83: *Ramsey (Sandown class)*

Fast patrol

Class	Ship	Pennant No.	Commissioned	Displacement	Type	Homeport	Note
P2000 or Archer class	HMS Archer	P264	1985	54 tonnes	Patrol boat URNU	—	
	HMS Biter	P270	1986	54 tonnes	Patrol boat URNU	—	
	HMS Smiter	P272	1988	54 tonnes	Patrol boat URNU	—	
	HMS Pursuer	P273	1988	54 tonnes	Patrol boat URNU	—	
	HMS Blazer	P279	1988	54 tonnes	Patrol boat URNU	—	
	HMS Dasher	P280	1988	54 tonnes	Patrol boat URNU	—	
	HMS Puncher	P291	1988	54 tonnes	Patrol boat URNU	—	
	HMS Charger	P292	1988	54 tonnes	Patrol boat URNU	—	
	HMS Ranger	P293	1988	54 tonnes	Patrol boat URNU	—	
	HMS Trumpeter	P294	1988	54 tonnes	Patrol boat URNU	—	
	HMS Express	P163	1988	54 tonnes	Patrol boat URNU	—	
	HMS Example	P165	1985	54 tonnes	Patrol boat URNU	—	
	HMS Explorer	P164	1986	54 tonnes	Patrol boat URNU	—	
	HMS Exploit	P167	1988	54 tonnes	Patrol boat URNU	—	
	HMS Tracker	P274	1998	54 tonnes	Patrol boat	Clyde	[880]
	HMS Raider	P275	1998	54 tonnes	Patrol boat	Clyde	[881]
Scimitar class	HMS Scimitar	P284	2003	24 tonnes	Patrol boat	Gibraltar	[882]
	HMS Sabre	P285	2003	24 tonnes	Patrol boat	Gibraltar	[883]

The Royal Marines operate three Island-class fast patrol boats (*Mull*, *Rona* and *Eorsa*) from HMNB Clyde.

Figure 84: *Raider (Archer class)*

Figure 85: *Sabre (Scimitar class)*

Survey

Class	Ship	Pennant No.	Commissioned	Displacement	Type	Home-port	Note
Echo class	HMS *Echo*	H87	2003	3,740 tonnes	Multi-purpose survey	Devonport	
	HMS *Enterprise*	H88	2003	3,740 tonnes	Multi-purpose survey	Devonport	
—	HMS *Scott*	H131	1997	13,500 tonnes	Ocean survey	Devonport	
—	HMS *Protector*	A173	2011	5,000 tonnes	Icebreaker & survey	Devonport	
—	HMS *Magpie*	H130	2018	37 tonnes	Survey Motor Launch	Devonport	

The British Antarctic Survey operates two Royal Research Ships which work in conjunction with *Protector*.

Figure 86: *Echo (Echo class)*

Figure 87: *Scott*

Figure 88: *Protector*

Figure 89: *Magpie*

HMS *Excellent*
Static ship

Class	Ship	Pennant No.	Commissioned	Displacement	Type	Homeport	Note
Type 82 or *Bristol* class	HMS *Bristol*	D23	1973	7,100 tonnes	Guided missile destroyer	—	884

Figure 90: *Bristol (T82 Bristol class)*

Silhouettes

Silhouettes of major fleet units:

Queen Elizabeth

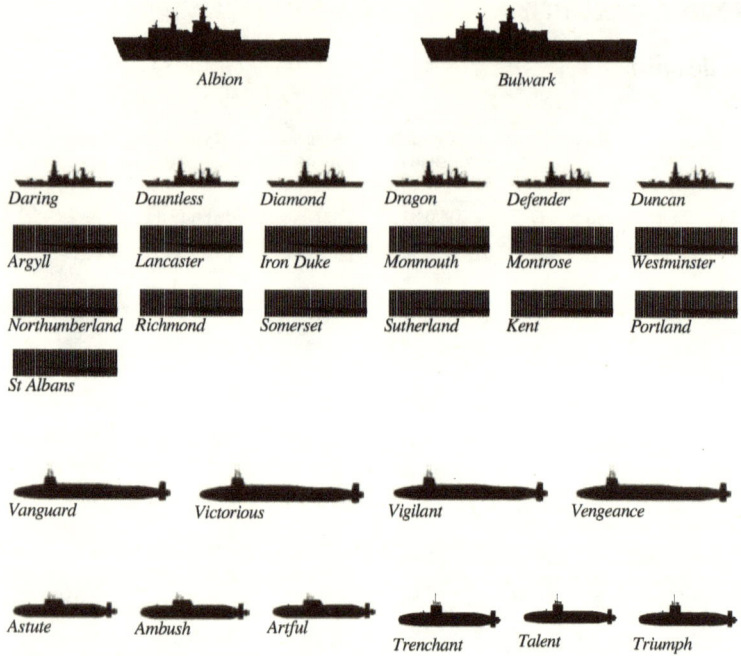

External links

- Royal Navy[885] (royalnavy.mod.uk)
- Royal Navy — The Equipment — Ships[886] (royalnavy.mod.uk)

Royal Navy Surface Fleet

	Royal Navy Surface FleetWikipedia:Citation needed
Active	1971-current
Country	United Kingdom
Branch	Royal Navy
Type	Fleet
Size	Command
Garrison/HQ	Portsmouth, England
Commanders	
Current commander	Rear-Admiral TBD

The **Surface Fleet**Wikipedia:Citation needed is the main Naval formation of the Royal Navy it consists of a collection of surface vessels (as opposed to submarines or aircraft). The surface fleet is administered by Rear-Admiral Paul Bennett. as the *Commander United Kingdom Maritime Forces and Rear Admiral Surface Ships.*

At present it consists of two flotillas based at HMNB Portsmouth and HMNB Devonport, both located on the south coast of England, and a flotilla based at HMNB Clyde, Faslane, Scotland. The Surface Fleet consists of a wide variety of vessels, ranging from aircraft carriers to mine countermeasures vessels to offshore patrol vessels, but the backbone of the fleet consists of destroyers (type 45) and frigates (type 23).

The surface fleet is continually engaged in numerous operations on a worldwide basis. Closer to home, the surface fleet also conducts Fishery Protection Patrols around UK waters, in a formal agreement with DEFRA. The Fishery Protection Squadron is the largest front line squadron in the Royal Navy.

History

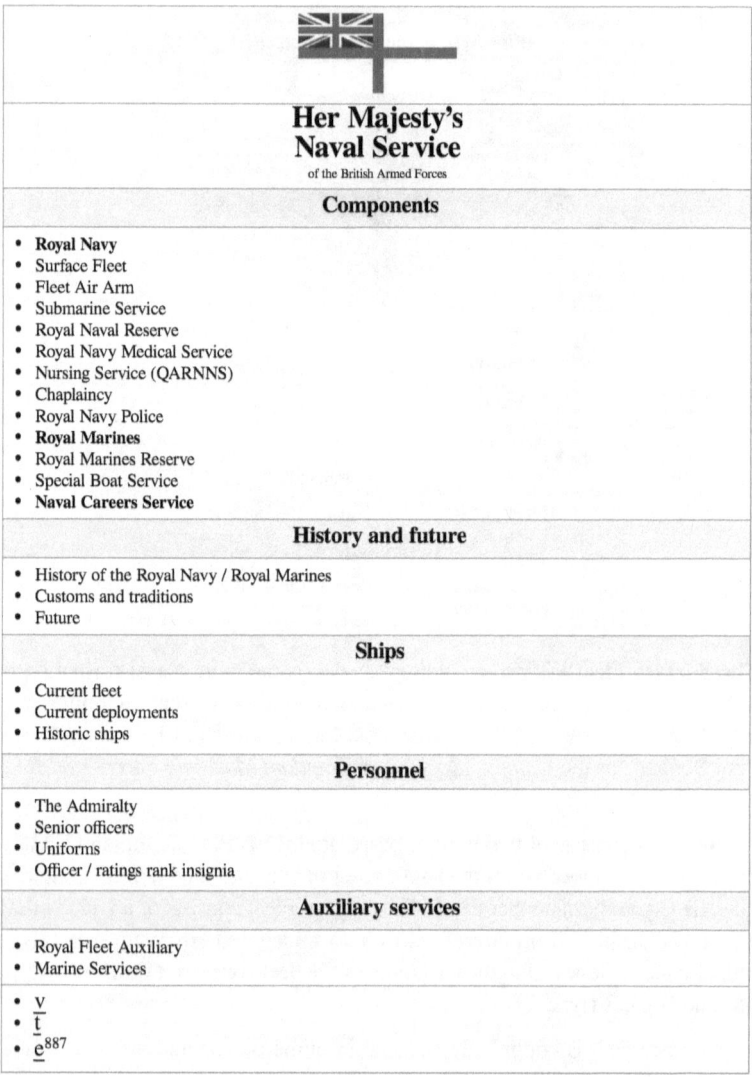

After World War Two, the Royal Navy re-established its pre-war pattern of fleet and command structure. The worldwide deployment of the navy was administered by the Admiralty until 1964 when this government ministry was amalgamated with the Ministry of Defence mainly using geographic commands. Each command usually consisted of either fleets, flotillas, squadrons and individual ships. Between 1954 and 1971 these commands were either abolished or merged into fewer but larger commands.

After 1951 the term flotilla applied to the higher command organisation of squadrons in the Home and Mediterranean Fleets. The squadrons of the Home Fleet were grouped under a Flag Officer, Flotillas, Home Fleet becoming the main seagoing flag officer. A similar arrangement applied to the Flag Officer, Flotillas, Mediterranean Fleet.[888] In the Far East the Flag Officer 5th Cruiser Squadron became Flag Officer 2nd in Command with similar seagoing duties.[889] Increasingly the term 'Submarine Flotilla' was used to describe the squadrons under command of the Flag Officer, Submarines.[890] In 1967 the Home and Mediterranean Fleets were merged to form the Western Fleet.

By the end of 1969 all remaining home commands were unified into a single office of the Commander-in-Chief, Naval Home Command, (CINCNAVHOME). The office was originally held by a four star admiral they responsible for administering the military unit Naval Home Command which was made up of all naval units that were not ships or submarines such as naval bases and establishments, and staff under the post.

In November 1971, further consolidation by the Ministry of Defence resulted in the Western Fleet being amalgamated with the Far East Fleet to form a single fleet command, commonly known as Fleet Command or FLEET. This command was initially administered by a four star admiral who held the title Commander-in-Chief Fleet, they were based at Northwood Headquarters, Middlesex, England. It was supported by Naval Home Command.[891] Between 1971 and 2002 the Fleet or British Fleet was divided into five major sub-commands administered by five flag officers, Flag Officer, Carriers and Amphibious ships (previously known as Flag Officer, Aircraft Carriers, Flag Officer, First Flotilla, Flag Officer, Second Flotilla, Flag Officer, Surface Fleet and Flag Officer, Third Flotilla.[892] In 1992 Fleet Headquarters moved to Portsmouth.

Between 1990 and 1992 the system was changed the Third Flotilla was abolished and the remaining First, Second Flotilla's were re-designated under new names known as the Surface Flotilla Command under the Flag Officer, Surface Flotilla (FOSF) who was - responsible for operational readiness and training[893] and the other United Kingdom Task Group (Command) under the Flag Officer, UK Task Group (FOUKTG) who would - command any deployed task group.[894]

In 2001 both of these commands were unified into a single command known as United Kingdom Maritime Forces Command responsible for administering the SURFACE FLEET under the Commander United Kingdom Maritime Forces then reporting to (CINCFLEET). He administered three sub-commands called, UK Task Group, Carrier Strike Group and DepCom UK Maritime Forces Command each of these are commanded by a Commodore. In 2012 the posts of (CINCNAVHOME) and (CINCFLEET) were abolished leading to the creation of a single fleet high command, administered by a Fleet Commander, (COMMFLEET) holding Vice-Admiral Rank who is currently based at headquarters Navy Command in Portsmouth, England. In 2015 Faslane Flotilla came under the command of the re-established post of Rear-Admiral Submarines who reports to the Fleet Commander.

Of note: Devonport and Portsmouth Flotillas are currently administered by the Assistant Chief of the Naval Staff (Support), (ACNS Spt).

Commander in Chief Fleet

In 1971, with the withdrawal of British forces from East of Suez, the Far East and Western fleets of the Royal Navy were unified under a single Commander-in-Chief Fleet, a member of both the Admiralty and Navy Boards he was initially a four star admiral based at HMS Warrior, a land base at Northwood in Middlesex and, from 2004, based at HMS Excellent at Portsmouth. Thereafter there were just two Commanders-in-Chief, the various fleet commands. In April 2012, the role was re-designated Fleet Commander and Deputy Chief of the Naval Staff.

Fleet Commander

Established 2012 the Fleet Commander and member of the Admiralty Board and Navy Board he is responsible for the operation, resourcing and training of the ships, submarines and aircraft, and personnel, of the Naval Service. He provides ships, submarines and aircraft ready for operations he the current post holder is he is based at Navy Command and is a three star admiral.

The Fleet 1971-1981

Included:

Carriers and Amphibious Ships

Included:

Office of the Flag Officer, Carriers and Amphibious Ships, (FOCAS) - 12.79 re-titled Flag Officer, Third Flotilla, (FO3FLOT) - reporting to (CINCFLEET)

1st Flotilla

Included:[895]

Office of the Flag Officer 1st Flotilla, (FO1FLOT) - reporting to (CINCFLEET), (1971–1990)

Second Flotilla

Included:[896]

Office of the Flag Officer, Second Flotilla, (FO2FLOT), (Cruiser flagship) - reporting to (CINCFLEET), (1971–1990)

Flag officers commanding

- Rear-Admiral David Williams: November 1971-March 1972
- Rear-Admiral Andrew J. Miller: March 1972-March 1973
- Rear-Admiral Richard P. Clayton: March 1973-December 1974
- Rear-Admiral John D.E. Fieldhouse: December 1974-October 1976
- Rear-Admiral William D.M. Staveley: October 1976-March 1977
- Rear-Admiral Martin La T. Wemyss: March 1977-December 1978
- Rear-Admiral Peter M. Stanford: December 1978-October 1980
- Rear-Admiral Nicholas J.S. Hunt: October 1980-November 1981

Third Flotilla

Included:[897]

Flag officers commanding

Office of the Flag Officer, Third Flotilla, (FO3FLOT) - reporting to (CINCFLEET), (1979–1992)

- Rear-Admiral Peter G.M. Herbert: November 1979-December 1979
- Vice-Admiral Sir John M.H. Cox: December 1979 – 1981

The Fleet 1981-2002

First Flotilla

Included:[898]

Office of the Flag Officer, First Flotilla, based at HMNB Portsmouth, (1971–1990)

Flag officers commanding

- Rear-Admiral Sir John F. Woodward: July 1981-April 1983
- Rear-Admiral J. Jeremy Black: April 1983-April 1984
- Rear-Admiral Robin I.T. Hogg: April 1984-October 1986
- Vice-Admiral John B. Kerr: October 1986-July 1988
- Vice-Admiral John F. Coward: July 1988-September 1989
- Vice-Admiral A. Peter Woodhead: September 1989 – 1990 - re-designated (FOSFLOT)

Second Flotilla

Included:[899]

Office of the Flag Officer, Second Flotilla, based at HMNB Devonport, (1971–1992)

Flag officers commanding

- Rear-Admiral Robert W. F. Gerken: November 1981-October 1983
- Rear-Admiral D. Benjamin Bathurst: October 1983-April 1985
- Rear-Admiral W. Richard S. Thomas: April 1985-December 1986
- Rear-Admiral Guy F. Liardet: December 1986-March 1988
- Rear-Admiral A. Peter Woodhead: March 1988-August 1989
- Rear-Admiral Peter C. Abbott: August 1989-January 1991
- Rear-Admiral John R. Brigstocke: January 1991-April 1992

Third Flotilla

Included:[900]

Office of the Flag Officer, Third Flotilla, (FO3FLOT), based at HMNB Portsmouth - reporting to (CINCFLEET), (1979–1992)

Flag officers commanding

- Vice-Admiral Sir John M.H. Cox: December 1981-March 1982
- Rear-Admiral Derek R. Reffell: March 1982-August 1983
- Vice-Admiral Sir Richard G.A. Fitch: August 1983-October 1985
- Vice-Admiral Sir J.Julian R. Oswald: October 1985-April 1987
- Rear-Admiral Hugo M. White: April 1987-October 1988
- Vice-Admiral Sir Alan Grose: October 1988-March 1990
- Vice-Admiral the Hon. Sir Nicholas J. Hill-Norton: March 1990-April 1992

Surface Flotilla

Included:[901]

Office of the Flag Officer, Surface Flotilla, (FOSF) - reporting to (CINCFLEET), (1990–1991)

Flag officers commanding

- Vice-Admiral A. Peter Woodhead: 1990-September 1991
- Rear-Admiral A. Bruce Richardson: September 1991-April 1992
- Vice-Admiral the Hon. Sir Nicholas J. Hill-Norton: April–November 1992
- Vice-Admiral Sir Michael C. Boyce: November 1992-April 1995
- Vice-Admiral Sir John R. Brigstocke: April 1995-July 1997
- Rear-Admiral Peter M. Franklyn: July 1997-April 2000
- Rear-Admiral Ian A. Forbes: April 2000-November 2001
- Rear-Admiral Alexander K. Backus: November 2001 – 2002

United Kingdom Task Group

Included:[902]

Office of the Commander, United Kingdom Task Group - reporting to (CINCFLEET)

Commanders

- Rear-Admiral John R. Brigstocke: April 1992-September 1993
- Rear-Admiral Michael P. Gretton: September 1993-December 1994
- Rear-Admiral Peter M. Franklyn: December 1994-February 1996
- Rear-Admiral Alan W.J. West: February 1996-October 1997
- Rear-Admiral Ian A. Forbes: October 1997-February 2000
- Rear-Admiral Stephen R. Meyer: February 2000-May 2001

The Surface Fleet 2002-current

United Kingdom Maritime Forces command

Included:

Office of the Commander United Kingdom Maritime Forces, (1993-current) - reporting to (CINCFLEET) to 2012 then Fleet Commander

Note the post holders formal title is Commander United Kingdom Maritime Forces and Rear Admiral Surface Ships.

Flag officers commanding

- Rear Admiral James Burnell-Nugent (2001–2002)
- Rear Admiral David Snelson (2002–2004)
- Rear Admiral Charles Style (2004–2005)
- Rear Admiral Neil Morisetti (2005–2007)
- Rear Admiral George Zambellas (2007–2008)
- Rear Admiral Philip Jones (2008–2009)
- Rear Admiral Peter Hudson (2009–2011)
- Rear Admiral Duncan Potts (2011–2013)
- Rear Admiral Robert Tarrant (2013–2014)
- Rear Admiral Tony Radakin (2014–2016)
- Rear Admiral Alex Burton (2016–2017)
- Rear Admiral Paul Bennett (2017–2018)

Commander Amphibious Task Group

Included:[903]

Commodores in Post

- Commodore Roy W. Halliday: August 1971-September 1973
- Commodore David T. Smith: September 1973-October 1975
- Commodore Richard D. Franklin: October 1975-February 1977
- Commodore Derek R. Reffell: June 1978-October 1979
- Commodore Christopher J. Isacke: October 1979-May 1981
- Commodore Michael C. Clapp: May 1981-February 1983
- Commodore Peter G. V. Dingemans: February 1983-January 1985
- Commodore John Garnier: January-July 1985
- Commodore E.S. Jeremy Larken: July 1985-December 1987
- Commodore Brian W. Turner: December 1987-April 1990
- Commodore Peter J. Grindal: April 1990-1992
- Commodore Richard A.Y. Bridges: 1992-1994
- Commodore Paul B.C. Canter: 1994-October 1996
- Commodore Paul D. Stone: October 1996-1998
- Commodore Niall S.R. Kilgour: 1998-July 2001
- Commodore A.James G. Miller: July 2001-September 2003
- Commodore Christopher J. Parry: September 2003-January 2005
- Commodore George M. Zambellas: January 2005-August 2006
- Commodore Philip A. Jones: August 2006-2008
- Commodore Peter D. Hudson: 2008-May 2009
- Commodore Paul M. Bennett: May 2009-January 2011
- Commodore John M. L. Kingwell: January-November 2011
- Commodore Patrick A. McAlpine: November 2011-February 2014

- Commodore Jeremy P. Kyd: February 2014-February 2015
- Commodore Martin J. Connell: February 2015-May 2016
- Commodore Andrew P. Burns: May 2016-May 2018
- Commodore James M.B. Parkin: May 2018-present

Included:[904]

Commander UK Task Group, (COMUKTG) - reporting to COMUKMARFOR, (2001–2011)

Commodores commanding

- Commodore Hugh A.H.G. Edleston: April 2001-January 2002
- Commodore James R. Fanshawe: January–December 2002
- Commodore Richard D. Leaman: January–June 2003
- Commodore Anthony J. Rix: November 2003-January 2006
- Commodore Bruce N.B. Williams: January 2006-December 2007
- Commodore Duncan L. Potts: December 2007-December 2008
- Commodore James A. Morse: December 2008-January 2011

Note: COMUKTG post renamed Deputy Commander UK Maritime Forces in January 2011.

Deputy Commander UK Maritime Forces

Included:[905]

Deputy Commander UK Maritime Forces, (DCOMUKMARFOR) - reporting to COMUKMARFOR, (2011-2016).

Commodores in Post

- Commodore Simon J. Ancona: January–June 2011
- Commodore John R.H. Clink: June 2011-October 2012
- Commodore Jeremy J.F.Blunden: October 2012-February 2015
- Commodore Guy A. Robinson: February 2015-September 2016

Carrier Strike Group

Included:[906]

Commodores commanding

- Commodore Alan D. Richards: 2006-July 2007
- Commodore Thomas A. Cunningham: July 2007-April 2009
- Commodore Simon J. Ancona: April 2009-January 2011
- Post in abeyance January 2011-February 2015
- Commodore Jeremy P. Kyd: February 2015-September 2016
- Commodore Andrew Betton: September 2016-present

References

- Brown, David (1987). The Royal Navy and Falklands War. Barsley, England: Pen and Sword. ISBN 9781473817791.
- MOD "Surface fleet: (2017) Royal Navy". www.royalnavy.mod.uk. Ministry of Defence, London, England.
- Roberts, John (2009). Safeguarding the Nation: The Story of the Modern Royal Navy. Barnsley, England: Seaforth Publishing. ISBN 9781848320437.
- Smith, Gordon. (2015) "Royal Navy Organisation and Ship Deployment 1947-2013: * Smith, Gordon. (2015) "Royal Navy Organisation and Ship Deployment 1947-2013: FLEET ORGANISATION 1955-1971". www.naval-history.net.
- Smith, Gordon. (2015) "Royal Navy Organisation and Ship Deployment 1947-2013: Summary of Fleet Organisation 1972-1981". www.naval-history.net.
- Smith, Gordon. (2015) "Royal Navy Organisation and Ship Deployment 1947-2013: FLEET ORGANISATION, 1981-2002". www.naval-history.net.
- Treacher, Sir John (2004). Life at Full Throttle. Barnsley, England: Pen and Sword. ISBN 9781844151349.
- The Navy Directory: (2017) KEY PERSONNEL: Seniority Lists of Officers on the Active List. (PDF). royalnavy.mod.uk. MOD, UK.

External links

- Royal Navy Surface Fleet official website[907]
- MaritimeQuest Royal Navy Index[908]

Fleet Air Arm

Fleet Air Arm	
Founded	1914 (As the Royal Naval Air Service) 1924 (as the naval branch of the Royal Air Force) 1937 (as part of Naval Service)
Country	🇬🇧
Allegiance	Queen Elizabeth II
Branch	Royal Navy
Size	5,000 personnel Approx. 174 aircraft[909]
Part of	Naval Service
Engagements	Second World War Korean War Operation Musketeer (Suez Crisis) Falklands War Gulf War Afghanistan War Iraq War
Website	[910]-FAA
Commanders	
Rear Admiral Fleet Air Arm Assistant Chief of Naval Staff (Aviation, Amphibious Capability and Carriers)	Rear Admiral Keith Blount CB OBE FRAeS RN
Commodore-in-Chief	HRH Prince Andrew, Duke of York
Insignia	
Roundels	
White Ensign	
Badge	
Aircraft flown	

Attack	Wildcat HMA2
Patrol	Merlin HM2 Wildcat HMA2
Reconnaissance	Commando Wildcat AH1
Trainer	King Air Tutor Hawk
Transport	Commando Merlin HC3/3A/i3/4/4A

Her Majesty's Naval Service
of the British Armed Forces

Components

- **Royal Navy**
- Surface Fleet
- Fleet Air Arm
- Submarine Service
- Royal Naval Reserve
- Royal Navy Medical Service
- Nursing Service (QARNNS)
- Chaplaincy
- Royal Navy Police
- **Royal Marines**
- Royal Marines Reserve
- Special Boat Service
- **Naval Careers Service**

History and future

- History of the Royal Navy / Royal Marines
- Customs and traditions
- Future

Ships

- Current fleet
- Current deployments
- Historic ships

Personnel

- The Admiralty
- Senior officers
- Uniforms
- Officer / ratings rank insignia

Auxiliary services

- Royal Fleet Auxiliary
- Marine Services

Fleet Air Arm

- v
- t
- e[911]

The **Fleet Air Arm** (**FAA**) is the branch of the British Royal Navy responsible for the operation of naval aircraft. The Fleet Air Arm currently operates the AgustaWestland Merlin, Westland Sea King, and AgustaWestland Wildcat helicopters and the BAE Hawk. Helicopters such as the Lynx and Westland Wasp have been deployed on smaller vessels since 1964, taking over the roles once performed by biplanes such as the Fairey Swordfish.

The Fleet Air Arm was formed in 1924 as an organisational unit of the Royal Air Force which was then operating the aircraft embarked on RN ships – the Royal Naval Air Service having been merged with the British Army's Royal Flying Corps in 1918, to form the Royal Air Force – and did not come under the direct control of the Admiralty until mid-1939. During the Second World War, the Fleet Air Arm operated aircraft on ships as well as land-based aircraft that defended the Royal Navy's shore establishments and facilities.

History

Beginnings

British naval flying started in 1909, with the construction of an airship for naval duties. In 1911 the Royal Navy graduated its first aeroplane pilots at the Royal Aero Club flying ground at Eastchurch, Isle of Sheppey under the tutelage of pioneer aviator George Bertram Cockburn. In May 1912, naval and army aviation were combined to become the Royal Flying Corps (RFC). The Naval Wing of the RFC lasted until July 1914 when the Royal Navy reformed its air branch, under the Air Department of the Admiralty, naming it the Royal Naval Air Service (RNAS).Wikipedia:Citation needed

By the outbreak of the First World War, in August 1914, the RNAS had more aircraft under its control than the remaining RFC.Wikipedia:Citation needed The roles of the RNAS were fleet reconnaissance, patrolling coasts for enemy ships and submarines, attacking enemy coastal territory and defending Britain from enemy air raids, along with deployment along the Western Front. In April 1918 the RNAS, which at this time had 67,000 officers and men, 2,949 aircraft, 103 airships and 126 coastal stations, merged with the RFC to form the Royal Air Force.

Figure 91: *An elephant pulling a Supermarine Walrus aircraft into position at a Fleet Air Arm station in India (c. June 1944).*

Fleet Air Arm

On 1 April 1924, the Fleet Air Arm of the Royal Air Force was formed, encompassing those RAF units that normally embarked on aircraft carriers and fighting ships. The year was significant for British naval aviation as only weeks before the founding of the Fleet Air Arm, the Royal Navy had commissioned HMS *Hermes*, the world's first ship to be designed and built as an aircraft carrier. Over the following months RAF Fleet Air Arm Fairey IIID reconnaissance biplanes operated off Hermes, conducting flying trials.

On 24 May 1939 the Fleet Air Arm was returned to Admiralty control under the "Inskip Award" (named after the Minister for Co-ordination of Defence overseeing the British re-armament programme) and renamed the Air Branch of the Royal Navy. At the onset of the Second World War, the Fleet Air Arm consisted of 20 squadrons with only 232 aircraft. By the end of the war the strength of the Fleet Air Arm was 59 aircraft carriers, 3,700 aircraft, 72,000 officers and men and 56 Naval air stations.

During the war, the FAA operated fighters, torpedo bombers and reconnaissance aircraft. Following the Dunkirk evacuation and the commencement of the Battle of Britain, the Royal Air Force soon found itself critically short of fighter pilots. In the summer of 1940, the RAF had just over 800 fighter pilots and as personnel shortages worsened; the RAF turned to the Admiralty to ask

Fleet Air Arm

Figure 92: *Hawker Sea Fury of No. 804 Squadron launched off HMS Glory during the Korean War, June 1951*

for help from the Fleet Air Arm. Fleet Air Arm crews under RAF Fighter Command were either seconded individually to RAF fighter squadrons or entire as with 804 and 808 Naval Air Squadrons. The former provided dockyard defence during the Battle of Britain with Sea Gladiators.

In British home waters and out into the Atlantic Ocean, operations against Axis shipping and submarines in support of the RN were mounted by RAF Coastal Command with large patrol bombers, flying boats and land-based fighter-bombers. The aircraft carrier had replaced the battleship as the capital ship of the RN and its aircraft were now its principal offensive weapons. The top scoring fighter ace with 17 victories was Commander Stanley Orr, the Royal Marine ace was Ronald Cuthbert Hay with 13 victories. A number of Royal Marines were FAA pilots during the war.

Notable Fleet Air Arm operations during the war included the Battle of Taranto, the sinking of the *Bismarck*, Operation Tungsten against the *Tirpitz* and Operation Meridian against oil plants in Sumatra.

Post-war history

After the war the FAA needed to fly jet aircraft from their carriers. The jet aircraft of the era were considerably less effective at low speeds than propeller aircraft, but propeller aircraft could not effectively fight jets at the high speeds

Figure 93: *Phantom FG.1 of 892 NAS aboard HMS Ark Royal in 1972*

Figure 94: *Two Sea Harriers from 800 Naval Air Squadron approach the flight deck of U.S. Navy aircraft carrier USS Dwight D. Eisenhower in 1984.*

flown by jet aircraft. The FAA took on its first jet, the Sea Vampire, in the late 1940s. The Sea Vampire was the first jet credited with taking off and landing on a carrier. The Air Arm continued with high-powered prop aircraft alongside the new jets resulting in the FAA being woefully outpowered during the Korean War. Nevertheless, jets were not yet wholly superior to propeller aircraft and a flight of ground attack Hawker Sea Furies downed a MiG-15 and damaged others in an engagement.

As jets became larger, more powerful and faster they required more space to take off and land. The US Navy simply built much larger carriers. The Royal Navy had a few large carriers built and completed after the end of the war but another solution was sought. This was partly overcome by the introduction of a Royal Navy idea to angle the flight deck away from the centre line so that the aircraft landing had a clear run away from the usual forward deck park. An associated British invention, intended to provide more precise optical guidance to aircraft on final approaching the deck, was the Fresnel lens optical landing aid. Another Royal Navy invention was the use of a steam-powered catapult to cater for the larger and heavier aircraft (both systems were adopted by the US Navy).

Defence cuts across the British armed forces during the 1960s and 1970s led to the withdrawal of existing Royal Navy aircraft carriers, transfer of Fleet Air Arm fixed-wing jet strike aircraft such as the F-4K (FG.1) Phantom II and Buccaneer S.2 to the Royal Air Force, and cancellation of large replacement aircraft carriers, including the CVA-01 design. The last conventional carrier to be retired was HMS *Ark Royal* in 1978.[912] A new series of small carriers, the *Invincible* class anti-submarine warfare ships (known as "through deck cruisers") were built and equipped with the Sea Harrier a derivative of the Hawker Siddeley Harrier VTOL aircraft. These carriers incorporated an upswept forward section of the flight deck that deflected the aircraft upward on launch and permitted heavier loads to be carried by the Harrier, for example in weaponry, and the system was used extensively in the Falklands War.

End of the Cold War

At the end of the Cold War in 1989 the Fleet Air Arm was under the command of the Flag Officer Naval Air Command, a Rear Admiral based at RNAS Yeovilton.

- **Flag Officer Naval Air Command** (FONAC), at RNAS Yeovilton
  - **RNAS Prestwick**:
    - 819 Naval Air Squadron, (Anti-submarine, 12x Sea King HAS.5)
    - 826 Naval Air Squadron, (Anti-submarine, 12x Sea King HAS.6)
    - HMS Gannet SAR Flight, (Search & Rescue, 8x Sea King HU.5)
  - **RNAS Yeovilton**:

- 707 Naval Air Squadron, (Air Assault, 10x Sea King HC.4)
- 800 Naval Air Squadron, (12x Sea Harrier FA.2)
- 801 Naval Air Squadron, (12x Sea Harrier FA.2)
- 845 Naval Air Squadron, (Air Assault, 10x Sea King HC.4)
- 846 Naval Air Squadron, (Air Assault, 10x Sea King HC.4)
- 899 Naval Air Squadron, (Training, 24x Sea Harrier FA.2)
- Fleet Requirements and Aircraft Direction Unit, (Aggressor Squadron, Canberra TT.18, Hawker Hunter GA.11)
- **RNAS Culdrose**:
  - 705 Naval Air Squadron, (Basic Helicopter Training, 38x Gazelle HT.2)
  - 706 Naval Air Squadron, (Sea King Training, 12x various types of Sea King)
  - 750 Naval Air Squadron, (Observer Training, Jetstream T2)
  - 771 Naval Air Squadron, (Search & Rescue, 12x Sea King HU.5)
  - 814 Naval Air Squadron, (Anti-submarine, 12x Sea King HAS.5)
  - 820 Naval Air Squadron, (Anti-submarine, 12x Sea King HAS.6)
  - 824 Naval Air Squadron, (Anti-submarine, 12x Sea King HAS.6) (disbanded August 1989)
  - 849 Naval Air Squadron, (Airborne early warning and control, 10x Sea King AEW.2A, 4x Sea King AEW.5)
- **RNAS Portland**:
  - 702 Naval Air Squadron, (Aircrew & Maintenance Training, 24x Lynx HAS.3S)
  - 772 Naval Air Squadron, (Air Assault, 10x Sea King HC.4)
  - 810 Naval Air Squadron, (Anti-submarine, 12x Sea King HAS.6)
  - 815 Naval Air Squadron, (Frigate & Destroyer Helicopters, 32x Lynx HAS.3S, most deployed on frigates and destroyers at sea)
  - 829 Naval Air Squadron, (Frigate & Destroyer Helicopters, 32x Lynx HAS.3S, most deployed on frigates and destroyers at sea)

Fleet Air Arm Inventory 1989

The inventory of the Fleet Air Arm in 1989 consisted of the following aircraft:

- **Combat aircraft**:
  - 42x Sea Harrier FRS.1/F(A).2
  - 2x/2x Sea Harrier T.4A/T.4N
- **Helicopters**:
  - 60+ Sea King HAS.5
  - 31+ Sea King HAS.6
  - 10x Sea King AEW.2A
  - 33x Sea King HC.4
  - 80+ Lynx HAS.3S

Fleet Air Arm

Figure 95: *A formation of four Sea Harrier FA.2s from 801 NAS in 2005.*

- 23x/8x Gazelle HT.2/HT.3
- **Trainers**:
  - 3x Canberra TT.18
  - 14x Chipmunk T.10
  - 5x Hunter T.8M
  - 12x/9x Hunter GA.11/T8
  - 19x Jetstream T.2
- **Liaison**:
  - 16x Dassault Falcon 20 (Civil-registered)

Post Cold War

In 2000 the Sea Harrier force was merged with the RAF's Harrier GR7 fleet to form Joint Force Harrier. The Fleet Air Arm began withdrawing the Sea Harrier from service in 2004 with the disbandment of 800 NAS. 801 NAS disbanded on 28 March 2006 at RNAS Yeovilton (HMS Heron). 800 and 801 NAS were then combined to form the Naval Strike Wing, flying ex-RAF Harrier GR7 and GR9s. On 1 April 2010, NSW reverted to the identity of 800 Naval Air Squadron. The Harrier GR7 and GR9 retired from service in December 2010 following the Strategic Defence and Security Review 2010.

Two new *Queen Elizabeth* class carriers able to operate the F-35B short take-off and landing variant of the US Lockheed Martin Lightning II aircraft are under construction. In the Strategic Defence and Security Review 2015, it was announced that the carriers would enter service "from 2018". The current procurement plan is for a force of 138 F-35 aircraft, which are intended to be operated by both the RAF and FAA from a common pool, in the same manner as the Joint Force Harrier. With the introduction of the F-35, the Fleet Air Arm will eventually return to the operation of fixed-wing strike aircraft at sea. In 2013, an initial cadre of Royal Air Force and Royal Navy pilots and aircraft maintenance personnel were assigned to the U.S. Marine Corps' Marine Fighter Attack Training Squadron 501 (VMFAT-501), part of the U.S. Air Force's 33rd Fighter Wing at Eglin Air Force Base, Florida, for training on the F-35B. 809 Naval Air Squadron will be the first FAA unit to operate the F-35B and will be based at RAF Marham.

Helicopters

Helicopters also became important combat platforms since the Second World War. Initially used in the search and rescue role, they were later developed for anti-submarine warfare and troop transport; during the 1956 Suez Crisis they were used to land Royal Marine Commando forces, the first time this had ever been done in combat.[913] Originally operated only from carriers, the development of the Westland Wasp in the 1960s allowed helicopters to operate on all ships of frigate size or larger. Wasps, Sea Kings and Wessex helicopters all played an active part in the 1982 Falklands War, while Lynx helicopters played an attack role against Iraqi patrol boats in the 1991 Gulf War and Commando Sea King HC4s as well as the Lynx HMA Mk 8 from HMS Argyll, assisted in suppressing rebel forces in the British intervention in the Sierra Leone Civil War in 2000.

Museums

The Fleet Air Arm has a museum near RNAS Yeovilton (HMS Heron) in Somerset, England at which many of the great historical aircraft flown by the Service are on display, along with aircraft from other sources. There is also a Fleet Air Arm museum inside the Museum of Transport and Technology (MOTAT) in Auckland, New Zealand. On display there is a full-size replica Fairey Swordfish, along with historic items and memorabilia.

The FAA today

Personnel

In 1938, Admiralty Fleet Orders 2885 announced the formation of an Air Branch of the Royal Naval Reserve. Thirty three unmarried men signed up for eighteen months full-time flying training; however, before these first volunteers were able to gain their wings Britain was at war. At the end of hostilities in 1945 the RNVR(A) was 46,000 strong, with over 8,000 aircrew. Post war the RNVR(A) comprised 12 dedicated reserve squadrons, grouped regionally into Air Divisions. However, defence cuts in 1957 disbanded the five Air Divisions, and the following year the RNVR was merged with the RNR. The RNR Air Branch was commissioned at RNAS Yeovilton on 16 July 1980, and shortly afterwards 38 ex-regular aircrew began refresher training. Today the Air Branch comprises approx 250 ex-regular service Officers and Ratings, covering all aviation trades, tasked to support the Fleet Air Arm.

As of 1 December 2013, the Regular Fleet Air Arm has a reported strength of 5,000 personnel, which represents approximately 20% of the Royal Navy's total strength (excluding Royal Marines). The Assistant Chief of Naval Staff (Aviation & Carriers), the professional head, who is also Rear Admiral Fleet Air Arm, is Rear Admiral Keith Blount, who relieved the previous incumbent, Rear Admiral R. G. Harding OBE, in May 2015.

Aircraft

The FAA operates fixed wing and rotary wing aircraft. It uses the same designation system for aircraft as the RAF. Three types of fixed wing aircraft are operated by the FAA for training purposes: pilot training is carried out using the Grob Tutor while, from March 2011, observer training is done using four Avenger T1 Beechcraft King Air 350ER. The third type is the Hawk T1/1A, which is used to simulate enemy aircraft for training purposes including AEW Fighter Control, air to air combat and ship attack.

Today the largest section of the FAA is the rotary wing section. Its aviators fly four types of helicopters, and within each type there are usually several marks/variants which carry out different roles. Pilots designated for rotary wing service train at the Defence Helicopter Flying School, RAF Shawbury. The School is a tri-Service organisation consisting of civilian and military instructors (including Naval instructors and a Naval Air Squadron) that take the student from basic flying through to more advanced flying such as instrument flying, navigation, formation and captaincy. The oldest aircraft in the fleet is the Westland Sea King, which performs missions in several variants. The Sea King HC4 serves as a medium lifter and troop transporter in support of

Figure 96: *The Wildcat HMA2 will become the standard small shipborne helicopter in the FAA, replacing the Lynx*

Figure 97: *A Merlin HM1 of 824 NAS alongside a Sea King ASaC7 of 849 NAS*

the Royal Marines. The HU5 model operates in the Search and rescue role and the ASaC7 variant operates in the AEW role. Intermediate in age is the Westland Lynx. The Lynx AH9A serves the FAA in observation and transport roles. Along with the Sea King HC4s, they equip the RN Commando Helicopter Force, which provides airborne support to 3 Commando Brigade of the Royal Marines.

To replace the Sea King in the Commando role, the Fleet Air Arm received the Merlin HC3/HC3A fleet previously operated by the RAF. These aircraft were transferred to the Royal Navy in September 2014 and will be ship optimised and redesignated as HC4s/HC4As, under the Merlin Life Sustainment Programme (MLSP) that was placed on contract in December 2013.

The surface combatants of the Royal Navy have their helicopters provided for the most part by the Lynx HMA8 aircraft. The Lynxes primarily have anti-submarine warfare and anti-surface vessel roles. They are able to fire the Sea Skua anti-surface missile, which was used to combat the Iraqi Navy in the 1991 Gulf War. It can be armed with Stingray air launched torpedoes and depth charges for anti-submarine warfare, as well as heavy calibre machine guns. The Lynx was originally envisaged for surface combatants that were too small for the Sea King, but now equips most frigates and destroyers of the Royal Navy. The Fleet Air Arm is introducing a total of 28 AW159 Wildcat HMA2 helicopters to replace the Lynx HMA8 in use in the Ship's Flights of the Royal Navy's escorts – this will perform a range of roles including anti-surface and anti-submarine warfare and airborne surveillance.

The AgustaWestland Merlin is the FAA's primary Anti-Submarine Warfare (ASW) helicopter, having replaced the Sea King HAS6 in the role. It is presently being upgraded from HM1 to HM2 standard and is deployed with various ships of the Royal Navy.

Future aircraft

Currently the Fleet Air Arm is an all rotary wing force. However, the introduction of the F-35B Lightning II will see a restoration of fixed wing, front-line operations. An initial order of 48 airframes was made in 2012 to equip the air wings of the planned two Queen Elizabeth-class aircraft carriers, with the operation split between the FAA and the Royal Air Force, as was the case with Joint Force Harrier. 809 Naval Air Squadron was announced as the second UK unit to fly the F-35B, the first being 617 Squadron RAF, and will be the first Fleet Air Arm unit to operate the aircraft. It is understood that at least two further frontline squadrons will stand up in the future alongside 809, 617, 17(R) Test and Evaluation Squadron and an RAF-numbered Operational Conversion Unit, creating a front-line fleet of four squadrons in addition to the OCU and

Figure 98: *The Fleet Air Arm plans to operate the F-35B from the Queen Elizabeth-class aircraft carriers.*

OEU. Under the Strategic Defence and Security Review of November 2015, the UK Government made a commitment to buying 138 F-35B, with at least 24 available for carrier use by 2024.Wikipedia:Citation needed

There is a project to replace the Sea King ASaC7 in the Airborne Surveillance and Control (ASaC) mission. Known as 'Crowsnest', the Assessment Phase for this project is under contract and involves competitive proposals for implementing the ASaC capability in a platform based upon the new Merlin HM2 helicopter. The Main Gate for the project is in 2017, a £269 million agreement in early 2017 was made by the MOD.

MOD DE&S signed a £30 million contract for the Boeing Insitu ScanEagle on 20 June 2013, to provide small, unmanned surveillance aircraft to equip RN warships and RFA ships. The Royal Navy's first UAV entered service with 831 Maritime Unmanned Aerial System (Mar UAS) Flight in December 2013 and is based at RNAS Culdrose.

Squadrons and flights

A Fleet Air Arm flying squadron is formally titled Naval Air Squadron (NAS), a title used as a suffix to the squadron number. The FAA assigns numbers in the 700–799 range to training and operational conversion squadrons and numbers in the 800–899 range to operational squadrons. Exceptions to the 700-799 include operational conversion squadrons which also hold some form of operational commitment where they are then titled 800-899. During WWII the 1700 and 1800 ranges were also used for operational squadrons.

Fleet Air Arm

Squadrons active in the FAA are:

Unit	Type	Aircraft	Base	Role	Notes
Flying Squadrons					
700X Naval Air Squadron	UAV	Scan Eagle RM1	RNAS Culdrose	Remotely Piloted Aircraft System shipborne flights	Provides HQ function for ScanEagle flights and serve as evaluation unit for any future UAV systems selected by the
				RPAS future trials unit	
703 Naval Air Squadron	Fixed-wing	Tutor T1	RAF Barkston Heath	Elementary flying training	Part of the Defence Elementary Flying Training School
705 Naval Air Squadron	Rotary	Juno HT1	RAF Shawbury	Basic and Advanced Single Engine helicopter training	Part of tri-service Defence Helicopter Flying School alongside 660 Squadron AAC and 60 Squadron RAF
727 Naval Air Squadron	Fixed-wing	Tutor T1	RNAS Yeovilton	Pilot grading and Air Experience/Elementary Flying Training	
736 Naval Air Squadron	Fixed wing	Hawk T1/T1A	RNAS Culdrose	Air combat simulated training	Formerly FRADU
750 Naval Air Squadron	Fixed-wing	Avenger T1	RNAS Culdrose	Observer grading and training	
809 Naval Air Squadron	Fixed-wing	F-35B Lightning	RAF Marham	Carrier-borne fighter/strike	To reform in April 2023.
814 Naval Air Squadron	Rotary	Merlin HM2	RNAS Culdrose	Anti-submarine warfare	Merged with 829 NAS in 2018
815 Naval Air Squadron	Rotary	Wildcat HMA2	RNAS Yeovilton	Small ship flights	
820 Naval Air Squadron	Rotary	Merlin HM2	RNAS Culdrose	Anti-submarine warfare	
824 Naval Air Squadron	Rotary	Merlin HM2	RNAS Culdrose	Conversion Training (Merlin ASW)	
825 Naval Air Squadron	Rotary	Wildcat HMA2	RNAS Yeovilton	Conversion Training (Wildcat)	Formed by merger of 700W NAS and 702 NAS in August 2014
845 Naval Air Squadron	Rotary	Merlin HC3A/-HC4	RNAS Yeovilton	Very High Readiness Medium lift	Part of CHF
846 Naval Air Squadron	Rotary	Merlin HC3/-HCi3	RNAS Yeovilton	Extremely High Readiness Medium lift	Part of CHF

				Operational Conversion Training (Merlin Commando)	
847 Naval Air Squadron	Rotary	Wildcat AH1	RNAS Yeovilton	Battlefield reconnaissance and support	Part of CHF
849 Naval Air Squadron	Rotary	Sea King ASaC.7	RNAS Culdrose	Airborne surveillance	Amalgamated with 854 NAS and 857 NAS in 2015 To convert to Merlin Crowsnest in 2018
Non-flying squadrons					
1700 Naval Air Squadron	Rotary & fixed-wing		RNAS Culdrose	Flight Deck activities, Logistic and Catering Support, Operations, Engineering Support, even medical assistance	Technical support Formerly Maritime Aviation Support Force (MASF)
1710 Naval Air Squadron	Rotary & fixed-wing		HMNB Portsmouth	Specialist aircraft repair, modification and scientific support	Technical support
Flights					
Royal Navy Historic Flight	Fixed-wing	number of historic aircraft	RNAS Yeovilton	Heritage education and public display	

An additional flying unit of the Royal Navy is the FOST Helicopter Support Unit based at HMS *Raleigh* in Cornwall. This unit is not part of the Fleet Air Arm, but is directly under the control of Flag Officer Sea Training, operated by a civilian contractor. The Royal Navy will share both operational and training duties on the Lightning II with the RAF under a banner organization called the **Lightning Force**, which will operate in the same manner as Joint Force Harrier.Wikipedia:Citation needed

Notable members

- Vice-Admiral Richard Bell Davies (1886–1966) – the first naval aviator to receive the VC and the first naval aviator of the Fleet Air Arm to reach flag rank
- Vice-Admiral Sir Lumley Lyster (1888–1957) – drew up attack plan in 1935 that was used for the Battle of Taranto five years later
- Admiral Sir Reginald Portal (1894–1983) – naval aviator who was the younger brother of Marshal of the Royal Air Force Lord Portal (1893–1971)

Figure 99: *Vice-Admiral Richard Bell Davies, first naval aviator to receive the VC and the first naval aviator of the Fleet Air Arm to reach flag rank.*

- Captain Henry Fancourt (1900–2004) – a pioneering aviator, he had a distinguished career in naval aviation until 1949. Worked for Short Bros and Hartland.
- Ralph Richardson (1902–1983) – English stage and screen actor, volunteered as a navy pilot during Second World War and rose to the rank of Lieutenant-Commander in the Air Branch.
- Admiral of the Fleet Sir Caspar John (1903–1984) – First Sea Lord 1960–63 and the first British naval aviator to reach the highest rank within the RN.
- Admiral Sir Walter Couchman (1905–1981) – naval observer who earned his pilot's wings too, he led the fly-past for the Coronation Fleet Review in June 1953.
- Laurence Olivier (1907–1989) – English stage and screen actor and director, volunteered as a navy pilot during the Second World War and rose to the rank of Lieutenant in the Air Branch.
- Duncan Hamilton – English Grand Prix driver and winner of the 1953 24 Hours of Le Mans.
- Lieutenant Commander (A) Eugene Esmonde (1909–1942) – posthumously awarded the Victoria Cross for leading 825 Naval Air Squadron Swordfish torpedo bombers in an attack on German capital ships during

the "Channel Dash".
- Michael Hordern (1911–1995) – actor, served as fighter controller during World War II.
- Jeffrey Quill (1913–1996) – RAF officer and Spitfire test pilot (Vickers-Armstrongs) who served five months with Fleet Air Arm as T/Lt.Cdr RNVR in 1944–5, helping to develop better carrier deck-landings with the Supermarine Seafire, the naval version of the Spitfire.
- Kenneth More (1914–1982) – actor, including films such as *Reach for the Sky* and *Sink the Bismarck*.
- Commander Charles Lamb (1914–1981) – author of the Second World War Fleet Air Arm autobiography *War in a Stringbag*.
- Vice-Admiral Sir Peter Compston (1915–2000) – served briefly in the British Army, then in the RAF for two years, before transferring as a pilot to the Royal Navy in 1938.
- Admiral Sir (Leslie) Derek Empson (1918–1997) – naval pilot who joined the Royal Navy as a naval rating. In his flying career, executed 782 aircraft carrier landings without a mishap.
- Rear-Admiral Cedric Kenelm Roberts (1918–2011) – (always known as 'Chico') a distinguished naval pilot who joined the Royal Navy as a naval rating in 1940. He was personal pilot to Vice-Admiral Lumley Lyster in 1943, commanded three Naval Air Squadrons and was shot down during the Korean War. Later, he commanded three Naval Air Stations and ended his naval flying career as Flag Officer Naval Flying Training 1968–71.
- Lieutenant-Commander Charles Wines ("Charlie Wines") (1917–1991) – joined the Royal Navy as a Supply Assistant, flew Swordfish torpedo bomber as a rating pilot in the Second World War. Commissioned as a pilot in 1944 he later spent more than twenty years, in the same job as a serving and retired officer, as the FAA Drafting Officer and as such the career manager for thousands of FAA ratings.
- Rear-Admiral Dennis Cambell (1907–2000) – inventor of the angled flight deck for aircraft carriers in 1951.
- Rear-Admiral Nick Goodhart (1919–2011) – inventor of the mirror-sight deck landing system for aircraft carriers in 1951.
- Captain Eric "Winkle" Brown (1919–2016) – holds the world record for the most types of aircraft flown by an individual (487 types). As a test pilot he made the first ever jet landing on an aircraft carrier in December 1945.
- Lieutenant Commander John Moffat (1919–) – crippled the German battleship *Bismarck* on 26 May 1941.
- Admiral Sir John Treacher (1924–) – naval pilot who was promoted Rear-Admiral at the age of 45 and held four important flag appointments before

leaving the Royal Navy in 1977, despite many expecting him to become First Sea Lord, for a career in business. Was at the helm of Westland during the political drama of the 1980s.
- Admiral Sir Ray Lygo (1924–2012) – naval pilot who joined the Royal Navy as a naval rating in 1942 and who reached First Sea Lord in 1978, led a successful career in industry and was Chief Executive and Deputy Chairman of British Aerospace in the 1980s.
- Sir George Martin (1926–2016) – record producer for The Beatles.
- Admiral of the Fleet Sir Ben Bathurst (1936–) – First Sea Lord 1993–95 and the last Royal Navy officer to be promoted to five-star rank.
- Rear-Admiral Sir Robert Woodard KCVO (c.1939–) – naval aviator commanded two Naval Air Squadrons, two warships, a Naval Air Station, the Clyde submarine base and ended his career as the Flag Officer Royal Yachts 1990–95, the only aviator to command the Royal Yacht HMY *Britannia*.
- Commander Nigel David "Sharkey" Ward (1943-) – commanded 801 Naval Air Squadron during the 1982 Falklands War.
- Rear-Admiral Iain Henderson (c.1948–) – the first officer, and first naval officer, to hold the modern appointment of Air Officer Commanding 3 Group 2000–01.
- Vice-Admiral His Excellency Sir Adrian Johns (c.1952–) is the first naval aviator to hold the post of Governor of Gibraltar.
- Commander Prince Andrew, Duke of York (1960–) – served during the Falklands War 1982 and for some years afterwards.
- Captain Brian Young (1930-2009) – former Sea Hawk pilot, later commanded the task group for Operation Paraquet during the Falklands War.

Some 64 naval pilots and 9 observers have reached flag rank in the Royal Navy and 4 Royal Marines pilots general rank in the Royal Marines. Four of these admirals with pilot's 'wings' were air engineering officers (test pilots) and two were supply officers; two of the non-executive officers reached four-star rank: a supply officer, Admiral Sir Brian Brown (1934–), and a Royal Marine, General Sir Peter Whiteley (1920–).

- At least 21 naval Air Engineer Officers (AEOs) have reached flag rank (including the four test pilots (see above)).

References

Works cited

- Ray Sturtivant & Theo Ballance, *The Squadrons of the Fleet Air Arm*, first edition 1994, Air Britain, Kent UK, ISBN 0-85130-223-8.

Bibliography

<templatestyles src="Template:Refbegin/styles.css" />

- Hackett, James, ed. (3 February 2010). *The Military Balance 2010.* London: Routledge for International Institute for Strategic Studies. ISBN 1-85743-557-5.
- Darling, Kev (2009). *Fleet Air Arm Carrier War: The History of British Naval Aviation.* Barnsley: Pen & Sword Aviation. ISBN 978-1-84415-903-1.
- Manning, Charles, ed. (2000). *Fly Navy: The View From the Cockpit 1945–2000.* Barnsley: Leo Cooper. ISBN 085052-732-5.

External links

 Wikimedia Commons has media related to *Fleet Air Arm*.

- Fleet Air Arm website[910]
- Fleet Air Arm Rating Aircrewmans Association[914]
- Fleet Air Arm Association[915]
- Fleet Air Arm Officers' Association[916]
- Fleet Air Arm Aircraft Handlers Association[917]

Royal Marines

Corps of Royal Marines	
Badge	
Founded	28 October 1664
Country	🇬🇧 United Kingdom[918]
Branch	Royal Navy
Type	Marines
Role	Expeditionary & amphibious warfare
Size	7,760 Royal Marines 530 Royal Marines Reserve
Naval Staff Offices	Whitehall, London, England
Nickname(s)	"Royals" "Bootnecks" "The Commandos" "Jollies"
Motto(s)	"Per Mare, Per Terram" (Latin) "By Sea, By Land"
Colours	Blue, Gold, Green, Red
March	Quick: "A Life on the Ocean Wave" Slow: "Preobrajensky"
Engagements	
Website	www.royalnavy.mod.uk/royalmarines[919]
Commanders	
Captain General	HRH The Duke of Sussex
First Sea Lord	Admiral Sir Philip Jones
Commandant General	Major General Charles Stickland
Insignia	

Non-ceremonial flag	

Her Majesty's Naval Service
of the British Armed Forces

Components

- **Royal Navy**
- Surface Fleet
- Fleet Air Arm
- Submarine Service
- Royal Naval Reserve
- Royal Navy Medical Service
- Nursing Service (QARNNS)
- Chaplaincy
- Royal Navy Police
- **Royal Marines**
- Royal Marines Reserve
- Special Boat Service
- **Naval Careers Service**

History and future

- History of the Royal Navy / Royal Marines
- Customs and traditions
- Future

Ships

- Current fleet
- Current deployments
- Historic ships

Personnel

- The Admiralty
- Senior officers
- Uniforms
- Officer / ratings rank insignia

Auxiliary services

- Royal Fleet Auxiliary
- Marine Services

- v
- t
- e^{920}

The **Corps of Royal Marines** (**RM**) is the amphibious light infantry of the Royal Navy. The Royal Marines were formed in 1755 as the Royal Navy's infantry troops. However, the marines can trace their origins back to the formation of the English Army's "Duke of York and Albany's maritime regiment of Foot" at the grounds of the Honourable Artillery Company on 28 October 1664.

As a highly specialised and adaptable light infantry force, the Royal Marines are trained for rapid deployment worldwide and capable of dealing with a wide range of threats. The Royal Marines are organised into a light infantry brigade (3 Commando Brigade) and a number of separate units, including 1 Assault Group Royal Marines, 43 Commando Royal Marines formerly Fleet Protection Group Royal Marines (previously the Comacchio Group), and a company strength commitment to the Special Forces Support Group. The Corps operates in all environments and climates, though particular expertise and training is spent on amphibious warfare, arctic warfare, mountain warfare, expeditionary warfare, and its commitment to the UK's Rapid Reaction Force.

Throughout its history, the Royal Marines have seen action in a number of major wars often fighting beside the British Army – including the Seven Years' War, the Napoleonic Wars, the Crimean War, World War I and World War II. In recent times the Corps has been largely deployed in expeditionary warfare roles such as the Falklands War, the Gulf War, the Bosnian War, the Kosovo War, the Sierra Leone Civil War, the Iraq War and the War in Afghanistan. The Royal Marines have close international ties with allied marine forces, particularly the United States Marine Corps and the Netherlands Marine Corps (Dutch: *Korps Mariniers*).[921,922] Today, the Royal Marines are an elite fighting force within the British Armed forces, having undergone many substantial changes over time.[923]

History

The Royal Marines traces its origins back to 28 October 1664 when at the grounds of the Honourable Artillery Company "the Duke of York and Albany's maritime regiment of foot" was first formed.

Early British Empire

On 5 April 1755, *His Majesty's Marine Forces*, fifty Companies in three Divisions, headquartered at Chatham, Portsmouth, and Plymouth, were formed by Order of Council under Admiralty control. Initially all field officers were Royal Navy officers as the Royal Navy felt that the ranks of Marine field officers were largely honorary. This meant that the furthest a Marine officer could advance was to lieutenant colonel. It was not until 1771 that the first Marine was promoted to colonel. This attitude persisted well into the 1800s. During the rest of the 18th century, they served in numerous landings all over the

Figure 100: *Major General John Tupper His Majesty's Marine Forces.*

world, the most famous being the landing at Belle Île on the Brittany coast in 1761. They also served in the American War of Independence, notably in the Battle of Bunker Hill led by Major John Pitcairn.

In 1788 a detachment of four companies of marines, under Major Robert Ross, accompanied the First Fleet to protect a new colony at Botany Bay (New South Wales). Due to an error the Fleet left Portsmouth without its main supply of ammunition, and were not resupplied until the Fleet docked in Rio de Janeiro midway through the voyage.[924] One scholar has claimed that the Marines deliberately spread smallpox among Australia's indigenous population in order to reduce its military effectiveness, but this is not corroborated by contemporaneous records of the settlement and most researchers attribute the indigenous smallpox outbreak to other causes.

In 1802, largely at the instigation of Admiral the Earl St. Vincent, they were titled the *Royal Marines* by King George III. The *Royal Marines Artillery* (RMA) was formed as a separate unit in 1804 to man the artillery in bomb ketches. These had been manned by the Army's Royal Regiment of Artillery, but a lawsuit by a Royal Artillery officer resulted in a court decision that Army officers were not subject to Naval orders. As RMA uniforms were the blue of the Royal Regiment of Artillery they were nicknamed the "Blue Marines" and

Figure 101: *Private of Marines, 1815.*

the Infantry element, who wore the scarlet uniforms of the British infantry, became known as the "Red Marines", often given the semi-derogatory nickname "Lobsters" by sailors. A fourth division of the Royal Marines, headquartered at Woolwich, was formed in 1805.

During the Napoleonic Wars the Royal Marines participated in every notable naval battle on board the Royal Navy's ships and also took part in multiple amphibious actions. Marines had a dual function aboard ships of the Royal Navy in this period; routinely, they ensured the security of the ship's officers and supported their maintenance of discipline in the ship's crew, and in battle, they engaged the enemy's crews, whether firing from positions on their own ship, or fighting in boarding actions. In the Caribbean theatre volunteers from freed French slaves on Marie-Galante were used to form Sir Alexander Cochrane's first Corps of Colonial Marines. These men bolstered the ranks, helping the British to hold the island until reinforcements arrived. This practice was repeated during the War of 1812, where escaped American slaves were formed into Cochrane's second Corps of Colonial Marines. These men were commanded by Royal Marines officers and fought alongside their regular Royal Marines counterparts at the Battle of Bladensburg. Throughout the war Royal Marines units raided up and down the east coast of America including up the Penobscot River and in the Chesapeake Bay. They fought in the Battle

Figure 102: *Royal Marines parade in the streets of Chania, Cretan State, in spring 1897, following British occupation during the Greco-Turkish War.*

of New Orleans and later helped capture Fort Bowyer in Mobile Bay in what was the last action of the war.

In 1855 the Infantry forces were renamed the *Royal Marines Light Infantry* (RMLI). During the Crimean War in 1854 and 1855, three Royal Marines earned the Victoria Cross, two in the Crimea and one in the Baltic. In 1862 the name was slightly altered to *Royal Marine Light Infantry*. The Royal Navy did not fight any other ships after 1850 and became interested in landings by Naval Brigades. In these Naval Brigades, the function of the Royal Marines was to land first and act as skimishers ahead of the sailor Infantry and Artillery. This skirmishing was the traditional function of Light Infantry.[925] For most of their history, British Marines had been organised as fusiliers. In the rest of the 19th Century the Royal Marines served in many landings especially in the First and Second Opium Wars (1839–1842 and 1856–1860) against the Chinese. These were all successful except for the landing at the Mouth of the Peiho in 1859, where Admiral Sir James Hope ordered a landing across extensive mud flats.

The Royal Marines also played a prominent role in the Boxer Rebellion in China (1900), where a Royal Marine earned a Victoria Cross.

Pursuing a career in the Marines had been considered social suicide through much of the 18th and 19th centuries since Marine officers had a lower standing than their counterparts in the Royal Navy. An effort was made in 1907 through the common entry or "Selborne Scheme" to reduce the professional differences between RN and RM officers through a system of common entry that provided for an initial period of service where both groups performed the same roles and underwent the same training.

World wars

First World War

During the First World War, in addition to their usual stations aboard ship, Royal Marines were part of the Royal Naval Division which landed in Belgium in 1914 to help defend Antwerp and later took part in the amphibious landing at Gallipoli in 1915. It also served on the Western Front. The Division's first two commanders were Royal Marine Artillery Generals. Other Royal Marines acted as landing parties in the Naval campaign against the Turkish fortifications in the Dardanelles before the Gallipoli landing. They were sent ashore to assess damage to Turkish fortifications after bombardment by British and French ships and, if necessary, to complete their destruction. The Royal Marines were the last to leave Gallipoli, replacing both British and French troops in a neatly planned and executed withdrawal from the beaches.

The Royal Marines also took part in the Zeebrugge Raid in 1918. Five Royal Marines earned the Victoria Cross in the First World War, two at Zeebrugge, one at Gallipoli, one at Jutland and one on the Western Front.

Between the wars

After the war Royal Marines took part in the allied intervention in Russia. In 1919, the 6th Battalion RMLI mutinied and was disbanded at Murmansk. The Royal Marine Artillery (RMA) and Royal Marine Light Infantry (RMLI) were amalgamated on 22 June 1923.[926] Post-war demobilisation had seen the Royal Marines reduced from 55,000 (1918) to 15,000 in 1922 and there was Treasury pressure for a further reduction to 6,000 or even the entire disbandment of the Corps. As a compromise an establishment of 9,500 was settled upon but this meant that two separate branches could no longer be maintained. The abandonment of the Marine's artillery role meant that the Corps would subsequently have to rely on Royal Artillery support when ashore, that the title of Royal Marines would apply to the entire Corps and that only a few specialists would now receive gunnery training. As a form of consolation the dark blue and red uniform of the Royal Marine Artillery now became the full dress of the entire Corps. Royal Marine officers and SNCO's however continue to wear the historic scarlet in mess dress to the present day. The ranks of private, used

Figure 103: *British Commandos in action during Operation Archery, Norway.*

by the RMLI, and gunner, used by the RMA, were abolished and replaced by the rank of Marine.[927]

Second World War

During the Second World War, a small party of Royal Marines were first ashore at Namsos in April 1940, seizing the approaches to the Norwegian town preparatory to a landing by the British Army two days later. The Royal Marines formed the Royal Marine Division as an amphibiously trained division, parts of which served at Dakar and in the capture of Madagascar. After the assault on the French naval base at Antsirane in Madagascar was held up, fifty Sea Service Royal Marines from HMS Ramilles commanded by Captain Martin Price were landed on the quay of the base by the British destroyer HMS Anthony after it ran the gauntlet of French shore batteries defending Diego Suarez Bay. They then captured two of the batteries, which led to a quick surrender by the French.[928]

In addition the Royal Marines formed Mobile Naval Base Defence Organisations (MNBDOs) similar to the United States Marine Corps Defense Battalions. One of these took part in the defence of Crete. Royal Marines also served in Malaya and in Singapore, where due to losses they were joined with remnants of the 2nd Battalion, Argyll and Sutherland Highlanders to form the

Figure 104: *Men of No 4 (Army) Commando engaged in house to house fighting with the Germans at Riva Bella, near Ouistreham.*

"Plymouth Argylls". The Royal Marines formed one Commando (A Commando) which served at Dieppe. One month after Dieppe, most of the 11th Royal Marine Battalion was killed or captured in an ill staged amphibious landing at Tobruk in Operation Agreement. Again, the Marines were involved with the Argyll and Sutherland Highlanders, this time the 1st Battalion. In 1942 the Infantry Battalions of the Royal Marine Division were re-organised as Commandos, joining the British Army Commandos. The Division command structure became a Special Service Brigade command. The support troops became landing craft crew and saw extensive action on D-Day in June 1944.

A total of four Special Service Brigades (later Commando brigade) were raised during the war, and Royal Marines were represented in all of them. A total of nine RM Commandos (Battalions) were raised during the war, numbered from 40 to 48. 1 Commando Brigade had just one RM Battalion, No 45 Commando. 2 Commando Brigade had two RM battalions, Nos 40 and 43 Commandos. 3 Commando Brigade also had two, Nos 42 and 44 Commandos. 4 Commando Brigade was entirely Royal Marine after March 1944, comprising Nos 41, 46, 47 and 48 Commandos. 1 Commando Brigade took part in first in the Tunisia Campaign and then assaults on Sicily and Normandy, campaigns in the Rhineland and crossing the Rhine. 2 Commando Brigade was involved in the Salerno landings, Anzio, Comacchio, and operations in the Argenta Gap. 3

Figure 105: *Royal Marine Commandos attached to 3rd Division move inland from Sword Beach on the Normandy coast, 6 June 1944.*

Commando Brigade served in Sicily and Burma. 4 Commando Brigade served in the Battle of Normandy and in the Battle of the Scheldt on the island of Walcheren during the clearing of Antwerp.

In January 1945, two further RM Brigades were formed, 116th Brigade and 117th Brigade. Both were conventional Infantry, rather than in the Commando role. 116th Brigade saw some action in the Netherlands, but 117th Brigade was hardly used operationally. In addition one Landing Craft Assault (LCA) unit was stationed in Australia late in the war as a training unit. In 1946 the Army Commandos were disbanded, leaving the Royal Marines to continue the Commando role (with supporting Army elements). A number of Royal Marines served as pilots during the Second World War. It was a Royal Marines officer who led the attack by a formation of Blackburn Skuas that sank the Königsberg. Eighteen Royal Marines commanded Fleet Air Arm squadrons during the course of the war, and with the formation of the British Pacific Fleet were well-represented in the final drive on Japan. Captains and Majors generally commanded squadrons, whilst in one case Lt. Colonel R.C. Hay on HMS *Indefatigable* was Air Group Co-ordinator from HMS *Victorious* of the entire British Pacific Fleet.

Throughout the war Royal Marines continued in their traditional role of providing ships detachments and manning a proportion of the guns on Cruisers

Figure 106: *Royal Marines during an exercise in Scotland.*

and Capital Ships. They also provided the crew for the UK's Minor Landing craft, and the Royal Marines Armoured Support Group manned Centaur IV tanks on D Day; one of these is still on display at Pegasus Bridge.

Only one Marine (Corporal Thomas Peck Hunter of 43 Commando) was awarded the Victoria Cross in the Second World War for action at Lake Comacchio in Italy. Hunter was the most recent RM Commando to be awarded the medal. The Royal Marines Boom Patrol Detachment under Blondie Haslar carried out Operation Frankton and provided the basis for the post-war continuation of the SBS.

Post-colonial era

The Corps underwent a notable change after 1945 however, when the Royal Marines took on the main responsibility for the role and training of the British Commandos. The Royal Marines have an illustrious history, and since their creation in 1942 Royal Marines Commandos have engaged on active operations across the globe, every year, except 1968.[929] Notably they were the first ever military unit to perform an air assault insertion by helicopter, during the Suez Crisis in 1956.[930] They were also part of the land element during the 1982 Falklands War.

Cold War

During the Cold War the Royal Marines were earmarked to reinforce NATO's northernmost command Allied Forces North Norway. Therefore, 3 Commando Brigade began to train annually in Northern Norway and had large stores of vehicles and supplies pre-positioned there. At the end of the Cold War in 1989 the structure of the Royal Marines was as follows:

- **Commandant General Royal Marines**, London
  - **3 Commando Brigade**, Plymouth
    - 40 Commando, Taunton
    - 42 Commando, Bickleigh
    - 45 Commando, Arbroath
    - 29 Commando Regiment, Royal Artillery, Plymouth, one battery in Arbroath, (18x L118 light guns)
    - 4 Assault Squadron, Plymouth (4x LCU Mk.9, 4x LCVP Mk.4, 2x Centurion BARV), served aboard HMS *Fearless* (L10)
    - 539 Assault Squadron, Plymouth (4x LCU Mk.9, 4x LCVP Mk.4, 2x Centurion BARV), served aboard HMS *Intrepid* (L11)
    - 59 Independent Commando Squadron, Royal Engineers, Plymouth, one troop in Arbroath
    - 3 Commando Brigade Air Squadron, RNAS Yeovilton, (12x Gazelle AH.1, 6x Lynx AH.1)
    - 2 Raiding Squadron, Royal Marines (Reserve), Plymouth
    - 131 Independent Commando Squadron, Royal Engineers (V), Plymouth
    - 289 Commando Battery, Royal Artillery (V), Plymouth (6x L118 light guns)
  - Special Boat Service, Poole, under operational control of United Kingdom Special Forces
  - Comacchio Group, HMNB Clyde, guarded HMNB Clyde and the UK's naval nuclear weapons stored at RNAD Coulport
  - Royal Marines Police, Plymouth
  - Commando Training Centre Royal Marines, Lympstone
  - Royal Marines Reserve (RMR), Plymouth
    - RMR Bristol, Bristol
    - RMR London, Wandsworth
    - RMR Merseyside, Liverpool
    - RMR Scotland, Edinburgh
    - RMR Tyne, Newcastle

Note: "(V)" denotes British Army reserve units.

Figure 107: *Royal Marines in Sangin, Afghanistan, 2010*

Today

Personnel

The Royal Marines are part of the Naval Service and under the full command of Fleet Commander. The rank structure of the corps is similar to that of the British Army with officers and other ranks recruited and initially trained separately from other naval personnel. Since 2017 women have been able to serve in all roles in the Royal Marines. On average, 1,200 recruits attend training courses at the Commando Training Centre Royal Marines every year.

At its height in 1944 during the Second World War, more than 70,000 people served in the Royal Marines. Following the Allied victory the Royal Marines were quickly reduced to a post-war strength of 13,000. When National Service finally came to an end in 1960, the Marines were again reduced, but this time to an all Commando-trained force of 9,000 personnel.[931] As of October 2014 the Royal Marines had a strength of 7,760 Regular[932] and 750 Royal Marines Reserve, giving a combined component strength of around 8,510 personnel. The Royal Marines are the only European marine force capable of conducting amphibious operations at brigade level.

Equipment

Infantry The basic infantry weapon of the Royal Marines is the L85A2 assault rifle, sometimes fitted with the L123A3 underslung grenade launcher. Support fire is provided by the L110A1 light machine gun, the L7A2 General Purpose Machine Gun (GPMG) and the L111A1 heavy machine gun (which is often mounted on an armoured vehicle); indirect fire by the L16A2 81mm mortar. Sniper rifles used include the L115A3, produced by Accuracy International. More recently the L129A1 has come into service as the designated marksman rifle. Other weapons include the Javelin Anti-Tank missile, the L107A1 pistol, the L131A1 pistol and the Fairbairn-Sykes Fighting Knife.

Armour The Royal Marines maintain no heavy armoured units, instead, they operate a fleet of lightly armoured and highly mobile vehicles intended for amphibious landings or rapid deployment. The primary armoured fighting vehicle operated by the Armoured Support Group is the BvS 10 Viking All Terrain Armoured Vehicle.[933] Other, lighter vehicles include the Land Rover Wolf Armoured Patrol Vehicle, the Jackal (MWMIK) Armoured Vehicle and the Pinzgauer High Mobility All Terrain Vehicle.[934]

Artillery Field artillery support is provided by 29th Commando Regiment Royal Artillery of the British Army using the L118 Light Gun, a 105 mm towed howitzer. The regiment is Commando-trained.

Aviation The Commando Helicopter Force of the Fleet Air Arm provides transport helicopters in support of the Royal Marines. It currently uses both Merlin HC4/4A medium-lift transport and Wildcat AH1 attack helicopters to provide direct aviation support for the Corps. In addition, the Royal Air Force provides Chinook heavy-lift and Puma HC2 medium-lift transport helicopters.

Vessels The Royal Marines operate a varied fleet of military watercraft designed to transport troops and material from ship to shore or conduct river or estuary patrols. These include the 2000TDX Landing Craft Air Cushion, the Mk10 Landing Craft Utility, the Mk5 Landing Craft Vehicle Personnel and the SDV Mk8 Mod 1 Swimmer Delivery Vehicle for special forces. Other smaller amphibious craft such as the Offshore Raiding Craft, Rigid Raider and Inflatable Raiding Craft are in service in much greater numbers.

Figure 108: *Royal Marines equipped for Arctic warfare during an exercise in Norway.*

Figure 109: *BvS 10 Vikings of the Royal Marines Armoured Support Group on exercise.*

Figure 110: *Royal Marines Landing Craft Utility (LCU) Mk10.*

Figure 111: *A Royal Marines Landing Craft Vehicle Personnel (LCVP) Mk5.*

Figure 112: *Royal Marines Landing Craft Air Cushion (LCAC).*

Formation and structure

The overall head of the Royal Marines is Her Majesty Queen Elizabeth II, in her role as Commander-in-Chief of the British Armed Forces. The ceremonial head of the Royal Marines is the Captain General Royal Marines (equivalent to the Colonel-in-Chief of a British Army regiment). The current Captain-General is Prince Harry, Duke of Sussex. Full Command of the Royal Marines is vested in the Fleet Commander (FLTCDR) with the Commandant General Royal Marines, a major-general, embedded within the Navy Command Headquarters (NCHQ) as Commander UK Amphibious Force (COMUKAMPHIBFOR).

The operational capability of the corps comprises a number of battalion-plus sized units, of which five are designated as "commandos":

- 40 Commando (known as *Forty* Commando) based at Norton Manor Barracks, Taunton, Somerset, England
- 42 Commando (known as *Four Two* Commando) based at Bickleigh Barracks, Plymouth, Devon, England
- 43 Commando Fleet Protection Group Royal Marines based at HM Naval Base Clyde, Helensburgh, Argyll and Bute (Previously Comacchio Group).
- 45 Commando (known as *Four Five* Commando) based at RM Condor, Arbroath, Angus, Scotland

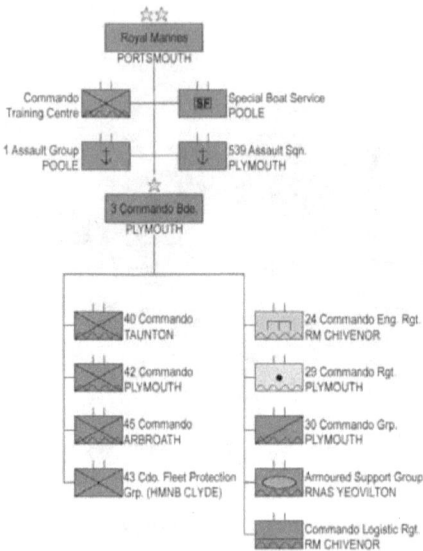

Figure 113: *Operational structure of the Royal Marines.*

- 30 Commando Information Exploitation Group based at Stonehouse Barracks, Plymouth
- Commando Logistic Regiment based at RM Chivenor, Devon
- 24 Commando Engineer Regiment based at RM Chivenor, Devon
- Royal Marines Armoured Support Group (RMASG) is an element of the Royal Marines that operates the Viking BvS 10 All Terrain Vehicle. It is based at RNAS Yeovilton in Somerset.
- Special Boat Service based at RM Poole, Dorset (although Full Command is retained by CINCFLEET, Operational Command of SBS RM is assigned to Director Special Forces).
- 1 Assault Group Royal Marines based at RM Tamar, Devonport.

Each Commando Unit will rotate through one of three roles every six months.

- Lead Commando – This unit will be the first unit called upon in case of short-notice operations anywhere around the world.
- Force Generating – Training (Force Generating) to assume the role of Lead Commando
- Standing task – general duties unit

With the exception of the 43 Commando Fleet Protection Group and Commando Logistic Regiment, which are each commanded by a full colonel, each

Figure 114: *Insignia of 3 Commando*

of these units is commanded by a lieutenant-colonel of the Royal Marines, who may have sub-specialised in a number of ways throughout their career.[935]

3 Commando Brigade

Operational command of the five commandos and the Commando Logistics Regiment is delegated to 3 Commando Brigade Royal Marines, of which they are a part. Based at Stonehouse Barracks, the brigade exercises control as directed by either CINCFLEET or the Permanent Joint Headquarters. As the main combat formation of the Royal Marines, the brigade has its own organic capability to it in the field, 30 Commando Information Exploitation Group, a battalion sized formation providing information operations capabilities, life support and security for the Brigade Headquarters.

43 Commando Fleet Protection Group Royal Marines, responsible for the security of the United Kingdom's nuclear deterrent and other security-related duties was originally outside the brigade however from April 2012 it moved into it. It also provides specialist boarding parties and snipers for the Royal Navy worldwide, for roles such as embargo enforcement, counter-narcotics, counter-piracy and counter-insurgency activities of the Royal Navy. It is the largest unit in the brigade, at 790 strong.

Independent elements

The independent elements of the Royal Marines are:[936]

- Commando Training Centre: This is the training unit for the entire corps, and consists of three separate sections:

Figure 115: *A Royal Marines team boards US Navy destroyer USS O'Bannon.*

- Commando Training Wing: This is the initial basic commando training section for new recruits to the Royal Marines, and the UK Forces All Arms Commando Course.
- Specialist Wing: This provides specialist training in the various trades which Marines may elect to join once qualified and experienced in a Rifle Company.
- Command Wing: This provides command training for both officers and NCOs of the Royal Marines.
- 1 Assault Group Royal Marines: Provides training in the use of landing craft and boats, and also serves as a parent unit for the three assault squadrons permanently embarked on the Royal Navy's amphibious ships.
  - 4 Assault Squadron—HMS *Bulwark*
  - 6 Assault Squadron—HMS *Albion*
- Special Boat Service (SBS) are naval special forces and under operational command of Director Special Forces, UK Special Forces Group. It is commanded by a lieutenant colonel qualified as a swimmer canoeist. SBS responsibilities include water-borne operations, maritime counter-terrorism and other special forces tasks.
- Royal Marines Band Service provides regular bands for the Royal Navy and provides expertise to train RN Volunteer Bands. Musicians have an important secondary roles as medics, field hospital orderlies, CBRN

specialists and any other roles that may be required of them. Personnel may not be commando trained, usually wearing the dark blue beret instead of green; until 2017, the band service was the only branch of the Royal Marines to admit women.

Structure of a commando

File:Royal Marine and Albanian Commando.jpg

The Commando Flash and dagger worn on the sleeve

The three commando units are each organised into six companies, further organised into platoon-sized troops, as follows:

Command company

- Main HQ
- Tactical HQ
- Reconnaissance Troop with a sniper section
- Mortar Troop
- Anti-Tank (AT) Troop
- Medium Machine Gun Troop

2X Close Combat Companies

- Company Headquarters
- 3X Close Combat Troops

Figure 116: *A Royal Marine RIB 'Underslinging', from an RAF Chinook as a method of quick extraction and insertion of waterborne personnel*

2X Stand Off Companies

- Company Headquarters
- Heavy Machine Gun (HMG) Troop
- AT Troop
- Close Combat Troop.

Logistic Company

- A Echelon 1
- A Echelon 2
- FRT (Forward Repair Team)
- RAP (Regimental Aid Post)
- B Echelon

In general a rifle company Marine will be a member of a four-man fire team, the building block of commando operations. A Royal Marine works with his team in the field and shares accommodation if living in barracks. This structure is a recent development, formerly Commandos were structured similarly to British Army light Infantry Battalions.[937]

Amphibious Task Group

Formerly known as the Amphibious Ready Group, the Amphibious Task Group (or ATG) is a mobile, balanced amphibious warfare force, based on a Commando Group and its supporting assets, that can be kept at high readiness to deploy into an area of operations. The ATG is normally based around specialist amphibious ships, most notably HMS *Ocean*, the largest ship in the British fleet. *Ocean* was designed and built to accommodate an embarked commando and its associated stores and equipment. The strategy of the ATG is to wait "beyond the horizon" and then deploy swiftly as directed by HM Government. The whole amphibious force is intended to be self-sustaining and capable of operating without host-nation support. The concept was successfully tested in operations in Sierra Leone.[938]

Commando Helicopter Force

The Commando Helicopter Force (CHF) forms part of the Fleet Air Arm. It comprises three helicopter squadrons and is commanded by the Joint Helicopter Command.[939] It consists of both Royal Navy (RN) and Royal Marines personnel. RN personnel need not be commando trained. The CHF is neither under the permanent control of 3 Commando Brigade nor that of the Commandant General Royal Marines, but rather is allocated to support Royal Marines units as required. It uses both Merlin HC4/4A medium-lift and Wildcat AH1 light transport/reconnaissance helicopters to provide aviation support for the Royal Marines.

Commando Forces 2030 & Maritime Operations Commando

On 11 April 2017 the First Sea Lord, Admiral Sir Philip Jones, announced that the Royal Marines were to be restructured. The Royal Marines will be able to deploy a specialist Maritime Operations Commando from the three combat units as part of the Commando Forces 2030 strategy.

Selection and training

Royal Marines are required to undergo one of the longest and most physically demanding specialist infantry training regimes in the world. Recruit training lasts for 32 weeks for Marines and 60 weeks for officers. Potential recruits must be male and aged 16 to 32 (18 to 25 for Commissioned Officers); however by the end of 2018 women will be permitted to apply after the ban on women in Ground Close Combat roles was lifted in July 2016. and they must

Figure 117: *A Royal Marine stands beside a tree to sight in his weapon during a training exercise.*

Figure 118: *Royal Marines snipers displaying their L115A1 rifles*

first undertake a series of interviews, medical tests, an eye/sight test, psychometric tests and a PJFT (Pre-joining fitness test).[940] Once a potential recruit passes these, enlisted recruits undertake a 3-day selection course called PRMC (Potential Royal Marine Course) and potential officers undertake POC (Potential Officer Course) – both take place at the Commando Training Centre Royal Marines (CTCRM) in Lympstone, Devon. Officers must also take the Admiralty Interview Board (AIB).[941] Upon passing the 3-day course, recruits then start basic recruit training (RT) at CTCRM. Unlike in many countries, enlisted Marines and officer Marines often train together for the first 32 weeks. A large proportion of training is carried out on Dartmoor's inhospitable terrain and Woodbury Common woodland.

Throughout the recruit training, Royal Marines learn and develop many military skills such as weapons handling, marksmanship and proficiency with different firearms, personal administration, marching and parade ground skills, map reading and navigation, physical fitness and mental toughness development, fieldcraft skills such as camouflage and stalking, basic survival techniques, patrolling and sentry duty development, unarmed and armed close quarters combat (CQC), first aid, underwater escape, chemical biological radiological nuclear (CBRN) training, military communications and signals, teamwork skills, amphibious landings training, and leadership skills for officers to name a few.

The best recruit to finish training is awarded the Kings Badge. King George V directed that his Royal Cypher, surrounded by a laurel wreath, would be known as the King's Badge, and would be awarded to the best all round recruit in the King's Squad, provided that he was worthy of the honour. The badge was to be carried on the left shoulder, and worn in every rank. The King's Badge is not awarded to every squad, and is only presented if a recruit measures up to the very exacting standards required.

Throughout his career, a Marine can specialise in a number of different roles upon completion of their respective courses after spending 1–2 years as a general duties (GD) Marine. Examples of some specialisations and different courses includes the mountain leader (ML), physical training instructor (PTI), Assault Engineer (AE), military police (MP), sniper course, medical assistant, pilot, reconnaissance operator (RO), drill instructor, driver, clerk, chef, signaller, combat intelligence, armourer, and heavy weapons training. Royal Marines can also apply for swimmer canoeist/Special Boat Service selection (SBS) or any other branch of the UKSF.[942] All Royal Marines will also conduct training exercises on differing military skills on a regular basis including development in mountain, arctic, jungle, amphibious and desert warfare. They can also be involved in exchange training programs with other countries

Figure 119: *Royal Marine Beret Badge*

forces – particularly the United States Marine Corps and the Netherlands Marine Corps/Korps Mariniers.

Museum

The Royal Marines Museum is in the course of relocating from Eastney Barracks to Portsmouth Dockyard.

Customs and traditions

The Royal Marines have a proud history and unique traditions. With the exceptions of "Gibraltar" and the laurel wreath for the Battle of Belle Island, their colours (flags) do not carry battle honours in the manner of the regiments of the British Army or of the US Marine Corps, but rather the "globe itself" as a symbol of the Corps.

The heraldic crest of the Royal Marines commemorates the history of the Corps. The Lion and Crown denotes a Royal regiment. King George III conferred this honour in 1802 "in consideration of the very meritorious services of the Marines in the late war." The "Great Globe itself" was chosen in 1827 by King George IV in place of Battle honours to recognise the Marines' service

Figure 120: *Memorial for H Barley of the Royal Marine Engineers*

and successes in multiple engagements in every quarter of the world. The laurels are believed to honour the gallantry they displayed during the investment and capture of Belle Isle, off Lorient, in April–June 1761. The word *Gibraltar* refers to the Capture of Gibraltar by a force of Anglo-Dutch Marines in 1704 and the subsequent defence of the strategic fortress throughout a nine-month siege against a numerically superior Franco-Spanish force. Their determination and valour throughout the siege led to a contemporary report published in *The Triumphs of Her Majesty's Arms* in 1707 to announce:

> *Encouraged by the Prince of Hesse, the garrison did more than could humanly be expected, and the English Marines gained an immortal glory*
>
> *— referred to by Paul Harris Nicolas, Historical record of the Royal marine forces*

There are no other battle honours displayed on the colours of the four battalion-sized units of the current Corps. The Latin motto "Per Mare Per Terram" translates into English as "By Sea By Land". Believed to have been first used in 1775 this motto describes the Royal Marines ability in fighting both afloat on-board ships of the Royal Navy, as well as ashore in their many land engagements. The fouled anchor, incorporated into the emblem in 1747, is the badge of the Lord High Admiral and shows that the Corps is part of the Naval Service.

Figure 121: *Royal Marines on Parade in the City of London marking the 350th anniversary of the Corps in 2014*

The regimental quick march of the Corps is "A Life on the Ocean Wave", while the slow march is the march of the Preobrazhensky Regiment, awarded to the Corps by Admiral of the Fleet Earl Mountbatten of Burma on the occasion of the Corps's tercentenary in 1964. Lord Mountbatten was Life Colonel Commandant of the Royal Marines until his murder by the IRA in 1979.

The Royal Marines are allowed by the Lord Mayor of the City of London to march through the City as a regiment in full array. This dates to the charter of Charles II that allowed recruiting parties of the Admiral's Regiment of 1664 to enter the City with drums beating and colours flying.

Uniforms

The modern Royal Marines retain a number of distinctive uniform items. These include the green "Lovat" service dress worn with the green beret, the dark blue parade dress worn with either the white Wolseley Pattern Helmet (commonly referred to as "pith helmet") or white and red peaked cap, the scarlet and blue mess dress for officers and senior non-commissioned officers and the white hot-weather uniform of the Band Service.

For historical information regarding Marine uniforms, see *Uniforms of the Royal Marines*.

Ranks and insignia

See also: Royal Marines officer ranks and Royal Marines other ranks

NATO code	OF-10	OF-9	OF-8	OF-7	OF-6	OF-5	OF-4	OF-3	OF-2	OF-1	OF-1	OF(D)	Student officer
United Kingdom (Royal Marines) (Edit)	Captain General Royal Marines	General	Lieutenant-General	Major-General	Brigadier	Colonel	Lieutenant-Colonel	Major	Captain	Lieutenant	Second Lieutenant	Officer Cadet	*No equivalent*

NATO Code	OR-9	OR-8	OR-7	OR-6	OR-5	OR-4	OR-3	OR-2	OR-1
United Kingdom (Royal Marines) (Edit)					*No equivalent*			*No equivalent*	No insignia
	Warrant officer class 1	Warrant officer class 2	Colour sergeant	Sergeant		Corporal	Lance corporal		Marine

Associations with other regiments and marines corps

Argyll and Sutherland Highlanders

Early connections date from Balaclava in the Crimean War and Lucknow during the Indian Mutiny, but the main association stems from World War II. In July 1940, after the fall of Dunkirk, the 5th Battalion, Argyll and Sutherland Highlanders served with the Royal Marine Brigade for over a year. When the battleships HMS *Prince of Wales* and HMS *Repulse* were sunk in December 1941, the Royal Marines survivors joined up with the remnants of the 2nd Battalion, in the defence of Singapore. They formed what became known as 'The Plymouth Argylls', after the association football team, since both ships were Plymouth manned. Most of the Highlanders and Marines who survived the bitter fighting were taken prisoner by the Japanese. The Royal Marines inter-unit rugby football trophy is the 'Argyll Bowl', presented to the Corps by the Regiment in 1941.

Princess of Wales's Royal Regiment

The fore-bearer regiments of the Princess of Wales's Royal Regiment, 31st (Huntingdonshire) Regiment of Foot was initially raised as amphibious troops. They served as Marines for a period. To this day one officer from the Royal Marines serves with the PWRR and Vice Versa. Also the Royal Marine Lanyard is worn by all ranks in Service Dress and Number 2 Dress uniform and barrack dress of PWRR.

Barbados Defence Force

Close links have existed between the Royal Marines and the Barbados Defence Force since 1985 when a bond was established following a series of cross-training exercises in the Caribbean. The Alliance was approved by HM the Queen in 1992.

Netherlands Marine Corps

The Royal Marines have close links with the Royal Netherlands Marine Corps, with whom they conduct NATO exercises throughout the year. Formed during the Anglo-Dutch Wars in 1665, the Dutch Marines distinguished themselves in raids on the English coast, where it is likely they met their future counterparts. Units of the Royal Netherlands Marine Corps work in close co-operation with 3 Commando Brigade of the Royal Marines. Operational units of the Royal Netherlands Marine Corps are fully integrated into this brigade. This integration is known as the United Kingdom-Netherlands Landing Force and is a component of the United Kingdom-Netherlands Amphibious Force as a key strike force during the Cold War to strengthen the Nordic area.

9th Light Armoured Marine Brigade

The 9eme BIMa (9th Marine Infantry Brigade) is a Marine infantry brigade which is one of the two designated amphibious brigades in France. It is unique in being the only 'all Marine' Brigade in the French Army; the other amphibious brigade, 6eme Light Armoured Brigade, is composed of a mix of cap badges. 9 BIMa is also a light armoured brigade, formed of two Marine infantry regiments (2 and 3 Regiments d'Infanterie de Marine- 2/3 RIMa) and a tank battalion.

Bibliography

- Akins, Thomas Beamish (1895). *History of Halifax*. Brookhouse Press. ISBN 978-1298600462.
- Brooks, Richard; Little, Matthew (2008). *Tracing Your Royal Marine Ancestors: A Guide for Family Historians*. Pen & Sword, Barnsley. ISBN 978-1844158690.
- Chappell, Mike (2004). *Wellington's Peninsula Regiments (2): The Light Infantry*. Oxford: Osprey Publishing. ISBN 1-84176-403-5.
- Chartrand, Rene (2002). *Colonial American Troops, 1610–1774*. **1**. Osprey Publishing. ISBN 978-1841763248.
- Edye, Lourenço (1893). *The Historical Records of the Royal Marines*[943]. **v. 1**. London: Harrison & Sons.
- Francis, David (1975). *The First Peninsular War: 1702–1713*. Ernest Benn. ISBN 978-0510002053.
- Gleig, George Robert (1827). *The campaigns of the British army at Washington and New Orleans in the years 1814-1815*. John Murray, London.
- Heidler, David; Heidler, Jeanne (2004). *Encyclopedia of the War Of 1812*. Naval Institute Press. ISBN 1591143624.

- Moore, John (1989). *The First Fleet Marines*. University of Queensland Press. ISBN 0702220655.
- Mountbatten, Lord Louis (1943). *Combined Operations: The Official Story Of The Commandos*. New York, The Macmillan Company.
- Nicolas, Paul (1845). *Historical record of the Royal marine forces*. Thomas and Boone, London.
- Lenihan, Padraig. *Consolidating Conquest, Ireland 1603-1727*. Pearson Education. ISBN 978-0582772175.
- Thompson, Julian (2001). *The Royal Marines, From Sea Soldiers to a Special Force*. Pan Books. ISBN 978-0330377027.
- Carter, B L (2013). *A Short history of The Royal Marines*. Royal marines Historical Society. ISBN 978-1908123053.

External links

 Wikimedia Commons has media related to *Royal Marines*.

- Royal Marines[944] on Royal Navy website
- Royal Marines[945] website
- Royal Marines Band Service[946] website
- Royal Marines Volunteer Cadet Corps (RMVCC) Portsmouth[947] website
- Download Royal Marines Registers of Service[948] (1842–1925). The National Archives official website
- Potential Royal Marines Commando forum[949] (for men wishing to join)
- "Rum Ration": The Navy Network[950] – unofficial website for the Royal Navy, Royal Marines, and Royal Fleet Auxiliary
- Royal Marines Museum[951] website
- Marine Society[952] website
- Royal Navy ranks, professions, and trades in World War 2, including Royal Marines[953]
- Royal Navy Battle Honours including Royal Marine Corps Memorable Dates, 1939–1945[954]
- Royal Marines Badges of Rank & Other Insignia[955]

Standing Royal Navy deployments

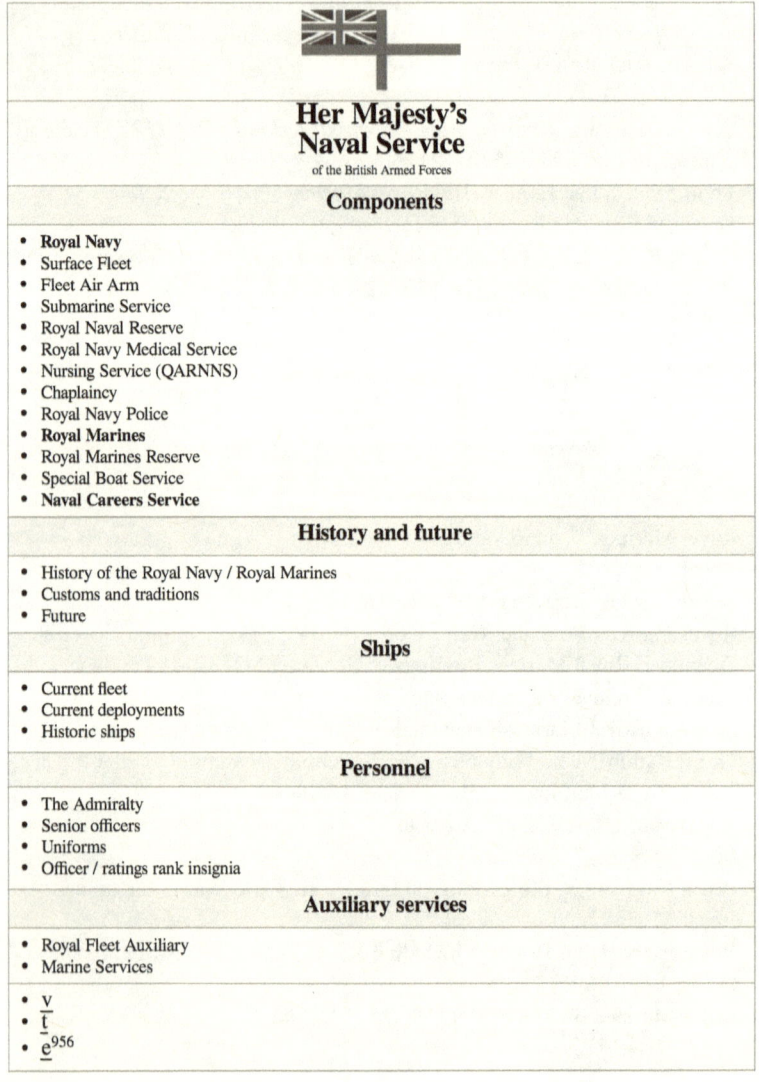

Her Majesty's Naval Service of the British Armed Forces
Components
• **Royal Navy** • Surface Fleet • Fleet Air Arm • Submarine Service • Royal Naval Reserve • Royal Navy Medical Service • Nursing Service (QARNNS) • Chaplaincy • Royal Navy Police • **Royal Marines** • Royal Marines Reserve • Special Boat Service • **Naval Careers Service**
History and future
• History of the Royal Navy / Royal Marines • Customs and traditions • Future
Ships
• Current fleet • Current deployments • Historic ships
Personnel
• The Admiralty • Senior officers • Uniforms • Officer / ratings rank insignia
Auxiliary services
• Royal Fleet Auxiliary • Marine Services
• $\underline{v}$ • $\underline{t}$ • $\underline{e}^{956}$

Standing Royal Navy deployments is a list of operations and commitments undertaken by the United Kingdom's Royal Navy on a worldwide basis. The following list details these commitments and deployments sorted by region and in alphabetical order. Routine deployments made by the Navy's nuclear-powered submarines and their location of operations is classified.

Figure 122: *Protector on Antarctic Patrol*

Atlantic

Antarctic Patrol

Antarctic Patrol is undertaken by the Royal Navy's Icebreaker and survey ship, HMS *Protector*, in the South Atlantic Ocean. Its primary mission is *"surveying and gathering data on the seas around Antarctica"* while also providing support to the British Antarctic Survey operation stationed in and around the British Antarctic Territory.[957] Two Royal Research Ships of the Merchant Navy are also stationed in the region; RRS James Clark Ross and RRS Ernest Shackleton.

Atlantic Patrol Tasking North

Formerly known as the **West Indies Guard Ship**. This is the Royal Navy's commitment to secure and protect the interests of the United Kingdom and British Overseas Territories in the regions of the North Atlantic and the Caribbean. The deployment primarily conducts counter narcotics missions and provides humanitarian assistance during hurricane season.[958]

This tasking was augmented by Operation Ruman in 2017 as a result of damage caused by Hurricane Irma.

The task is typically carried out by a single warship, or more recently by a River class patrol vessel or a Royal Fleet Auxiliary vessel.[959] As of April 2018, the RFA Mounts Bay (L3008) is assigned.

Figure 123: *Clyde patrols off West Falkland*

Atlantic Patrol Tasking South

The Royal Navy maintains a permanent presence in the South Atlantic and West Africa to provide *"ongoing protection and reassurance to British interests"* such as the sovereignty of the Falkland Islands and South Georgia, while also supporting British Forces South Atlantic Islands. The commitment consists of two warships; either a guided-missile destroyer or frigate accompanied by a Royal Fleet Auxiliary vessel.[960]

Falkland Islands Patrol Task

The Falkland Islands Patrol Task consists of a single warship (an Offshore Patrol Vessel) stationed around the EEZ of the Falkland Islands. It forms part of British Forces South Atlantic Islands and aims to reassure the inhabitants of the region and maintain British sovereignty.

HMS *Clyde* has been permanently assigned to the task since her commission.[961] *Clyde* uses the deepwater naval base facilities of East Cove Military Port at Mare Harbour, East Falkland.

Figure 124: *Royal Marines during the annual Cold Weather Training exercise in the Norwegian Arctic*

Standing NATO Maritime Group 1

The Standing NATO Maritime Group 1 is part of the wider NATO Response Force, its standard area of operations is the Atlantic Ocean.[962] As of January 2016, the type 23 frigate HMS *Iron Duke* was the latest British contribution to the task force.[963]

British and Northern European Waters

Cold Weather Training

Cold Weather Training is a Royal Navy commitment to the annual Norwegian-led exercise in the Arctic regions. Its purpose is to build and strengthen military ties and to enable the Royal Marines and Royal Navy sailors to "fight and win" in extreme conditions.[964]

Faslane Patrol Boat Squadron

The Faslane Patrol Boat Squadron (FPBS) provides force protection in around the waters of HMNB Clyde, where the Royal Navy's nuclear-powered submarine fleet is based. The squadron currently consists of HMS *Tracker* and HMS *Raider*.

Figure 125: *Fleet Ready Escort HMS Dragon escorting the Russian aircraft carrier, Admiral Kuznetsov, through the English Channel*

Fishery Protection

The Fishery Protection Squadron is charged with protecting the British fishing industry, providing security to the oil and gas fields in the North Sea and other duties in the United Kingdoms Exclusive economic zone. It consists of one warship; the offshore patrol vessels HMS *Mersey*.[965]

Fleet Ready Escort

The Fleet Ready Escort (FRE) is a single warship maintained at high readiness for deployment at short notice anywhere in the world. The FRE consists of either a guided-missile destroyer or a frigate. As of January 2014, this commitment has been 'gapped' by the Royal Navy twice; for 19 days in 2011 and 18 days in 2012.[966]

Flag Officer Sea Training

Training in UK Home Waters is essential for preparing both crews and ships before overseas deployment. Flag Officer Sea Training (FOST) is responsible for making sure that both Royal Navy and Royal Fleet Auxiliary ships are fit for operational propose after rigorous exercises and readiness inspections. This commitment is ongoing 365 days a year.[967]

As of May 2018 RFA Tidespring (A136) is assigned to FOST.

Joint Warrior

Exercise Joint Warrior is a Royal Navy (and wider British Armed Forces) commitment to engage in an biannual tri-service exercise (including multinational NATO forces) intended to achieve enhanced military effect. It is the largest military exercise in Europe.[968]

Towed Array Patrol Ship

Towed Array Patrol Ship (TAPS) is a standing task for reactive anti-submarine patrol duties in support of the Continuous At Sea Deterrent (Trident). A Type 23 frigate is maintained at high readiness for this task 365 days a year.

East of Suez

This is a list of operations and commitments presently undertaken by the Royal Navy East of Suez in the Red Sea, Gulf of Aden, Persian Gulf, Arabian Sea, the wider Indian Ocean and the Far East:

Combined Task Force

The Royal Navy regularly contributes to two multinational coalitions; Combined Task Force 150 and Combined Task Force 151. Combined Task Force 150 is focused on maritime security and counter-terrorism; while Combined Task Force 151 is charged with anti-piracy missions.[969]

Humanitarian Missions

The Royal Navy remains committed to providing humanitarian aid where possible. During the 2004 Indian Ocean earthquake and tsunami the Royal Navy responded by deploying RFA *Diligence* and the frigate HMS *Chatham* with Westland Lynx helicopters to provide assistance.[970] In 2014, the Royal Navy deployed HMS *Echo* (a multi-role hydrographic survey ship) and HMS *Tireless* (a nuclear-powered fleet submarine) to search for the missing Malaysia Airlines Flight 370 in the Indian Ocean Region.[971]

Operation Atalanta

Operation Atalanta is a European Union multinational task force charged to combat terrorism and piracy off the Horn of Africa and Somalia. Operational headquarters are located in the United Kingdom at Northwood Headquarters, London.[972] British ships in the region are usually assigned to CTF.

In November 2017 Charles Stickland (Major General of the Royal Marines) was appointed as CO of Operation Atalanta.

Figure 126: *A Trident II D-5 ballistic missile launched from a Vanguard-class submarine*

Operation Kipion

Operation Kipion is an ongoing maritime presence in the Gulf and Indian Ocean by the Royal Navy to protect and secure the nation's many political and commercial interests. The enduring commitment usually consists of an escort (a guided-missile destroyer or frigate), a supporting Royal Fleet Auxiliary ship and several other ships with various roles.[973] Operation Kipion was formerly known as the Armilla patrol during the 1980s and 1990s.

Operation Kipion Mine Countermeasures

The Royal Navy maintains a permanent presence in the Gulf consisting of mine countermeasure vessels. It provides continued support to the region ensuring the "*safe flow of trade and oil*".[974] Typically the mine countermeasure vessels are supported by a Royal Fleet Auxiliary ship acting as a 'mothership'.

Global

Continuous At Sea Deterrent

The Continuous At Sea Deterrent (CASD) (*or* Trident) is provided by the Royal Navy's four Vanguard-class submarines which deploy on a continuous

Figure 127: *LPH HMS Ocean during the JEF(M) Amphibious Task Group in October 2016*

basis around the globe. The Vanguard-class are each armed with a maximum of 16 Trident II D-5 submarine-launched ballistic missiles and 48 nuclear warheads.[975]

International Partnerships

The Royal Navy remains committed to working with its International Partners around the globe. The principal purpose of these partnerships is to reassure allied nations, to share intelligence and expertise, to build trust and ultimately provide security across the worlds oceans.[976] Examples of such International Partnerships of which the Royal Navy plays a leading role include; the maritime component of the Anglo-French Combined Joint Expeditionary Force (CJEF), the North Atlantic Treaty Organization, AUSCANNZUKUS, the European Maritime Force and the Five Power Defence Arrangements. The United Kingdom is a member of RIMPAC also, although it hasn't participated in way of deploying a surface ship in several years.

Joint Expeditionary Force (Maritime)

Joint Expeditionary Force (Maritime) (JEF(M)) -formerly the Response Force Task Group (RFTG) created under the 2010 Strategic Defence and Security Review- is the Royal Navy's amphibious expeditionary task group maintained at high-readiness and available at short notice to respond to unexpected global events. In addition to amphibious operations, the JEF(M) can undertake a diverse range of activities such as evacuation operations, disaster relief or humanitarian aid.[977] The composition of the JEF(M) generally consists of several large amphibious warfare ships (both RN and RFA) and replenishment ships from the Royal Fleet Auxiliary.

To demonstrate the operational readiness and global reach of the JEF(M), the Royal Navy deploys the amphibious task group on annual large scale international exercises, primarily in the Mediterranean and Indian Ocean.[978,979] As an international deployment, the JEF(M) gets the chance to engage in "intense" exercises with foreign and allied navies, such as (for example) the Royal Navy of Oman.[980]

NATO Mine Countermeasures

This is the Royal Navy's commitment to support NATO MCM operations in the Baltic, Northern European Waters, the Atlantic and the Mediterranean Sea (though it is capable of deploying globally if needed). There are two organisational structures; Standing NATO Mine Countermeasures Group 1 and Standing NATO Mine Countermeasures Group 2.[981]

Mediterranean

Gibraltar Squadron

The Gibraltar Squadron consists of two fast patrol boats; HMS *Scimitar* and HMS *Sabre*. They provide force protection for NATO or coalition warships entering the naval facilities of Gibraltar and conduct maritime security in the surrounding British territorial waters.[982]

Standing NATO Maritime Group 2

The Royal Navy routinely provides a single warship to the Standing NATO Maritime Group 2 (part of the NATO Response Force). The standard area of operations for the Standing NRF Maritime Group 2 is the Mediterranean Sea.. In 2017, HMS *Duncan* deployed as flagship of the group, HM Ships *Diamond* and *Ocean* also took on the role prior to *Duncan* resuming her duties in early 2018 till July 2018.[983]

Figure 128: *Merlin HC3 of 846 NAS with HMS Scimitar in British territorial waters off Gibraltar*

Special Purpose Task Group

In April 2016, *IHS Jane's* reported that the Royal Navy had formed a new marine task group, named the Special Purpose Task Group (SPTG), in December 2015. The task group is reportedly 150-strong and centred around Zulu Company of 45 Commando Royal Marines. It conducts counter-trafficking, counter-terrorism operations as well as providing support to United Kingdom Special Forces. The SPTG's first operational deployment was in January 2016 to the Mediterranean on board RFA Mounts Bay (L3008). Additional personnel from 29 Regiment Royal Artillery, 17 Port and Maritime Regiment of the Royal Logistic Corps, 24 Engineer Regiment, and 30 (Information Exploitation) Commando Royal Marines were attached to provide specialist capabilities and expertise.

Pacific

Humanitarian Missions

Although the Royal Navy no-longer maintains a permanent naval presence in the Pacific Ocean, it is always committed to providing humanitarian aid where possible. When Typhoon Haiyan struck the Philippines in late 2013, the Royal Navy deployed HMS *Daring* and HMS *Illustrious* as part of the United Kingdom's humanitarian aid mission to the region (known as Operation Patwin).[984]

Other

As of late 2014, warships deployed on the Atlantic Patrol Tasking South have routinely extended their operations into the South Pacific. The latest warship to be deployed is HMS *Lancaster*, departing the United Kingdom on 21 March 2015 for a 9-month deployment to the region.[985] *Lancaster* relieved HMS *Dragon* which had been deployed since October 2014.[986] In April 2016, the Royal Navy successfully attained Observer membership of the Western Pacific Naval Symposium (WPNS).[987]

External links

- Royal Navy: Operations[988] (royalnavy.mod.uk)

List of Royal Navy shore establishments

Ships of the Royal Navy

- *Ships by name*:
- A
- B
- C
- D–F
- G–H
- I–L
- M–N
- O–Q
- R–T
- U–Z

- fleet aircraft carriers
- escort aircraft carriers
- seaplane carriers
- amphibious assault shipping
- battlecruisers
- dreadnought battleships
- pre-dreadnought battleships
- ironclads
- bomb vessels
- breastwork monitors
- corvettes and sloops
- cruisers
- destroyers
- torpedo boats
- fireships
- frigates
- gun-brigs
- gunboats and gunvessels
- mine countermeasure vessels
- monitors
- patrol and attack craft
- royal yachts
- ships of the line

- submarines
- support ships
- survey vessels
- shore establishments
- hospitals and hospital ships
- air stations
- aircraft wings
- fleets and major commands
- squadrons and flotillas
- early English ships (1409–1660)
- early Scots ships (1329–1707)
- v
- t
- e[989]

This is a **list of shore establishments (or *stone frigates*) of the Royal Navy and Royal Naval Reserve**.

Current Royal Navy shore establishments

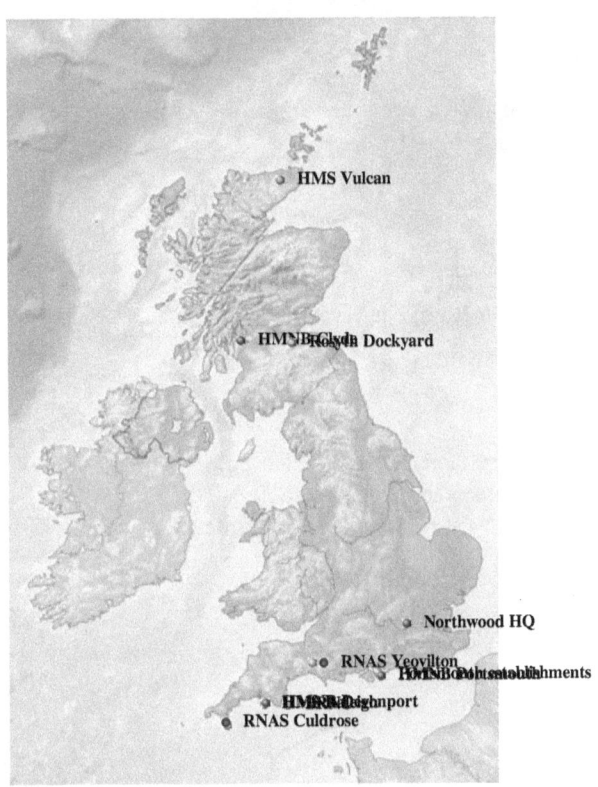

File:United Kingdom relief location map.jpg

Royal Navy bases and establishments in the United Kingdom (Portsmouth establishments: **HMS Collingwood, HMS Excellent, HMS Sultan, HMS Temeraire, Institute of Naval Medicine**)

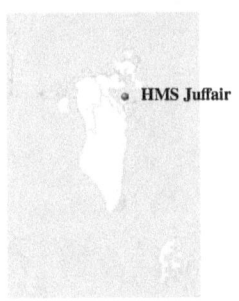

File:Bahrain adm location map.svg

Royal Navy support facility in Bahrain

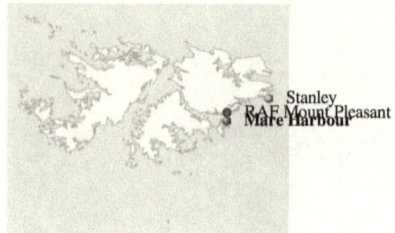

File:Falkland Islands location map.svg

Mare Harbour, the base for Royal Navy vessels in the Falkland Islands & South Atlantic

Naval bases

- HMS *Drake* (HMNB Devonport, Devonport, Devon)
- HMS *Nelson* (HMNB Portsmouth, Portsmouth)
- HMS *Neptune* (HMNB Clyde, Faslane, Dunbartonshire)

Air stations

- HMS *Seahawk* (RNAS Culdrose, Cornwall)
  - RNAS Predannack
- HMS *Heron* (RNAS Yeovilton, Somerset)
  - RNAS Merryfield
- HMS *GANNET* Prestwick, Ayrshire

Training establishments

- HMS *Collingwood* (Fareham, Hampshire)
- HMS *Dartmouth* (Britannia Royal Naval College, Dartmouth, Devon)
  - Includes *Hindostan* as static training ship
- HMS *Excellent* (Whale Island, Portsmouth)
  - Includes *Bristol* as static training ship
- HMS *Raleigh* (Torpoint, Cornwall)
  - Includes *Brecon* as static training ship
- HMS *Sultan* (Gosport, Hampshire)
- HMS *Temeraire* (Portsmouth)

List of Royal Navy shore establishments 305

Other

- HMS *Caledonia*, Rosyth Dockyard, Rosyth, Fife
- HMS *Saker* Administrative aggregation of Royal Navy personnel based in the United States
- Institute of Naval Medicine (Alverstoke, Hampshire) INM[990]
- Northwood Headquarters (Northwood, Middlesex, England), formerly HMS *Warrior*. Operational HQ for Commander in Chief Fleet

Defence Munitions Centres

Formerly Royal Naval Armaments Depot and formally elements of Defence Equipment and Support.

- DM Beith
- RNAD Coulport
- DM Crombie
- DM Gosport

Testing establishments

- Vulcan Naval Reactor Test Establishment (HMS *Vulcan*) (Dounreay, Thurso, Caithness)

Overseas naval facilities

- HMS *Juffair* (Mina Salman Port, Bahrain)
- East Cove Military Port (Mare Harbour, Falkland Islands)
- Port of Gibraltar (Gibraltar)

De facto overseas naval facilities

- Diego Garcia (British Indian Ocean Territory)
- Naval Party 1022 (Sembawang, Singapore)[991]

Current Royal Marines establishments

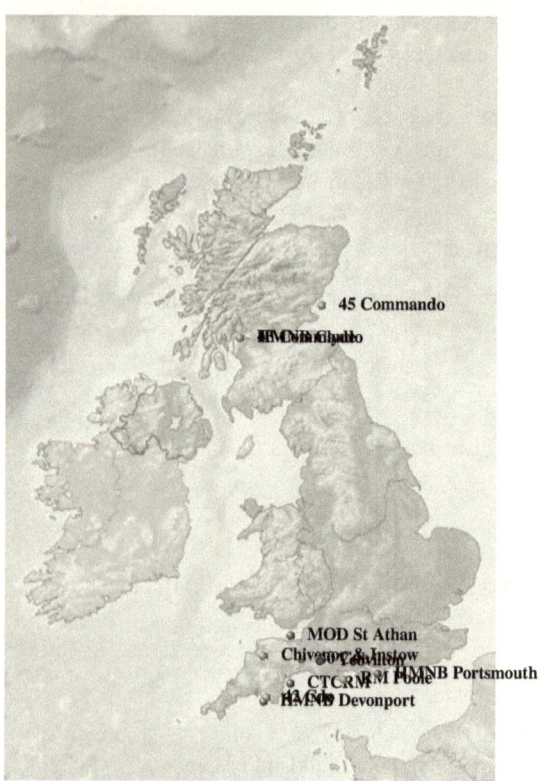

File:United Kingdom relief location map.jpg

Royal Marines Establishments - Green: **RM Units**, Blue: **Royal Navy Establishments**, Red: **Training**, Roundel: **Fleet Air Arm station**

- Commando Training Centre Royal Marines, Lympstone, Devon
- Stonehouse Barracks, Plymouth, Devon - Headquarters 3 Commando Brigade
- RM Poole, Hamworthy Barracks, Poole, Dorset
- RM Condor, Arbroath, Angus - 45 Commando
- Norton Manor Camp, Taunton, Somerset - 40 Commando
- Bickleigh Barracks, Plymouth, Devon - 42 Commando
- RM Chivenor, Braunton, Devon
- Arromanches Camp, Instow, Devon.

Significant RM presences are also located in:

- HM Naval Base Portsmouth

- HM Naval Base Clyde - 43 Commando
- MOD St Athan
- RNAS Yeovilton - Commando Helicopter Force

Royal Marines Band Service

- HMS Nelson - Portsmouth Band and School of Music
- HMS Raleigh - Plymouth Band
- HMS Collingwood - Collingwood Band
- HMS Caledonia - Scotland Band
- Comando Training Center - CTC Band

The RMBS also have 8 Royal Navy Volunteer Bands under a Bandmaster from the Band Service at:HMS Seahawk, HMS Heron, HMS Collingwood, Northwood, HMS Sultan, HMS Drake, HMS Nelson and HMS Neptune. Another Volunteer Band, baced out of Britannia Royal Naval College, doesn't have a RMBS bandmaster.

Current Royal Naval Reserve units and establishments

The modern Royal Naval Reserve has fifteen Units (with 3 satellite units). These are:

- HMS *Calliope*, Gateshead, Tyne & Wear, England
- HMS *Cambria*, Cardiff, Wales
  - Tawe Division (Swansea)
- HMS *Ceres*, Leeds, West Yorkshire, England
- HMS *Dalriada*, Glasgow, Scotland
- HMS *Eaglet*, Liverpool, England
- HMS *Forward*, Birmingham, England
- HMS *Flying Fox*, Bristol, England
- HMS *Ferret*, Chicksands, Bedfordshire, England
- HMS *Hibernia*, Lisburn, Northern Ireland
- HMS *King Alfred*, Whale Island, Portsmouth, Hampshire, England
- HMS *President*, by Tower Bridge, London E1, England
  - Medway Division (Chatham, Kent)
- HMS *Scotia*, Rosyth, Fife, Scotland (Within the grounds of HMS Caledonia)
  - Tay Division (Dundee)
- HMS *Sherwood*, Nottingham, England
- HMS *Vivid*, HMNB Devonport, Plymouth, Devon, England
- HMS *Wildfire*, Northwood, Middlesex, England

Former shore establishments

Former naval bases

- HMNB Rosyth, (Fife, UK)
- HMNB Chatham (Kent, UK)
- Woolwich Dockyard
- Deptford Dockyard
- Queenstown
- Portland Dockyard
- Scapa Flow
- Pembroke Dockyard
- Sheerness Dockyard
- Simon's Town Dockyard, South Africa
- Trincomalee Dockyard
- Malta H.M. Dockyard, H.M. Dockyard School Plus apprenticeships
- Kingston Royal Naval Dockyard
- Amherstburg Royal Naval Dockyard
- Esquimalt Royal Navy Dockyard
- Penetanguishene Naval Yard
- Naval Shipyards, York (Upper Canada)

Former air stations

- RNAS Lee-on-Solent (HMS Daedalus) (previously HMS Ariel) Lee-on-the-Solent, Hampshire, England
- HMS *Kestrel*, World War II Royal Naval Air Station at Worthy Down, Hampshire[992]
- RNAS Lossiemouth (HMS Fulmar) Lossiemouth, Moray 1946 -1972
- HMS *Jackdaw II*, Dunino Kingsbarns Fife Satellite airfield of Crail
- RNAS Donibristle, Fife 1917 - 1959 (also known as RAF Donibristle)
- HMS *Osprey*, naval air station, (Portland, Dorset, England) ASDIC training; Flag Officer Sea Training; RNAS Portland (Lynx helicopter)
- HMS *Robin*, Grimsetter, Kirkwall, Orkney, RNAS Grimsetter
- HMS *Siskin*, Gosport Hampshire, Now HMS *Sultan*
- HMS *Tern*, Twatt Orkney RNAS Twatt
- HMS *Nuthatch*, RNAS Anthorn
- HMS Goldcrest, Brawdy. Pembrokeshire.

Former Royal Naval Hospitals

- RNH Bermuda.
- RNH Bighi, Malta
- RNH Gibraltar, Gibraltar
- RNH Gillingham, in Medway, Kent
- RNH Greenwich[993], in London
- RNH Haslar, Gosport, England
- RNH Mauritius
- RNH Mtarfa, Malta
- RNH Plymouth[994], known as Stonehouse, Devonport, England
- RNH Portland, Dorset.
- RNH Simon's Town, South Africa
- Royal Naval Hospital (Hong Kong) - now Ruttonjee Hospital in Hong Kong, China
- RNH Trincomalee, Trincomalee, Sri Lanka (Ceylon)

Former shore bases

A to D

- HMS *Abastor*, Tilbury
- HMS *Abatos*, the bombed-out Supermarine factory, Woolston, Southampton
- HMS *Afrikander*, Base depot ship, Simon's Town, South Africa
- HMS *Aggressive*, Coastal Forces Motor Launch (ML) and Steam Gun Boat base, Newhaven, East Sussex
- HMS *Allenby*, Combined Operations base, Folkestone
- HMS *Ambrose*, Headquarters of 9th Submarine Flotilla (1940–1946), Dundee
- HMS *Anderson*, listening station of the Far East Combined Bureau, Colombo, Ceylon
- HMS *Ararat* (later HMS *Brontosaurus*), Combined Training Centre, Castle Toward, Toward, Argyll
- HMS *Arbella*, Combined Operations Landing Craft Training Establishment, Boston, Lincolnshire
- HMS *Appledore*, Combined Operations base and training establishment, Fremington Camp, Fremington, Devon
- HMS *Appledore II*, Combined Operations base, Ilfracombe
- HMS *Ariel* (formerly HMS *Kestrel*), RNAS Worthy Down, Winchester, Hampshire
- HMS *Ariel*, Royal Naval Aircraft Training Establishment, Culcheth, Warrington, Cheshire

- HMS *Armanillo*, Combined Operations RN Beach Commando training centre, Glenfinnart
- HMS *Asbury*, shore based transit accommodation, Asbury Park, New Jersey
- HMS *Atlantic Isle*, U-boat monitoring station, Tristan da Cunha during WWII
- HMS *Attack*, Coastal Forces MLs and storage, RN Dockyard, Portland
- HMS *Avalon*, St. John's, Newfoundland and Labrador, Canada
- HMS *Badger*, HQ of Flag Officer Harwich and Coastal Forces base (1939–1946), Harwich
- HMS *Baldur* (also HMS *Baldur II*), Accommodation and accounting, Iceland
- HMS *Beaver*, HQ, Flag Officer-in-Charge, Humber, (1 October 1940 - July 1945) - (base A.O. at Grimsby)
- HMS *Beaver II*, Coastal Forces MLs, Immingham
- HMS *Bee*, Coastal Forces MLs working up base, Weymouth (1942–1943), then Holyhead, Wales (1943–1945)
- HMS *Beehive*, Coastal Forces MTBs and MGBs, Boomer Hall, Felixstowe, Suffolk
- HMS *Bellerophon*, Portsmouth, Hampshire
- HMS *Benbow*, Trinidad
- HMS *Birnbeck*, Secret weapons research and testing (1941–1946), Birnbeck Pier, Weston-super-Mare
- HMS *Bluebird III*, (formerly HMS *Allenby*, possibly), Folkestone
- HMS *Boscawen*, Naval Police Patrol HQ, Portland, Dorset
- HMS *Britannia III*, Coastal Forces Motor Torpedo Boat & Motor Gun Boats, Dartmouth
- HMS *Brontosaurus* (formerly HMS *Ararat*), Combined Operations landing craft crew training, Castle Toward, Toward, Argyll
- HMS *Cabbala*, Training establishment for WRNS W/T operators, at Lowton near Warrington[995]
- HMS *Caledonia*, Rosyth, Fife
- HMS *Cambridge* (1956), Wembury, Devon
- HMS *Caroline* (1914), Coastal Forces MLs, Belfast
- HMS *Centurion*, Gosport, Hampshire
- HMS *Centurion*, Haslemere, Surrey
- HMS *Ceres* (formerly HMS *Demetrius*), Wetherby, Yorkshire
- HMS *Ceres*, Yeadon, West Yorkshire
- HMS *Cicala*, Coastal Forces MTBs & MGBs, Dartmouth
- HMS *Claverhouse*, Coastal Forces MLs, Leith
- HMS *Cochrane* (formerly RNAS Donibristle/HMS *Merlin*), Rosyth, Fife

List of Royal Navy shore establishments 311

- HMS *Copra*, Combined Operations Pay, Ratings and Accounts, The Moorings, Largs
- HMS *Cricket*, Landing Craft training base, River Hamble, Hampshire
- HMS *Dalriada*, Royal Naval Reserve base, Greenock, Inverclyde,
- HMS *Dalriada*, Royal Naval Reserve base, Inverkip, Inverclyde,
- HMS *Dartmouth II*, Coastal Forces MTBs, MGBs & MLs, Dartmouth
- HMS *Defiance*, Torpedo school, Devonport, Devon
- HMS *Defiance*, Fleet Maintenance Base, Devonport
- HMS *Dinosaur I*, HQ for tank landing craft training, Troon, Ayrshire
- HMS *Dinosaur II*, Landing craft and work-up base, Irvine, Ayrshire
- HMS *Dorlin*, Combined Operations RN Beach Signals and Royal Signals sections battle training, Dorlin House, Acharacle, Argyll
- HMS *Dolphin*, Gosport, Hampshire
- HMS *Dryad*, former location of the Maritime Warfare School, Southwick, Hampshire
- HMS *Duke*, Basic Training Establishment, Malvern, 1944-1945. The Telecommunications Research Establishment moved into *Duke* in 1946 (renamed in turn the Radar Research Establishment, the Royal Radar Establishment and the Royal Signals and Radar Establishment) and is now a QinetiQ research site.
- HMS *Dundonald I*, Holding and training base for RN Beach Commandos, Gailes Camp, Auchengate, Troon, Ayrshire
- HMS *Dundonald II*, Combined Signal School (CSS), Auchingate, Troon, Ayrshire

E to K

- HMS *Egmont*, Naval HQ, Fort St Angelo, Birgu, Malta
- HMS *Ferret* (later HMS *Sea Eagle*), Convoy escort base and anti-submarine training, Londonderry, Northern Ireland
- HMS *Fervent*, Coastal Forces MTBs, MGBs & MLs, Ramsgate
- HMS *Fisgard*, artificer and engineer training (1848–1983), Torpoint, Cornwall
- HMS *Flora III*, Coastal Forces MLs, Invergordon, Scotland
- HMS *Flycatcher*, HQ of Mobile Naval Air Bases during World War II, Ludham then Middle Wallop. RNAS Kai Tak from 1947.
- HMS *Flowerdown*, Y-station at RAF Flowerdown
- HMS *Foliot I*, Landing craft accounting base, Plymouth
- HMS *Foliot III*, Combined Operations holding base, Buckleigh, Plymouth
- HMS *Forest Moor*, HF receiver station, Nidderdale, Harrogate
- HMS *Forte IV*, Coastal Forces MLs, Falmouth
- HMS *Forward*, Command and radar plotting centre, Newhaven

- HMS *Forward II* (later HMS *Aggressive*), Coastal Forces MTBs, Newhaven
- HMS *Fox*, Coastal Forces MTBs & MLs, Lerwick, Scotland
- HMS *Ganges*, Boys' Training Establishment, Shotley, Ipswich, Suffolk
- HMS *Glendower* WWII training establishment, Butlin's Pwllheli holiday camp, Caernarfonshire
- HMS *Golden Hind*, WW2 RN Barracks, Sydney, Australia
- HMS *Gosling*, Royal Naval Air Establishment, Risley, Warrington, Cheshire, was a collection of 5 camps responsible for various aspects of training FAA personnel
- HMS *Gunner*, Auxiliary Patrol base, Lerwick, Shetland
- HMS *Haig*, Rye
- HMS *Hannibal*, Algiers
- HMS *Helder*, Landing craft training, Brightlingsea
- HMS *Helicon*, Scapa Flow diversionary anchorage, 1939–40, Arctic convoys concentration point, 1942–44, Loch Ewe
- HMS *Highflyer*, Trincomalee, Ceylon
- HMS *Hornet*, Coastal Forces Depot MTB, Gosport, Hampshire
- HMS *Inskip*, Inskip, Preston, Lancashire
- HMS *Jackdaw*, RNAS Crail, Fife
- HMS *James Cook*, Combined Operations Beach Training Establishment, Glen Caladh, Nr Tighnabruaich, Argyll
- HMS *Jufair*, Bahrain
- HMS *Kestrel* (later HMS *Ariel*), Royal Naval Air Station and General Service Establishment, Worthy Down, near Winchester, England
- HMS *King Alfred*, WWII RNVR officer training centre, Hove, Sussex

L to R

- HMS *Lanka*, Colombo, Ceylon
- HMS *Lizard*, Combined Operations landing craft base, Shoreham
- HMS *Lochailort*, Combined Operations officer training, Inverailort House, Lochailort, Inverness-shire
- HMS *Lochinvar*, Fleet Minesweeper base, Port Edgar, South Queensferry
- HMS *Louisburg* (also HMS *Roseneath*), Combined Operations, Roseneath, Dunbartonshire
- HMS Lynx, HQ, Naval Officer-in-Charge, Dover & CO HMS Lynx, (10 July 1945 - April 1946)
- HMS *Macaw*, Bootle, Cumbria, England. FAA aircrew reception centre.
- HMS *Malabar*, Bermuda
- HMS *Manatee*, Landing craft, Yarmouth, Isle of Wight
- HMS *Mastodon*, Landing craft, Exbury House, Southampton
- HMS *Mauritius*, Mauritius

List of Royal Navy shore establishments 313

- HMS Martelo, HQ Naval Officer-in-Charge, Lowestoft, (1 October 1945 - April 1946)
- HMS *Medina*, Landing craft and Fleet Air Arm, Puckpool, Ryde, Isle of Wight
- HMS *Mentor*, Lews Castle, Stornoway, Western Isles
- HMS *Mercury*, Communications school, Petersfield, Hampshire
- HMS *Midge*, Great Yarmouth
- HMS Minos, HQ Naval Officer-in-Charge, Lowestoft, (5 May 1942 - 1 October 1945)
- HMS *Monck*, Combined Training HQ, Largs, Ayrshire
- HMS *Monck*, Combined Operations Carrier Training, Port Glasgow
- HMS *Monck*, Roseneath, Dunbartonshire
- HMS *Monck*, HQ Flag Officer Greenock, Greenock
- HMS Nemo, HQ Naval Officer-in-Charge, Brightlingsea, (June 1940 - May 1945)
- HMS *Newt*, Landing craft base, Newhaven
- HMS *Nile*, Alexandria, Egypt (1939–1946)
- HMS *Nimrod*, Anti-submarine warfare training from early 1940, Campbeltown, Argyll
- HMS *Northney* (HMS *Northney I*, HMS *Northney II*, HMS *Northney III* and HMS *Northnney IV*), Landing craft training base, Hayling Island
- HMS *Osprey*, (from January 1941), Asdic training, advanced courses for officers, Dunoon, Argyll
- HMS *Owl*, RNAS Fearn, Fearn, Ross-shire
- HMS *Pasco*, Combined Operations landing craft signals training, Glenbranter Camp, Glenbranter, Strachur, Argyll
- HMS *Pembroke*, HQ, Commander-in-Chief, the Nore, (RN base, Chatham) Chatham, Kent
- HMS *Pembroke*, HQ, Admiral-Superintendent, Chatham Dockyard, Chatham, Kent
- HMS *Pembroke*, HQ, Commodore-in-Command, Royal Naval Barracks, Chatham, Chatham, Kent
- HMS *Phœnicia*, Manoel Island, Malta
- HMS *Phoenix*, Tipner, Portsmouth, Hampshire
- HMS *President* (parts later spun out as HMS *St Vincent*), Admiralty accounting base, Furse House, 37 Queen's Gate Terrace, London SW7
- HMS President II, HQ, Liaison Officer for Naval Reserve and Merchant Navy Duties, London, (8 February 1938 - August 1939)
- HMS *Prosperine*, Lyness, Orkney
- HMS *Pyramus*, Kirkwall, Orkney
- HMS Queen Charlotte WWII land based gunnery school, Shore Rd., Ainsdale Southport, Lancashire

- HMS *Quebec*, Combined Operations training, Inverary, Argyll
- HMS *Return*, Tokyo, Japan - now British Embassy in Tokyo
- HMS *Robertson*, Holding base for RM landing craft personnel, Kitchener Camp, Richborough, Kent
- HMS *Rooke*, Gibraltar
- HMS *Roseneath* (also HMS *Louisburg*), Combined Operations, Roseneath, Dunbartonshire
- HMS *Royal Albert*, Wireless Station (SIGINT), Cuxhaven, Germany. Post-WWII
- HMS *Royal Arthur*, Petty Officers' training school, Butlins Skegness, later Corsham, Wiltshire
- HMS *Royal Charlotte*, Wireless Station (SIGINT), Cuxhaven, Germany. Post-WWII
- Royal Naval College, Greenwich, London

S to Z

- HMS *St Angelo*, Naval HQ, Fort St Angelo, Birgu, Malta
- HMS *St Barbara*, Bognor Regis, Sussex, anti-aircraft firing range and gunnery training school
- HMS *St Christopher*, Coastal Forces training base, Fort William, Inverness-shire
- HMS *St George*, Gosport, Hampshire
- HMS *St Vincent* (1927–1969), Boys and Juniors Training Establishment, Gosport, Hampshire
- HMS *St Vincent* (1992–1998), Communications centre, Whitehall, London
- HMS *Salford*, RNR Communications Training Centre, Salford
- HMS *Sanderling*, RNAS Abbotsinch, Abbotsinch, Glasgow
- HMS *Scotia*, Basic training, 1942, from 1959 RNR Rosyth, Butlin's Ayr, South Ayrshire
- HMS *Sea Eagle* (formerly HMS *Ferret*), Eglinton, County Londonderry, Northern Ireland
- HMS *Sea Serpent*, Bracklesham Bay and Birdham, near Chichester
- HMS *Seahawk*, Coastal Forces training base, Ardrishaig, Argyll
- HMS *Sembawang* (Singapore Naval Base), was the Royal Navy's biggest dockyard and its base of operations in the Far East from 1939 until 1971. HMS *Terror* (1945–1971) was the barracks next to the naval base, while the nearby HMS *Simbang* was a RN Air Station.
- HMS *Sheba*, Aden
- HMS *Spartiate*, Western Approaches Command, St Enoch's Hotel, Glasgow
- HMS *Squid*, Tank landing craft repair base, Southampton

- HMS *Squid II*, Landing craft squadron staff, Westcliff Hall Hotel, Hythe
- HMS *Standard*, WWII training establishment for men who would otherwise be discharged, Kielder, Northumberland
- HMS *Stopford*, Landing craft working-up base, Bo'ness
- HMS *Talbot*, Manoel Island, Malta
- HMS *Tamar*, Base operated from 1897 to 1997 at two locations in Hong Kong
- HMS *Tarlair*, Hydrophone training school during World War I, Hawkcraig near Aberdour
- HMS *Thunderer*, Royal Naval Engineering College, Keyham and Manadon, Plymouth, Devon
- HMS *Tormentor*, Landing craft operational base, Hamble, Southampton
- HMS *Tormentor II* Training camp, Cowes, Isle of Wight
- HMS *Tullichewan* (previously HMS *Spartiate* II), Holding base for Combined Operations, Tullichewan Castle Camp, Balloch, Loch Lomond, Scotland
- HMS *Turtle*, Combined Operations training, Poole, Dorset
- HMS *Uva*, Diyatalawa, Ceylon
- HMS *Valkyrie II*, Training establishment for HO ratings, Isle of Man
- HMS *Varbel*, X class submarine training, Port Bannatyne Hydropathic Hotel, Port Bannatyne, Isle of Bute, Scotland
- HMS *Varbell II*, X class submarine advanced training, Ardtaraig House, Loch Striven, Argyll, Scotland
- HMS Vectis (shore establishment), Cowes Castle, Seaview, Isle of Wight
- HMS *Vernon*, Portsmouth, Hampshire
- HMS *Wagtail*, RNAS Ayr
- HMS *Warren*, Combined Operations senior officer training, Largs, Ayrshire
- HMS *Wasp*, Coastal Forces HQ, Lord Warden Hotel, Dover
- HMS Watchful, HQ, Flag Officer-in-Charge, Yarmouth, (14 April 1942 - July 1945)
- HMS *Westcliffe*, Flotilla training, Southend
- HMS *Westcliffe II*, Combined Operations holding base for RM landing craft personnel, Burnham-on-Crouch, Essex
- HMS *Wildfire*, Chatham, Kent
- HMS *Wildfire II* (1939–1940), Combined Operations base, Sheerness
- HMS *Wildfire III* (1940–1946), Combined Operations base, Sheerness
- HMS *Woolvestone*, Landing craft base, Ipswich
- HMS Yeoman, HQ, Flag Officer-in-Charge, London, (3 February 1942 - July 1945)
- HMS Yeoman, HQ, Naval Officer-in-Charge, , London, (1-30, April, 1946)

Other

- Bedhampton Camp, former non airfield satellite of RNAS Lee-on-Solent (HMS Daedalus).
- Yarmouth Roads, former fleet anchorage off Great Yarmouth, Norfolk, England (1294-1815)

Royal Naval Armaments Depots

- RNAD Broughton Moor, Cumbria, England
- RNAD Crombie, Fife
- RNAD Dean Hill, Salisbury, Wiltshire, England
- RNAD Gosport including Priddy's Hard, Hampshire, England

Royal Naval Stores Depots

Include:

- RNSD Almondbank/RNAW Almondbank/RNAW Perth, Almondbank, Perth & Kinross - now a Eurocopter installation.
- RNSD Coventry, Warwickshire, England
- RNSD Copenacre, England. (1940-1995),
- RNSD Eaglescliffe, Teesside, England
- RNSD Llangennech, Llangennech, Carmarthenshire, Wales, (1945-1995)
- RNSD Lathalmond, Dunfermline, Scotland
- RNSD Trecwn, Trecwn, Pembrokeshire, West Wales
- RNSD Woolston, Woolston, Southampton, Hampshire, England

Royal Navy Aircraft Yards

- RNAY Wroughton, Aircraft storage and maintenance unit, Wroughton, Swindon, England

Further reading

- *Shield of Empire - The Royal Navy and Scotland*, Brian Lavery, Birlinn 2007 ISBN 978-1-84158-513-0

External links

- Coastal Forces Shore establishments[996]
- Combined Operations Training Establishments[997]

Customs and traditions of the Royal Navy

There are many customs and traditions associated with the Royal Navy of the United Kingdom, many of these traditions have carried on to other Commonwealth navies, such as Canada, Australia and New Zealand. These include formal customs including separate crests associated with ships, ensigns and fleet reviews. There are also several less formal customs and traditions including Naval slang commonly referred to as Jack Speak and the traditional games of Uckers and Euchre. Winston Churchill probably never dismissed the customs of the Royal Navy as "nothing but rum, sodomy and the lash".

Heraldry

Ensigns

Commissioned ships and submarines wear the White Ensign at the stern whilst alongside during daylight hours and at the main-mast whilst under way. When alongside, the Union Jack is flown from the jackstaff at the bow, but can only be flown underway on special circumstances, i.e. when dressed with masthead flags (when it is flown at the jackstaff), to signal a court-martial is in progress (when it is flown from the starboard yardarm), or to indicate the presence of an Admiral of the Fleet, including the Lord High Admiral or the Monarch (when it is flown from the highest hoist).

Ships badges

The Royal Navy assigns badges to every ship, submarine, squadron and shore establishment. Prior to the age of steam ships, ships were identified by their figurehead. With the removal of the figurehead, ships badges and mottos were created to graphically represent the ships. The official process for creating the badge was initiated by Charles ffoulkes after World War I who was appointed as the Admiralty Advisor on Heraldry. Soon after his appointment The Ships' Badges Committee was established. This was amalgamated in 1983 with the Ships' Names Committee (founded in 1913) to create the Ships' Names and Badges Committee. The Naval Crown adorns the top of all the badges. The frame is gold rope. Originally, different classes of ships had different shapes, but currently all ships and submarines have a circular design. Shore establishments have an offset square design.

Fleet reviews

The Fleet Review is an irregular tradition of assembling the fleet before the monarch. For example, at the most recent Review on 28 June 2005 to mark the bi-centenary of the Battle of Trafalgar, 167 ships of the RN, and 30 other nations, were present. The fleet review in 2005 showed the marked contrast between the size of the Navy in 2005 compared to the last review in 1977. In total the Royal Navy had 67 ships on display, with the largest ship present being the French carrier *Charles De Gaulle* at over 200 feet longer than HMS *Invincible*.

Service nicknames

Nicknames for the service include *The Andrew* or *Andrew Miller* (of uncertain origin, possibly after a zealous press ganger) and *The Senior Service*. It is also referred to as the *Grey Funnel Line*: ship owning companies, or lines, painted their steam ship's funnels in distinctive colours such as Cunard's red and black or the eponymous Blue Funnel Line, and the Royal Navy's funnels are plain grey.

Naval salute

Originally subordinates would remove their headgear to a superior. In a book called *New Art of War*, printed in 1740, it is stated that;

> When the King or Captain General is being saluted each Officer is to time his salute so as to pull off his hat when the person he salutes is almost opposite him.

Queen Victoria instituted the hand salute in the Navy to replace uncovering when she sent for certain officers and men to Osborne House to thank them for rendering help to a distressed German ship, and did not like to see men in uniform without headdress.Wikipedia:Citation needed During the age of sail, ships' officers were always worried about mutiny and it therefore became custom that whenever an officer approached, the rating would prove that he was not armed.Wikipedia:Citation needed This was done by knuckling the forehead and later evolved into the modern Navy salute with the hand at 45 degrees, palm facing in. The reason that the palm faces in is because sailors' hands were covered in tar from the sheets and rigging and it was considered unseemly to show an officer or a member of the Royal family a dirty palm.Wikipedia:Citation needed

Toasts

The Toasts of the Royal Navy are a set of traditional drinking toasts.

Day	Toast
Sunday	"Absent friends"
Monday	"Our ships at sea"
Tuesday	"Our men" (changed in 2013 to "Our sailors")
Wednesday	"Ourselves"
Thursday	"A bloody war or a sickly season"
Friday	"A willing foe and sea-room"
Saturday	"Our wives and sweethearts" (Usually with the reply "May they never meet!"; changed in 2013 to "Our families")

In June 2013 the Tuesday and Saturday toasts were officially changed under orders from the Second Sea Lord, Vice-Admiral David Steel, to reflect the fact that women have been at sea in the Royal Navy for nearly two decades. Officially the Tuesday toast is now "our sailors" and the Saturday toast is "our families". However, the majority of personnel prefer the traditional toasts and they are still overwhelmingly used.

While most of these toasts are self-explanatory, "a bloody war or a sickly season" refers to the desire and likelihood of being promoted when many people die: during war or sickness.

The toasts are typically given by the youngest officer present at the mess dinner.[998]Wikipedia:Citing sources#What information to include By tradition, these toasts are proposed immediately after the loyal toast, on the relevant day of the week. The Navy traditionally makes the loyal toast seated, due to the evident danger of low deckheads on wooden sailing ships.

Affiliation

Ships will engage in a number of affiliations. It is often misunderstood that ships are named after places when normally they are associated with the local lord e.g. the Duke of Marlborough. There were however a number of vessels named after places during World War II after schools, cadet units and charities. At one time every Sea Cadet unit in the UK had an affiliated ship (with the exception of Kettering, which is affiliated with 800 Naval Air Squadron; Yeovilton, now disbanded; and Yeovil unit which, due to its location on RNAS *Yeovilton* (HMS *Heron*), is affiliated with 848 Helicopter Squadron). However, now that Sea Cadet units outnumber Royal Navy vessels, this is no longer possible.

Naval slang

The RN has evolved a rich volume of slang, known as *Jack-speak*. Nowadays the British sailor is usually *Jack* (or *Jenny*) rather than the more historical *Jack Tar*, which is an allusion to either the former requirement to tar long hair or the tar-stained hands of sailors. Nicknames for a British sailor, applied by others, include *Matelot* (pronounced "matlow", and derived from mid 19th century (nautical slang): from French, variant of matenot which was also taken from the Middle Dutch mattenoot 'bed companion', because sailors had to share hammocks in twos, and *Limey*, from the Lime-juice given to British sailors to combat scurvy - mainly redundant in use within the Royal Navy. Royal Marines are fondly known as *Bootnecks* or often just as *Royals*.

Uckers and Euchre

Uckers is a two player board game similar to Ludo that is traditionally played in the Royal Navy. It is fiercely competitive and rules differ between ships and stations (and between other services).

Euchre, pronounced you-ker, is a card game also played on board ships, in naval establishments and also in pubs in Cornwall and Devon. It is similar to Trumps, and equally competitive. Euchre involves nominated partners, is played only with the nine card and higher, apart from the two of spades - called the "Benny" - (making 25 cards in all) and uses the eight and seven cards as a score board. The winner is the first team to score 15.

Songs and marches

There are several songs that are commonly associated with the Royal Navy including "Heart of Oak" (the official quick march) and "Rule, Britannia!"

External links

- Royal Navy Life and Customs in World War 2[999]
- Officer/Rating Relationships in the Royal Navy 1941-1972 by Lt Cdr G Mason RN Rtd[1000]

British Army

British Army

<indicator name="good-star"> ⊕ </indicator>

British Army	
Founded	1660[1001]
Country	🇬🇧 United Kingdom[1002]
Type	Army
Role	Land warfare
Size	81,500 Regular[1003] 27,000 Army Reserve[1004]
Part of	British Armed Forces
Patron	Elizabeth II
Website	www.army.mod.uk[1005]
Commanders	
Chief of the General Staff	General Mark Carleton-Smith
Commander Field Army	Lieutenant-General Patrick Sanders CBE DSO
Army Sergeant Major	WO1 Glenn Haughton OBE
Insignia	
War flag[1006]	
Non-ceremonial flag	

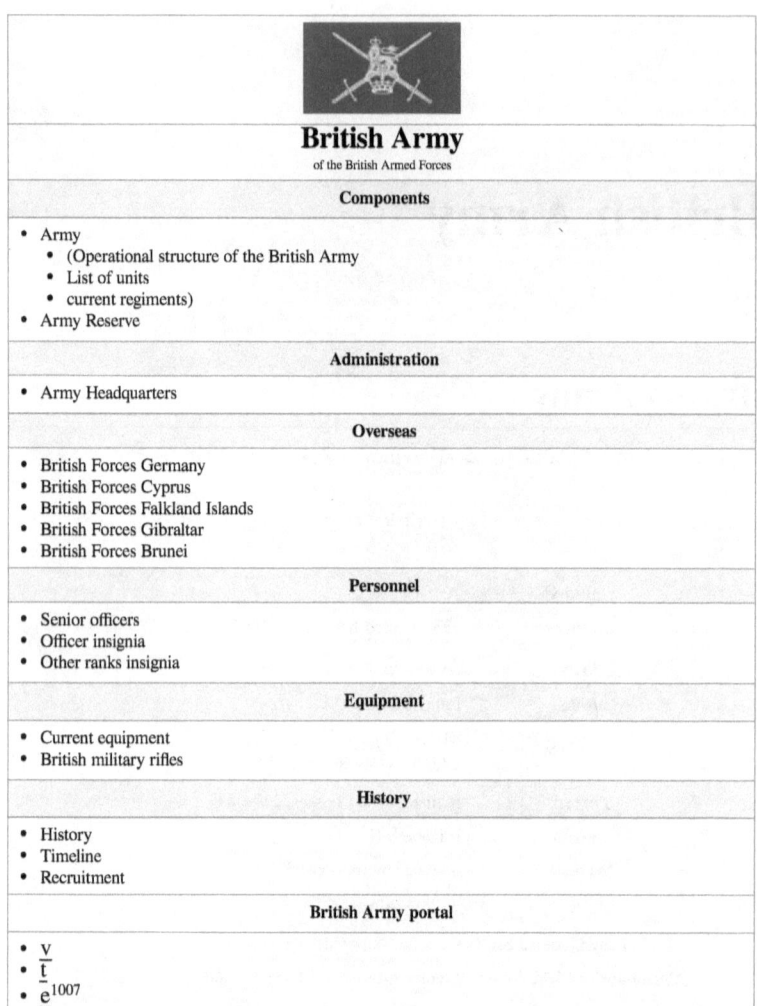

The **British Army** is the principal land warfare force of the United Kingdom, a part of British Armed Forces. As of 2018, the British Army comprises just over 81,500 trained regular (full-time) personnel and just over 27,000 trained reserve (part-time) personnel.

The modern British Army traces back to 1707, with an antecedent in the English Army that was created during the Restoration in 1660. The term "British Army" was adopted in 1707 after the Acts of Union between England and Scotland. Although all members of the British Army are expected to swear (or affirm) allegiance to Elizabeth II as their commander-in-chief, the Bill of

Figure 129: *Lord General Thomas Fairfax, the first commander of the New Model Army*

Rights of 1689 requires parliamentary consent for the Crown to maintain a peacetime standing army; hence the reason it is not called the "Royal Army". Therefore, Parliament approves the Army by passing an Armed Forces Act at least once every five years. The Army is administered by the Ministry of Defence and commanded by the Chief of the General Staff.

The British Army has seen action in major wars between the world's great powers, including the Seven Years' War, the Napoleonic Wars, the Crimean War and the First and Second World Wars. Britain's victories in these decisive wars allowed it to influence world events and establish itself as one of the world's leading military and economic powers. Since the end of the Cold War the British Army has been deployed to a number of conflict zones, often as part of an expeditionary force, a coalition force or part of a United Nations peacekeeping operation.

History

Formation

Until the English Civil War, England never had a standing army with professional officers and careerist corporals and sergeants. It relied on militia organized by local officials, or private forces mobilized by the nobility, or on hired

Figure 130: *Lord Protector Oliver Cromwell*

mercenaries from Europe.[1008] From the later Middle Ages until the English Civil War, when a foreign expeditionary force was needed, such as the one that Henry V of England took to France and that fought at the Battle of Agincourt (1415), the army, a professional one, was raised for the duration of the expedition.

During the English Civil War, the members of the Long Parliament realised that the use of county militia organised into regional associations (such as the Eastern Association), often commanded by local members of parliament (both from the House of Commons and the House of Lords), while more than able to hold their own in the regions which Parliamentarians controlled, were unlikely to win the war. So Parliament initiated two actions. The Self-denying Ordinance, with the notable exception of Oliver Cromwell, forbade members of parliament from serving as officers in the Parliamentary armies. This created a distinction between the civilians in Parliament, who tended to be Presbyterian and conciliatory to the Royalists in nature, and a corps of professional officers, who tended to Independent politics, to whom they reported. The second action was legislation for the creation of a Parliamentary-funded army, commanded by Lord General Thomas Fairfax, which became known as the New Model Army (originally new-modelled Army).[1009]

While this proved to be a war winning formula, the New Model Army, being organized and politically active, went on to dominate the politics of the

Interregnum and by 1660 was widely disliked. The New Model Army was paid off and disbanded at the Restoration of the monarchy in 1660. For many decades the excesses of the New Model Army under the Protectorate of Oliver Cromwell was a horror story and the Whig element recoiled from allowing a standing army.[1010] The militia acts of 1661 and 1662 prevented local authorities from calling up militia and oppressing their own local opponents. Calling up the militia was possible only if the king and local elites agreed to do so.

Charles II and his Cavalier supporters favoured a new army under royal control; and immediately after the Restoration began working on its establishment.[1011] The first English Army regiments, including elements of the disbanded New Model Army, were formed between November 1660 and January 1661[1012] and became a standing military force for Britain (financed by Parliament).[1013] The Royal Scots and Irish Armies were financed by the parliaments of Scotland and Ireland. Parliamentary control was established by the Bill of Rights 1689 and Claim of Right Act 1689, although the monarch continued to influence aspects of army administration until at least the end of the nineteenth century.[1014]

After the Restoration Charles II pulled together four regiments of infantry and cavalry, calling them his guards, at a cost of £122,000 from his general budget. This became the foundation of the permanent English Army. By 1685 it had grown to 7,500 soldiers in marching regiments, and 1,400 men permanently stationed in garrisons. A rebellion in 1685 allowed James II to raise the forces to 20,000 men. There were 37,000 in 1678, when England played a role in the closing stage of the Franco-Dutch War. After William and Mary's accession to the throne England involved itself in the War of the Grand Alliance, primarily to prevent a French invasion restoring James II (Mary's father). In 1689, William III expanded the army to 74,000, and then to 94,000 in 1694. Parliament was very nervous, and reduced the cadre to 7000 in 1697. Scotland and Ireland had theoretically separate military establishments, but they were unofficially merged with the English force.[1015,1016]

By the time of the 1707 Acts of Union, many regiments of the English and Scottish armies were combined under one operational command and stationed in the Netherlands for the War of the Spanish Succession. Although all the regiments were now part of the new British military establishment, they remained under the old operational-command structure and retained much of the institutional ethos, customs and traditions of the standing armies created shortly after the restoration of the monarchy 47 years earlier. The order of seniority of the most-senior British Army line regiments is based on that of the English army. Although technically the Scots Royal Regiment of Foot was raised in 1633 and is the oldest Regiment of the Line, Scottish and Irish regiments were only allowed to take a rank in the English army on the date of their arrival

Figure 131: *John Churchill, 1st Duke of Marlborough, was one of the first generals in the British Army and fought in the War of the Spanish Succession.*

in England (or the date when they were first placed on the English establishment). In 1694, a board of general officers was convened to decide the rank of English, Irish and Scots regiments serving in the Netherlands; the regiment which became known as the Scots Greys were designated the 4th Dragoons because there were three English regiments raised prior to 1688, when the Scots Greys were first placed in the English establishment. In 1713, when a new board of general officers was convened to decide the rank of several regiments, the seniority of the Scots Greys was reassessed and based on their June 1685 entry into England. At that time there was only one English regiment of dragoons, and the Scots Greys eventually received the British Army rank of 2nd Dragoons.[1017]

British Empire (1700–1914)

After 1700 British continental policy was to contain expansion by competing powers such as France and Spain. Although Spain was the dominant global power during the previous two centuries and the chief threat to England's early transatlantic ambitions, its influence was now waning. The territorial ambitions of the French, however, led to the War of the Spanish Succession and the Napoleonic Wars.

Figure 132: *The Duke of Wellington and Field Marshal von Blücher's triumph over Napoleon Bonaparte at the Battle of Waterloo*

Although the Royal Navy is widely regarded as vital to the rise of the British Empire, the British Army played an important role in the formation of colonies, protectorates and dominions in the Americas, Africa, Asia, India and Australasia. British soldiers captured strategically-important territories, and the army was involved in wars to secure the empire's borders and support friendly governments. Among these actions were the Seven Years' War, the American Revolutionary War, the Napoleonic Wars, the First and Second Opium Wars, the Boxer Rebellion, the New Zealand Wars, the Sepoy Rebellion of 1857, the first and second Boer Wars, the Fenian raids, the Irish War of Independence, interventions in Afghanistan (intended to maintain a buffer state between British India and the Russian Empire) and the Crimean War (to keep the Russian Empire at a safe distance by aiding Turkey). Like the English Army, the British Army fought the kingdoms of Spain, France (including the Empire of France) and the Netherlands for supremacy in North America and the West Indies. With native and provincial assistance, the army conquered New France in the North American theatre of the Seven Years' War and suppressed a Native American uprising in Pontiac's War.[1018] The British Army was defeated in the American Revolutionary War, losing the Thirteen Colonies but retaining The Canadas and The Maritimes as British North America.

The British Army was heavily involved in the Napoleonic Wars, participating in a number of campaigns in Europe (including continuous deployment in the Peninsular War), the Caribbean, North Africa and North America. The war between the British and the First French Empire of Napoleon Bonaparte stretched around the world; at its peak in 1813, the regular army contained over 250,000 men. A coalition of Anglo-Dutch and Prussian armies under the

Figure 133: *In the 1879 Battle of Rorke's Drift, a small British force repelled an attack by overwhelming Zulu forces; eleven Victoria Crosses were awarded for its defence.*

Duke of Wellington and Field Marshal von Blücher finally defeated Napoleon at Waterloo in 1815.

The English were involved politically and militarily in Ireland since receiving the Lordship of Ireland from the pope in 1171. The campaign of English republican Protector Oliver Cromwell involved uncompromising treatment of the Irish towns (most notably Drogheda and Wexford) which supported the Royalists during the English Civil War. The English Army (and the subsequent British Army) remained in Ireland primarily to suppress Irish revolts or disorder. In addition to its conflict with Irish nationalists, it was faced with the prospect of battling Anglo-Irish and Ulster Scots in Ireland who were angered by unfavourable taxation of Irish produce imported into Britain. With other Irish groups, they raised a volunteer army and threatened to emulate the American colonists if their conditions were not met. Learning from their experience in America, the British government sought a political solution. The British Army fought Irish rebels—Protestant and Catholic—primarily in Ulster and Leinster (Wolfe Tone's United Irishmen) in the 1798 rebellion.[1019]

In addition to battling the armies of other European empires (and its former colonies, the United States, in the War of 1812), the British Army fought the Chinese in the first and second Opium Wars and the Boxer Rebellion, Māori tribes in the first of the New Zealand Wars, Nawab Shiraj-ud-Daula's forces and British East India Company mutineers in the Sepoy Rebellion of 1857, the Boers in the first and second Boer Wars, Irish Fenians in Canada during

Figure 134: *British World War I Mark I tank; the guidance wheels behind the main body were later scrapped as unnecessary. Armoured vehicles of the era required considerable infantry and artillery support. (Photo by Ernest Brooks)*

the Fenian raids and Irish separatists in the Anglo-Irish War. The increasing demands of imperial expansion and the inadequacy and inefficiency of the underfunded British Army, Militia, Yeomanry and Volunteer Force after the Napoleonic Wars led to the late-19th-century Cardwell and Childers Reforms, which gave the army its modern shape and redefined its regimental system. The 1907 Haldane Reforms created the Territorial Force as the army's volunteer reserve component, merging and reorganising the Volunteer Force, Militia and Yeomanry.

World Wars (1914–1945)

Great Britain has been challenged by other powers, primarily the German Empire and the Third Reich during the 20th century. A century earlier it vied with Napoleonic France for global pre-eminence, and Hannoverian Britain's natural allies were the kingdoms and principalities of northern Germany. By the middle of the 19th century, Britain and France were allies in preventing Russia's appropriation of the Ottoman Empire (although the fear of French invasion led shortly afterwards to the creation of the Volunteer Force. By the first decade of the 20th century, the United Kingdom was allied with France (by the Entente Cordiale) and Russia (which had a secret agreement with France

Figure 135: *Infantrymen of the Middlesex Regiment with horse-drawn Lewis gun carts returning from the trenches near Albert, France in September 1916. In the background is a line of supply lorries.*

for mutual support in a war against the Prussian-led German Empire and the Austro-Hungarian Empire).

When the First World War broke out in August 1914 the British Army sent the British Expeditionary Force (BEF), consisting mainly of regular army troops, to France and Belgium. The fighting bogged down into static trench warfare for the remainder of the war. In 1915 the army created the Mediterranean Expeditionary Force to invade the Ottoman Empire via Gallipoli, an unsuccessful attempt to capture Constantinople and secure a sea route to Russia.[1020]

World War I was the most devastating in British military history, with nearly 800,000 men killed and over two million wounded. Early in the war, the BEF was virtually destroyed and was replaced first by volunteers and then a conscript force. Major battles included those at the Somme and Passchendaele. Advances in technology saw the advent of the tank (and the creation of the Royal Tank Regiment) and advances in aircraft design (including the creation of the Royal Flying Corps) which would be decisive in future battles. Trench warfare dominated Western Front strategy for most of the war, and the use of chemical weapons (disabling and poison gases) added to the devastation.

Figure 136: *Led by their piper, men of the 7th Battalion, Seaforth Highlanders (part of the 46th (Highland) Brigade), advance during Operation Epsom on 26 June 1944.*

The Second World War broke out in September 1939 with the Russian and German Army's invasion of Poland. British assurances to the Poles led the British Empire to declare war on Germany. As in the First World War, a relatively-small BEF was sent to France and hastily evacuated from Dunkirk as the German forces swept through the Low Countries and across France in May 1940.

After the US entered the war and the British Army recovered from its earlier defeats, it defeated the Germans and Italians at the Second Battle of El Alamein in North Africa in 1942–1943 and helped drive them from Africa. It then fought through Italy[1021] and, with the help of American, Canadian, Australian, New Zealand, Indian and Free French forces, took part in the D-Day invasion of Normandy on 6 June 1944; nearly half the Allied soldiers were British.[1022] In the Far East, the British Army rallied against the Japanese in the Burma Campaign and regained the British Far Eastern colonial possessions.[1023]

Postcolonial era (1945–2000)

After the Second World War the British Army was significantly reduced in size, although National Service continued until 1960. This period saw decolonisation begin with the partition and independence of India and Pakistan, followed by the independence of British colonies in Africa and Asia. Although the British Army was a major participant in Korea in the early 1950s and Suez in 1956, during this period Britain's role in world events was reduced and the army was downsized. The British Army of the Rhine, consisting of I (BR) Corps, remained in Germany as a bulwark against Soviet invasion. The Cold War continued, with significant technological advances in warfare, and the army saw the introduction of new weapons systems. Despite the decline of the British Empire, the army was engaged in Aden, Indonesia, Cyprus, Kenya and Malaya. In 1982, the British Army and the Royal Marines helped liberate the Falkland Islands during the conflict with Argentina after that country's invasion of the British territory.

In the three decades following 1969, the army was heavily deployed in Northern Ireland's Operation Banner to support the Royal Ulster Constabulary (later the Police Service of Northern Ireland) in their conflict with republican paramilitary groups. The locally recruited Ulster Defence Regiment was formed, becoming home-service battalions of the Royal Irish Regiment in 1992 before it was disbanded in 2006. Over 700 soldiers were killed during the Troubles. Following the 1994–1996 IRA ceasefires and since 1997, demilitarisation has been part of the peace process and the military presence has been reduced.[1024] On 25 June 2007 the 2nd Battalion of the Princess of Wales's Royal Regiment left the army complex in Bessbrook, County Armagh, ending the longest operation in British Army history.

Persian Gulf War

The British Army contributed 50,000 troops to the coalition which fought Iraq in the Persian Gulf War, and British forces controlled Kuwait after its liberation. Forty-seven British military personnel died during the war.

Balkan conflicts

The army was deployed to Yugoslavia in 1992. Initially part of the United Nations Protection Force, in 1995 its command was transferred to the Implementation Force (IFOR) and then to the Stabilisation Force in Bosnia and Herzegovina (SFOR); the commitment rose to over 10,000 troops. In 1999, British forces under SFOR command were sent to Kosovo and the contingent increased to 19,000 troops. Between early 1993 and June 2010, 72 British military personnel died during operations in the former Yugoslavian countries of Bosnia, Kosovo and Macedonia.

Figure 137: *Wrecked and abandoned vehicles along the Highway of Death*

The Troubles

Although there have been permanent garrisons in Northern Ireland throughout its history, the British Army was deployed as a peacekeeping force from 1969 to 2007 in Operation Banner. Initially, this was (in the wake of unionist attacks on nationalist communities in Derry[1025] and Belfast)[1026] to prevent further loyalist attacks on Catholic communities; it developed into support of the Royal Ulster Constabulary (RUC) and its successor, the Police Service of Northern Ireland (PSNI) against the Provisional Irish Republican Army (PIRA).[1027] Under the 1998 Good Friday Agreement, there was a gradual reduction in the number of soldiers deployed.[1028] In 2005, after the PIRA declared a ceasefire, the British Army dismantled posts, withdrew many troops and restored troop levels to those of a peace-time garrison.[1029]

Operation Banner ended at midnight on 31 July 2007 after about 38 years of continuous deployment, the longest in British Army history. According to an internal document released in 2007, the British Army had failed to defeat the IRA but made it impossible for them to win by violence. Operation Helvetic replaced Operation Banner in 2007, maintaining fewer service personnel in a more-benign environment. From 1971 to 1997, a total of 763 British military personnel were killed during the Troubles.[1030] About 300 deaths during the conflict were attributed to the British Army, including paramilitary troops and civilians.

Figure 138: *Royal Anglian Regiment in Helmand Province*

Recent history (2000–present)

War in Afghanistan

In November 2001, as part of Operation Enduring Freedom with the United States, the United Kingdom invaded Afghanistan to topple the Taliban in Operation Herrick. The 3rd Division were deployed in Kabul to assist in the liberation of the capital and defeat Taliban forces in the mountains. In 2006 the British Army began concentrating on fighting Taliban forces and bringing security to Helmand Province, with around 9,500 British troops (including marines, airmen and sailors) deployed at its peak—the second-largest force after that of the US.[1031] In December 2012 Prime Minister David Cameron announced that the combat mission would end in 2014, and troop numbers gradually fell as the Afghan National Army took over the brunt of the fighting. Between 2001 and 26 April 2014 a total of 453 British military personnel died in Afghan operations. Operation Herrick ended with the handover of Camp Bastion on 26 October 2014, but the British Army maintains a deployment in Afghanistan as part of Operation Toral.

Figure 139: *British soldiers from the 1st Battalion, Royal Regiment of Fusiliers battlegroup engage Iraqi positions with an 81mm mortar south of Basra.*

Iraq War

In 2003 the United Kingdom was a major contributor to the invasion of Iraq, sending a force of over 46,000 military personnel. The British Army controlled southern Iraq, maintained a peace-keeping presence in Basra. All British troops were withdrawn from Iraq by 30 April 2009, after the Iraqi government refused to extend their mandate. One hundred seventy-nine British military personnel died in Iraqi operations. The British Armed Forces returned to Iraq in 2014 as part of Operation Shader to counter the Islamic State (ISIL).

UK Operations/Military Aid to the Civil Authorities

The British Army maintains a standing liability to support the civil authorities in certain circumstances, usually in either niche capabilities (e.g. explosive ordance removal) or in general support of the civil authorities when their capacity is exceeded. In recent years this has been seen as Army personnel supporting the civil authorities in the face of the 2001 United Kingdom foot-and-mouth outbreak, the 2002 Firefighters strike, widespread flooding in 2005, 2007, 2009, 2013 and 2014 and most recently supporting the security services on Operation Temperer following the 2017 Manchester Arena bombing.

Modern army

Personnel

The British Army has been a volunteer force since national service ended during the 1960s. Since the creation of the part-time, reserve Territorial Force in 1908 (renamed the Army Reserve in 2014) the full-time British Army has been known as the Regular Army. In January 2018 there were just over 81,500 trained Regulars and 27,000 Army Reservists.

Following the Strategic Defence and Security Review 2010 (SDSR) and the Strategic Defence and Security Review 2015 the British Army adopted an evolving structure (known as Army 2020 Refine) that would see the number of Regular personnel set at 82,000 and see an increase in the number of Reservists to 30,000. This would bring the ratio of regular to part-time personnel in line with the US and Canada and better integrate the Army Reserve into the Regular Army.

In addition to the active Regular and Reserve force all former Regular Army personnel may be recalled for duty if required (known as the Regular Reserve)[1032]. The Regular Reserve has two categories: A and D. Category A is mandatory, with the length of time in the category dependent on time spent in Regular Army service. Category D is voluntary, and consists of personnel who are no longer required to serve in category A. Regular Reserves in both categories serve under a fixed-term reserve contract and may report for training or service overseas and at home, similar to the Army Reserve.[1033] In 2007, there were 121,800 Regular Reserves, of which 33,760 served in categories A and D.[1034] Beginning in April 2013, the full Regular Reserve strength was no longer reported—only those serving in categories A and D (30,000 in 2015).[1035]

The table below illustrates British Army personnel figures from 1710 to 2010. The Army Reserve (Territorial Army) was established in 1908.

British Army strength[1036] 1918 & 1945, 1920, 1930, 1950, 1960, 1970, 1980–2000, 2010,[1037,1038] 2015</ref>							
(1707–1800)		(1801–1921)		(1921– Present)			
Year	Regular Army	Year	Regular Army	Year	Regular Army	Army Reserve	Total
1710	70,000	1810	226,000	1921	*Interwar period*		—
1720	20,000	1820	114,000	1930			—
1730	20,000	1830	106,000	1945ᵇ	3,120,000	Included in Regular	3,120,000

1740	55,000	1840	130,000	1950	364,000	83,000	**447,000**
1750	27,000	1850	151,000	1960	258,000	120,000	**387,000**
1760	87,000	1860	215,000	1970	176,000	80,000	**256,000**
1770	48,000	1870	185,000	1980	159,000	63,000	**222,000**
1780	79,000	1880	165,000	1990	153,000	73,000	**226,000**
1790	84,000	1890	210,000	2000	110,000	45,000	**155,000**
1800	163,000	1900	275,000	2010	113,000	29,000	**142,000**
		1918a	3,820,000	2015	83,360	29,603	**112,990**

- a ^ End of the First World War
- b ^ End of the Second World War

Equipment

Infantry

The British Army's basic infantry weapon is the L85A2 or L85A3 assault rifle, sometimes equipped with an L17A2 under-barrel grenade launcher or other attachments with the Picatinny rail. The rifle has several variants, including the L86A2, the Light Support Weapon (LSW) and the L22A2 carbine (issued to tank crews). These weapons are usually equipped with iron sights or an optical SUSAT, although optical sights have been purchased to supplement these.

Support fire is provided by the FN Minimi light machine gun and the L7 general-purpose machine gun (GPMG), and indirect fire is provided by L16 81mm mortars. The L129A1 sharpshooter rifle was brought into service during the war in Afghanistan to meet an urgent operational requirement. Sniper rifles include the L118A1 7.62 mm, L115A3 and the AW50F, all manufactured by Accuracy International. Other weapons, such as the L128A1 (Benelli M4) combat shotgun, may be temporarily used.

Armour

The army's main battle tank is the Challenger 2.[1039,1040] It is supported by the Warrior Infantry Fighting Vehicle as the primary armoured personnel carrier and the many variants of the Combat Vehicle Reconnaissance (Tracked) and the FV430 series, which had its engines and armour upgraded as the Bulldog. Light armoured units often utilise the Supacat "Jackal" MWMIK and Coyote for reconnaissance and fire support.

Figure 140: *The Blues and Royals Trooping the Colour in 2007*

Artillery

The army has three main artillery systems: the Multi Launch Rocket System (MLRS), the AS-90 and the L118 light gun. The MLRS, first used in Operation Granby, has an 85-kilometre (53 mi) range. The AS-90 is a 155 mm self-propelled armoured gun with a 24-kilometre (15 mi) range. The L118 light gun is a 105 mm towed gun used in support of 16 Air Assault Brigade, 3 Commando Brigade of the Royal Marines and the Adaptive Force.[1041] To identify artillery targets, the army operates weapon locators such as the MAMBA Radar and utilises artillery sound ranging. For air defence it uses the Short-Range Air Defence (SHORAD) Rapier FSC missile system, widely deployed since the Falklands War, and the Very Short-Range Air Defence (VSHORAD) Starstreak HVM (high-velocity missile) launched by a single soldier or from a vehicle-mounted launcher.[1042]

Protected mobility

Where armour is not required or mobility and speed are favoured the British Army utilises protected patrol vehicles, such as the Panther variant of the Iveco LMV, the Foxhound, and variants of the Cougar family (such as the Ridgeback, Husky and Mastiff). For day-to-day utility work the army commonly uses the Land Rover Wolf, which is based on the Land Rover Defender.

Engineers, utility and signals

Specialist engineering vehicles include bomb-disposal robots and the modern variants of the Armoured Vehicle Royal Engineers, including the Titan bridge-layer, Trojan combat-engineer vehicle, Terrier Armoured Digger and Python Minefield Breaching System. Day-to-day utility work uses a series of support vehicles, including six-, nine- and fifteen-tonne trucks (often called "Bedfords", after a historic utility vehicle), heavy-equipment transporters (HET), close-support tankers, quad bikes and ambulances. Tactical communication uses the Bowman radio system, and operational or strategic communication is controlled by the Royal Corps of Signals.

Aviation

The Army Air Corps (AAC) provides direct aviation support, with the Royal Air Force providing support helicopters. The primary attack helicopter is the Westland WAH-64 Apache, a licence-built, modified version of the US AH-64 Apache which replaced the Westland Lynx AH7 in the anti-tank role. Other helicopters include the Westland Gazelle (a light surveillance aircraft), the Bell 212 (in jungle "hot and high" environments) and the AgustaWestland AW159 Wildcat, a dedicated intelligence, surveillance, target acquisition, and reconnaissance (ISTAR) helicopter. The Eurocopter AS 365N Dauphin is used for special operations aviation,[1043] and the Britten-Norman Islander is a light, fixed-wing aircraft used for airborne reconnaissance and command and control. The army operates two unmanned aerial vehicles ('UAV's) in a surveillance role: the small Lockheed Martin Desert Hawk III and the larger Thales Watchkeeper WK450.

Figure 141: *Challenger II main battle tank*

Figure 142: *Warrior IFV*

Figure 143: *AS-90*

Figure 144: *Guided Multiple Launch Rocket System (GMLRS)*

Figure 145: *AgustaWestland Apache*

Figure 146: *L85A2 assault rifle*

Current deployments

Low-intensity operations

Location	Date	Details
Afghanistan	2015	Operation Toral: The army maintains a deployment of 500 personnel in support of NATO's Resolute Support Mission.
Iraq	2014	Operation Shader: The army has personnel stationed in Iraq as part of the ongoing military intervention against ISIL, primarily to assist in the training of Iraqi security forces. With other elements of the British Armed Forces, there were 275 army personnel in 2016.
Cyprus	1964	Operation Tosca: There were 275 troops deployed as part of the UNFI-CYP in 2016.
Sierra Leone	1999	International Military Assistance Training Team: The British Army were deployed to Sierra Leone for Operation Palliser in 1999, under United Nations resolutions, to aid the government in quelling violent uprisings by militiamen. Troops remain in the region to provide military support and training to the Sierra Leone government. British troops also provided support during the 2014 West African Ebola virus epidemic.
Baltic states	2017	NATO Response Force: The British Army will deploy up to 800 troops in 2017 as part of its commitment to NATO to counter perceived Russian aggression against the Baltic states.

Permanent overseas postings

Location	Date	Details
Belize	1949	British Army Training and Support Unit Belize: British troops were based in Belize from 1949 to 1994. Belize's neighbour, Guatemala, claimed the territory and there were a number of border disputes. At the request of the Belize government, British troops remained in Belize after independence in 1981 as a defence force. Although the main training unit was meant to be mothballed after the Strategic Defence and Security Review, in 2015 it continued to be in use.
Bermuda	1701	Royal Bermuda Regiment: British troops have been based in Bermuda since 1701, and home defence is now provided by the Royal Bermuda Regiment.
Brunei	1962	British Forces Brunei: One battalion of the Royal Gurkha Rifles, British Garrison, Training Team Brunei (TTB) and 7 Flight AAC. A Gurkha battalion has been maintained in Brunei since the Brunei Revolt in 1962 at the request of Sultan Omar Ali Saifuddin III. Training Team Brunei (TTB) is the Army's jungle-warfare school, and a small number of garrison troops support the battalion. 7 Flight AAC provides helicopter support to the Gurkha battalion and TTB.
Canada	1972	British Army Training Unit Suffield: A training centre in Alberta prairie for the use of British Army and Canadian Forces under agreement with the government of Canada. British forces conduct regular, major armoured training exercises every year, with helicopter support provided by 29 (BATUS) Flight AAC.
Cyprus	1960	Two resident infantry battalions, Royal Engineers and Joint Service Signals Unit at Ayios Nikolaos as part of British Forces Cyprus. The UK retains two Sovereign Base Areas on Cyprus after the rest of the island's independence, which are forward bases for deployments to the Middle East. Principal facilities are Alexander Barracks at Dhekelia and Salamanca Barracks at Episkopi.[1044]
Falkland Islands	1982	Part of British Forces South Atlantic Islands: The British Army contribution consists of an infantry company group and an Engineer Squadron. Previously, a platoon-sized Royal Marines Naval Party was the military presence. After the war in 1982 between Argentina and the UK, the garrison was enlarged and bolstered with a base at RAF Mount Pleasant on East Falkland.[1045]
Germany	1945–2020	Part of British Forces Germany: Home of the 1st (UK) Armoured Division. British forces remained in Germany after the end of the Second World War. The forces were reduced considerably after the end of the Cold War and in October 2010, Prime Minister David Cameron announced large cuts in defence; all UK troops currently in Germany will leave by 2020.[1046]
Gibraltar	1704	Part of British Forces Gibraltar: A British Army garrison is provided by an indigenous regiment, the Royal Gibraltar Regiment.[1047]
Kenya	2010	British Army Training Unit Kenya: The army has a training centre in Kenya, under an agreement with the Kenyan government, which provides training facilities for three infantry battalions per year.

Structure

Arms of the British Army
Combat Arms
• Royal Armoured Corps • Infantry • Guards Division • Scottish, Welsh and Irish Division • King's Division • Queen's Division • Parachute Regiment • Royal Gurkha Rifles • The Rifles • Special Air Service • Army Air Corps • Special Reconnaissance Regiment
Combat Support Arms
• Royal Artillery • Royal Engineers • Royal Corps of Signals • Intelligence Corps
Combat Services
• Royal Army Chaplains' Department • Royal Logistic Corps • Army Medical Services • Royal Army Medical Corps • Royal Army Dental Corps • Royal Army Veterinary Corps • Queen Alexandra's Royal Army Nursing Corps • Royal Electrical and Mechanical Engineers • Adjutant General's Corps • Educational and Training Services Branch • Army Legal Services Branch • Provost Branch (Royal Military Police) • Military Provost Staff • Military Provost Guard Service) • Small Arms School Corps • Royal Army Physical Training Corps • General Service Corps • Corps of Army Music
• v • t • e[1048]

Army Headquarters is located in Andover, Hampshire. The army's structure is broadly similar to the Royal Navy and Royal Air Force, in that the four-star (general-equivalent) field commands have been eliminated. Under the Army 2020 Command structure, the Chief of the General Staff is in charge of Army

Headquarters. There are four lieutenant-general posts in Army headquarters: the Deputy Chief of the General Staff, the Commander Field Army, the Commander Home Command and the Commander Allied Rapid Reaction Corps. Army Headquarters is responsible for providing forces at operational readiness for employment by the Permanent Joint Headquarters.

The command structure is hierarchical, with divisions and brigades controlling groups of units. Major units are regiment- or battalion-sized, and minor units are company-sized units (or platoons). All units are Regular (full-time) or Army Reserve (part-time).

Naming conventions of units differ for historical reasons, creating some confusion; the term "battalion" in the infantry is synonymous with a cavalry, artillery or engineer regiment, and the infantry "company" is synonymous with an engineer or cavalry squadron and an artillery battery. The table below illustrates the different names for equivalent units.

Infantry	Cavalry	Artillery	Engineers
Regiment (two or more battalions grouped for administration)	No equivalent	No equivalent	No equivalent
Battalion	Regiment	Regiment	Regiment
Company	Squadron	Battery	Squadron
Platoon	Troop	Troop	Troop

Adding to the confusion is the tendency of units (again for historical reasons) to misuse titles for larger administrative structures. Although the Royal Artillery consists of 13 Regular regiments (equivalent to infantry battalions), it calls itself the Royal Regiment of Artillery when referring to the units as a whole. The Royal Logistic Corps and Intelligence Corps are not corps-sized, but corps in this instance are administrative branches consisting of several battalions or regiments.

Operational structure

The field forces of the British Army after the Army 2020 reforms are organised in garrison as:

- Reaction forces: A modified 16 Air Assault Brigade and an armoured division (3rd Division) of three armoured infantry brigades (1st, 12th and 20th Armoured Infantry Brigades). In 2020, this division will reorganise and consist of two armoured infantry brigades and two strike brigades.

Figure 147: *Challenger 2, Warrior, AS90, MLRS and Stormer of the Yorkshire Battlegroup*

- Adaptive forces: The 1st Division, consisting of seven infantry brigades. In 2020, the adaptive force will consist of specialised infantry battalions who will train, advise, assist, mentor and accompany operations by indigenous forces.
- Force Troops Command: Nine brigades of supporting units which supplement the reaction and adaptive forces.

For operational tasks the most common unit is the battlegroup, formed around a combat unit and supported by units (or sub-units) from other areas. An example of a battlegroup in the Reactive Force (e.g. the 1st Brigade) would be two companies of armoured infantry (e.g. from the 1st Battalion of the Mercian Regiment), one squadron of heavy armour (e.g. A Squadron of the Royal Tank Regiment), a company of engineers (e.g. B Company of the 22nd Engineer Regiment), a battery of artillery (e.g. D Battery of the 1st Regiment of the Royal Horse Artillery) and smaller attachments from medical, logistic and intelligence units. Typically organised and commanded by a battlegroup headquarters and named after the unit which provided the most combat units, in this example it would be the 1 Mercian Battlegroup). This creates a self-sustaining mixed formation of armour, infantry, artillery, engineers and support units, typically 600 to 1,000 soldiers commanded by a lieutenant colonel.

The table below demonstrates how three or four battlegroups make up a brigade and three or four brigades make up a division. A division is currently the largest unit the British Army is capable of deploying independently, although it could be grouped with three or four other divisions from a multi-national coalition to form a corps.

Type of unit	Division	Brigade	Battle-group	Battalion, Regiment	Company, Squadron	Platoon, Troop	Section	Fire Team
Contains	3 brigades	3–4 battalions (battlegroups)	Combined arms unit	4–6 companies	3 platoons	3 sections	2 fire teams	4 individuals
Personnel	15,000	5,000	700–1,000	720	120	30	8–10	4
Commanded by	Maj-Gen	Brig	Lt Col	Lt Col	Maj	Capt, Lt or 2nd Lt	Cpl	LCpl

Special forces

The British Army contributes two of the three special forces formations to the United Kingdom Special Forces directorate: the Special Air Service and Special Reconnaissance Regiments. The Special Air Service consists of one regular-army and two reserve regiments. The regular regiment, 22 SAS, has its headquarters and depot in Hereford and consists of five squadrons (A, B, D, G and Reserve) and a training wing. 22 SAS is supported by two reserve regiments: 21 SAS and 23 SAS—collectively, the Special Air Service (Reserve) (SAS [R])—under the command of the 1st Intelligence, Surveillance and Reconnaissance Brigade.[1049]

The Special Reconnaissance Regiment (SRR), formed in 2005, performs close reconnaissance and special surveillance tasks. The Special Forces Support Group, under the operational control of the Director of Special Forces, provides operational manoeuvring support to the United Kingdom Special Forces.

Local units

The British Army historically included many units from what are now separate Commonwealth *realms*. When the English Empire was established in North America, Bermuda, and the West Indies in the early Seventeenth Century there was no standing English Army, only the Militia, and this was extended to the colonies. Colonial Militias defended colonies single-handedly at first against Indigenous peoples and European competitors. Once the standing English Army, later the British Army, came into existence, the colonial Militias fought side-by-side with it in a number of wars, including the Seven Years' War. Some of the colonial Militias rebelled during the American War of Independence. Militia fought alongside the regular British Army (and Native allies) in defending British North America from their former countrymen during the American War of 1812. With the growth of the Empire around

Figure 148: *SAS cap badge*

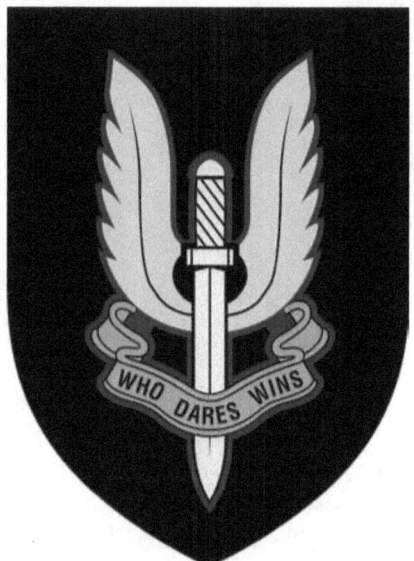

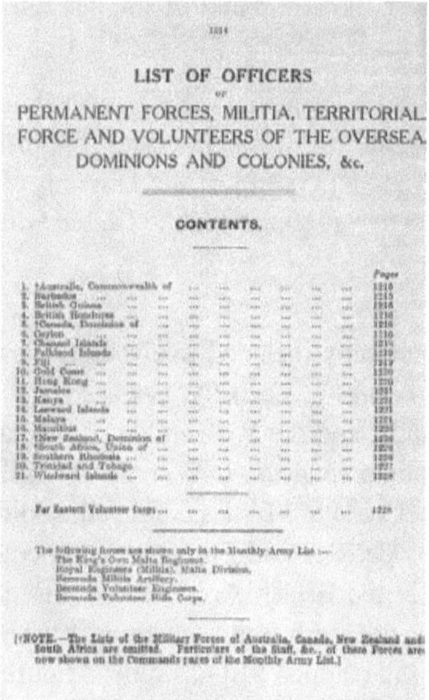

LIST OF OFFICERS
OF
PERMANENT FORCES, MILITIA, TERRITORIAL FORCE AND VOLUNTEERS OF THE OVERSEA DOMINIONS AND COLONIES, &c.

CONTENTS.

		Pages
1.	*Australia, Commonwealth of	[illegible]
2.	Barbados	1215
3.	British Guiana	[illegible]
4.	British Honduras	[illegible]
5.	*Canada, Dominion of	[illegible]
6.	Ceylon	[illegible]
7.	Channel Islands	[illegible]
8.	Falkland Islands	[illegible]
9.	Fiji	[illegible]
10.	Gold Coast	1220
11.	Hong Kong	[illegible]
12.	Jamaica	1221
13.	Kenya	[illegible]
14.	Leeward Islands	[illegible]
15.	Malaya	[illegible]
16.	Mauritius	[illegible]
17.	*New Zealand, Dominion of	[illegible]
18.	*South Africa, Union of	[illegible]
19.	Southern Rhodesia	[illegible]
20.	Trinidad and Tobago	1227
21.	Windward Islands	1228
	Far Eastern Volunteer Corps	1228

The following forces are shown only in the Monthly Army List :—
The King's Own Malta Regiment.
Royal Engineers (Militia), Malta Division.
Bermuda Militia Artillery.
Bermuda Volunteer Engineers.
Bermuda Volunteer Rifle Corps.

[*NOTE.—The Lists of the Military Forces of Australia, Canada, New Zealand and South Africa are omitted. Particulars of the Staff, &c., of these Forces are now shown on the Commands pages of the Monthly Army List.]

Figure 149: *1939 Dominion and Colonial Regiments*

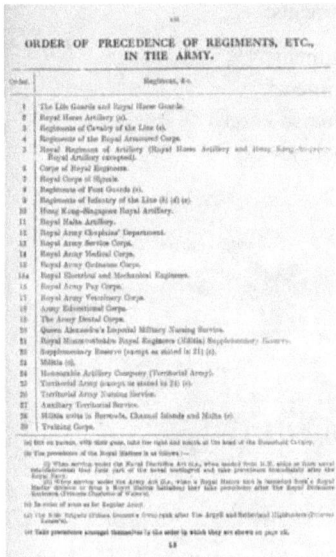

Figure 150: *1945 Order of Precedence of the British Army*

the world, *Non-European* (i.e., non-white, except for officers) units were recruited in many colonies and protectorates, but most were deemed auxiliaries and not part of the British Army. The West India Regiments were an exception, as they were fully incorporated into the British Army, but were kept outside of Europe and non-whites were denied commissions. Locally raised units in strategically-located colonies (including Bermuda, Gibraltar, Malta) and the Channel Islands were generally more fully integrated into the British Army as evident from their appearances in British Army Lists, unlike units such as King's African Rifles. The larger colonies (Australia, New Zealand, Canada, South Africa, et cet.) mostly achieved Commonwealth Dominion status before or after the First World War and were granted granted full legislative independence in 1931. While remaining within the British Empire, this placed their governments on a par with the British Government, and hence their military units comprised separate armies (e.g. the Australian Army), although Canada retained the term Militia for its military forces until the Second World War. From the 1940s, these Dominions and many colonies chose full independence, usually becoming Commonwealth realms (as member states of the Commonwealth are known today).

Units raised in self-governing and Crown colonies that are part of the British Realm remain under UK control. The UK retains responsibility for the defence of the fourteen remaining British Overseas Territories, of which four have locally raised regiments:

- Royal Bermuda Regiment[1050]
- Royal Gibraltar Regiment[1051]
- Falkland Islands Defence Force
- Royal Montserrat Defence Force

Figure 151: *Falkland Islands Defence Force on parade in June 2013*

Figure 152: *Detachment of the Falkland Islands Defence Force in ceremonial dress*

Figure 153: *John Fitzgerald Kennedy, escorted by a Bermuda Militia Artillery officer, inspects a Bermuda Rifles guard in 1961, four years before the units amalgamated*

Figure 154: *WO1 Herman Eve, RSM of the Royal Bermuda Regiment in 1992*

Figure 155: *Bandsmen of the Royal Bermuda Regiment*

Figure 156: *Royal Bermuda Regiment on parade*

Figure 157: *Changing of the guard, Royal Gibraltar Regiment (2012)*

Figure 158: *Royal Gibraltar Regiment in London, April 2012*

Figure 159: *One of the most recognisable recruiting posters of the British Army; from World War I, with Lord Kitchener*

Recruitment

Although the army primarily recruits within the United Kingdom, it accepts applications from Commonwealth citizens and (occasionally) those from friendly nations who meet certain criteria. In 2016, it was decided to open all roles to women in 2018; women had not been permitted to join the Combat Arms. The British Army is an equal-opportunity employer (with some exceptions due to its medical standards), and does not discriminate based on race, religion or sexual orientation.

The minimum age is 16 (after the end of GCSEs), although soldiers under 18 may not serve in operations. The maximum recruitment age was raised in January 2007 from 26 to 33 years, and the maximum age for Army Reserve soldiers is higher. A soldier would traditionally enlist for a term of 22 years, although recently there has been a shift towards 12-year terms with a 22-year option. A soldier is not normally permitted to leave until they have served for at least four years, and must give 12 months' notice.

Figure 160: *New College buildings at Royal Military Academy Sandhurst*

Oath of allegiance

All soldiers must take an oath of allegiance upon joining the Army, a process known as attestation. Those who wish to swear by God use the following words:

> *I, [soldier's name], swear by Almighty God that I will be faithful and bear true allegiance to Her Majesty Queen Elizabeth II, her heirs and successors and that I will as in duty bound honestly and faithfully defend Her Majesty, her heirs and successors in person, crown and dignity against all enemies and will observe and obey all orders of Her Majesty, her heirs and successors and of the generals and officers set over me.*

Others replace the words "swear by Almighty God" with "solemnly, sincerely and truly declare and affirm".

Training establishments

Royal Military Academy Sandhurst (RMAS) is the officer-training school, and Royal School of Artillery (RSA) trains the Royal Artillery. Royal School of Military Engineering (RSME) trains the Corps of Royal Engineers.

The Army Training Regiment, Grantham provides training for Army Reserve recruits, and the Army Training Regiment, Pirbright provides training for the Army Air Corps, the Royal Artillery, the Royal Corps of Signals, the Royal Logistic Corps, the Royal Electrical and Mechanical Engineers, the Adjutant General's Corps, the Royal Army Medical Corps and the Intelligence Corps.

The Army Training Regiment, Winchester trains the Royal Armoured Corps, the Army Air Corps, the Royal Artillery, the Royal Engineers, the Royal Corps of Signals, the Royal Logistic Corps, the Royal Electrical and Mechanical Engineers, the Adjutant General's Corps, the Royal Army Medical Corps and the Intelligence Corps.

There is an Infantry Training Centre at Catterick and an Infantry Battle School in Brecon. Other training centres are the Army Foundation College (Harrogate) and Army Training Units.

Flags and ensigns

The army's official flag is the 3:5 ratio Union Jack, although a non-ceremonial flag flies at the Ministry of Defence building in Whitehall and is often used at recruiting and military events and exhibitions. It represents the army on the Cenotaph at Whitehall in London, the UK memorial to its war dead. Each British Army unit has a set of flags, known as the colours—normally a Regimental Colour and a Queen's Colour (the Union Jack).

Figure 161: *Official Army flag*

Figure 162: *Non-ceremonial army flag; "Army", in gold letters, sometimes appears below the badge.*

Figure 163: *Ensign for general use by the Royal Logistic Corps*

Figure 164: *Ensign flown by the Royal Logistic Corps from vessels commanded by commissioned officers*

Figure 165: *Ensign of the Corps of Royal Engineers*

Ranks, specialisms and insignia

Officers

NATO code	OF-10	OF-9	OF-8	OF-7	OF-6	OF-5	OF-4	OF-3	OF-2	OF-1		OF(D)	Student officer
🇬🇧 United Kingdom (Edit)													*No equivalent*
	Field Marshal[1052]	General	Lieutenant-General	Major-General	Brigadier	Colonel	Lieutenant-Colonel	Major	Captain	Lieutenant	Second Lieutenant	Officer Cadet	
Abbreviation:	FM	Gen	Lt Gen	Maj Gen	Brig	Col	Lt Col	Maj	Capt	Lt	2Lt	OCdt	

[203]Rank in abeyance.

Enlisted

NATO Code	OR-9	OR-8	OR-7	OR-6	OR-5	OR-4	OR-3	OR-2	OR-1
🇬🇧 United Kingdom (Edit)						No equivalent			No insignia
	Warrant officer class 1	Warrant officer class 2	Staff/Colour sergeant	Sergeant		Corporal	Lance corporal	Private (or equivalent)	
Abbreviation:	WO1	WO2	S/Sgt / C/Sgt	Sgt		Cpl / Bdr /L/-Sgt	L/Cpl / L/-Bdr	Pte	

Each regiment and corps has distinctive insignia, such as a cap badge, beret, tactical recognition flash or stable belt. Many units also call soldiers of different ranks by different names; a NATO OR-1 (private) is called a guardsman in Guards regiments, a gunner in artillery units and a sapper in engineer units. These names do not affect a soldier's pay or role.

Uniforms

The British Army uniform has sixteen categories, ranging from ceremonial uniforms to combat dress to evening wear. No. 8 Dress, the day-to-day uniform, is known as "Personal Clothing System – Combat Uniform" (PCS-CU) and consists of a Multi-Terrain Pattern (MTP) windproof smock, a lightweight jacket and trousers with ancillary items such as thermals and waterproofs. The army has introduced tactical recognition flashes (TRFs); worn on the right arm of a combat uniform, the insignia denotes the wearer's regiment or corps.

Working headdress is typically a beret, whose colour indicates its wearer's type of regiment. Beret colours are:

- Khaki—Foot Guards, Honourable Artillery Company, Princess of Wales's Royal Regiment, Royal Anglian Regiment
- Light grey—Royal Scots Dragoon Guards, Queen Alexandra's Royal Army Nursing Corps
- Brown—King's Royal Hussars
- Black—Royal Tank Regiment

- Dark (rifle) green—The Rifles, Royal Gurkha Rifles
- Maroon—Parachute Regiment
- Beige—Special Air Service
- Sky blue—Army Air Corps
- Cypress green—Intelligence Corps
- Scarlet—Royal Military Police
- Green—Adjutant General's Corps
- Navy blue—All other units

In addition to working dress, the army has a number of parade uniforms for ceremonial and non-ceremonial occasions. The most-commonly-seen uniforms are No.1 Dress (full ceremonial, seen at formal occasions such as at the changing of the guard at Buckingham Palace) and No.2 Dress (Service Dress), a brown uniform worn for non-ceremonial parades.

Bibliography

- Bates, Gill (2010). *Rising Star: China's New Security Diplomacy.* Brookings Institution Press. p. 25[1053]. ISBN 978-0-8157-0453-9.
- BBC staff (6 January 2007). "Recruitment Age for Army Raised"[1054]. BBC News. Archived[1055] from the original on 18 November 2010.
- Beevor, Antony (1990). *Inside the British Army.* London: Chatto & Windus. ISBN 0-7011-3466-6.
- Buchanan, Michael (27 November 2008). "Irish swell ranks of UK military"[1056]. BBC.
- Burnside, Iain (19 May 2010). "Songs for squaddies: the war musical Lads in Their Hundreds"[1057]. The Guardian.
- Cassidy, Robert M (2006). *Counterinsurgency and the global war on terror: military culture and irregular war.* Greenwood Publishing Group. ISBN 0-275-98990-9.
- Chisholm, Hugh, ed. (1911). "Constantinople". *Encyclopædia Britannica.* **7** (11th ed.). Cambridge University Press. p. 3.
- Chandler, David; Beckett, Ian, eds. (2003). *The Oxford History of the British Army.* Oxford Paperbacks.
- Connolly, Sean J. (1998). *The Oxford Companion to Irish history.* Oxford: Oxford University Press. p. 505. ISBN 978-0-19-211695-6.
- Ensor, (Sir) Robert (1980) [1936]. *England: 1870–1914. (The Oxford History of England).* **XIV** (Revised ed.). Oxford: Oxford University Press. ISBN 0-19-821705-6.
- Fremont-Barnes, Gregory (2009). *Who Dares Wins – The SAS and the Iranian Embassy Siege 1980.* Osprey Publishing. ISBN 1-84603-395-0.

- French, David. *Army, Empire, and Cold War: The British Army and Military Policy, 1945–1971* (2012) DOI:10.1093/acprof:oso/9780199548231.001.0001
- Gilbert, Martin (2005). *Churchill and America*. Simon & Schuster. p. 301[1058]. ISBN 0-7432-9122-0.
- Heyman, Charles (2009). *The Armed Forces of the United Kingdom 2010–2011*. Pen & Sword. ISBN 978-1-84884-084-3.
- Holmes, Richard (2002). *Redcoat: The British soldier in the Age of Horse and Musket*. HarperCollins. pp. 48,55–57,59–65,177–8. ISBN 978-0-00-653152-4.
- Holmes, Richard (2011). *Soldiers: Army Lives and Loyalties from Redcoat to Dusty Warriors*. HarperCollins.
- Mallinson, Allan (2009). *The Making of the British Army*. Bantam Press. ISBN 978-0-593-05108-5.
- McGarrigle, Heather (6 December 2010). "British army sees more Irish recruits"[1059]. *Belfast Telegraph*.
- McKernan, Michael (2005). *Northern Ireland in 1897–2004 Yearbook 2005*. Stationery Office. p. 17. ISBN 978-0-9546284-2-0.
- Miller, John (2000). *James II*. Yale University Press. ISBN 978-0-300-08728-4.
- Norton-Taylor, Richard (5 April 2008). "Commonwealth recruitment caps & current commonwealth troop levels"[1060]. *The Guardian*. London. Archived[1061] from the original on 18 November 2010.
- OED staff (June 2013). "Rupert, n.". *Oxford English Dictionary*[1062] (Online ed.). Oxford University Press.
- OED staff (June 2013). "Taffy, n.2". *Oxford English Dictionary*[1063] (Online ed.). Oxford University Press.
- Ripley, Tim (10 December 2008). "UK Army Air Corps received Dauphins". *Jane's Defence Weekly*. **45** (50): 10.
- Rogers, Colonel H.C.B. (1968). *Battles and Generals of the Civil Wars*. Seeley Service & Company.
- Royal Scots Greys (1840). *Historical record of the Royal regiment of Scots dragoons: now the Second, or Royal North British dragoons, commonly called the Scots greys, to 1839*. p. 56[1064]–57.
- Sharrock, David (10 September 2008). "Irish recruits sign up for British Army in cross-border revolution"[1065]. London: The Times.
- SMH Military correspondent (26 October 1939). "British Army Expansion"[1066]. *The Sydney Morning Herald*. p. 5. Retrieved 18 June 2010.
- Taylor, AJP (1976). *The Second World War an illustrated history*. Penguin books. ISBN 0-14-004135-4.
- Taylor, Claire; Brooke-Holland, Louisa (28 February 2012). "Armed Forces Redundancies"[1067] (PDF). House of Commons. Retrieved 13 May

2012.

- Warwick, Nigel W. M. (2014). *In every place: The RAF Armoured Cars in the Middle East 1921–1953*. Rushden, Northamptonshire, England: Forces & Corporate Publishing Ltd. ISBN 978-0-9574725-2-5.

External links

 Wikimedia Commons has media related to *British Army*.

- British Army Website[1068]

List of equipment of the British Army

British Army
of the British Armed Forces
Components
<ul><li>Army<ul><li>(Operational structure of the British Army</li><li>List of units</li><li>current regiments)</li></ul></li><li>Army Reserve</li></ul>
Administration
<ul><li>Army Headquarters</li></ul>
Overseas
<ul><li>British Forces Germany</li><li>British Forces Cyprus</li><li>British Forces Falkland Islands</li><li>British Forces Gibraltar</li><li>British Forces Brunei</li></ul>
Personnel
<ul><li>Senior officers</li><li>Officer insignia</li><li>Other ranks insignia</li></ul>
Equipment
<ul><li>Current equipment</li><li>British military rifles</li></ul>
History

- History
- Timeline
- Recruitment

British Army portal

- v
- t
- e[1069]

This is a **list of equipment of the British Army** currently in use. It includes small arms, combat vehicles, aircraft, watercraft, artillery and transport vehicles. The primary task of the British Army is to help defend the interests of the United Kingdom, but it can also serve as part of a North Atlantic Treaty Organisation (NATO) force, or a United Nations (UN) or any other multi-national force. To meet its commitments, the equipment of the army is constantly updated and modified. To meet any shortage or requirement on operations, the army can request equipment under an Urgent Operational Requirement (UOR), which supplements planned equipment programmes.

Infantry section equipment

The infantry section normally has two four-man infantry fire teams. On operations, each fire team is usually equipped with the following:

Weapons

- L85A2 rifle
- L85A2 rifle with L123A2 UGL (underslung grenade launcher)
- L129A1 sharpshooter rifle or L86A2 Light Support Weapon (LSW)
- L110A2 Minimi light machine gun
- AT4 84mm anti-tank weapon
- L72A9 light anti-structure munition
- L84 White phosphorus smoke grenades
- L109A1 High explosive grenades
- L132A1 Smoke grenades

Vision systems

- Sight Unit Small Arms, Trilux (SUSAT) or SpecterOS[1070] Lightweight Day Sights (LDS)
- Advanced Combat Optical Gunsight (ACOG) to be used with the L129A1 rifle
- Image intensified Common Weapon Sights
- Laser Light Module Vario Ray Adaptive Target Acquisition Modules[1071]
- TAM-14 small Thermal Imaging System
- Head mounted Night Vision System (HNVS), based on the American AN/PVS-14.
- VIPER 2+ thermal imaging weapon sights
- Commander's target locating systems (CTLS)

Communications equipment

- Personal Role Radio (PRR) - one issued to each member.
- Bowman secure VHF Radio

Weapons

Firearms

Name	Origin	Type	Cartridge	Image	Details
L105A1 & L106A1, L117A1, L117A1	Germany Switzerland	Semi-automatic pistol	9×19mm		Variants of the SIG Sauer P226 were purchased as an interim weapon to replace the L9A1 Browning under an Urgent Operational Requirement (UOR) for use in Afghanistan. Although purchased as an interim weapon, they will continue to be used until the end of their life cycles.[1072]
L131A1, L137A1	Austria	Semi-automatic pistol	9×19mm		Adopted as the new standard issue pistol to replace the L9A1 Browning, and eventually, the SIG Sauer P226. The Glock 17 is a sidearm used for close combat with a magazine capacity of 17 9mm rounds. Over 25,000 were purchased.

L85A2, L85A3, L22A2	UK	Assault rifle	5.56×45mm		Standard issue assault rifle. Can be fitted with SUSAT, ACOG, Elcan SpecterOS 4X or Thermal Viper 2 sights. The LLM-Vario Ray laser aiming module and the L123 Underslung Grenade Launcher (UGL) can also be attached. A shortened carbine, the L22A2, is used primarily by vehicle and helicopter crews for self-defence. On the 11th of April, the British Ministry of Defense officially announced the adaptation of the L85A3, which is an upgrade to the L85A2 which features a number of changes, including a new handguard. The L85's in service are currently being upgraded to the new A3 standard.
L119A1, L119A2	Canada	Assault rifle	5.56×45mm		Used by the pathfinder group of the Parachute Regiment, UKSF, the Royal Military Police Close Protection Unit and 43 Commando Royal Marines. Attachments include the L17A1. It has been upgraded from the A1 to the A2 variant.
L86A2	UK	Light support weapon	5.56×45mm		Standard issue light support weapon based on the L85A2 assault rifle. It features a longer barrel, a bipod and a shoulder strap for greater range and accuracy. The L86A2 is capable of a high rate of accurate rapid fire at ranges up to 1,000 meters. It is being upgraded with picatinny rails and a new muzzle, stock and bipod.
L129A1	USA	Sharpshooter rifle	7.62×51mm		The primary designated marksman rifle, equipped with an ACOG optical sight for long-range engagements. There is also a Sniper Support Weapon version fitted with a 12x Schmidt & Bender scope and a suppressor for use by the second man in each sniper team.
L2A1	Germany	Sharpshooter rifle	7.62×51mm		Battle rifle used by the Royal Military Police Close Protection Unit and UKSF.

List of equipment of the British Army

M16A2/-M203	USA	Assault rifle	5.56x45mm		Seen used by SAS during Gulf War.
L91A1, L92A1, L80A1, L90A1	Germany	Submachine gun	9mm		Used by UKSF and the Royal Military Police Close Protection Unit.[1073] The weapon comes in multiple variants, from the standard L91A1 and the suppressed L92A1 (pictured), to the more easily concealable L80A1 and L90A1, which are stockless and have vertical foregrips.
L128A1	Italy	Semi-automatic shotgun	12-gauge		Standard issue combat shotgun used by the "point man" of an infantry section. The L128A1 has a capacity of eight rounds and a maximum effective range of 140 m (460 ft) for solid shot and 40 m (130 ft) for buckshot.
L74A1	USA	Pump-action shotgun	12-gauge		Used by UKSF as a breaching shotgun.
L118A1 L118A1 AWC	UK	Sniper rifle	7.62×51mm		Entered service in 1985, has an effective range of around 800 meters and is designed to perform in both desert and arctic conditions. The L118A1 has largely been replaced in front-line service by the L129A1 and the L115A3. The L118A1 AWC is used exclusively by the SAS.[1074]
L115A3	UK	Sniper rifle	.338 Lapua Magnum		Primary sniper rifle. It is equipped with a 25x scope, a suppressor, a folding stock, a five-round .338 Lapua Magnum magazine and has an effective range in excess of 1,100 m (3,600 ft). Corporal of Horse Craig Harrison currently holds the record for the 2nd longest recorded sniper shot in history at 2,475 meters (2,707 yd) with this rifle.

Name	Origin	Type	Cartridge	Image	Details
L121A1	UK	Anti-material rifle	.50 BMG		The L121A1 (AW50F) is intended to engage a variety of targets, including radar installations, light vehicles (including light armoured vehicles), field fortifications, boats and ammunition dumps. The standard ammunition combines a penetrator with high-explosive and incendiary effects in a single round. It is used by the SAS.
AI AX50	UK	Anti-material rifle	.50 BMG		Long range anti-material rifle based on the DNA of the AW50. The Accuracy International AX50 is a stand alone .50 BMG anti-material rifle variant that replaced the AW50.
L135A1 LRPAS	USA	Anti-material rifle	.50 BMG		Recoil-operated, semi-automatic anti-material rifle. The British Army uses the M82A1 under the L135A1 Long Range Precision Anti Structure Rifle designation.

Machine guns

Name	Origin	Type	Cartridge	Image	Details
L108A1, L110A2, L110A3 Minimi 7.62	Belgium	Light machine gun	5.56mm 7.62mm		The 5.56mm "FN Minimi" and "FN Minimi Para" is the designated light machine gun (LMG). The LMG is belt-fed and equipped with a fixed, folding bipod. One LMG is issued per four man infantry fireteam for sustained suppressive fire out to 300 m. The Minimi 7.62mm is the latest version of the weapon to enter front-line service, however the army is reviewing whether to retain the Minimi in dismounted close combat infantry platoons.
L7A2	Belgium	General-purpose machine gun	7.62mm		The designated GPMG for sustained fire out to 1,800 m. Used by two-men teams in specialised machine gun platoons for battalion-level fire support. Mounted on most vehicles within the British Army, including helicopters.
L111A1	USA	Heavy machine gun	.50 BMG		The L111A1 is the British Army version of the American M2 Browning. It can be attached to both armoured and soft-skin vehicles, or a ground-mount tripod. The weapon has an effective range of 2,000 m.

Name	Origin	Type	Calibre	Details
L134A1	Germany	Grenade machine gun	40mm	The L134A1 is used for the suppression of enemy infantry and can be mounted on both armoured vehicles and tripods. It combines the advantages of a HMG and a mortar in one; delivering a high rate of fire with fragmentation effect. The weapon has a 320rpm rate of fire and an effective range of 1,500 m (4,900 ft)-2,000 m (6,600 ft).

Explosives

Name	Origin	Type	Detonation	Image	Details
L109A1	Switzerland	Frag grenade	Fuse		British version of the Swiss HG 85 Grenade. It differs from the original in that it has a matte black safety clip similar to the American M67 grenade. It has a 3-4 second fuse, contains 155g of high explosive and has a lethal range of 10 m (33 ft).
M18 Claymore mine	USA	Anti-personnel mine	Remote		Used for specialist and defensive purposes. It has seen use in Afghanistan. It will be replaced with the Fixed Directional Fragmentation Weapon (FDFW), a Finnish designed mine that has yet to be formally identified.[1075] Procurement began in 2014[1076]
L9A8 Bar Mine	UK	Anti-tank mine	Pressure		Primary anti-tank mine. During the Gulf War, it was found to be highly resistant to mine ploughs, simply rotating under it to detonate below the vehicle, disabling some M60 tanks of the USMC after Iraq captured L9s from the Kuwaiti Army.

Indirect fire weapons

Name	Origin	Type	Calibre	Image	Details
M6-895	Austria	Mortar	60mm		Procured as an UOR. It can be fired in both the direct and indirect roles at a rate of 1–12 rounds a minute and can also be operated in the hand-held mode. Around 1,900 of these 60mm mortars were purchased as a UOR to replace the older 51mm Mortar that served on operations.

L16A2	United Kingdom Canada	Mortar	81mm		Operated by a three-man team. It is often vehicle-borne; in mechanised infantry battalions it is mounted and fired from a Bulldog armoured vehicle. Around 470 are in service.

Portable anti-material weapons

Name	Origin	Type	Warhead	Image	Details
MBT LAW	Sweden United Kingdom	Anti-tank weapon	150mm		Disposable, man-portable, short range fire-and-forget anti-tank guided missile system. It is designed to "knock out any main battle tank in just one shot by striking it from above".
FGM-148 Javelin	USA	Anti-tank weapon	127mm		Man-portable medium range anti-tank missile system. It fires a High Explosive Anti Tank (HEAT) warhead and is capable of penetrating explosive-reactive armour.
ILAW	Sweden	Anti-tank weapon	84mm		Small quantities of AT4 CS HP projectiles have been purchased.
L2A1 ASM	Israel	Anti-structure weapon	90mm		Disposable, man-portable guided anti-structure weapon. It is designed to destroy hardened structures, such as bunkers, buildings and other fixed positions.
Starstreak MAN-PAD	UK	Anti-air weapon	22mm x 3		Alongside the LML and Stormer mounted versions, the British Armed Forces also possess the high speed Starstreak Missile on a shoulder mounted and man portable launcher. This can also be used as a surface attack weapon, capable of penetrating the frontal armour of even IFVs.

Personal equipment

Protective equipment

A British Army infantryman showing full combat dress and standard personal kit (front and back views)

The standard helmet in service is the Mk.7, which replaced the older Mk 6 helmet. The Mk.7 helmet is equipped with a new harness that keeps the helmet more stable on the head when night vision equipment is fitted. It is also better integrated with new weapon sights, making it easier to use in a variety of fighting positions.

Since 2006, troops in Afghanistan (and until 2009 Iraq), have been issued with Osprey body armour. This has provided much better protection than previous body armour systems. The new Mk 4 'Osprey Assault' body armour, which replaced the older Osprey vests, provides the same ballistic protection, while improving the comfort of personnel on operations in Afghanistan. It has all the stopping power of the previous body armour, but is closer fitting, less bulky and is easier to move in. It is specifically developed to meet the British Army's requirements, using cutting edge materials and manufacturing technology.

Both the Mk 7 helmet and the Osprey armour are slated to be replaced by the Virtus system. The Virtus vest is even closer fitting and lighter than the Opsrey Mk 4, and features a quick-release mechanism to aid safe extraction from hazardous situations such as burning vehicles, and a dynamic weight distribution system which, when linked to a user's waist belt, aids in spreading the load of the armour and a bergen or other backpack across the back, shoulders, and hips. The Virtus helmet provides increased blunt impact protection, is specially shaped to allow effective weapon usage while in a prone position, and features a permanent night vision mount and a scalable counterweight attached to the helmet's rear in order to ease strain on the user's neck.

In January 2015, over 300,000 General Service Respirators had been delivered to replace the in-service S10 respirator. These respirators are also used by the Royal Navy, Royal Air Force and Royal Fleet Auxiliary.

Figure 166: *A British Army sniper showing full combat dress and personal kit.*

Multi-Terrain Pattern

The Multi-Terrain Pattern is designed and intended to perform consistently across a wide range of environments. A wide range of camouflage colours were trialled in Britain, Cyprus, Kenya and Afghanistan, ultimately the Crye's "Multicam" pattern was determined to be the best performing, across the widest range of environments (by a significant margin) and was subsequently selected as the basis for the new British MTP camouflage, and combined with the existing British DPM pattern. The MTP pattern itself was not trialled against other patterns and its adoption was based solely on its similarity to the original Crye Multicam pattern.

Boots

In 2012 the MOD purchased a newly designed range of brown combat boots from Haix, Alt-Berg, and other manufacturers for the Army, Royal Navy and RAF to replace the black and desert combat footwear previously worn. Five different boots, developed to match the Multi-Terrain Pattern uniform, are available to Armed Forces personnel depending on where they are based and what role they are in. Each of the five boot types comes in two different styles, with personnel being able to wear the particular style they find most comfortable. Black boots have been retained for wear with most non-camouflage uniforms as well as units on parade in full dress uniform, such as regiments performing ceremonial duties in central London.

- Desert Combat – worn by dismounted troops conducting medium to high levels of activity in desert type environments with temperatures exceeding 40 °C
- Desert Patrol – worn by drivers/armoured troops conducting lower levels of activity in desert type environments exceeding 40 °C
- Temperate Combat – worn by dismounted troops for medium to high levels of activity in temperate (European) climates
- Patrol – worn by mounted troops (drivers/armoured troops) taking part in lower levels of activity in temperate (European) climates
- Cold Wet Weather – worn by dismounted troops for medium to high levels of activity in temperatures down to –20 °C.

Before the adoption of the brown boots, British troops were issued with desert combat boots manufactured by Meindl[1077] and Lowa for use in Afghanistan. Both boots remain listed as part of the MOD's 'Black Bag' of operational clothing despite their official replacement by the brown boots, and may be worn by individual soldiers in lieu of the issue footwear.

Bayonet

The current British L3A1 bayonet has a hollow handle that fits over the L85 rifle's muzzle and slots that line up with those on the flash eliminator. The blade is offset to the side of the handle to allow the bullet to pass beside the blade. It can also be used as a multi-purpose knife and wire-cutter when combined with its scabbard. The scabbard also has a sharpening stone and folding saw blade.

Personal Role Radio

A Personal Role Radio (PRR) is distributed to every member of an eight-strong infantry section.

Personal Load Carrying Equipment

PLCE being used during training exercises

Soldiers need to carry ammunition, water, food and protective equipment. They use Personal Load Carrying Equipment (PLCE), a tough, modular system of camouflaged belt, yoke and pouches. To this can be added two small rucksacks and a large rucksack for additional carrying capacity, when required.

Figure 167: *Challenger 2, Warrior, AS90, MLRS and Stormer of 1 YORKS battlegroup*

The PLCM is due to be upgraded to the new VIRTUS tactical vest next year, with testing with selected units currently taking place.

PLCE is now very unlikely to be spotted on the front-lines due to the introduction of Osprey body armour, though MTP versions do exist and, due to its durability and the quantity produced, the webbing is often seen in use during training exercises.

Future Integrated Soldier Technology

The Future Integrated Soldier Technology (FIST) is a programme under development by the Ministry of Defence. The programme is designed to achieve enhanced military effect through the used of advanced technologies improving the situational awareness, lethality and survivability of soldiers. Ultimately, the programme is part of the wider British Armed Forces doctrine of network-enabled capability. 35,000 sets of kit are expected to be bought and issued between 2015 and 2020. This equipment is designed to bring the British infantryman up to standards and link with new technology currently employed, including the new underslung grenade launcher for the SA80 and the deployed Bowman communications network. It is not intended that every soldier be equipped with FIST: instead, unit commanders will request FIST kits as necessary so that they can be tailored to the situation and mission aims.

Vehicles

Armoured

Name	Origin	Type	Number	Image	Details

Challenger 2	UK	Main battle tank	331		Equips three regular and one Yeomanry (reserve) Armoured Regiments of the Royal Armoured Corps. A Challenger 2 Life Extension Project (LEP) is planned, and will include new optronics, situational awareness and fire control systems. In 2010 due to budget cuts, 118 tanks were withdrawn from service. Of these, 70 were put in storage and 48 were converted to Driver Training Tanks.
CVR(T)	UK	Armoured fighting vehicle	654[1078]		Recce (201), APC, command and ARV variants equip three Armoured Cavalry Regiments of the Royal Armoured Corps and their REME detachments. APC and command variants also in use with the Royal Artillery, while an ambulance variant is operated by the 1st Armoured Medical Regiment. Some variants have been partially replaced by the Iveco LMV, entire family to be replaced by 589 Ajax (Scout SV) starting 2017.
Warrior	UK	Armoured fighting vehicle	769		Equips six battalions of Armoured Infantry and their REME detachments. A small number are also used by the Royal Artillery for command and observation. Under the £1bn Warrior Capability Sustainment Programme (WCSP) awarded to Lockheed Martin UK, the Warrior will be upgraded and receive an improved turret and new stabilised 40mm CTA International cannon.
Bulldog	UK	Armoured fighting vehicle	895		
Mastiff Ridgeback Wolfhound	United States United Kingdom	Protected mobility vehicle	396 168 125		The 6×6 Mastiff and 4×4 Ridgback equip three battalions of Heavy Protected Mobility Infantry, the vehicles can be equipped with either a 12.7mm heavy machine gun or a 40mm grenade machine gun. The 6×6 Wolfhound is a protected tactical support variant of the Mastiff.

Name	Origin	Type	Number	Image	Details
Jackal Coyote	UK	Protected mobility vehicle	437 71		The 4×4 Jackal equips three Light Cavalry Regiments of the Royal Armoured Corps. The vehicle is also used for convoy protection and various configurations exist for the SAS too. The 6×6 Coyote is a protected tactical support variant of the jackal.
Foxhound	UK	Protected mobility vehicle	399		Equips six battalions of Light Protected Mobility Infantry.
Husky	USA	Protected mobility vehicle	311		Protected tactical support vehicle.
RWMIK Land Rover	UK	Protected patrol vehicle	371[1079]		The Revised Weapons Mounted Installation Kit equips three Yeomanry (reserve) Light Cavalry Regiments of the Royal Armoured Corps. The vehicle is also used for convoy protection and various configurations exist for the SAS too.
Snatch Land Rover	UK	Protected patrol vehicle	364		Based on the "Heavy Duty Chassis", which features much higher levels of armour and protection against IED's.
Panther	Italy	Command and liaison	401		Armoured command and liaison vehicle for commanders and officers in various cavalry and armoured formations.
TPz Fuchs	Germany	CBRN reconnaissance	11		Equips Falcon Squadron, Royal Tank Regiment.[1080]

Artillery and air-defence

Name	Origin	Type	Number	Image	Details
GMLRS	USA	Rocket artillery	35		The Guided Multiple Launch Rocket System (GMLRS), nicknamed the '70 km Sniper' or 'GSRS (Grid Square Removal System)', provides pinpoint accuracy, delivering a 200 lb high-explosive warhead to its target. It has twice the range of other artillery systems used by the British Army. Operated by the: 1st Regiment Royal Horse Artillery, 19th Regiment Royal Artillery and the 26th Regiment Royal Artillery.

L131 AS-90	UK	Self-propelled artillery	89		The L131 AS-90 is a 155mm self-propelled howitzer and is the largest piece of field artillery in the British Army. The L131 is operated by three field regiments of the Royal Horse Artillery and Royal Artillery, including the: 1st Regiment Royal Horse Artillery, 19th Regiment Royal Artillery and the 26th Regiment Royal Artillery.
L118 Light Gun	UK	Towed howitzer	126		The L118 Light Gun is used by the 3rd, 4th, 7th and the 29th field artillery regiments of the British Army. It can be towed by a medium-weight vehicle (such as a Pinzgauer) or carried around the battlefield underslung by Chinook helicopter.
Rapier	UK	Surface-to-air missile system	24		The Rapier Field Standard C is a Short Range Air Defence System (SHORAD), which is compact, mobile and air-portable, making it suitable for world-wide operations. It is a 24-hour, all-weather guided weapon system with the capability to engage two targets at once. Operated by the 16th Regiment Royal Artillery across four batteries, one of which is permanently based in the Falkland Islands.
Starstreak SP HVM	UK	Surface-to-air missile system	62		The Starstreak SP HVM is mounted on the Alvis Stormer AFV with an 8-round launcher and internal stowage for a further 12 missiles. The Starstreak HVM (High Velocity Missile) is designed to counter threats from very high performance, low-flying aircraft and fast 'pop up' strikes by helicopters. Operated by 12th Regiment Royal Artillery.
Starstreak LML	UK	Surface-to-air missile system	145		The Starstreak Lightweight Multiple Launcher (LML) is a short-range, highly mobile air defence system that holds three missiles ready for firing and can be used as either a stationary launch unit or mounted on a light vehicle, such as a Land Rover. Starstreak can also be used as a surface attack weapon, capable of penetrating the frontal armour of even IFV's. Operated by 12th Regiment Royal Artillery.

Mobile artillery monitoring battlefield radar

The Mobile Artillery Monitoring Battlefield Radar (or Mobile Artillery Monitoring Battlefield Asset) is a counter-battery radar. It detects enemy artillery projectiles fired by one or more weapons and from their trajectories locates the position of the weapon that fired it. It has a detection range of up to 30 km and can process up-to 100 projectiles simultaneously. It is mounted on a Bandvagn 206 (Bv206) all-terrain vehicle. Five vehicles are operated by the 5th Regiment Royal Artillery.

Exactor

The Exactor is a previously classified purchase of the Rafael Spike-NLOS missile system. The system is primarily used for precise indirect counter barrage attacks at long ranges (30 km (19 mi)) where the GMLRS would result in too much collateral damage. It originally consisted of six Mk2 or Mk4 missiles mounted on an M113 chassis, of which 12 were purchased directly from the Israeli Defence Force with a further two chassis leased.

In 2010, the United Kingdom hired Rafael to produce an improved Mk 5 missile and also ditched the M-113 based launchers as they were poorly air-conditioned and difficult to keep running. These new missiles were mounted on a simpler flatbed trailer containing four missiles each. This new system was dubbed the Exactor 2 by the U.K. Ministry of Defence.[1081] 18 such systems now exist within the Royal Artillery in six batteries of three

Centurion

Centurion is a C-RAM system based on the 20mm Phalanx CIWS, originally acquired for used in Basra, Iraq. It is operated by 16th Regiment Royal Artillery, and intended to intercept incoming rockets, shells and mortars out to a 1.2km square area.[1082] They are maintained by Babcock International in the United Kingdom. A total of 10 sets were purchased in 2005[1083] but since then 4 have been reconverted back to the maritime variant[1084]

Engineering and logistics

Name	Origin	Type	Number	Image	Details
Trojan	UK	Assault breacher vehicle	32		Trojan is based on the Challenger 2 chassis and is designed to breach through enemy defences, such as walls or fortifications, and clear paths through minefields. The Trojan is equipped with the Python Minefield Breaching System.
Titan	UK	Armoured vehicle-launched bridge	33		The Titan is an armoured bridge launcher based on the Challenger 2 chassis with the capability to deploy a bridge up to 60 meters long.

List of equipment of the British Army

CRARRV	UK	Armoured recovery vehicle	75		Based on the Challenger 1 chassis and is designed to recover and repair damaged or incapacitated tanks.
Terrier	UK	Combat engineering vehicle	60		Provides mobility support (obstacle and route clearance), counter-mobility (digging of anti-tank ditches and other obstacles) and survivability (digging of trenches and Armoured Fighting Vehicle slots).
Alvis Unipower	UK	Tank bridge transporter	139		The Tank bridge transporter (TBT) has the same cross-country performance as a tank even when fully loaded. It can carry 1 × No 10 Bridge or 2 × No 12 Bridges (Close Support Bridge) of the BR90 family of bridges. It can deploy, drop off and load bridges independently, but it cannot recover them.
M3 Amphibious Rig	Germany	Amphibious bridging vehicle	37		The M3 Amphibious Rigs are vehicles operated by a 3-man crew. The M3 Rigs can drive into the water, open up and join together to create a bridge of varying length. A 100m bridge can be constructed using 8 rigs.
Buffalo	USA	Talisman counter-IED	19[1085]		Mine resistant ambush protected (MRAP) armoured vehicle, which forms part of the British Army's Talisman counter-IED system.
JCB HMEE	UK	Talisman counter-IED	17		Heavily armoured excavator. It forms part of the Talisman counter-IED system. The MoD has committed to bring the HMEE along with all related Talisman elements (Minewolf, Tarantula Hawk, Buffalo, Panama and Talon) into the core budget.[1086]
Oshkosh HET	USA	Heavy equipment transporter	91		The Oshkosh HET 1070F is the Heavy Equipment Transporter (HET) of the British Army. The Heavy Equipment Transporters are capable of carrying a 72-tonne Main Battle Tank and are responsible for the strategic transportation of armoured vehicles over land.

MTVR	USA	Close support tanker	357[1087]		The Oshkosh Wheeled Tanker forms the backbone of the British Army's bulk fuel and water transportation. The Tanker can be fitted with enhanced blast-proof armour for driver protection and General Purpose Machine Guns.
MAN SV	Germany	Support vehicle	7,484		The MAN family of support vehicles are gradually replacing all 4-tonne, 8-tonne and 14-tonne cargo vehicles currently in service. They have good mobility and the ability to be fitted with armour and General Purpose Machine Guns.
Leyland, Foden	UK	DROPS	1,217		The Leyland MMLC is the Medium Mobility Load Carrier (MMLC) using a standard pallet and rack system and forms the logistic backbone of the British Army. The Foden IMMLC is the Improved Medium Mobility Load Carrier and is used primarily as an ammunition carrier in support of AS90 155mm self-propelled guns.

C vehicle fleet

The job of the Royal Engineers is to restrict the enemy's ability to advance, while also allowing friendly combat forces the freedom to maneuver as necessary. Other tasks undertaken are bomb disposal, the construction of fortifications, runways, roads and bridges and the improvement of existing infrastructure to support operations - such as improving existing roads for logistic convoys. To achieve this, the Royal Engineers operate a large and diverse fleet of vehicles. At present, the C vehicle fleet is provided by a private finance initiative (PFI) and consists of some 2,500 vehicles of over 160 types of "earthmoving plant, Engineer Construction Plant (ECP) and rough terrain Materials Handling Equipment (MHE)".

The provider of the PFI is Amey Lex Consortium (ALC), which was awarded a 15-year contract in 2005 for £600 million. The handing over of the C vehicle fleet to a PFI has improved overall efficiency, with ALC selecting common chassis for multiple roles and significantly reducing equipment types. This has led to reduced training needs in personnel, commonality of spares and an overall reduction in the logistic footprint and cost of maintenance.[1088] ALC maintains the fleet at various degrees of readiness, with a large pool of the vehicles being modified and adapted for military use - however, the majority of the fleet is maintained at commercial standards. The fleet is dispersed worldwide to accommodate both existing and future operations. When in use, the vehicles are essentially being "hired on an ad hoc basis". To help sustain the C vehicle fleet on operations, the PFI includes a logistics support package.[1089]

Miscellaneous

Name	Origin	Type	Number	Image	Details
Pinzgauer	Austria	All-terrain truck	190		The Pinzgauer is a 4×4 and 6×6 tactical support vehicle used by the Royal Artillery to tow artillery pieces, such as the Rapier and L118 Light gun.
Mowag Duro	Switzerland	All-terrain truck	190		118 Duro II and 48 Duro III are operated by communications and intelligence units. A further six Duro II and 18 Duro III are tasked with mine clearance and bomb disposal units - these have become known as Tellar and Citizen in British Army service.[1090,1091]
Land Rover Wolf	UK	Utility vehicle	12,000[1092]		The Land Rover Wolf is a militarised version of the Land Rover Defender. They can be found in service with the British Army worldwide, and can be armed with one 12.7mm Heavy Machine Gun and a 7.62mm General Purpose Machine Gun. The Land Rover Wolf is designated as a Truck Utility Light (TUL) and Medium (TUM).
Land Rover Pulse	UK	Battlefield ambulance	116		The Land Rover Pulse battlefield ambulance has full medical facilities with the capacity to hold up to six seated casualties or four casualties on stretchers. The Vehicle can be airlifted.

All-terrain vehicles

There are a number of all-terrain vehicles in service with the British Army. The Supacat ATMP is a lightweight 6×6 used by airborne and air-mobile forces. It can carry up to 8 troops with a standard NATO pallet of stores and ammunition. The Springer all-terrain vehicle is a light-role 4×2 load carriage platform, which can self-load a 1-ton pallet. Each vehicle is equipped with an 8,000 lb (3,600 kg) self-recovery winch and sand ladders, which act as loading ramps for a cargo pallet.[1093] Approximately 900 Grizzly 450 quad bikes are used as light transport for things such as mortars, ammunition and general supplies. Finally, the Harley Davidson MT350E and Honda R250 motorcycles are used by dispatch riders and for a variety of liaison and traffic control tasks.

Figure 168: *A Supacat ATMP, kitted out for operations in Afghanistan*

Special forces

The Special forces maintain a unique fleet of vehicles to support their covert operations. In 2001, 65 Supacat High Mobility Transporter (HMT) 400 vehicles were ordered under Project Minacity after being in development for a special forces protected vehicle requirement since the late 1990s. The Minacity vehicles entered service in 2003 in Afghanistan. In 2008, 24 Australian Bushmaster armoured vehicles were purchased under a UOR for the SAS in Iraq providing all-round protection unlike the Minacity with an exposed crew. It is fitted with additional armour, counter-IED electronics, and a .50 calibre machine gun mounted in a RWS.[1094] In addition, other vehicles known to be in service are: 60 Toyota Hilux for special forces mobility; and 78 ACMAT VLRAs as tactical support vehicles to resupply and sustain special forces on operations.[1095] In August 2016, the BBC reported that the Jankel Toyota Land Cruiser-based Al-Thalab long range patrol vehicle was being used in Syria.

Aircraft

Type	Origin	Class	Role	Introduced	In service	Total	Notes
AgustaWestland Apache	UK	Rotorcraft	Attack	2004	50	67	
AgustaWestland AW159 Wildcat	UK	Rotorcraft	Utility	2014	34	34	
Bell 212	Canada	Rotorcraft	Utility	1995	5	5	
Britten-Norman Defender	UK	Propeller	Patrol	2003	9	9	
Britten-Norman Islander	UK	Propeller	Patrol	1997	3	7	
Eurocopter AS365 Dauphin II	France	Rotorcraft	SAS	2009	5	5	
Thales Watchkeeper WK450	UK	UAV	ISR	2014	50	50	
Westland Gazelle	UK	Rotorcraft	Patrol	1974	34	34	

Figure 169: *AgustaWestland Apache*

Watercraft

Raiding craft

The raiding craft in service with the British Army are operated in large numbers, predominately with the Royal Engineers and the Royal Logistic Corps, for supporting both bridging and amphibious operations. These craft are highly versatile and often find themselves serving in environments ranging from the Arctic to the tropics.[1096]

Mk.4 Workboat

Four boats in service,[1097] operated by the Royal Logistic Corps as small tugs and general purpose work-boats in support of amphibious operations. They have a displacement of 48 tonnes and a maximum speed of 10 knots.

Mexeflotes

Mexeflotes are amphibious landing raft operated by the Royal Logistic Corps for amphibious operations and are designed to deliver both armoured vehicles and material from ship to shore. They are deployed on the 16,160 tonne Bay-class landing ships of the Royal Fleet Auxiliary.

Future equipment

Ajax Scout SV

'Future Protected Vehicle' - concept

- The Future Integrated Soldier Technology is a suite of equipment capable of enhancing an infantryman's effectiveness as part of the Future Soldier programme.
- The Future Rapid Effect System was a planned family of medium-weight armoured vehicles intended to replace the CVR(T) series of vehicles. This has been replaced by the Scout SV known as "Ajax" in British service and its variants.

- An Armoured Battlefield Support Vehicle (ABSV) will replace some vehicles, such as the mortar carriers, in armoured infantry units
- The Land Ceptor Missile system will replace the Rapier by 2020.
- The MAN Support vehicle is currently being introduced into service. There will be 6,928 cargo vehicles, including unit support tankers, 288 recovery vehicles and 69 recovery trailers. Deployment is planned for 2014.[1098]
- UK MOD has a requirement to acquire a new Modular Assault Rifle System (MARS) for deployment with certain military units from 2014.[1099]
- A new body armour system known as Virtus is under development as a replacement for the Osprey vest and Mk. 7 helmet.
- The MoD has a requirement for a new multi role vehicle under the Multi Role Vehicle-Protected requirement with main gate expected in 2017. At DSEI 2015 General Dynamics UK announced that they would offer variants of their Ocelot (Foxhound) and Eagle vehicles for the requirement.[1100] In July 2017, the US DSCA notified the US Congress of a possible sale of 2,747 JLTV vehicles and accessories to the UK.
- The British Army wants to purchase 8x8 wheeled armoured fighting vehicles to replace the Mastiff and Ridgeback in British Service. This program used to be part of FRES UV, later named simply UV (Utility Vehicle) and now known as Mechanised Infantry Vehicle (MIV). This vehicle is intended to equip the 4 "heavy protected mobility" battalions under Army 2020 Refine. They will also be part of the 2 Strike Brigades proposed under the Strategic Defence and Security Review 2015.
- Senior army officers and procurement officials are looking at either upgrading the Challenger 2 or outright replacing it. At DSEI 2015, army officials expressed their concern with the Challenger 2's armament and its inevitable obsolescence in coming years. Other causes of concern are the Challengers engine and electronics. The army stated that they had been in discussions with armoured fighting vehicle manufacturers about the future of the tank and its potential replacement. A later Defense News article said that the British Army would still proceed with its Challenger 2 LEP, citing that a replacement at the present would be too costly. On 22 December 2016, an assessment phase award was awarded to BAE Systems and Rheinmetall Land Systeme GmbH to progress the Challenger 2 Life Extension Project.
- Under the Non-Articulated Vehicle – Protected (NAV-P) program, the MoD is looking for a successor to the DROPS vehicles.[1101]

External links

- Equipment - British Army[1102] - Official British Army website managed by the Ministry of Defence.
- Equipment on the British Army Rumour Service[1103] - The British Military Open Encyclopedia.
- Defence Suppliers Directory[1104] - Defence industry database.
- Discover Military - British Army[1105]
- British Special Forces & Elite Units[1106] - Information on equipment used by the SAS and other UK special forces.

Structure of the British Army

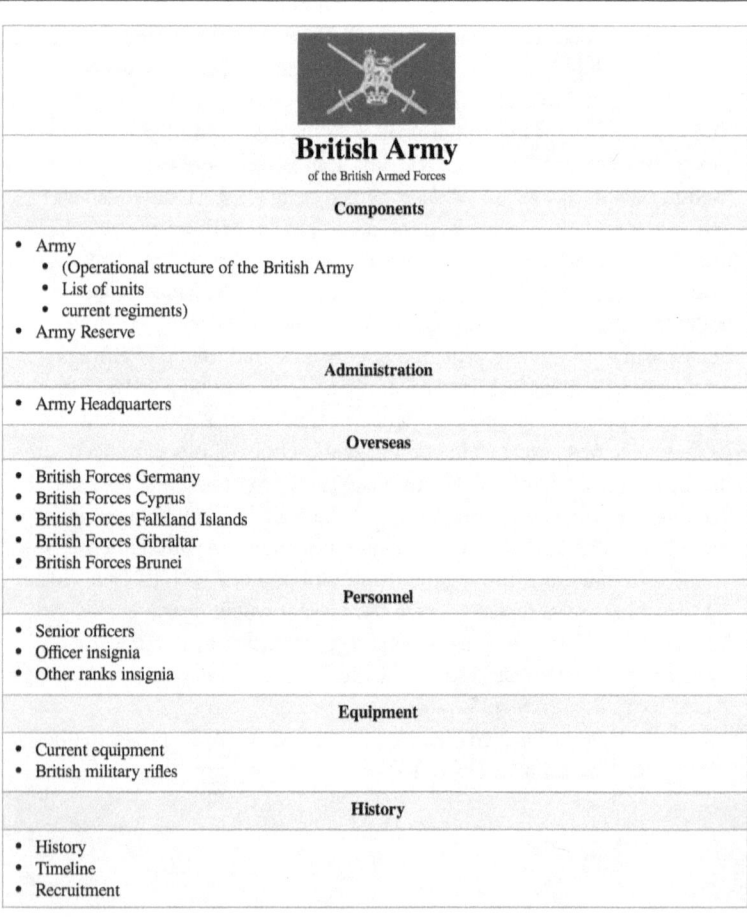

British Army
of the British Armed Forces
Components

• Army
  • (Operational structure of the British Army)
  • List of units
  • current regiments)
• Army Reserve

Administration
• Army Headquarters
Overseas
• British Forces Germany • British Forces Cyprus • British Forces Falkland Islands • British Forces Gibraltar • British Forces Brunei
Personnel
• Senior officers • Officer insignia • Other ranks insignia
Equipment
• Current equipment • British military rifles
History
• History • Timeline • Recruitment

British Army portal
- v - t - e[1107]

The **structure of the British Army** is broadly similar to that of the Royal Navy and Royal Air Force, in that the four-star (general-equivalent) field commands have been eliminated. Army Headquarters is located in Andover, Hampshire. As the top-level budget holder, this organisation is responsible for providing forces at operational readiness for employment by the Permanent Joint Headquarters. There is a Commander Field Army and a personnel and UK operations command, Home Command.

The command structure is hierarchical with divisions and brigades controlling groupings of units from an administrative perspective. Major Units are regiment or battalion-sized with minor units being either company sized sub-units or platoons. All units within the service are either Regular (full-time) or Army Reserve (full-time or casual), or a combination with sub-units of each type.

Naming conventions of units differ for traditional British historical reasons, creating a significant opportunity for confusion; an infantry battalion is equivalent to a cavalry regiment. An infantry regiment is an administrative and ceremonial organisation only, and may include several battalions. For operational tasks, a battle group will be formed around a combat unit, supported by units or sub-units from other areas. An example would be a squadron of tanks attached to an armoured infantry battle group, together with a reconnaissance troop, artillery battery and engineering support.

Since the 1957 Defence Review, the structure of the Army has consistently shrunk. A comparison of the List of British Army Regiments (1962), the List of British Army Regiments (1994) and the List of British Army Regiments (2008) will show the steep decline in the number of infantry and armoured regiments. Since 1990, reductions have been almost constant, through succeeding defence reviews: Options for Change (1990), Front Line First (1994), the Strategic Defence Review of 1998, Delivering Security in a Changing World (2003), and the Strategic Defence and Security Review of 2010. However, the 2015 Review indicated no change from the personnel number targets set in 2010.

Army Headquarters

Through a major army reorganisation effective 1 November 2011, the Chief of the General Staff took direct command of the Army through a new structure, based at Andover[1108] and known as "Army Headquarters".[1109,1110]

Reporting to the Chief of the General Staff are four lieutenant-generals: the Deputy Chief of the General Staff; the Commander Field Army (CFA); the Commander Home Command (CHC), and Commander Allied Rapid Reaction Corps. The CFA is responsible for generating and preparing forces for current and contingency operations; he commands 1st (United Kingdom) Division, 3rd (United Kingdom) Division, and Force Troops Command (FTC). CHC is responsible for commanding a wide variety or organisations that both contribute to the administrative running of the Army (i.e. the Army Personnel Centre (APC) in Glasgow), and focuses on the 'home base' (i.e. Regional Command).

Formations

Commands

A command is a military formation that handles a specific task or region, and can direct forces as large as multiple corps or as little as a few battalions. Previously the Army had regional commands in the UK, including Aldershot Command, Eastern Command, Northern Command, Scottish Command, Southern Command and Western Command. In addition, there were functional commands, such as Anti-Aircraft Command (disbanded in the 1950s), and overseas commands, such as Middle East Command. Gradually, these were consolidated into a land command in the UK, Headquarters UK Land Forces, and a land command in Germany, British Army of the Rhine. Eventually, both were merged into Land Command and later, Field Army.

From 1995, UK commands and later districts were replaced by regenerative divisions. 2nd Division, 4th Division, 5th Division and London District acted as regional commands within the UK reporting to Commander Regional Forces. Scotland District was absorbed by 2nd Division in 2000. The divisions were responsible for training subordinate formations and units under their command for operations in the UK, such as Military Aid to the Civil Community, as well as training units for overseas deployments. 2nd, 4th and 5th Divisions were replaced by Support Command on 1 November 2011.[1111]

London District includes many units with significant ceremonial roles. The Queen's Guard at Buckingham Palace and Windsor Castle is primarily mounted by the two Foot Guards Battalions and one Line Infantry Battalion, together with the Foot Guards Incremental companies: Nijmegen Company, Grenadier Guards, No 7 Company, Coldstream Guards, and F Company, Scots Guards. The guard at Horse Guards is normally drawn from the Household Cavalry Mounted Regiment (HCMR). The Honourable Artillery Company carries out public duties in the City of London. The HAC and the King's Troop, Royal Horse Artillery provide gun salutes in London. Under the General Officer Commanding Scotland, public duties in Edinburgh are the responsibility of a new incremental company, Balaklava Company, 5th Battalion, the Royal Regiment of Scotland (Argyll and Sutherland Highlanders), formed after the reduction of the Argylls from battalion status.

Corps

British Army lists
Commands and Army groups
Field armies in the First World War
Field armies in the Second World War
Corps in the First World War
Corps in the Second World War
Divisions in the First World War
Divisions in the Second World War
Brigades in the First World War
Brigades in the Second World War
Royal Armoured Corps Regiments in Second World War
Royal Artillery Batteries
Regiments of Foot
Regiments in 1881
Territorial Force Units in 1908
Yeomanry Regiments converted to Royal Artillery
Regiments in 1962
Regiments in 1994
Regiments in 2008
Territorial Army units in 2012

Present-day Regiments
Nicknames of regiments

A corps, in the sense of a field fighting formation, is a formation of two or more divisions, potentially 50,000 personnel or more. While the British Army has no standing corps headquarters, forces are allocated through a number of multinational arrangements to the North Atlantic Treaty Organisation (NATO) and European commitments, providing much of the headquarters capability and framework for the multinational Allied Rapid Reaction Corps. The last purely British corps, I (BR) Corps, disbanded in Germany after the end of the Cold War.

The word corps is also used for administrative groupings by common function, such as the Royal Armoured Corps and Army Air Corps. Various Combat Support Arms and Services are referred to in the wider sense as a Corps, such as the Royal Corps of Signals.

Divisions

A division is a formation of three or four brigades, around twenty thousand personnel, commanded by a Major General.

The British Army has two deployable divisions, capable of deploying the headquarters and subordinate formations immediately to operations.

- 1st (United Kingdom) Division
- 3rd (United Kingdom) Division

London District is responsible for the maintenance of capability for the defence of the capital and the provision of ceremonial units and garrisons for the Crown Estate in London, such as the Tower of London.

Several infantry regiments are organised into four administrative divisions based on the type of infantry unit or traditional recruiting areas:

- Guards Division
- Scottish, Welsh and Irish Division
- King's Division
- Queen's Division

Brigades

A brigade contains three or four battalion-sized units, around 5,000 personnel, and is commanded by a one star officer, a Brigadier. The brigade will contain a wide range of military disciplines allowing the conduct of a spectrum of military tasks.

The brigade would be required to deploy up to three separate battlegroups, the primary tactical formation employed in British doctrine. The battlegroup is a mixed formation built around the core of one unit, an armoured regiment or infantry battalion, with sub-units providing artillery, engineers, logistics, aviation, etc., as required.

Combat formations include:

- 4th Infantry Brigade
- 7th Infantry Brigade
- 11th Infantry Brigade
- 38th Infantry Brigade
- 51st Infantry Brigade
- 160th Infantry Brigade
- 1st Armoured Infantry Brigade
- 12th Armoured Infantry Brigade
- 20th Armoured Infantry Brigade
- 16 Air Assault Brigade

There are also several non-combat focused service support units of brigade size.

Order of precedence

The British Army parades according to the order of precedence, from right to left, with the unit at the extreme right being highest on the order. The Household Cavalry has the highest precedence, unless the Royal Horse Artillery parades with its guns.

Army 2020

In 2010, the incoming government conducted a defence review. Those elements affecting the army were released as part of the Future British Army Structure (Next Steps) publication,[1112] which was superseded by the "Army 2020" concept announced in 2012. Under Army 2020 the army will be divided into:

- **Reaction forces** comprising a modified 16 Air Assault Brigade and an armoured division (3rd (UK) Division) of three armoured infantry brigades. These will be the 1st, 12th and 20th Armoured Infantry Brigades.[1113]
- **Adaptive forces** comprising a division (1st (UK) Division) of seven infantry brigades, three of which (the 4th, 7th, and 51st) will be deployable. This will be assisted by another 2-star command, Support Command (United Kingdom)[1114,1115,1116]
- **Force troops and logistics** support comprising eight brigades.

All units from Germany will gradually move back to the UK. The basing plan was released on 5 March 2013. This positions 3rd (UK) Division as the head of the Reaction Force. 1st (UK) Division is the division in charge of the Adaptable Force being based in York. This basing plan locates all three Reaction Force Brigades, along with the three Armoured Regiments and the six Armoured Infantry Battalions, in the Salisbury Plain training area.[1117]

Refinements to the plans following the 2015 Strategic Defence and Security Review became known as "Army 2020 Refine".

Arms and services

Combat Arms

The Combat Arms are the "teeth" of the British Army, infantry, armoured and aviation units which engage in close action.

Household Cavalry and Royal Armoured Corps

Regiments of line cavalry and the Royal Tank Regiment together form the Royal Armoured Corps which has units equipped with either main battle tanks, light armour for reconnaissance, or lightly armoured vehicles for the light cavalry role. An additional reconnaissance regiment is provided by the Household Cavalry Regiment, of the Household Cavalry, which administratively is not considered to be part of the RAC, but is included among the RAC order of battle for operational tasking.

Armoured Regiments	Armoured Cavalry Regiments	Light Cavalry Regiments
The King's Royal Hussars	Household Cavalry Regiment	1st The Queen's Dragoon Guards
The Queen's Royal Hussars (Queen's Own and Royal Irish)	The Royal Dragoon Guards	The Royal Scots Dragoon Guards (Carabiniers and Greys)
The Royal Tank Regiment	The Royal Lancers (Queen Elizabeth's Own)	The Light Dragoons

Infantry

The Infantry is divided for administrative purposes into four 'divisions', with battalions being trained and equipped to operate in one of six main roles:

- Air Assault Infantry
- Armoured Infantry
- Light Infantry
- Mechanised Infantry
- Specialised Training Infantry
- Public Duties

Under the arms-plot system, a battalion would spend between two and six years in one role, before re-training for another. Following a review of the operation of the army, it has been demonstrated that this system is inefficient and is being phased out, with battalions specialising in role—this will see armoured infantry, mechanised infantry and air assault battalions remaining in a single posting; however, light infantry battalions will continue to be periodically rotated between postings. Personnel will be "trickle posted" between battalions of the same regiment as required, and to further their careers.

Guards Division	Scottish, Welsh and Irish Division	King's Division	Queen's Division
1st Bn, Grenadier Guards	1st, 2nd, 3rd & 4th Bn, The Royal Regiment of Scotland	1st & 2nd Bn, The Duke of Lancaster's Regiment (King's Lancashire and Border)	1st & 2nd Bn, The Princess of Wales's Royal Regiment (Queen's and Royal Hampshires)
1st Bn, Coldstream Guards	1st Bn, The Royal Welsh	1st & 2nd Bn The Yorkshire Regiment (14th/-15th, 19th and 33rd/76th Foot)	1st Bn, The Royal Regiment of Fusiliers
1st Bn, Scots Guards	1st Bn, The Royal Irish Regiment (27th (Inniskilling) 83rd and 87th and The Ulster Defence Regiment)	1st & 2nd Bn, The Mercian Regiment (Cheshire, Worcesters and Foresters, and Staffords)	1st & 2nd Bn, The Royal Anglian Regiment
1st Bn, Irish Guards			The Royal Gibraltar Regiment
1st Bn, Welsh Guards			

Three further infantry units in the regular army are not grouped within the various infantry divisions:

- 1st, 2nd & 3rd Bn, The Parachute Regiment

- 1st & 2nd Bn, The Royal Gurkha Rifles
- 1st, 2nd, 3rd, 4th & 5th Bn, The Rifles

The role of the Royal Gibraltar Regiment is limited to the defence of Gibraltar.

The three senior regiments of foot guards, plus the Royal Regiment of Scotland, each maintain an additional reinforced company that retains custody of the colours of battalions that are in suspended animation:

- Nijmegen Company, Grenadier Guards (ex 2nd Bn, Grenadier Guards)
- No. 7 Company, Coldstream Guards (ex 2nd Bn, Coldstream Guards)
- F Company, Scots Guards (ex 2nd Bn, Scots Guards)
- Balaklava Company, Argyll & Sutherland Highlanders, The Royal Regiment of Scotland (ex 5th Bn, The Royal Regiment of Scotland)

Brigade of Gurkhas

The Royal Gurkha Rifles is the largest element of the Brigade of Gurkhas, which includes its own support arms. These units are affiliated to the equivalent British units, but have their own unique cap badges.

- Support units of the Brigade of Gurkhas
  - Queen's Gurkha Engineers:
    - 69 Field Squadron, 36 Engineer Regiment, Royal Engineers
    - 70 Field Support Squadron, 36 Engineer Regiment, Royal Engineers
  - Queen's Gurkha Signals:
    - 246 Gurkha Signal Squadron, 2 Signal Regiment, Royal Signals
    - 248 Gurkha Signal Squadron, 22 Signal Regiment, Royal Signals
    - 250 Gurkha Signal Squadron, 30 Signal Regiment, Royal Signals
  - 10 Queen's Own Gurkha Logistic Regiment RLC

Special Forces

- Special Air Service – The Regular Army's special forces formation is a single, battalion sized unit, 22nd SAS Regiment.
- Special Forces Support Group – A tri-service unit formed around 1st Battalion, Parachute Regiment and enhanced with personnel from Combat Support Services, the Royal Marines and RAF Regiment. SFSG is designed to provide support to Special Forces operations.
- Special Reconnaissance Regiment – A tri-service element of the United Kingdom Special Forces alongside the SAS and Special Boat Service.

Note: UKSF is considered a joint organisation and as such falls outside the Army chain of command.

Combat Support Arms

The Combat Support Arms provide direct support to the Combat Arms and include artillery, engineer, signals and aviation.

Royal Regiment of Artillery

The Royal Artillery consists of 13 Regular Regiments and 5 Reserve Regiments along with the ceremonial King's Troop. Although not part of the Royal Regiment of Artillery the Honourable Artillery Company shares some of the same capabilities. Four of the Regular Regiments retain the cap badge, or "cypher", and traditions of the Royal Horse Artillery, although this naming convention has no link to the role that they undertake. The Royal Artillery undertakes six different roles:

Home Defence (Ceremonial)	Air Defence	Close Support (AS90 & MRLS)	Close Support (L118 Light Gun)	Surveillance and Target Acquisition (STA)	Unmanned Aerial Systems (UAS)	Training
King's Troop, RHA	12 Regiment RA	1st Regiment RHA	7th (Para) Regiment RHA	5 Regiment RA	32 Regiment RA	14 Regiment RA
	16 Regiment RA	19 Regiment RA	29 (Cdo) Regiment RA	Honourable Artillery Company (HAC)	47 Regiment RA	
		26 Regiment RA	3rd Regiment RHA			
			4 Regiment RA			

Corps of Royal Engineers

The Royal Engineers is a corps of 15 regiments in the regular army providing military engineering (civil engineering, assault engineering and demolition) capabilities to the field army and facilities management expertise within garrisons.

Regiments are associated with Brigade level formations with a number of independent squadrons and support groups associated with specific tasks:

The Royal School of Military Engineering (RSME) comprises two recruit training regiments:

- 1 RSME Regiment – Construction Engineer School
- 3 RSME Regiment – Combat Engineer School

The remainder are field regiments attached to various deployable formations:

- 21 Engineer Regiment

- 22 Engineer Regiment
- 23 Parachute Engineer Regiment
- 24 Commando Engineer Regiment
- 26 Engineer Regiment
- 32 Engineer Regiment
- 33 Engineer Regiment (EOD)
- 35 Engineer Regiment
- 36 Engineer Regiment
- 39 Engineer Regiment
- 42 Engineer Regiment (Geographic)

Royal Corps of Signals

The Royal Signals is a corps of 10 Regiments and 13 independent squadrons which provides communications and information systems support to formations of Brigade level and above. Below the Brigade level support is provided by *Battalion Signallers* drawn from the parent unit. Within the deployable brigades, the Signal Regiment also provides support to the HQ function including logistics, life support and force protection capabilities.

- 1st Signal Regiment
- 2nd Signal Regiment
- 3rd (United Kingdom) Division Signal Regiment
- 10th Signal Regiment
- 11th (Royal School of Signals) Signal Regiment
- 14th Signal Regiment (Electronic Warfare)
- 15th Signal Regiment (Information Support)
- 16th Signal Regiment
- 18th (UKSF) Signal Regiment
- 21st Signal Regiment
- 22nd Signal Regiment
- 30th Signal Regiment

Army Air Corps

The Army Air Corps provides battlefield air support with six regiments and four independent squadrons and flights:

- 1 Regiment Army Air Corps
- 2 Regiment Army Air Corps
- 3 Regiment Army Air Corps
- 4 Regiment Army Air Corps
- 5 Regiment Army Air Corps
- 7 (Training) Regiment Army Air Corps
- 657 Squadron (RAF Odiham)

- 658 Squadron (Stirling Lines)
- 7 Flight (Brunei)
- 25 Flight (AAC Middle Wallop)

Intelligence Corps

The Intelligence Corps provides intelligence support including collection, interpretation and counter-intelligence capabilities with three battalions and a joint service group:

- 1 Military Intelligence Battalion
- 2 Military Intelligence Battalion
- 4 Military Intelligence Battalion
- 15 (UK) Psychological Operations Group

Combat Service Support Arms

The Combat Service Support Arms provide sustainment and support for the Combat and Combat Support Arms. Whilst CSS personnel are not intended to close with and engage opposition forces, the fluidity of the modern battlefield means that these personnel are likely to be engaged in close combat at times, particularly when associated with Battle Groups.

Royal Logistic Corps

The Royal Logistic Corps is the largest single corps in the British Army:

- 1 Close Support Logistic Regiment RLC
- 3 Close Support Logistic Regiment RLC
- 4 Close Support Logistic Regiment RLC
- 6 Force Logistic Regiment RLC
- 7 Force Logistic Regiment RLC
- 9 Theatre Logistic Regiment RLC
- 10 Queen's Own Gurkha Logistic Regiment RLC
- 11 Explosive Ordnance Disposal Regiment RLC
- 13 Air Assault Support Regiment RLC
- 17 Port and Maritime Regiment RLC
- 25 Training Support Regiment RLC
- 27 Theatre Logistic Regiment RLC
- 29 Postal Courier & Movement Regiment RLC

Corps of Royal Electrical and Mechanical Engineers

The Royal Electrical and Mechanical Engineers is a corps that provides maintenance support to equipment and vehicles. Most units will have either a Light Aid Detachment (LAD) or Workshop (Wksp) attached. Seven battalions provide support to formations of brigade level and above:

- 1 Close Support Battalion REME
- 2 Close Support Battalion REME
- 3 Close Support Battalion REME
- 4 Close Support Battalion REME
- 5 Force Support Battalion REME
- 6 Close Support Battalion REME
- 7 Aviation Support Battalion REME

Medical services

The Army Medical Services provide primary and secondary care for the armed forces in fixed locations and whilst deployed on operations. Personnel are attached to a parent unit, one of five field regiments or the defence medical services. The AMS comprises four different Corps providing the range of medical and veterinary care, with the Royal Army Medical Corps also providing the administrative framework for the regiments.

- Royal Army Medical Corps
  - 1st Armoured Medical Regiment
  - 2nd Medical Regiment
  - 3 Medical Regiment
  - 4 Armoured Medical Regiment
  - 5 Armoured Medical Regiment
  - 16 Medical Regiment
  - 225 Medical Regiment
  - 253 Medical Regiment
  - 22 Field Hospital
  - 33 Field Hospital
  - 34 Field Hospital
  - 254 Medical Regiment
- Royal Army Dental Corps
- Queen Alexandra's Royal Army Nursing Corps
- Royal Army Veterinary Corps
  - 1 Military Working Dog Regiment

Adjutant General's Corps

The Adjutant General's Corps provides administrative, police and disciplinary and educational support to the army. The AGC is an amalgamation with three of the constituent units retaining their previous cap badge. Personnel from the AGC administrative and educational specialisations serve in attached posts to establishments or units of other arms. The police and disciplinary activities retain their own cap badges and act as discrete bodies. The Corps as a whole is divided into four separate branches:

- **Staff and Personnel Branch**: The SPS branch is the largest part of the AGC and has responsibility for providing most administrative functions, including finance, IT support, human resources. The SPS branch was formed by the amalgamation of the Royal Army Pay Corps with elements of the Royal Army Ordnance Corps and Women's Royal Army Corps.
- **Education and Training Services Branch**: The ETS branch provides for the educational needs of all serving personnel. These cover both professional development within the army, and wider personal development. The ETS branch was formed through the renaming of the Royal Army Educational Corps.
- **Army Legal Services Branch**: The ALS branch provides legal advice to the army and to individuals requiring representation at Courts Martial. It is one of the smallest individual units, numbering 120 professionally qualified lawyers. All of its members are officers. The ALS branch retains the cap badge and traditions of the Army Legal Corps.
- **Provost Branch**: The Provost branch consists of three separate elements:
  - **Military Provost Staff**: The MPS is the element of the provost branch responsible for administering military correctional facilities. The MPS is one of the few elements in the army that does not recruit directly; instead, its members are volunteers from other branches of the army. The MPS retains the cap badge and traditions of the Military Provost Staff Corps.
  - **Royal Military Police**: The RMP provides the army's policing services, both in peacetime and in wartime. Units of the RMP are trained to deploy with the Field Army in the event of mobilisation. The RMP provides two regular regiments and supplements Army Reserve regiments with one Provost company each. A further provost company is trained in the air assault mission and is permanently attached to 16 Air Assault Brigade. The Corps also provides a number of specialist capabilities, such as the Special Investigation Branch, Close Protection Teams and special escort capabilities.
    - 1 Regiment, Royal Military Police
    - 3 Regiment, Royal Military Police

- **Military Provost Guard Service**: The MPGS is a unit dedicated to the guarding of military installations, allowing the army to replace civilian guards with trained soldiers. The MPGS has responsibilities at installations belonging to all three services.

Other services

- Royal Army Physical Training Corps
- Corps of Army Music
- Royal Army Chaplains' Department
- Small Arms School Corps

Training

Training in the Regular Army differs for soldiers and officers but in general takes place in at least two phases:

Phase one training is basic military training for all new recruits. Here candidates learn the basic standards of military performance including operation in the field, weapon handling, personal administration, drill etc.

- Prospective officers attend the Royal Military Academy Sandhurst, where they undergo basic training in soldiering, defence policy and the structure of government, administration, command and leadership. The Commissioning Course for new entry officers lasts 44 weeks. Some specialist branches, Medical and Legal, undergo a short course which provides basic military training.
- Infantry soldiers undergo a 26-week course at the Infantry Training Centre at Catterick Garrison which combines phase one and phase two training.
- Soldiers in other specialisations undergo the 14-week Army Development Course at the Army Training Centre, Pirbright or the Army Training Regiment at Winchester
- Junior Soldiers (Under 18) at the Army Foundation College in Harrogate undergo either 23 or 46 weeks training (Junior Soldiers with trades complete 23 weeks and infantry Junior Soldiers complete 46 weeks)

Phase two training is specific to the trade that the soldier or officer will follow and is conducted in a branch specialised school. Phase two training enables the individual to join an operational unit prepared to contribute to operational effectiveness. These schools are under the direction of the parent corps or arm of the service, as illustrated above, with the Infantry Training Centre being formed of two training battalions.

Units of the Army Reserve

Combat Arms

Armour

The four armoured regiments of the Army Reserve operate in two roles - provision of crew replacements for armoured regiments, and Light Cavalry (reconnaissance):

- Royal Yeomanry
- Royal Wessex Yeomanry
- Queen's Own Yeomanry
- Scottish and North Irish Yeomanry

Infantry

- 52nd Lowland, 6th Battalion The Royal Regiment of Scotland
- 51st Highland, 7th Battalion The Royal Regiment of Scotland
- 3rd Battalion, The Princess of Wales's Royal Regiment
- The London Regiment
- 4th Battalion, The Duke of Lancaster's Regiment
- 5th Battalion, The Royal Regiment of Fusiliers
- 3rd Battalion, The Royal Anglian Regiment
- 4th Battalion, The Yorkshire Regiment
- 4th Battalion, The Mercian Regiment
- 3rd Battalion, The Royal Welsh
- 2nd Battalion, The Royal Irish Regiment
- 4th Battalion, The Parachute Regiment
- 6th Battalion, The Rifles
- 7th Battalion, The Rifles

Special Air Service

- 21st Special Air Service Regiment (Artists)
- 23rd Special Air Service Regiment

Combat Support

Honourable Artillery Company

- Honourable Artillery Company

Royal Artillery

- 101 (Northumbrian) Regiment RA - MLRS
- 103 Regiment RA - Light Gun
- 104 Regiment RA - UAV
- 105 Regiment RA - Light Gun
- 106 (Yeomanry) Regiment RA - Air Defense

Royal Engineers

- The Engineer and Logistic Staff Corps – Specialist industry knowledge (invitation only, industry leaders)
- Royal Monmouthshire Royal Engineers (Militia) – Field Regiment
- 71 Engineer Regiment
- 75 Engineer Regiment

Note: Although the Royal Monmouthshire Royal Engineers is part of the Royal Engineers order of battle, it is a separate regiment with its own cap badge, regimental colours and traditions.

Royal Signals

- 32 (Scottish) Signal Regiment
- 37 (Wessex and Welsh) Signal Regiment
- 39 (Skinners) Signal Regiment
- 71 (Yeomanry) Signal Regiment
- 63 (SAS) Signal Squadron

Army Air Corps

- 6 Regiment, Army Air Corps

Intelligence Corps

- 3 Military Intelligence Battalion
- 5 Military Intelligence Battalion
- 6 Military Intelligence Battalion
- 7 Military Intelligence Battalion

Combat Service Support

Royal Electrical and Mechanical Engineers

- 101 Battalion, REME
- 102 Battalion, REME
- 103 Battalion, REME
- 104 Battalion, REME
- 105 Battalion, REME
- 106 Battalion, REME

Royal Logistic Corps

- 150 Regiment
- 151 Regiment
- 152 (North Irish) Regiment
- 154 (Scottish) Regiment
- 156 Regiment
- 157 (Welsh) Regiment
- 158 Regiment
- 159 Regiment
- 162 Regiment
- 165 Port and Maritime Regiment
- 167 Catering Support Regiment
- 383 Commando Petroleum Troop

Army Medical Services

- 201 (Northern) Field Hospital
- 202 (Midlands) Field Hospital
- 203 (Welsh) Field Hospital
- 204 (North Irish) Field Hospital
- 205 (Scottish) Field Hospital
- 207 (Manchester) Field Hospital
- 208 (Liverpool) Field Hospital
- 212 (Yorkshire) Field Hospital
- 217 (London) General Hospital
- 243 (Wessex) Field Hospital
- 256 (City of London) Field Hospital
- 306 Hospital Support Regiment
- 335 Medical Evacuation Regiment
- Medical Operational Support Group

External links and sources

- Official Army Website[1118]
- SaBRE[1119]
- British Monarchy and the British Army[1120]
- A Guide to Appointments and Invitations for Defence Staffs within High Commissions and Embassies in London, UK Ministry of Defence, June 2005 edition
- Operations in the UK: The Defence Contribution to Resilience (Interim Joint Doctrine Publication 2)

Recruitment in the British Army

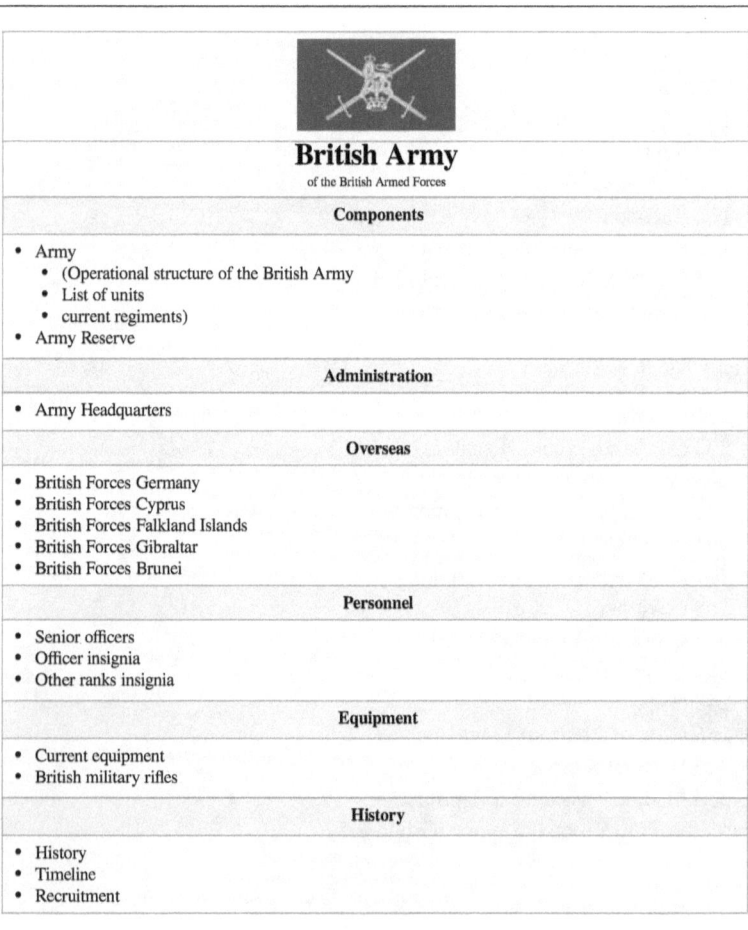

British Army portal
• v • t • e[1121]

The British Army came into being with the unification of the Kingdoms of England and Scotland into the Kingdom of Great Britain in 1754. The new British Army incorporated Regiments that had already existed in England and Scotland. The Army has traditionally relied on volunteer recruits, the only exceptions to this being during the latter part of the First World War until 1919, and then again during the Second World War when conscription was brought in during the war and stayed until 1960.

18th and 19th centuries

At the beginning of the 18th century, the standing strength of the British Army was reduced after the Treaty of Ryswick, and stood at 7,000 troops at home and 14,000 based overseas,[1122] with recruits ranging from 17 to 50 years of age. The army was kept small by the government during peacetime, mainly due to the fear that the army would be unduly influenced by the Crown or used to depose the government. The Bill of Rights of 1689 specifies that Parliamentary authority is needed to maintain a standing army in peacetime.

For much of the 18th century, the army was recruited in a wide variety of places, and many of its recruits were mercenaries from continental Europe, including Danes, Hessians and Hanoverians.[1123] These mercenaries were hired out by other rulers on contracted terms. Other regiments were formed of volunteers such as French Huguenots. By 1709, during the War of the Spanish Succession, the British Army totalled 150,000 men, of whom 81,000 were foreign mercenaries. The rest of the army consisted of natives of the British Isles who, apart from the officers, were mainly recruited from the poorest sections of society. Each regiment was responsible for the recruitment of its own troops, and individual colonels would lead recruiting parties on tours of the towns and villages. This was emphasized by a popular play of the time called *The Recruiting Officer*.[1124] Other powers were given by the British government to allow the forcible enlistment of vagrants and vagabonds. Some of these powers were abused by recruiting officers desperate to fill their quotas, although a legalized Royal Navy press-gang system would not be implemented yet, even though normal recruiting methods failed to supply the required annual influx of troops, as the army was not a popular profession, with low pay, flogging and other barbarous disciplinary measures. The army's recruiting methods and treatment of its soldiers would remain the same for the rest of the 18th century.

Figure 170: *Press gang, British caricature of 1780*

During the American Revolutionary War, a policy similar to the Royal Navy's Press Gangs was introduced. Two acts were passed, the Recruiting Act 1778 and the Recruiting Act 1779, for the impressment of individuals. For some men this would have been for being drunk and disorderly. The chief advantages of these acts was in the number of volunteers brought in under the apprehension of impressment. To avoid impressment, some recruits incapacitated themselves by cutting off the thumb and forefinger of the right hand. Both acts were repealed in 1780. The British Government also released criminals and debtors from prison on the condition they joined the army. Three entire regiments during the American Revolution were raised from this early release programme.[1125] Of the Volunteer recruits, some would find they had been enticed to take the King's shilling under false pretenses and many men would find they had signed to a lifetime in the army.

After the defeat of Great Britain by the American revolutionaries, the British Army fell into dereliction (it should be noted that the army in 1775 was in a poor state anyway), morale and discipline were low, and troops levels fell.[1126] The Army was neglected as never before and its total strength in 1793 stood at 40,000 men.[1127]

Figure 171: *British Army recruitment poster during the Napoleonic wars offering both limited and unlimited (long-term) service*

Napoleonic wars

The United Kingdom's struggle with France during the Napoleonic wars required the British Army to expand rapidly. Ordinary recruiting methods failed to supply the number of men required to fill the Army ranks. The main methods used for recruiting were: private individuals were recruited for their own interests, volunteers from the militia and placing obligations on communities to enlist. Generals called for conscription for the first time in British History, although this was never enacted for the regular army.[1128] During this period, Great Britain was at a disadvantage to her enemy, as due to the Industrial Revolution potential recruits were instead drawn to the cities to earn more money in the many factories now being built in the country, while France was still largely an agrarian society.

Competition from civilian occupations was intense and highlighted in the disparity in pay; where a private could earn 7s per week in 1806, a dockworker could expect to earn 28s.[1129] However soldiers would expect to supplement this meagre income with promotion and loot on campaign. During the early phases of the war, joining the Army could still mean effectively joining for life, which was frequently brutally cut short. For instance, a posting to the Caribbean in 1790 was seen as a near death sentence, as thousands of men died or were disabled by disease there.[1130] The Army still struggled to raise the troops required to replace the discharged, wounded and dead as the war against France continued. As early as 1794, 18,596 soldiers died on active service and another 40,639 men were discharged. This would remain a constant theme during the Napoleonic wars, and the British Army also used foreign volunteers, such as French Royalists, Germans, Greeks and Corsicans to supplement its forces. In 1813 one fifth of the army, 52,000 men, were such volunteers.[1131] The British Army in 1813 contained over 250,000 men,[1132] though this was much larger in comparison to the army at the beginning of the war, the all volunteer British army was still much smaller than that of France, which with conscription had an army over 2.6 million.

Reform

From 1798 onwards, structural, training and logistical reforms implemented or authorised by the Duke of York (as commander-in-chief of the army) slowly improved the lot of the ordinary soldier. York oversaw a crackdown on corruption[1133] and removed the threat of corporal punishment for a large number of petty offences (while it was still retained for serious derelictions of duty). He also stamped down on the abuse of buying officer commissions, making it necessary for officers to serve two full years before either promotion or purchase to captain and six years before becoming a major[1134] The establishment of the Royal Military Academy for officers was instigated due to York's influence,[1135] while regular recruits to the army were allowed to join under contract for limited periods, rather than for life. Men such as Sir John Moore, Thomas Sydney Beckwith and Rowland Hill characterised the new breed of officers who sought to improve the relationship between officers and men, motivating troops through mutual respect, reward and promotion rather than by relying on punishment. The Shorncliffe System for light infantry was established, being devised by Lt-Col Kenneth Mackenzie, and trained soldiers to think for themselves and act on initiative while the light infantry officers drilled alongside the men fostering comradeship. In addition, the introduction of new tactical and organisational flexibility contributed a great deal to the successes of the Peninsula and Waterloo.

Post-Napoleonic army

After the victory in the Napoleonic wars, there followed 40 years of peace in Europe during which the army would again revert to its peacetime role. The Army that won the war was again neglected in the peace. The Government's immediate priority was to cut taxes, to lessen the burden of taxation on the economy, which had remained high over the previous 20 years, to pay for the expensive war that enabled Britain to be victorious over France. The British

Army funding would be cut drastically in the short term, but as became evident this would apply for the next 40 years. The budget was cut from £43 million in 1815, to £10.7 million in 1820, £8 million in 1836 and only rose slightly 10 years later to £9.5 million.[1136] With the budget cuts, troop levels were inevitably cut from 233,592 men in 1815 to 102,529 men by 1828. There were further reductions in 1838, after which troop strength stood at 91,388.[1137] With the constant cuts, recruiting parties would achieve their reduced recruiting targets with greater ease.

1870 reforms

The army during peacetime was deliberately kept small and the recruitment methods would only change once the Cardwell reforms were implemented in the 1870s. The Crimean War nevertheless highlighted several defects and weaknesses in the Army's organisation. Although in theory, 70,000 soldiers were stationed in Britain, it was found that this number included several units in transit from distant outposts of the Empire, and some underdeveloped recruits and many old soldiers whose constitution had been ruined by harsh climate and disease and who were no longer capable of serving in the field. As a result, the provision of an expeditionary force of only 25,000 in the Crimea stripped Britain of almost every trained soldier.[1138]

Some of the Cardwell's reforms included the abolition of sale of commissions, the banning of flogging and other measures, such as reducing the length of service, to make recruitment more appealing. An Enlistment Act saw a change in the terms of enlistment, which could at last produce some trained reserves and also made soldiering a more tempting career. A Localisation Scheme resulted in the pairing of single-battalion regiments via administrative depots on a county-based system.

Officers and royalty

Officers of the British army prior to the late 18th century were mainly recruited from a narrow segment of society, with a majority coming from the landed gentry and the aristocracy or often officers were from families with a military tradition. (This contrasted with the Navy, whose officers were more often from a middle-class background.) The second son of King George III, Prince Frederick, Duke of York and Albany, did much to improve the standard of officer recruitment from his position as Commander in Chief of the Army (from 1795 to 1809, then from 1811 to 1827). The sale of commissions, finally abolished in the Cardwell reforms in 1868-1874, and the further Childers Reforms. In spite of its abolition, the status of an officer being from a privileged background and that of another rank being from a less privileged one has, for the most part remained.

Figure 172: *Army Parade with Prince Harry*

The Royal Family traditionally had its members serve in the Armed Forces, usually with the Royal Navy though many have served with the Army. This occasionally warped operations in the field, for example at the Battle of Tel el-Kebir, where Wolseley was forced to leave an entire brigade of Guards in reserve to avoid harm coming to Queen Victoria's third son, the Duke of Connaught.[1139] The tradition has continued into the 21st century, with Prince Harry and Prince William both joining the Army as officers. However, Royals are no longer deliberately kept out of harm's way; Prince Harry saw active service in Afghanistan until the publicity posed a threat to the troops serving with him, while Prince Andrew served as a front-line helicopter pilot with the Royal Navy during the Falklands War.

Foreign Royals have also served in the Army, such as Eugène Bonaparte, the son of Napoléon III, who was commissioned into the Royal Artillery, but was killed in 1879 while serving in South Africa during the Anglo-Zulu War. Later in the 20th century, King Abdullah II of Jordan served as a Second Lieutenant with the 13th/18th Royal Hussars (Queen Mary's Own), and Sultan Qaboos bin Said al Said of Oman served with the Cameronians (Scottish Rifles).

Figure 173: *British Volunteer recruits in London, August 1914, who would form Kitchener's New Army*

First World War

At the start of 1914, the British Army had a reported strength of 710,000 men including reserves, of which 247,432 were regular troops, also including 80,000 regular troops formed as the British Expeditionary Force.[1140] The recruitment drive would be spearheaded by Lord Kitchener once war had been declared in August 1914.

It was abundantly clear that the army that the Kaiser had referred to as a "contemptible little army" would need thousands more recruits. Young Britons answered the call, for King and Country, and voluntarily joined the British Army. By early 1915 much of the regular army had been killed and were now replaced by the part-time volunteers of the Territorial Force and Kitchener's new volunteer army. A feature of the volunteer army was the Pals battalions, recruited from single communities or even factories, who were allowed to serve together. The Kitchener recruitment campaign had proved to be very successful, as on 1 September 1914, over 30,000 men enlisted.[1141] With each day passing, thousands more were clamouring to be taken. The British Government soon realized the main drawback of this campaign, as opposed to the French and German conscriptions, which selected each individual men, a high proportion of men from skilled industries left their works, which would prove

Figure 174: *World War I recruitment poster*

to be costly in the war effort. A better-controlled enlistment program would be required.

The Military Service Bill was enacted with effect from January 1916 and specified that men from the ages of 18 to 41 were liable to be called up for service unless they were married (or widowed with children), or else served in one of a number of reserved professions. By the end of World War I, almost a quarter of the total male population of the United Kingdom of Great Britain and Ireland had joined up, over five million men.

Inter-war period 1919-38

After the Great war and the inevitable defence cuts that would follow, the army was reduced in size, and by 1920 had fallen to a strength of 370,000. There were a number of factors for the reductions in the size of British Army, and the cuts to the budget of the Army. The army now had competition from the new armed service, the Royal Air Force, which could patrol far greater land areas, and keep the far flung corners of the Empire policed from the sky at a relatively cheaper cost. The defence budget for the army was repeatedly cut yearly, as in 1923 the army defence budget was 43.5 million pounds sterling, and during the Great Depression in 1932 to just under 36 million pounds sterling. Only with the rise of Germany, would the budget for the British army again increase, by

Figure 175: *Inter-war period recruitment poster*

1938 to 123 million pounds sterling; the army again started a rapid recruitment program.[1142]

Second World War

Further information: Conscription in the United Kingdom during Second World War

The pre-war army was an all-volunteer army and recruits were allotted to the corps of their wishes. The only pre-conditions placed on candidates were an interview with a recruiting officer, who could only glean partial information on a recruit, a medical examination, and some educational tests. If these requirements were met, the recruit was posted to the arm of his choice, there was no scientific selection process unlike the rapidly growing German army. This led to men being allocated to the wrong or unsuitable corps. The Secretary of State for War, Leslie Hore-Belisha attempted to address these problems, and the wider problems of the British army.[1143] The process of allocating men would remain ad hoc at the start of the war. The army would be without the quotas of men required from skilled professions and trades, which modern warfare demanded. With the army being the least popular service compared to the navy and airforce, a higher proportion of army recruits were said to be dull and backward.[1144]

Figure 176: *Skilled men were required to join the 1st Assault Brigade Royal Engineers manning this modified Churchill tank, and to carry out combat engineering and other technical support*

The following memorandum to the Executive Committee of the Army Council highlighted the growing concern.

> *'The British Army is wasting manpower in this war almost as badly as it did in the last war. A man is posted to a Corps almost entirely on the demand of the moment and without any effort at personal selection by proper tests.'*[1145]

Only with the creation of the Beveridge committee in 1941, and their subsequent findings in 1942, would the situation of skilled men not being assigned correctly, be addressed. The findings led directly to the creation of the General Service Corps, and would remain in place long after the war.[1146] Hore-Belisha had sought permission to introduce conscription in 1938 but was rebuffed by Neville Chamberlain, who would not agree to increased defence spending. In early 1939, he was finally allowed to introduce conscription to meet the threat of Germany, with the Military Training Act of 27 April 1939. The act required all men aged 20 and 21 to take six months military training. This act was extended on the declaration of the war, to include all fit men between the ages of 18 and 41. Conscription was gradually brought in, starting in October 1939 and applying to all fit men between 20–23, and the age group was increased as the war continued.

At the start of the Second World War, the British Army Strength stood at 897,000 men including reserves. By the end of 1939, the strength of the British Army stood at 1.1 million men, and further increased to 1.65 million men during June 1940. By the end of the war and the final demobilisations in 1946, over 3.5 million men had been enlisted in the British Army.

The Local Defence Volunteers was formed early in 1940. Very large numbers of civilians too old or too young for the Army, or barred from serving if they were in reserved occupations, volunteered for the new force. The organisation was eventually renamed the "Home Guard" and was to be part of the defence of Britain in the advent of a German invasion of Britain.

From National Service to all-professional army

As with the previous World War, the end of wartime conscription saw the army reduced in size and reverting to its peacetime role of maintaining the Empire. In 1947, British India was given Independence, which meant the loss of the British Indian Army and thousands of volunteer soldiers. The British Government had relied on the British Indian Army for Imperial matters. Now, without this army, the regular British Army was judged to be too small for the demands of an impending Cold War and maintaining the Empire. To meet this demand, which volunteers alone would not, peacetime conscription was enacted by the government and passed by the House of Commons in 1947. In the United Kingdom, it is this period of peacetime conscription that is usually referred to as 'National Service'. It remains the only period of peacetime conscription in UK history, apart from the periods immediately before and after World War II. The majority of National Servicemen went into the Army and, by 1951, National Servicemen made up half the force, leading to a reduced level of voluntary recruitment to the regular army. The last intake of National Servicemen took place in 1960, with the last National Serviceman being demobbed on 16 May 1963. The army reverted to an all professional volunteer service, which it remains to this day.

The decision to abolish National Service was taken in 1957 with the 1957 Defence White Paper, which led to an enormous reduction in the number of soldiers between 1958–63, from about 330,000 to 165,000 by the end of National Service. In the decades that followed, cuts in the Army were the constant theme, although they were never on a large scale until the end of the cold war. Between 1963 and 1992, strength was reduced to 153,000. In 1990, the Government started another defence review, which concluded with the Defence White Paper of 1992. In a post-Soviet world, the white paper would again further reduce the army by 50,000,[1147] effectively ending the British Army of the Rhine. The current strength of the British army is approximately 102,000 regular personnel.

Figure 177: *A British Army recruitment centre.*

Present day

The Army mainly recruits within the United Kingdom, and normally has a recruitment target of around 25,000 soldiers per year. Low unemployment in Britain has resulted in the Army having difficulty in meeting its target, and in the early years of the 21st century there has been a marked increase in the number of recruits from mostly Commonwealth countries.

The minimum recruitment age is 16 years, after the end of GCSEs, although soldiers may not serve on operations below 18 years; the maximum recruitment age was raised in January 2007 from 26 to 33 years. The normal term of engagement is 22 years; and, once enlisted, soldiers are not normally permitted to leave until they have served at least four years. Soldiers are now Enlisted on a 24-year engagement known as versatile engagement (VEng). After 22 years service a soldier may be offered a 2-year extension. After the 2 years the soldier or officer maybe after a further 2 years service and thereafter until they reach 55 years of age.

Figure 178: *This First World War poster, urges men from the Dominions of the British Empire to enlist in the war effort.*

Empire and Commonwealth

During both World Wars, subjects throughout the British Empire volunteered to help the United Kingdom. During World War I, the Dominions raised their own armies, but were under the British command structure, and very much integrated into the British fighting forces. Over 2.5 million men, which included Canada sending 418,000 men overseas, Australia sending 322,000, South Africa sending 230,000, New Zealand sending 124,000, and other volunteers from the Crown Colonies.

During peacetime, British Empire soldiers were usually recruited into indigenous regiments, such as the Hong Kong Volunteer Defence Corps, to garrison their own land, thus ensuring that the Army did not have to allocate its own units to garrison the territories. One of the oldest regiments raised from the empire was the West India Regiment, which was raised in 1795, and was formed as an integral part of the regular British Army. The recruits of the West India Regiment were originally raised from freed slaves from North America and by the purchase of slaves in the West Indies; the regiment was disbanded in 1927. The Fiji Infantry Regiment, which was raised in 1920 and consisted of a single battalion, garrisoned the Pacific territory. One of the largest units

Figure 179: *An Australian World War I recruitment poster*

was the multi-battalion Royal West African Frontier Force, which garrisoned British West Africa and included The Nigeria Regiment.

British Indian Army

The largest of the colonial military forces was the British Indian Army. Up to Indian independence, this was a volunteer army, raised from the native population and staffed by British officers. The Indian Army served both as a security force in India itself and, particularly during the World Wars, in other theatres. The Indian Army proved a very useful adjunct to British forces wherever it served. Recruitment was entirely voluntary; about 1.3 million men served in the First World War, many on the Western Front, and 2.5 million in the Second. Initially the soldiers and NCOs were Indian, with British officers, but later Indian officers were promoted King's Commissioned Indian Officer.

Gurkhas

The Gurkhas has been employed as an integral part of the Indian Army since the early 19th century. After Indian independence, some Gurkha units were transferred to the British Army. There are approximately 3,500 Gurkhas currently serving in the British Army. Joining the British Army is one of the few ways Nepalese people have of escaping poverty and earning a good salary. As

Recruitment in the British Army

Figure 180: *Indian troops on the western front*

Figure 181: *A British Gurkha unit*

Figure 182: *Irish Volunteers of the 10th (Irish) Division's Basingstoke, 1915*

a result, each year, there are thousands of applicants, as in 2007 when over 17,349 applied for just 230 posts. In some years, there are over 60,000 applying to join, and from 2010, women were allowed to join for the first time. Candidates must be between 17½ and 21 years of age.

Irish regiments

Irishmen have served in large numbers with the British army since its inception in the early 18th century and into the Seven Years' War, the Napoleonic Wars and beyond. During this time, 20 to 40 percent of soldiers in English regiments of the Army were Irish born which, together with a high proportion of Scots, meant there were, on occasion, more Irish soldiers than English in some English regiments.[1148,1149]</ref> Levels would remain high, although recruitment steadily dropped from the period of the Irish Famine until 1900, but the Irish would remain over represented compared to the size of the population. At the turn of the 20th century, the number of Irish volunteers reduced, as the criticism by nationalists of recruitment to the army grew. Over 28,000 Irishmen served in the army during the Second Boer War, but by 1910 recruitment levels had fallen to 9 percent and for the first time were below Ireland's share of the UK population. During World War I, over 200,000 Irish soldiers volunteered to serve; many recruits from the new Southern state were known as National Volunteers. During World War II, over 70,000 were recruited from the Republic of Ireland and 38,000 from Northern Ireland.[1150]

Figure 183: *Johnson Beharry VC was born in Grenada*

The importance of the Irish in the British Army was summed up by Rudyard Kipling, who lost his son, Lt John Kipling of the Irish Guards, in World War I,

> *"For where there are Irish there's bound to be fighting, And when there's no fighting it's Ireland no more."*

Present Commonwealth & foreign recruitment

In 2008, Commonwealth origin volunteers comprised approximately 6.7% of the Army's total strength. In total, 6,600 foreign soldiers from 42 countries were represented in the Army, not including Gurkhas, i.e. Nepalis. After Nepal, the nation with most citizens in the British Army was Fiji, with 1,900, followed by Jamaica and Ghana with 600 each; soldiers also came from more prosperous countries, such as Australia, New Zealand and South Africa. There are also volunteers from the Republic of Ireland - the level of recruitment amongst Irish nationals has been increasing, and figures for recruitment in Northern Ireland reveal that 16% came from south of the border during 2008. With Levels growing year on year since 2005 and up from 5% in 2006.

The Ministry of Defence subsequently capped the number of recruits from Commonwealth countries at 10% of any corps or regiment in the Army, although this did not affect the Gurkhas. The cap was debated, as some feared

Figure 184: *One of the most famous recruiting posters of the British Army; from World War I featuring Kitchener.*

the army's "Britishness" was being diluted, and employing too many could make the army seem as employing too many mercenaries.

In 1998 previous restrictions on the enlistment of Commonwealth citizens in the British Army had been lifted, following recruiting difficulties amongst British citizens. Under the new provisions Commonwealth citizens were permitted to enlist directly in any one of the British services and significant numbers did so in subsequent years. However, in 2013 the previous restraints were reintroduced with immediate effect, in the context of reduced establishment numbers. From July 2013, all Commonwealth citizens except for those from Ireland, Cyprus, and Malta must have resided for 5 years in the UK before being allowed to join. As of May 2016, commonwealth citizens can enlist in the British army in limited roles without meeting the residence requirements.

Notes

Sources

- Chandler, David; Beckett, I.F.W. (2003). *The Oxford History of the British Army*[1151]. Oxford Paperbacks. ISBN 978-0-19-280311-5.

- Clayton, Tim (2014). *Waterloo. Four Days that Changed Europe's Destiny*. Abacus. ISBN 9780349123011.
- Cookson, J.E. (1997). *The British Armed Nation, 1793-1815*[1152]. Oxford University Press. ISBN 0-19-820658-5.
- Crang, Jeremy (2000). *The British army and the People's War, 1939-1945*[1153]. Manchester: Manchester University Press. ISBN 978-0-7190-4741-1.
- Farwell, Byron (1973). *Queen Victoria's little wars*. Wordsworth Editions. ISBN 1-84022-216-6.
- Lindsay, J. O (1957). *The New Cambridge Modern History: Vol. 7: The Old Regime*[1154]. Cambridge University. ISBN 978-0-521-04545-2.
- McElwee, William (1974). *The Art of War: Waterloo to Mons*. London: Purnell. ISBN 0-253-31075-X.
- Vane, The Hon. W L (1913). *The Durham Light Infantry. The United Red and White Rose*. Naval and Military Press. ISBN 9781845741464.
- Young, Peter; Lawford, J.P. (1970). *History of the British Army*. Littlehampton Book Services. ISBN 0-213-00050-4.
- Simes, Thomas (1776). *The Military Guide for Young Officers*. London: Humphprey's, Bell & Aitkin.

External links

- Official **British Army Recruitment** website[1155]
- BBC article: "Recruitment in the British Army"[1156] — *including on 'Taking the King's Shilling.'*
- BBC article: "Recruitment at the start of World War II"[1157]
- Recruiting Instructions[1158] — from *The Military Guide for Young Officers*, 1776, Thomas Simes.

List of British Army installations

This is a **list of British Army Installations** in the United Kingdom and overseas. British overseas bases are concentrated in Cyprus, Brunei, Kenya, the South Atlantic and Germany.

Overseas installations

Afghanistan

The UK commitment to the current NATO "Resolute Support" mission in Afghanistan, the UK element of which is known as Operation Toral, is based at Qargha just outside Kabul.

Name	Part of	Country	County	Opened	Description
Afghan National Army Officer Academy (ANAOA) (Camp Qargha)	Operation Toral	Afghanistan	Kabul	2015	The training academy is modelled on the military academy at Sandhurst and is currently training around 530 officer cadets. This will be the UK's lasting legacy to the Afghan Army.

Belize

Name	Part of	Country	County	Opened	Description
Price Barracks	British Army Training Support Unit Belize (BATSUB)	Belize	Belize District		A small permanent team maintains 25 Service Family Accommodation quarters, enough accommodation for 600 troops on exercise and various associated buildings, as well as three satellite camps in the Baldy Beacons area of Belize.

List of British Army installations 425

Baldy Beacon and Guacamollo Bridge Training Areas	British Army Training Support Unit Belize (BATSUB)	Belize	Belize District		
Mountain Pine Ridge Training Area	British Army Training Support Unit Belize (BATSUB)	Belize	Belize District		

British Overseas Territories

Bermuda

Name	Part of	Country	Region	Opened	Description
Warwick Camp (Bermuda)	Royal Bermuda Regiment	Bermuda		1869	HQ of the Royal Bermuda Regiment

British Indian Ocean Territory

Name	Part of	Country	Region	Opened	Description
Permanent Joint Operating Base (PJOB) Diego Garcia	British Forces British Indian Ocean Territory	British Indian Ocean Territory	Diego Garcia	1966	

Falkland Islands

Name	Part of	Country	Region	Opened	Description
Mount Pleasant Complex	British Forces South Atlantic Islands	Falklands Islands	East Falkland	1985	HQ for British Force South Atlantic Islands with approximately 1000 army personnel permanently deployed.
Falklands Defence Force HQ, Stanley	British Forces South Atlantic Islands	Falkland Islands	East Falkland		

Gibraltar

British Forces Gibraltar (BFG) maintains the garrison at Gibraltar.

Name	Part of	Country	Region	Opened	Units
Devil's Tower Camp	British Forces Gibraltar	Gibraltar		1942	Regimental headquarters for the Royal Gibraltar Regiment
Four Corners Estate	British Forces Gibraltar	Gibraltar			
Tunnels of Gibraltar	British Forces Gibraltar	Gibraltar		1782	34 Miles of tunnels offer a unique training ground for British Forces Gibraltar. Whilst expansion of the network ceased in 1968 and some areas have been turned over to the Civil Administration of Gibraltar, most of the network remains in MOD ownership.

Sovereign Base Areas of Akrotiri and Dhekelia

The two British enclaves in the Republic of Cyprus act as platforms for the projection of British military assets in the Eastern Mediterranean and the Middle East. The enclaves serve as centres for regional communications monitoring from the eastern Mediterranean through the Middle East to Iran. Facilities within the retained areas also support British military activities on retained sites in the Republic of Cyprus and provide unique training opportunities.

Western Sovereign Base Area

Name	Part of	Country	Region	Opened	Units
Episkopi Cantonment	British Forces Cyprus	Sovereign Base Areas of Akrotiri and Dhekelia	Western Sovereign Base Area	Sovereign Base Areas established in 1960	Home to HQ British Forces Cyprus
Paramali North and South Quarters	British Forces Cyprus	Sovereign Base Areas of Akrotiri and Dhekelia	Western Sovereign Base Area	Sovereign Base Areas established in 1960	

Eastern Sovereign Base Area

Name	Part of	Country	Region	Opened	Units
Alexander Barracks	British Forces Cyprus	Sovereign Base Areas of Akrotiri and Dhekelia	Eastern Sovereign Base Area	Sovereign Base Areas established in 1960	
Ayios Nikolaos Station	British Forces Cyprus	Sovereign Base Areas of Akrotiri and Dhekelia	Eastern Sovereign Base Area	Sovereign Base Areas established in 1960	The Joint Service Signal Unit (JSSU), a static communications organisation maintaining secure links from Cyprus to the rest of the world. The station is a significant centre for GCHQ's collection of signals data and intelligence from the Eastern Mediterranean region and Middle East.
Dhekelia Airfield	British Forces Cyprus	Sovereign Base Areas of Akrotiri and Dhekelia	Eastern Sovereign Base Area		A small airfield whose primary role is as a British Army Helicopter Base.
Dhekelia Cantonment	British Forces Cyprus	Sovereign Base Areas of Akrotiri and Dhekelia	Eastern Sovereign Base Area	Sovereign Base Areas established in 1960	Headquarters of the Eastern Sovereign Base Area, a resident infantry battalion, an engineer squadron, and various logistic units, as well as UK-based civilians and dependents.
Nightingale Barracks	British Forces Cyprus	Sovereign Base Areas of Akrotiri and Dhekelia	Eastern Sovereign Base Area		

Brunei

Around 2000 Army personnel, largely from the 1st Battalion Royal Gurkha Rifles, are stationed in Brunei (Britain's largest remaining east of Suez deployment). Medicine Lines, Tuker Lines and Scout Base are close to the town of Seria whilst Sittang Camp's more isolated placement in Tutong District reflects its role as a Jungle Training Centre.

Name	Part of	Country	County	Opened	Description
Sittang Camp (jungle training facility)	British Forces Brunei	Brunei	Tutong District	1959	British Army Jungle Warfare Training School
Medicina Lines	British Forces Brunei	Brunei	Belait District	1959	
Tuker Lines	British Forces Brunei	Brunei	Belait District	1959	Hosts the Garrison HQ
Scout Base (7 Flt AAC Helicopter Base)	British Forces Brunei	Brunei	Belait District	1959	Brunei support troops

Canada

Following the withdrawal of the RAF from CFB Goose Bay, the sole British deployment in Canada is the Army Training Unit at Suffield.

Name	Part of	Country	County	Opened	Units
CFB Suffield	British Army Training Unit Suffield	Canada	Alberta	In use by the British Army Since 1971.	A large army training ground

Cyprus

In addition to the Sovereign Base Areas of Akrotiri and Dhekelia, the 1960 Treaty of Establishment between the United Kingdom and the Republic of Cyprus granted the UK the right to permanently make use of 40 further sites on the island for military purposes.

Name	Part of	Country	County	Opened	Units
Berengaria Village Married Quarters	British Forces Cyprus	Cyprus	Limassol		The Harakis Borehole and the Berengaria village pipeline are also retained to supply water.
Troodos Leave Camp	British Forces Cyprus	Cyprus	Troodos		Accommodation is used by BFC, visiting troops and youth services in support of adventurous training. Site also contains married quarters, NAAFI and Works Unit. Contiguous with RAF Troodos.

List of British Army installations

British East Mediterranean Relay Station	British Forces Cyprus	Cyprus	Zygi		Used by the Foreign and Commonwealth Office to broadcast BBC World Service programming to Israel and the Arabic Speaking World.
Kissousa Headwaters, Reservoir and Pumping Station	British Forces Cyprus	Cyprus	Limassol		A secure water supply for the Akrotiri Sovereign Base Area

Three retained army facilities are not currently in use by British Forces Cyprus as a result of the Cyprus Conflict.

Name	Part of	Country	County	Opened	Units
Famagusta Joint Services Port Utility	British Forces Cyprus	Cyprus	Famagusta		Lies in Northern Cyprus and therefore not currently in use.
Famagusta Family Shop and NAAFI HQ	British Forces Cyprus	Cyprus	Famagusta		Lies in Northern Cyprus and therefore not currently in use.
Famagusta NAAFI Transport Yard	British Forces Cyprus	Cyprus	Famagusta		Lies in Northern Cyprus and therefore not currently in use.

Britain also makes a permanent contribution to the United Nations Peacekeeping Force in Cyprus.

Name	Part of	Country	County	Opened	Units
Blue Beret Camp	United Nations Peacekeeping Force in Cyprus	Cyprus	Nicosia	1964	Groups of British soldiers are deployed as part of the nine-member United Nations Force which patrols the UNPA to prevent a resurgence of violence between Greek and Turkish Cypriot communities. They are operationally distinct from British Forces Cyprus

Germany

In 2010 approximately 25,000 British soldiers were permanently based in western Germany, a legacy of WWII and the Cold War. Facilities in Germany are no longer strategically useful, therefore British Forces began withdrawing from Germany in 2010; in 2015 21,500 troops remained in the country. The deployment will have been phased out by 2020, although concentrations of installations and troops in the Paderborn / Bielefeld / Gütersloh area and at Mansergh Barracks will remain until late in the decade.

Paderborn

Name	Garrison	Country	County	Expected Closure	Units
Normandy Barracks	Westfalen	Germany	North Rhine-Westphalia	N/A	20th Armoured Infantry Brigade, 1 MWD and 110 Provost Company RMP
Dempsey Barracks	Westfalen	Germany	North Rhine-Westphalia	N/A	1 Armoured Medical Regiment
Barker Barracks	Westfalen	Germany	North Rhine-Westphalia	N/A	3 Armoured Close Support Battalion
Athlone Barracks	Westfalen	Germany	North Rhine-Westphalia	N/A	The Queen's Royal Hussars
Alanbrooke Barracks	Westfalen	Germany	North Rhine-Westphalia	N/A	5th Battalion The Rifles

Bielefeld and Gütersloh

Name	Garrison	Country	County	Expected Closure	Units
Antwerp Barracks	Westfalen	Germany	North Rhine-Westphalia	N/A	20th Armoured Brigade.
Mansergh Barracks	Westfalen	Germany	North Rhine-Westphalia	N/A	26th Regiment Royal Artillery.
Normandy Barracks	Westfalen	Germany	North Rhine-Westphalia	N/A	Personnel Recovery Centre.
Bielefeld Station	Rhine	Germany	North Rhine-Westphalia	Not expected to be vacated before 2019.	HQ British Forces Germany.

Nepal

The British Army presence in Nepal is related to the Brigade of Gurkhas. British Gurkhas Nepal manages the recruitment of soldiers, the care of families and ensures the rights of veterans.

Name	Garrison	Country	County	Opened	Notes
HQ Jawalakhel, Patan	British Gurkhas Nepal	Nepal	Kathmandu		The Headquarters British Gurkhas Nepal and the Kathmandu station, which is the focal point for organisation of transit to and from Nepal, the welfare of serving soldiers and payment of pensions.

List of British Army installations

Name	Garrison	Country	County	Opened	Notes & Units
Pokhara Camp	British Gurkhas Nepal	Nepal			The British Gurkha Camp in Pokhara is the main recruitment centre, where the annual selection course is run. Pokhara is also the location of the main pension records and houses the headquarters of the Gurkha Welfare Trust.
Dharan Station	British Gurkhas Nepal	Nepal			A small station intended to assist BGN operations in eastern Nepal. It is used primarily as a movement base and regional recruiting centre.

Sierra Leone

Name	Garrison	Country	County	Opened	Notes & Units
IMATT HQ, Leicester Peak	IMATT (International Military Advisory and Training Team)	Sierra Leone	Freetown	1999	Facility for training the Republic of Sierra Leone Armed Forces

Iraq

Name	Part of	Country	County	Opened	Units
Al Asad Base		Iraq	Al Anbar Governate		

Kenya

The British Army presence in Kenya is based around the British Army Training Unit Kenya (BATUK).

Name	Part of	Country	County	Opened	Units
The Nanyuki Show Ground (NSG) and Training Area	British Army Training Unit Kenya	Kenya	Laikipia County		BATUK HQ and main training area.
Kahawa Barracks, Nairobi	British Army Training Unit Kenya	Kenya	Nairobi		BATUK Rear area base and Depot.

International Mine Action Training Centre	The British Peace Support Team East Africa	Kenya	Nairobi County	2005	The IMATC is a joint British and Kenyan venture aimed at alleviating the suffering caused by landmines and explosive remnants of war, by providing high quality Mine Action Training
Peace Training Support Centre	The British Peace Support Team East Africa	Kenya	Nairobi County	2005	

United Kingdom

Name	Garrison	Country	County	Opened	Notes & Units
Alanbrooke Barracks / RAF Topcliffe		England	North Yorkshire	1972	4th Regiment Royal Artillery
Albemarle Barracks		England	Northumberland	1970	39th Regiment Royal Artillery
Alexander Barracks		England	Surrey	1875	Army Training Centre, Pirbright
Aliwal Barracks	Tidworth Camp	England	Wiltshire		2nd Royal Tank Regiment King's Royal Hussars
Allenby Barracks		England	Dorset	1899	Armour Centre
Alma Lines	Catterick	England	North Yorkshire		The Royal Dragoon Guards
Arnhem Barracks	Aldershot	England	Hampshire	1965	
Assaye Barracks	Tidworth	England	Wiltshire		1st Regiment Royal Horse Artillery
Baker Barracks		England	West Sussex	1984	12th Regiment Royal Artillery 47th Regiment Royal Artillery
Beachley Barracks		England	Gloucestershire	1915	1st Battalion, The Rifles
Beach-head Lines	Catterick	England	North Yorkshire		
Battlesbury Barracks		England	Wiltshire		1st Battalion the Yorkshire Regiment
Beacon Barracks		England	Staffordshire	2006	22 Signal Regiment
Berechurch Hall Camp	Colchester	England	Essex		Military Corrective Training Centre

List of British Army installations

Bhurtpore Barracks	Tidworth	England	Wiltshire		19th Regiment Royal Artillery
Bourlon Barracks	Catterick	England	North Yorkshire		1st Battalion, The Scots Guards The Highlanders, 4th Battalion, Royal Regiment of Scotland
Blandford Camp		England	Dorset	1724	11 (Royal School of Signals) Signal Regiment 15 Signal Regiment
Brock Barracks		England	Berkshire	1881	
Brompton Barracks		England	Kent	1812	Royal School of Military Engineering (Chatham)
Browning Barracks	Aldershot	England	Hampshire	1964	
Bruneval Barracks	Aldershot	England	Hampshire	1965	
Buller Barracks	Aldershot	England	Hampshire	1970	
Cambrai Lines	Catterick	England	North Yorkshire		The Queen's Royal Lancers
Cameron Barracks		Scotland	Inverness-shire	1884	
Campion Lines	Bulford Camp	England	Wiltshire		HQ Special Investigation Branch
Carver Barracks		England	Essex	1974	33 Engineer Regiment (EOD) 101 (City of London) Engineer Regiment (Explosive Ordnance Disposal)
Cavalry Barracks, Hounslow		England	London	1793	1st Battalion, Welsh Guards
Cawdor Barracks		Wales	Pembrokeshire	1944	14 Signal Regiment (Electronic Warfare)
Chetwynd Barracks		England	Nottinghamshire	1919	49 (East) Brigade
Claro Barracks		England	North Yorkshire		21 Engineer Regiment
Clayton Barracks (Thornhill Barracks)	Aldershot	England	Hampshire	1928	
Clive Barracks		England	Shropshire	1976	1st Battalion, The Royal Irish Regiment
Combermere Barracks		England	Berkshire	1804	Household Cavalry Regiment
Copthorne Barracks		England	Shropshire	1881	143 (West Midlands) Brigade
Dale Barracks		England	Cheshire	1939	

Dalton Barracks		England	Oxfordshire	1992	3 Logistic Support Regiment 4 Logistic Support Regiment 12 Logistic Support Regiment
Deepcut Barracks		England	Surrey	1903	25 Training Support Regiment Defence College of Logistics
Delhi Barracks	Tidworth	England	Wiltshire		HQ 1st Mechanized Brigade 215 Signal Squadron 4 (Close Support) Battalion REME 6 (Close Support) Battalion REME
Denison Barracks		England	Berkshire	1949	42 Engineer Regiment (Geographic)
Dering Lines		Wales	Powys	1939	Infantry Battle School
Dreghorn Barracks		Scotland	Edinburgh	1939	Royal Scots Borderers
Duchess of Kent Barracks	Aldershot	England	Hampshire	1969	
Elizabeth Barracks		England	Surrey	1875	Army Training Centre, Pirbright
Fenham Barracks		England	Tyne & Wear	1806	'D' Squadron (The Northumberland Hussars) 201 (Northern) Field Hospital
Fort George		Scotland	Inverness-shire	1757	
Forthside Barracks		Scotland	Stirlingshire	1899	
Fulwood Barracks		England	Lancashire	1848	42 (North West) Brigade
Gamecock Barracks		England	Warwickshire	1959	30 Signal Regiment
Gaza Barracks	Catterick	England	North Yorkshire		3 Medical Regiment
Gibraltar Barracks, Surrey		England	Surrey		Royal School of Military Engineering (Minley)
Gibraltar Barracks, Suffolk		England	Suffolk		Regimental HQ Royal Anglian Regiment
Glencorse Barracks		Scotland	Midlothian	1803	Royal Highland Fusiliers
Goojerat Barracks	Colchester	England	Essex		156 Provost Company
Gordon Barracks		Scotland	Aberdeenshire	1935	
Hammersley Barracks	Aldershot	England	Hampshire	1964	Royal Army Physical Training Corps (RAPTC)
Howe Barracks		England	Kent		

Hyde Park Barracks		England	London	1795	Household Cavalry Mounted Regiment
Imjin Barracks		England	Gloucestershire	2010	Allied Rapid Reaction Corps
Imphal Barracks		England	North Yorkshire	1880	15th Infantry Brigade
Invicta Park Barracks		England	Kent	1936	36 Engineer Regiment
Jellalabad Barracks	Tidworth	England	Wiltshire		HQ 43 (Wessex) Brigade
Kendrew Barracks		England	Rutland	2012	2nd Battalion, Royal Anglian Regiment 7 Regiment
Kinloss Barracks		Scotland	Moray	2012	39 Engineer Regiment
Kiwi Barracks	Bulford	England	Wiltshire		4th Battalion, The Rifles
Lucknow Barracks	Tidworth	England	Wiltshire		2nd Battalion, The Royal Welsh (Royal Regiment of Wales)
Maindy Barracks		Wales	Cardiff	1877	3rd Battalion, The Royal Welsh (Royal Regiment of Wales)
Marne Barracks	Catterick	England	North Yorkshire	1994	1st Battalion, The Mercian Regiment 5th Regiment Royal Artillery
McGrigor Barracks	Aldershot	England	Hampshire		
Megiddo Lines	Catterick	England	North Yorkshire		1 (Close Support) Battalion REME
Merville Barracks	Colchester	England	Essex		2nd Battalion, Parachute Regiment 3rd Battalion, Parachute Regiment
Mooltan Barracks	Tidworth	England	Wiltshire		1st Battalion, Royal Regiment of Fusiliers
Normandy Barracks	Aldershot	England	Hampshire	1965	
Palace Barracks, Holywood		Northern Ireland	Down	1886	Royal Irish Regiment
Piave Lines	Catterick	England	North Yorkshire		
Picton Barracks	Bulford	England	Wiltshire		HQ 3rd Division
Prince Philip Barracks		England	Hampshire		School of Electrical and Mechanical Engineers
Prince William of Gloucester Barracks		England	Lincolnshire	1976	5 Training Regiment

Quebec Barracks	Aldershot	England	Hampshire		
Queen Elizabeth Barracks		England	North Yorkshire		
Redford Barracks		Scotland	Edinburgh	1915	3rd Battalion, The Rifles
Regent's Park Barracks		England	London	1896	20 Transport Squadron
Rhine Barracks	Aldershot	England	Hampshire	1965	
Roberts Barracks		England	Wiltshire		32nd Regiment Royal Artillery
Robertson Barracks		England	Norfolk	1995	1st The Queen's Dragoon Guards
Rock Barracks		England	Suffolk	2006	23 Engineer Regiment (Air Assault)
Royal Artillery Barracks		England	London	1802	2nd Battalion, Princess of Wales's Royal Regiment
Sam Domingo Barracks Formerly Louisburg Barracks	Aldershot	England	Hampshire		Central Volunteer Headquarters REME
Shorncliffe Army Camp		England	Kent		2 (South East) Brigade
Sir John Moore Barracks		England	Hampshire	1986	ATR Winchester
Somme Barracks		England	South Yorkshire	1907	1st Battalion, The Duke of Lancaster's Regiment
St George's Barracks		England	Rutland	2006	16th Regiment Royal Artillery
Stirling Barracks		England	Wiltshire		14th Regiment Royal Artillery
Swinton Barracks	Tidworth (Perham Down)	England	Wiltshire		22 Engineer Regiment 26 Engineer Regiment
The Barracks, Brecon		Wales	Powys	1805	160th (Wales) Brigade
Thiepval Barracks		Northern Ireland	Antrim	1954	38th (Irish) Infantry Brigade
Travers Barracks	Aldershot	England	Hampshire		27 Theatre Logistic Regiment
Unijack Barracks		England	North Yorkshire	1947	Army Foundation College, Harrogate
Vauxhall Barracks		England	Oxfordshire		11 Explosive Ordnance Disposal Regiment RLC
Victoria Barracks		England	London	1853	1st Battalion, Coldstream Guards

Walcheren Barracks		Scotland	Glasgow	1967	
Ward Barracks	Bulford	England	Wiltshire		
Weeton Barracks		England	Lancashire		2nd Battalion the Duke of Lancaster's Regiment
Wellington Barracks		England	London	1833	
Whittington Barracks		England	Staffordshire	1877	Defence Medical Services
Wyvern Barracks		England	Devon	1800	

External links

- "Parliamentary Questions and Answers - name and location of each Regular and Territorial Army Infantry Battalion"[1159]. Think Defence. 2 February 2011.

Selection and Training in the British Army

Selection and training in the British Army is the process by which candidates for service are identified, inducted and brought onto the trained strength. The process is the responsibility of the Adjutant General, the personnel director for the Army based at Trenchard Lines in Wiltshire.

Selection

Candidates for all three of the British Armed Forces are first handled through Armed Forces Career Offices, which are located in major conurbations around the United Kingdom supporting the respective recruitment functions. Candidates for enlistment may be aged between 15 years, 7 months (for enlistment from age 16) and 32. Candidates for officer entry may be aged between 18 and 29.

Regular Army training

Candidates for the Army undergo common training, beginning with initial military training, to bring all personnel to a similar standard in basic military skills, and further specialist training is delivered according to the Regiment or Corps for which the individual has been identified as a candidate. Completion of Phase 2 training brings the individual onto the trained strength; however, each of the British Armed Forces will continue to deliver specialist and generalist training throughout the individual's career.

Much training in the British Armed Forces has been accredited by various awarding bodies, resulting in the opportunity to gain civilian qualifications through service training activities.

Phase 1

Phase 1 training features basic training for all new recruits. For other ranks, this is the **Common Military Syllabus (Recruits)** (CMSR). CMSR covers the skills and fitness needed to survive and operate in a field environment, and seeks to imbue the ethos and principles of the British Army. The trainee is required to demonstrate competence in thirteen training objectives over the fourteen-week course. Officers undertake the **Commissioning Course**, which covers the basic aspects of soldiering as well as command, leadership and management. The standard course for new Direct Entry Officers lasts 44 weeks. Professionally qualified officers (those that have joined the army having already gained a professional qualification, such as doctors, lawyers or chaplains) undergo a shorter, ten-week course.[1160] The **Late Entry Officers Course** is a four-week course for already serving soldiers that have been chosen for commissioning as officers.[1161]

There are five training establishments for Phase 1 training in the Regular Army:

Title	Name	Course length	Attendees
Officers			
Royal Military Academy Sandhurst	Sandhurst	44 wk	All Arms Direct Entry Officers
		10 wk	Professionally Qualified Officers
		4 wk	Late Entry Officers
Other Ranks			
Army Foundation College	Harrogate	49 wk	(ages 16–17½) • Royal Armoured Corps/Household Cavalry • Royal Artillery • some Royal Logistic Corps roles
		23 wk	(ages 16–17½) for those joining courses with longer Phase 2 training – these are: • Royal Electrical and Mechanical Engineers • Royal Engineers • Royal Signals • Adjutant General's Corps • Royal Army Medical Corps • Army Air Corps • and some Royal Logistic Corps roles

Selection and Training in the British Army

Army Training Regiment	Pirbright	14 wk	• Corps of Royal Electrical and Mechanical Engineers • Army Air Corps • Royal Regiment of Artillery • Royal Corps of Signals • Royal Logistic Corps • Adjutant General's Corps • Royal Army Medical Corps • Intelligence Corps • Corps of Army Music
Army Training Regiment	Winchester	14 wk	• Royal Armoured Corps • Army Air Corps • Royal Regiment of Artillery • Corps of Royal Engineers • Royal Corps of Signals • Royal Logistic Corps • Adjutant General's Corps • Royal Army Medical Corps • Intelligence Corps
Infantry Training Centre	Catterick	26 wk	Infantry Regiments

Phase 1 training is intended to bring all recruits to a base level of military competency, capable of operating in the field, providing force protection, operational security and displaying the other characteristics of a member of the British Army. For officers, this also includes the professional competencies required for command. During this period, recruits pass in and receive their regimental berets; they then pass out and continue to phase 2 to undergo job training. The training embeds the core values:

- Courage
- Discipline
- Respect for others
- Integrity
- Loyalty
- Selfless commitment

Phase 2

The second phase involves the new officer or soldier training for the branch of the service they wish to specialise in, and then undergoing specific training. This is with one of the specialist schools located around the country:

Name	Location	Arm	Comments
Infantry Training Centre	Catterick	Infantry	Combined Phase 1 and 2
Armour Centre	Bovington Camp	Royal Armoured Corps Household Cavalry	
Royal School of Artillery	Larkhill	Royal Artillery	
Army Aviation Centre	Middle Wallop	Army Air Corps	
Royal School of Military Engineering	Chatham	Royal Engineers	
Royal School of Signals	Blandford Camp	Royal Corps of Signals	
Defence School of Electronic and Mechanical Engineering	Lyneham	Royal Electrical and Mechanical Engineers	
Defence College of Logistics	various	Royal Logistic Corps	
Defence Medical Services Training Centre	Whittington Barracks	Royal Army Medical Corps	
Defence School of Personnel Administration	Worthy Down Barracks	Adjutant General's Corps	
Defence College of Policing and Guarding	Southwick Park	Royal Military Police	
Royal Military School of Music	Kneller Hall	Corps of Army Music	
Joint Intelligence Training Group	Chicksands	Intelligence Corps	

Infantry Training Centre

Since 2001, infantry training for other ranks is undertaken as a single 26-week course (28 weeks for the parachute regiment, or any of the five guards regiments) at the Infantry Training Centre at Catterick Garrison, as opposed to being divided into Phase 1 and Phase 2 training. The ITC is divided into four battalions; these are divided into companies, each of which are responsible for one of the infantry's administrative divisions:

- 1st Infantry Training Battalion is responsible for training soldiers destined to join the regiments of the Queen's Division, Prince of Wales' Division, the Royal Irish Regiment and The Rifles, King's Division and the Royal Regiment of Scotland. The 1st Battalion has five training companies:
  - Queen's Division Company
  - Prince of Wales's Division Company
  - Rifles Training Company
  - King's Division Company
  - Royal Regiment of Scotland Training Company

- 2nd Infantry Training Battalion has responsibility for training recruits who will join one of the regiments of the Guards Division, the Parachute Regiment and the Brigade of Gurkhas. 2 ITB is also responsible for the Phase 2 training for junior entry recruits from the Army Foundation College, as well as training for the infantry elements of the Army Reserve.
  - Guards Training Company
  - Parachute Regiment Training Company
  - Gurkha Training Company
  - Anzio Company
- The ITC Support Battalion is the ITC's primary support unit, dealing with logistic and medical support. The battalion is structured to provide maximum support throughout the ITC and consists of the following departments:
  - Headquarter (HQ) Company
  - Hook VC Company (discharged soldiers)
  - Gym
  - Army School of Ceremonial
  - Army School of Bagpipe Music and Highland Drumming
  - Quartermaster's (QMs) Department
  - G7 Training
  - 400 Troop, Royal Logistic Corps

Further infantry training, as well as Phase 2 training for new infantry officers, is undertaken at the Infantry Battle School and the Specialist Weapons School.

Army Reserve training

Soldiers

For Army Reserve soldiers, recruit training is in two phases: Phase 1, also known as the Common Military Syllabus (Reserve) (CMS(R)) Course, and Phase 2, special-to-arm training.

Phase 1

In Phase 1, recruits cover the Common Military Syllabus 14 (CMS14). Part 'a' is a series of four training weekends at Army Training Units (ATUs), formerly known as Regional Training Centres (RTCs). At some ATUs the Phase 1a is also run as a consolidated course. For all Army Reserve soldiers, Phase 1 concludes with a two-week training course (Phase 1b) normally held at an Army Training Regiment; infantry recruits then undertake their Phase 2 training at Catterick. Recruits to the 4th Battalion, The Parachute Regiment and the Honourable Artillery Company complete their equivalent of CMS(R) within their own units.

Phase 2

Phase 2 is a further period of special-to-arm training specific to the type of unit the recruit is joining. This is normally conducted by the Arm or Service that the recruit is joining, for example for infantry units, Phase 2 consists of the two-week Combat Infantryman's Course (Reserve) (CIC (Res)) held at the Infantry Training Centre, Catterick.

Officers

To gain a commission, potential officers have to pass through four modules of training, which together form the Army Reserve Commissioning Course.

Module A consists of basic field training and elementary military skills. This can be completed at either a UOTC over a number of weekends, or over two weeks at the Royal Military Academy Sandhurst (RMAS).

Module B covers training in Tactics, Leadership, Doctrine and Navigation, both in theory and in practice, with a focus on the section battle drills and the platoon combat estimate. This training can either be spread over ten weekends at a UOTC, or two weeks at the RMAS.

Module C builds on the Tactics, Leadership, Doctrine and Navigation taught in Module B, with a greater focus on the theory behind these constructs. CBRN training is also added at this point, and Officer Cadets undergo a number of field exercises to test their military and leadership skills. Module C can only be undertaken at the RMAS.

Module D: once the Officer Cadet has completed their Army Officer Selection Board, they can complete this final module, after which they will become commissioned officers in the British Army. Based at the RMAS, this module consists primarily of a prolonged field exercise, followed by drill training in preparation for the passing out parade.

On successful completion of Module D, the Officer Cadets receive their Commission and become Second Lieutenants. Further training that is required prior to them being considered for operational deployment and promotion to Lieutenant includes:

Post Commissioning Training (formerly known as Module 5), again run at an OTC, over three weekends.

Special To Arm training is specific to the type of unit the subaltern is joining, and covers a two-week period. This is increasingly integrated with the tactics phase of a Regular training course. For example, the Platoon Commander's Battle Course held at the Infantry Battle School in Brecon, which is integrated with Regular training, or the Yeomanry Tactics Course held at the Land Warfare Centre in Warminster, which is not.

External links

 Wikimedia Commons has media related to *Selection and training in the British Army*.

- Training in the Army[1162] at army.mod.uk

Royal Air Force

Royal Air Force

Royal Air Force	
	Badge of the Royal Air Force
Founded	1 April 1918 (100 years)
Country	United Kingdom
Allegiance	Elizabeth II
Type	Air force
Role	Aerial warfare
Size	33,240 active personnel 832 operational aircraft 1,940 RAuxAF 2,220 reserve personnel[1163]
Air Staff Offices	Whitehall, London
Motto(s)	Latin: *Per Ardua ad Astra* "Through Adversity to the Stars"
March	Royal Air Force March Past
Website	www.raf.mod.uk[1164]
Commanders	
Chief of the Air Staff	Air Chief Marshal Sir Stephen Hillier KCB CBE DFC

Notable commanders	Lord Trenchard Lord Portal
Insignia	
Ensign	
Logo	
Roundels	
Fin flashes	
Pilot's Brevet	
Aircraft flown	
Attack	• Eurofighter Typhoon • General Atomics MQ-9A Reaper • General Atomics MQ-9B Protector • Lockheed Martin F-35 Lightning II • Panavia Tornado GR4
Fighter	• Eurofighter Typhoon • Lockheed Martin F-35 Lightning II
Trainer helicopter	• Bell Griffin HT1 • Eurocopter Squirrel HT1
Utility helicopter	• Aérospatiale SA 330 Puma HC2 • Leonardo AW109SP GrandNew • Bell Griffin HAR2 • Boeing Chinook HC4/5/6/6A
Reconnaissance	• Beechcraft Shadow R1 • Boeing E-3D Sentry AEW1 • Boeing RC-135W Airseeker • General Atomics MQ-9A Reaper • Panavia Tornado GR4A • Raytheon Sentinel R1
Trainer	• BAE Hawk T1/T2 • Beechcraft Super King Air • Grob Viking T1 • Grob Tutor T1 • Short Tucano T1

Transport	• Airbus Voyager KC2/KC3 • Airbus A400M Atlas C1 • Boeing C-17 Globemaster III • BAe 146 CC2/C3 • Lockheed Martin C-130J Hercules C4/C5

The **Royal Air Force** (**RAF**) is the United Kingdom's aerial warfare force. Formed towards the end of the First World War on 1 April 1918, it is the oldest independent air force in the world. Following victory over the Central Powers in 1918 the RAF emerged as, at the time, the largest air force in the world.[1165] Since its formation, the RAF has taken a significant role in British military history. In particular, it played a large part in the Second World War where it fought its most famous campaign, the Battle of Britain.[1166]

The RAF's mission is to support the objectives of the British Ministry of Defence (MoD), which are to "provide the capabilities needed: to ensure the security and defence of the United Kingdom and overseas territories, including against terrorism; to support the Government's foreign policy objectives particularly in promoting international peace and security". The RAF describe its mission statement as "... [to provide] An *agile*, *adaptable* and *capable* Air Force that, person for person, is second to none, and that makes a decisive air power contribution in support of the UK Defence Mission". The mission statement is supported by the RAF's definition of air power, which guides its strategy. Air power is defined as "the ability to project power from the air and space to influence the behaviour of people or the course of events".

Today the Royal Air Force maintains an operational fleet of various types of aircraft, described by the RAF as being "leading-edge" in terms of technology.[1167] This largely consists of fixed-wing aircraft, including: fighter and strike aircraft, airborne early warning and control aircraft, ISTAR and SIGINT aircraft, aerial refueling aircraft and strategic and tactical transport aircraft. The majority of the RAF's rotary-wing aircraft form part of the tri-service Joint Helicopter Command in support of ground forces. Most of the RAF's aircraft and personnel are based in the UK, with many others serving on operations (principally over Iraq and Syria) or at long-established overseas bases (Ascension Island, Cyprus, Gibraltar, and the Falkland Islands). Although the RAF is the principal British air power arm, the Royal Navy's Fleet Air Arm and the British Army's Army Air Corps also deliver air power which is integrated into the maritime, littoral and land environments.

History

Origins

While the British were not the first to make use of heavier-than-air military aircraft, the RAF is the world's oldest independent air force: that is, the first air force to become independent of army or navy control. Following publication of the "Smuts report" prepared by Jan Smuts the RAF was founded on 1 April 1918, with headquarters located in the former Hotel Cecil, during the First World War, by the amalgamation of the Royal Flying Corps (RFC) and the Royal Naval Air Service (RNAS). At that time it was the largest air force in the world. After the war, the service was drastically cut and its inter-war years were relatively quiet, with the RAF taking responsibility for the control of Iraq and executing a number of minor actions in other parts of the British Empire. The RAF's naval aviation branch, the Fleet Air Arm, was founded in 1924 but handed over to Admiralty control on 24 May 1939.

The RAF developed the doctrine of strategic bombing which led to the construction of long-range bombers and became its main bombing strategy in the Second World War.[1168]

Second World War

The RAF underwent rapid expansion prior to and during the Second World War. Under the British Commonwealth Air Training Plan of December 1939, the air forces of British Commonwealth countries trained and formed "Article XV squadrons" for service with RAF formations. Many individual personnel from these countries, and exiles from occupied Europe, also served with RAF squadrons. By the end of the war the Royal Canadian Air Force had contributed more than 30 squadrons to serve in RAF formations, similarly, approximately a quarter of Bomber Command's personnel were Canadian. Additionally, the Royal Australian Air Force represented around nine percent of all RAF personnel who served in the European and Mediterranean theatres.

In the Battle of Britain in 1940, the RAF (supplemented by 2 Fleet Air Arm Squadrons, Polish, Czecho-Slovak and other multinational pilots and ground personnel) defended the skies over Britain against the numerically superior German Luftwaffe. In what is perhaps the most prolonged and complicated air campaign in history, the Battle of Britain contributed significantly to the delay and subsequent indefinite postponement of Hitler's plans for an invasion of the United Kingdom (Operation Sea Lion). In the House of Commons on 20 August, prompted by the ongoing efforts of the RAF, Prime Minister Winston Churchill eloquently made a speech to the nation, where he said "Never in the field of human conflict was so much owed by so many to so few".

Figure 185: *A late-war version of the Spitfire, which played a major role in the Battle of Britain.*

Figure 186: *The Avro Lancaster heavy bomber was extensively used during the strategic bombing of Germany.*

Figure 187: *The Handley Page Victor bomber was a strategic bomber of the RAF's V bomber force used to carry both conventional and nuclear bombs.*

The largest RAF effort during the war was the strategic bombing campaign against Germany by Bomber Command. While RAF bombing of Germany began almost immediately upon the outbreak of war, under the leadership of Air Chief Marshal Harris, these attacks became increasingly devastating from 1942 onward as new technology and greater numbers of superior aircraft became available. The RAF adopted night-time area bombing on German cities such as Hamburg and Dresden, and developed precision bombing techniques for specific operations, such as the "Dambusters" raid by No. 617 Squadron,[1169] or the Amiens prison raid known as Operation Jericho.

Cold War era

Following victory in the Second World War, the RAF underwent significant re-organisation, as technological advances in air warfare saw the arrival of jet fighters and bombers. During the early stages of the Cold War, one of the first major operations undertaken by the Royal Air Force was in 1948 and the Berlin Airlift, codenamed Operation Plainfire. Between 26 June and the lifting of the Russian blockade of the city on 2 May, the RAF provided 17% of the total supplies delivered during the event, using Avro Yorks, Douglas Dakotas flying to Gatow Airport and Short Sunderlands flying to Lake Havel.

Figure 188: *The Avro Vulcan was a strategic bomber used during the Cold War to carry conventional and nuclear bombs.*

Before Britain developed its own nuclear weapons the RAF was provided with American nuclear weapons under Project E. However following the development of its own arsenal, the British Government elected on 16 February 1960 to share the country's nuclear deterrent between the RAF and submarines of the Royal Navy, first deciding on 13 April to concentrate solely on the air force's V bomber fleet. These were initially armed with nuclear gravity bombs, later being equipped with the Blue Steel missile. Following the development of the Royal Navy's Polaris submarines, the strategic nuclear deterrent passed to the navy's submarines on 30 June 1969. With the introduction of Polaris, the RAF's strategic nuclear role was reduced to a tactical one, using WE.177 gravity bombs. This tactical role was continued by the V bombers into the 1980s and until 1998 by Tornado GR1s.[1170,1171]

For much of the Cold War the primary role of the RAF was the defence of Western Europe against potential attack by the Soviet Union, with many squadrons based in West Germany. With the decline of the British Empire, global operations were scaled back, and RAF Far East Air Force was disbanded on 31 October 1971.[1172] Despite this, the RAF fought in many battles in the Cold War period. In June 1948 the RAF commenced Operation Firedog against Malayan terrorists during the Malayan Emergency. Operations continued for the next 12 years until 1960 with aircraft flying out of RAF Tengah and RAF Butterworth. The RAF played a minor role in the Korean War, with flying boats taking part. From 1953 to 1956 the RAF Avro Lincoln squadrons carried out anti-Mau Mau operations in Kenya using its base at RAF Eastleigh. The Suez Crisis in 1956 saw a large RAF role, with aircraft operating from RAF Akrotiri and RAF Nicosia on Cyprus and RAF Luqa and RAF Hal Far on Malta as part of Operation Musketeer. The Konfrontasi against Indonesia in the early 1960s did see use of RAF aircraft, but due to a combination of deft diplomacy and selective ignoring of certain events by both sides, it never developed into a full-scale war.

One of the largest actions undertaken by the RAF during the cold war was the air campaign during the 1982 Falklands War, in which the RAF operated alongside the Fleet Air Arm. During the war, RAF aircraft were deployed in the mid-Atlantic at RAF Ascension Island and a detachment from No. 1 Squadron was deployed with the Royal Navy, operating from the aircraft carrier HMS *Hermes*.[1173,1174] RAF pilots also flew missions using the Royal Navy's Sea Harriers in the air-to-air combat role. Following a British victory, the RAF remained in the South Atlantic to provide air defence to the Falkland Islands, based at RAF Mount Pleasant (built 1984).

Recent history

With the end of the Cold War and the collapse of the Soviet Union, the RAF's focus has returned to delivering expeditionary air power.[1175] Since 1990 the RAF has been involved in several large-scale operations, including: the 1991 Gulf War, the 1999 Kosovo War, the 2001 War in Afghanistan,[1176] the 2003 invasion and war in Iraq and the 2011 intervention in Libya.

The RAF's 90th anniversary was commemorated on 1 April 2008 by a flypast of 9 Red Arrows and four Typhoons along the Thames, in a straight line from just south of London City Airport Tower Bridge, the London Eye, the RAF Memorial and (at 13.00) the Ministry of Defence building.

Four major defence reviews have been conducted since the end of the Cold War: the 1990 Options for Change, the 1998 Strategic Defence Review, the 2003 Delivering Security in a Changing World and the 2010 Strategic Defence and Security Review. All four defence reviews have resulted in steady reductions in manpower and numbers of aircraft, especially combat aircraft such as fast-jets. As part of the latest 2010 Strategic Defence and Security Review, the BAE Systems Nimrod MRA4 maritime patrol aircraft was cancelled due to over spending and missing deadlines. Other reductions saw total RAF manpower reduced by 5,000 personnel to a trained strength of 33,000 and the early retirement of the Joint Force Harrier aircraft, the Harrier GR7/GR9.

In recent years fighter aircraft on Quick Reaction Alert (QRA) have been increasingly required to scramble in response to efforts made by the Russian Air Force to approach British airspace.[1177] On 24 January 2014 in the Houses

Figure 189: *Typhoons and Red Arrows flypast for the 90th Anniversary of the RAF, 2008*

Figure 190: *A Typhoon on QRA intercepts a Russian Tupolev Tu-95 bomber approaching UK airspace.*

of Parliament, Conservative MP and Minister of State for the Armed Forces, Andrew Robathan, announced that the RAF's QRA force had been scrambled almost thirty times in the last three years: eleven times during 2010, ten times during 2011 and eight times during 2012.[1178]

RAF Coningsby in Lincolnshire and RAF Lossiemouth in Moray both provide Quick Reaction Alert, or QRA, and scramble their fighter jets within minutes to meet or intercept aircraft which give cause for concern. Lossiemouth generally covers the northern sector, while Coningsby provides QRA in the south. Typhoon pilot Flight Lieutenant Noel Rees describes how QRA duty works. "At the start of the scaled QRA response, civilian air traffic controllers might see on their screens an aircraft behaving erratically, not responding to their radio calls, or note that it's transmitting a distress signal through its transponder. Rather than scramble Typhoons at the first hint of something abnormal, a controller has the option to put them on a higher level of alert, 'a call to cockpit'. In this scenario the pilot races to the hardened aircraft shelter and does everything short of starting his engines".[1179]

On 4 October 2015, a final stand-down saw the end of more than 70 years of RAF Search and Rescue provision in the UK. The RAF and Royal Navy's Westland Sea King fleets, after over 30 years of service, were retired. A civilian contractor, Bristow Helicopters, took over responsibility for UK Search and Rescue, under a Private Finance Initiative with newly purchased Sikorsky S-92 and AgustaWestland AW189 aircraft. The new contract means that all UK SAR coverage is now provided by Bristow aircraft.

In 2018 the RAF's vision of a future constellation of imagery satellites was initiated through the launch of the Carbonite-2 technology demonstrator. The 100 kg Carbonite-2 uses commercial off-the-shelf (COTS) components to deliver high-quality imagery and 3D video footage from space.

Structure

Royal Air Force

- **Royal Air Force**
- RAF Regiment
- RAF Volunteer Reserve
- RAF Medical Services
- Nursing Service (PMRAFNS)
- Royal Auxiliary Air Force
- RAF Police

History

- History
- Timeline

Aircraft

- List of RAF aircraft

Structure

- Air Command
- No. 1 Group
- No. 2 Group
- Joint Force Air Component Headquarters (JFACHQ)
- No. 22 Group
- No. 38 Group
- Stations

Personnel

- Officer ranks
- Other ranks

- $\underline{v}$
- $\underline{t}$
- $\underline{e}^{1180}$

The professional head of the RAF is the Chief of the Air Staff (CAS). The CAS heads the Air Force Board, which is a committee of the Defence Council. The Air Force Board is the management board of the RAF and consists of several high-ranking officers.

Authority is delegated from the Air Force Board to the RAF's commands. While there were once individual commands responsible for bombers, fighters, training, etc., now only the Air Command exists, headquartered at RAF High Wycombe. As this command is headed by the Chief of the Air Staff himself, it does not operate in way previous commands did with their own separate Air Officers Commanding and staff remote from Whitehall.

Groups

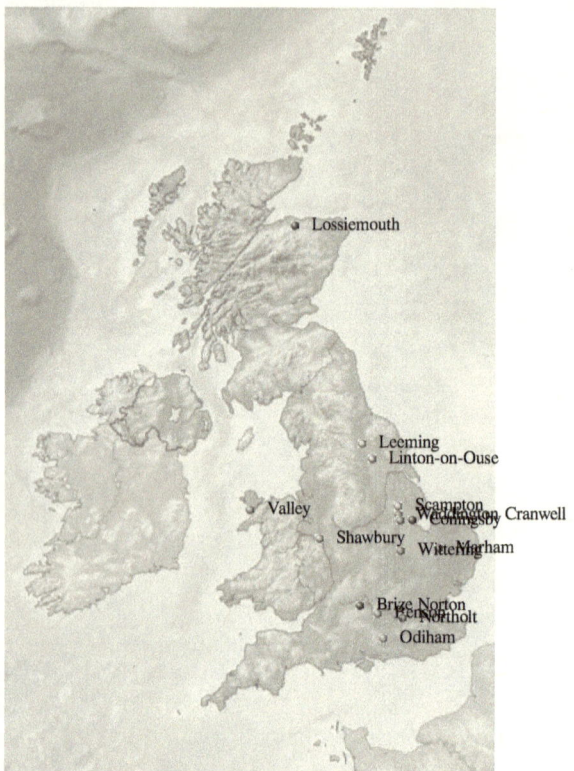

File:United Kingdom relief location map.jpg

Main bases of the Royal Air Force 2018:
- Typhoon ● Tornado ● Hawk T1A ● Hawk T2 ● Tucano T1
- ISTAR ● Transport ● Helicopters ● Basic Trainers ● VIP

Groups are the subdivisions of operational commands; these are responsible for certain types of operation or for operations in limited geographical areas:

- No. 1 Group (Air Combat): controls the fast-jet force and the RAF's intelligence, surveillance, target acquisition, and reconnaissance (ISTAR) capabilities, as well as the following stations: RAF Boulmer, RAF Coningsby, RAF Fylingdales, RAF Lossiemouth, RAF Marham, RAF Scampton, RAF Spadeadam and RAF Waddington.
- No. 2 Group (Air Combat Support): controls the Air Mobility aircraft and the RAF's Force Protection assets as well as the following stations: RAF Benson, RAF Brize Norton, RAF Odiham and RAF Northolt.

Figure 191: *Phased Array Ballistic Missile Early Warning System at RAF Fylingdales.*

- No. 11 Group (Multi-domain operations group): will lead air and space operations.
- No. 22 Group (Training): responsible for the supply of qualified and skilled personnel, as well as the following stations: RAF College Cranwell, RAF Cosford, RAF Halton, RAF Linton-on-Ouse, RAF Shawbury, MOD St Athan, RAF St Mawgan and RAF Valley.
- No. 38 Group (Air Combat Service Support): responsible for engineering and logistics, communications and medical operations, as well as the following stations: RAF High Wycombe and RAF Wittering.
- No. 83 Group (Expeditionary Air): the RAF's operational headquarters in the Middle East, responsible for UK air operations in the Operations KIPION and SHADER Joint Operating Areas (JOAs) of some eight million square miles.

Stations

An RAF station is ordinarily subordinate to a group; it is commanded by a group captain and it is sub-divided into administrative wings, each under a wing commander, as follows:

- Operations wing
- Forward support wing

- Depth support wing
- Tactical imagery support wing
- Base support wing

Wings

As well as administrative wings, the RAF has formed Expeditionary Air Wings (EAWs), each under a wing commander, to support operations; wings currently active are as follows:

- No. 34 Expeditionary Air Wing, based at RAF Waddington: delivers ISTAR operations
- No. 38 Expeditionary Air Wing, based at RAF Brize Norton: delivers air transport operations
- No. 121 Expeditionary Air Wing based at RAF Coningsby: delivers multi role operations
- No. 135 Expeditionary Air Wing based at RAF Leeming: delivers fighter operations
- No. 138 Expeditionary Air Wing based at RAF Marham: delivers fighter operations
- No. 140 Expeditionary Air Wing based at RAF Lossiemouth: delivers fighter operations
- No. 901 Expeditionary Air Wing based in the middle east: delivers voice and data systems
- No. 902 Expeditionary Air Wing based in the middle east: delivers helicopter services
- No. 903 Expeditionary Air Wing based at RAF Akrotiri: delivers operations against ISIL
- No. 906 Expeditionary Air Wing based in the middle east: delivers transport services

Squadrons

A flying squadron is an aircraft unit which carries out the primary tasks of the RAF. RAF squadrons are somewhat analogous to the regiments of the British Army in that they have histories and traditions going back to their formation, regardless of where they are based, which aircraft they are operating, etc. They can be awarded standards and battle honours for meritorious service. Whilst every squadron is different, most flying squadrons are commanded by a wing commander and, for a fast-jet squadron, have an establishment of around 12 aircraft.

Training Schools

The RAF Schools consist of the squadrons and support apparatus that train new aircrew to join front-line squadrons. The schools separate individual streams, but group together units with similar responsibility or that operate the same aircraft type. Some schools operate with only one Squadron, and have an overall training throughput which is relatively small; some, like 3 FTS, have responsibility for all Elementary Flying Training (EFT) in the RAF, and all RAF aircrew will pass through its squadrons when they start their flying careers. 2 FTS and 6 FTS do not have a front-line training responsibility – their job is to group the University Air Squadrons and the Volunteer Gliding Squadrons together. 2 FTS's commanding officer holds the only full-time flying appointment for a Group Captain in the RAF, although he is a reservist.

- Central Flying School – CFS standardises flying training across the air force and ensures standards and safety are maintained.
- No. 1 Flying Training School – Basic Fast Jet Training (BFJT), based at RAF Linton-on-Ouse
- No. 2 Flying Training School – Gliding training, based at RAF Syerston
- No. 3 Flying Training School – Elementary Flying Training, based at RAFC Cranwell with a squadron at RAF Wittering.
- No. 4 Flying Training School – Advanced Fast Jet Training (AFJT), based at RAF Valley
- No. 6 Flying Training School – Flight training for the University Air Squadrons, based at RAF stations throughout the UK

The British military operate a number of joint training organisations based at RAF Stations:

- Defence Elementary Flying Training School – Elementary Flying Training for Royal Navy and Army Air Corps students, based at RAF Barkston Heath
- Defence Helicopter Flying School – Basic helicopter training, based at RAF Shawbury.
- Defence College of Technical Training – Several different specialist areas: aeronautical engineering, electro and mechanical engineering, and communication and information systems.
  - Defence College of Aeronautical Engineering. Comprising:
    - Royal Naval Air Engineering and Survival Equipment School.
    - DCAE (Lyneham)
    - No 1 School of Technical Training, Royal Air Force
  - Defence College of Electro-Mechanical Engineering. Comprising:
    - Royal Naval School of Marine Engineering
    - 8 Battalion Royal Electrical and Mechanical Engineers

Figure 192: *RAF Mount Pleasant, home to No. 1435 Flight providing air defence for the Falkland Islands*

- No 4 School of Technical Training, Royal Air Force
- Defence School of Communications and Information Systems. Comprising:
  - 11th (Royal School of Signals) Signal Regiment
  - No 1 Radio School, Royal Air Force
- Defence School of Marine Engineering.

Flights

A flight is a sub-division of a squadron. Flying squadrons are often divided into two flights, e.g., "A" and "B", each under the command of a squadron leader. Administrative squadrons on a station are also divided into flights and these flights are commanded by a junior officer, often a flight lieutenant. Because of their small size, there are several flying units formed as flights rather than squadrons. For example, No. 1435 Flight is based at RAF Mount Pleasant in the Falkland Islands, maintaining air defence cover with four Eurofighter Typhoon aircraft.

Figure 193: *Members of the RAF Regiment on parade, 2013*

Personnel

At its height in 1944 during the Second World War, more than 1,100,000 personnel were serving in the RAF. The longest-lived founding member of the RAF was Henry Allingham, who died on 18 July 2009 aged 113.

As of 1 January 2015, the Royal Air Force numbered some 34,200 Regular[1181] and 1,940 Royal Auxiliary Air Force[1182] personnel, giving a combined component strength of 36,140 personnel. In addition to the active elements of the Royal Air Force, (Regular and Royal Auxiliary Air Force), all ex-Regular personnel remain liable to be recalled for duty in a time of need, this is known as the Regular Reserve. In 2007 there were 33,980 Regular Reserves of the Royal Air Force, of which 7,950 served under a fixed-term reserve contract.[1183] Publications since April 2013 no-longer report the entire strength of the Regular Reserve, instead they only give a figure for Regular Reserves who serve under a fixed-term reserve contract.[1184] They had a strength of 7,120 personnel in 2014.[1185]

Figures provided by the International Institute for Strategic Studies from 2012 showed that Royal Air Force pilots achieve a relatively high number of flying hours per year when compared with other major NATO allies such as France and Germany. RAF pilots achieve 210 to 290 flying hours per year.[1186] French and German Air Force pilots achieved only 180 and 150 flying hours across their fleets respectively.[1187]

Officers

Officers hold a commission from the Sovereign, which provides the legal authority for them to issue orders to subordinates. The commission of a regular officer is granted after successfully completing the 24-week-long Initial Officer Training course at the RAF College, Cranwell, Lincolnshire.

To emphasize the merger of both military and naval aviation when the RAF was formed, many of the titles of officers were deliberately chosen to be of a naval character, such as flight lieutenant, wing commander, group captain, and air commodore.

Other ranks

Other ranks attend the Recruit Training Squadron at RAF Halton for basic training. The titles and insignia of other ranks in the RAF were based on that of the Army, with some alterations in terminology. Over the years, this structure has seen significant changes: for example, there was once a separate system for those in technical trades, and the ranks of chief technician and junior technician continue to be held only by personnel in technical trades. RAF other ranks fall into four categories: Warrant Officers, Senior Non-Commissioned Officers, Junior Non-Commissioned Officers and Airmen. All Warrant Officers in the RAF are equal in terms of rank, but the most senior Non-Commissioned appointment is known as the Chief of the Air Staff's Warrant Officer.

Branches and trades

- RAF pilots and weapon systems officers (WSO) (formerly known as navigators) are commissioned officers of the Flying Branch. i.e., Fg(P) or Fg(WSO). Formerly in the General Duties branch, which is now reserved for wing commanders and above from any previous branch.
- Non-commissioned (NCO) aircrew known as weapon systems operators (WSOp), fulfil the specialist roles of air engineer (E), air electronics operator (AEOp), air loadmaster (ALM) and air signaller (S). Though they are now known collectively as weapon systems operators, individual trade specialisations remain. Commissioned officer specialists are promoted from within branch to become Fg(WSO).

The majority of the members of the RAF serve in support roles on the ground:

- Aerospace Battle Managers(Officers), Aerospace Systems Managers/Operators(Other Ranks) (formally Fighter Controllers(FC)) control RAF and NATO aircraft. The FC control the interception of enemy aircraft while the ATC provide air traffic services at RAF stations and to the majority of en-route military aircraft in UK airspace.

Figure 194: *A Tornado WSO of No. 12 Squadron*

Figure 195: *An RAF Regiment Gunner*

- RAF Flight Operations Officers are involved with the planning and co-ordination of all Flying Operations. Flight Operations Officers can be found in every RAF Flying Station and Squadron.
- RAF Intelligence Officers and Intelligence Analysts support all operational activities by providing timely and accurate indicators and warnings. They conduct detailed all source military intelligence fusion and analysis by utilising classified and open source information including imagery, human and communications (signals) intelligence. Intelligence is used to inform commanders of the assessed capabilities and intentions of the enemy for strategic / operational planning and targeting. They also tailor the information to brief aircrews for mission planning and other tactical units (such as RAF Regiment) for Force Protection.
- The RAF Regiment is the RAF's infantry unit, its officers and gunners defend RAF airfields from attack. The RAF Regiment is also responsible for CBRN defence and training the rest of the RAF in ground defence.
- RAF Police are the military police of the RAF.
- Engineering Officers and technicians are employed to maintain and repair the equipment used by the RAF. This includes routine preparation for flight and maintenance on aircraft, arming aircraft with weapons, as well as deeper level repair work on aircraft systems, IT systems, ground-based radar, vehicles, ground support equipment, etc.
- Flight Operations Officers assist in the planning, tasking, co-ordination and monitoring of air operations.
- Logistics Officers manage the movement of the people, transport and equipment necessary to keep aircraft flying. They are the custodians of the supply chain; responsible for catering within the UK, and on exercises and operations overseas; purchase and store equipment/fuel and operate IT systems that manage RAF Logistics.
- Personnel Branch officers (Support and Training specialisations) and associated trades (Personnel Support and Physical Training Instructor) are involved with human resources management, training management, physical education, parachute instruction, media handling, infrastructure management, accounts, administration of Service law, personnel and recruitment.
- RAF Medical Branch provides healthcare at home and on deployed operations, including aeromedical evacuation services. Medical officers are the doctors of the RAF and have specialist expertise in aviation medicine to support aircrew and their protective equipment. Medical officers can go on aeromedical evacuations, providing vital assistance on search-and-rescue missions or emergency relief flights worldwide. RAF Medical Officers are either based in primary care on operations or on RAF stations in the UK or in one of six Ministry of Defence Hospital Units (MDHU's)

around the UK as specialist practitioners.
- RAF Chaplains Branch provides spiritual and moral support for RAF personnel and their families.
- RAF Legal Branch provides legal advice on discipline / criminal law and operations law.

Specialist training and education

The Royal Air Force operates several units and centres for the provision of non-generic training and education. These include the Royal Air Force Leadership Centre and the Royal Air Force Centre for Air Power Studies, both based at RAF Cranwell, and the Air Warfare Centre, based at RAF Waddington and RAF Cranwell. NCO training and developmental courses occur at RAF Halton and officer courses occur at the Joint Services Command and Staff College at Shrivenham.

Aircraft

British military aircraft designations generally comprise a *type name* followed by a *mark number* which includes an alphabetical *rôle prefix*. For example, the *Typhoon F2* was designated as a fighter by the 'F', and the second variant of the type to be produced:

Combat Air

The Eurofighter Typhoon FGR4 is the RAF's air defence fighter aircraft, with a total of six squadrons based across RAF Coningsby and RAF Lossiemouth, following the retirement of the Panavia Tornado F3 in late March 2011. Their task is to defend UK airspace. In October 2007 it was announced that MoD Boscombe Down, RNAS Culdrose and RAF Marham would also be used as Quick Reaction Alert bases from early 2008, offering around-the-clock fighter coverage for the South and South West of UK airspace when a direct threat has been identified.[1188]

The RAF has five front-line and one reserve Typhoon units; 3 (Fighter) Squadron, XI Squadron and 29 (Reserve) Squadron (Operational Conversion Unit) based at RAF Coningsby, with 1 (Fighter) Squadron, II (Army Cooperation) Squadron and 6 Squadron based at RAF Lossiemouth. On 23 November 2015 it was announced that two additional front-line Typhoon squadrons will be formed consisting of Tranche 1 versions.

The mainstay of the strike fleet are the squadrons of Tornado GR4s. These supersonic aircraft can carry a wide range of weaponry, including Storm Shadow cruise missiles, laser-guided bombs and the ASRAAM missile.[1189] Since June

2008, the Eurofighter Typhoon FGR4 has also been capable of being deployed operationally in the air-to-ground role.[1190] The RAF has two operational Tornado units, with IX (Bomber) Squadron and 31 Squadron based at RAF Marham. With the aircraft type nearing its retirement and replacement by the F-35, the RAF Lossiemouth-based 15 (Reserve) Squadron (the Tornado Operational Conversion Unit) was disbanded in March 2017.

The Tornado was previously supplemented by the Harrier GR7/GR9 in the strike and close air support roles, and to counter enemy air defences. The Harrier fleet was withdrawn in December 2010 following the Strategic Defence and Security Review 2010; the Tornado GR4 is due to retire in March 2019 and be replaced by the Eurofighter Typhoon and F-35 Lightning II. On 23 November 2015 it was announced that a total of 138 F-35Bs will be ordered.

Typhoon FGR4

Tornado GR4

On 20 September 2015, *The Sunday Times* reported that the number of fast jet squadrons would increase due to threats posed by Islamic State and Russia. This was later officially confirmed by the government in its 2015 Strategic Defence and Security Review (SDSR) which outlined the government's commitment to 138 F-35 Lightning IIs and two additional Typhoon squadrons. On 4 December 2015, Chief of the Air Staff Air Chief Marshal Sir Andrew Pulford announced his plans for one more combat squadron, in addition to the three outlined in the SDSR, to bring the total number of combat squadrons to ten.

Intelligence, Surveillance, Target Acquisition, and Reconnaissance (ISTAR)

The Sentry AEW1, based at RAF Waddington, provides airborne early warning to detect incoming enemy aircraft and to co-ordinate the aerial battlefield.

The Sentinel R1 (formally known as ASTOR – Airborne STand-Off Radar) provides a ground radar-surveillance platform based on the Bombardier Global Express long range business jet. These were supplemented in 2009 by four (a fifth was added later) Beechcraft Shadow R1 aircraft equipped for the ISTAR role over Afghanistan. Three more Shadow aircraft will be procured as per the 2015 Defence Review. The Tornado GR4A is fitted with cameras and sensors in the visual, infra-red and radar ranges of the spectrum.

Ten MQ-9A Reaper Unmanned aerial vehicles have been purchased to support operations in Iraq and Afghanistan. They are operated by No. 39 Squadron RAF based at Creech Air Force Base and 13 Squadron at RAF Waddington.

Three Boeing RC-135W Rivet Joint replaced the Nimrod R1 fleet in the signals intelligence role. The Nimrod fleet was retired in 2011, the RAF co-manned aircraft of the US Air Force until the three RC-135s entered service between 2014 and 2017. The aircraft will be Boeing KC-135 Stratotanker tankers converted to RC-135W standard in the most complex combined Foreign Military Sales case and co-operative support arrangement that the UK has undertaken with the United States Air Force since the Second World War. Airseeker received its first operational deployment in August 2014, when it was deployed to the Middle East to fly missions over Iraq and Syria as part of Operation Shader.

Sentry AEW1

Sentinel R1

RC-135W Rivet Joint

Shadow R1

MQ-9A Reaper

Helicopters

An important part of the work of the RAF is to support the British Army by ferrying troops and equipment at the battlefield. However, RAF helicopters are also used in a variety of other roles, including support of RAF ground units and heavy-lift support for the Royal Marines. The support helicopters are organised into the tri-service Joint Helicopter Command (JHC), along with helicopters of the British Army and Royal Navy.

The large twin-rotor Chinook, based at RAF Odiham provides heavy-lift support and is supported by the Puma HC2 medium-lift helicopter based at RAF Benson. The Griffin HAR.2s based at RAF Akrotiri in the Cyprus Sovereign Base Areas, the only remaining dedicated helicopter Search and Rescue force in the RAF. However, all UK military helicopter aircrew routinely train and practice the skills necessary for Search and Rescue, and the support helicopters based in the UK are available to the Government under Military Aid to the Civil Authorities in case they are needed. The AW109 Grand New aircraft of

32 (the Royal) Squadron also provide VIP transport and military helicopter capabilities.

Chinook HC2

Puma HC2

Bell Griffin HAR2

Air Mobility

The RAF operate the Boeing C-17 Globemaster III in the heavy strategic airlift role, originally leasing four from Boeing. These were purchased, followed by a fifth delivered on 7 April 2008 and a sixth delivered on 8 June 2008. The new aircraft entered frontline use within days rather than weeks. The MoD said there was "a stated departmental requirement for eight" C-17s and a seventh was subsequently ordered, to be delivered in December 2010. In February 2012 the purchase of an eighth C-17 was confirmed; the aircraft arrived at RAF Brize Norton in May 2012.

More routine strategic airlift transport tasks are carried out by the Airbus A330 MRTT, known as the Voyager in RAF service. The first Voyager arrived in the UK for testing at MoD Boscombe Down in April 2011, and entered service in April 2012. The Voyager received approval from the MoD on 16 May 2013 to begin air-to-air refuelling flights and made its first operational tanker flight on 20 May 2013 as part of a training sortie with Tornado GR4s. By 21 May 2013, the Voyager fleet had carried over 50,000 passengers and carried over 3,000 tons of cargo. A total of 14 Voyagers are due to form the fleet, with 9 allocated to sole RAF use. As the Voyagers lack a refueling boom, the RAF has requested a memorandum of understanding (MoU) with the USAF allowing the UK access to tankers equipped with refueling booms for its Boeing RC-135W Airseeker SIGINT aircraft.

Shorter range, tactical-airlift transport is provided by the Lockheed Martin C-130J Hercules, known as Hercules C4 and C5 in RAF service and based at RAF Brize Norton in Oxfordshire. The draw-down of the Hercules C5 fleet has begun with the final aircraft planned to retire in 2019. The fourteen C4 extended variants are scheduled to retire on 31 March 2035. The Airbus A400M Atlas replaced the RAF's fleet of Hercules C1/C3 (C-130K) transport aircraft which were withdrawn from service on 31 December 2012 and will also replace the C4/C5 variants. Originally, 25 aircraft were ordered, although the total is now 22.

No. 32 (The Royal) Squadron replaced the Queen's Flight in 1995 and operate the Agusta A109 and BAe 146 CC2 in the general air transport and VIP transport roles. The squadron is based at RAF Northolt in west London. Aircraft operate with a priority for military needs over VIP transport. Two additional BAe 146s were purchased in March 2012 from TNT Airways and were refitted by Hawker Beechcraft on behalf of BAE Systems for tactical freight and personnel transport use. The aircraft, designated as the BAe 146 C Mk 3, arrived in Afghanistan in April 2013.

C-17A Globemaster III

Atlas C1 (A400M)

Hercules C5 (C-130J)

Voyager KC3 (A330 MRTT)

BAe 146 CC2

BAe 146 C3

Training aircraft

Elementary Flying Training, as well as Multi-Engine Lead-In training, is conducted on the Tutor T1. Basic fast jet training is provided on the Tucano T1 and initial helicopter training on the Squirrel HT1, at which stage aircrew gain their 'wings'. Multi-Engine aircrew, weapon systems officer (WSO) and weapon systems operator (WSOp) students are trained on the King Air to gain their wings before a posting to an Operational Conversion Unit. Advanced jet flying training is now provided on Hawk T2 for fast jet aircrew and helicopter pilots complete a course on the Griffin HT1, before they are sent to their OCU, which trains them on a specific aircraft type in preparation for service with a front-line squadron. The OCUs use modified operational aircraft, such as the Typhoon T3, as well as sophisticated simulators and ground training.

The Tutor equips the fourteen University Air Squadrons, which provide University students an opportunity to undertake an RAF training syllabus based loosely on EFT to get them to and beyond solo standard. These units are co-located with Air Experience Flights, which share the same aircraft and facilities and provide air experience flying to the Air Training Corps and CCF. The Volunteer Gliding Squadrons also provide air experience flying to cadets using the Viking TX1 conventional glider. Due to an airworthiness issue in April 2014, the Viking fleet and the Vigilant T1 aircraft were grounded for a

two-year period, although Viking operations have subsequently resumed. The Vigilant was unexpectedly withdrawn from service in May 2018, a year earlier than planned. A contract tender was initiated in February 2018 to replace this capability starting in 2022.

Two of the ten T-6 Texan II trainers due as part of the UK Military Flight Training System were delivered in February 2018, forming the nucleus of the unit to be operated at RAF Valley. The aircraft are jointly operated by the Royal Air Force and Ascent Flight Training to provide lead-in training for RAF and Royal Navy fighter pilots prior to advanced training on the Hawk.

100 Squadron operates the Hawk T1 to support other fast jets and in support of ground unit training, as an aggressor aircraft. The Squadron fulfils the role of enemy aircraft in air combat training or to provide more assets in joint exercises.

Tutor T1

Tucano T1

Hawk T1

King Air T1

Viking T1

Future aircraft

The F-35B Lightning II is intended to enter service around 2020 under the Joint Combat Aircraft programme.[1191] On 19 July 2012 the Defence Secretary, Philip Hammond, in a speech in the USA, indicated that the UK would initially receive 48 F-35B to equip the Navy's carrier fleet and would announce at a later date what the final numbers would be. Jon Thompson, MOD Permanent Secretary, told the House of Commons Defence Select Committee, in late 2012: "Our commitment over the first 10 years is for 48 F-35B". An order for the first 14 aircraft on top of the four already procured for operational test and evaluation is expected later in 2013. The first four of 14 production aircraft were ordered in November 2014.[1192] Six further aircraft were ordered on 3 November 2015, with expected delivery in 2016. In November 2015, the government commitment to order 48 F-35B aircraft by 2023,[1193] 24 of which will be available for carrier duties. The 2015 Strategic Defence and Security Review stated the intent for the UK to purchase 138 F-35 aircraft over

the life of the programme. The first F-35 aircraft arrived at RAF Fairford in Gloucestershire on 29 June 2016 after a Transatlantic crossing involving air to air refuelling.

On 5 October 2015, it was announced that the Scavenger programme had been replaced by **"Protector"**, a new requirement for at least 20 systems. On 7 October 2015, it was revealed that Protector will be a Certifiable derivative of the MQ-9B SkyGuardian with enhanced range and endurance. In July 2018, a General Atomics US Civil registered MQ-9B SkyGuardian was flown from North Dakota to RAF Fairford for the Royal International Air Tattoo where it was given RAF markings. It was formally announced by the Chief of Air Staff that No. 31 Squadron RAF would become the 1st Sqn to operate the Protector RG1.

In July 2014 the House of Common Defence Select Committee released a report on the RAF future force structure that envisaged a mixture of unmanned and manned platforms, including further F-35, Protector RG1, a service life extension for the Typhoon (which would otherwise end its service in 2030) or a possible new manned aircraft.

In November 2015, the Government confirmed in its Strategic Defence and Security Review that nine Boeing P-8 Poseidon aircraft will be purchased for surveillance, anti-submarine and anti-surface ship warfare, filling a capability gap in maritime patrol that had been left since the cancellation of the Nimrod MRA4 programme in the 2010 SDSR.

In July 2018 at the Farnborough Airshow, the Defence Secretary announced a £2bn investment for BAe Systems, MBDA and Leonardo to develop a new British 5th Generation Fighter to replace Typhoon in 2035 under Project TEMPEST.

Boeing P-8 Poseidon

F-35 Lightning II

UK Military Flying Training System

The UK's military flying training has been civilianised through a public-private partnership, which puts training output in the hands of a civilian contractor, known as Ascent Flight Training, a consortium of Lockheed Martin and Babcock International. The main elements of the system are fixed- and rotary-wing training from ab-initio all the way to Operational Conversion Units, which prepare aircrew for a specific frontline platform.

Fixed wing

The new process uses three new fixed wing aircraft, the Grob 'Prefect' elementary trainer, the Beechcraft T-6 Texan II basic fast jet trainer, and the Embraer Phenom 100 multi-engine trainer. The aircraft have been procured to reduce the training gap between the older generation Tutor T1, Tucano T1 and King Air T1 aircraft, and the RAF's modern frontline aircraft, including advanced systems and glass cockpits. MFTS also relies far more on synthetic training to deliver aircrew to the front line, where advanced synthetic training is commonplace. Basic Fast Jet training is undertaken on the Texan, and advanced training is done on the BAE Systems Hawk T2, the contract for which had been separated from the rest of the UK MFTS contract, under the auspices of the Advanced Fast Jet Trainer programme.

Prefect T1

Texan T1

BAE Hawk T2

Phenom T1

Rotary

In May 2016, it was announced that the RAF would see delivery of 29 Airbus H135 and 3 Airbus H145 helicopters for use as training aircraft. It was announced by Air Marshal Sean Reynolds, the Senior Responsible Owner for UKMFTS, that "Aircrew across the three Services will continue to conduct their basic and advanced rotary training at RAF Shawbury and Army Air Corps Middle Wallop. Aircrew selected for training in mountain and maritime helicopter operations will receive instruction at RAF Valley".

Symbols, flags, emblems and uniform

Following the tradition of the other British fighting services, the RAF has adopted symbols to represent it, use as rallying devices for members and promote esprit de corps. British aircraft in the early stages of the First World War carried the Union Flag as an identifying feature; however, this was easily

Figure 196: *Royal Air Force Ensign*

Figure 197: *Queen's Colour*

confused with Germany's Iron Cross motif. In October 1914, therefore, the French system of three concentric rings was adopted, with the colours reversed to a red disc surrounded by a white ring and an outer blue ring.[1194] The relative sizes of the rings have changed over the years and during World War II an outer yellow ring was added to the fuselage roundel. Aircraft serving in the Far East during World War II had the red disc removed to prevent confusion with Japanese aircraft. Since the 1970s, camouflaged aircraft carry low-visibility roundels, either red and blue on dark camouflage, or washed-out pink and light blue on light colours. Most uncamouflaged training and transport aircraft retain the traditional red-white-blue roundel.

The Latin motto of the RAF, "Per Ardua ad Astra", is usually translated as "Through Adversity to the Stars",[1195] but the RAF's official translation is "Through Struggle to the Stars". The choice of motto is attributed to a junior officer named J S Yule, in response to a request from a commander of the RFC, Colonel Sykes, for suggestions.

The Badge of the Royal Air Force was first used in August 1918. In heraldic terms it is: "In front of a circle inscribed with the motto Per Ardua Ad Astra and ensigned by the Imperial Crown an eagle volant and affronte Head lowered and to the sinister". Although there have been debates among airmen over the years whether the bird was originally meant to be an albatross or an eagle, the consensus is that it was always an eagle.

Ceremonial functions and display

Red Arrows

The Red Arrows, officially known as the Royal Air Force Aerobatic Team, is the aerobatics display team of the Royal Air Force based at RAF Scampton, with under-review plans to move to RAF Waddington. The team was formed in late 1964 as an all-RAF team, replacing a number of unofficial teams that had been sponsored by RAF commands. The Red Arrows badge shows the aircraft in their trademark *Diamond Nine* formation, with the motto *Éclat*, a French word meaning "brilliance" or "excellence".

Initially, they were equipped with seven Folland Gnat trainers inherited from the RAF Yellowjacks display team. This aircraft was chosen because it was less expensive to operate than front-line fighters. In their first season, they flew at 65 shows across Europe. In 1966, the team was increased to nine members, enabling them to develop their *Diamond Nine* formation. In late 1979, they switched to the BAE Hawk trainer. The Red Arrows have performed over 4,700 displays in 56 countries worldwide.

Figure 198: *The Red Arrows in formation with an F35B and a pair of Typhoons at the Royal International Air Tattoo in 2016.*

Royal Air Force music

Headquarters Royal Air Force Music Services, located at RAF Northolt, supports professional musicians who attend events around the globe in support of the RAF. The Central Band of the Royal Air Force was established in 1920. Other bands include the Band of the Royal Air Force College, the Band of the Royal Air Force Regiment and the Band of the Royal Auxiliary Air Force

Current deployments

Country	Dates	Deployment	Details
Gibraltar	1940s–present	RAF Gibraltar	Although there are no permanently stationed aircraft, RAF aircraft (e.g. transports) make regular visits.
Cyprus	1940–present	RAF Akrotiri	As part of British Forces Cyprus, the RAF have aircraft which can be deployed from Cyprus as part of the intervention against ISIL.
Qatar	2005–present	RAF Al Udeid	An RAF RC-135 Rivet Joint aircraft is based at Al Udeid which is currently in use as a Middle Eastern base for the RAF as well as being the headquarters for the RAF contribution to Operation Shader.

Afghanistan	2001–present	Operation Toral	The UK continues to contribute to NATO's Resolute Support Mission with the RAF providing Puma HC2s.
Norway	1960s–present	Bardufoss Air Station	RAF fighter and/or helicopter squadrons undergo winter-training in Norway.
Ascension Island	1982–present	RAF Ascension Island	The island is used as an air bridge between the UK and the Falkland Islands.
Falkland Islands	1982–present	RAF Mount Pleasant	As part of British Forces South Atlantic Islands, the RAF has two Chinook helicopters based at Mount Pleasant.

Bibliography

- International Institute for Strategic Studies; Hackett, James (ed.) (3 February 2010). *The Military Balance 2010*. London: Routledge. ISBN 1857435575.
- International Institute for Strategic Studies; Hackett, James (ed.) (7 March 2012). *The Military Balance 2012*. London: Routledge. ISBN 1857436423.
- Robertson, Bruce (1967). *Aircraft Markings of the World 1912-1967*. London: Harleyford. ISBN 978-0900435096.
- Shores, Christopher (1969). *Finnish Air Force, 1918–1968*. Reading, Berkshire, UK: Osprey Publications Ltd. ISBN 0-85045-012-8.

External links

Wikimedia Commons has media related to *Royal Air Force*.

Wikimedia Commons has media related to *Aircraft of the air force of the United Kingdom*.

- Official website[1196]
- RAF Reservist Support Service[1197]
- RAF Museum[1198]
- RAF Benevolent Fund[1199]
- The RAF channel on YouTube[1200]

List of Royal Air Force groups

This is a **list of Royal Air Force groups**. The group is a formation just below command level.

There are currently only five groups in operation: No. 1 Group, No. 2 Group, No. 22 Group, No. 38 Group and No. 83 Group.

Group	Dates active	Notes
No. 1 Group RAF	1918–1926 1927–1939 1940–present	Originally formed on 1 April 1918, it was renumbered No. 21 Group on 12 April 1926. Reformed on 25 August 1927 by renaming the Air Defence Group, but disbanded on 22 December 1939. Reformed on 22 June 1940 in Bomber Command, post-war it operated the Thor ballistic missile. From 1968 it operated bomber and strike aircraft of Strike Command. Since January 2000 it has been responsible for UK air defence operations.
No. 2 Group RAF	1918–1920 1936–1947 1948–1958 1993–1996 2000–present	Formed as No. 2 (Training) Group on 1 April 1918, it was disbanded on 31 March 1920. Reformed as No. 2 (Bombing) Group, Bomber Command on 20 March 1936. In May 1943 it was transferred to the 2nd Tactical Air Force, Fighter Command, until the formation of the Allied Expeditionary Air Force. Disbanded on 1 May 1947, but reformed on 1 December 1948 as part of the British Air Force of Occupation. It rejoined 2nd TAF on 1 September 1951, and was disbanded on 15 November 1958. Reformed on 1 April 1993 by renaming RAF Germany, then disbanded on 1 April 1996 when absorbed into No. 1 Group. Reformed on 7 January 2000 to control air transport, air-to-air refuelling and airborne early warning within the RAF. On 1 April 2006 it absorbed No. 3 Group.
No. 3 Group RAF	1918–1921 1923–1926 1936–1967 2000–2006	No. 3 Group was first formed on 10 May 1918, and disbanded on 31 August 1921. It was reformed from No. 11 Wing on 1 April 1923 and disbanded when renumbered as No. 23 (Training) Group on 12 April 1926. Reformed on 1 May 1936 as No. 3 (Bomber) Group, Bomber Command. From 1959 to 1963 it operated the Thor ballistic missile, then V bomber squadrons until disbanded in 1967. It was reformed on 1 April 2000 to control the Joint Force Harrier and Maritime resources. By 2004 it was also responsible for Air Battle Management, but was disbanded on 1 April 2006, and its functions taken over by No 2 Group.
No. 4 Group RAF	1918–1919 1937–1948	Originally formed on 1 April 1918, but disbanded on 24 March 1919. It was reformed on 1 April 1937 as No. 4 (Bomber) Group, Bomber Command. Transferred to Transport Command on 7 May 1945, and disbanded on 2 February 1948.
No. 5 Group RAF	1918–1919 1937–1945	Formed on 1 April 1918, but disbanded on 15 May 1919. Reformed on 1 September 1937 as No. 5 (Bomber) Group, Bomber Command. Disbanded on 15 December 1945.

List of Royal Air Force groups 483

No. 6 Group RAF	1918 1924–1926 1936–1939 1942–1945	No. 6 (Equipment) Group was formed on 1 April 1918, but was renamed Technical Group on 15 August 1918. It was reformed in Italy as No. 6 (Adriatic) Group on 27 September 1918, but reduced to No. 66 Wing on 20 December 1918. Reformed as No. 6 (Fighter) Group on 1 May 1924, and disbanded 20 May 1926. Reformed as No. 6 (Auxiliary) Group on 1 May 1936 by renaming No. 1 (Air Defence Group). Transferred to Bomber Command on 14 July 1936, and renamed No. 6 (Bomber) Group on 1 January 1939, but became No. 91 Group on 11 May 1942. Reformed as part of the Royal Canadian Air Force on 25 October 1942, and disbanded on 31 August 1945.
No. 7 Group RAF	1918–1919 1919–1926 1940–1942 1944–1945	Formed on 1 April 1918 from Southern Training Brigade, renamed No. 7 (Training) Group on 8 August, and disbanded on 16 August 1919. Reformed by reducing South-Western Area to Group status on 20 September 1919, and disbanded on 12 April 1926. Reformed on 15 July 1940 as No. 7 (Operational Training) Group, Bomber Command. Renamed No. 92 Group on 11 May 1942. Reformed on 1 November 1944 to control Heavy Conversion Units until disbanded on 21 December 1945.
No. 8 Group RAF	1918–1919 1941–1942 1943–1945	Formed in April 1918, renamed No. 8 (Training) Group on 8 August, and disbanded on 15 May 1919. Reformed as No. 8 (Bomber) Group on 1 September 1941, but disbanded on 28 January 1942. The Pathfinder Force was renamed No. 8 (Pathfinder Force) Group on 13 January 1943, and disbanded on 15 December 1945.
No. 9 Group RAF	1918–1919 1940–1944	Formed on 1 April 1918, renamed No. 9 (Operations) Group on 8 August, and disbanded on 15 May 1919. Reformed on 9 August 1940 as No. 9 (Fighter) Group, Fighter Command, to cover the North-West England and Northern Ireland. Absorbed into No. 12 Group on 15 September 1944.
No. 10 Group RAF	1918–1932 1940–1945	Formed on 1 April 1918, renamed No. 10 (Operations) Group on 8 August, and disbanded on 18 January 1932. Reformed on 1 June 1940 as No. 10 (Fighter) Group to cover South-West England. Absorbed into No. 11 Group on 2 May 1945.
No. 11 Group RAF	1918–1920 1936–1960 1961–1963 1968–1996	Formed on 1 April 1918 as No. 11 (Equipment) Group, and disbanded on 17 May 1918. It was reformed on 22 August 1918, but reduced to No. 11 Wing in May 1920. Reformed on 1 May 1936 as No. 11 (Fighter) Group by renaming Fighting Area, and transferred to Fighter Command on 14 July 1936. Disbanded on 31 December 1960, but reformed on 1 January 1961 by renaming No. 13 Group. Renamed No. 11 (Northern) Sector on 1 April 1963. Reformed on 1 April 1968 within Strike Command to take over the role of Fighter Command. Renamed No. 11 (Air Defence) Group in January 1986. Amalgamated with No. 18 Group on 1 April 1996. It will be reformed post 2018, as a "multi-domain operations group" to ensure the service thinks and acts in a networked way.
No. 12 Group RAF	1918–1919 1937–1963	Formed in April 1918, renamed No. 12 (Training) Group on 8 August, becoming RAF (Cadet) College on 1 November 1919. Reformed on 1 April 1937 as No. 12 (Fighter) Group to cover the Midlands and North of England. Renamed No 12 (Northern) Sector on 31 March 1963.

No. 13 Group RAF	1918–1961	Formed on 1 April 1918, renamed No. 13 (Training) Group on 8 August 1918, and merged into No. 3 Group on 18 October 1919. Reformed on 15 March 1939 as No. 13 (Fighter) Group to cover the North of England and Scotland, and disbanded on 20 May 1946. Reformed on 16 May 1955, and disbanded on 31 December 1961 by being renamed No. 11 Group.
No. 14 Group RAF	1918–1919 1940–1943	Formed on 1 April 1918 by renaming the Milford Haven Anti-Submarine Group, renamed No. 14 (Operations) Group on 8 August, and disbanded on 19 May 1919. Reformed on 20 January 1940 as No. 14 (Fighter) Group by renaming No. 60 Wing in France, and disbanded on 22 June 1940. Reformed in June 1940 to cover Scotland, and disbanded on 15 July 1943.
No. 15 Group RAF	1918–1919 1939–1945	No. 15 (Equipment) Group was formed on 1 April 1918, and disbanded by 27 September 1918 when it was reformed as No. 15 (Aegean) Group to control 62 and 63 Wings until disbanded on 1 September 1919. Reformed on 15 March 1939 as No. 15 (General Reconnaissance) Group, Coastal Command. Disbanded on 1 August 1945.
No. 16 Group RAF	1918–1920 1936–1946	Formed on 1 April 1918 by renaming Northern Training Brigade, renamed No. 16 (Training) Group on 8 August, and disbanded on 7 February 1920. Reformed on 1 December 1936 as No. 16 (Reconnaissance) Group, Coastal Command. Disbanded by being reduced to No. 16 Wing on 8 March 1946.
No. 17 Group RAF	1918–1919 1936–1945	Formed in No. 4 Area in April 1918 and transferred to North-Eastern Area on 8 May 1918. (Training) added on 8 August 1918. Disbanded 18 October 1919. Reformed 1 December 1936 as No. 17 (Training) Group in Coastal Command. Order of battle on 6 June 1944 included No.s 4,5,6,7,9, 131, 132 OTUs and No. 1674 Heavy Conversion Unit. Disbanded 1 September 1945.
No. 18 Group RAF	1918–1919 1938–1996	First formed on 1 April 1918, it was disbanded 18 October 1919. It was reformed on 1 September 1938 as No. 18 (Reconnaissance) Group of Coastal Command. It was disbanded when merged with No. 11 Group on 1 April 1996 to form No. 11/18 Group.
No. 11/18 Group RAF	1996–2000	Formed in 1996 as part of Strike Command, combining No. 11 and 18 Groups. In 2000 its assets were transferred to No. 1 and 3 Groups.
No. 19 Group RAF	1918 1941–1969	Formed in April 1918 as No. 19 (Equipment) Group in York, but disbanded in June. Reformed in early 1941 as No. 19 (General Reconnaissance) Group, Coastal Command, at Mount Wise, Plymouth, relocating to RAF Mount Batten in 1947. Became HQ Southern Maritime Air Region in November 1969.
No. 20 Group RAF	1918–1919 1939–1943	Originally formed on 1 April 1918, but disbanded in September 1919. Reformed in November 1939 as No. 20 (Training) Group, Training Command. Transferred to Technical Training Command in May 1940. Absorbed into No. 22 (Training) Group, August 1943.

List of Royal Air Force groups

No. 21 Group RAF	1918 1926–1934 1938–1955	The group was formed on 1 April 1918 at Montrose within No. 5 Area, but disbanded on being absorbed into No. 20 Group RAF on 1 July 1918. It reformed as No 21 (Training) Group, on 12 April 1926 when No 1 Group was renamed. Part of Inland Area, it disbanded on 1 February 1934. Reformed as No 21 (Training) Group within Training Command and based at Cranwell. It was transferred to Flying Training Command on 27 May 1940 and was responsible for the RAF College and the Service Flying Training Schools from the Midlands northwards. In 1947 and 1953, absorbed No. 91 Group RAF and No. 54 Group RAF, before disbanding in 1955.
No. 22 Group RAF	1918–1919 1926–1940 1943–1972 2006–present	Formed on 1 April 1918 as No. 22 (Operations) Group, in Scotland, and disbanded on 30 May 1919. Reformed on 12 April 1926 from No. 7 Group as No. 22 (Army Co-operation) Group and on 1 December 1940 expanded to become Army Cooperation Command. Reformed on 1 August 1943 as No. 22 (Training) Group, Technical Training Command, until disbanded on 31 January 1972. Reformed on 30 October 2006 as No. 22 (Training) Group when Training Group was renamed.
No. 23 Group RAF	1918 1926–1975	Formed on 1 April 1918 as No. 23 (Equipment) Group, but disbanded in May. Reformed as No. 23 (Training) Group on 12 April 1926 by re-numbering No. 3 Group. Transferred to Training Command on 1 May 1936, and to Flying Training Command on 27 May 1940. Disbanded on 2 May 1975.
No. 24 Group RAF	1918–1919 1936–1975	Formed on 26 June 1918 from No. 46 and 48 Wings. Disbanded 13 June 1919. Reformed on 10 July 1936 as No. 24 (Training) Group, Training Command, and transferred to Technical Training Command on 27 May 1940, becoming No. 24 (Technical Training) Group. Disbanded on 29 December 1975.
No. 25 Group RAF	1918–1920 1937–1948	Formed on 12 August 1918 as No. 25 (Operations) Group, but disbanded in 1920. Reformed on 1 February 1937 when the Armament Group was renamed No. 25 (Armament) Group, Training Command. Transferred to Flying Training Command on 27 May 1940, and disbanded on 15 April 1948.
No. 26 Group RAF	1918–1919 1937–1939 1940–1946	Formed in Egypt as No. 26 (Training) Group in November 1918, but disbanded in 1919. Reformed on 1 December 1937 by renaming the Superintendent of the Reserve and Inspector of Civil Flying Training Schools within Training Command to control Elementary and Reserve Flying Training Schools. Renamed No. 50 (Reserve) Group and transferred to Reserve Command, 3 February 1939. Reformed on 12 February 1940 as No. 26 (Signals) Group in Training Command, and transferred to Technical Training Command on 27 May 1940. Transferred to Bomber Command on 10 February 1942, and amalgamated with No. 60 (Signals) Group to form No. 90 (Signals) Group on 25 April 1946.
No. 27 Group RAF	1918–1919 1941–1958	Originally formed on 29 August 1918 at RAF Bircham Newton as part of the Independent Air Force, and disbanded on 19 May 1919. Reformed on 26 May 1941 as No. 27 (Signals Training) Group, Technical Training Command. Disbanded on 1 October 1958.
No. 28 Group RAF	1918–1919 1942–1950	Formed as No. 28 (Orkney & Shetland Islands) Group under the Commander-in-Chief of the Grand Fleet on 13 July 1918, and disbanded on 15 April 1919. Reformed as No. 28 (Technical Training) Group, Technical Training Command, on 1 November 1942. Disbanded on 6 March 1950.

No. 29 Group RAF	1918–1922 1942–1945	Briefly formed as No 29 (Training) Group in Egypt in early November 1918. Reformed on 27 November 1918 as No. 29 (Operations) Group under Commander-in-Chief of the Grand Fleet. Renamed No. 29 (Fleet) Group in August 1919. Transferred to Coastal Area on 15 September 1919, and disbanded on 31 March 1922. Reformed on 1 July 1942 as No. 29 (Flying Training) Group, Flying Training Command, splitting off from No. 25 Group. Re-absorbed into No. 25 Group in July 1945.
No. 30 Group RAF	1918–1919 1937–1945	Formed at Salonika in August 1918 as No. 30 (Operational) Group, but reduced and renamed No. 16 Wing on 7 April 1919. Reformed on 17 March 1937 as No. 30 (Balloon Barrage) Group, Fighter Command. Transferred to Balloon Command on 1 November 1938, and disbanded on 7 January 1945. Headquartered at Chessington, near Surbiton, Surrey, when in Balloon Command.
No. 31 Group RAF	1918–1919 1939–1941	Formed in Mesopotamia in August 1918 as No. 31 (Operational) Group, and disbanded in April 1919. Reformed on 1 April 1939 as No. 31 (Balloon Barrage) Group in Balloon Command. Disbanded on 13 November 1941.
No. 32 Group RAF	1939–1944	Formed on 1 March 1939 as No. 32 (Balloon Barrage) Group, Balloon Command. Disbanded on 15 November 1944. Headquartered at Claverton Manor, Claverton, near Bath, Somerset.
No. 33 Group RAF	1939–1944	Formed as No. 33 (Balloon Barrage) Group, Balloon Command, on 1 March 1939. Disbanded on 4 September 1944. Headquartered at Parkhead House, Abbey Lane, Sheffield, Yorkshire.
No. 34 Group RAF	1939–1944	Formed as No. 34 (Balloon Barrage) Group, Balloon Command, on 7 April 1940. Disbanded on 19 July 1943. Headquartered at Tor House, Corstorphine Road, Edinburgh.
No. 38 Group RAF	1943–1951 1960–1983 1992–2000 2014–present	Formed on 11 October 1943 as No. 38 (Airborne Force) Group, Fighter Command. On 1 June 1945 became part of RAF Transport Command, and was disbanded on 1 February 1951. Reformed on 1 January 1960 as No. 38 (Air Support) Group, Transport Command. it was transferred to Strike Command on 1 July 1972, and disbanded on 17 November 1983. Reformed 1 November 1992 as part of Strike Command, and disbanded on 1 April 2000. No. 38 Group was reformed on 2 July 2014, bringing together the RAF's Engineering, Logistics, Communications and Medical Operations units. It is headquartered at RAF Wittering, Lincolnshire.
No. 40 Group RAF	1939–1961	Formed on 3 January 1939 as No. 40 (Maintenance) Group, Maintenance Command. Responsible for all equipment except bombs and explosives. Disbanded on 28 July 1961.
No. 41 Group RAF	1939–1961	Formed on 1 January 1939 as No. 41 (Maintenance) Group, Maintenance Command. Responsible for supply and allocation of aircraft. Disbanded on 21 July 1961.
No. 42 Group RAF	1939–1956	Formed on 1 January 1939 as No. 42 (Maintenance) Group, Maintenance Command. On 17 April 1939 the group assumed responsibility for all ammunition and fuel depots. It was disbanded on 2 January 1956.
No. 43 Group RAF	1939–1956	Formed on 1 January 1939 as No. 43 (Maintenance) Group, Maintenance Command. On 21 September 1939 it assumed responsibility for the salvage of aircraft and equipment. Disbanded on 2 January 1956.

List of Royal Air Force groups

No. 44 Group RAF	1941–1946	No. 44 (Ferry Service) Group was formed on 15 August 1941 from the Overseas Air Movements Control Unit of Ferry Command. Transferred to Transport Command on 25 March 1943, and disbanded on 14 August 1946.
No. 45 Group RAF	1943–1946	No. 45 (Atlantic Ferry) Group was formed 1 April 1943 from Ferry Command when it was reduced to a Group within Transport Command. It was renamed No. 45 (Transport) Group in June 1944, and transferred to Coastal Command on 1 January 1946. Reduced to No. 45 Wing on 15 February 1946.
No. 46 Group RAF	1944–1950 1972–1976	Formed on 17 January 1944 as No. 46 (Transport) Group, but disbanded on 15 October 1949. It was reformed on 1 November 1949 when No. 47 (Transport) Group was renamed, and disbanded on 31 March 1950. It was reformed on 1 September 1972 as No. 46 (Strategic Support) Group, Strike Command, to take over the transport role of Air Support Command. It was merged with No. 38 Group on 1 January 1976.
No. 47 Group RAF	1945–1949	No. 47 (Transport) Group was formed on 1 January 1945 from No. 116 Wing. In June 1946 it controlled RAF Bourn – no units; RAF Holmsley South – 246 Sqn; RAF Lyneham – 511 Sqn, 2 GCA Unit; RAF Merryfield – no units; RAF Oakington – 242 Sqn; RAF Stradishall – 51 Sqn; RAF Waterbeach – 59 Sqn, 220 Sqn; 53 Sqn (Upwood) 47 Comm Flt (Little Staughton). It was renamed No. 46 Group on 1 November 1949.
No. 48 Group RAF	1945–1946	No. 48 (Transport) Group was formed on 29 October 1945, and disbanded on 15 May 1946.
No. 50 Group RAF	1939–1947	No. 50 (Training) Group was formed on 1 February 1939 by renaming No. 26 (Training) Group and transferring it to Reserve Command. It was transferred to Flying Training Command on 27 May 1940, and disbanded 31 May 1947.
No. 51 Group RAF	1939–1945	No. 51 (Training) Group was formed on 11 May 1939 as part of Reserve Command. It was transferred to Flying Training Command on 27 May 1940, and disbanded 14 July 1945.
No. 52 Group RAF		No. 52 (Training) Group was due to form in March 1939 in Reserve Command, but not activated.
No. 53 Group RAF		No. 53 (Training) Group was due to form in March 1939 in Reserve Command, but not activated.
No. 54 Group RAF	1939–1946 1951–1953	No. 54 (Training) Group was formed 30 August 1939 in Reserve Command to control Initial Training Wings. It was transferred to Flying Training Command on 27 May 1940, and disbanded on 17 June 1946. It was reformed on 1 April 1951 to control Initial Training Wings and Grading Schools. All units were transferred to No. 21 Group on 24 June 1953. Disbanded 10 July 1953.
No. 60 Group RAF	1940–1946	No. 60 (Signals) Group was formed on 23 March 1940 to control RDF (Radar) Stations and other Radio units in Fighter Command. Amalgamated with No. 26 (Signals) Group to form No. 90 (Signals) Group on 25 April 1946.

Group	Dates	Description
No. 61 Group RAF	1940 1946–1959	No. 61 Group was first formed on 1 July 1940 in Northern Ireland, and was raised to Command status and renamed RAF in Northern Ireland on 1 August 1940. Reformed as No. 61 (Eastern Reserve) Group on 2 May 1946 within Reserve Command, it was renamed No. 61 (Eastern) Group on 1 August 1950 and transferred to Home Command. It was renamed No. 61 (Southern Reserve) Group on 1 January 1957, and disbanded 31 May 1959.
No. 62 Group RAF	1946–1957	No. 62 (Southern Reserve) Group was formed on 15 May 1946 within Reserve Command, and renamed No. 62 (Southern) Group on 1 August 1950 when transferred to Home Command. It was absorbed into No. 61 Group on 1 January 1957.
No. 63 Group RAF	1946–1957	No. 63 (Western & Welsh Reserve) Group was formed on 2 May 1946 within Reserve Command, and renamed No. 63 (Western & Welsh) Group on 1 August 1950 when transferred to Home Command. It was disbanded on 1 February 1957.
No. 64 Group RAF	1946–1958/9	No. 64 (Northern Reserve) Group was formed on 2 May 1946 within Reserve Command, and was renamed No. 64 (Northern) Group on 1 August 1950 when transferred to Home Command. It was disbanded in 1958 or 1959.
No. 65 Group RAF	1946–1950/1	No. 65 (London Reserve) Group was formed on 2 May 1946 within Reserve Command, and renamed No. 65 (London) Group on 1 August 1950 when transferred to Home Command. It was disbanded in 1950 or 1951.
No. 66 Group RAF	1946–1956/7	No. 66 (Scottish Reserve) Group was formed on 2 May 1946 within Reserve Command and renamed No. 66 (Scottish) Group on 1 August 1950 when transferred to Home Command. It was disbanded in 1956 or 1957.
No. 67 Group RAF	1950–1957	No. 67 (Northern Ireland Reserve) Group was formed on 31 March 1950 from RAF in Northern Ireland. It was renamed No. 67 (Northern Ireland) Group on 1 August 1950 when transferred to Home Command. It was disbanded on 28 February 1957.
No. 70 Group RAF	1940–1955	No. 70 (Army Co-Operation Training) Group was formed on 25 November 1940 from No. 22 (Army Co-operation) Group, Fighter Command. It was transferred to Army Cooperation Command on 1 December 1940, and to Air Defence of Great Britain on 1 June 1943, and finally disbanded on 17 July 1945. Order of battle on 1 June 1944, mostly target-towing Hurricanes.
No. 71 Group RAF	1940–1941	No. 71 (Army Co-Operation) Group was formed on 25 November 1940 from No. 22 (Army Co-operation) Group, Fighter Command. It was transferred to Army Cooperation Command on 1 December 1940, and disbanded on 14 August 1941.
No. 72 Group RAF	1942–1943	No. 72 (Army Co-Operation Training) Group was formed on 16 September 1942 within Army Cooperation Command. It was disbanded on 1 August 1943.
No. 81 Group RAF	1940–1943 1952–1958	No. 81 (Training) Group was formed on 16 December 1940 in Fighter Command to control Fighter Operational Training Units, and was disbanded on 20 April 1943. Reformed as part of Fighter Command in January 1952 to control the command's training units. Disbanded in 1957.
No. 82 Group RAF	1941–1942	No. 82 (Fighter) Group was formed on 21 July 1941, and absorbed into RAF in Northern Ireland on 15 October 1942.

List of Royal Air Force groups

No. 83 Expeditionary Air Group RAF	1943–1946 1952–1958 2006–present	Formed on 1 April 1943 as No. 83 (Composite) Group, 2nd Tactical Air Force, and was absorbed into No. 84 Group on 21 April 1946. Reformed on 9 July 1952 as No. 83 Group, part of the British Air Forces of Occupation in Germany, until disbanded on 16 June 1958. Reformed as No. 83 Expeditionary Air Group on 1 April 2006 in the Middle East to support operations in the region.
No. 84 Group RAF	1943–1947	No. 84 (Composite) Group was formed on 15 July 1943 within 2nd Tactical Air Force. It was disbanded on 15 December 1947.
No. 85 Group RAF	1943–1946 1948–1950	No. 85 Group was formed on 17 December 1943 within 2nd Tactical Air Force from wings of the RAF Airfield Construction Service. It was renamed No. 85 (Base) Group on 14 February 1944, and reduced to the status of No. 85 Wing on 1 July 1946. It was reformed on 1 December 1948, and disbanded on 1 July 1950.
No. 87 Group RAF	1945–1956	No. 87 (Transport) Group was formed on 17 February 1945, and renamed No. 87 (Transport) Group on 15 July 1945. Allocated to 2nd Tactical Air Force/British Air Forces of Occupation, it was reduced to the status of No. 87 Wing on 15 July 1946.
No. 88 Group RAF	1945	No. 88 (Fighter) Group was formed in Edinburgh on 7 May 1945 for operations in Norway, and was finally disbanded on 31 December 1945.
No. 90 Group RAF	1946–1958 1969–1973	No 26. Group and No 60. Group were amalgamated to form No 90. (Signals) Group on 24 April 1946 under the administrative control of British Air Forces of Occupation and Transport Command. It became an Independent Group in 1951 or 1952. It was raised to RAF Signals Command on 3 November 1958, reverting to Group status on 1 January 1969 within Strike Command. It was transferred to Maintenance Command on 1 September 1972 and disbanded on 31 August 1973, becoming part of RAF Support Command.
No. 91 Group RAF	1942–1947	No. 91 (Training) Group was formed on 11 May 1942 by renaming No. 6 Group. It was renamed No. 21 Group on 1 May 1947.
No. 92 Group RAF	1942–1945	No. 92 (Training) Group was formed on 11 May 1942 by renaming No. 7 Group. It was disbanded on 15 July 1945.
No. 93 Group RAF	1942–1945	No. 93 (Training) Group was formed on 15 June 1942, and disbanded on 14 February 1945.
No. 100 Group RAF	1943–1945	No. 100 (Special Duties) Group was formed on 3 December 1943 within Bomber Command for electronic warfare and countermeasures. It was disbanded on 17 December 1945.
No. 106 Group RAF	1944–1946	In June 1943, No. 1 PRU was formed into No. 106 Wing, with five squadrons (Nos. 540 to 544 inclusive) and an Operational Training Unit. The Wing was elevated to Group status in April 1944 as No. 106 (Photo Reconnaissance) Group, with two Spitfire (541 & 542) and two Mosquito (540 & 544) squadrons. It was disbanded on 15 August 1946.

No. 200 Group RAF	1939–1942	No. 200 (Coastal) Group was formed on 25 September 1939 under the control of HQ RAF Mediterranean to control units operating from Gibraltar. It was transferred to Coastal Command in November/December 1940, and renamed AHQ Gibraltar on 1 May 1942.
No. 201 Group RAF	1939–1944	No. 201 (General Reconnaissance) Group was formed on 18 September 1939 from the General Reconnaissance Group, Middle East. It was renamed No. 201 (Naval Co-operation) Group on 3 October 1941, and absorbed into Air Defence Eastern Mediterranean on 1 February 1944.
No. 202 Group RAF	1939–1941 1944	No. 202 (Operations) Group was formed on 21 September 1939 by renaming RAF Egypt Group, and was absorbed in No. 204 Group on 12 April 1941. It was reformed on 26 May 1941, and renamed AHQ Egypt on 1 December 1941. It was reformed on 11 July 1944 to administer RAF units involved on Operation Dragoon, and was disbanded on 7 November 1944.
No. 203 Group RAF	1940–1945	No. 203 (Maintenance) Group was formed on 17 August 1940 from HQ RAF Sudan. It was renamed No. 203 (Training) Group on 10 May 1943, and disbanded on 28 February 1945.
No. 204 Group RAF	1941	No. 204 (Operations) Group was formed on 12 April 1941 by renaming HQ RAF Cyrenaica. It was renamed AHQ Western Desert on 21 October 1941.
No. 205 Group RAF	1941–1956	No. 205 (Heavy Bomber) Group was formed on 23 October 1941 by renaming No. 257 Wing. It was disbanded on 15 April 1956.
No. 206 Group RAF	1941–1946 1951–1954	No. 206 (Maintenance) Group was formed on 1 September 1941 by renaming Maintenance Group, and was disbanded on 28 February 1946. Reformed on 1 June 1951 as No. 206 (Base Maintenance) Group, it was disbanded on 31 August 1954.
No. 207 Group RAF	1941–1942	No. 207 (General Purpose) Group was formed on 15 December 1941 by renaming AHQ East Africa, reverting to AHQ East Africa on 16 November 1942.
No. 209 Group RAF	1942–1944	No. 209 (Fighter) Group was formed on 15 December 1942 by upgrading No. 263 Wing. It was disbanded on 15 November 1944.
No. 210 Group RAF	1943–1945	No. 210 (Fighter) Group was formed on 1 May 1943, and was disbanded on 1 May 1944. It was reformed on 6 July 1944 to control coastal air forces in North Africa and Western Mediterranean, and transferred to AHQ Malta in January 1945. It was disbanded on 25 April 1945.
No. 211 Group RAF	1941–1945	No. 211 (Medium Bomber) Group was formed on 10 December 1941 by renaming Nucleus Group Western Desert. It was disbanded on 3 February 1942. Reformed as No. 211 (Offensive Fighter) Group on 12 March 1942, but reduced to 'Z' Sector, Northwest African Air Forces on 17 September 1943.
No. 212 Group RAF	1942–1946	No. 212 (Fighter Control) Group was formed on 1 December 1942, as part of the Western Desert Air Force. It was later transferred to AHQ Egypt, and eventually disbanded on 31 January 1946.
No. 213 Group RAF	1941–1943	No. 213 (Operational) Group was formed on 15 December 1941 by renaming Advanced AHQ Levant. It was disbanded on 15 November 1943.

List of Royal Air Force groups

No. 214 Group RAF	1942–1945	No. 214 Group was formed on 1 January 1942 as part of AHQ Iraq, and was merged with No. 217 Group on 30 November 1942. Reformed on 15 April 1943 as No. 214 (Maintenance) Group, it was disbanded on 31 December 1945.
No. 215 Group RAF	1942–1943	No. 215 (General Reconnaissance) Group was formed on 1 May 1942 at Basrah. It was disbanded on 1 November 1943.
No. 216 Group RAF	1942–1946	No. 216 (Ferry) Group was formed on 21 May 1942, and was renamed No. 216 (Air Transport and Ferry) Group on 9 September 1942. It was disbanded on 26 October 1946.
No. 217 Group RAF	1942–1943 1943–1944	No. 217 (Paiforce) Group was formed on 18 September 1942 from Persian Group, and was disbanded on 1 May 1943. Reformed on 3 November 1943 within RAF Middle East, it was disbanded on 29 February 1944.
No. 218 Group RAF	1942–1943 1943–1946	No. 218 (Maintenance) Group was formed on 1 October 1942, and disbanded on 17 April 1943. Reformed on 30 November 1943, it was disbanded on 20 June 1946.
No. 219 Group RAF	1942–1944 1946	No. 219 (Fighter) Group was formed on 6 December 1942 as No. 219 (Fighter) Group, subordinate to AHQ Eastern Mediterranean, and was disbanded on 27 July 1944. It was reformed on 1 March 1946 by amalgamating AHQ Eastern Mediterranean, AHQ Egypt and No. 206 Group. It was amalgamated with No. 205 Group on 1 December 1946.
No. 221 Group RAF	1941–1942 1942–1945	No. 221 Group was formed on 21 April 1941 in Burma. Later renamed BURGROUP, it reverted to No. 221 Group on 15 December 1941. In February 1942 it was again renamed, this time as NORGROUP. It was disbanded on 12 March 1942. Reformed on 12 March 1942 as a composite group in India, and later renamed first as No. 221 (Bomber) Group and then as No. 221 (Tactical) Group. It was disbanded on 30 September 1945.
No. 222 Group RAF	1941–1945	No. 222 (General Reconnaissance) Group was formed on 1 September 1941. It was renamed AHQ Ceylon on 15 October 1945.
No. 223 Group RAF	1941 1942–1945	No. 223 Group was formed on 9 August 1941 by renaming AHQ Far East. Renamed NORGROUP on 24 November 1941. Reformed on 1 May 1942 as No. 223 (Composite) Group by renumbering No. 1 (Indian) Group. Renamed No. 1 (Indian) Group on 15 August 1945.
No. 224 Group RAF	1942–1945 1957–1968	No. 224 (Fighter) Group was formed on 3 January 1942, but was disbanded on 28 March 1942. Reformed on 1 April 1942, and renamed No. 224 (Tactical) Group on 1 December 1942. Disbanded by renaming as AHQ Malaya on 30 September 1945. Reformed on 31 August 1957 from AHQ Malaya, it was disbanded on 1 October 1968.
No. 225 Group RAF	1942 1942–1945	No. 225 (Bomber) Group was formed on 17 January 1942 by renaming No. 223 Group. It was disbanded on 28 March 1942. Reformed as No. 225 (Composite) Group on 20 April 1942. It absorbed No. 2 (Indian) Group on 12 April 1942. Renamed No. 2 (Indian) Group on 1 October 1945.

No. 226 Group RAF	1942 1942–1946	No. 226 (Fighter) Group was formed on 18 January 1942 in Singapore. After the surrender the number was reused to control fighters in defence of Java. Not formally disbanded, but ceased to exist in March 1942. It was reformed on 9 May 1942 as No. 226 (Maintenance) Group, and was disbanded on 31 July 1946.
No. 227 Group RAF	1942–1946	No. 227 (Training) Group was formed on 6 June 1942. It was renumbered No. 4 (Indian) Group on 1 May 1946.
No. 228 Group RAF	1943 1945–1946	No. 228 Group was formed on 22 February 1943, and disbanded on 15 May 1943. Reformed on 27 February 1945 as No. 228 (Administrative) Group, and renumbered, No. 3 (Indian) Group on 1 May 1946.
No. 229 Group RAF	1943–1947	No. 229 (Transport) Group was formed on 16 December 1943 from No. 179 Wing. It was disbanded on 31 March 1947.
No. 230 Group RAF	1943–1945 1952–1953	No. 230 (Maintenance) Group was formed on 15 December 1943, and absorbed into AHQ Burma on 16 May 1945. It was reformed on 1 April 1952, and renamed AHQ Singapore on 16 February 1953.
No. 231 Group RAF	1943–1945	No. 231 (Bomber) Group was formed on 13 December 1943. It was disbanded on 30 September 1945.
No. 232 Group RAF	1945–1946	No. 232 (Transport) Group was formed in March 1945, and was disbanded on 15 August 1946. Officially a Transport Command Group, operating under control of HQ Air Command South East Asia.
No. 233 Group RAF	1945–1946	No. 233 Group was formed on 28 March 1945, but was disbanded on 30 June 1946. It was planned to control RAF units allocated to Operation Roger.
No. 238 Group RAF	1945	No. 238 (Airborne Assault) Group was formed on 20 April 1945, and was reduced to No. 238 Wing on 11 September 1945.
No. 241 Group RAF	1942	No. 241 (Special Operations) Group was formed on 1 January 1942 in London, intended for operations in the Far East. It was disbanded on 14 July 1942 without becoming operational.
No. 242 Group RAF	1942–1944	No. 242 Group was formed on 24 August 1942 in North Africa. It was disbanded on 14 September 1944.
No. 246 Group RAF	1943	No. 246 Group was formed on 3 July 1943, but was disbanded on 9 August 1943. It was formed on to control RAF units for the proposed defence of Portuguese airfields.
No. 247 Group RAF	1943–1946	No. 247 Group was formed in October 1943 within Coastal Command to control units operating from the Azores. It was disbanded on 1 March 1946.
No. 300 Group RAF	1945–1946	Formed in Australia in late 1944 as No. 300 Wing, becoming No. 300 (Transport) Group on 24 April 1945. It was reduced to wing status on 31 March 1946. Officially part of Transport Command, it operated under control of HQ Air Command South East Asia to support the British Pacific Fleet.
No. 333 Group RAF	1942	No. 333 (Special Operational) Group was formed on 1 September 1942 for Operation Torch, and became Eastern Air Command on 19 November 1942.

List of Royal Air Force groups

Air Defence Group RAF	1927	Air Defence Group was formed on 18 July 1927 by renaming HQ Special Reserve and Auxiliary Air Force. It was renamed No. 1 Air Defence Group on 25 August 1927.
Armament Group RAF	1934–1937	Armament Group was formed on 1 February 1934. Transferred to Training Command on 1 May 1936, it was renamed No. 25 Group on 1 December 1937.
Experimental Group RAF	1918–1919	Experimental Group was formed on 16 August 1918 to control RAF experimental establishments. It was disbanded on 1 January 1919.
Firth of Forth Group RAF	1918–	Firth of Forth Group was formed on 1 November 1918 to control RAF bases at Turnhouse, Rosyth and Donibristle.
Technical Group RAF	1918–	Technical Group was formed in November 1918 to control 2, 7, 8 & 10 Aircraft Acceptance Parks.
Training Group RAF	1994–2006	Training Group (Defence Agency) was formed on 1 April 1994 within Personnel and Training Command. Became Chief Executive, Training Group Defence Agency and AOC, Training Group in 1996 or 1997. Disbanded by being renamed No. 22 (Training) Group on 30 October 2006.
Indian Group RAF	1921–1922	Formed on 1 January 1921 when RAF India Command was demoted to group status. It was reorganised in October 1921, divided into four wings from two, although the number of squadrons were not increased. It ceased to exist when re-raised to command status on 1 April 1922.
No. 1 (Indian) Group RAF	1928–1947	Part of Royal Air Force, India.
No. 2 (Indian) Group RAF	1940–1947	Part of Royal Air Force, India.
No. 3 (Indian) Group RAF		Part of Royal Air Force, India.

List of Royal Air Force stations

This **list of RAF Stations** is a list of all current Royal Air Force stations (military air bases), airfields, and administrative headquarters of the Royal Air Force. Also included are airfields operated by the Ministry of Defence but no longer considered as RAF stations, MOD air weapons ranges and stations operated by the US Visiting Forces.

RAF stations and MOD airfields in the UK
Royal Air Force (RAF)

Airbus A-330 Voyager at RAF Brize Norton.

Eurocopter Squirrel HT1 at RAF Shawbury.

RAF front-line operations are focussed on seven main operating bases (MOB's) -

- RAF Coningsby, RAF Marham and RAF Lossiemouth (Air Combat)
- RAF Waddington (Intelligence, Surveillance Target Acquisition and Reconnaissance (ISTAR))
- RAF Brize Norton (Air Transport)
- RAF Benson and RAF Odiham (Support Helicopter operating under Joint Helicopter Command)

Operations are supported by numerous other flying and non-flying stations, with activity focussed at RAF Honington which coordinates Force Protection and RAF Leeming and RAF Wittering which have a support enabler role.

Stations such as RAF Cranwell and RAF Valley form part of the UK Military Flying Training System which is dedicated to training air-crew for all three UK

Figure 199: *RAF Cranwell College Hall*

armed services. Specialist ground crew training is focused at RAF Cosford and MOD St. Athan.

The Control and Reporting Centre (CRC) at RAF Boulmer is tasked with compiling a Recognised Air Picture of UK air space and providing tactical control of the Quick Reaction Alert Force. In order to achieve this Boulmer is supported by a network of seven Remote Radar Heads (RRHs) and a Remote Radio Site (RRS) spread the length of the UK.

Ministry of Defence (MOD)

Several former RAF stations are still owned by the Ministry of Defence (MOD) and are operated by QinetiQ in the test and evaluation role. The main facility providing this role is MOD Boscombe Down which still has a significant RAF presence.

A small number of former RAF stations, still owned by the MOD but no longer considered as stations, are regularly used by the RAF as relief landing grounds (RLGs) or training areas.

British Army barracks such as at Kinloss and Leuchars are listed as they perform a RLG role for the RAF.

Name	Constituent country	County	Units and purpose
MOD Aberporth	Wales	Ceredigion	Former RAE Aberporth, operated by QinetiQ on behalf of the MOD as a test & evaluation range.
RAF Barkston Heath	England	Lincolnshire	• Relief landing ground predominately used by Grob Tutor T1s of No. 3 Flying Training School (3 FTS) operating from RAF Cranwell. • From January 2018 the airfield will provide tri-service elementary flight training using the Grob Prefect T1 as part of the UK Military Flying Training System.
RAF Barnham	England	Suffolk	• Non-flying station which is a satellite site of RAF Honington and provides domestic accommodation and training facilities for the RAF Regiment. • The MOD is expected to close and dispose of RAF Barnham by 2020.
RRH Benbecula	Scotland	Comhairle nan Eilean Siar	Remote Radar Head forming part of the UK Air Surveillance and Control System which is managed from RAF Boulmer. The station was formerly known as RAF Benbecula.
RAF Benson	England	Oxfordshire	Home of the RAF's Puma Support Helicopter Force fleet operating under Joint Helicopter Command, comprising No. 33 Squadron and No. 230 Squadrons operating the Westland Puma HC2 and No. 28 (AC) Squadron operating the Puma and Boeing Chinook HC4.
MOD Boscombe Down	England	Wiltshire	Test & evaluation airfield operated by QinetiQ on behalf of the MOD. Home to the Aircraft Test and Evaluation Centre, Empire Test Pilots School, Rotary Wing Test and Evaluation Squadron and the Joint Aircraft Recovery and Transportation Squadron.
RAF Boulmer	England	Northumberland	Non-flying station, home to the UK Air Surveillance and Control Systems (UKASCS) Force Command, RAF School of Aerospace Battle Management and a NATO Control and Reporting Centre responsible for monitoring UK airspace.
RAF Brize Norton	England	Oxfordshire	The RAF's largest station, home to the strategic and tactical air-transport and air-to-air refuelling fleets (Boeing C-17A Globemaster, Lockheed Martin C-130 Hercules C4/5, Airbus Voyager KC2/KC3 and the Airbus A400M Atlas).
RRH Brizlee Wood	England	Northumberland	Remote Radar Head forming part of the UK Air Surveillance and Control System which is managed from RAF Boulmer. The station was formerly known as RAF Brizlee Wood.
RRH Buchan	Scotland	Aberdeenshire	Remote Radar Head forming part of the UK Air Surveillance and Control System which is managed from RAF Boulmer The station was formerly known as RAF Buchan.

List of Royal Air Force stations

Chetwynd Airfield	England	Shropshire	Former RAF station, now an unmanned grass airfield used for training purposes by helicopters of the Defence Helicopter Flying School from RAF Shawbury.
RAF Coningsby	England	Lincolnshire	• Eurofighter Typhoon FGR4 main operating base with No. 3 Squadron and No. 11 Squadron both contributing to the Quick Reaction Alert (Interceptor) South capability, whereas No. 29 Squadron is the Typhoon operational conversion unit. • No. 41 Squadron operate the Panavia Tornado GR4 and Typhoon for test and evaluation purposes and the Battle of Britain Memorial Flight operate a fleet of historic aircraft in the flying display role.
RAF Cosford	England	Shropshire	• Training establishment, home to the Defence School of Aeronautical Engineering (DSAE) Headquarters, No. 1 School of Technical Training, the RAF Aerosystems Engineer and Management Training School, No. 1 Radio School and the RAF School of Physical Training. • Flying units include the University of Birmingham Air Squadron, No. 8 Air Experience Flight and No. 633 Volunteer Gliding Squadron. • Royal Air Force Museum Cosford.
RAF Cranwell	England	Lincolnshire	• Training establishment, home to RAF College Cranwell, the Officer and Aircrew Selection Centre and Air Cadets Headquarters. • Flying units comprise the Central Flying School responsible for training flying instructors, the headquarters and flying squadrons of No. 3 Flying Training School (Beechcraft King Air B200 and Grob Tutor T1) and No. 6 Flying Training School also flying the Tutor.
RAF Digby	England	Lincolnshire	Non-flying station providing specialist communications support under command of Defence Intelligence. Station personnel are drawn from all three UK armed forces and the US military. Home to the Joint Services Signals Organisation Headquarters, Joint Signals Service Unit (Digby), No. 591 Signals Unit and the Aerial Erector School.
RAF Fylingdales	England	North Yorkshire	Non-flying station providing an uninterrupted ballistic missile early warning and space surveillance capability to the UK and US Governments.
RAF Halton	England	Buckinghamshire	• Training establishment comprising the Recruit Training Squadron, Airmens Command Squadron, International Defence Training, Supply and Management Training Wing, Specialist Training Squadron and several other RAF and joint support units. • A grass airfield provides a base for No. 613 Volunteer Gliding Squadron and several RAF flying clubs. • The MOD is expected to close and dispose of RAF Halton by 2022.
MOD Hebrides	Scotland	Comhairle nan Eilean Siar	Former RAF Benbecula, operated by QinetiQ on behalf of the MOD as a test and evaluation range.

RAF Henlow	England	Bedfordshire	• Support station, home to several RAF and Joint Forces Command units including the RAF Centre of Aviation Medicine, the Joint Arms Control Implementation Group (JACIG), elements of Engineering Operations under Information Systems & Services (ISS), Defence Cultural Specialist Unit, the Band of the Queen's Division and specialist units of the RAF Police. • A grass airfield provides a base for No. 616 Volunteer Gliding Squadron and two flying clubs. • The MoD is expected to close and dispose of RAF Henlow by 2022.
RAF High Wycombe	England	Buckinghamshire	Non-flying administrative support station, home to Headquarters RAF Air Command, No. 1 Group, No. 2 Group, No. 22 Group and No. 38 Group.
RAF Honington	England	Suffolk	• Support station, home to the vast majority of the RAF Regiment including the RAF Force Protection Headquarters and Force Protection Centre, and numerous RAF Regiment squadrons including No. 20 Wing in the Chemical Biological Radiological and Nuclear role. The station also hosts RAF Police Headquarters and No. 3 RAF Police Wing. • No. 611 Volunteer Gliding Squadron is the only flying unit.
Keevil Airfield	England	Wiltshire	Former RAF station, now an unmanned airfield used for training purposes predominately by aircraft from RAF Brize Norton. Has also been used by the British Army for ground exercises and by Joint Helicopter Command.
Kinloss Barracks	Scotland	Moray	Relief Landing Ground (RLG) for RAF Lossiemouth, maintained by a small number of RAF personnel. Formerly RAF Kinloss, the station is now a British Army barracks.
Kirknewton Airfield	Scotland	Midlothian	Former RAF station, now home to No. 661 Volunteer Gliding Squadron flying the Grob Viking T1.
RAF Leeming	England	North Yorkshire	• Home to No. 100 Squadron operating the BAE Systems Hawk T1 in the mixed target facilities role and the Northumbrian Universities Air Squadron and No. 11 Air Experience Flight which are both equipped with the Grob Tutor T1. • Non flying units include No. 90 Signals Unit, No. 2 Force Protection Wing, No. 34 Squadron RAF Regiment, No. 609 (West Riding) Auxiliary Squadron and the Joint Forward Air Controllers Training and Standards Unit (JFACTSU).
Leuchars Station	Scotland	Fife	Relief Landing Ground (RLG) for RAF Lossiemouth, maintained by a small number of RAF personnel operating the airfield and air traffic control radar. The former RAF station is now a British Army barracks but continues to accommodate the East of Scotland Universities Air Squadron and No. 12 Air Experience Flight (both flying the Grob Tutor T1) and No. 612 (County of Aberdeen) Squadron (Royal Auxiliary Air Force) in the medical support role.

RAF Linton-on-Ouse	England	North Yorkshire	Training station home to No. 72 Squadron operating the Shorts Tucano T1 as part of No. 1 Flying Training School (1 FTS). Yorkshire Universities Air Squadron and No. 9 Air Experience Flight operate the Grob Tutor T1 and No. 642 Volunteer Gliding Squadron the Grob Vigilant T1. With the transfer of the fast jet flying programme to RAF Valley, the MoD announced in July 2018 that Linton-on-Ouse would be closed by 2020.
Little Rissington Airfield	England	Gloucestershire	Former RAF station, home to No. 637 Volunteer Gliding Squadron and used for military exercises.
RAF Lossiemouth	Scotland	Moray	• Eurofighter Typhoon FGR4 main operating base with No. 1 Squadron, No. 2 (AC) Squadron and No. 6 Squadron all contributing to the Quick Reaction Alert (Interceptor) North capability. No. 5 Force Protection Wing HQ, No. 51 Squadron RAF Regiment and No. 2622 (Highland) Squadron (RAuxAF) operate in the airfield defence role. • The RAF's new P-8A Poseidon aircraft is expected to be based at Lossiemouth from 2020 and a new Typhoon squadron is expected to be formed by April 2019.
RAF Marham	England	Norfolk	• Tornado GR4/4A main operating base. Home to No. 12 Squadron, No. 9 Squadron and No. 31 Squadron. Non-flying units include the Tactical Imagery-Intelligence Wing, No. 3 Force Protection Wing HQ, No. 93 Expeditionary Armament Squadron and No. 2620 (County of Norfolk) Squadron (RAuxAF). • From 2018 Marham will be home to the RAF's new Lockheed Martin F-35 Lightning II aircraft which is to initially be operated by No. 617 Squadron.
RAF Mona	Wales	Isle of Anglesey	Relief Landing Ground (RLG) for Hawk T1As operating from RAF Valley.
RRH Neatishead	England	Norfolk	Remote Radar Head forming part of the UK Air Surveillance and Control System which is managed from RAF Boulmer. The station was formerly known as RAF Neatishead. Part of the site is now the RAF Air Defence Radar Museum.
RAF Northolt	England	Greater London	• Home of No. 32 (The Royal) Squadron operated the BAe 146 and Augusta 109 in the Command Support Air Transport role. The station is also home to No. 63 Squadron (Queen's Colour Squadron) RAF Regiment, No. 600 (City of London) Squadron (RAuxAF), No. 1 AIDU (Aeronautical Information Documents Unit) and the Headquarters Music Services and the Central Band of the RAF. • A number of other military units are based at Northolt, including the British Forces Post Office and No. 621 (Explosive Ordnance Disposal) Squadron of Royal Logistics Corps.

RAF Odiham	England	Hampshire	Home of the RAF's Chinook fleet operating under Joint Helicopter Command, comprising No. 18 Squadron, and No. 27 Squadrons. No. 7 Squadron operates its Chinooks alongside No. 657 Squadron of the Army Air Corps (flying the Westland Lynx AH9A) as part of the Joint Special Forces Aviation Wing which has its headquarters at Odiham. No. 618 Volunteer Glider Squadron operates the Grob Viking T1.
RRH Portreath	England	Cornwall	Remote Radar Head forming part of the UK Air Surveillance and Control System which is managed from RAF Boulmer. The station was formerly known as RAF Portreath.
RRS Saxa Vord	Scotland	Shetland Islands	Remote Radio Site forming part of the UK Air Surveillance and Control System which is managed from RAF Boulmer. The site was brought back to full operational capability in 2018, although with no permanent personnel.
RAF Scampton	England	Lincolnshire	Home of the RAF Aerobatic Team (The Red Arrows) flying the BAE Systems Hawk T1A. Non-flying units include No. 1 Air Control Centre and the RAF Mobile Meteorological Unit. In July 2018, the MoD announced that Scampton would close by 2022; all units would be relocated to other RAF Bases.
RAF Shawbury	England	Shropshire	Home of the tri-service Defence Helicopter Flying School, comprising 60(R) Squadron, No. 660 Squadron Army Air Corps and 705 Naval Air Squadron, flying the Eurocopter Squirrel HT1 and Bell Griffin HT1. Elements of the Central Flying School (Helicopter) Squadron train helicopter flying instructors and the School of Air Operations Control (SAOC) trains air traffic controllers for the RAF and Royal Navy.
MOD St. Athan	Wales	Vale of Glamorgan	Training station, home to No. 4 School of Technical Training and the University of Wales Air Squadron flying the Grob Tutor T1.
RAF St Mawgan	England	Cornwall	Non-flying station with the airfield part now operating as Cornwall Newquay Airport. The station is home to the tri-service Defence Survival Training Organisation and No. 505 (Wessex) Squadron RAuxAF. It is also used by the Defence Infrastructure Organisation to accommodate personnel utilising the Defence Training Estate within the south west of England.
RRH Staxton Wold	England	North Yorkshire	Remote Radar Head forming part of the UK Air Surveillance and Control System which is managed from RAF Boulmer. The station was formerly known as RAF Staxton Wold.
RAF (U) Swanwick	England	Hampshire	RAF (Unit) Swanwick is the military element of London Area Control Centre. The unit also operates the UK's Distress and Diversion Cell and provides air traffic control services for RAF Northolt.
RAF Syerston	England	Nottinghamshire	Home of No. 2 Flying Training School headquarters, the Central Gliding School and No. 644 Volunteer Gliding Squadron.

List of Royal Air Force stations

Ternhill Airfield	England	Shropshire	Former RAF station, now an unmanned airfield used for training purposes by helicopters of the Defence Helicopter Flying School from RAF Shawbury.
RAF Topcliffe	England	North Yorkshire	Unmanned Relief Landing Ground for Shorts Tucano T1s operating from RAF Linton-on-Ouse. Home to No. 645 Volunteer Gliding Squadrons flying the Grob Vigilant T1.
RRH Trimingham	England	Norfolk	Remote Radar Head, satellite station of RRH Neatishead.
RAF Valley	Wales	Isle of Anglesey	• Training station home to No. 4 Squadron operating the BAE Systems Hawk T2 and as part of No. 4 Flying Training School. No. 202 Squadron, part of the Defence Helicopter Flying School, operates the Bell Griffin HT2 in the maritime and mountains flying skills training role. The station is also home to the RAF Mountain Rescue Service headquarters. • The airfield incorporates Anglesey Airport.
RAF Waddington	England	Lincolnshire	• Main operating base, home to the RAF's Intelligence, Surveillance, Target Acquisition and Reconnaissance (ISTAR) operations. No. 5(AC) Squadron operate the Sentinel R1, No. 8 Squadron the Boeing Sentry AEW1, No. 13 Squadron the General Atomics MQ-9 Reaper, No. 14 Squadron the Beechcraft Shadow R1, No. 51 Squadron the Boeing RC-135V Rivet Joint. No. 54 Squadron is the ISTAR training unit and 56 Squadron is the ISTAR test and evaluation unit. • Non-flying squadrons include No. 2503 (County of Lincoln) Squadron RAuxAF Regiment the RAF Air Battlespace Training Centre, RAF Air Warfare Centre, the headquarters of the intelligence reserves and No. 7006 (VR) Intelligence Squadron.
MOD West Freugh	Scotland	Dumfries and Galloway	Former RAF station, operated by QinetiQ on behalf of the MOD as a test and evaluation range. The airfield is disused and unlicensed but available for military exercises.
RAF Weston-on-the-Green	England	Oxfordshire	Force Development Training Centre, used by No. 1 Parachute Training School (based at nearby RAF Brize Norton) as a parachute drop-zone.
Defence CBRN Centre, Winterbourne Gunner	England	Wiltshire	The Defence Chemical Biological Radiological and Nuclear (CBRN) Centre is managed by RAF Air Command. It is responsible for all training issues related to CBRN warfare for the UK armed forces.
RAF Wittering	England	Cambridgeshire and Northamptonshire	• Support station accommodating elements of the RAF A4 Force which supports deployed and expeditionary air operations. The A4 force comprises a variety of units under No. 42 (Expeditionary Support) Wing and No. 85 (Expeditionary Logistics) Wing. • Flying units consist of No. 16 Squadron of No. 3 Flying Training School and No. 115 Squadron, University of London Air Squadron, Cambridge University Air Squadron and No. 5 Air Experience Flight of No. 6 Flying Training School, all flying the Grob Tutor T1.

RAF Wood-vale	England	Merseyside	Training station home to Liverpool University Air Squadron, Manchester and Salford Universities Air Squadron, No. 10 Air Experience Flight all flying the Grob Tutor T1 and No. 631 Volunteer Gliding Squadron flying the Grob Vigilant T1. The Station is also home to No. 611 (West Lancashire) Squadron RAuxAF.
RAF Wyton	England	Cambridgeshire	Non-flying station operated under Joint Forces Command. Home to the Joint Forces Intelligence Group (JFIG), the Defence Intelligence Fusion Centre (DIFC), No. 42 Engineer Regiment (Geographic) of the British Army.

RAF stations operated by the United States Visiting Forces

At the invitation of the UK Government, the United States has had military forces (US Visiting Forces) permanently stationed in the UK since the Second World War. The 1951 NATO Status of Forces Agreement and the Visiting Forces Act 1952, along with other bilateral acts, establishes the legal status of the USVF in the UK. Several military sites within England are made available for the USVF's purposes. An RAF commander is present at the main USVF sites and is normally of the rank of squadron leader, whereas a US colonel will normally command US personnel at each station. The role of the RAF commander is to liaise with the US base commander and act as head of establishment for Ministry of Defence employees. The use of UK bases for combat operations by the United States is a joint decision by both governments.

The United States Air Force (USAF) 501st Combat Support Wing manages and supports operations at RAF Alconbury, RAF Croughton, RAF Fairford, RAF Menwith Hill, RAF Molesworth and RAF Welford.

In January 2017 the US Department of Defence announced through their *European Infrastructure Consolidation* programme that they would be withdrawing from RAF Mildenhall, and activities at RAF Alconbury and RAF Molesworth would be moved to RAF Croughton. In April 2017 it was reported by the US European Command was reviewing the decision to close these stations.

List of Royal Air Force stations

Figure 200: *A United States Air Force CV-22B Osprey at RAF Mildenhall.*

Name	Constituent country	County	Units and purpose
RAF Alconbury	England	Cambridgeshire	- Non-flying station home to the USAF 423rd Air Base Group (part of the 501st Combat Support Wing) which provides services and accommodation to support operations at RAF Molesworth and the Joint Warfare Centre, Stavanger in Norway. - In 2015 the US Department of Defence announced the US withdrawal from the station.
RAF Barford St John	England	Oxfordshire	Non-flying station operated as a signals intelligence relay station by the USAF. The facility is a satellite station of RAF Croughton and controlled remotely.
RAF Croughton	England	Northamptonshire	Non-flying station operated as a signals intelligence facility by the USAF and US intelligence agencies. The station is operated by the USAF 422nd Air Base Group (part of the 501st Combat Support Wing).
RAF Fairford	England	Gloucestershire	- Forward operating airfield predominately used by USAF heavy bombers such as the B-1B Lancer, B-2A Spirit and B-52H Stratofortress. The station is operated by the USAF 420th Air Base Squadron, 422nd Air Base Group (part of the 501st Combat Support Wing). - The Royal International Air Tattoo, the world's largest military air show, is held at Fairford annually in July.

RAF Feltwell	England	Norfolk	Non-flying station, operated as a space intelligence facility by the USAF 18th Intelligence Squadron (Detachment 4), part of the 544th Intelligence, Surveillance and Reconnaissance Group. Feltwell is parented by the 48th Fighter Wing at RAF Lakenheath.
RAF Lakenheath	England	Suffolk	• Home to the USAF 48th Fighter Wing operating the F-15C/D and F-15E. The wing comprises the 492d Fighter Squadron (FS), 493d FS and the 494th FS. The station is also home to the 56th Rescue Squadron operating the HH-60G Pave Hawk in the combat search and rescue role. • The F-35A Lightning II is expected to be based at the station from 2020.
RAF Menwith Hill	England	North Yorkshire	Joint UK/US signals intelligence gathering station which functions primarily as a field station of the US National Security Agency. Operations are supported by the USAF 421st Air Base Squadron which is part of the 501st Combat Support Wing.
RAF Mildenhall	England	Suffolk	• Home to the USAF 100th Air Refuelling Wing operating the KC-135R Stratotanker, the 352nd Special Operations Wing operating the CV-22 Osprey, MC-130J Commando II and MC-130H Combat Talon II. The 95th Reconnaissance Squadron supports RC-135 Rivet Joint and OC-135 Open Skies, aircraft when deployed to Europe and operating from the station. • In 2015 the US Department of Defence announced the US withdrawal from the station by 2023.
RAF Molesworth	England	Cambridgeshire	• Non-flying station, home to the Joint Intelligence Operations Center Europe (JIOCEUR) Analytic Center operated by the US Defense Intelligence Agency and the J2 Directorate which provides US Africa Command with intelligence. The station is supported by the USAF 423rd Air Base Group (part of the 501st Combat Support Wing). • In 2015 the US Department of Defence announced the US withdrawal from the station by 2021 with operations transferring to RAF Croughton.
RAF Welford	England	Berkshire	Non-flying station used as ammunition depot in support of bomber operating from RAF Fairford. The station is operated by the USAF 420th Munitions Squadron (part of the 501st Combat Support Wing).

MOD air weapons ranges

Air weapons ranges (AWR) within the UK, previously operated by the RAF, are the responsibility of the Service Delivery (SD) part of the Defence Infrastructure Organisation (DIO). QinetiQ were awarded a three-year contract by the DIO in 2010 to manage the ranges but this role was taken over by Landmarc Support Services (an Interserve company) in 2014 as part of a contract covering the wider MoD Defence Training Estate.

Name	Constituent country	County	Units and purpose
DIO (SD) Cape Wrath	Scotland	Highland	Parented by DIO (SD) Tain.
DIO (SD) Donna Nook Air Weapons Range	England	Lincolnshire	Parented by RAF Coningsby.
DIO (SD) Holbeach Air Weapons Range	England	Lincolnshire	Parented by RAF Marham.
DIO (SD) Pembrey Sands Air Weapons Range	Wales	Carmarthenshire	
DIO (SD) Tain Air Weapons Range	Scotland	Highland	Parented by RAF Lossiemouth.
RAF Spadeadam	England	Cumbria	Electronic warfare range.

RAF stations and locations overseas

Permanent Joint Operating Bases

The UK operate Permanent Joint Operating Bases (PJOB's) in the four British Overseas Territories of Ascension Island, Cyprus, Falkland Islands and Gibraltar. The PJOB's contribute to the physical defence and maintenance of sovereignty of the British Overseas Territories and enable the UK to conduct expeditionary military operations. Although command and oversight of the PJOB's is provided by Joint Forces Command, the airfield elements are known as RAF stations.

Semi-permanent operations

The RAF have a semi-permanent presence at several overseas locations. Active military operations in the Middle East are supported by Expeditionary Air Wings which have been established at foreign airfields in the United Arab Emirates and Qatar. The RAF have a presence within Eastern European countries on a rotational basis as part of the NATO's Baltic Air Policing and Southern Air Policing missions.

Two squadrons are located within the United States to support close cooperation with the USAF in the operation of the MQ-9A Reaper and development of the F-35A Lighting II.

Figure 201: *A RAF Harrier GR9 over RAF Akrotiri in 2010.*

Name	Country	Units and purpose
RAF Akrotiri	Sovereign Base Areas of Akrotiri and Dhekelia	• Permanent Joint Operating Base acting as a strategic staging airfield to support British military operations in the Middle East. It is operated by the Cyprus Operations Support Unit (COSU). • No. 903 Expeditionary Air Wing was established in December 2014 to support combat and support aircraft on detachment to the airfield as part of Operation Shader. • No. 84 Squadron operate the Griffin HAR2 helicopter.
Al Minhad Air Base	United Arab Emirates	No. 906 Expeditionary Air Wing was established in January 2013 to provide a Middle East air transport and refuelling hub.[1201]
Al Udeid Air Base	Qatar	No. 83 Expeditionary Air Group was established in April 2006 as the headquarters for all RAF assets in the Middle East and is responsible for UK air operations as part of Operation Kipon and Operation Shader.
RAF Ascension Island	Saint Helena, Ascension and Tristan da Cunha	Permanent Joint Operating Base predominantly operating as an air-bridge between RAF Brize Norton in Oxfordshire and RAF Mount Pleasant in the Falkland Islands. Also used by the United States Air Force (USAF) and NASA as a communications and satellite tracking station.
MCAS Beaufort	United States	No. 617 Squadron personnel are training on the Lockheed Martin F-35 Lightning II, embedded within VMFAT-501 of the US Marine Corps. The squadron is expected to transfer to RAF Marham in mid 2018.

List of Royal Air Force stations 507

RRH Byron Heights	Falkland Islands	Remote Radar Head located on West Falkland.
Creech Air Force Base	United States	No. 39 Squadron operate the MQ-9A Reaper.
Edwards Air Force Base	United States	No. 17(R) Squadron formed at Edwards in April 2013 to test and evaluate the Lockheed Martin F-35 Lightning II.
RAF Gibraltar	Gibraltar	Permanent Joint Operating Base acting as a strategic staging airfield. Also functions as Gibraltar International Airport which comprises a civilian passenger terminal operated by Government of Gibraltar.
RRH Mount Alice	Falkland Islands	Remote Radar Head located on West Falkland.
RRH Mount Kent	Falkland Islands	Remote Radar Head located on East Falkland.
RAF Mount Pleasant	Falkland Islands	Permanent Joint Operating Base opened in 1985 after the Falklands War. No. 905 Expeditionary Air Wing operates four permanently based Typhoon FGR4s, one Voyager KC2, one Hercules C5 and two Chinook HC4s.
RAF Troodos	Cyprus	Signals intelligence gathering and radar station located in the Troodos Mountains, outside the Sovereign Base Areas. Operated by golf section of the Joint Service Signal Unit (Cyprus).

Map of stations within the UK

Map of the United Kingdom showing active RAF stations, Ministry of Defence (MOD) airfields (non Royal Navy or Army Air Corps), MOD air weapons ranges and RAF stations occupied by the United States Visiting Forces (USVF).

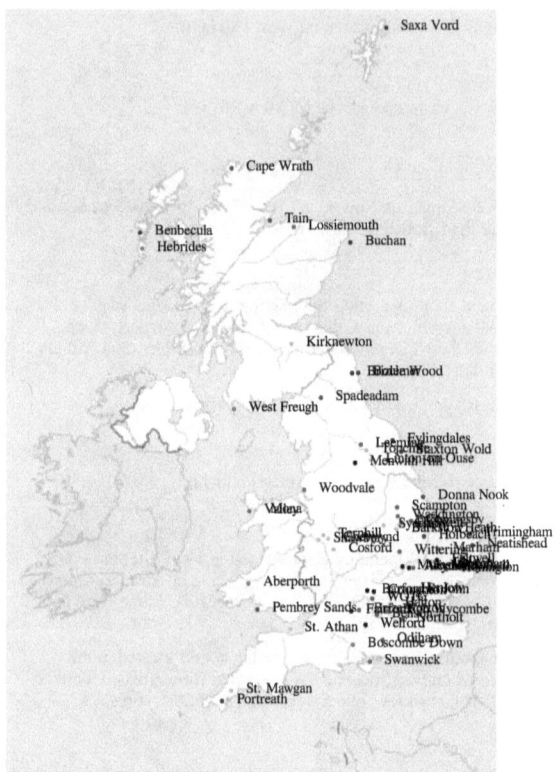

File:United Kingdom adm location map.svg

● Flying Station ● Training Station ● Support Station ● UK Air Surveillance And Control System Sites ● Air Weapons Range ● MOD Aeronautical Test and Evaluation Site ● US Air Force Installation
WOTG = Weston-on-the-Green, LN = Lakenheath

References

Bibliography

<templatestyles src="Template:Refbegin/styles.css" />

- Halley, James J. *The Squadrons of the Royal Air Force*. Tonbridge, Kent, UK: Air-Britain (Historians) Ltd., 1980. ISBN 0-85130-083-9.
- Halley, James J. *The Squadrons of the Royal Air Force & Commonwealth, 1981-1988*. Tonbridge, Kent, UK: Air-Britain (Historians) Ltd., 1988. ISBN 0-85130-164-9.

- Jefford, C.G, MBE,BA ,RAF (Retd). *RAF Squadrons, a Comprehensive Record of the Movement and Equipment of all RAF Squadrons and their Antecedents since 1912.* Shrewsbury, Shropshire, UK: Airlife Publishing, 1988. ISBN 1-84037-141-2.
- Rawlings, John. *Fighter Squadrons of the RAF and their Aircraft.* London: Macdonald and Jane's Publishers Ltd., 1969 (second edition 1976). ISBN 0-354-01028-X.

External links

- RAF Stations[1202] official web page listing current Royal Air Force stations
- Current functions of RAF bases[1203]
- UK "Secret Bases"[1204]
- gallery of RAF images ServicePals.com[1205]
- Subterranea Britannica[1206] - Cold War
- Pastscape Search English Heritage records[1207]

List of Royal Air Force aircraft squadrons

Squadrons are the main form of flying unit of the Royal Air Force (RAF). These include Royal Flying Corps (RFC) and Royal Naval Air Service (RNAS) squadrons incorporated into the RAF when it was formed on 1 April 1918, during the First World War. Other squadrons of the RAF include those from Commonwealth air forces which have served within the RAF structure and squadrons of the Fleet Air Arm before it transferred to the Royal Navy in 1939.

Some squadrons have an individual tradition of presenting their squadron number in Roman numerals or using a suffix to their squadron number (such as "(F)" for "Fighter", "(B)" for "Bomber" or "(AC)" for "Army Co-operation") to indicate a past or present role. An example would be No. 18 (Bomber) Squadron RAF which currently actually operates the heavy-lift Chinook helicopter. However, these practices have, at least in the past, been deprecated at higher levels and generally only apply to certain squadrons with long traditions, especially those numbered from 1-20.[1208]

Flying training units and operational evaluation squadrons have generally been (Reserve) squadrons, although they are regular active-duty units. The policy of the (Reserve) numberplate was rescinded in February 2018, to coincide with the renaming of 22 (Training) Group to just 22 Group in line with other RAF Groups.

Some Squadron names include the location they were originally formed.

Figure 202: *Typhoons representing the RAF Typhoon squadrons - 1 Sqn, 2 Sqn, 3 Sqn, 6 Sqn, 29 Sqn, 11 Sqn, 41 Sqn, 1435 Flight, and BOB75 in the centre to commemorate the Battle of Britain*

Regular RFC, RNAS, and RAF squadrons (Nos. 1–299)

Squadrons in **Bold Type** are currently active

Nos. 1–50

- **No. 1 (Fighter) Squadron RAF** (Typhoon FGR4)
- **No. II (Army Cooperation) Squadron RAF** (Typhoon FGR4)
- **No. 3 (Fighter) Squadron RAF** (Typhoon FGR4)
- **No. IV Squadron RAF** (Hawk T2)
- **No. V (Army Cooperation) Squadron RAF** (Sentinel R1)
- **No. 6 Squadron RAF** (Typhoon FGR4)
- **No. 7 Squadron RAF** (Chinook HC4)
- **No. VIII Squadron RAF** (Sentry AEW1)
- **No. IX (Bomber) Squadron RAF** (Tornado GR4)
- **No. 10 Squadron RAF** (Voyager KC2/KC3)
- **No. XI (Fighter) Squadron RAF** (Typhoon FGR4)
- **No. 12 (Bomber) Squadron RAF** (Tornado GR4)
- **No. XIII Squadron RAF** (MQ-9 Reaper)

List of Royal Air Force aircraft squadrons

- **No. 14 Squadron RAF** (Shadow R1)
- No. XV Squadron
- **No. 16 Squadron RAF** (Tutor T1)
- **No. XVII Squadron RAF** (F-35B Lightning Test & Evaluation Squadron)
- **No. 18 (Bomber) Squadron** (Chinook HC2)
- No. 19 Squadron RAF
- No. 20 Squadron RAF
- No. 21 Squadron RAF
- No. 22 Squadron RAF
- No. 23 Squadron RAF
- **No. XXIV (Commonwealth) Squadron RAF** (Hercules C4/5)
- No. 25 Squadron RAF
- No. 26 (South African) Squadron RAF
- **No. 27 Squadron RAF** (Chinook HC2)
- **No. 28 Squadron RAF** (Chinook HC4/6 and Puma HC2 OCU)
- **No. 29 Squadron RAF** (Typhoon T3 and FGR4 OCU)
- **No. 30 Squadron RAF** (Hercules)
- **No. 31 Squadron RAF** (Tornado GR4)
- **No. 32 (The Royal) Squadron RAF** (BAe 146 & AW109)
- **No. 33 Squadron RAF** (Puma HC2)
- No. 34 Squadron RAF
- No. 35 (Madras Presidency) Squadron RAF
- No. 36 Squadron RAF
- No. 37 Squadron RAF
- No. 38 Squadron RAF
- **No. 39 Squadron RAF** (MQ-9 Reaper)
- No. 40 Squadron RAF
- **No. 41 Squadron RAF** (Typhoon Test & Evaluation Squadron)
- No. 42 Squadron RAF
- No. 43 (China-British) Squadron RAF
- No. 44 (Rhodesia) Squadron RAF
- **No. 45 Squadron RAF** (King Air)
- No. 46 (Uganda) Squadron RAF
- **No. 47 Squadron RAF** (Hercules)
- No. 48 Squadron RAF
- No. 49 Squadron RAF
- No. 50 Squadron RAF

Nos. 51–66

- **No. 51 Squadron RAF** (Airseeker)
- No. 52 Squadron RAF
- No. 53 Squadron RAF
- **No. 54 Squadron RAF** (Sentry/Sentinel ISTAR OCU)
- No. 55 Squadron RAF
- **No. 56 (Punjab) Squadron RAF** (AIR C2ISR OEU)
- **No. LVII Squadron RAF** (Grob 120TP Prefect)
- No. 58 Squadron RAF
- No. 59 Squadron RAF
- **No. 60 Squadron RAF** (Griffin HT1)
- No. 61 Squadron RAF
- No. 62 Squadron RAF
- No. 63 Squadron RAF
- No. 64 Squadron RAF
- No. 65 (East India) Squadron RAF
- No. 66 Squadron RAF

Nos. 67–71

During the First World War, in order to avoid confusion with similarly-numbered British flying squadrons, units of the separate Australian Flying Corps were known for administrative purposes as 67, 68, 69, and 71 squadrons. Since the Second World War these numbers have always been used by RAF units.

However, the designation 70 (or LXX) Squadron has always been used for RFC/RAF units.

- No. 67 Squadron
  - 1916–18: No. 1 Squadron, Australian Flying Corps
  - From 1941: No. 67 Squadron RAF
- No. 68 Squadron
  - 1916–18: No. 2 Squadron, Australian Flying Corps
  - From 1941: No. 68 Squadron RAF
- No. 69 Squadron RAF
  - 1916–18: No. 3 Squadron Australian Flying Corps
  - From 1941: No. 69 Squadron RAF
- **No. LXX Squadron RAF** (Atlas)
- No. 71 Squadron
  - 1916–18: No. 4 Squadron Australian Flying Corps
  - From 1940: No. 71 Squadron RAF (staffed by US volunteers in 1940–42)

List of Royal Air Force aircraft squadrons

Nos. 72–100

- **No. 72 (Basutoland) Squadron RAF** (Tucano T1)
- No. 73 Squadron RAF
- No. 74 (Trinidad) Squadron RAF
- No. 75 (New Zealand) Squadron RAF
- No. 76 Squadron RAF
- No. 77 Squadron RAF
- No. 78 Squadron RAF
- No. 79 (Madras Presidency) Squadron RAF
- No. 80 Squadron RAF
- No. 81 Squadron RAF
- No. 82 (United Provinces) Squadron RAF
- No. 83 Squadron RAF
- **No. 84 Squadron RAF** (Griffin HAR2)
- No. 85 Squadron RAF
- No. 86 Squadron RAF
- No. 87 (United Provinces) Squadron RAF
- No. 88 (Hong Kong) Squadron RAF
- No. 89 Squadron RAF
- No. 90 Squadron RAF
- No. 91 (Nigeria) Squadron RAF
- **No. 92 (East India) Squadron RAF** Tactics and Training Squadron
- No. 93 Squadron RAF
- No. 94 Squadron RAF
- No. 95 Squadron RAF
- No. 96 Squadron RAF
- No. 97 (Straits Settlements) Squadron RAF
- No. 98 Squadron RAF
- **No. 99 (Madras Presidency) Squadron RAF** (C-17 Globemaster)
- **No. 100 Squadron RAF** (Hawk T1)

Nos. 101–150

- **No. 101 Squadron RAF** (Voyager KC2/K3C)
- No. 102 (Ceylon) Squadron RAF
- No. 103 Squadron RAF
- No. 104 Squadron RAF
- No. 105 Squadron RAF
- No. 106 Squadron RAF
- No. 107 Squadron RAF
- No. 108 Squadron RAF
- No. 109 Squadron RAF

- No. 110 (Hyderabad) Squadron RAF
- No. 111 Squadron RAF
- No. 112 Squadron RAF
- No. 113 Squadron RAF
- No. 114 (Hong Kong) Squadron RAF
- **No. 115 Squadron RAF** (Tutor T1)
- No. 116 Squadron RAF
- No. 117 Squadron RAF
- No. 118 Squadron RAF
- No. 119 Squadron RAF
- No. 120 Squadron RAF
- No. 121 (Eagle) Squadron RAF later 335th Fighter Squadron USAAF[1209]
- No. 122 (Bombay) Squadron RAF
- No. 123 (East India) Squadron RAF
- No. 124 (Baroda) Squadron RAF
- No. 125 (Newfoundland) Squadron RAF
- No. 126 (Persian Gulf) Squadron RAF
- No. 127 Squadron RAF
- No. 128 Squadron RAF
- No. 129 (Mysore) Squadron RAF
- No. 130 (Punjab) Squadron RAF
- No. 131 (County of Kent) Squadron RAF
- No. 132 (City of Bombay) Squadron RAF
- No. 133 (Eagle) Squadron
- No. 134 Squadron RAF
- No. 135 Squadron RAF
- No. 136 Squadron RAF
- No. 137 Squadron RAF
- No. 138 Squadron RAF
- No. 139 (Jamaica) Squadron RAF
- No. 140 Squadron RAF
- No. 141 Squadron RAF
- No. 142 Squadron RAF
- No. 143 Squadron RAF
- No. 144 Squadron RAF
- No. 145 Squadron RAF
- No. 146 Squadron RAF
- No. 147 Squadron RAF
- No. 148 Squadron RAF
- No. 149 (East India) Squadron
- No. 150 Squadron RAF

Nos. 151–200

- No. 151 Squadron RAF
- No. 152 (Hyderabad) Squadron RAF
- No. 153 Squadron RAF
- No. 154 (Motor Industries) Squadron RAF
- No. 155 Squadron RAF
- No. 156 Squadron RAF
- No. 157 Squadron RAF
- No. 158 Squadron RAF
- No. 159 Squadron RAF
- No. 160 Squadron RAF
- No. 161 Squadron RAF
- No. 162 Squadron RAF
- No. 163 Squadron RAF
- No. 164 (Argentine British) Squadron RAF
- No. 165 (Ceylon) Squadron RAF
- No. 166 Squadron RAF
- No. 167 (Gold Coast) Squadron RAF
- No. 168 Squadron RAF
- No. 169 Squadron RAF
- No. 170 Squadron RAF
- No. 171 Squadron RAF
- No. 172 Squadron RAF
- No. 173 Squadron RAF
- No. 174 (Mauritius) Squadron RAF
- No. 175 Squadron RAF
- No. 176 Squadron RAF
- No. 177 Squadron RAF
- No. 178 Squadron RAF
- No. 179 Squadron RAF
- No. 180 Squadron RAF
- No. 181 Squadron RAF
- No. 182 Squadron RAF
- No. 183 (Gold Coast) Squadron RAF
- No. 184 Squadron RAF
- No. 185 Squadron RAF
- No. 186 Squadron RAF
- No. 187 Squadron RAF
- No. 188 Squadron RAF
- No. 189 Squadron RAF
- No. 190 Squadron RAF
- No. 191 Squadron RAF

- No. 192 Squadron RAF
- No. 193 (Fellowship of the Bellows) Squadron RAF
- No. 194 Squadron RAF
- No. 195 Squadron RAF
- No. 196 Squadron RAF
- No. 197 Squadron RAF
- No. 198 Squadron RAF
- No. 199 Squadron RAF
- No. 200 Squadron RAF

Nos. 201–250

The first squadrons to carry numbers above 200 were former RNAS squadrons that were renumbered upon amalgamation with 200 added to their RNAS squadron number. Independent flights of the RNAS were grouped together in squadrons and given numbers in the 200 series.

- No. 201 Squadron RAF
- **No. 202 Squadron RAF - (Griffin/AW139)**
- No. 203 Squadron RAF
- No. 204 Squadron RAF
- No. 205 Squadron RAF
- **No. 206 Squadron RAF** - Atlas & Hercules OEU
- No. 207 Squadron RAF
- No. 208 Squadron RAF
- No. 209 Squadron RAF
- No. 210 Squadron RAF
- No. 211 Squadron RAF
- No. 212 Squadron RAF
- No. 213 (Ceylon) Squadron RAF
- No. 214 (Federated Malay States) Squadron RAF
- No. 215 Squadron RAF
- No. 216 Squadron RAF
- No. 217 Squadron RAF
- No. 218 (Gold Coast) Squadron RAF
- No. 219 (Mysore) Squadron RAF
- No. 220 Squadron RAF
- No. 221 Squadron RAF
- No. 222 (Natal) Squadron RAF
- No. 223 Squadron RAF
- No. 224 Squadron RAF
- No. 225 Squadron RAF
- No. 226 Squadron RAF

- No. 227 Squadron RAF
- No. 228 Squadron RAF
- No. 229 Squadron RAF
- **No. 230 Squadron RAF** (Puma HC2)
- No. 231 Squadron RAF
- No. 232 Squadron RAF
- No. 233 Squadron RAF
- No. 234 (Madras Presidency) Squadron RAF
- No. 235 Squadron RAF
- No. 236 Squadron RAF
- No. 237 Squadron RAF second formation as No. 237 (Rhodesia) from No. 1 Squadron Southern Rhodesian Air Force
- No. 238 Squadron RAF
- No. 239 Squadron RAF
- No. 240 Squadron RAF
- No. 241 Squadron RAF
- No. 242 (Canadian) Squadron RAF
- No. 243 Squadron RAF
- No. 244 Squadron RAF
- No. 245 (Northern Rhodesia) Squadron RAF
- No. 246 Squadron RAF
- No. 247 Squadron (China-British) Squadron RAF
- No. 248 Squadron RAF
- No. 249 (Gold Coast) Squadron RAF
- No. 250 (Sudan) Squadron RAF

Nos. 251–299

- No. 251 Squadron RAF
- No. 252 Squadron RAF
- No. 253 (Hyderabad State) Squadron RAF
- No. 254 Squadron RAF
- No. 255 Squadron RAF
- No. 256 Squadron RAF
- No. 257 (Burma) Squadron RAF
- No. 258 Squadron RAF
- No. 259 Squadron RAF
- No. 260 Squadron RAF
- No. 261 Squadron RAF
- No. 262 Squadron RAF
- No. 263 (Fellowship of the Bellows) Squadron RAF
- No. 264 (Madras Presidency) Squadron RAF
- No. 265 Squadron RAF

- No. 266 (Rhodesia) Squadron RAF
- No. 267 (Malta) Squadron RAF
- No. 268 Squadron RAF
- No. 269 Squadron RAF
- No. 270 Squadron RAF
- No. 271 Squadron RAF
- No. 272 Squadron RAF
- No. 273 Squadron RAF
- No. 274 Squadron RAF
- No. 275 Squadron RAF
- No. 276 Squadron RAF
- No. 277 Squadron RAF
- No. 278 Squadron RAF
- No. 279 Squadron RAF
- No. 280 Squadron RAF
- No. 281 Squadron RAF
- No. 282 Squadron RAF
- No. 283 Squadron RAF
- No. 284 Squadron RAF
- No. 285 Squadron RAF
- No. 286 Squadron RAF
- No. 287 Squadron RAF
- No. 288 Squadron RAF
- No. 289 Squadron RAF
- No. 290 Squadron RAF
- No. 291 Squadron RAF
- No. 292 Squadron RAF
- No. 293 Squadron RAF
- No. 294 Squadron RAF
- No. 295 Squadron RAF
- No. 296 Squadron RAF
- No. 297 Squadron RAF
- No. 298 Squadron RAF
- No. 299 Squadron RAF

Nos. 300–352

Squadrons in the 300–352 series were staffed during the Second World War by volunteers from countries in occupied Europe. In some cases, these RAF squadrons and personnel were regarded by a relevant government-in-exile as serving concurrently with its air force.

Similarly, in 1940–42, three "Eagle Squadrons" were composed of volunteers from the USA: No. 71 (Eagle) Squadron, later 334th Fighter Squadron USAAF; No. 121 (Eagle) Squadron, later 335th Fighter Squadron USAAF and No. 133 (Eagle) Squadron, later 336th Fighter Squadron USAAF.

Polish (300–309)

See also Squadrons Nos. 315–318, 663 and Polish Fighting Team (under Other)

- No. 300 "Land of Masovia" Polish Bomber Squadron (*Ziemi Mazowieckiej*)
- No. 301 "Land of Pomerania" Polish Bomber Squadron (*Ziemi Pomorskiej*)
- No. 302 "City of Poznań" Polish Fighter Squadron (*Poznański*)
- No. 303 "Kosciuszko" Polish Fighter Squadron (*Warszawski im. Tadeusza Kościuszki*)
- No. 304 "Land of Silesia" Polish Bomber Squadron (*Ziemi Śląskiej im. Ks. Józefa Poniatowskiego*)
- No. 305 "Land of Greater Poland" Polish Bomber Squadron (*Ziemi Wielkopolskiej im. Marszałka Józefa Piłsudskiego*)
- No. 306 "City of Toruń" Polish Fighter Squadron (*Toruński*)
- No. 307 "City of Lwów" Polish Fighter Squadron (*Lwowskich Puchaczy*)
- No. 308 "City of Kraków" Polish Fighter Squadron (*Krakowski*)
- No. 309 "Land of Czerwień" Polish Fighter-Reconnaissance Squadron (*Ziemi Czerwieńskiej*)

Czechoslovakian (310–313)

- No. 310 (Czechoslovak) Squadron
- No. 311 (Czechoslovak) Squadron
- No. 312 (Czechoslovak) Squadron
- No. 313 (Czechoslovak) Squadron

(Note: the RAF has never had a flying unit named 314 Squadron, although it has used the number for No. 314 Technical Services Unit. A proposed 314 Squadron was allocated squadron code "UY" during the period April to September 1939, but was never formed.)

Polish (315–318)

See also Squadrons Nos. 300–309, 663 and Polish Fighting Team (under Other)

- No. 315 "City of Dęblin" Polish Fighter Squadron (*Dębliński*)
- No. 316 "City of Warsaw" Polish Fighter Squadron (*Warszawski*)
- No. 317 "City of Wilno" Polish Fighter Squadron (*Wileński*)
- No. 318 "City of Gdańsk" Polish Fighter-Reconnaissance Squadron (*Gdański*)

Note: the RAF never had a No. 319 Squadron; the "Polish Fighting Team" was attached to No. 145 Fighter Squadron. A proposed 319 Squadron was allocated squadron codes VE for the period April to September 1939. There was also 663 Artillery Observation Squadron; No. 138 Special Duty Squadron Polish Flight "C" and No. 1586 Polish Special Duty Flight.

Dutch (320–325)

- No. 320 (Netherlands) Squadron
- No. 321 (Netherlands) Squadron
- No. 322 (Dutch) Squadron

Note: Nos. 323 to 325 Squadrons were not formed, but allocated Squadron Codes GN, PQ and EA respectively for the period April to September 1939. However these numbers were used for post-war Royal Netherlands Air Force squadrons.

French (326–329)

See also Nos. 340–347 Squadron

- No. 326 (GC 2/7 *Nice*)
- No. 327 (GC 1/3 *Corse*)
- No. 328 (GC 1/7 *Provence*)
- No. 329 (GC 1/2 *Cigognes*)

Norwegian (330–334)

- No. 330 Squadron RAF
- No. 331 Squadron RAF
- No. 332 Squadron RAF
- No. 333 Squadron RAF
- No. 334 Squadron RAF

Greek (335–339)

- No. 335 Squadron RAF
- No. 336 Squadron RAF

Note: Nos: 337–339 never formed,[1210] but were allocated Squadron Codes OK, ML and KN respectively for the period April to September 1939. The Royal Hellenic Air Force 13th Light Bomber Squadron was also under RAF command in World War II.

French (340–347)

See also Nos. 326–329 Squadron

- No. 340 (GC 4/2 *Ile de France*)
- No. 341 (GC 3/2 *Alsace*)
- No. 342 (GB 1/20 *Lorraine*)
- No. 343 (Flotille 7E)
- No. 344 (Flotille 1E)
- No. 345 (GC 2/2 *Berry*)
- No. 346 (GB 2/23 *Guyenne*)
- No. 347 (GB 1/25 *Tunisie*)

Note: No. 348 Squadron was not formed,[1211] but Squadron codes letters FR were allocated for the period April to September 1939.

Belgian (349–350)

- No. 349 Squadron RAF
- No. 350 Squadron RAF

Yugoslavian (351–352)

- No. 351 (Jugoslav) Squadron RAF
- No. 352 (Jugoslav) Squadron RAF

Nos. 353–361

- No. 353 Squadron RAF
- No. 354 Squadron RAF
- No. 355 Squadron RAF
- No. 356 Squadron RAF
- No. 357 Squadron RAF
- No. 358 Squadron RAF
- No. 360 Squadron RAF
- No. 361 Squadron RAF

Note: Nos. 362–399 Squadrons were not formed.[1212]

Article XV squadrons of World War II (Nos. 400–490)

Under Article XV of the British Commonwealth Air Training Plan, the air forces of Australia, Canada and New Zealand formed squadrons for service under RAF operational control. Most were new formations, however some had already existed prior to the creation of Article XV and had already been operational during the war, including combat operations.

Royal Canadian Air Force (400–443)

- No. 400 Squadron RCAF (City of Toronto)
- No. 401 Squadron RCAF (Ram)
- No. 402 Squadron RCAF (City of Winnipeg)
- No. 403 Squadron RCAF (Wolf)
- No. 404 Squadron RCAF (Buffalo)
- No. 405 Squadron RCAF (Vancouver)
- No. 406 Squadron RCAF (Lynx)
- No. 407 Squadron RCAF (Demon)
- No. 408 Squadron RCAF (Goose)
- No. 409 Squadron RCAF (Nighthawk)
- No. 410 Squadron RCAF (Cougar)
- No. 411 Squadron RCAF (Grizzly Bear)
- No. 412 Squadron RCAF (Falcon)
- No. 413 Squadron RCAF (Tusker)
- No. 414 Squadron RCAF (Sarnia Imperials)
- No. 415 Squadron RCAF (Swordfish)
- No. 416 Squadron RCAF (City of Oshawa)
- No. 417 Squadron RCAF (City of Windsor)
- No. 418 Squadron RCAF (City of Edmonton)
- No. 419 Squadron RCAF (Moose)
- No. 420 Squadron RCAF (Snowy Owl)
- No. 421 Squadron RCAF (Red Indian)
- No. 422 Squadron RCAF (Flying Yachtsman)
- No. 423 Squadron RCAF (Bald Eagle)
- No. 424 Squadron RCAF (Tiger)
- No. 425 Squadron RCAF (Alouette)
- No. 426 Squadron RCAF (Thunderbird)
- No. 427 Squadron RCAF (Lion)
- No. 428 Squadron RCAF (Ghost)
- No. 429 Squadron RCAF (Bison)
- No. 430 Squadron RCAF (City of Sudbury)

- No. 431 Squadron RCAF (Iroquois)
- No. 432 Squadron RCAF (Leaside)
- No. 433 Squadron RCAF (Porcupine)
- No. 434 Squadron RCAF (Bluenose)
- No. 435 Squadron RCAF (Chinthe)
- No. 436 Squadron RCAF (Elephant)
- No. 437 Squadron RCAF (Husky)
- No. 438 Squadron RCAF (Wildcat)
- No. 439 Squadron RCAF (Westmount)
- No. 440 Squadron RCAF (City of Ottawa and Beaver)
- No. 441 Squadron RCAF (Silver Fox)
- No. 442 Squadron RCAF (Caribou)
- No. 443 Squadron RCAF (Hornet)

Note: Although squadron numbers 444 to 449 were also reserved for the RCAF, it did not use them during the Second World War.

Royal Australian Air Force (450–467)

- No. 450 Squadron RAAF
- No. 451 Squadron RAAF
- No. 452 Squadron RAAF
- No. 453 Squadron RAAF
- No. 454 Squadron RAAF
- No. 455 Squadron RAAF
- No. 456 Squadron RAAF
- No. 457 Squadron RAAF
- No. 458 Squadron RAAF
- No. 459 Squadron RAAF
- No. 460 Squadron RAAF
- No. 461 Squadron RAAF
- No. 462 Squadron RAAF
- No. 463 Squadron RAAF
- No. 464 Squadron RAAF
- No. 466 Squadron RAAF
- No. 467 Squadron RAAF

Note: Although squadron numbers 465 and 468 to 479 were also reserved for the RAAF during the Second World War, it did not use them.

Royal New Zealand Air Force (485–490)

- No. 485 Squadron RNZAF
- No. 486 Squadron RNZAF
- No. 487 Squadron RNZAF
- No. 488 Squadron RNZAF
- No. 489 Squadron RNZAF
- No. 490 Squadron RNZAF

Note: Although the squadron numbers 491 to 499 were reserved for RNZAF units during the Second World War, no such squadrons were formed.

Royal Auxiliary Air Force squadrons (Nos. 500–509)

Formed as "Special Reserve" squadrons but absorbed into the Royal Auxiliary Air Force

- No. 500 (County of Kent) Squadron
- **No. 501 (County of Gloucester) Squadron**
- **No. 502 (Ulster) Squadron**
- No. 503 (City of Lincoln) Squadron
- **No. 504 (County of Nottingham) Squadron**
- **No. 505 (Wessex) Squadron**

Note: No. 505, 506, 507, 508 and 509 Squadrons allocated Squadron codes YF, FS, GX, DY and BQ respectively for the period April to September 1939, but were never formed.

Regular RAF squadrons (Nos. 510–598)

- No. 510 Squadron RAF
- No. 511 Squadron RAF
- No. 512 Squadron RAF
- No. 513 Squadron RAF
- No. 514 Squadron RAF
- No. 515 Squadron RAF
- No. 516 Squadron RAF
- No. 517 Squadron RAF
- No. 518 Squadron RAF
- No. 519 Squadron RAF
- No. 520 Squadron RAF
- No. 521 Squadron RAF
- No. 524 Squadron RAF

List of Royal Air Force aircraft squadrons

- No. 525 Squadron RAF
- No. 526 Squadron RAF
- No. 527 Squadron RAF
- No. 528 Squadron RAF
- No. 529 Squadron RAF
- No. 530 Squadron RAF
- No. 531 Squadron RAF
- No. 532 Squadron RAF
- No. 533 Squadron RAF
- No. 534 Squadron RAF
- No. 535 Squadron RAF
- No. 536 Squadron RAF
- No. 537 Squadron RAF
- No. 538 Squadron RAF
- No. 539 Squadron RAF
- No. 540 Squadron RAF
- No. 541 Squadron RAF
- No. 542 Squadron RAF
- No. 543 Squadron RAF
- No. 544 Squadron RAF
- No. 547 Squadron RAF
- No. 548 Squadron RAF
- No. 549 Squadron RAF
- No. 550 Squadron RAF
- No. 567 Squadron RAF
- No. 569 Squadron RAF
- No. 570 Squadron RAF
- No. 571 Squadron RAF
- No. 575 Squadron RAF
- No. 576 Squadron RAF
- No. 577 Squadron RAF
- No. 578 Squadron RAF
- No. 582 Squadron RAF
- No. 586 Squadron RAF
- No. 587 Squadron RAF
- No. 595 Squadron RAF
- No. 597 Squadron RAF
- No. 598 Squadron RAF

Note: No No. 599 Squadron seems to have been formed. There were to have been Reserve squadrons using numbers *551–566* which would have been created by adding 500 to existing Operational Training Unit designations.[1213] In

Advanced Training Squadrons (550–565)

In the event of a German Invasion the Operational Training Units would have been re-formed into the Squadrons below, under plans as part of *Operation Saracen*, formulated in Spring 1942, which were later revised as *Operation Banquet*. Some reserve Squadron numbers were used by their respective OTU's during operational tasks until at least May 1944.

- No. 550 Squadron RAF – Air Fighting Development Unit (*Banquet*)
- No. 551 Squadron RAF – 51 Operational Training Unit (*Saracen* and *Banquet*)
- No. 552 Squadron RAF – 51 Operational Training Unit (*Saracen* and *Banquet*)
- No. 553 Squadron RAF – 53 Operational Training Unit (*Saracen* and *Banquet*)
- No. 554 Squadron RAF – 53 Operational Training Unit (*Saracen* and *Banquet*)
- No. 555 Squadron RAF – 55 Operational Training Unit (*Saracen* and *Banquet*)
- No. 556 Squadron RAF – 56 Operational Training Unit (*Saracen* and *Banquet*)
- No. 557 Squadron RAF – 57 Operational Training Unit (*Saracen* and *Banquet*)
- No. 558 Squadron RAF – 58 Operational Training Unit (*Saracen* and *Banquet*)
- No. 559 Squadron RAF – 59 Operational Training Unit (*Saracen* and *Banquet*)
- No. 560 Squadron RAF – 56 Operational Training Unit (*Banquet*)
- No. 561 Squadron RAF – 61 Operational Training Unit (*Saracen* and *Banquet*)
- No. 562 Squadron RAF – 57 Operational Training Unit (*Banquet*)
- No. 563 Squadron RAF – 58 Operational Training Unit (*Banquet*)
- No. 564 Squadron RAF – 59 Operational Training Unit (*Banquet*)
- No. 565 Squadron RAF – 61 Operational Training Unit (*Banquet*)

Royal Auxiliary Air Force Squadrons (600–616)

- **No. 600 (City of London) Squadron**
- **No. 601 (County of London) Squadron**
- **No. 602 (City of Glasgow) Squadron**
- **No. 603 (City of Edinburgh) Squadron**
- No. 604 (County of Middlesex) Squadron
- **No. 605 (County of Warwick) Squadron**
- **No. 606 (Chiltern) Squadron**
- **No. 607 (County of Durham) Squadron**
- No. 608 (North Riding) Squadron
- **No. 609 (West Riding) Squadron**
- No. 610 (County of Chester) Squadron
- **No. 611 (West Lancashire) Squadron**
- **No. 612 (County of Aberdeen) Squadron**
- No. 613 (City of Manchester) Squadron
- **No. 614 (County of Glamorgan) Squadron**
- No. 614A Squadron
- No. 615 (County of Surrey) Squadron
- No. 616 (South Yorkshire) Squadron

Note: No. 606 Squadron RAF was allocated Squadron codes BG for the period April to September 1939, but was not formed. A non-flying No. 606 Helicopter Support Squadron of the RAuxAF was later formed in 1999.[1214]

Regular RAF squadrons (Nos. 617–650)

- **No. 617 Squadron RAF** ("The Dambusters") (F-35B Lightning))
- No. 618 Squadron RAF
- No. 619 Squadron RAF
- No. 620 Squadron RAF
- No. 621 Squadron RAF
- **No. 622 Squadron RAF**
- No. 623 Squadron RAF
- No. 624 Squadron RAF
- No. 625 Squadron RAF
- No. 626 Squadron RAF
- No. 627 Squadron RAF
- No. 628 Squadron RAF
- No. 630 Squadron RAF
- No. 631 Squadron RAF
- No. 635 Squadron RAF
- No. 639 Squadron RAF

- No. 640 Squadron RAF
- No. 644 Squadron RAF
- No. 650 Squadron RAF

Note: Nos. 629, 632–634, 636–638, 641–643 and 645–649 were never formed,[1215] but some were allocated Squadron codes for the period April to September 1939 – 629 (LQ), 632 (LO), 636 (VZ), 637 (UK), 638 (PZ), 641 (EV), 645 (KF), 646 (YG), 647 (ZS), 648 (YT) and 649 (HA). However a fictitious "633 Squadron" was featured in the eponymous novel and film. In addition, a fictitious 641 Squadron featured in the film "Mosquito Squadron". Also, RAF Volunteer Gliding Squadrons (formerly Volunteer Gliding Schools until 2005) have been numbered in the range 611 to 671 since 1955.

Air Observation Post squadrons

These squadrons were formed during the Second World War to perform artillery spotting and liaison roles, in co-operation with Army units. Most AOP squadron aircrew were provided by the Army. Nos. 661–664 and 666 Squadron were re-formed as Royal Auxiliary Air Force units in 1949. Nos. 651, 652 and 656 Squadron were transferred to the Army Air Corps in 1957.[1216]

- No. 651 (AOP) Squadron RAF
- No. 652 (AOP) Squadron RAF
- No. 653 (AOP) Squadron RAF
- No. 654 (AOP) Squadron RAF
- No. 655 (AOP) Squadron RAF
- No. 656 (AOP) Squadron RAF
- No. 657 (AOP) Squadron RAF
- No. 658 (AOP) Squadron RAF
- No. 659 (AOP) Squadron RAF
- No. 660 (AOP) Squadron RAF
- No. 661 (AOP) Squadron RAF
- No. 662 (AOP) Squadron RAF
- No. 663 (AOP) Squadron RAF (Polish)
- No. 664 (AOP) Squadron RCAF (Canadian) – reformed in 1949 as No. 664 Squadron RAuxAF
- No. 665 (AOP) Squadron RCAF (Canadian)
- No. 666 (AOP) Squadron RCAF (Canadian) – reformed in 1949 as No. 666 Squadron RAuxAF

Regular RAF squadrons (Nos. 667–695)

- No. 667 Squadron RAF
- No. 668 Squadron RAF
- No. 669 Squadron RAF
- No. 670 Squadron RAF
- No. 671 Squadron RAF
- No. 672 Squadron RAF
- No. 673 Squadron RAF
- No. 679 Squadron RAF
- No. 680 Squadron RAF
- No. 681 Squadron RAF
- No. 682 Squadron RAF
- No. 683 Squadron RAF
- No. 684 Squadron RAF
- No. 691 Squadron RAF
- No. 692 (Fellowship of the Bellows) Squadron
- No. 695 Squadron RAF

Note: Nos. 693–694 and 696–699 Squadrons were never formed.

Fleet Air Arm squadrons

While still under the control of the RAF, flights of the Fleet Air Arm were organized into squadrons with numbers in the 700 and 800 range. The range 700 to 750 had been previously used for Fleet Air Arm Catapult Flight numbers.[1217]

- No. 712 Squadron
- No. 715 Squadron
- No. 718 Squadron
- No. 800 Squadron
- No. 801 Squadron
- No. 802 Squadron
- No. 803 Squadron
- No. 810 Squadron
- No. 811 Squadron
- No. 812 Squadron
- No. 813 Squadron
- No. 814 Squadron
- No. 820 Squadron
- No. 821 Squadron
- No. 822 Squadron

- No. 823 Squadron
- No. 824 Squadron
- No. 825 Squadron

These squadrons were transferred to the Royal Navy in 1939, becoming Naval Air Squadrons (NAS).[1218] The 700 and 800 range of squadron numbers continued to be used by the Royal Navy for newly formed Naval Air Squadrons.

Training Depot Stations

Training Depot Stations (TDS) were still in use after the formation of the RAF in 1918.

- No. 1 Training Depot Station
- No. 2 Training Depot Station
- No. 3 Training Depot Station
- No. 4 Training Depot Station
- No. 5 Training Depot Station
- No. 6 Training Depot Station
- No. 7 Training Depot Station
- No. 8 Training Depot Station
- No. 9 Training Depot Station
- No. 10 Training Depot Station
- No. 11 Training Depot Station
- No. 12 Training Depot Station
- No. 13 Training Depot Station
- No. 14 Training Depot Station
- No. 15 Training Depot Station
- No. 16 Training Depot Station
- No. 17 Training Depot Station
- No. 18 Training Depot Station
- No. 19 Training Depot Station
- No. 20 Training Depot Station
- No. 21 Training Depot Station
- No. 22 Training Depot Station
- No. 23 Training Depot Station
- No. 24 Training Depot Station
- No. 25 Training Depot Station
- No. 26 Training Depot Station
- No. 27 Training Depot Station
- No. 28 Training Depot Station
- No. 29 Training Depot Station
- No. 30 Training Depot Station

- No. 31 Training Depot Station
- No. 32 Training Depot Station
- No. 33 Training Depot Station
- No. 34 Training Depot Station
- No. 35 Training Depot Station
- No. 36 Training Depot Station
- No. 37 Training Depot Station
- No. 38 Training Depot Station
- No. 39 Training Depot Station
- No. 40 Training Depot Station
- No. 41 Training Depot Station
- No. 42 Training Depot Station
- No. 43 Training Depot Station
- No. 44 Training Depot Station
- No. 45 Training Depot Station
- No. 46 Training Depot Station
- No. 47 Training Depot Station
- No. 48 Training Depot Station
- No. 49 Training Depot Station
- No. 50 Training Depot Station
- No. 51 Training Depot Station
- No. 52 Training Depot Station
- No. 53 Training Depot Station
- No. 54 Training Depot Station
- No. 55 Training Depot Station
- No. 56 Training Depot Station
- No. 57 Training Depot Station
- No. 58 Training Depot Station
- No. 59 Training Depot Station
- No. 60 Training Depot Station
- No. 61 Training Depot Station
- No. 98 Depot Squadron
- No. 99 Depot Squadron
- No. 190 (Depot) Squadron
- No. 191 (Depot) Squadron
- No. 192 (Depot) Squadron
- No. 198 (Depot) Squadron
- No. 199 (Depot) Squadron
- No. 201 Training Depot Station
- No. 202 Training Depot Station
- No. 203 Training Depot Station
- No. 204 Training Depot Station

- No. 205 Training Depot Station
- No. 206 Training Depot Station
- No. 207 Training Depot Station
- No. 208 (Temporary) Training Depot Station
- No. 209 (Seaplane) Training Depot Station
- No. 210 Training Depot Station
- No. 211 Training Depot Station
- No. 212 Training Depot Station
- No. 213 Training Depot Station

University Air Squadrons

The majority of Universities in the United Kingdom are, or have been, represented by University Air Squadrons where under-graduates can sample the Royal Air Force and learn to fly, as well as take advantage of scholarship schemes. They operate the **Tutor T.1**.

- Aberdeen University Air Squadron
- Aberystwyth University Air Squadron
- Aberdeen, Dundee and St. Andrews University Air Squadron
- Belfast University Air Squadron
- Birmingham University Air Squadron
- **Bristol University Air Squadron** - (RAF Colerne)
- **Cambridge University Air Squadron** - (RAF Wittering)
- Cardiff University Air Squadron
- Derby University Air Squadron
- Durham University Air Squadron
- East Lowlands University Air Squadron
- **East Midlands University Air Squadron** - (RAFC Cranwell)
- **East of Scotland Universities Air Squadron** - (Glasgow Airport)
- Edinburgh University Air Squadron
- Exeter University Air Squadron
- Glasgow University Air Squadron
- Hull University Air Squadron
- Leeds University Air Squadron
- **Liverpool University Air Squadron** - (RAF Woodvale)
- London University Air Squadron - (RAF Wittering)
- **Manchester and Salford Universities Air Squadron** - (RAF Woodvale)
- Manchester University Air Squadron
- **Northern Ireland University Air Squadron** - (JHFS Aldergrove)
- **Northumbrian Universities Air Squadron** - (RAF Leeming)
- Nottingham University Air Squadron
- **Oxford University Air Squadron** - (RAF Benson)

List of Royal Air Force aircraft squadrons 533

- Perth University Air Squadron
- Queen's University Air Squadron
- St. Andrews University Air Squadron
- St. Andrews and Dundee Universities Air Squadron
- **Southampton University Air Squadron** - (MOD Boscombe Down)
- Swansea University Air Squadron
- **Universities of Glasgow and Strathclyde Air Squadron** - (Leuchars Station)
- **University of Birmingham Air Squadron** - (RAF Cosford)
- University of Liverpool Air Squadron
- **University of London Air Squadron** - (RAF Wittering)
- **University of Wales Air Squadron** - (MOD St Athan)
- Wales University Air Squadron
- Wolverhampton University Air Squadron
- Yatesbury University Air Squadron
- **Yorkshire Universities Air Squadron** - (RAF Linton-on-Ouse)

Volunteer Gliding Squadrons

Initially formed as Volunteer Gliding Schools, these squadrons retained their gliding school numbers when reformed as squadrons. Conflicts with the main Squadron numbers resolved by the VGS suffix. These Squadrons operate the **Viking TX.1** glider.

- 611 Volunteer Gliding Squadron formerly 102 GS
- 612 Volunteer Gliding Squadron formerly 104 GS
- 613 Volunteer Gliding Squadron formerly 122 GS
- **614 Volunteer Gliding Squadron** formerly 142 GS, 146 GS and 147 GS - (MDPGA Wethersfield)
- **615 Volunteer Gliding Squadron** formerly 141 GS and 168 GS - (RAF Kenley)
- 616 Volunteer Gliding Squadron formerly 106 GS
- 617 Volunteer Gliding Squadron
- 618 Volunteer Gliding Squadron formerly 146 GS and 168 GS
- **621 Volunteer Gliding Squadron** - (RAF Hullavington)
- **622 Volunteer Gliding Squadron** formerly 89 GS - (Trenchard Lines)
- 624 Volunteer Gliding Squadron formerly 84 GS
- 625 Volunteer Gliding Squadron formerly 83 GS
- **626 Volunteer Gliding Squadron** formerly 82 GS - (RNAS Predannack)
- **631 Volunteer Gliding Squadron** formerly 186 GS - (RAF Woodvale)
- **632 Volunteer Gliding Squadron** formerly 45 GS - (RAF Ternhill)
- 633 Volunteer Gliding Squadron
- 634 Volunteer Gliding Squadron formerly 68 GS

- 635 Volunteer Gliding Squadron
- 636 Volunteer Gliding Squadron
- **637 Volunteer Gliding Squadron** - (RAF Little Rissington)
- 642 Volunteer Gliding Squadron formerly 23 GS
- 643 Volunteer Gliding Squadron formerly 107 EGS (merged with 644 VGS)
- **644 Volunteer Gliding Squadron** formerly 29 EGS - (RAF Syerston)
- **645 Volunteer Gliding Squadron** formerly 26 GS - (RAF Topcliffe)
- **661 Volunteer Gliding Squadron** formerly 1 EGS - (RAF Kirknewton)
- 662 Volunteer Gliding Squadron formerly 2 GS and 5 GS
- 663 Volunteer Gliding Squadron
- 664 Volunteer Gliding Squadron
- **HQ No. 2 Flying Training School RAF** - (RAF Syerston)
- **Central Gliding School** - (RAF Syerston)

Independent Flights

The RAF maintains a number of independent flights, some on a permanent basis, others on an ad-hoc basis as required. For a full list, see List of Royal Air Force aircraft independent flights.

- **Battle of Britain Memorial Flight** - 6 x Spitfire (various Marks), 2 x Hurricane, 1 x Lancaster, 1 x Dakota, 2 x Chipmunk - (RAF Coningsby)
- **1310 Flight** - 2 x Chinook HC.2s - (RAF Mount Pleasant)
- **1312 Flight** - 1 x Voyager KC.2, 1 x Hercules C.3 - (RAF Mount Pleasant)
- **1435 Flight** - 4 x Typhoon FGR.4 - (RAF Mount Pleasant)

Air Experience Flights

These units are co-located with UAS units (or regular Air Force units) to pool resources and share aircraft. Air Experience Flights provide flying experience to Royal Air Force Air Cadets and other air-minded youth groups such as Air Scouts and the Girls Venture Corps Air Cadets.

- **No. 1 Air Experience Flight** - (MOD St Athan) - Wales UAS
- **No. 2 Air Experience Flight** - (RAF Boscombe Down) - Southampton UAS
- **No. 3 Air Experience Flight** - (RAF Colerne) - Bristol UAS
- **No. 4 Air Experience Flight** - (Glasgow Airport) - Glasgow & Strathclyde UAS
- **No. 5 Air Experience Flight** - (RAF Wittering) - London/Cambridge/East Midlands UAS

- **No. 6 Air Experience Flight** - (RAF Benson) - Oxford UAS
- **No. 7 Air Experience Flight** - (RAF Cranwell)
- **No. 8 Air Experience Flight** - (RAF Cosford) - Birmingham UAS
- **No. 9 Air Experience Flight** - (RAF Linton-on-Ouse) - Yorkshire UAS
- **No. 10 Air Experience Flight** - (RAF Woodvale) - Liverpool/Manchester UAS
- **No. 11 Air Experience Flight** - (RAF Leeming) - Northumbrian UAS
- **No. 12 Air Experience Flight** - (RAF Leuchars) - East of Scotland UAS

Other Squadrons

The Royal Air force and Royal flying corps has always comprised a certain number of non-numbered Squadrons to fulfil special duties, experimental or one-off tasks.

- Air Command Southeast Asia (Internal Air Service) Squadron
- Air Council Inspection Squadron
- Air Despatch Letter Service Squadron
- Air Training Squadron
- All-Weather Development Squadron
- All-Weather Fighter Combat Squadron
- Andover Training Squadron
- Antler Squadron
- Arrow Squadron
- Artillery Co-operation Squadron
- Auxiliary Fighter Squadron (Malaya)
- Auxiliary Fighter Squadron (Singapore)
- Singapore Squadron
- B-29 Training Squadron
- Burmese Conversion Squadron
- Composite Fighting Squadron
- Composite Royal Naval Air service/Royal Flying Corps Squadron
- Communications Electronics Basic Training Squadron
- Demonstration Squadron
- Development Squadron, Gosport
- Elementary Flying Training Squadron
- Experimental Armament Squadron
- Far East Air Force Examining Squadron
- Far East Air Force Training Squadron
- Ferry Squadron
- Ferry Support Squadron
- Floatplane Training Squadron
- Flying Selection Squadron

- Glider Exercise Squadron
- Glider Training Squadron
- Ground Controlled Approach Squadron
- Guided Weapons Development Squadron
- No.1 Guided Weapons Trials Squadron
- Headquarters Service Ferry Pools/Squadron
- Home Defence Squadron
- Hong Kong Auxiliary Squadron
- Hong Kong Fighter Squadron
- Javelin Instrument Rating Squadron
- Joint Trials and Training Squadron
- Kuala Lumpur Fighter Squadron
- Kuala Lumpur Squadron
- Low Level and Air Defence Training Squadron - See No. 6 Flying Training School RAF
- Low Flying Operations Squadron
- Multi-Engine Training Squadron - See No. 6 Flying Training School RAF
- Nimrod Line Squadron
- Offensive Support Role Support Squadron
- Parachute Exercise Squadron
- Penang Squadron
- Penang Fighter Squadron
- Radar Research Squadron
- Refresher Flying Squadron
- Reserve Training Squadron
- Royal Air Force College Air Squadron
- Royal Naval Fighter Squadron
- Seaplane Squadron, Alexandria
- Seaplane Squadron, Port Said
- Seaplane Training Squadron
- Sentry Training Squadron
- Service Ferry Squadron
- Service Ferry Training Squadron
- Signals Command Development Squadron
- Signals Squadron
- Southeast Asia (Internal Air Service) Squadron
- Special Installation Squadron
- Special Transport Squadron
- No. 1 Torpedo Training Squadron
- Training Squadron, Sylt
- Western Union Examining Squadron
- UK Mobile Air Movements Squadron

List of Royal Air Force aircraft squadrons 537

- No. 1435 Squadron RAF
- 'B' Squadron
- 'B' Squadron, Aegean
- 'C' Squadron, Aegean
- 'D' Squadron, Aegean
- 'S' Squadron
- 'T' Squadron, Egypt
- 'X' (Canadian) Reserve Squadron
- 'X' Squadron
- 'X' Squadron, Egypt
- 'Y' (Canadian) Reserve Squadron
- 'Y' Squadron, Egypt - See No. 4 Flying Training School RAF
- 'Y' Squadron, Iraq - See No. 4 Flying Training School RAF
- 'Z' Squadron, Aegean
- 'Z' Squadron, Egypt

Communication Squadrons

To allow rapid transport of Air Officers, staff and other important people many units and Headquarters operated communication Sections, Flights, Squadrons or wings.

- Aden Communication Squadron
- Aden Protectorate Communication and Support Squadron
- Air Command Far East and Air Headquarters Malaya Communication Squadron
- Air Component Field Force Communication Squadron
- Air Defence of Great Britain Communication Squadron
- Air Division Communication Squadron
- Air Forces Gulf Communication Squadron
- Air Headquarters Burma Communication Squadron
- Air Headquarters East Africa Communication Squadron
- Air Headquarters Hong Kong Communication Squadron
- Air Headquarters India Communication Squadron
- Air Headquarters Italy Communication Squadron
- Air Headquarters Malaya Communication Squadron
- Air Headquarters Malta Communication Squadron
- Air Headquarters Netherlands East Indies Communication Squadron
- Allied Air Forces Central Europe Communication Squadron
- Allied Expeditionary Air Force Communication Squadron
- 2nd Allied Tactical Air Force Communication Squadron
- Base Air Forces, Southeast Asia Communication Squadron
- Bengal/Burma Communication Squadron

- Bomber Command Communication Squadron
- Bomber/Fighter/Coastal Command Communication Squadron
- British Air Forces of Occupation Communication Squadron
- British Air Forces Southeast Asia Communication Squadron
- British Commonwealth Air Communication Squadron
- Burma Communication Squadron
- Coastal Command Communication Squadron
- Colerne Communication Squadron
- Communication Squadron, GHQ Royal Flying Corps, France
- Communication Squadron, GHQ Royal Air Force, France
- Communication Squadron, Hendon
- Far East Communication Squadron
- Fighter Command Communication Squadron
- Flying Training Command Communication Squadron
- No. 2 Group Communication Squadron
- No. 83 Group Communication Squadron
- No. 84 Group Communication Squadron (Air 29/2354)
- No. 85 Group Communication Squadron
- No. 88 Group Communication Squadron
- No. 221 Group Communication Squadron
- No. 232 Group Communication Squadron
- No. 238 Group Communication Squadron
- Headquarters Air Command Southeast Asia (Communication) Squadron
- Headquarters British Forces Aden Communication Squadron
- Headquarters Communication Squadron, Royal Air Force
- Headquarters Communication Squadron, Royal Flying Corps
- Headquarters Middle East Air Force Communication Squadron
- Headquarters Middle East Communication Squadron
- Headquarters Royal Air Force Burma Communication Squadron
- Headquarters Royal Air Force Northern Ireland Communication Squadron
- Home Command Communication Squadron
- Maintenance Command Communication Squadron
- Maintenance Command Communication and Ferry Squadron
- Malaya Communication Squadron
- Malta Communication and Target Towing Squadron
- Mediterranean and Middle East Communication Squadron
- Metropolitan Communication Squadron
- Middle East Communication Squadron
- Northern Communication Squadron
- Reserve Command Communication Squadron
- Royal Air Force Bengal/Burma Communication Squadron
- Royal Air Force Germany Communication Squadron

- Southeast Asia Communication Squadron
- Southern Communication Squadron
- Strike Command Communication Squadron
- Special Communication Squadron
- No. 1 (Communication) Squadron
- No. 2 (Communication) Squadron
- No. 3 (Communication) Squadron
- No. 4 (Communication) Squadron
- No. 5 (Communication) Squadron
- No. 6 (Communication) Squadron
- No. 7 (Communication) Squadron
- No. 8 (Communication) Squadron
- Supreme Commander's Headquarters (Air) Communication Squadron
- Supreme Headquarters Allied Expeditionary Force (RAF) Communication Squadron
- Tactical Air Force (Burma) Communication Squadron
- 2nd Tactical Air Force Communication Squadron
- 3rd Tactical Air Force Communication Squadron
- 2nd Tactical Communication Squadron
- Training Commands Communication Squadron
- Transport Command Communication Squadron
- Turnhouse Communication Squadron
- West Africa Command Communication Squadron
- West Africa Communication Squadron
- West Africa Transport and Communication Squadron
- Western Communication Squadron
- No. 85 Wing Communication Squadron

Barrage Balloon Squadrons of the Auxiliary Air Force

- No. 901 (County of London) Balloon Squadron AAF
- No. 902 (County of London) Balloon Squadron AAF
- No. 903 (County of London) Balloon Squadron AAF
- No. 904 (County of Surrey) Balloon Squadron AAF
- No. 905 (County of Surrey) Balloon Squadron AAF
- No. 906 (County of Middlesex) Balloon Squadron AAF
- No. 907 (County of Middlesex) Balloon Squadron AAF
- No. 908 (County of Essex) Balloon Squadron AAF
- No. 909 (County of Essex) Balloon Squadron AAF
- No. 910 (County of Essex) Balloon Squadron AAF
- No. 911 (County of Warwick) Balloon Squadron AAF
- No. 912 (County of Warwick) Balloon Squadron AAF
- No. 913 (County of Warwick) Balloon Squadron AAF

- No. 914 (County of Warwick) Balloon Squadron AAF
- No. 915 (County of Warwick) Balloon Squadron AAF
- No. 916 (County of Warwick) Balloon Squadron AAF
- No. 917 (County of Warwick) Balloon Squadron AAF
- No. 918 (County of Derby) Balloon Squadron AAF
- No. 919 (West Lancashire) Balloon Squadron AAF
- No. 920 Balloon Squadron AAF
- No. 921 (West Lancashire) Balloon Squadron AAF
- No. 922 (West Lancashire) Balloon Squadron AAF
- No. 923 (West Lancashire) Balloon Squadron AAF
- No. 924 Balloon Squadron AAF
- No. 925 (East Lancashire) Balloon Squadron AAF
- No. 926 (East Lancashire) Balloon Squadron AAF
- No. 927 (County of Gloucester) Balloon Squadron AAF
- No. 928 Balloon Squadron AAF
- No. 929 Balloon Squadron AAF
- No. 930 (Hampshire) Balloon Squadron AAF
- No. 931 (Hampshire) Balloon Squadron AAF
- No. 932 (Hampshire) Balloon Squadron AAF
- No. 933 (Hampshire) Balloon Squadron AAF
- No. 934 (County of Devon) Balloon Squadron AAF
- No. 935 (County of Glamorgan) Balloon Squadron AAF
- No. 936 (County of Northumberland) Balloon Squadron AAF
- No. 937 (County of Northumberland) Balloon Squadron AAF
- No. 936/937 Balloon Squadron AAF
- No. 938 (County of Northumberland) Balloon Squadron AAF
- No. 939 (West Riding) Balloon Squadron AAF
- No. 940 (West Riding) Balloon Squadron AAF
- No. 941 (West Riding) Balloon Squadron AAF
- No. 942 (East Riding) Balloon Squadron AAF
- No. 943 (East Riding) Balloon Squadron AAF
- No. 942/943 (East Riding) Balloon Squadron AAF
- No. 944 (East Riding) Balloon Squadron AAF
- No. 945 (City of Glasgow) Balloon Squadron AAF
- No. 946 (City of Glasgow) Balloon Squadron AAF
- No. 947 (City of Glasgow) Balloon Squadron AAF
- No. 948 Balloon Squadron AAF
- No. 949 Balloon Squadron AAF
- No. 950 Balloon Squadron AAF
- No. 951 Balloon Squadron AAF
- No. 952 Balloon Squadron AAF
- No. 953 Balloon Squadron AAF

List of Royal Air Force aircraft squadrons 541

- No. 954 Balloon Squadron AAF
- No. 955 Balloon Squadron AAF
- No. 956 Balloon Squadron AAF
- No. 957 Balloon Squadron AAF
- No. 958 Balloon Squadron AAF
- No. 959 Balloon Squadron AAF
- No. 960 Balloon Squadron AAF
- No. 961 Balloon Squadron AAF
- No. 962 Balloon Squadron AAF
- No. 963 Balloon Squadron AAF
- No. 964 Balloon Squadron AAF
- No. 965 Balloon Squadron AAF
- No. 966 Balloon Squadron AAF
- No. 967 Balloon Squadron AAF
- No. 968 Balloon Squadron AAF
- No. 969 Balloon Squadron AAF
- No. 970 Balloon Squadron AAF
- No. 971 Balloon Squadron AAF
- No. 972 Balloon Squadron AAF
- No. 973 Balloon Squadron AAF
- No. 974 Balloon Squadron AAF
- No. 975 Balloon Squadron AAF
- No. 976 Balloon Squadron AAF
- No. 977 Balloon Squadron AAF
- No. 978 Balloon Squadron AAF
- No. 979 Balloon Squadron AAF
- No. 980 Balloon Squadron AAF
- No. 981 Balloon Squadron AAF
- No. 982 Balloon Squadron AAF
- No. 983 Balloon Squadron AAF
- No. 984 Balloon Squadron AAF
- No. 985 Balloon Squadron AAF
- No. 986 Balloon Squadron AAF
- No. 987 Balloon Squadron AAF
- No. 988 Balloon Squadron AAF
- No. 989 Balloon Squadron AAF
- No. 990 Balloon Squadron AAF
- No. 991 Balloon Squadron AAF
- No. 992 (Mobile) Balloon Squadron AAF
- No. 993 (Mobile) Balloon Squadron AAF
- No. 994 (Mobile) Balloon Squadron AAF
- No. 995 (Mobile) Balloon Squadron AAF

- No. 996 Balloon Squadron AAF
- No. 997 Balloon Squadron AAF
- No. 998 Balloon Squadron AAF
- No. 999 Balloon Squadron AAF

1219

Squadron codes

Most units of the Royal Air Force are identified by alphabetical (or similar) characters, known as a "squadron code", that is painted on all aircraft belonging to that unit. When individual units are assigned unusually large numbers of aircraft, multiple squadron codes have been used.

Other air forces, especially those from other Commonwealth countries, have often used similar systems of identification. During the Second World War, when units from other air forces were attached to the RAF – such as the Article XV squadrons (also known as "400 series squadrons") – their squadron codes were often changed, to avoid confusion with RAF units.

Historically, the codes have usually been two letters of the alphabet, painted on the rear fuselage next to the RAF roundel. These formed a suffix or prefix to the call sign of each aircraft (on the other side of the roundel) which was usually a single letter (e. g. "G for George"). In general, when an aircraft is lost or withdrawn from use, its call sign has been applied to its replacement or another aircraft.

References

- Halley, James J. *The Squadrons of the Royal Air Force & Commonwealth 1918–1988*. Tonbridge, Kent, UK: Air Britain (Historians) Ltd., 1988. ISBN 0-85130-164-9.
- Jefford, C.G. *RAF Squadrons, a Comprehensive record of the Movement and Equipment of all RAF Squadrons and their Antecedents since 1912*. Shropshire, UK: Airlife Publishing, 1988 (second edition 2001). ISBN 1-85310-053-6.
- Lake, Alan. "Flying Units of the RAF".Airlife Publishing. Shrewsbury. 1999. ISBN 1-84037-086-6

External links

- a list of current squadrons from the RAF website[1220]

List of Royal Air Force schools

This is a list of schools within the Royal Air Force, empire flying training scheme, civilian and service elementary training schemes, as well as gliding schools.

Schools

The Royal Air Force operated many schools to train aircrew in the many and various skills required to operate an air force.

Air Gunners School

- No. 1 Air Gunners School RAF
- No. 2 Air Gunners School RAF
- No. 3 Air Gunners School RAF
- No. 4 Air Gunners School RAF
- No. 5 Air Gunners School RAF
- No. 6 Air Gunners School RAF
- No. 7 Air Gunners School RAF
- No. 8 Air Gunners School RAF
- No. 9 Air Gunners School RAF
- No. 10 Air Gunners School RAF
- No. 11 Air Gunners School RAF
- No. 12 Air Gunners School RAF
- No. 13 Air Gunners School RAF

Air Navigation School

- No. 1 Air Navigation School RAF
- No. 2 Air Navigation School RAF
- No. 3 Air Navigation School RAF
- No. 4 Air Navigation School RAF
- No. 5 Air Navigation School RAF
- No. 6 Air Navigation School RAF
- No. 7 Air Navigation School RAF
- No. 10 Air Navigation School RAF
- No. 31 Air Navigation School RAF
- No. 32 Air Navigation School RAF
- No. 33 Air Navigation School RAF

Air Observers School

- No. 1 Air Observers School RAF
- No. 2 Air Observers School RAF
- No. 3 Air Observers School RAF
- No. 4 Air Observers School RAF
- No. 5 Air Observers School RAF
- No. 6 Air Observers School RAF
- No. 7 Air Observers School RAF
- No. 8 Air Observers School RAF
- No. 9 Air Observers School RAF
- No. 10 Air Observers School RAF
- No. 24 Combined Air Observers School RAF

Air Observers Navigation School

- No. 1 Air Observers Navigation School RAF
- No. 2 Air Observers Navigation School RAF
- No. 3 Air Observers Navigation School RAF
- No. 4 Air Observers Navigation School RAF
- No. 5 Air Observers Navigation School RAF
- No. 6 Air Observers Navigation School RAF
- No. 7 Air Observers Navigation School RAF
- No. 8 Air Observers Navigation School RAF
- No. 9 Air Observers Navigation School RAF
- No. 10 Air Observers Navigation School RAF
- No. 11 Air Observers Navigation School RAF

Bombing and Gunnery School

- No. 1 Bombing and Gunnery School RAF
- No. 2 Bombing and Gunnery School RAF
- No. 3 Bombing and Gunnery School RAF
- No. 4 Bombing and Gunnery School RAF
- No. 5 Bombing and Gunnery School RAF
- No. 6 Bombing and Gunnery School RAF
- No. 7 Bombing and Gunnery School RAF
- No. 8 Bombing and Gunnery School RAF
- No. 9 Bombing and Gunnery School RAF
- No. 10 Bombing and Gunnery School RAF
- No. 24 Bombing and Gunnery School RAF
- No. 31 Bombing and Gunnery School RAF

List of Royal Air Force schools

Civil Air Navigation School

- No. 1 Civil Air Navigation School RAF
- No. 2 Civil Air Navigation School RAF
- No. 3 Civil Air Navigation School RAF
- No. 4 Civil Air Navigation School RAF
- No. 5 Civil Air Navigation School RAF
- No. 6 Civil Air Navigation School RAF
- No. 7 Civil Air Navigation School RAF
- No. 8 Civil Air Navigation School RAF
- No. 9 Civil Air Navigation School RAF
- No. 10 Civil Air Navigation School RAF

Fighting School

- No. 1 Fighting School RAF
- No. 2 Fighting School RAF
- No. 3 Fighting School RAF
- No. 4 Fighting School RAF
- No. 5 Fighting School RAF

Lancaster Finishing School

- No. 1 Lancaster Finishing School RAF
- No. 3 Lancaster Finishing School RAF
- No. 5 Lancaster Finishing School RAF
- No. 6 Lancaster Finishing School RAF

Middle East Training School

- No. 1 Middle East Training School RAF
- No. 2 Middle East Training School RAF
- No. 3 Middle East Training School RAF
- No. 4 Middle East Training School RAF
- No. 5 Middle East Training School RAF

Radio School

- No. 1 Radio School RAF
- No. 2 Radio School RAF
- No. 3 Radio School RAF
- No. 4 Radio School RAF
- No. 6 Radio School RAF
- No. 10 Radio School RAF
- No. 11 Radio School RAF
- No. 12 Radio School RAF
- No. 14 Radio School RAF

Signals School

- No. 1 Signals School RAF
- No. 2 Signals School RAF
- No. 3 Signals School (India) RAF
- No. 3 Signals School RAF
- No. 4 Signals School RAF

Technical Training schools

- No. 1 School of Technical Training RAF
- No. 2 School of Technical Training RAF
- No. 3 School of Technical Training RAF
- No. 4 School of Technical Training RAF
- No. 5 School of Technical Training RAF
- No. 11 School of Technical Training RAF
- No. 16 (Polish) School of Technical Training RAF

Aerial Fighting and Gunnery schools

- No. 1 School of Aerial Fighting and Gunnery RAF
- No. 2 School of Aerial Fighting and Gunnery RAF
- No. 3 School of Aerial Fighting and Gunnery RAF
- No. 4 School of Aerial Fighting and Gunnery RAF

Navigation and Bomb Dropping schools

- No. 1 School of Aerial Navigation and Bomb Dropping RAF
- No. 2 School of Aerial Navigation and Bomb Dropping RAF
- No. 3 School of Aerial Navigation and Bomb Dropping RAF
- No. 4 School of Aerial Navigation and Bomb Dropping RAF
- No. 1 School of Navigation and Bomb Dropping RAF
- No. 2 School of Navigation and Bomb Dropping RAF
- No. 3 School of Navigation and Bomb Dropping RAF
- No. 4 School of Navigation and Bomb Dropping RAF

Recruit Training schools

- No. 1 School of Recruit Training RAF
- No. 2 School of Recruit Training RAF
- No. 3 School of Recruit Training RAF
- No. 4 School of Recruit Training RAF
- No. 5 School of Recruit Training RAF
- No. 6 School of Recruit Training RAF
- No. 7 School of Recruit Training RAF
- No. 8 School of Recruit Training RAF
- No. 9 School of Recruit Training RAF
- No. 10 School of Recruit Training RAF

List of Royal Air Force schools 547

- No. 11 School of Recruit Training RAF
- No. 12 School of Recruit Training RAF
- No. 13 School of Recruit Training RAF
- No. 15 School of Recruit Training RAF

Various Schools

- No. 1 (Auxiliary) School of Aerial Gunnery RAF
- No. 1 (Coastal) Engine Control Demonstration Unit RAF
- No. 1 (Middle East) Central Gunnery School RAF
- No. 1 (Observers) School of Aerial Gunnery RAF
- No. 1 (Training) Wireless School RAF
- No. 1 Air Armament School RAF
- No. 1 Air Electronics School RAF
- No. 1 Air Gunnery School RAF
- No. 1 Air Gunnery School (India) RAF
- No. 1 Air Signallers School RAF
- No. 1 Basic Air Navigation School RAF
- No. 1 Beam Approach School RAF
- No. 1 Blind Approach School RAF
- No. 1 Coastal Defence Training Unit RAF
- No. 1 Electrical and Wireless School RAF
- No. 1 General Service Training School RAF
- No. 1 Grading School RAF
- No. 1 Ground Defense Gunners School RAF
- No. 1 Initial Training School RAF
- No. 1 Marine Observers School RAF
- No. 1 Observers School RAF
- No. 1 Officers Advanced Training School RAF
- No. 1 Parachute and Glider Training School RAF
- No. 1 Parachute School RAF
- No. 1 Parachute Training School RAF
- No. 1 School of Aerial Fighting RAF
- No. 1 School of Air Navigation RAF
- No. 1 School of Army Co-operation RAF
- No. 1 School of General Reconnaissance RAF
- No. 1 School of Photography RAF
- No. 1 Torpedo Refresher School RAF
- No. 2 (Auxiliary) School of Aerial Gunnery RAF
- No. 2 Air Armament School RAF
- No. 2 Air Signallers School RAF
- No. 2 Aircrew Grading School RAF
- No. 2 Basic Air Navigation School RAF

- No. 2 Electrical and Wireless School RAF
- No. 2 Grading School RAF
- No. 2 Marine Observers School RAF
- No. 2 Observers School RAF
- No. 2 Officers Advanced Training School RAF
- No. 2 School of Administration Training
- No. 2 School of Aerial Fighting RAF
- No. 2 School of Air Navigation RAF
- No. 2 School of Army Co-operation RAF
- No. 2 School of General Reconnaissance RAF
- No. 2 Torpedo Refresher School RAF
- No. 2 Wireless School RAF
- No. 24 Bombing, Gunnery and Air Navigation School RAF
- No. 29 Elementary Navigation and Air Gunnery School (Southern Rhodesia) RAF
- No. 3 (Auxiliary) School of Aerial Gunnery RAF
- No. 3 Electrical and Wireless School RAF
- No. 3 Parachute Training School RAF
- No. 3 Radio Direction Finding School RAF
- No. 3 School of General Reconnaissance RAF
- No. 4 (Auxiliary) School of Aerial Gunnery RAF
- No. 4 Parachute Training School RAF
- No. 44 Training School RAF
- No. 50 Initial Training School RAF
- No. 93 Group Screened Pilots School RAF
- Administrative Apprentice Training School
- Advanced Air Firing School
- Advanced Bombing and Gunnery School (Middle East)
- Advanced Training School
- Aerial Erector School RAF
- Aerial Fighting and Gunnery School
- Aerial Fighting School, Heliopolis
- Air Armament School
- Air Electronics and Air Engineers School
- Air Electronics School
- Air Electronics, Engineer and Loadmaster School
- Air Fighting School (Middle East)
- Air Landing School
- Air Navigation and Bombing School
- Air Navigation School, India
- Air Navigation School
- Air Observation Post School

List of Royal Air Force schools

- Air Observers School, North Coates
- Air Pilotage School
- Airborne Interception School
- Airborne Interception/Air-to-Surface Vessel School
- Aircraft Direction School
- Aircrew Officers Training School
- Airfield Controllers School
- All-Weather Fighter Leaders School
- Anti U-Boat Devices School
- Armament and gunnery School
- Army Co-operation School
- Artillery and Infantry Co-operation School
- Artillery Observation School, Egypt
- Artillery Observation School
- Belgian Training School
- Blind Approach School
- Bomber Command Bombing School
- Central Air Traffic Control School
- Central Gunnery School (Middle East)
- Central Gunnery School
- Central Landing School
- Central Navigation and Control School
- Central Navigation School
- Central Squadron and Flight Commanders School
- Chinese Air Force Cadet School
- Coastal Command Anti U-Boat Devices School
- Coastal Command Flying Instructors School
- Coastal Command Gunnery School
- Coastal Command Instructors School
- Coastal Command Landplane Pilots Pool - See No. 1 (Coastal) Operational Training Unit RAF
- Coastal Command Tactical Development Unit
- Coastal Defence Development Unit
- Control and Reporting School
- Day and Night Bombing Observation School
- Electrical and Wireless School
- Empire Air Armament School
- Empire Air Navigation School
- Empire Central Flying School
- Empire Radio School
- Empire Test Pilots School
- Fighter Command Control and Reporting School

- Fighter Leaders School
- Fighter Weapons School
- Fleet School of Aerial Fighting and Gunnery
- Fleet School of Aerial Fighting and Gunnery
- Franco-Belgium Air Training School
- General Reconnaissance and Air Navigation School (India)
- General Reconnaissance School
- Grand Fleet School of Aerial Fighting and Gunnery
- Ground Defence Gunners School
- India Detachment, Chinese Air Force Cadet School
- Light Aircraft School
- Machine Gun School
- Marine Observers School, Aldeburgh
- Marine Observers School, Leysdown
- Navigation School
- Navigation Training School
- NCO Training School
- Observers School of Reconnaissance and Aerial Photography
- Officers Advanced Training School
- Parachute Training Centre
- Parachute Training School (India)
- Pilots and Observers Aerial Gunnery and Aerial Fighting School
- Rhodesian Central Flying School
- Royal Air Force (Belgian) Training School
- Royal Air Force (Middle East) Central Gunnery School
- Royal Air Force (Middle East) Gunnery School
- Royal Air Force and Army Co-operation School
- Royal Air Force and Navy Co-operation School
- Royal Air Force School of Army Co-operation
- Royal Air Force School of Aviation Medicine
- Royal Air Force School of Catering
- Royal Air Force School, India
- Royal Naval Air Service Gunnery School
- School for Anti-Submarine Inshore Patrol Observers
- School for Marine Operational Pilots
- School for Wireless Operators
- School of Aerial Co-operation with Coastal Artillery
- School of Aerial Fighting (Canada)
- School of Aerial Fighting and Bomb Dropping
- School of Aerial Fighting, Heliopolis
- School of Aerial Gunnery and Bombing
- School of Aerial Gunnery, (Canada)

List of Royal Air Force schools

- School of Aerial Gunnery, Aboukir
- School of Aerial Gunnery, Hythe
- School of Aerial Gunnery, Loch Doon
- School of Aerial Gunnery, Marske
- School of Aerial Gunnery, New Romney
- School of Aerial Gunnery, Turnberry
- School of Aerial Navigation
- School of Air Navigation
- School of Air Pilotage
- School of Air Sea Rescue
- School of Air Support
- School of Air Traffic Control
- School of Air Transport
- School of Army Co-operation
- School of Artillery Co-operation (Canada)
- School of Aviation Medicine
- School of Control and Reporting
- School of Fighter Control
- School of General Reconnaissance
- School of Land/Air Warfare
- School of Naval Co-operation and Aerial Navigation
- School of Naval Co-operation
- School of Photography, Maps and Reconnaissance
- School of Photography
- Secretarial Branch Training School
- Specialised Low Attack Instructors School (India)
- Specialised Low Attack Instructors School
- Staff Navigators School (Middle East)
- Strike Command Bombing School
- Temporary Air Observer's School
- Test Pilots School
- The Officers Advanced Training School
- Torpedo Aeroplane School
- Torpedo Bombing School
- Torpedo Maintenance School
- Torpedo Training School
- Wireless and Observers School
- Wireless School, Brooklands
- Wireless School, Egypt
- Wireless School
- Wireless Telephony School
- WRAF Clerical Trades Training School

Flying training schools

To train pilots for the Royal Air Force, there have been many flying training schools, which are listed here.

Numbered schools

British Flying Training School

- No. 1 British Flying Training School RAF
- No. 2 British Flying Training School RAF
- No. 3 British Flying Training School RAF
- No. 4 British Flying Training School RAF
- No. 5 British Flying Training School RAF
- No. 6 British Flying Training School RAF
- No. 7 British Flying Training School RAF

Central Flying School

- No. 2 Central Flying School RAF
- No. 3 Central Flying School RAF - Planned but never formed.

Advanced Flying School

- No. 201 Advanced Flying School RAF
- No. 202 Advanced Flying School RAF
- No. 203 Advanced Flying School RAF
- No. 204 Advanced Flying School RAF
- No. 205 Advanced Flying School RAF
- No. 206 Advanced Flying School RAF
- No. 207 Advanced Flying School RAF
- No. 208 Advanced Flying School RAF
- No. 209 Advanced Flying School RAF
- No. 210 Advanced Flying School RAF
- No. 211 Advanced Flying School RAF
- No. 215 Advanced Flying School RAF

Basic Flying Training School

- No. 1 Basic Flying Training School RAF
- No. 2 Basic Flying Training School RAF
- No. 3 Basic Flying Training School RAF
- No. 4 Basic Flying Training School RAF
- No. 5 Basic Flying Training School RAF

(Basic) Flying Training School

- No. 2 (Basic) Flying Training School RAF
- No. 3 (Basic) Flying Training School RAF

(Advanced) Flying Training School

- No. 4 (Advanced) Flying Training School RAF
- No. 5 (Advanced) Flying Training School RAF
- No. 6 (Advanced) Flying Training School RAF
- No. 8 (Advanced) Flying Training School RAF
- No. 9 (Advanced) Flying Training School RAF
- No. 10 (Advanced) Flying Training School RAF
- No. 14 (Advanced) Flying Training School RAF

Elementary and Reserve Flying Training School

- No. 1 Elementary and Reserve Flying Training School RAF
- No. 2 Elementary and Reserve Flying Training School RAF
- No. 3 Elementary and Reserve Flying Training School RAF
- No. 4 Elementary and Reserve Flying Training School RAF
- No. 5 Elementary and Reserve Flying Training School RAF
- No. 6 Elementary and Reserve Flying Training School RAF
- No. 7 Elementary and Reserve Flying Training School RAF
- No. 8 Elementary and Reserve Flying Training School RAF
- No. 9 Elementary and Reserve Flying Training School RAF
- No. 10 Elementary and Reserve Flying Training School RAF
- No. 11 Elementary and Reserve Flying Training School RAF
- No. 12 Elementary and Reserve Flying Training School RAF
- No. 13 Elementary and Reserve Flying Training School RAF
- No. 14 Elementary and Reserve Flying Training School RAF
- No. 15 Elementary and Reserve Flying Training School RAF
- No. 16 Elementary and Reserve Flying Training School RAF
- No. 17 Elementary and Reserve Flying Training School RAF
- No. 18 Elementary and Reserve Flying Training School RAF
- No. 19 Elementary and Reserve Flying Training School RAF
- No. 20 Elementary and Reserve Flying Training School RAF
- No. 21 Elementary and Reserve Flying Training School RAF
- No. 22 Elementary and Reserve Flying Training School RAF
- No. 23 Elementary and Reserve Flying Training School RAF
- No. 24 Elementary and Reserve Flying Training School RAF
- No. 25 Elementary and Reserve Flying Training School RAF
- No. 26 Elementary and Reserve Flying Training School RAF
- No. 27 Elementary and Reserve Flying Training School RAF
- No. 28 Elementary and Reserve Flying Training School RAF
- No. 29 Elementary and Reserve Flying Training School RAF
- No. 30 Elementary and Reserve Flying Training School RAF
- No. 31 Elementary and Reserve Flying Training School RAF
- No. 32 Elementary and Reserve Flying Training School RAF

- No. 33 Elementary and Reserve Flying Training School RAF
- No. 34 Elementary and Reserve Flying Training School RAF
- No. 35 Elementary and Reserve Flying Training School RAF
- No. 36 Elementary and Reserve Flying Training School RAF
- No. 37 Elementary and Reserve Flying Training School RAF
- No. 38 Elementary and Reserve Flying Training School RAF
- No. 39 Elementary and Reserve Flying Training School RAF
- No. 40 Elementary and Reserve Flying Training School RAF
- No. 41 Elementary and Reserve Flying Training School RAF
- No. 42 Elementary and Reserve Flying Training School RAF
- No. 43 Elementary and Reserve Flying Training School RAF
- No. 44 Elementary and Reserve Flying Training School RAF
- No. 45 Elementary and Reserve Flying Training School RAF
- No. 46 Elementary and Reserve Flying Training School RAF
- No. 47 Elementary and Reserve Flying Training School RAF
- No. 48 Elementary and Reserve Flying Training School RAF
- No. 49 Elementary and Reserve Flying Training School RAF
- No. 50 Elementary and Reserve Flying Training School RAF
- No. 51 Elementary and Reserve Flying Training School RAF
- No. 52 Elementary and Reserve Flying Training School RAF
- No. 53 Elementary and Reserve Flying Training School RAF
- No. 54 Elementary and Reserve Flying Training School RAF
- No. 55 Elementary and Reserve Flying Training School RAF
- No. 56 Elementary and Reserve Flying Training School RAF
- No. 57 Elementary and Reserve Flying Training School RAF
- No. 58 Elementary and Reserve Flying Training School RAF
- No. 59 Elementary and Reserve Flying Training School RAF

Elementary Flying Training School

- No. 1 Elementary Flying Training School (India)
- No. 1 Elementary Flying Training School RAF
- No. 2 Elementary Flying Training School RAF
- No. 3 Elementary Flying Training School RAF
- No. 4 Elementary Flying Training School RAF
- No. 5 Elementary Flying Training School RAF
- No. 6 Elementary Flying Training School RAF
- No. 7 Elementary Flying Training School RAF
- No. 8 Elementary Flying Training School RAF
- No. 9 Elementary Flying Training School RAF
- No. 10 Elementary Flying Training School RAF
- No. 11 Elementary Flying Training School RAF
- No. 12 Elementary Flying Training School RAF

List of Royal Air Force schools 555

- No. 13 Elementary Flying Training School RAF
- No. 14 Elementary Flying Training School RAF
- No. 15 Elementary Flying Training School RAF
- No. 16 Elementary Flying Training School RAF
- No. 17 Elementary Flying Training School RAF
- No. 18 Elementary Flying Training School RAF
- No. 19 Elementary Flying Training School RAF
- No. 20 Elementary Flying Training School RAF
- No. 21 Elementary Flying Training School RAF
- No. 22 Elementary Flying Training School RAF
- No. 23 Elementary Flying Training School RAF
- No. 24 Elementary Flying Training School RAF
- No. 25 Elementary Flying Training School RAF
- No. 25 Elementary Flying Training School (Southern Rhodesia) RAF
- No. 26 Elementary Flying Training School RAF
- No. 26 Elementary Flying Training School (Southern Rhodesia) RAF
- No. 27 Elementary Flying Training School RAF
- No. 27 Elementary Flying Training School (Southern Rhodesia) RAF
- No. 28 Elementary Flying Training School RAF
- No. 28 Elementary Flying Training School (Southern Rhodesia) RAF
- No. 28 Elementary Flying Training School RAF
- No. 29 Elementary Flying Training School RAF
- No. 30 Elementary Flying Training School RAF
- No. 30 Elementary Flying Training School (Kenya) RAF
- No. 31 Elementary Flying Training School RAF
- No. 32 Elementary Flying Training School RAF
- No. 33 Elementary Flying Training School RAF
- No. 34 Elementary Flying Training School (Canada) RAF
- No. 35 Elementary Flying Training School (Canada) RAF
- No. 36 Elementary Flying Training School (Canada) RAF

Flying Instructors School

- No. 1 Flying Instructors School RAF
- No. 1 Flying Instructors School (Advanced) RAF
- No. 2 Flying Instructors School RAF
- No. 2 Flying Instructors School (Advanced) RAF
- No. 3 Flying Instructors School (Advanced) RAF
- No. 4 Flying Instructors School RAF
- No. 4 Flying Instructors School (Elementary) RAF
- No. 4 Flying Instructors School (Supplementary) RAF
- No. 5 Flying Instructors School RAF
- No. 5 Flying Instructors School (Elementary) RAF

- No. 5 Flying Instructors School (Supplementary) RAF
- No. 6 Flying Instructors School RAF
- No. 6 Flying Instructors School (Elementary) RAF
- No. 6 Flying Instructors School (Supplementary) RAF
- No. 7 Flying Instructors School RAF
- No. 7 Flying Instructors School (Advanced) RAF
- No. 11 Flying Instructors School RAF
- No. 10 Flying Instructors School (Elementary) RAF
- No. 12 Flying Instructors School (Operational) RAF
- No. 33 Flying Instructors School, Southern Rhodesia RAF

Flying Refresher School

- No. 101 Flying Refresher School RAF
- No. 102 Flying Refresher School RAF
- No. 103 Flying Refresher School RAF
- No. 104 Flying Refresher School RAF

Flying Training School

- No. 1 (Indian) Flying Training School
- No. 1 Flying Training School RAF
- No. 2 Flying Training School RAF
- No. 3 Flying Training School RAF
- No. 4 Flying Training School RAF
- No. 5 Flying Training School RAF
- No. 6 Flying Training School RAF
- No. 7 Flying Training School RAF
- No. 8 Flying Training School RAF
- No. 9 Flying Training School RAF
- No. 10 Flying Training School RAF
- No. 11 Flying Training School RAF
- No. 12 Flying Training School RAF
- No. 13 Flying Training School RAF
- No. 14 Flying Training School RAF
- No. 15 Flying Training School RAF
- No. 19 Flying Training School RAF
- No. 20 Flying Training School RAF
- No. 21 Flying Training School RAF
- No. 22 Flying Training School RAF
- No. 207 Flying Training School RAF
- No. 211 Flying Training School RAF

Refresher School

- No. 1 Refresher School RAF
- No. 1 Refresher Flying Training School RAF

Reserve Flying School

- No. 1 Reserve Flying School RAF
- No. 2 Reserve Flying School RAF
- No. 3 Reserve Flying School RAF
- No. 4 Reserve Flying School RAF
- No. 5 Reserve Flying School RAF
- No. 6 Reserve Flying School RAF
- No. 7 Reserve Flying School RAF
- No. 8 Reserve Flying School RAF
- No. 9 Reserve Flying School RAF
- No. 10 Reserve Flying School RAF
- No. 11 Reserve Flying School RAF
- No. 12 Reserve Flying School RAF
- No. 13 Reserve Flying School RAF
- No. 14 Reserve Flying School RAF
- No. 15 Reserve Flying School RAF
- No. 16 Reserve Flying School RAF
- No. 17 Reserve Flying School RAF
- No. 18 Reserve Flying School RAF
- No. 19 Reserve Flying School RAF
- No. 20 Reserve Flying School RAF
- No. 21 Reserve Flying School RAF
- No. 22 Reserve Flying School RAF
- No. 23 Reserve Flying School RAF
- No. 24 Reserve Flying School RAF
- No. 25 Reserve Flying School RAF

School of Special Flying

- No. 1 School of Special Flying RAF
- No. 2 School of Special Flying RAF

Service Flying Training School

- No. 1 (Indian) Service Flying Training School
- No. 1 Service Flying Training School RAF
- No. 2 Service Flying Training School RAF
- No. 3 Service Flying Training School RAF
- No. 4 Service Flying Training School RAF
- No. 5 Service Flying Training School RAF

- No. 6 Service Flying Training School RAF
- No. 7 Service Flying Training School RAF
- No. 8 Service Flying Training School RAF
- No. 9 Service Flying Training School RAF
- No. 10 Service Flying Training School RAF
- No. 11 Service Flying Training School RAF
- No. 12 Service Flying Training School RAF
- No. 13 Service Flying Training School RAF
- No. 14 Service Flying Training School RAF
- No. 15 Service Flying Training School RAF
- No. 16 (Polish) Service Flying Training School RAF
- No. 17 Service Flying Training School RAF
- No. 20 Service Flying Training School RAF
- No. 21 Service Flying Training School RAF
- No. 22 Service Flying Training School RAF
- No. 23 Service Flying Training School RAF
- No. 31 Service Flying Training School RAF
- No. 32 Service Flying Training School RAF
- No. 33 Service Flying Training School RAF
- No. 34 Service Flying Training School RAF
- No. 35 Service Flying Training School RAF
- No. 36 Service Flying Training School RAF
- No. 37 Service Flying Training School RAF
- No. 38 Service Flying Training School RAF
- No. 39 Service Flying Training School RAF
- No. 41 Service Flying Training School RAF

Other Schools

- Advanced Flying School (India)
- Central Flying School (India)
- Central Flying School (Southern Rhodesia)
- Chinese Elementary Flying Training School
- Defence Helicopter Flying School
- Elementary and Reserve Flying Training School, Kenya
- Empire Flying School
- Flying Boat Instructors School, El Khanka
- Flying Instructors School (India)
- Flying Instructors School, The Curragh
- Flying Instructors School, Upavon
- Flying Instructors Training School
- Flying Refresher School
- Instructors School

- Joint Elementary Flying Training School
- Midland Area Flying instructors School
- Midland Area School of Special Flying
- Netheravon Flying School
- Northeastern Area Flying Instructors School
- Northern Area Flying Instructors School
- Northwestern Area Flying Instructors School
- Refresher Flying Training School
- Reserve Flying School, Brough
- Reserve Flying School, Coventry
- Reserve Flying School, Filton
- Reserve Flying School, Hamble
- Reserve Flying School, Renfrew
- Reserve Flying School, Stag Lane
- Royal Air Force College Service Flying Training School
- Royal Navy Elementary Flying Training School
- School of Refresher Flying
- School of Special Flying (Canada)
- School of Special Flying, Gosport
- Southeastern Area Flying Instructors School
- Southwestern Area Flying Instructors School

Gliding schools

As well as powered aircraft, the Royal Air Force has operated a large number of gliders both for military tasks and for Cadet training.

Regular Gliding Schools

- No. 1 Elementary Gliding Training School RAF
- No. 2 Elementary Gliding Training School RAF
- No. 3 Elementary Gliding Training School RAF

Volunteer Gliding Schools

- Air Cadet Central Gliding School

References

Bibliography

- Halley, James J. *The Squadrons of the Royal Air Force & Commonwealth 1918-1988*. Tonbridge, Kent, UK: Air Britain (Historians) Ltd., 1988. ISBN 0-85130-164-9.
- Jefford, C.G. *RAF Squadrons, a Comprehensive record of the Movement and Equipment of all RAF Squadrons and their Antecedents since 1912*. Shropshire, UK: Airlife Publishing, 1988 (second edition 2001). ISBN 1-85310-053-6.
- Lake, Alan. "Flying Units of the RAF". Airlife Publishing. Shrewsbury. 1999. ISBN 1-84037-086-6

List of active United Kingdom military aircraft

This is a list of military aircraft currently in service with the Armed Forces of the United Kingdom.

Royal Air Force

Type	Origin	Class	Role	Introduced	In service	Total	Notes
Leonardo GrandNew	Italy	Rotorcraft	Transport	2016	1	1	Used for transportation of senior military commanders or government ministers
Airbus A400M Atlas	Spain	Propeller	Transport	2014	20	20	Two on order
Airbus Voyager	Spain	Jet	Tanker / Transport	2011	14	14	
Beechcraft King Air	USA	Propeller	Trainer	2004	7	7	To be replaced as part of the new Ascent UK Military Flight Training System detailed below
Qinetiq Zephyr	UK	Solar	ISTAR	2017	3	7	
Beechcraft Shadow R1	USA	Propeller	ISTAR	2009	5	6	

List of active United Kingdom military aircraft 561

Bell Griffin HAR2	Canada	Rotor-craft	Utility	2003	3	3	Used for SAR duties in Akrotiri Cyprus
Boeing Chinook	USA	Rotor-craft	Transport	1980	60	66	
Boeing C-17A Globemaster III	USA	Jet	Transport	2001	8	8	
Boeing Sentry AEW1	USA	Jet	AEW&C	1990	6	7	
Boeing Airseeker R1	USA	Jet	SIGINT	2013	3	3	
British Aerospace 146	UK	Jet	Transport	1995	4	6	
British Aerospace Hawk T1	UK	Jet	Trainer	1976	35	175	Used in the aggressor role by 100 squadron and the Red Arrows
British Aerospace Hawk T2	UK	Jet	Trainer	2009	28	28	Used as an advanced fast jet lead-in trainer
Eurofighter Typhoon	UK	Jet	Multi-role	2007	120	140	Of the 22 two seat trainer aircraft 16 Tranche 1's are to be scrapped under the RTP (reduce to produce) requirement which started in late 2016
General Atomics MQ-9 Reaper	USA	UAV	ISR / attack	2007	10	10	
Grob Tutor T1	Germany	Propeller	Basic Trainer	1999	90	91	To be replaced as part of the new Ascent UK Military Flight Training System detailed below[1221]
Grob Viking TX1	Germany	Glider	Trainer	1990	73	73	
Lockheed C-130J Hercules	USA	Propeller	Transport	2000	18	24	Shorter C5 variant being withdrawn as part of SDSR 2015 to leave 13 of the C4 variant after one was lost after a mission against ISIS
Lockheed Martin F-35B Lightning II	USA	Jet	Multi-role	2013	15	22	Joint operated with Fleet Air Arm.
Panavia Tornado GR4	UK	Jet	Attack	1979	25	142	OSD Q1 2019
Raytheon Sentinel R1	Canada / USA	Jet	ISTAR	2008	4	5	

Short Tucano T1	UK	Propeller	Trainer	1989	78	130	To be replaced as part of the new Ascent UK Military Flight Training System detailed below
Westland Puma HC2	UK	Rotorcraft	Transport	1971	23	24	

RAF Battle of Britain Memorial Flight

Type	Origin	Class	Role	Introduced	In service	Total	Notes
Avro Lancaster (*PA474*)	UK	Propeller	Bomber	1942	1		1 B.I
De Havilland Canada Chipmunk	UK	Propeller	Trainer	1946	2	753	2 T.10
Douglas Dakota	USA	Propeller	Transport	1942	1		1 C.3
Hawker Hurricane	UK	Propeller	Fighter	1937	2	14533	2 Mk IIc
Supermarine Spitfire	UK	Propeller	Fighter	1938	6	20341	1 Mk IIa, 1 Mk Vb, 1 LF.IXe, 1 LF.XVIe, 2 PR.XIX

Fleet Air Arm

Type	Origin	Class	Role	Introduced	In service	Total	Notes
AgustaWestland AW159 Wildcat	UK	Rotorcraft	Attack	2014	28	28	
AgustaWestland AW101 Merlin	UK	Rotorcraft	Transport	2000	55	71	Split 30 Mk2 and 25 Mk4/4A. The Mk4/4A are undergoing a capability upgrade and will be fully delivered by 2020
Westland Sea King ASaC7	UK	Rotorcraft	AEW	1979	7	7	OSD Q3 2018
Eurocopter AS365 Dauphin II	France	Rotorcraft	Utility	1999	2	2	Used as transport of instructors as part of FOST training
British Aerospace Hawk T1	UK	Jet	Trainer	1994	14	14	Used in the aggressor role by 736 squadron

Beechcraft Avenger	USA	Propeller	Trainer	2011	4	4	To be replaced as part of the new Ascent UK Military Flight Training System detailed below
Grob Tutor T1	Germany	Propeller	Basic Trainer	2002	5	5	To be replaced as part of the new Ascent UK Military Flight Training System detailed below
Lockheed Martin F-35B Lightning II	USA	Jet	Multirole	2013	-	-	To be Jointly operated with Royal Air Force

Royal Navy Historic Flight

Type	Origin	Class	Role	Introduced	In service	Total	Notes
de Havilland Chipmunk	UK	Propeller	Trainer	1946	1		1 T.10
Fairey Swordfish	UK	Propeller	Torpedo-bomber	1936	2		2 Mk.I/-II
Hawker Sea Fury	UK	Propeller	Fighter-bomber	1945	1		1 FB11
Hawker Sea Hawk	UK	Jet	Fighter-bomber	1953	1		1 FGA6

Army Air Corps

Type	Origin	Class	Role	Introduced	In service	Total	Notes
AgustaWestland Apache	UK	Rotorcraft	Attack	2004	50	67	
AgustaWestland AW159 Wildcat	UK	Rotorcraft	Attack	2014	34	34	
Bell 212	Canada	Rotorcraft	Attack	1995	5	5	Used by No.7 Flight and No.25 Flight AAC in Brunei and Kenya in support of TTB and BATUK
Britten-Norman Defender	UK	Propeller	Patrol	2003	9	9	
Britten-Norman Islander	UK	Propeller	Patrol	1997	6	6	
Eurocopter AS365 Dauphin II	France	Rotorcraft	SAS	2009	5	5	

Thales Watch-keeper WK450	UK	UAV	ISR	2014	105	105	
Westland Gazelle	UK	Rotor-craft	Patrol	1974	24	26	to be retired in 2025. The two additional units are currently undergoing work to bring them back into service

UK Military Flying Training System

The contractors providing the new UK Military Flying Training System will eventually operate 38 fixed wing aircraft and 32 helicopters on the military register, but the aircraft are initially civilian-registered.

Type	Origin	Class	Role	Introduced	In service	Total	Notes
Grob Prefect T1	Germany	Propeller	Basic Trainer	2018	23	23	ISD expected early 2019
Beechcraft Texan T1	USA	Propeller	Trainer	2018	4	10	ISD expected early 2019
Embraer Phenom 100	Brazil	Jet	Trainer	2018	5	5	ISD expected mid 2018
Airbus H135 Juno	Germany	Rotor-craft	Trainer	2018	29	29	ISD 1 April 2018
Airbus H145 Jupiter	Germany	Rotor-craft	Trainer	2018	3	3	ISD 1 April 2018

Empire Test Pilots' School

Type	Origin	Class	Role	Introduced	In service	No.	Notes
Agusta AW109	Italy	Rotor-craft	Utility		2		1222
Avro RJ	UK	Jet	Transport		2		
British Aerospace Hawk	UK	Jet	Trainer / experimental		3		
JAS 39 Gripen	Sweden	Jet	Trainer		1		1223
Short Tucano T1	UK	Propeller	Trainer		2		
Airbus H125	France	Rotor-craft	Trainer	Mar 2018	1		
Grob G 120TP	Germany	Propeller	Basic Trainer	Nov 2017	1		
Pilatus PC-21	Switzerland	Propeller	Advanced Trainer	Jan 2018	1		

List of active United Kingdom military aircraft

Figure 203: *Tri-service badge of the United Kingdom's armed forces.*

Ministry of Defence

As well as the military services a number of defence contractors operate military aircraft on behalf of the Ministry of Defence.

Type	Origin	Class	Role	Introduced	In service	Total	Notes
Agusta AW109	Italy	Rotorcraft	Utility		1		QinetiQ Boscombe Down.
Eurofighter Typhoon	UK	Jet	Multi-role		2		BAE Systems, Warton.
Hawker Hunter	UK	Jet	Fighter		3		Hawker Hunter Aviation.
Lockheed Martin F-35B Lightning II	USA	Jet	Multi-role	2013	3	3	Lockheed Martin, United States.
Panavia Tornado	UK	Jet	Attack		2		BAE Systems, Warton.
Westland Sea King	UK	Rotorcraft	Utility		1		QinetiQ Boscombe Down.

External links

- United Kingdom Defence Statistics - 2014[1224] (gov.uk)
- United Kingdom Defence Statistics - 2013[1225] (dasa.mod.uk)

AirTanker Services

AirTanker

IATA	ICAO	Callsign
9L	TOW	TOWLINE

Founded	2007
Commenced operations	2013
AOC #	2388
Hubs	RAF Brize Norton
Focus cities	Birmingham Airport
Fleet size	14
Parent company	Airbus (40%) Rolls-Royce plc (20%) Cobham plc (13.33%) Babcock International (13.33%) and Thales Group (13.33%)
Headquarters	RAF Brize Norton, United Kingdom
Website	www<wbr/>.airtanker<wbr/>.co<wbr/>.uk[1226]

AirTanker Services, operating as **AirTanker**, is a British charter airline which operates charter flights using reserve aerial refuelling aircraft.

In 2008 the Ministry of Defence signed the Future Strategic Tanker Aircraft (FSTA) contract with AirTanker to provide the Royal Air Force (RAF) with an air transport and air-to-air refuelling capability. As well as supporting the RAF, AirTanker holds a United Kingdom Civil Aviation Authority Type A Operating Licence, permitting it to carry passengers, cargo and mail on aircraft with 20 or more seats.[1227]

Following the granting of an operating licence the airline flew its first charter flight to RAF Akrotiri in Cyprus for the UK Ministry of Defence in January 2013.[1228] After delays in certification, its first operational refuelling flight took place on 20 May 2013.

Figure 204: *Airbus Voyager of the RAF, owned by Airtanker, arrives at the 2016 RIAT, England*

From May 2015, AirTanker leased one aircraft to Thomas Cook Airlines to be deployed on holiday routes. The contract will initially run for three years and involve mainly long haul flights from Glasgow, Manchester and London Stansted Airport. Their first commercial flight took place on 1 May 2015 from Manchester to Cancun and Punta Cana for Thomas Cook Airlines using an Airbus A330.

On 30 September 2016, AirTanker reached the final establishment phase milestone in the Future Strategic Tanker Aircraft (FSTA) programme with the achievement of Full Service Date on time and on budget delivering all 14 Aircraft.

AirTanker also provides twice-weekly flights from RAF Brize Norton to RAF Mount Pleasant on the Falkland Islands mainly for military personnel, though fare-paying passengers are also allowed to travel.

Fleet

As of December 2017 the AirTanker fleet comprises the following:[1229]

Figure 205: *An AirTanker Airbus Voyager*

AirTanker Fleet

Aircraft	In service	Orders	Notes
Airbus A330-200	4	—	Aircraft are damp and wet leased to other operators when not required to support the Royal Air Force requirements. 1 leased year round to Thomas Cook Airlines 1 wet-leased seasonally to TUI Group and damp-leased to Thomas Cook seasonally 1 leased to Jet2.com seasonally[1230]
Airbus Voyager (A330 MRTT)	10	—	Multi-Role Tanker Aircraft operated for the Royal Air Force under military regulations under the FSTA contract.
Total	**14**	**0**	

External links
Official website[1231]

Future of the Royal Air Force

The planning for the **future of the Royal Air Force** involves supporting ongoing British military operations, the introduction of new aircraft types, greater focus on network enabled capability and increasing interoperability with members of NATO.

F-35 Lightning II

The Lockheed Martin F-35 Lightning II is a family of single-seat, single-engine, fifth generation multirole fighters under development to perform ground attack, reconnaissance, and air defence missions with stealth capability. It was selected for the UK's Joint Combat Aircraft requirement in 2001 and is expected to enter service with the Royal Navy and the RAF from around 2020, having been selected initially to replace the Royal Navy's Sea Harrier fighter, and latterly the existing Tornado GR.4 and Harrier GR.9 fleets (the latter already having been retired in late 2010), operating principally from the Queen Elizabeth class aircraft carriers.[1232] It will be the main component of the RAF's manned strike capability, and marks the return of a carrier-borne strike capability for the Fleet Air Arm for the first time in nearly a decade.

The version initially selected was the Short Take Off Vertical Landing (STOVL) variant of the F-35, known as the F-35B. However, on 19 October 2010, David Cameron announced that the UK would change their order to the F-35C CATOBAR carrier variant for both the RAF and Navy. The F-35C variant features larger wings with folding wingtips and larger wing and tail control surfaces for improved low-speed control. This gives it a greater range and the ability to carry a larger and more diverse payload than the F-35B.

In May 2012, it was announced that the government had reverted to the previous plan to operate the Short Take Off Vertical Landing F-35B, due to rising estimated shipbuilding costs associated with the CATOBAR variant F-35C, and an earlier estimated in-service date for the F-35B.[1233]

The delivery of the UK's first F-35B was made on 19 July 2012 at Fort Worth, Texas, for flight trials by the RAF and Royal Navy.

In 2015, the government's Strategic Defence and Security Review confirmed a planned order of 138 F-35s, with 24 of them to be available for carrier duties by 2023.

Current & Future Units:

Figure 206: *A Royal Air Force F-35B in flight.*

- **17(R) Squadron**, Edwards Air Force Base. 17(R) Squadron is the F-35B Operational Evaluation Unit.
- 617 Squadron, RAF Marham. 617 Squadron (The Dambusters), will be the first operational British F-35 unit in 2019.
- Additional unnamed frontline Squadron
- 207 Squadron - Operational Conversion Unit

Additionally, 809 Naval Air Squadron and another as-yet unnamed Fleet Air Arm squadron, both to be based at RAF Marham, will also operate the F-35.

Typhoon

It was announced in the 2015 Strategic Defence and Security Review that the Royal Air Force would retain its Tranche 1 Typhoons and use them to stand up an additional two squadrons. It was also announced that the aircraft would remain in service until 2040, ten years longer than previously planned. The Government also promised to invest further in Typhoon air-to-ground capabilities and in a new active electronically scanned array(AESA) radar, as well as completing integration of the Storm Shadow and Brimstone missiles with the Typhoon.

Frontline Units

- **1(F) Squadron**

Figure 207: *RAF Typhoon*

- **2(AC) Squadron**
- **3(F) Squadron**
- **6 Squadron**
- **XI Squadron**
- 2 additional squadrons (UK MOD announced on 14 Dec 2017 that No. 12 Squadron will be one of the two squadrons. In July 2018, it was stated that IX(B) Squadron would be the second. IX(B) Squadron was to form as a Typhoon-equipped squadron based at RAF Lossiemouth in the second-half of 2018. No. 12 Squadron would re-equip with Typhoon at RAF Coningsby, likely in 2019.)

Operational Conversion Units
- **29 Squadron**

Figure 208: *A mockup of BAE Mantis.*

Unmanned Aerial Vehicles

Protector

The Protector programme (formerly known as Scavenger) will supply a next-generation medium-altitude, long-endurance (MALE) UAV to replace the current General Atomics MQ-9 Reaper UAVs.

In June 2011, it was announced that BAE Systems and Dassault Aviation would collaborate on an aircraft called Telemos. It was suggested that BAE Systems would supply the airframe and guidance based on BAE Mantis, with a payload from Thales and integration by Dassault. However, the project was effectively abandoned in 2012 after Dassault pursued a collaboration with EADS Cassidian and Alenia Aermacchi instead.

In October 2015, Prime Minister David Cameron announced the purchase of more than 20 Protector UAVs which would be delivered by the end of the decade. This was later confirmed in the 2015 Strategic Defence and Security Review. As of mid-2018, the in-service date had slipped to 2024. The exact platform selected for Protector was not disclosed, but in February 2016, Christopher Ames of General Atomics Aeronautical Systems claimed that it would be a Certifiable Predator B. Air Commodore Peter Grinsted of the Ministry of Defence later confirmed that it would be an enhanced variant of Predator B, designed to be compatible with NATO airworthiness standards. He confirmed that it would also come with the extended wing and fuel tanks of the ER (Extended Range) version, giving an increased endurance of over 40 hours. In April 2016, the Ministry of Defence confirmed it would seek to acquire the Certifiable Predator B through a Foreign Military Sales contract with the U.S. Department of Defense.

According to MBDA, the Royal Air Force intends to arm the aircraft with Brimstone missiles.

Figure 209: *A model of BAE Taranis.*

Future Combat Air System (FCAS)

The Future Combat Air System (FCAS) (also known as the Unmanned Combat Air System (UCAS)) aims to deliver an unmanned combat aerial vehicle (UCAV) by 2030. FCAS will be built in cooperation with France, utilizing technology from the BAE Taranis and Dassault nEUROn technology demonstrators. Development of full-scale prototypes is expected to begin by 2017. In the Royal Air Force, FCAS will be expected to operate alongside Typhoons and F-35 Lightning IIs.

As a UCAV, FCAS will utilize stealth technology to reduce its radar cross-section (its radar signature is reportedly the size of a dragonfly). It will feature a high degree of autonomy, enabling it to complete a large part of its missions without human control. It will have a 16-metre (50 ft) wingspan and two internal weapon bays.

According to Bernard Gray of the Ministry of Defence, technology from FCAS could also be incorporated onto a manned platform. Other officials have also insisted that a manned option for FCAS has not been ruled out. According to a House of Commons Defence Select Committee (DSC) report, a new "clean-sheet" manned fighter design has not been ruled out, nor has the option to buy further or upgrade existing aircraft.

At the 2018 Farnborough Airshow, U.K. Defence Secretary Gavin Williamson announced Team Tempest, a joint program office consisting of government divisions alongside BAE Systems, Leonardo, MBDA and Rolls-Royce would be developing a new design of fighter aircraft with UK£2 billion (US$2.6 billion) in funding, by 2025. This will develop new technologies and means of production under the Future Combat Air System Technology Initiative (FCAS TI)). It is likely to involve technology from Italy and Sweden using Grippen E, and is also likely to leverage on the UK's Eurofighter Typhoon experience.[1234]

Zephyr

Leading up to the Strategic Defence and Security Review 2015, Prime Minister David Cameron announced that "British-designed unmanned aircraft will be constructed to fly at the very edge of the earth's atmosphere and allow us to observe our adversaries for weeks on end, providing critical intelligence for our forces." Gareth Jennings of *IHS Jane's* identified this as the solar-powered Qinetiq Zephyr. The Ministry of Defence confirmed an initial order for two Zephyr aircraft in February 2016 for demonstration purposes. In August 2016, the MOD confirmed a purchase of a third Zephyr.

Transport and air-to-air refuelling

Atlas

Future transport capability will rely on the Airbus A400M Atlas, of which 22 are to be used to replace the Hercules C1/C3 (C-130K) aircraft.

The Airbus A400M will increase the airlift capacity and range compared with the aircraft it was originally set to replace, the older versions of the Hercules and Transall. Cargo capacity is expected to double over existing aircraft, both in payload and volume, and range is increased substantially as well. The cargo box is 17.71 m long excluding ramp, 4.00 m wide, and 3.85 m high. The height is 4.00 m aft of the wing and the ramp is 5.40 m long. The Airbus A400M will operate in many configurations including cargo transport, troop transport, Medical evacuation, and electronic surveillance. The aircraft is intended for use on short, soft landing strips and for long-range, cargo transport flights.

Current & Future Units

- **70 Squadron**, based at RAF Brize Norton. The first A400M unit.
- 24 Squadron, the OCU Squadron that trains Atlas crews.[1235]
- 30 Squadron will be the second operational A400M following retirement of part of the Hercules fleet.

Figure 210: *The first A400M on final approach, during its fourth flight on 15 January 2010.*

Figure 211: *RAF C130J-30s, based at RAF Brize Norton*

Hercules

Strategic Defence and Security Review 2015 included a reprieve for some of the Hercules fleet, with the Government announcing "We will upgrade and extend the life of our C130J aircraft, allowing them to support a range of operations until 2030". It had been reported that the Army's senior leadership was unhappy with the retirement of the Hercules aircraft, due to uncertainty regarding the A400M's and C-17's effectiveness in some tactical roles. The

Figure 212: *The first Royal Air Force RC-135W arrives at RAF Waddington in November 2013.*

2015 Strategic Defence and Security Review envisioned a fleet of 14 C130J aircraft (the variant of which was not explicitly made clear).

- 24 Squadron
- 30 Squadron

Voyager

Fourteen Voyager air-to-air refuelling aircraft are in service as of 2016[1236], with one fitted for transport of the Prime Minister, senior cabinet officials and the Royal Family.

- 10 Squadron
- 101 Squadron

Signals Intelligence

Air Seeker

A total of three Boeing RC-135 *Rivet Joint* signals intelligence aircraft, ordered to replace the Nimrod R1 which was retired in 2011, are now in service as of 2017.[1237] These became known as Air Seeker when they entered RAF service in 2014. The aircraft is an extensively modified Boeing C-135 Stratolifter with onboard sensors which enable the crew to detect, identify and geolocate signals throughout the electromagnetic spectrum. The crew can then forward information in a variety of formats to a wide range of consumers via the onboard secure communications suite.

- 51 Squadron

Sentinel R1

The 2015 Strategic Defence and Security Review announced that the Sentinel R1 would remain in service "until the next decade" with the intention that it be withdrawn by 2025.

- V(AC) Squadron

Shadow R1

The 2015 Strategic Defence and Security Review stated that the Shadow R1 would remain in service until "at least" 2030. An additional two aircraft would also be procured for a total of eight in service by 2025.

- 14 Squadron

Project SOLOMON

In 2004, the Royal Air Force initiated Project DABINETT, an integrated architecture to collect, process and disseminate intelligence from manned and unmanned aircraft such as Sentinel and Watchkeeper. Initial Gate was approved in January 2008; when assessment phase contracts were awarded to BAe INSYTE and Lockheed Martin UK. In February 2010, it had been renamed Project SOLOMON. Phase I concentrates on disseminating information over the UK Defence Information Infrastructure networks, with Initial Operating Capability in March 2012 and Full Operating Capability in March 2015. There, however, has been no progress since then.

Maritime Patrol

Poseidon

One of the most anticipated announcements in the Strategic Defence and Security Review 2015 was the purchase of a maritime patrol aircraft to replace the capability lost after the cancellation of the Nimrod MRA.4 in 2010. The review announced that the UK planned to acquire 9 **Boeing P-8 Poseidon** aircraft, which would be based at RAF Lossiemouth in Scotland by 2025. The aircraft will include an "overland surveillance capability", which could eventually replace the surveillance capability lost by the retirement of the Sentinel R1 in 2025. The RAF plans to operate its P-8s with U.S. weapons such as MK54 torpedoes and Harpoon anti-ship missiles initially, with a possible transition

Figure 213: *The Royal Air Force plans to acquire 9 P-8 Poseidon aircraft.*

onto British weapons in the future. The first RAF P-8 squadron will be 120 Squadron, standing up in April 2018 while the second will be 201 Squadron, standing up in 2021.

Future Units
- 120 Squadron
- 201 Squadron

Helicopters

Chinook

On 16 December 2009, the Ministry of Defence announced that 22 Chinook helicopters would be added to the current Chinook fleet, bringing the total number in service to 70 by 2013. However, in 2010, the order was reduced to 14. The new aircraft will enter service from late 2014 onwards. In 2006, the retirement dates for the HC2 and HC2A fleets were scheduled for 2015 and 2025, respectively, however with upgrades to a digital cockpit and digital automatic flight control system the types are expected to be flying until 2040.

- **7 Squadron**
- **18(B) Squadron**
- **27 Squadron**

Figure 214: *An RAF Chinook HC2 in 2009.*

Puma

A total of 24 Puma HC1's have been upgraded to HC2 standard to prolong their lives until 2025.

- 33 Squadron
- 230 Squadron

Training

The training provided to Royal Air Force aircrew is evolving, through a shift towards contractor-provided training, and increasing use of simulators to supplement flying time. The aircraft currently in use are approaching the end of their working lives. In order to fund new aircraft, the training system is being outsourced to the private sector, over a 25-year Private Finance Initiative valued at £6 billion. The consortium running the new **UK Military Flying Training System** is a partnership between Lockheed Martin and Babcock International, is known as Ascent Flight Training. The current generation training aircraft will be replaced over the next few years:

Training Phase	Current	Replacement	Base
Elementary Flying Training	Tutor T.1	Grob G 120TP	RAF Cranwell, RAF Wittering
Basic Fast Jet Training	Tucano T.1	Beechcraft T-6 Texan II	RAF Linton-on-Ouse
Advanced Fast Jet Training	Hawk T.1/T.2	Hawk T.2	RAF Valley
Multi-Engine Training	Beechcraft King Air	Embraer Phenom 100	RAF Cranwell
Basic Gliding Training	Viking T.1	None identified	RAF Syerston and various locations
Basic Helicopter Flying Training	Eurocopter Squirrel HT.1	Eurocopter H135	RAF Shawbury
Advanced Helicopter Flying Training	Bell Griffin HT.1	Eurocopter H145	RAF Shawbury

Wikipedia:Citation needed

Missiles

- The Royal Air Force has signed a contract to receive the Meteor BVRAAM missile for its tranche 2 and 3 Eurofighter Typhoons and future F-35 Lightning IIs. It will replace the AMRAAMs currently in service except for the tranche 1 Typhoons as they are not able to use it. It will be fitted on the Eurofighter Typhoon by the end of 2018 and the F-35B in 2024.[1238,1239,1240]
- The 2015 Strategic Defence and Security Review announced further investment into the Storm Shadow and Brimstone missiles.
- In March 2016, the Ministry of Defence extended the assessment phase contract for the SPEAR 3 missile programme, which aims to deliver a "mini-cruise missile" capable of attacking stationary and moving targets.

Countermeasures

- In September 2016, an initial £2.5m batch order for the British-developed BriteCloud DRFM jammer was placed with Leonardo-Finmeccanica. If trials of the system prove successful, it could begin to be fitted to the Royal Air Force's fast-jet fleet by mid-2017.[1241]

Others

No. 601 Squadron, Royal Auxiliary Air Force will reform to tap into the talents of leaders from industry, academia and research to advise and shape and inspire the RAF.

Ministry of Defence

Ministry of Defence (United Kingdom)

Ministry of Defence

Department overview	
Formed	1 April 1964 (As modern department)
Jurisdiction	United Kingdom
Headquarters	Main Building, Whitehall, Westminster, London 51°30′14″N 0°07′30″W[1242] Coordinates: 51°30′14″N 0°07′30″W[1242]
Employees	56,860 civilian staff (October 2015)[1243]
Annual budget	£46 billion; FY 2017–18 (≈$64 billion)[1244]
Minister responsible	• Gavin Williamson, Secretary of State for Defence
Department executives	• General Sir Nick Carter, Chief of the Defence Staff • Stephen Lovegrove, Permanent Secretary
Child agencies	• Defence Electronics and Components Agency • Defence Science and Technology Laboratory • United Kingdom Hydrographic Office
Website	mod.uk[1245]

United Kingdom

The **Ministry of Defence** (**MoD** or **MOD**) is the British government department responsible for implementing the defence policy set by Her Majesty's Government and is the headquarters of the British Armed Forces.

The MOD states that its principal objectives are to defend the United Kingdom of Great Britain and Northern Ireland and its interests and to strengthen international peace and stability.[1247] With the collapse of the Soviet Union and the end of the Cold War, the MOD does not foresee any short-term conventional military threat; rather, it has identified weapons of mass destruction, international terrorism, and failed and failing states as the overriding threats to Britain's interests.[1248] The MOD also manages day-to-day running of the armed forces, contingency planning and defence procurement.

History

During the 1920s and 1930s, British civil servants and politicians, looking back at the performance of the state during World War I, concluded that there was a need for greater co-ordination between the three services that made up the armed forces of the United Kingdom—the Royal Navy, the British Army and the Royal Air Force. The formation of a united ministry of defence was rejected by David Lloyd George's coalition government in 1921; but the Chiefs of Staff Committee was formed in 1923, for the purposes of inter-service co-ordination. As rearmament became a concern during the 1930s, Stanley Baldwin created the position of Minister for Co-ordination of Defence. Lord Chatfield held the post until the fall of Neville Chamberlain's government in 1940;

his success was limited by his lack of control over the existing Service departments and his limited political influence.

Winston Churchill, on forming his government in 1940, created the office of Minister of Defence to exercise ministerial control over the Chiefs of Staff Committee and to co-ordinate defence matters. The post was held by the Prime Minister of the day until Clement Attlee's government introduced the Ministry of Defence Act of 1946. The new ministry was headed by a Minister of Defence who possessed a seat in the Cabinet. The three existing service Ministers—the First Lord of the Admiralty, the Secretary of State for War and the Secretary of State for Air—remained in direct operational control of their respective services, but ceased to attend Cabinet.

From 1946 to 1964 five Departments of State did the work of the modern Ministry of Defence: the Admiralty, the War Office, the Air Ministry, the Ministry of Aviation, and an earlier form of the Ministry of Defence. These departments merged in 1964; the defence functions of the Ministry of Aviation Supply merged into the Ministry of Defence in 1971.

Ministers

The Ministers in the Ministry of Defence are as follows:

Minister	Rank	Portfolio
The Rt Hon. Gavin Williamson CBE MP	Secretary of State	Overall responsibility for the department and its strategic direction
The Rt Hon. The Earl Howe PC	Minister of State	Department spokesman in the House of Lords, commemorations and ceremonies; Efficiency Programme; EU relations, including Brexit; Lawfare; ceremonial duties, medallic recognition and protocol policy and casework; commemorations; engagement with retired senior defence personnel and wider opinion formers; community engagement; arms control and proliferation, including export licensing; UK Hydrographic Office; Statutory Instrument Programme; Australia, Far East; defence fire and rescue; London estate; Defence Medical Services; museums and heritage; ministerial correspondence and PQs
The Rt Hon. Mark Lancaster TD MP	Minister of State for the Armed Forces	Operations; operational legal matters; force generation and international defence engagement including: operations and operational legal policy; force generation (including exercises); manning, recruitment and retention of regulars; cyber; Permanent Joint Operating Bases; Northern Ireland; international defence engagement; Africa and Latin America; operational public inquiries, inquests, safety and security

The Rt Hon. Tobias Ellwood MP	Parliamentary Under-Secretary of State for Defence People and Veterans	Civilian and service personnel policy; veterans policy including resettlement, transition, charities and Veterans Board; Armed Forces People Programme; mental Health; DIO better defence estate; armed forces pay, pensions and compensation; Armed Forces Covenant; service justice; welfare and service families; youth and cadets; security and safety including vetting (non-operations); inquiries and inquests (operations and non-operations); environment and sustainability; equality, diversity and inclusion
Stuart Andrew MP	Minister for Defence Procurement	Equipment plan delivery, the nuclear enterprise, defence equipment and support reform, defence exports, innovation, science and technology (including Dstl), information computer technology, the Gulf, the Single Source Regulations Office, and Scotland and Wales

Senior military and civilian officials

Chiefs of the Defence Staff

The Chief of the Defence Staff (CDS) is the professional head of the British Armed Forces and the most senior uniformed military adviser to the Secretary of State for Defence and the Prime Minister.

The CDS is supported by the Vice Chief of the Defence Staff (VCDS) who deputises and is responsible for the day-to-day running of the armed services aspect of the MOD through the Central Staff, working closely alongside the Permanent Secretary. They are joined by the professional heads of the three British armed services (Royal Navy, British Army and Royal Air Force) and the Commander of Joint Forces Command. All personnel sit at OF-9 rank in the NATO rank system.

Together the Chiefs of Staff form the Chiefs of Staff Committee with responsibility for providing advice on operational military matters and the preparation and conduct of military operations.

The current Chiefs of Staff are as follows.

- Chief of the Defence Staff – General Sir Nick Carter
- Vice-Chief of the Defence Staff – General Sir Gordon Messenger
- First Sea Lord and Chief of the Naval Staff – Admiral Sir Philip Jones (Head of the Royal Navy)
- Chief of the General Staff – General Mark Carleton-Smith (Head of the British Army)
- Chief of the Air Staff – Air Chief Marshal Sir Stephen Hillier (Head of the Royal Air Force)
- Commander of Joint Forces Command – General Sir Christopher Deverell

Figure 215: *Air Chief Marshal Sir Stuart Peach, the Chief of the Defence Staff.*

Other senior military officers

The Chief of Staff is supported by several other senior military personnel at OF-8 rank.

- Chief of Defence People – Lieutenant General Richard Nugee
- Deputy Chief of Defence Staff (Military Capability) – Lieutenant-General Mark Poffley
- Director General MOD Saudi Armed Forces Projects – Air Marshal Ian Morrison
- Director General Defence Safety Authority – Air Marshal Richard Garwood
- Deputy Chief of Defence Staff (Military Strategy and Operations) – Lieutenant-General Mark Carleton-Smith
- Defence Senior Adviser Middle East

Additionally, there are a number of Assistant Chiefs of Defence Staff, including the Assistant Chief of the Defence Staff (Reserves and Cadets) and the Defence Services Secretary in the Royal Household of the Sovereign of the United Kingdom, who is also the Assistant Chief of Defence Staff (Personnel).

Permanent Secretary and other senior officials

The Ministers and Chiefs of the Defence Staff are supported by several civilian, scientific and professional military advisors. The Permanent Under-Secretary of State for Defence (generally known as the Permanent Secretary) is the senior civil servant at the MOD. Their role is to ensure that it operates effectively as a government department and has responsibility for the strategy, performance, reform, organisation and the finances of the MOD. The role works closely with the Chief of the Defence Staff in leading the organisation and supporting Ministers in the conduct of business in the Department across the full range of responsibilities.

- Permanent Under-Secretary of State – Stephen Lovegrove
- Director General Finance – Cat Little
- Director General Head Office and Commissioning Services – Julie Taylor
- Director General Nuclear – Julian Kelly
- Director General Security Policy – Peter Watkins
- MOD Chief Scientific Adviser – Professor Hugh Durrant-Whyte
- MOD Chief Scientific Adviser (Nuclear) – Professor Robin Grimes
- Lead Non-Executive Board Member – Sir Gerry Grimstone
- Non-Executive Defence Board Member and Chair of the Defence Audit Committee – Graham Williams
- Non-Executive Defence Board Member and Chair of the Defence Equipment and Support Board – Paul Skinner
- Non-Executive Defence Board Member and Chair of the People Committee – Danuta Gray

Defence policy

The 1998 *Strategic Defence Review* and the 2003 *Delivering Security in a Changing World* white paper outlined the following posture for the British Armed Forces –

- The ability to support three simultaneous small- to medium-scale operations, with at least one as an enduring peace-keeping mission (e.g. Kosovo). These forces must be capable of representing Britain as lead nation in any coalition operations.
- The ability, at longer notice, to deploy forces in a large-scale operation while running a concurrent small-scale operation.

The MOD has since been regarded as a leader in elaborating the post-Cold War organising concept of "defence diplomacy". As a result of the Strategic Defence and Security Review 2010, Prime Minister David Cameron signed a 50-year treaty with French President Nicolas Sarkozy that would have the two countries co-operate intensively in military matters. The UK is establishing air and naval bases in the Persian Gulf, located in the UAE and Bahrain. A presence in Oman is also being considered.

The Strategic Defence and Security Review 2015 included £178 billion investment in new equipment and capabilities. The review set a defence policy with four primary missions for the Armed Forces:

- Defend and contribute to the security and resilience of the UK and Overseas Territories.
- Provide the nuclear deterrent.
- Contribute to improved understanding of the world through strategic intelligence and the global defence network.
- Reinforce international security and the collective capacity of our allies, partners and multilateral institutions.

The review stated the Armed Forces will also contribute to the government's response to crises by being prepared to:

- Support humanitarian assistance and disaster response, and conduct rescue missions.
- Conduct strike operations.
- Conduct operations to restore peace and stability.
- Conduct major combat operations if required, including under NATO Article 5.

Current threats

Following the end of the Cold War, the threat of direct conventional military confrontation with other states has been replaced by terrorism. In 2009, Sir Richard Dannatt, then head of the British Army, predicted British forces to be involved in combating "predatory non-state actors" for the foreseeable future, in what he called an "era of persistent conflict". He told the Chatham House think tank that the fight against al-Qaeda and other militant Islamist groups was "probably the fight of our generation".

Dannatt criticised a remnant "Cold War mentality", with military expenditures based on retaining a capability against a direct conventional strategic threat; He said currently only 10% of the MOD's equipment programme budget between 2003 and 2018 was to be invested in the "land environment" – at a time when Britain was engaged in land–based wars in Afghanistan and Iraq.

The Defence Committee – Third Report "Defence Equipment 2009" cites an article from the *Financial Times* website[1249] stating that the Chief of Defence Materiel, General Sir Kevin O'Donoghue, had instructed staff within Defence Equipment and Support (DE&S) through an internal memorandum

Figure 216: *The plaque outside the South Door of the MoD's Main Building.*

to re-prioritise the approvals process to focus on supporting current operations over the next three years; deterrence related programmes; those that reflect defence obligations both contractual or international; and those where production contracts are already signed. The report also cites concerns over potential cuts in the defence science and technology research budget; implications of inappropriate estimation of Defence Inflation within budgetary processes; underfunding in the Equipment Programme; and a general concern over striking the appropriate balance over a short-term focus (Current Operations) and long-term consequences of failure to invest in the delivery of future UK defence capabilities on future combatants and campaigns. The then Secretary of State for Defence, Bob Ainsworth MP, reinforced this re-prioritisation of focus on current operations and had not ruled out *"major shifts"* in defence spending. In the same article, the First Sea Lord and Chief of the Naval Staff, Admiral Sir Mark Stanhope, acknowledged that there was not enough money within the defence budget and it is preparing itself for tough decisions and the potential for cutbacks. According to figures published by the London *Evening Standard* the defence budget for 2009 is *"more than 10% overspent"* (figures cannot be verified) and the paper states that this had caused Gordon Brown to say that the defence spending must be cut.[1250] The MOD has been investing in IT to cut costs and improve services for its personnel. As of 2017 there is concern that defence spending may be insufficient to meet defence needs.[1251]

Figure 217: *A British armed forces careers office in Oxford*

Governance and departmental organisation

Governance

Defence is governed and managed by several committees committee.

- The Defence Board is the main MOD corporate board chaired by the Secretary of State and responsible for top level leadership and management across defence. The board's membership comprises the Secretary of State, the Armed Forces Minister, the Permanent Secretary, the Chief and Vice Chief of the Defence Staff, the Chief of Defence Materiel, Director General Finance and three non-executive board members.
- The Defence Council provides the formal legal basis for the conduct of defence in the UK through a range of powers vested in it by statute and Letters Patent. It too is chaired by the Secretary of State, and its members are ministers, the senior officers and senior civilian officials.

Departmental organisation

The following organisations come under the control of the MOD.

Top level budgets

The MOD comprises seven top-level budgets. The head of each organisation is personally accountable for the performance and outputs of their particular organisation.

- Navy Command - Royal Navy
- Army Command - British Army
- Air Command - Royal Air Force
- Joint Forces Command
- Head Office and Corporate Services (HOCS)
- Defence Infrastructure Organisation (DIO)
- Director General Nuclear

Bespoke trading entity

- Defence Equipment and Support (DE&S)

Executive agencies

- Defence Electronics and Components Agency (DECA)
- Defence Science and Technology Laboratory (Dstl)
- UK Hydrographic Office (UKHO) – also has trading fund status.
- Submarine Delivery Agency (SDA) – created in April 2017 and to be fully functional by April 2018.

Executive non-departmental public bodies

- National Museum of the Royal Navy
- National Army Museum
- Royal Air Force Museum
- Single Source Regulations Office (SSRO)

Advisory non-departmental public bodies

- Advisory Committee on Conscientious Objectors
- Advisory Group on Military Medicine
- Armed Forces Pay Review Body
- Defence Nuclear Safety Committee
- Independent Medical Expert Group
- National Employer Advisory Board
- Nuclear Research Advisory Council
- Scientific Advisory Committee on the Medical Implications of Less-Lethal Weapons
- Veterans Advisory and Pensions Committees

Ad-hoc advisory group

- Central Advisory Committee on Compensation

Other bodies

- Commonwealth War Graves Commission
- Defence Academy of the United Kingdom
- Defence Sixth Form College
- Defence and Security Media Advisory Committee
- Fleet Air Arm Museum
- Independent Monitoring Board for the Military Corrective Training Centre (Colhester)
- Reserve Forces' and Cadets' Associations
- Royal Hospital Chelsea
- Royal Marines Museum
- Royal Navy Submarine Museum
- Service Complaints Ombudsman
- Service Prosecuting Authority
- United Kingdom Reserve Forces Association

Public corporations

- The Oil and Pipelines Agency (OPA)

Support organisation

- Defence Business Services (DBS)

In addition, the MOD is responsible for the administration of the Sovereign Base Areas of Akrotiri and Dhekelia in Cyprus.

Property portfolio

The Ministry of Defence is one of the United Kingdom's largest landowners, owning 227,300 hectares of land and foreshore (either freehold or leasehold) at April 2014, which was valued at "about £20 billion". The MOD also has "rights of access" to a further 222,000 hectares. In total, this is about 1.8% of the UK land mass. The total annual cost to support the defence estate is "in excess of £3.3 billion".

The defence estate is divided as training areas & ranges (84.0%), research & development (5.4%), airfields (3.4%), barracks & camps (2.5%), storage & supply depots (1.6%), and other (3.0%). These are largely managed by the Defence Infrastructure Organisation.

Figure 218: *The MoD Main Building, Whitehall, London*

Main Building

The headquarters of the MOD are in Whitehall and is known as MOD Main Building. This structure is neoclassical in style and was originally built between 1938 and 1959 to designs by Vincent Harris to house the Air Ministry and the Board of Trade. A major refurbishment of the building was completed under a Private Finance Initiative contract by Skanska in 2004.[1252] The northern entrance in Horse Guards Avenue is flanked by two monumental statues, *Earth* and *Water*, by Charles Wheeler. Opposite stands the Gurkha Monument, sculpted by Philip Jackson and unveiled in 1997 by Queen Elizabeth II. Within it is the Victoria Cross and George Cross Memorial, and nearby are memorials to the Fleet Air Arm and RAF (to its east, facing the riverside).

Henry VIII's wine cellar at the Palace of Whitehall, built in 1514–1516 for Cardinal Wolsey, is in the basement of Main Building, and is used for entertainment. The entire vaulted brick structure of the cellar was encased in steel and concrete and relocated nine feet to the west and nearly 19 feet (5.8 m) deeper in 1949, when construction was resumed at the site after World War II. This was carried out without any significant damage to the structure.

Controversies

Fraud

The most notable fraud conviction has been that of Gordon Foxley, Director of Ammunition Procurement at the Ministry of Defence from 1981 to 1984. Police claimed he received at least £3.5m in total in corrupt payments, such as substantial bribes from overseas arms contractors aiming to influence the allocation of contracts.

Germ and chemical warfare tests

A government report covered by *The Guardian* newspaper in 2002 indicated that between 1940 and 1979, the Ministry of Defence "turned large parts of the country into a giant laboratory to conduct a series of secret germ warfare tests on the public" and many of these tests "involved releasing potentially dangerous chemicals and micro-organisms over vast swathes of the population without the public being told." The Ministry of Defence claims that these trials were to simulate germ warfare and that the tests were harmless. However, families who have been in the area of many of the tests are experiencing children with birth defects and physical and mental handicaps and many are asking for a public inquiry. The report estimated these tests affected millions of people, including during one period between 1961 and 1968 where "more than a million people along the south coast of England, from Torquay to the New Forest, were exposed to bacteria including *e.coli* and *bacillus globigii*, which mimics anthrax." Two scientists commissioned by the Ministry of Defence stated that these trials posed no risk to the public. This was confirmed by Sue Ellison, a representative of the Defence Science and Technology Laboratory at Porton Down who said that the results from these trials "will save lives, should the country or our forces face an attack by chemical and biological weapons." Asked whether such tests are still being carried out, she said: "It is not our policy to discuss ongoing research." It is unknown whether or not the harmlessness of the trials was known at the time of their occurrence.Wikipedia:Citation needed

Chinook HC3 helicopters

> "...the most incompetent procurement of all time...might as well have bought eight turkeys."
>
> — Parliamentary public accounts committee

The MOD was criticised for spending £240m on eight Boeing Chinook HC3 helicopters which only started to enter service in 2010, many years after they were ordered in 1995 and delivered in 2001. A National Audit Office report reveals that the helicopters have been stored in air conditioned hangars in Britain since their 2001 Wikipedia:Please clarify delivery, while troops in Afghanistan have been forced to rely on helicopters which are flying with safety faults. By the time the Chinooks are airworthy, the total cost of the project could be as much as £500m.

In April 2008, a £90m contract was signed with Boeing for a "quick fix" solution, so they could fly by 2010: QinetiQ would downgrade the Chinooks—stripping out some of their more advanced equipment.

Territorial Army cuts

In October 2009, the MOD was heavily criticized for withdrawing the bi-annual non-operational training £20m budget for the Territorial Army (TA), ending all non-operational training for 6 months until April 2010. The government eventually backed down and restored the funding. The TA provides a small percentage of the UK's operational troops. Its members train on weekly evenings and monthly weekends, as well as two-week exercises generally annually and occasionally bi-annually for troops doing other courses. The cuts would have meant a significant loss of personnel and would have had adverse effects on recruitment.[1253]

Overspending

In 2013 it was found that the Ministry of Defence had overspent on its equipment budget by £6.5bn on orders that could take up to 39 years to fulfil. The Ministry of Defence has been criticised in the past for poor management and financial control, investing in projects that have taken up to 10 and even as much as 15 years to be delivered.

Bibliography

- Chester, D. N and Willson, F. M. G. *The Organisation of British Central Government 1914–1964*: Chapters VI and X (2nd edition). London: George Allen & Unwin, 1968.

External links

 Wikimedia Commons has media related to *Ministry of Defence (United Kingdom)*.

- Official website[1254]
- www.mod.uk Archived Website[1255]
- Defence Relationship Management[1256]
- Defencemanagement.com[1257]

Appendix

References

[1] Parliament http://www.parliament.uk/business/news/2012/march/speaker-addresses-hm-the-queen/ Speaker addresses Her Majesty Queen Elizabeth II, 20 March 2012

[2] Figure is current as of 1 May 2016. It includes 150,620 Regular and 2,850 Gurkhas, but excludes personnel of the Military Provost Guard Service, Regular Reserves called up for duty and the Sponsored Reserves. UNIQ-ref-0-e98eb6ef29254262-QINU

[3] Figure is current as of 1 April 2015. It includes 35,200 Volunteer Reserve personnel, UNIQ-ref-1-e98eb6ef29254262-QINU 44,600 Regular Reserve and 2,050 Sponsored Reserves. Does not include 6,590 personnel of the University Service Units. Parliament http://www.parliament.uk/business/news/2012/march/speaker-addresses-hm-the-queen/ Speaker addresses Her Majesty Queen Elizabeth II, 20 March 2012

[4] https://www.gov.uk/government/uploads/system/uploads/attachment_data/file/661480/autumn_budget_2017_web.pdf Autumn Budget 2018 Budget (22 November 2017) – see page 5

[5] Exchange rate as of 4 February 2018

[6] Also referred to as the *Armed Forces of the United Kingdom*.

[7] The Mission of the Armed Forces http://www.armedforces.co.uk/mod/listings/l0002.html, armedforces.co.uk

[8]

[9] Nelson's Navy: The Ships, Men, and Organization, 1793-1815 Brian Lavery

[10]

[11] Herwig p. 48–50

[12] Colman (2005), *A 'Special Relationship'?: Harold Wilson, Lyndon B. Johnson, and Anglo-American Relations' at the Summit', 1964–68*, p77

[13] Focus on Europe http://www.raf.mod.uk/rafcms/mediafiles/F21E81DC_E902_D3CE_488720FE8488434D.pdf, raf.mod.uk

[14] Johnman & Gorst (1997), *The Suez Crisis*, p166

[15] Lider (1985), *British Military Thought After World War II*, p525

[16] Lee (1996), *Aspects of British Political History 1914–1995*, 273

[17] Pierre (1972), *Nuclear Politics: the British experience with an independent strategic force: 1939–1970*, p100

[18] Hack (2000), *Defence and Decolonisation in South-East Asia: Britain, Malaya, Singapore, 1941–1968*, p285

[19] Chandler & Beckett (2003), p345

[20] Vanguard to Trident 1945–2000 http://www.royal-navy.mod.uk/server/show/nav.3867 , royal-navy.mod.uk

[21] Kennedy (2004), *British Naval Strategy East of Suez, 1900–2000: Influence and Actions*, p193

[22] Chandler & Beckett (2003), p421

[23] Chandler & Beckett (2003), pp350–351

[24] Frantzen (2005), *Nato And Peace Support Operations, 1991–1999: Policies And Doctrines*, p104

[25] UK Armed Forces Deaths: Operational deaths post World War II 3 September 1945 to 17 February 2016 https://www.gov.uk/government/uploads/system/uploads/attachment_data/file/512070/20160331_UK_Armed_Forces_Operational_deaths_post_World_War_II.O.pdf, Ministry of Defence, gov.uk, Published 31 March 2016

[26] Forces Queen and Armed Forces https://www.royal.uk/search?tags[0]=Queen%20and%20Armed%20, royal.uk.

[27] The current structure of defence management in Britain was set in place in 1964 when the modern day Ministry of Defence (MoD) was created (an earlier form had existed since 1940). The MoD assumed the roles of the Admiralty, the War Office and the Air Ministry.

[28] MOD civilian personnel quarterly report: 2015 https://www.gov.uk/government/statistics/mod-civilian-personnel-quarterly-report-2015, gov.uk, 1 October 2015

[29] Hansard (1998), House of Commons Written Answers https://publications.parliament.uk/pa/cm199798/cmhansrd/vo980512/text/80512w06.htm, publications.parliament.uk

[30] Other Personnel includes personnel of the Military Provost Guard Service, Regular Reserves called up for duty and the Sponsored Reserves.Figure is current as of 1 May 2016. It includes 150,620 Regular and 2,850 Gurkhas, but excludes personnel of the Military Provost Guard Service, Regular Reserves called up for duty and the Sponsored Reserves.Figure is current as of 1 April 2015. It includes 35,200 Volunteer Reserve personnel,https://www.gov.uk/government/uploads/system/uploads/attachment_data/file/661480/autumn_budget_2017_web.pdf Autumn Budget 2018 Budget (22 November 2017) – *see page 5* 44,600 Regular Reserve and 2,050 Sponsored Reserves. Does not include 6,590 personnel of the University Service Units.Exchange rate as of 4 February 2018

[31] //en.wikipedia.org/w/index.php?title=British_Armed_Forces&action=edit

[32] gov.uk MoD – monthly personnel report https://www.gov.uk/government/uploads/system/uploads/attachment_data/file/527838/Monthly_service_personnel_statistics-May_2016.pdf, table 1 page 4. 1 May 2016.

[33] UK Service Personnel is a term used by the Ministry of Defence, and comprises UK Regulars, the Brigade of Gurkhas, the Volunteer Reserve and Other Personnel (I.e the Military Provost Guard Service, Regular Reserves called up for duty and the Sponsored Reserves).

[34] gov.uk MoD – reserves and cadet strengths https://www.gov.uk/government/uploads/system/uploads/attachment_data/file/314795/uk_reserve_force_cadets_2014.pdf, table 4 page 13. See note 2. April 2014.

[35] gov.uk MoD – reserves and cadet strengths https://www.gov.uk/government/uploads/system/uploads/attachment_data/file/435444/20150615_TSP7Apr15-O.pdf, table 1a-page 10. 12 July 1690.

[36] gov.uk MoD – Quarterly Location Statistics https://www.gov.uk/government/uploads/system/uploads/attachment_data/file/522654/20160504-QLS_Front_Page_April16.pdf, 1 April 2016

[37] RUSI Briefing Paper https://rusi.org/system/files/RUSIBriefingPaperSept2011.pdf, Is the UK Defence Budget Crisis Really Over?. Malcolm Chalmers. Published September 2011, P. 18

[38] Royal Navy – Continuous at sea deterrent http://www.royalnavy.mod.uk/news-and-latest-activity/operations/global/continuous-at-sea-deterrent, royalnavy.mod.uk, Accessed 6 December 2014

[39] House of Commons Hansard - Written Statements - Nuclear Deterrent https://publications.parliament.uk/pa/cm201415/cmhansrd/cm150120/wmstext/150120m0001.htm#15012039000004, publications.parliament.uk, 20 January 2015

[40] Permanent Joint Operating Bases (PJOBs) https://www.gov.uk/government/publications/permanent-joint-operating-bases-pjobs/permanent-joint-operating-bases-pjobs, www.gov.uk, 12 December 2012

[41] ("*The White Ensign is still flying above the operations of Naval Party 1022 (NP1022), based at Sembawang Wharves in Singapore.*")

[42] The Royal Gibraltar Regiment http://www.1rg.gi/theregiment/regular/operations.qxp , 1rg.gi

[43] More soldiers from Royal Gibraltar Regiment in overseas duties in regiment's history http://www.panorama.gi/archive/050110/updates.htm#More%20soldiers, www.panorama.gi

[44]

[45] Fleet Command and Organisation http://www.armedforces.co.uk/navy/listings/l0006.html, armedforces.co.uk

[46] Hampshire (1975), *The Royal Navy Since 1945: its transition to the nuclear age*, p248

[47] BBC News (2002), UK's mountain warfare elite http://news.bbc.co.uk/1/hi/uk/1593996.stm, news.bbc.co.uk

[48] The Commando Role for 1 RIFLER http://www.army.mod.uk/infantry/regts/the_rifles/rifles_hq/commando_role.htm, army.mod.uk

[49] Commando Logistic Regiment https://www.royalnavy.mod.uk/static/content/2540.html, royalnavy.mod.uk

[50] Army Command reorganization http://www.dmilt.com/index.php?option=com_content&view=article&id=2506:uk-army-command-reorganization&catid=1:europe&Itemid=57 Defence Marketing Intelligence, 10 November 2011

[51] Higher Command http://www.army.mod.uk/structure/142.aspx

[52] Divisions and Brigades http://www.army.mod.uk/unitsandorgs/divisions_brigades/index.htm, army.mod.uk
[53] Number of Regiments, Infantry battalions & Major Headquarters, in the Regular & Territorial Army at 1 April each year http://www.dasa.mod.uk/natstats/ukds/2006/c3/table32.html, dasa.mod.uk
[54] The Mercian Regiment was formed in August 2007, to become the final regiment created as a result of the infantry amalgamations under FAS
[55] Arms and Services http://www.army.mod.uk/unitsandorgs/arms_and_services/index.htm, army.mod.uk
[56] RAF – Structure http://www.raf.mod.uk/structure/ , raf.mod.uk
[57] Transforming the Royal Air Force http://www.raf.mod.uk/rafcms/mediafiles/628864A8_ EC65_BEBF_C4C64EC02534493A.pdf , raf.mod.uk
[58] Royal Air Force Squadrons http://www.raf.mod.uk/structure/squadrons.cfm, raf.mod.uk
[59] Aircraft Order of Battle http://www.scramble.nl/uk.htm, scramble.nl
[60] Royal Air Force – Equipment http://www.raf.mod.uk/equipment, raf.mod.uk
[61] The Royal Air Force Regiment http://www.raf.mod.uk/structure/rafregiment.cfm, raf.mod.uk
[62] RAF Regiment http://www.armedforces.co.uk/raf/listings/l0041.html, armedforces.co.uk
[63] Evans (2005), How British Army is fast becoming foreign legion http://www.timesonline.co.uk/tol/news/uk/article589974.ece, timesonline.co.uk
[64] BBC News (2007), Recruitment Age for Army Raised http://news.bbc.co.uk/1/hi/uk/6236345.stm, news.bbc.co.uk
[65] UK Armed Forces Quarterly Personnel Report https://www.gov.uk/government/uploads/system/uploads/attachment_data/file/310468/quarterly_personnel_report_apr14.pdf, gov.uk, 1 April 2014
[66] Women in the Armed Forces http://www.mod.uk/DefenceInternet/FactSheets/WomenInTheArmedForces.htm, mod.uk
[67] Tornados and Taliban are all in a day's work http://www.thisisdevon.co.uk/news/Tornados-Taliban-day-s-work-Nikki-navigator/article-1652922-detail/article.html . This is Devon (2009-12-29). Retrieved on 2013-08-24.
[68] https://www.gov.uk/government/organisations/ministry-of-defence
[69] https://web.archive.org/web/20091204170712/http://da.mod.uk/mk
[70] http://www.royalnavy.mod.uk/
[71] http://www.royalnavy.mod.uk/our-organisation/the-fighting-arms/royal-marines
[72] http://www.army.mod.uk/
[73] http://www.raf.mod.uk/
[74] //en.wikipedia.org/w/index.php?title=Template:Royal_Navy&action=edit
[75] Swanton, p. 39
[76] Savage, p. 84
[77] Savage, p. 86
[78] Savage, p. 93
[79] Savage, p. 107
[80] Sarah Foot, *Æthelstan: the first king of England* (2011). p. 165
[81] Swanton, p. 119
[82] Swanton, p. 138
[83] Swanton, p. 160
[84] Swanton, p. 168
[85] Swanton, p. 190
[86] Swanton, p. 196
[87] Graham Cushway, *Edward III and the War at Sea: The English Navy, 1327–1377* (Boydell Press, 2011)
[88] Wagner, p. 322
[89] Arthur Nelson, *The Tudor navy: the ships, men and organisation, 1485–1603* (2001) p. 36
[90] David Loades, and Charles S. Knighton, eds. *The Navy of Edward VI and Mary I* (Ashgate, 2013).
[91] Robert Hutchinson, *The Spanish Armada* (Macmillan, 2014).

[92] Julian S. Corbett, *Drake and the Tudor Navy, With a History of the Rise of England as a Maritime Power* (2 vol 1898) online https://books.google.com/books?id=qs0gAAAAMAAJ
[93] Geoffrey Parker, "The 'Dreadnought' Revolution of Tudor England", *Mariner's Mirror*, Aug 1996, Vol. 82 Issue 3, pp 269–300
[94] Geoffrey Parker, "Why the Armada Failed", *History Today*, May 1988, Vol. 38 Issue 5, pp 26–33
[95] Hutchinson, *The Spanish Armada* (2014).
[96] Winfield, xviii
[97] Barrow, p. 375.
[98] Macdougall, Norman, *James IV*, Tuckewell (1997), 235.
[99] Hay, Denys, *Letters of James V*, HMSO (1954), 26, date of sale 2 April 1514, ?o.s.
[100] Wills, pp. 27-28
[101] Fissel, p. 126-127
[102] Coward 2002, p. 134
[103] Rodger 2004, pp. 76-7
[104] "It can hardly be denied that the Dutch raid on the Medway vies with the Battle of Majuba in 1881 and the Fall of Singapore in 1942 for the unenviable distinctor of being the most humiliating defeat suffered by British arms." – Charles Ralph Boxer: *The Anglo-Dutch Wars of the 17th Century*, Her Majesty's Stationery Office, London (1974), p.39
[105] *Articles of War, 1661, 1749 and 1866 /* (1982)
[106] Ollard, 1984, ch.16
[107] Pemsel, p. 59
[108] Marley, p. 24
[109] Reid 2002, pp. 88–90
[110] Lavery 2012, pp. 126-128
[111] Marshall (1828), Supplement, Part 3, pp.384-88
[112] Theodore Roosevelt, *The naval war of 1812* (1883) online edition http://www.gutenberg.org/dirs/etext05/8trnv10.txt
[113] [[USN http://www.msc.navy.mil/sealift/2004/May/perspective.htm] website]
[114] *The Andrew And The Onions: The Story Of The Royal Navy In Bermuda, 1795–1975*, Lt. Commander Ian Strannack, The Bermuda Maritime Museum Press, The Bermuda Maritime Museum, P.O. Box MA 133, Mangrove Bay, Bermuda MA BX.
[115] Roger Parkinson, *The Late Victorian Navy: The Pre-Dreadnought Era and the Origins of the First World War*, (2008)
[116] Harbottle and Bruce, p. 10
[117] "The Progress of the Japanese War", 4 October 1863, *The New York Times*
[118] Heathcote, p. 120
[119] Royle, p. 606
[120] Day and McNeil, p. 694
[121] Grantham, p. 73
[122] Gardner 2004, p. 154
[123] Lyon p. 8, 9
[124] Pugh, Philip *The Cost of Seapower, the Influence of Money on Naval Affairs from 1815 to the Present Day*, pub Conway, 1986, page 34.
[125] Saibene, Marc *Les Cuirasses Redoutable, Devastation, Courbet, Programme de 1872*, pub Marines edition, pages 72 and 77.
[126] Ranft, Bryan (ed.), *Ironclad to Trident, 100 Years of Defence Commentary, BRASSEYS's 1886–1986*, Brassey's Defence Publishing (part of the Pergamon Group), 1986.
[127] Sondhaus, p. 161.
[128] Jon Tetsuro Sumida, "Geography, Technology, and British Naval Strategy in the Dreadnought Era." Naval War College Review 2006 59(3), p. 89–102.
[129] Brooks, p. 239.
[130] Robert K. Massie, 1991 p. 471
[131] Gardiner, Gray, and Budzbon, p. 86
[132] Herwig p. 48–50
[133] The British Battle-Fleet, Fred T. Jane [1912], p354

[134] UK Retail Price Index inflation figures are based on data from Clark, Gregory (2017). "The Annual RPI and Average Earnings for Britain, 1209 to Present (New Series)" https://measuringworth.com/ukearncpi/. *MeasuringWorth*. Retrieved 6 November 2017.
[135] Harold F. Williamson, *The American Petroleum Industry: the Age of Energy 1899–1959* (1963) 2:267
[136] Marriott, p. 35
[137] Royal Navy in World War 2 http://www.naval-history.net/xDKWW2-3908-01RNships.htm:
[138] " HMS *Hood* 1920 http://www.royalnavy.mod.uk/history/ships/hms-hood-1920/index.htm". Royal Navy
[139] Kennedy, 1989, pp. 570-1
[140] Ballantyne, p. 204
[141] created from data found at and Conways *All the World's Fighting Ships 1947–1995*
[142] https//books.google.com
[143] https//books.google.lk
[144] https://books.google.com/books?id=BHu7AAAAIAAJ
[145] https://books.google.com/books?id=mtwTAAAAIAAJ&dq=1882+alexandria+bombardment
[146] http://www.history.ac.uk/reviews/review/1706
[147] //doi.org/10.14296/RiH/2014/1706
[148] https://books.google.com/books?id=ZOGoCgAAQBAJ&dq=George+Clark++Later+Stuarts+1660-1714&source=gbs_navlinks_s
[149] http://www.royal-navy.org/
[150] http://www.royalnavy.mod.uk/history
[151] http://www.pbenyon.plus.com/Naval_History/Index.html
[152] http://www.nationalarchives.gov.uk/documentsonline/adm196.asp
[153] http://www.nationalarchives.gov.uk/documentsonline/seamenswills.asp
[154] http://www.nationalarchives.gov.uk/documentsonline/royal-navy-service.asp
[155] http://www.worldwar1atsea.net
[156] http://www.naval-history.net/
[157] https//books.google.com
[158] //en.wikipedia.org/w/index.php?title=Template:British_Army&action=edit
[159] //en.wikipedia.org/w/index.php?title=History_of_the_British_Army&action=edit
[160] Mallinson, p.2
[161] Asquith 1981, p. 3.
[162] Mallinson 2009, p. 17.
[163] Churchill 1956, p. 200.
[164] Mallinson, p. 30
[165] As no system is improvised, a precedent for the innovation was to be found in the history of England. Two regiments created in the reign of Henry VIII, still subsist, the *Gentlemen Pensioners* and the *Yeomen of the Guard* formed in those days a sort of transition between the system of accidental armies and permanent armies . The core of Gentlemen Pensioners consisted exclusively of noblemen. In the reign of William IV (17 March 1834) they took the name of Gentlemen at Arms; they are now a ceremonial of body guard who attend at great public ceremonies. The "Yeomen of the Guard" (officers of the King's household) do duty at the Palaces in a uniform of the time of Henry VIII .
[166] Colburn 1860, p. 566.
[167] Colburn 1860, pp. 566–567.
[168] Colburn 1860, p. 567.
[169] UK Statute Law Database http//www.statutelaw.gov.uk
[170] Royal Scots Greys 1840, pp. 56-57.
[171] Mallinson, p. 40
[172] Mallinson, p. 43
[173] Le Mesurier, p. 50
[174] John Armstrong at Oxford Dictionary of National Biography http://www.oxforddnb.com/view/article/659?docPos=4
[175] Mallinson, p. 100

[176] Regimental Museum of the Queen's Lancashire Regiment http://www.qlrmuseum.co.uk/Short%20History.htm
[177] The People's War http://www.bbc.co.uk/ww2peopleswar/stories/87/a8675887.shtml BBC
[178] The Infantry Battalion http://www.thediehards.co.uk/infantry_battalion.htm
[179] Reid, pp. 85-87
[180] Mallinson, p. 104
[181] History and Uniform of the 60th (Royal American) Regiment of Foot, 1755-1760 http://www.militaryheritage.com/60thregt.htm
[182] The Battle of Culloden 1746 http://www.britishbattles.com/battle_of_culloden.htm
[183] Mallinson, p. 106
[184] Anderson, pp. 211-212
[185] Hopson's Grenadiers http://www.militaryheritage.com/40thregt.htm
[186] Mallinson, p. 110
[187] Mallinson, p. 105
[188] Anderson, p. 453
[189] Pontiac's War http://www.umbc.edu/che/tahlessons/pdf/Pontiacs_War(PrinterFriendly).pdf Baltimore County Public Schools
[190] Mallinson, p. 118
[191] Chartrand, p. 11
[192] Mallinson, p. 131
[193] Mallinson, p. 129
[194] Chappell, p. 8
[195] Chandler & Beckett, p. 132
[196] Haythornthwaite (1987), p. 6
[197] Ferguson, p. 15
[198] Peter Burroughs, "An Unreformed Army? 1815–1868", in David Chandler, editor, *The Oxford History of the British Army* (1996), pp 183-84
[199] Orlando Figes, *The Crimean War* (2010) pp 469-71
[200] Survey of a post-medieval 'squatter' occupation site and 19th century military earthworks at Hungry Hill, Upper Hale, near Farnham, p. 251 http://ads.ahds.ac.uk/catalogue/adsdata/arch-379-1/ahds/dissemination/pdf/vol_92/Surrey_Arch_Vol_92_245-254.pdf
[201] Cassidy, p 78
[202] Cassidy, p 79
[203] Chappell, p 4
[204] Chappell, p 3
[205] Ensor, pp. 525–526
[206] Tucker & Roberts, p. 504
[207] Tucker & Roberts (2005), p. 505
[208] Mark I tank https://web.archive.org/web/20071014050900/http://www.bbc.co.uk/history/worldwars/wwone/nonflash_tank.shtml
[209] Willmott & Kindersley, p. 91
[210] Mallinson, p. 322
[211] Stevens, F.A., *The Machine Gun Corps : a short history*. Tonbridge : F.A. Stevens, 1981.
[212] Royal Corps of Signals - Heritage http://www.army.mod.uk/signals/heritage/default.aspx
[213] Irish Regiments in World War I http://www.waterfordcountymuseum.org/exhibit/web/Display/article/31/6/
[214] *Military Innovation in the Interwar Period*, Murray, Williamson & Millett, Allen R., Cambridge University Press (1996),
[215] Technology, Doctrine and Debate: The evolution of British Army Doctrine between the Wars p. 29 http://www.army.forces.gc.ca/caj/documents/vol_07/iss_1/caj_vol7.1_06_e.pdf *Canadian Army Journal*, Vol. 7.1, Spring 2004
[216] Queen, Estonians honour Britain's 'forgotten fleet' http://www.monstersandcritics.com/news/europe/features/article_1212989.php EPA/INGA Kundzina, 20 October 2006
[217] Lord Plumer http://www.kcl.ac.uk/lhcma/locreg/PLUMER.shtml Liddell Hart
[218] *The Original British Army of the Rhine* by Richard A. Rinaldi

[219] Sir Adrian Carton de Wiart http://www.oxforddnb.com/view/article/32316 *Oxford Dictionary of National Biography*
[220] Exploits of Somalia's national hero becomes basis for movie https://news.google.com/newspapers?nid=266&dat=19850615&id=5vsrAAAAIBAJ&sjid=gG0FAAAAIBAJ&pg=2508,6505397 Kentucky New Era, 15 June 1985
[221] Don't be too tragic about Ireland https://www.theguardian.com/news/1921/oct/12/mainsection.fromthearchive *The Guardian*, 12 October 1921
[222] Morris, 1999, p. 136
[223] Mallinson, p. 330
[224] Mallinson, p. 327
[225] Grant and Youens, p. 34
[226] Mallinson, p. 331
[227] The War, Day by Day https://news.google.com/newspapers?id=lE4RAAAAIBAJ&sjid=KJUDAAAAIBAJ&pg=7292,3736980&dq=army+britain+number&hl=en *Sydney Morning Herald*, 26 October 1939
[228] Mallinson, p. 335
[229] Fact file: Reserved Occupations http://www.bbc.co.uk/ww2peopleswar/timeline/factfiles/nonflash/a6652019.shtml BBC
[230] Mallinson, p. 345
[231] Fact file: British Army - Pre-war to Present http://www.bbc.co.uk/ww2peopleswar/timeline/factfiles/nonflash/a6648078.shtml?sectionId=0&articleId=6648078 BBC
[232] Taylor (1976), p. 157
[233] Taylor (1976), p. 191
[234] Taylor (1976), p. 210
[235] Taylor (1976), p. 227
[236] Mallinson, p. 371
[237] History of the United Nations https://www.un.org/aboutun/unhistory/
[238] The North Atlantic Treaty http://www.nato.int/cps/en/natolive/official_texts_17120.htm
[239] The Warsaw Pact, 1955 http://www.fordham.edu/halsall/mod/1955warsawpact.html
[240] Watson and Rinaldi, p. 31
[241] Wilton Park http://www.subbrit.org.uk/rsg/sites/w/wilton_park/ accessed November 2008
[242] Mallinson, p. 384
[243] Parker 2005, p. 224
[244] "Merged regiments and new brigading – many famous units to lose separate identity", *The Times*, 25 July 1957
[245] A Brief History of 145 Brigade http://www.army.mod.uk/documents/general/145Bde_history.pdf
[246] The Blues & Royals http://www.army.mod.uk/armoured/regiments/15461.aspx
[247] The King's Royal Hussars http://www.army.mod.uk/armoured/regiments/15461.aspx
[248] The Royal Regiment of Wales http://www.rrw.org.uk/
[249] The Royal Regiment of Fusiliers http://www.mikebooth2009.com/index.php?option=com_content&view=article&id=23&Itemid=69
[250] National Archives http://www.nationalarchives.gov.uk/catalogue/DisplayCatalogueDetails.asp?CATID=4283&CATLN=3&FullDetails=True&j=1
[251] Java (Withdrawal of Troops) http://hansard.millbanksystems.com/written_answers/1946/apr/16/java-withdrawal-of-troops *Hansard*, 16 April 1946
[252] Somerset Light Infantry http://www2.army.mod.uk/lightinfantry/history_traditions/county_regiments/somli.htm
[253] Clifford, Clark, *Counsel to the President: A Memoir*, 1991, P 20.
[254] Mallinson, p. 402
[255] Mallinson, p. 401
[256] Mallinson, p. 407
[257] Mallinson, p. 411
[258] Hugh McCabe http://cain.ulst.ac.uk/sutton/chron/1969.html
[259] Mallinson, p. 413
[260] Internment - A Chronology of the Main Events http://cain.ulst.ac.uk/events/intern/chron.htm

[261] History – Operation Motorman http://www.museumoffreederry.org/history-motorman.html , Museum of Free Derry. Retrieved 2007-09-02.
[262] O'Brien, p. 55
[263] S.I. No. 377/1999 — British-Irish Agreement Act, 1999 (Commencement) Order, 1999 http://www.irishstatutebook.ie/1999/en/si/0377.html
[264] Operation Banner http://www.armedforces.co.uk/mod/listings/l0018.html
[265] Taylor, Peter (24 July 2002). Six days that shook Britain https://www.theguardian.com/Archive/Article/0,4273,4467433,00.html. *The Guardian*
[266] Falklands Surrender Document http://www.britains-smallwars.com/Museum/Falklands/falkSurrenderDocument.html
[267] Defence (Options for Change) http://hansard.millbanksystems.com/commons/1990/jul/25/defence-options-for-change Hansard, 25 July 1990
[268] *The challenges to NATO: A British view* Sir John Weston, Permanent Representative of the United Kingdom on the North Atlantic Council http://www.nato.int/docu/review/1992/9206-2.htm
[269] Gurkha Brigade history http://www.britains-smallwars.com/malaya/gurkhaROH/history.html
[270] Strategic Defence Review http://www.mod.uk/NR/rdonlyres/65F3D7AC-4340-4119-93A2-20825848E50E/0/sdr1998_complete.pdf Presented to Parliament, 1998
[271] Strategic Defence Review: Joint Helicopter Command http://webarchive.nationalarchives.gov.uk/20060130230333/http://www.mod.uk/issues/sdr/jhc.htm
[272] Delivering Security in a Changing World http://www.mod.uk/NR/rdonlyres/051AF365-0A97-4550-99C0-4D87D7C95DED/0/cm6041I_whitepaper2003.pdf White Paper, 2004
[273] Mallinson, p. 445
[274] Mallinson, p. 446
[275] Mallinson, p. 447
[276] Mallinson, p. 448
[277] Mallinson, p. 478
[278] Mallinson, p. 451
[279] Mallinson, p. 454
[280] Mallinson, p. 463
[281] https://books.google.com/books?id=8lbzKJxqnWEC&lpg=PP1&pg=PA3#v=onepage&q&f=false
[282] https://www.amazon.com/Sickness-Suffering-Sword-1808-1815-Commanders-ebook/dp/B00CM100DW/
[283] https://archive.org/details/oxfordillustrate00davi
[284] http://www.americanrevolution.org/britisharmy.html
[285] https://books.google.com/books?id=8UEIAAAAQAAJ&pg=PA56#v=onepage&q&f=false
[286] https//books.google.com
[287] https://www.amazon.com/Oxford-History-British-Army/dp/0192803115/
[288] https://archive.org/details/cromwellsarmyah00firtgoog
[289] https://archive.org/search.php?query=creator%3A%28j.w.%20fortescue%29
[290] https://openlibrary.org/books/OL7073893M/A_history_of_the_British_army.
[291] https://books.google.com/books?id=ZOGoCgAAQBAJ&printsec=frontcover&source=gbs_ge_summary_r&cad=0#v=onepage&q&f=false
[292] https://books.google.com/books/about/Warrior_Race.html?id=JCaAcdQ2DCAC
[293] https://www.amazon.com/Women-British-Army-1907-1948-History/dp/0415390575/
[294] http://www.nas.gov.uk/guides/military.asp
[295] http://www.historyhome.co.uk/c-eight/ireland/irenorth.htm
[296] http://www.history.ac.uk/ihr/Focus/War/reviews/revgrantSM.html
[297] http://www.Britains-smallwars.com
[298] http://www.national-army-museum.ac.uk
[299] http://www.1914-1918.net
[300] https://web.archive.org/web/20060829135946/http://www.remuseum.org.uk/rem_his_history.htm
[301] http://dl.lib.brown.edu/libweb/collections/askb/
[302] http://www.sabre-mod.uk

303 The Finnish Air Force claims to be the first independent air force in the world. When it was founded on 6 March 1918, it consisted of one aircraft and was commanded by a junior officer. Shores, Christopher. *Finnish Air Force, 1918–1968*. Reading, Berkshire, UK: Osprey Publications Ltd., 1969. ().
304 Orange, p. 33
305 Lord Trenchard
306 Sir Christopher Bullock
307 de la Ferté 1960, p. 108
308 Sea Your History - Interwar: Fleet Air Arm http://www.seayourhistory.org.uk/content/view/454/613/
309 Till 1979
310 Tami Davis Biddle, "British and American Approaches to Strategic Bombing: Their Origins and Implementation in the World War II Combined Bomber Offensive," *Journal of Strategic Studies,* March 1995, Vol. 18 Issue 1, pp 91–144; Tami Davis Biddle, *Rhetoric and Reality in Air Warfare: The Evolution of British and American Ideas about Strategic Bombing, 1914–1945* (2002)
311 RCAF Archives http://www.rcaf.com/archives/archives_features/history/waryears.php
312 Robinson, 2005
313 Norwood, 2013, p. 237
314 RAF Museum British Military Aviation in 1952 http://www.rafmuseum.org.uk/milestones-of-flight/british_military/1952.cfm
315 Burnell, Brian. "Weapon detail and No.15 Squadron data for 1984." http://nuclear-weapons.info/images/1984.PNG *nuclear-weapons.info*. Retrieved 19 January 2011.
316 "Strategic Defence Review 1998: Full Report." http://www.mod.uk/NR/rdonlyres/65F3D7AC-4340-4119-93A2-20825848E50E/0/sdr1998_complete.pdf *Ministry of Defence,* 1998, p. 24.
317 Air of Authority – A History of RAF Organisation – Overseas Commands – Iraq, India and the Far East http://www.rafweb.org/Cmd_O3.htm
318
319 Ashworth 1989, p.26.
320 Evans 1998, pp. 74–75.
321 "Tornados Bound for Kandahar", *Air Forces Monthly*, August 2008 issue, p. 8.
322 From *Jane's Defence Weekly*, 16 March 2011, operational requirements forced the Royal Air Force to deploy one of its two remaining Nimrod R1s two weeks before they were due to be withdrawn.
323 Ministry of Defence, *Statement on Defence 1952*, HMSO, 1952
324 1998 Publication http://www.dasa.mod.uk/natstats/ukds/1998/ukds1998.pdf , dasa.mod.uk
325 Strength of UK Regular Forces by Service and whether trained or untrained at 1 April each year http://www.dasa.mod.uk/natstats/ukds/2006/c2/table27.html , dasa.mod.uk
326 Strength of the Reserve Forces at 1 April each year http://www.dasa.mod.uk/natstats/ukds/2006/c2/table214.html , dasa.mod.uk
327 UK Defence Statistics 2011 published 28 September 2011 http://www.dasa.mod.uk/ukds.pdf
328 UK Defence in Numbers, August 2015, p. 5 https://www.gov.uk/government/uploads/system/uploads/attachment_data/file/467482/20151013-UK_Defence_in_Numbers_screen.pdf
329 Including WRAF personnel
330 DASA statistics http://www.dasa.mod.uk/applications/newWeb/www/apps/publications/pubViewFile.php?content=170&date=2012-02-09&type=pdf&PublishTime=09:30:00
331 Does not includes numbers of personnel with liability for recall
332 DASA statistics http://www.dasa.mod.uk/applications/newWeb/www/apps/publications/pubViewFile.php?content=70&date=2012-05-17&type=pdf&PublishTime=09:30:00
333 Excludes University Air Squadron personnel
334 https://www.worldcat.org/oclc/223965469
335 https://web.archive.org/web/20070222132627/http://www.remuseum.org.uk/specialism/rem_spec_aero.htm
336 https://web.archive.org/web/20061218200955/http://www.remuseum.org.uk/rem_his_special.htm#aero
337 http://www.remuseum.org.uk/corpshistory/rem_corps_part8.htm#equip

[338] http://www.raf.mod.uk/history/
[339] Antony Beevor, Inside the British Army, Corgi Books, 1990, 186-7.
[340] //en.wikipedia.org/w/index.php?title=Template:Nuclear_weapons&action=edit
[341] Clark 1961, p. 9.
[342] Gowing 1964, pp. 17–18.
[343] Clark 1961, p. 5.
[344] Clark 1961, p. 11.
[345] Bernstein 2011, p. 240.
[346] Zimmerman 1995, p. 262.
[347] Gowing 1964, pp. 23–29.
[348] Farmelo 2013, pp. 15–24.
[349] Gowing 1964, pp. 37–39.
[350] Szasz 1992, pp. 3–5.
[351] Gowing 1964, pp. 39–41.
[352] Bernstein 2011, pp. 440–446.
[353] Clark 1961, pp. 54–56.
[354] Hewlett & Anderson 1962, pp. 39–40.
[355] Phelps 2010, pp. 282–283.
[356] Hewlett & Anderson 1962, p. 42.
[357] Gowing 1964, pp. 108–111.
[358] Phelps 2010, pp. 126–128.
[359] Zimmerman 1995, pp. 266–267.
[360] Bernstein 1976, pp. 206–207.
[361] Paul 2000, p. 26.
[362] Bernstein 1976, pp. 206–208.
[363] Bernstein 1976, p. 208.
[364] Gowing 1964, pp. 162–165.
[365] Hewlett & Anderson 1962, p. 277.
[366] Hewlett & Anderson 1962, pp. 285–286.
[367] Gowing 1964, pp. 340–342.
[368] Gowing 1964, pp. 250–256.
[369] Gowing 1964, pp. 226–227, 256–258.
[370] Jones 1985, pp. 246–247.
[371] Szasz 1992, pp. 148–151.
[372] Gowing 1964, pp. 260–268.
[373] Gowing 1964, pp. 236–239.
[374] Gowing 1964, p. 242.
[375] Jones 1985, p. 528.
[376] Szasz 1992, p. 64.
[377] Gowing & Arnold 1974a, p. 93.
[378] Goldberg 1964, p. 410.
[379] Paul 2000, pp. 72–73.
[380] Hewlett & Anderson 1962, pp. 457–458.
[381] Gott 1963, p. 240.
[382] Gowing & Arnold 1974a, pp. 73–77.
[383] Hewlett & Anderson 1962, p. 468.
[384] Gowing & Arnold 1974a, p. 92.
[385] Paul 2000, pp. 80–83.
[386] Paul 2000, p. 88.
[387] Jones 1985, pp. 576–578.
[388] Gowing & Arnold 1974a, pp. 106–108.
[389] Gowing & Arnold 1974a, pp. 105–108.
[390] Botti 1987, p. 61.
[391] Botti 1987, pp. 74–75.
[392] Farmelo 2013, p. 322.
[393] Gowing & Arnold 1974a, p. 21.

[394] Baylis & Stoddart 2015, p. 32.
[395] Wynn 1997, pp. 16–18.
[396] Gowing & Arnold 1974a, p. 174.
[397] Wynn 1997, pp. 6, 18.
[398] Gowing & Arnold 1974a, p. 216.
[399] Wynn 1997, pp. 11–12.
[400] Goldberg 1964, p. 417.
[401] Gowing & Arnold 1974a, pp. 40–41.
[402] Gowing & Arnold 1974a, pp. 176–179.
[403] Cathcart 1995, p. 21.
[404] Gowing & Arnold 1974a, pp. 181–184.
[405] Gowing & Arnold 1974a, pp. 211–213.
[406] Cathcart 1995, pp. 88–89.
[407] Cathcart 1995, pp. 24, 48, 57.
[408] Cathcart 1995, pp. 39–43.
[409] Gowing & Arnold 1974b, pp. 194–196.
[410] Gowing & Arnold 1974a, p. 41.
[411] Gowing & Arnold 1974b, pp. 370–371.
[412] Gowing & Arnold 1974b, p. 386.
[413] Gowing & Arnold 1974b, pp. 430–433.
[414] Gowing & Arnold 1974b, pp. 413–420.
[415] Gowing & Arnold 1974a, pp. 358–360.
[416] Gowing & Arnold 1974a, pp. 245–254.
[417] Hewlett & Duncan 1969, pp. 281–283.
[418] Wheeler 1985–1986, pp. 70–73.
[419] Young 2007, pp. 130–133.
[420] Baylis 1995, pp. 75–76.
[421] Aldrich 1998, pp. 333–339.
[422] Dawson & Rosecrance 1966, pp. 28–29.
[423] Goldberg 1964, pp. 409–429.
[424] Gowing & Arnold 1974b, p. 498.
[425] Cathcart 1995, pp. 138–140.
[426] Aylen 2015, p. 35.
[427] Wynn 1997, p. 92.
[428] Wynn 1997, pp. 55–56.
[429] Gowing & Arnold 1974a, pp. 234–235.
[430] Moore 2010, pp. 112–113, 256.
[431] Aylen 2015, pp. 49–50.
[432] Wynn 1997, p. 56.
[433] Wynn 1997, p. ix, 177.
[434] Brookes 1982, pp. 102, 132.
[435] Wynn 1997, p. 115.
[436] Spinardi 1997, pp. 547–582.
[437] Baylis 1995, pp. 86–87.
[438] Ball 1995, pp. 145–147.
[439] Baylis 1995, pp. 162–163.
[440] Baylis 1995, p. 145.
[441] Baylis 1995, pp. 160–163, 179–185.
[442] Arnold & Pyne 2001, p. 38.
[443] Bernstein 2010, pp. 43–46.
[444] Arnold & Pyne 2001, p. 39.
[445] Arnold & Pyne 2001, pp. 84–87.
[446] Arnold & Pyne 2001, p. 139.
[447] Arnold & Pyne 2001, p. 21.
[448] Arnold & Pyne 2001, pp. 145–146.
[449] Baylis 1994, p. 171.

[450] Hubbard & Simmons 2008, pp. 142–146.
[451] McIntyre 2006, p. 28.
[452] McIntyre 2006, pp. 29–30.
[453] Arnold & Pyne 2001, p. 147.
[454] Dombey & Grove 1992, pp. 8–9.
[455] Baylis 1994, pp. 167–168.
[456] McIntyre 2006, pp. 26–27.
[457] Moore 2010, pp. 103–105.
[458] Wynn 1997, pp. 242–243.
[459] Arnold & Pyne 2001, pp. 149–153.
[460] McIntyre 2006, pp. 34–36.
[461] Hubbard & Simmons 2008, p. 157.
[462] Hubbard & Simmons 2008, p. 162.
[463] Arnold & Pyne 2001, pp. 160–161.
[464] Arnold & Pyne 2001, pp. 160–162.
[465] Arnold & Pyne 2001, pp. 165–167.
[466] Hubbard & Simmons 2008, p. 170.
[467] Arnold & Pyne 2001, pp. 173–174.
[468] Baylis 1994, p. 170.
[469] Hewlett & Holl 1989, pp. 547–548.
[470] Arnold & Pyne 2001, pp. 177–182.
[471] Arnold & Pyne 2001, p. 191.
[472] Baylis 1995, pp. 48, 397–398.
[473] Ball 1995, pp. 71, 78–79.
[474] Baylis 1995, pp. 429–430.
[475] Gott 1963, p. 248.
[476] Bowie & Platt 1984, p. 43.
[477] Epstein 1966, p. 141.
[478] Moore 2010, p. 28.
[479] Baylis 1995, pp. 185–187.
[480] Wheeler 1985–1986, pp. 81–84.
[481] Baylis 1995, p. 416.
[482] Wheeler 1985–1986, p. 83.
[483] Baylis 1995, pp. 110–114.
[484] Wheeler 1985–1986, p. 82.
[485] Young 2007, p. 11.
[486] Stoddart 2014b, p. 195.
[487] Botti 1987, pp. 199–201.
[488] Arnold & Pyne 2001, p. 199.
[489] Botti 1987, pp. 224–225.
[490] Botti 1987, pp. 234–236.
[491] Botti 1987, p. 238.
[492] Macmillan 1971, p. 323.
[493] Ritchie 2015, p. 3.
[494] Moore 2010, p. 35.
[495] Ritchie 2015, p. 4.
[496] //en.wikipedia.org/w/index.php?title=Nuclear_weapons_and_the_United_Kingdom&action=edit
[497] Young 2016, p. 201.
[498] Paul 2000, pp. 200–201.
[499] Wynn 1997, pp. 254–256.
[500] Wynn 1997, p. 258.
[501] Baylis 1995, p. 258.
[502] Wynn 1997, p. 259.
[503] Moore 2010, p. 114.
[504] Moore 2010, pp. 98–99.

[505] Bronk 2014, p. 980.
[506] Wynn 1997, pp. 264–265.
[507] Moore 2010, pp. 114, 256.
[508] Young 2016, p. 212.
[509] Bronk 2014, pp. 978–980.
[510] Bronk 2014, p. 985.
[511] Wynn 1997, pp. 262–263.
[512] Young 2007, p. 994.
[513] Wynn 1997, pp. 266–267.
[514] Moore 2010, pp. 114, 210.
[515] Young 2016, pp. 213–214.
[516] Wynn 1997, pp. 371–372.
[517] Young 2016, pp. 98–99.
[518] Baylis & Stoddart 2015, p. 221.
[519] Moore 2010, pp. 48, 99–100.
[520] Wynn 1997, pp. 358–360.
[521] Wynn 1997, p. 362.
[522] Moore 2010, p. 126.
[523] Hawkings 2002, pp. 42–43.
[524] Moore 2010, pp. 132–133.
[525] Norris & Kristensen 2013, p. 73.
[526] Stoddart 2012, pp. 109, 313.
[527] MacDonald 2006, pp. 59–60.
[528] Moore 2010, p. 130.
[529] Moore 2010, p. 162.
[530] Moore 2010, pp. 221–222.
[531] Stoddart 2012, pp. 220, 314.
[532] Ritchie 2014, pp. 14–16.
[533] Moore 2010, pp. 89–90.
[534] Moore 2010, pp. 104–106.
[535] Moore 2010, pp. 113–116.
[536] Moore 2010, p. 217.
[537] Baylis 1995, pp. 286–288.
[538] Moore 2010, pp. 64–68.
[539] Moore 2010, pp. 118–120.
[540] Moore 2010, pp. 218–220.
[541] Grove 1987, p. 384.
[542] Moore 2010, pp. 168–169.
[543] Jones 2017, p. 371.
[544] Jones 2017, pp. 372–379.
[545] Harrison 1982, p. 30.
[546] Jones 2017, pp. 366–368.
[547] Jones 2017, pp. 380–381.
[548] Middeke 2000, p. 76.
[549] Dumbrell 2006, p. 174.
[550] Moore 2010, pp. 236–239.
[551] Jones 2017, pp. 413–415.
[552] Nailor 1988, pp. 91, 96.
[553] Grove 1987, p. 243.
[554] Ludlam 2008, p. 257.
[555] Stoddart 2012, p. 34.
[556] Middeke 2000, pp. 69–70.
[557] Stoddart 2012, pp. 153–160.
[558] Stoddart 2012, pp. 128–131.
[559] Baylis & Stoddart 2003, p. 128.
[560] Stoddart 2014a, p. 94.

561 Stoddart 2014a, pp. 100–101.
562 Stoddart 2014b, pp. 102–105.
563 Stoddart 2014b, pp. 97, 105.
564 Stoddart 2014b, pp. 197–202.
565 Stoddart 2014b, p. 52.
566 Chalmers 1999, p. 63.
567 Butler & Bromley 2001, p. 10.
568 Point 64, Strategic Defence Review http://www.mod.uk/NR/rdonlyres/65F3D7AC-4340-4119-93A2-20825848E50E/0/sdr1998_complete.pdf , Presented to Parliament by the Secretary of State for Defence, George Robertson, July 1998
569 Ritchie 2008, pp. 7–9.
570 Ritchie 2008, pp. 1–5.
571 Leonard 2014, pp. 210–214.
572 Atomic Weapons Tests in:
573 Sources give slightly varying dates for the request and selection of the site.
574 Arnold & Smith 2006, pp. 215–225.
575 Arnold & Pyne 2001, pp. 96–102.
576 Arnold & Pyne 2001, p. 236.
577 Arnold & Pyne 2001, pp. 195–196.
578 Baylis 2008, p. 462.
579 Wade 2008, p. 209.
580 House of Commons Debate, Nuclear Explosions (Prohibition and Inspections) Bill https://publications.parliament.uk/pa/cm199798/cmhansrd/vo971106/debtext/71106-22.htm#71106-22_head0, Hansard, 6 November 1997 : Column 455
581 Status of CTBT Ratification http://www.basicint.org/nuclear/CTBT/status.htm, British American Security Information Council, last updated on 14 June 2001
582 Wade 2008, p. 210.
583 Young 2007, pp. 118–119.
584 Young 2007, pp. 120–122.
585 Young 2007, pp. 123–124.
586 Young 2007, p. 130.
587 Young 2007, p. 133.
588 Young 2007, p. 58.
589 Grant 2011, pp. 58–62.
590 Wynn 1997, pp. 626–627.
591 Stoddart 2014b, p. 236.
592 Stoddart 2014b, pp. 211–217.
593 Stocker 2004, pp. 13–16.
594 Campbell 1982, p. 22.
595 Openshaw, Steadman & Greene 1983, p. 105.
596 Campbell 1982, pp. 53–54.
597 Wittner 2003, p. 294.
598 Campbell 1982, pp. 124–130.
599 Cocroft & Newsome 2009, p. 25.
600 Bowie & Platt 1984, pp. 63–70.
601 Epstein 1966, p. 145.
602 Arnold & Pyne 2001, p. 65.
603 Epstein 1966, p. 140.
604 Groom 1974, pp. 131–154.
605 Epstein 1966, pp. 146–156.
606 Scott 2012, pp. 116–118.
607 Chalmers 1999, p. 62.
608 Ritchie 2016, pp. 658–659.
609 //doi.org/10.1017/s0260210598003313
610 //www.jstor.org/stable/20097530
611 //www.worldcat.org/oclc/753874620

[612] //www.worldcat.org/oclc/70673342
[613] //doi.org/10.1179/1758120614Z.00000000054
[614] //www.worldcat.org/issn/1758-1206
[615] //www.worldcat.org/oclc/231678791
[616] //doi.org/10.1080/13619469408581287
[617] //www.worldcat.org/issn/1361-9462
[618] //doi.org/10.1080/0141-2390312331279718
[619] //www.worldcat.org/issn/0140-2390
[620] //doi.org/10.1080/01402390020247 26
[621] //www.worldcat.org/oclc/900506637
[622] //doi.org/10.2307/448105
[623] //www.jstor.org/stable/448105
[624] http://adsabs.harvard.edu/abs/2010PhP....12...36B
[625] //doi.org/10.1007/s00016-009-0001-1
[626] //www.worldcat.org/issn/1422-6944
[627] http://www.pugetsound.edu/files/resources/7579_Bernstein%20on%20Frisch%20Peierls%20May%202011.pdf
[628] http://adsabs.harvard.edu/abs/2011AmJPh..79..440B
[629] //doi.org/10.1119/1.3533426
[630] //www.worldcat.org/issn/0002-9505
[631] //www.worldcat.org/oclc/464084495
[632] https://www.rand.org/pubs/reports/R3085.html
[633] //www.worldcat.org/oclc/29212035
[634] //doi.org/10.1080/01402390.2013.770736
[635] //www.worldcat.org/issn/1743-937X
[636] http://www.basicint.org/sites/default/files/PUB010301.pdf
[637] //www.worldcat.org/oclc/78965689
[638] //www.worldcat.org/oclc/1027281129
[639] //www.worldcat.org/oclc/31241690
[640] //doi.org/10.1177/0967010699030001005
[641] //www.worldcat.org/issn/0967-0106
[642] //www.worldcat.org/oclc/824335
[643] http//research.historicengland.org.uk
[644] //www.worldcat.org/issn/1478-7008
[645] //doi.org/10.2307/2009841
[646] //www.jstor.org/stable/2009841
[647] https://www.lrb.co.uk/v14/n20/norman-dombey/britains-thermonuclear-bluff
[648] //www.worldcat.org/oclc/433341082
[649] //doi.org/10.1086/385523
[650] //www.worldcat.org/issn/0021-9371
[651] //www.jstor.org/stable/175321
[652] //doi.org/10.2307/2610825
[653] //www.jstor.org/stable/2610825
[654] //doi.org/10.2307/2611300
[655] //www.jstor.org/stable/2611300
[656] //www.worldcat.org/oclc/3195209
[657] //www.worldcat.org/oclc/611555258
[658] //www.worldcat.org/oclc/946341039
[659] http://www.airforcemag.com/MagazineArchive/Documents/2011/March%202011/0311victor.pdf
[660] //www.worldcat.org/oclc/462212978
[661] //www.worldcat.org/oclc/15081825
[662] //doi.org/10.1080/03071848208523423
[663] //www.worldcat.org/issn/0307-1847
[664] https://web.archive.org/web/20071005024725if_/http://www.awe.co.uk/Images/blue_peacock_tcm6-1992.pdf

[665] http://www.awe.co.uk/Images/blue_peacock_tcm6-1992.pdf
[666] https://www.governmentattic.org/5docs/TheNewWorld1939-1946.pdf
[667] //www.worldcat.org/oclc/637004643
[668] http://energy.gov/sites/prod/files/2013/04/f0/Hewlett%20and%20Duncan%20-%20Atomic%20Shield%20%28complete%29.pdf
[669] //www.worldcat.org/oclc/3717478
[670] http://blog.nuclearsecrecy.com/misc/1989-Hewlett-Holl-AtomsforPeaceandWar.pdf
[671] //www.worldcat.org/oclc/82275622
[672] //www.worldcat.org/oclc/436867016
[673] //www.worldcat.org/oclc/1005663721
[674] http://www.history.army.mil/html/books/011/11-10/CMH_Pub_11-10.pdf
[675] //www.worldcat.org/oclc/10913875
[676] //doi.org/10.1080/14443058.2014.895956
[677] //www.worldcat.org/oclc/845346116
[678] //doi.org/10.1111/j.1475-5661.2006.00196.x
[679] //www.worldcat.org/issn/0020-2754
[680] //www.jstor.org/stable/3804419
[681] //www.worldcat.org/oclc/198741
[682] http://www.mcintyre.plus.com/grapple/MegatonWeaponsMA.pdf
[683] https://muse.jhu.edu/article/9145
[684] //www.worldcat.org/issn/1520-3972
[685] //www.worldcat.org/oclc/428030700
[686] //www.worldcat.org/oclc/231046793
[687] //doi.org/10.1177/0096340213493260
[688] //www.worldcat.org/issn/0096-3402
[689] //www.worldcat.org/oclc/470911157
[690] //www.worldcat.org/oclc/43615254
[691] //www.worldcat.org/oclc/642846903
[692] https://bradscholars.brad.ac.uk/handle/10454/917
[693] //www.worldcat.org/oclc/682883281
[694] //www.worldcat.org/oclc/951512317
[695] //doi.org/10.1080/10736700.2017.1345517
[696] //www.worldcat.org/issn/1073-6700
[697] https://fas.org/wp-content/uploads/2015/03/2015-FAS-UK-NNPP-HEU-final2.pdf
[698] //doi.org/10.1080/07075332.2012.620242
[699] //www.worldcat.org/issn/0707-5332
[700] //doi.org/10.1177/030631297027004001
[701] //www.worldcat.org/issn/0306-3127
[702] //www.jstor.org/stable/285558
[703] https://ssi.armywarcollege.edu/pdffiles/PUB410.pdf
[704] //www.worldcat.org/oclc/56021256
[705] //www.worldcat.org/oclc/951512907
[706] //www.worldcat.org/oclc/870285634
[707] //www.worldcat.org/oclc/900698250
[708] //www.worldcat.org/oclc/23901666
[709] //www.jstor.org/stable/2618068
[710] //www.worldcat.org/oclc/249977055
[711] //www.worldcat.org/oclc/39225127
[712] //www.jstor.org/stable/30036432
[713] //doi.org/10.1162/jcws.2007.9.2.5
[714] //www.worldcat.org/oclc/942707047
[715] //doi.org/10.1177/096834459500200302
[716] https://web.archive.org/web/20140808060720/http://historyinpieces.com/british-nuclear-warheads-1953-2013
[717] http://historyinpieces.com
[718] http://sonicbomb.com/modules.php?name=Content&pa=showpage&pid=111

[719] http://www.sonicbomb.com
[720] http://www.basicint.org/nuclear/UK_Policy/main.htm
[721] https://web.archive.org/web/20060613203050/http://www.skomer.u-net.com/projects/nukes.htm
[722] http://www.mcis.soton.ac.uk/Site_Files/pdf/nuclear_history/Working_Paper_No_1.pdf
[723] Permanent Joint Operating Bases (PJOBs) https://www.gov.uk/government/publications/permanent-joint-operating-bases-pjobs/permanent-joint-operating-bases-pjobs, www.gov.uk, 12 December 2012
[724] ("*The White Ensign is still flying above the operations of Naval Party 1022 (NP1022), based at Sembawang Wharves in Singapore.*")
[725] http://www.bermudaregiment.bm/
[726] http://www.fig.gov.fk/fidf/
[727] http://royalgibraltarregiment.gi/
[728] https://www.youtube.com/watch?v=vQzcbuhra8s
[729] • English Empire (until 1707) • Kingdom of Scotland (until 1707) • British Empire (1707 – 20th century)
[730] Since April 2013, MoD publications no longer report the entire strength of the Regular Reserve, instead, only Regular Reserves serving under a fixed-term reserve contract are counted. These contracts are similar in nature to the Maritime Reserve.
[731] In Royal Navy parlance, "commissioned ships" invariably refers to both submarines and surface ships. Non-commissioned ships operated by or in support of Her Majesty's Naval Service are not included.
[732] Military Aircraft:Written question – 225369 (House of Commons Hansard) http://www.parliament.uk/business/publications/written-questions-answers-statements/written-question/Commons/2015-02-25/225369/, parliament.uk, March 2015
[733] http://royalnavy.mod.uk
[734] 1630–1707Middle Ages–17071707–1800
[735] 1545–1606Middle Ages–16061606–1800
[736] //en.wikipedia.org/w/index.php?title=Template:Royal_Navy&action=edit
[737] Rose, *Power at Sea*, p. 36
[738] Hyde-Price, *European Security*, pp. 105–106
[739] Axe, David (10 August 2016). The Decline of the Royal Navy http://www.maritime-executive.com/editorials/the-decline-of-the-royal-navy. Originally on Reuters. Retrieved 26 September 2017.
[740] Glaze, Ben (4 September 2017). Armed Forces recruitment crisis sees military "running to stand to still", warns report ordered by Downing Street https://www.mirror.co.uk/news/politics/armed-forces-recruitment-crisis-sees-11110597. *Mirror*. Retrieved 26 September 2017.
[741] Getting ship shape: IfM develops a fleet management tool for the Royal Navy http://www.ifm.eng.cam.ac.uk/news/helping-the-royal-navy-manage-its-fleet/#.UTCtHTBkuIU, University of Cambridge.
[742] Rodger, *Safeguard*, pp. 18–30
[743] Swanton, p. 138
[744] Swanton, pp. 154–65, 160–72
[745] Rodger, *Safeguard*, pp. 35–49
[746] Rodger, *Safeguard*, pp. 52–53, 117–30
[747] Rodger, *Safeguard*, pp. 93–99
[748] Rodger, *Safeguard*, pp. 91–97, 99–116, 143–44
[749] Nelson, *Tudor Navy*, p. 36
[750] P. F. Tytler, *History of Scotland, Volume 2* (London: Black, 1829), pp. 309–10.
[751] J. Hunter, *Last of the Free: A History of the Highlands and Islands of Scotland* (London: Random House, 2011), , pp. 106–111.
[752] A. Macquarrie, *Medieval Scotland: Kinship and Nation* (Thrupp: Sutton, 2004), , p. 147.
[753] N. A. M. Rodger, *The Safeguard of the Sea: A Naval History of Britain 660–1649* (London: Penguin UK, 2004), , pp. 74–75.
[754] P. J. Potter, *Gothic Kings of Britain: the Lives of 31 Medieval Rulers, 1016–1399* (Jefferson, NC: McFarland, 2008), , p. 157.

[755] A. Macquarrie, *Medieval Scotland: Kinship and Nation* (Thrupp: Sutton, 2004), , p. 153.
[756] N. A. M. Rodger, *The Safeguard of the Sea: A Naval History of Britain. Volume One 660–1649* (London: Harper, 1997) pp. 74–90.
[757] J. Grant, "The Old Scots Navy from 1689 to 1710", *Publications of the Navy Records Society*, 44 (London: Navy Records Society, 1913–14), pp. i–xii.
[758] S. Murdoch, *The Terror of the Seas?: Scottish Maritime Warfare, 1513–1713* (Leiden: Brill, 2010), , p. 10.
[759] Rodger *Command*, pp. 166–167
[760] E. P. Statham, *Privateers and Privateering* (Cambridge University Press, 2011), , pp. 19–20.
[761] N. Tranter, *The Story of Scotland* https//books.google.com (Neil Wilson, 2012), .
[762] Rodger, *Safeguard*, pp. 221–37
[763] Rodger, *Safeguard*, pp. 238–53, 281–86, 292–96
[764] Rodger, *Safeguard*, pp. 253–71
[765] Hart, Francis Rußel, *Admirals of the Caribbean*, Houghton Mifflin Co., 1922, pp. 28–32, describes a large privateer fleet of 25 ships commanded by Drake in 1585 that raided about the Spanish Caribbean colonies.
[766] Rodger, *Safeguard*, pp. 349–63
[767] Rodger, *Safeguard*, pp. 379–94, 482
[768] Rodger, *Command*, pp. 2–3, 216–17, 607
[769] Rodger, *Command*, pp. 6–8
[770] Rodger, *Command*, pp. 12–16
[771] Rodger, *Command*, pp. 16–18
[772] A. P. van Vliet, "The influence of Dunkirk privateering on the North Sea (herring) fishery during the years 1580–1650", in J. Roding and L. Heerma van Voss (eds.), *The North Sea and Culture (1550–1800)* (Leiden 1996), 150–165, esp. 156.
[773] Rodger, *Command*, pp. 67–76
[774] Rodger, *Command*, pp. 76–77
[775] Rodger, *Command*, pp. 80–85
[776] Rodger, *Command*, pp. 88–91
[777] Rodger, *Command*, pp. 142–52, 607–08
[778] Rodger, *Safeguard*, pp. 395–98; Rodger, *Command*, pp. 33–55, 95–122 Ollard, 1984, ch.16;
[779] N. Macdougall, *James IV* (Tuckwell, 1997), , p. 235.
[780] J. Grant, "The Old Scots Navy from 1689 to 1710", *Publications of the Navy Records Society*, 44 (London: Navy Records Society, 1913–14), pp. i–xii.
[781] T. Christopher Smout, *Scotland and the Sea* (Edinburgh: Rowman and Littlefield, 1992), , p. 45.
[782] S. Murdoch, *The Terror of the Seas?: Scottish Maritime Warfare, 1513–1713* (Leiden: Brill, 2010), , pp. 33–34.
[783] M. Merriman, *The Rough Wooings* (Tuckwell, 2000), p. 181.
[784] S. Murdoch, *The Terror of the Seas?: Scottish Maritime Warfare 1513–1713* (Leiden: Brill, 2010), , p. 50.
[785] J. E. A. Dawson, *Scotland Re-Formed, 1488–1587* (Edinburgh: Edinburgh University Press, 2007), , pp. 181–82.
[786] S. Murdoch, *The Terror of the Seas?: Scottish Maritime Warfare, 1513–1713* (Leiden: Brill, 2010), , p. 172.
[787] N. A. M. Rodger, *The Safeguard of the Sea: A Naval History of Britain 660–1649* (London: Penguin UK, 2004), , p. 197.
[788] John Strype, *Ecclesiastical Memorials*, vol. 3, part 2 (Oxford, 1822), p. 81.
[789] John Strype, *Ecclesiastical Memorials*, vol. 3 part 2 (Oxford, 1822), pp. 67–69, 86–87 https://books.google.com/books?id=upwNAAAAQAAJ&source=gbs_navlinks_s, and G. Buchanan, *History of Scotland*, trans Aikman, vol. 2 (1827), 396, bk. 16, cap. 19: R. Holinshed, Raphael, *Chronicles: Scotland*, vol. 5 (1808), p. 585.
[790] S. Murdoch, *The Terror of the Seas?: Scottish Maritime Warfare, 1513–1713* (Leiden: Brill, 2010), , p. 169.
[791] S. Murdoch, *The Terror of the Seas?: Scottish Maritime Warfare, 1513–1713* (Leiden: Brill, 2010), , p. 168.

[792] R. B. Manning, *An Apprenticeship in Arms: The Origins of the British Army 1585–1702* (Oxford: Oxford University Press, 2006), , p. 118.
[793] S. Murdoch, *The Terror of the Seas?: Scottish Maritime Warfare, 1513–1713* (Leiden: Brill, 2010), , p. 174.
[794] A. I. MacInnes and A. H. Williamson, eds., *Shaping the Stuart World, 1603–1714: The Atlantic Connection* (Brill, 2006), , p. 349.
[795]
[796] Rodger, *Command*, p. 608
[797] Rodger, *Command*, pp. 291–311, 408–25, 473–76, 484–88
[798] Rodger, *Command*, pp. 164–80
[799] Simms pp. 210–11
[800] Beatson, *Memoirs*, pp. 25–27
[801] Browning, *Austrian Succession*, p. 60
[802] Coxe, William. *Memoirs of the kings of Spain of the House of Bourbon*, Volume 3, London 1815. Coxe gives the overall loss of the expedition during the campaign as 20,000 lives lost; Reed Browning considers this "not implausible" (p. 382).
[803] Rodger, *Command*, pp. 234–56
[804] Rodger, *Command*, pp. 263–79, 284
[805] Rodger, *Command*, pp. 277–83
[806] Rodger, *Command*, pp. 284–87
[807] Rodger, *Command*, pp. 330–51
[808] Rodger, *Command*, pp. 351–52
[809] Rodger, *Command*, pp. 353–57
[810] Bown, Stephen R. *Scurvy: How a Surgeon, a Mariner and a Gentleman Solved the Greatest Medical Mystery of the Age of Sail*, Viking 2003.
[811] Parkinson, C. Northcote, *Britannia Rules – the classic age of naval history 1793–1815* (1977), pp. 15–19; Rodger, *Command*, pp. 427–33
[812] Parkinson, pp. 33–37, 45–49; Rodger, *Command*, pp. 435–36, 438–40, 456, 463
[813] Parkinson, pp. 40–45; Rodger, *Command*, pp. 445–50
[814] Parkinson, pp. 54–61; Rodger, *Command*, pp. 457–61
[815] Parkinson, pp. 75–82; Rodger, *Command*, pp. 468–71
[816] Parkinson, pp. 82–84; Rodger, *Command*, pp. 428–29, 435–36, 472
[817] Parkinson, pp. 91–114; Rodger, *Command*, pp. 528–44
[818] Parkinson, pp. 114, 117–18, 131–40; Rodger, *Command*, pp. 542–43, 545–48, 555–57
[819] Parkinson, pp. 120–21; Rodger, *Command*, p. 549
[820] Rodger, *Command*, pp. 564–72
[821] Rodger, *Command*, p. 562
[822] Sondhaus, p. 161.
[823] Margaret Macmillan, *The War That Ended Peace: The Road to 1914* (2013) cover 1890s to 1914; ch 5
[824] Osbourne, Eric W. (2004). *Britain's Economic Blockade of Germany, 1914–1919*. Routledge.
[825] Churchill, Winston.*The Second World War. Vol. 2, Their Finest Hour*.1949 Houghton Mifflin Company:p. 229
[826] " HMS Hood 1920 http://www.royalnavy.mod.uk/history/ships/hms-hood-1920/index.htm". Royal Navy
[827] Kennedy, 1989, pp. 570–71
[828] Eric J. Grove, *Vanguard to Trident*, Naval Institute Press/The Bodley Head, London, 1987
[829] https://www.royalnavy.mod.uk/news-and-latest-activity/news/2013/december/31/131231-duncan-service
[830] " HMS Richmond and HMS Enterprise rescue 541 migrants from the Med https://www.telegraph.co.uk/news/uknews/defence/11962766/HMS-Richmond-and-HMS-Enterprise-rescue-541-migrants-from-the-Med.html". *The Daily Telegraph*. 29 October 2015.
[831] https://www.bbc.co.uk/news/uk-scotland-glasgow-west-40660677
[832] https://www.gov.uk/government/news/ambitious-future-for-naval-shipbuilding-in-the-uk
[833] gov.uk MoD – regular personnel https://www.gov.uk/government/uploads/system/uploads/attachment_data/file/402652/MPR_January_2015.pdf, table 2-page 8. 1 January 2015.

[834] gov.uk MoD – quarterly personnel report https://www.gov.uk/government/uploads/system/uploads/attachment_data/file/402633/quarterly_personnel_report_jan15.pdf, table 2-page 7. 1 January 2015.

[835] dasa.mod – reserves and cadet strengths http://www.dasa.mod.uk/publications/personnel/military/reserves-and-cadets-strengths/2012-04-01/2012-revised.pdf, table 2-page 4. April 2012.

[836] dasa.mod – reserves and cadet strengths http://www.dasa.mod.uk/publications/personnel/military/reserves-and-cadets-strengths/2013-04-01/2013.pdf, table 2-page 12. See note 2. April 2013.

[837] gov.uk MoD – reserves and cadet strengths https://www.gov.uk/government/uploads/system/uploads/attachment_data/file/314795/uk_reserve_force_cadets_2014.pdf, table 2-page 11. April 2014.

[838] Life is breathed back in Lusty http://www.navynews.co.uk/news/1191-life-is-breathed-back-in-lusty.aspx

[839] //en.wikipedia.org/w/index.php?title=Royal_Navy&action=edit

[840] THE FLEET WELCOMES HMS DUNCAN, THE SIXTH AND FINAL TYPE 45 DESTROYER http://www.royalnavy.mod.uk/News-and-Events/Latest-News/2013/September/26/130926-Duncan-commissioned, 26 September 2013

[841] Royal Navy: Type 45 Destroyer http://www.royalnavy.mod.uk/The-Fleet/Ships/Destroyers/Type-45-Destroyers, 28 January 2014

[842] *Grafton* became *Almirante Lynch*, *Marlborough* became *Almirante Condell*, *Norfolk* became *Almirante Cochrane*

[843] Securing Britain in an Age of Uncertainty: The Strategic Defence and Security Review http://www.direct.gov.uk/prod_consum_dg/groups/dg_digitalassets/@dg/@en/documents/digitalasset/dg_191634.pdf?CID=PDF&PLA=furl&CRE=sdsr direct.gov.uk

[844] Royal Marines home page http://www.royalnavy.mod.uk/royalmarines/ on Royal Navy website

[845] Cougar http://www.royalnavy.mod.uk/operations-and-support/operations/auriga/index.htm . Royal Navy. Retrieved on 18 September 2011.

[846] Ministry of Defence | Defence News | Training and Adventure | Royal Navy ready for unforeseen global events http://www.mod.uk/DefenceInternet/DefenceNews/TrainingAndAdventure/RoyalNavyReadyForUnforeseenGlobalEvents.htm. Mod.uk (20 February 2007). Retrieved on 18 September 2011.

[847] Operations in the Gulf http://www.royalnavy.mod.uk/operations-and-support/operations/operations-in-the-gulf/index.htm. Royal Navy. Retrieved on 18 September 2011.

[848] United Kingdom Component Command UKMCC http://www.royalnavy.mod.uk/operations-and-support/operations/united-kingdom-component-command-ukmcc/index.htm. Royal Navy (15 June 2010). Retrieved on 18 September 2011.

[849] Commanding Officer http://www.royalnavy.mod.uk/operations-and-support/operations/iraqi-training-and-advisory-mission-navy/commanding-officer/index.htm. Royal Navy. Retrieved on 18 September 2011.

[850] CTF – Iraqi Maritime http://www.royalnavy.mod.uk/operations-and-support/operations/ctf-iraqi-maritime/index.htm

[851] Five Power Defence Arrangements (FPDA) http://ukinmalaysia.fco.gov.uk/en/about-us/working-with-malaysia/defence-new/five-power-defence-arrangements. Ukinmalaysia.fco.gov.uk (3 March 2009). Retrieved on 18 September 2011.

[852] European Union Naval Force Somalia – Operation Atalanta http://www.eunavfor.eu/. Eunavfor.eu. Retrieved on 18 September 2011.

[853] Parliament http://www.parliament.uk/business/news/2012/march/speaker-addresses-hm-the-queen/ Speaker addresses Her Majesty Queen Elizabeth II, 20 March 2012 [*"The daily example that You set, mirrored by our courageous armed forces of which You are Commander-in-Chief, is extraordinary."*]

[854] MoD Website: people – First Sea Lord and Chief of Naval Staff http://www.mod.uk/defenceinternet/aboutdefence/people/chiefsofstaff/firstsealordandchiefofnavalstaff.htm, accessed 23 July 2013

[855] British Forces Post Office – Ship/unit numbers http://www.bfpo.mod.uk/bfponumbers_ships.htm 4 February 2011

[856] most books on the subject of the Royal Danish Navy
[857] The Dress of the British Sailor HMSO 1957 Badges and Insignia if the British Armed Services published by Adam & Charles Black London 1974 BRD 81 Naval Service Uniform Regulations Chapter 3 (0317) 2009 Naval and Marine Badges and Insignia of WW2 Guido Rosignoli, Blandford Press
[858] //www.worldcat.org/oclc/937652092
[859] http://www.royalnavy.mod.uk/
[860] http://www.royal-navy.org/
[861] http://www.harry-tates.org.uk/
[862] http://3decks.pbwiki.com/
[863] http://www.seayourhistory.org.uk/
[864] http://www.royalmarinesmuseum.co.uk/
[865] http://www.wrecksite.eu/ownerBuilderView.aspx?3695
[866] http://www.navynews.co.uk/
[867] http://www.forcesreunited.org.uk/
[868] https://www.youtube.com/user/RoyalNavyOfficial
[869] https://www.youtube.com/user/TwoSixTV
[870] //en.wikipedia.org/w/index.php?title=Template:Royal_Navy&action=edit
[871] Serco Marine Services - Vessel Management http://www.sercomarine.com/our-services/defence/vessel-management/index.aspx , sercomarine.com, Retrieved 20 June 2014
[872] Launched in 1765 and commissioned in 1778, making *Victory* the world's oldest warship still in commission.
[873] All submarines of the Royal Navy are nuclear-powered.
[874] All submarines of the Royal Navy are nuclear-powered.
[875] *Queen Elizabeth* is the current Fleet Flagship.group=N
[876] *Bulwark* entered 'extended readiness' in late 2016.
[877] *Daring* is acting as a Harbour Training Ship.
[878] *Lancaster* was acting as a Harbour Training Ship until March 2017, when she was towed to Plymouth for refit.
[879] *Clyde* is a modified River-class OPV stationed in the British Overseas Territory of the Falkland Islands.
[880] Forms part of the Faslane Patrol Boat Squadron providing security to nuclear submarines entering and leaving the waters in and around HMNB Clyde.
[881] Forms part of the Faslane Patrol Boat Squadron providing security to nuclear submarines entering and leaving the waters in and around HMNB Clyde.
[882] Permanently based in the British Overseas Territory of Gibraltar. Forms part of the Gibraltar Squadron.
[883] Permanently based in the British Overseas Territory of Gibraltar. Forms part of the Gibraltar Squadron.
[884] *Bristol* is permanently docked at HMS *Excellent*. Formerly a guided missile destroyer, now modified to act as a static training and accommodation ship for both Royal Navy and Cadet personnel.
[885] http://www.royalnavy.mod.uk
[886] http://www.royalnavy.mod.uk/The-Fleet/Ships
[887] //en.wikipedia.org/w/index.php?title=Template:Royal_Navy&action=edit
[888] Smith.2015.
[889] Smith.2015.
[890] Smith.2015.
[891] Smith.2015.
[892] Smith.2015.
[893] Smith.2015.
[894] Smith.2015.
[895] Mackie.pp.215-217.
[896] Mackie.pp.215-217.
[897] Mackie.pp.215-217.
[898] Mackie.pp.215-217.
[899] Mackie.pp.215-217.
[900] Mackie.pp.215-217.

901 Mackie.p.215.
902 Mackie.p.218.
903 Mackie.p.219.
904 Mackie.p.218-219.
905 Mackie.p.218-219.
906 Mackie.p.218-219.
907 https://www.royalnavy.mod.uk/our-organisation/the-fighting-arms/surface-fleet
908 http://www.maritimequest.com/warship_directory/great_britain/pages/royal_navy_main_page.htm
909 Military Aircraft:Written question – 225369 (House of Commons Hansard) http://www.parliament.uk/business/publications/written-questions-answers-statements/written-question/Commons/2015-02-25/225369/, parliament.uk, March 2015
910 http://www.royalnavy.mod.uk/our-organisation/the-fighting-arms/fleet-air-arm
911 //en.wikipedia.org/w/index.php?title=Template:Royal_Navy&action=edit
912 Manning, p. 149
913 Darling, p. 224
914 http://www.aircrewman.org.uk
915 http://www.faaa.org.uk
916 http://www.fleetairarmoa.org
917 http://www.chockheads.co.uk
918 • England (1664–1707) • Great Britain (1707–1801)
919 http://www.royalnavy.mod.uk/royalmarines
920 //en.wikipedia.org/w/index.php?title=Template:Royal_Navy&action=edit
921 Royal Marines Train In Californian Desert http://www.mod.uk/DefenceInternet/DefenceNews/TrainingAndAdventure/RoyalMarinesTrainInCalifornianDesert.htm, mod.uk
922 Royal Netherlands Marine Corps http://www.royalnavy.mod.uk/The-Fleet/The-Royal-Marines/About-the-Royal-Marines/Royal-Netherlands-Marine-Corps, royalnavy.mod.uk
923 Thompson, p. 3
924 Moore 1987, p.41
925 Chappell, pp. 14–15
926 London Gazette http//www.gazettes-online.co.uk, 20 July 1923
927 London Gazette http//www.gazettes-online.co.uk, 16 October 1923
928 Mountbatten, p. 107
929 History of RM deployments http://www.royalnavy.mod.uk/royalmarines/units-and-deployments/3-commando-brigade/brigade-information/history
930 Royal Marines Museum – Suez deployment http://www.royalmarinesmuseum.co.uk/museumresearch/PDFs/Suez%201956.pdf (PDF)
931 Nicholas van der Bijl and Nick Bijl, *The Royal Marines 1939–93*, Osprey Publishing, 1995
932 gov.uk MoD – Royal Navy & Royal Marines quarterly pocket brief https://www.gov.uk/government/uploads/system/uploads/attachment_data/file/373597/20141029_RN_RM_Service_Quarterly_Pocket_Brief_Oct14.pdf, October 2014. See table 1.
933 IISS 2010, pp. 168
934 Joint Committees On Transportation Holds Public Hearing Re: Trans 123 http://www.wisconsin-pinzgauers.org/ www.wisconsin-pinzgauers.org
935 Bridge Card – 11 February 11 http://www.royalnavy.mod.uk/linkedfiles/referencelibrary/ref_library_docs/bridgecard11feb11.pdf
936 Other Units of the Royal marines http://www.royalnavy.mod.uk/royalmarines/units-and-deployments/other-royal-marine-units/ on Royal Navy website
937 Commando Units To Be Reshaped http://www.navynews.co.uk/articles/2000/0012/0000122901.asp#, Navy News article
938 comukamphibfor http://www.royal-navy.mod.uk/training-and-people/the-rn-today/navy-command-headquarters/fleet-battle-staff/comukamphibfor/index.htm
939 Commando Helicopter Force webpage http://www.royalnavy.mod.uk/operations-and-support/establishments/naval-bases-and-air-stations/rnas-yeovilton/commando-helicopter-force/
940 Recruitment Process Royal Marines http://www.royalnavy.mod.uk/Careers/How-To-Join/Recruitment-Process/Royal-Marines, royalnavy.mod.uk

[941] Admiralty Interview Board (pdf) http://www.royalnavy.mod.uk/Careers/Explore-Opportunities/~/media/Files/CNR-PDFs/Admiralty%20Interview%20Board.pdf, royalnavy.mod.uk

[942] Commando specialisations http://www.royalnavy.mod.uk/Careers/Maritime-Reserves/Royal-Marine-Reserves/Training-and-Education/Commando-specialisations, royalnavy.mod.uk

[943] https://books.google.com/books?id=sJdPAAAAYAAJ

[944] https://www.royalnavy.mod.uk/our-organisation/the-fighting-arms/royal-marines

[945] http://www.royalnavy.mod.uk/royalmarines/

[946] http://www.royalmarinesbands.co.uk/

[947] http://www.royalmarinescadetsportsmouth.co.uk/

[948] http://www.nationalarchives.gov.uk/documentsonline/royalmarines.asp

[949] http://www.royalmarines.uk/

[950] https://web.archive.org/web/20090107042128/http://rumration.co.uk/

[951] http://www.royalmarinesmuseum.co.uk/

[952] https://archive.is/20061008143134/http://www.mscos.ac.uk/

[953] http://www.naval-history.net/WW2aaRN-PayTables00Ranks-Badges.htm

[954] http://www.naval-history.net/WW2CampaignsRNHons.htm

[955] http://www.royalnavy.mod.uk/news-and-events/reference-library/~/media/files/navy-pdfs/news-and-events/naval%20publications/br%203book/an40e.pdf

[956] //en.wikipedia.org/w/index.php?title=Template:Royal_Navy&action=edit

[957] Antarctic Patrol http://www.royalnavy.mod.uk/news-and-latest-activity/operations/south-atlantic/antarctic-patrol, royalnavy.mod.uk, Retrieved 1 June 2014

[958] Atlantic Patrol Tasking North http://www.royalnavy.mod.uk/news-and-latest-activity/operations/north-atlantic/atlantic-patrol-tasking-north, royalnavy.mod.uk, Retrieved 1 June 2014

[959] Tony Skinner, 'RN cuts back Standing Task commitments,' Jane's Defence Weekly, 20 July 2005, p.12

[960] Atlantic Patrol Tasking South http://www.royalnavy.mod.uk/news-and-latest-activity/operations/south-atlantic/atlantic-patrol-tasking, royalnavy.mod.uk, Retrieved 1 June 2014

[961] Falkland Islands Patrol Task http://www.royalnavy.mod.uk/news-and-latest-activity/operations/south-atlantic/falkland-islands-patrol-vessel, royalnavy.mod.uk, Retrieved 1 June 2014

[962] Standing NATO Maritime Group 1 and 2 http://www.aco.nato.int/page13615814.aspx, aco.nato.int, Retrieved 2 June 2014

[963] HMS Iron Duke deploys http://www.royalnavy.mod.uk/news-and-latest-activity/news/2016/january/11/160111-iron-duke-deploys, royalnavy.mod.uk, January 2016

[964] Cold Weather Training http://www.royalnavy.mod.uk/news-and-latest-activity/operations/arctic-and-northern-european-waters/norway-cold-weather, royalnavy.mod.uk, Retrieved 2 February 2015

[965] Fishery Protection http://www.royalnavy.mod.uk/news-and-latest-activity/operations/uk-home-waters/fishery-protection

[966] House of Commons Hansard Written Answers https://publications.parliament.uk/pa/cm201314/cmhansrd/cm140127/text/140127w0002.htm#140127w0002.htm_wqn32 (publications.parliament.uk) 27 January 2014

[967] Training http://www.royalnavy.mod.uk/news-and-latest-activity/operations/uk-home-waters/training, royalnavy.mod.uk, Retrieved 2 June 2014

[968] Joint Warrior http://www.royalnavy.mod.uk/news-and-latest-activity/operations/uk-home-waters/joint-warrior, royalnavy.mod.uk, Retrieved 2 June 2014

[969] CTF 150 http://www.royalnavy.mod.uk/news-and-latest-activity/operations/indian-ocean/ctf-150, royalnavy.mod.uk, Retrieved 2 June 2014

[970] UK boosts help for tsunami victims https://www.theguardian.com/uk/2004/dec/31/tsunami2004.politics1, theguardian.com, 31 December 2004

[971] Search For MH370 http://www.royalnavy.mod.uk/news-and-latest-activity/operations/indian-ocean/mh370-search, royalnavy.mod.uk, Retrieved 2 June 2014

972 Spanish Ambassador Visits Operational Headquarters in the United Kingdom http://eunavfor.eu/the-spanish-ambassador-to-united-kingdom-visits-eu-naval-force-operational-headquarters/, eunavfor.eu, 28 May 2014
973 Operation Kipion http://www.royalnavy.mod.uk/news-and-latest-activity/operations/red-sea-and-persian-gulf/kipion, royalnavy.mod.uk, Retrieved 2 June 2014
974 Operation Kipion Mine Countermeasures http://www.royalnavy.mod.uk/news-and-latest-activity/operations/red-sea-and-persian-gulf/kipion-mcmv, royalnavy.mod.uk, Retrieved 27 April 2014
975 Continuous At Sea Deterrent http://www.royalnavy.mod.uk/news-and-latest-activity/operations/global/continuous-at-sea-deterrent, royalnavy.mod.uk, Retrieved 2 June 2014
976 International Partnerships http://www.royalnavy.mod.uk/what-we-do/international-partnerships, royalnavy.mod.uk, Retrieved 2 June 2014
977 Royal Navy ready for unforeseen global events https://www.gov.uk/government/news/royal-navy-ready-for-unforeseen-global-events, gov.uk, 9 May 2011
978 Royal Navy sails for annual 'Cougar' deployment http://www.royalnavy.mod.uk/news-and-latest-activity/news/2013/august/09/130809-cougar-13, royalnavy.mod.uk, 09 August 2013
979 Royal Navy set for Cougar 13 https://www.gov.uk/government/news/royal-navy-set-for-cougar-13, gov.uk, 08 August 2013
980 Royal Navy sharpens claws for Exercise Omani Cougar http://www.royalnavy.mod.uk/news-and-latest-activity/news/2013/october/25/131025-rn-sharpens-claws, royalnavy.mod.uk, 25 October 2013
981 NATO Mine Countermeasures http://www.royalnavy.mod.uk/news-and-latest-activity/operations/mediterranean-and-black-sea/nato-mcmv, royalnavy.mod.uk, Retrieved 2 June 2014
982 Gibraltar Squadron http://www.royalnavy.mod.uk/news-and-latest-activity/operations/mediterranean-and-black-sea/gibraltar-squadron, royalnavy.mod.uk, Retrieved 2 June 2014
983 https://www.royalnavy.mod.uk/news-and-latest-activity/news/2018/february/06/180206-hms-albion-deploys
984 Operation Patwin http://www.royalnavy.mod.uk/news-and-latest-activity/operations/pacific/patwin, royalnavy.mod.uk, Retrieved 2014
985 HMS Lancaster deploys http://www.royalnavy.mod.uk/news-and-latest-activity/news/2015/march/23/150323-hms-lancaster-deploys, royalnavy.mod.uk, Retrieved March 2015
986 HMS Dragon leaves Portsmouth on deployment http://www.royalnavy.mod.uk/news-and-latest-activity/news/2014/october/27/141027-hms-dragon-leaves-portsmouth-on-deployment, royalnavy.mod.uk,Retrieved 2015
987 Royal Navy joins partners in Asia-Pacific region http://www.royalnavy.mod.uk/news-and-latest-activity/news/2016/april/15/160415-asia-partnership, royalnavy.mod.uk, 15/04/2016
988 http://www.royalnavy.mod.uk/Operations/Current-Operations
989 //en.wikipedia.org/w/index.php?title=Template:Royal_Navy_ship_types&action=edit
990 http://www.royalnavy.mod.uk/The-Fleet/Medics-and-Chaplains/Medical-Services/Medical-Departments/Institute-Naval-Medicine
991 ("*The White Ensign is still flying above the operations of Naval Party 1022 (NP1022), based at Sembawang Wharves in Singapore.*")
992 Hampshire Railways Remembered. Kevin Robertson & Leslie Oppitz. 1988. p97
993 https://web.archive.org/web/20121017123254/http://veterans-uk.info/about_us/greenwich.html
994 https://web.archive.org/web/20130204011728/http://www.rnhstonehousereunion.org.uk/
995 Signal!: A History of Signalling in the Royal Navy, Barrie H. Kent, Permanent Publications, 2004 https://books.google.com/books?id=gGLm1lhzu8AC&pg=PA94
996 http://www.unithistories.com/units_british/RN_CoastalForces.html#Shore%20establishments
997 http://www.combinedops.com/Training%20EST%20UK.htm
998 A. Metaxas, "Metaxas' Personal Authoritative Manual on Naval Traditions"
999 http://www.naval-history.net/WW2aaNavalLife-Customs1.htm
1000 http://www.naval-history.net/xGM-Pers-Officer-Ratings.htm
1001 English/Scottish parliamentary control 1689, British parliamentary control 1707. UNIQ-ref-0-e98eb6ef29254262-QINU

[1002] • English Empire (1660–1707) • Kingdom of Scotland (1660–1707) • British Empire (1707–20th century)
[1003] Figure current as of 1 May 2018. Includes approx. 4000 soldiers who have completed basic Phase 1 training, but who have not completed trade-specific Phase 2 training
[1004] Figure current as of 1 May 2018.
[1005] https://www.army.mod.uk/
[1006] 1707–1800
[1007] //en.wikipedia.org/w/index.php?title=Template:British_Army&action=edit
[1008] David G. Chandler, ed., *The Oxford history of the British army* (1996) pp 24–45.
[1009] Rogers 1968, pp. 207–211.
[1010] Lord Macaulay *The History of England from the accession of James the Second* (C.H. Firth ed. 1913) 1:136-38
[1011] David Chandler, *The Oxford History of the British Army* (2003) p. 46. https://books.google.com/books?id=ZOgs8WpJI9AC&lpg=PA45&dq=british%20army%20founded%201660&pg=PA46#v=onepage&q=british%20army%20founded%201660&f=false
[1012] David Chandler, *The Oxford History of the British Army* (2003) p. 47. https://books.google.com/books?id=ZOgs8WpJI9AC&lpg=PA45&dq=british%20army%20founded%201660&pg=PA47#v=onepage&q=british%20army%20founded%201660&f=false
[1013] Mallinson, p.2
[1014] David Chandler, *The Oxford History of the British Army* (2003) p. xvi–xvii
[1015] Chandler, ed., *The Oxford history of the British army* (1996) pp 46–57.
[1016] Correlli Barnett, *Britain and her army, 1509–1970: a military, political and social survey* (1970) pp 90–98, 110–25.
[1017] Royal Scots Greys 1840, pp. 56–57.
[1018] Pontiac's War http://www.umbc.edu/che/tahlessons/pdf/Pontiacs_War(PrinterFriendly).pdf Baltimore County Public Schools
[1019] The 1798 Irish Rebellion http://www.bbc.co.uk/history/british/empire_seapower/irish_reb_01.shtml BBC
[1020] Chisholm 1911, p. 3.
[1021] Taylor 1976, p. 157.
[1022] Gilbert 2005, p. 301.
[1023] Taylor 1976, p. 210.
[1024] Army ending its operation in NI http://news.bbc.co.uk/1/hi/northern_ireland/6923342.stm BBC News, 31 July 2007
[1025] Bloomfield, K Stormont in Crisis (Belfast 1994) p 114
[1026] PRONI: Cabinet conclusions file CAB/4/1460
[1027] McKernan 2005, p. 17.
[1028] Army dismantles NI post http://news.bbc.co.uk/1/hi/northern_ireland/859388.stm BBC News, 31 July 2000
[1029] Army To Dismantle Tower Block Post http://www.skyscrapernews.com/news.php?ref=391 Skyscrapernews, 2 August 2005
[1030] Remembrance Day: Where they fell https://www.bbc.co.uk/news/uk-11743727 BBC News, 13 November 2010
[1031] UK sends 500 more to Afghanistan http://news.bbc.co.uk/1/hi/8305922.stm BBC News, 15 October 2009
[1032] British Army: Regular Reserve http://www.army.mod.uk/reserve/31789.aspx, 27 January 2014
[1033] dasa.mod – reserves and cadet strengths http://www.dasa.mod.uk/publications/personnel/military/reserves-and-cadets-strengths/2013-04-01/2013.pdf, table 3-page 13 – read note 2. April 2013.
[1034] dasa.mod – reserves and cadet strengths http://www.dasa.mod.uk/publications/personnel/military/reserves-and-cadets-strengths/2012-04-01/2012-revised.pdf, table 3-page 5. April 2012.
[1035] gov.uk MoD – reserves and cadet strengths https://www.gov.uk/government/uploads/system/uploads/attachment_data/file/435444/20150615_TSP7Apr15-O.pdf, table 1a-page 10. 1 April 2015.
[1036] 1710–1900,<ref name="Rasler"> (Figure 8.1 Change in the Size of the British Army 1650–1910)

[1037] (Table 2a – Strength of UK Armed Forces1 – full-time trained and untrained personnel)
[1038] (Table 1 – Strengths of All Services Reserves)
[1039] Challenger 2 http://www.baesystems.com/ProductsServices/l_and_a_ls_challenger.html BA Systems
[1040] "UKDS 2013" http://www.dasa.mod.uk/publications/equipment/CFE-vehicles-and-aircraft/2013/2013.pdf
[1041] 105 mm Light Gun http://www.baesystems.com/ProductsServices/l_and_a_ls_105mm_light_gun.html BAe Systems
[1042] Starstreak II sighted http://www.janes.com/events/exhibitions/dsei2007/sections/daily/day1/starstreak-ii-sighted.shtml Janes
[1043] Ripley 2008, p. 10.
[1044] Somme Barracks (Cyprus) http://hansard.millbanksystems.com/written_answers/2001/mar/26/somme-barracks-cyprus Hansard, 26 March 2001
[1045] Falklands Forces Have A Vital Role To Play https://web.archive.org/web/20110430045552/http://www.falklandnews.com/public/story.cfm?get=3878&source=7 Falkland Islands News Network, 3 May 2006
[1046] Defence review: Cameron unveils armed forces cuts https://www.bbc.co.uk/news/uk-politics-11570593, BBC News Retrieved 19 October 2010.
[1047] Royal Gibraltar Regiment trains in the UK http://www.mod.uk/DefenceInternet/DefenceNews/TrainingAndAdventure/RoyalGibraltarRegimentTrainsInTheUk.htm Defence News, 13 May 2010
[1048] //en.wikipedia.org/w/index.php?title=Template:British_Army_Arms&action=edit
[1049] Army Briefing Note 120/14, Newly formed Force Troops Command Specialist Brigades: "It commands all of the Army's Intelligence, Surveillance and Electronic Warfare assets, and is made up of units specifically from the former 1 Military Intelligence Brigade and 1 Artillery Brigade, as well as 14 Signal Regiment, 21 and 23 SAS®."
[1050] DefenceNews ArticleRoyal Anglian soldiers boost Bermuda Regiment http://www.mod.uk/DefenceInternet/DefenceNews/TrainingAndAdventure/RoyalAnglianSoldiersBoostBermudaRegiment.htm Defence News, 19 January 2011,
[1051] Royal Gibraltar Regiment trains in UK http://www.mod.uk/DefenceInternet/DefenceNews/TrainingAndAdventure/RoyalGibraltarRegimentTrainsInUk.htm Defence News, 12 May 2011
[1052] Title; Honorary or posthumous rank; war time rank; ceremonial rank
[1053] https://books.google.com/?id=lXkvEIUmg68C&pg=PA25&dq=%22nationalist+Boxers%22#v=onepage&q=%22nationalist%20Boxers%22&f=false
[1054] http://news.bbc.co.uk/1/hi/uk/6236345.stm
[1055] https://www.webcitation.org/5uKh1JTZ7?url=http://news.bbc.co.uk/1/hi/uk/6236345.stm
[1056] http://news.bbc.co.uk/1/hi/uk/7749793.stm
[1057] https://www.theguardian.com/stage/2010/may/19/war-musical-lads-in-their-hundreds
[1058] https//books.google.com
[1059] http://www.belfasttelegraph.co.uk/news/local-national/uk/british-army-sees-more-irish-recruits-15022631.html
[1060] https://www.theguardian.com/uk/2008/apr/05/military.defence
[1061] https://www.webcitation.org/5uKh00P9q?url=http://www.guardian.co.uk/uk/2008/apr/05/military.defence
[1062] http://www.oed.com/view/Entry/269065?redirectedFrom=rupert
[1063] http://www.oed.com/view/Entry/197006?rskey=1LEQ6y&result=2&isAdvanced=false
[1064] https://books.google.com/books?id=8UEIAAAAQAAJ&pg=PA56#v=onepage&q&f=false
[1065] http://www.timesonline.co.uk/tol/news/uk/article4724617.ece
[1066] https://news.google.com/newspapers?id=lE4RAAAAIBAJ&sjid=KJUDAAAAIBAJ&pg=7292,3736980&dq=army+britain+number&hl=en
[1067] http://www.parliament.uk/briefing-papers/SN05951.pdf
[1068] http://www.army.mod.uk/
[1069] //en.wikipedia.org/w/index.php?title=Template:British_Army&action=edit
[1070] SpecterOS™ 4X sight by Raytheon ELCAN selected for UK MoD FIST programme http://www.elcan.com/Our_Company/BulletinFiles/090910_UKMoDFIST_chooses_SpecterOS4x.php (elcan.com)

[1071] New Army Kit Helps Soldiers See More Clearly https://www.gov.uk/government/news/new-army-kit-helps-soldiers-see-more-clearly (gov.uk)
[1072] "British Military Adopts Glock 17 Generation 4" http://modernserviceweapons.com/?p=1687 - Modernserviceweapons.com, 12 January 2013
[1073] *The Illustrated Directory of 20th Century Guns.* Salamander Books Ltd.
[1074] Kommando International Special Operations Magazine, K-ISOM, Ausgabe 5, Mai/Juni 2009
[1075] Light Infantry and Regular-Reserve Integration http://www.sasc-comrades.org/Journal_docs/SECTION_3_14.pdf, sasc-comrades.org, Accessed 3 December 2014
[1076] http://ukarmedforcescommentary.blogspot.co.uk
[1077] House of Commons Hansard Written Answers for 13 Nov 2007 (pt 0010) http://www.parliament.the-stationery-office.com/pa/cm200708/cmhansrd/cm071113/text/71113w0010.htm
[1078] Hansard 2016 https://publications.parliament.uk/pa/cm201213/cmhansrd/cm120627/text/120627w0001.htm
[1079] House of Commons Hansard Written Answers https://publications.parliament.uk/pa/cm201314/cmhansrd/cm130904/text/130904w0001.htm#1309053000011 (publications.parliament.uk), September 2013
[1080] Defence Equipment and Support https://www.gov.uk/government/uploads/system/uploads/attachment_data/file/417372/20150326_DE_S_Corporate_Plan_Final.pdf, gov.uk, page 25
[1081] https://medium.com/war-is-boring/the-british-army-secretly-sent-israeli-missiles-in-iraq-and-afghanistan-3cc1f62437ea
[1082] Artillery Soldier Roles - British Army https://web.archive.org/web/20090331110726/http://www.army.mod.uk/artillery/career/8020.aspx
[1083] http://www.deagel.com/Artillery-Systems/Centurion_a001641004.aspx
[1084] UK MoD contracts Babcock Phalanx Work https://www.shephardmedia.com/news/imps-news/uk-mod-contracts-babcock-phalanx-work/
[1085] House of Commons Hansard Written Answers https://publications.parliament.uk/pa/cm201314/cmhansrd/cm140212/text/140212w0003.htm#140212187000022 (publications.parliament.uk), February 2014
[1086] WWL ships JCB military excavators to the UK http://www.2wglobal.com/www/newsFeatures/newsShowPages/show_wwwpress.jsp?newsRepository=wwwpress&oid=21146 (2wglobal.com)
[1087] House of Commons Hansard Written Answers https://publications.parliament.uk/pa/cm201213/cmhansrd/cm120627/text/120627w0001.htm (publications.parliament.uk), July 2012
[1088] ALC - C VEHICLE CAPABILITY (PDF) http://www.alcvehicles.com/pdfs/alc%20trifold%20v4%20final.pdf, alcvehicles.com
[1089] Army Vehicles and Equipment (PDF) http://www.army.mod.uk/documents/general/285986_ARMY_VEHICLESEQUIPMENT_V12.PDF_web.pdf , army.mod.uk
[1090] "Newest Munitions Disposal Vehicle Is Launched" http//webarchive.nationalarchives.gov.uk MoD Defence News
[1091] GD MOWAG's Duro Light Vehicle Family Racking Up Wins http://www.defenseindustrydaily.com/gd-mowags-duro-light-vehicle-family-racking-up-wins-01648/ (defenseindustry-daily.com)
[1092] "The Royal Logistic Corps" http://www.armedforces.co.uk/army/listings/l0146.html (www.armedforces.co.uk)
[1093] House of Commons Hansard Written Answers https://publications.parliament.uk/pa/cm201314/cmhansrd/cm140212/text/140212w0003.htm#140212187000022 (publications.parliament.uk), 12 February 2014
[1094] Neville (2011), p. 42
[1095] Jane's Defence Weekly, 16 April 2014, Page 26
[1096] British Army - Assault boats & landing craft http://www.army.mod.uk/equipment/23211.aspx, Retrieved 21 June 2014
[1097] *Storm* (WB41), *Diablo* (WB42), *Mistral* (WB43) and *Sirocco* (WB44)
[1098] Support Vehicle http://www.army.mod.uk/equipment/23268.aspx, army.mod.uk
[1099] Supply of Modular Assault Rifle System http://www.government-online.net/supply-of-modular-assault-rifle-system/, government-online.net

[1100] Defence Equipment and Support - Corporate Plan - 2016 - 2019 https://www.gov.uk/government/uploads/system/uploads/attachment_data/file/526950/DES_Corporate_Plan_201619-20160526.pdf Ministry of Defence.
[1101] http://www.dtic.mil/ndia/2014tactical/SessionIIIRafferty.pdf
[1102] http://www.army.mod.uk/equipment/equipment.aspx
[1103] http://www.arrse.co.uk/wiki/Category:Equipment
[1104] http://www.armedforces.co.uk/armyindex.htm
[1105] http://discovermilitary.com/?s=british+army
[1106] http://www.eliteukforces.info/
[1107] //en.wikipedia.org/w/index.php?title=Template:British_Army&action=edit
[1108] Correspondence from Army Secretariat http://www.whatdotheyknow.com/request/92060/response/228969/attach/3/20111121%20FOI%20Cross%20Response%20V2%20U.pdf
[1109] Army Command reorganization http://www.dmilt.com/index.php?option=com_content&view=article&id=2506:uk-army-command-reorganization&catid=1:europe&Itemid=57 Defence Marketing Intelligence, 10 November 2011
[1110] Higher Command http://www.army.mod.uk/structure/142.aspx
[1111] Charles Heyman, 'The British Army: A Pocket Guide 2012-2013', p.31
[1112] Briefing Paper SN06038 Defence Basing Review: Headline Decisions http://www.parliament.uk/briefing-papers/SN06038.pdf House of Commons Library
[1113] Army Basing Plan: The basing plan table labels them as "Armoured Infantry Brigades" https://www.gov.uk/government/uploads/system/uploads/attachment_data/file/136406/regular_army_basing_plan.pdf
[1114] Army Basing Plan: The basing plan table labels them in order https://www.gov.uk/government/uploads/system/uploads/attachment_data/file/136406/regular_army_basing_plan.pdf
[1115] Transforming the British Army Annex A http://www.rfca-yorkshire.org.uk/files/TransformingtheBritishArmyAnnexA.pdf
[1116] Transforming the British Army Annex C http://www.rfca-yorkshire.org.uk/files/TransformingtheBritishArmyAnnexC.pdf
[1117] Major Army sites - basing https://www.gov.uk/government/uploads/system/uploads/attachment_data/file/136421/major_army_sites_basing.pdf
[1118] http://www.army.mod.uk/structure/structure.aspx
[1119] http://www.sabre.mod.uk/
[1120] http://www.royal.gov.uk/MonarchUK/ArmedForces/QueenandtheArmedForces.aspx
[1121] //en.wikipedia.org/w/index.php?title=Template:British_Army&action=edit
[1122] Young, p.25 para 1
[1123] Young, p.25. para 4
[1124] Young, p.26, para 1
[1125] The New Cambridge Modern History: Vol. 7: The Old Regime, p. 183, para 4
[1126] The Oxford History of the British Army, p. 132, para 1
[1127] The Oxford History of the British Army, p.132, para 2
[1128] Cookson, Page 111, para 3
[1129] The Oxford History of the British Army, p.137, para 2
[1130] The Oxford History of the British Army, p.138, para 1
[1131] The Oxford History of the British Army, p.138, para 2
[1132] Chandler & Beckett, p. 132
[1133] The Oxford History of the British Army, p.143
[1134] Holmes, R. (2002) *Redcoat: The British Soldier in the Age of Horse and Musket* pg 158
[1135] The Oxford History of the British Army, p.147
[1136] *The Oxford History of the British Army*, p.163, para 3
[1137] The Oxford History of the British Army, p.164, para 2
[1138] McElwee, pp.71-73
[1139] Farwell, pp.157, 166
[1140] The Oxford History of the British Army, p.211, para 1
[1141] Young, p.216, para 3
[1142] The Oxford History of the British Army, p.258
[1143] Crang, p.5

[1144] Crang, p.6
[1145] Crang, p.9
[1146] Crang, p.11
[1147] The Oxford History of the British Army, p.343, para 1
[1148] Clayton p. 55
[1149] In 1800 the 68th Regiment, then ~700+ strong received 2600 volunteers from the Irish Militia, enough to form a second battalion. After training and transfers it arrived in the West Indies in 1801 with a total strength of 1860 men.<ref>Vane pp. 31-33
[1150] *The Oxford companion to Irish history*, Sean J. Connolly, p. 505
[1151] https//books.google.co.uk
[1152] https//books.google.co.uk
[1153] https://books.google.com/books?id=ky3gSOreBOIC&pg=PA18&dq=british+army+recruitment+world+war+ii&sig=ACfU3U0JjLJPFSiUB_bdFkBtbYPWs0nxlQ#PPA5,M1
[1154] https//books.google.co.uk
[1155] http://www.army.mod.uk/join/join.aspx
[1156] http://www.bbc.co.uk/education/beyond/factsheets/makhist/makhist7_prog8b.shtml
[1157] http://www.bbc.co.uk/ww2peopleswar/timeline/factfiles/nonflash/a1138664.shtml?sectionId=1&articleId=1138664
[1158] http://redsandrevs.co.uk/RS_recruitment.html
[1159] http://www.thinkdefence.co.uk/2011/02/parliamentary-questions-and-answers-02-feb-2011/
[1160] Professional Qualified Officers http://www.army.mod.uk/training_education/training/17071.aspx
[1161] Late Entry Officers Course http://www.army.mod.uk/training_education/training/17967.aspx
[1162] http://www.army.mod.uk/training_education/24344.aspx
[1163] Since April 2013, MoD publications no longer report the entire strength of the Regular Reserve, instead, only Regular Reserves serving under a fixed-term reserve contract are counted. These contracts are similar in nature to the RAuxAF.
[1164] http://www.raf.mod.uk/
[1165] Air Power and Colonial Control: The Royal Air Force, 1919–1939 https://books.google.com/books/about/Air_Power_and_Colonial_Control.html?id=9QYNAQAAIAAJ&redir_esc=y By David E. Omissi, Published 1 January 1990, Retrieved 1 February 2014. Page 8.
[1166] BBC: Fact File : The RAF http://www.bbc.co.uk/history/ww2peopleswar/timeline/factfiles/nonflash/a6649248.shtml, retrieved 1 February 2014
[1167] Royal Air Force: Our high-tech gear http://www.raf.mod.uk/careers/life-in-the-raf/our-hi-tech-gear/, retrieved 1 February 2014
[1168] Tami Davis Biddle, "British and American Approaches to Strategic Bombing: Their Origins and Implementation in the World War II Combined Bomber Offensive," *Journal of Strategic Studies*, March 1995, Vol. 18 Issue 1, pp 91–144; Tami Davis Biddle, *Rhetoric and Reality in Air Warfare: The Evolution of British and American Ideas about Strategic Bombing, 1914–1945* (2002)
[1169] Paul Brickhill, *The Dambusters*
[1170] Burnell, Brian. "Weapon detail and No.15 Squadron data for 1984." http://nuclear-weapons.info/images/1984.PNG *nuclear-weapons.info*. Retrieved 19 January 2011.
[1171] "Strategic Defence Review 1998: Full Report." http://www.mod.uk/NR/rdonlyres/65F3D7AC-4340-4119-93A2-20825848E50E/0/sdr1998_complete.pdf *Ministry of Defence*, 1998, p. 24.
[1172] Air of Authority – A History of RAF Organisation – Overseas Commands – Iraq, India and the Far East http://www.rafweb.org/Cmd_O3.htm
[1173] Ashworth 1989, p.26.
[1174] Evans 1998, pp. 74–75.
[1175] Royal Air Force: Expeditionary Air Force http://www.raf.mod.uk/organisation/ExpeditionaryAirForce.cfm , raf.mod.uk
[1176] *Tornados Bound for Kandahar*, Air Forces Monthly, August 2008 issue, p. 8.
[1177] RAF Typhoons intercept Russian bombers http://www.flightglobal.com/news/articles/picture-raf-typhoons-intercept-russian-bombers-363985/ (flightglobal.com), 27 October 2011
[1178] Hansard https://publications.parliament.uk/pa/cm201213/cmhansrd/cm130124/text/130124w0001.htm (publications.parliament.uk), 24 January 2014

[1179] UK Ministry of Defence press release 20 September 2012
[1180] //en.wikipedia.org/w/index.php?title=Template:RAF&action=edit
[1181] gov.uk MoD – regular personnel https://www.gov.uk/government/uploads/system/uploads/attachment_data/file/402652/MPR_January_2015.pdf, table 2 page 8. 1 January 2015.
[1182] gov.uk MoD – quarterly personnel report https://www.gov.uk/government/uploads/system/uploads/attachment_data/file/402633/quarterly_personnel_report_jan15.pdf, table 4 page 9. 1 January 2015.
[1183] dasa.mod – reserves and cadet strengths http://www.dasa.mod.uk/publications/personnel/military/reserves-and-cadets-strengths/2012-04-01/2012-revised.pdf, table 4 page 6. April 2012.
[1184] gov.uk MoD – reserves and cadet strengths https://www.gov.uk/government/uploads/system/uploads/attachment_data/file/314795/uk_reserve_force_cadets_2014.pdf, table 4 page 13. See note 2. April 2014.
[1185] gov.uk MoD – reserves and cadet strengths https://www.gov.uk/government/uploads/system/uploads/attachment_data/file/314795/uk_reserve_force_cadets_2014.pdf, table 4 page 13. April 2014.
[1186] IISS 2012, pp. 171
[1187] IISS 2012, pp. 111–120
[1188] *Air base in front line armed http://www.salisburyjournal.co.uk/display.var.1792468.0.air_base_in_front_line_fullyarmed.php – Salisbury Journal*, 29 October 2007
[1189] "UK retires ALARM missile" http://www.janes.com/article/32800/uk-retires-alarm-missile 21 January 2014
[1190] AirForcesMonthly.August 2008.p9
[1191] "U.K. Makes F-35 U-Turn to Cut Costs, Narrow Carrier-Defense Gap." https://www.bloomberg.com/news/2012-05-10/u-k-makes-f-35-u-turn-to-cut-costs-narrow-carrier-defense-gap.html *Bloomberg News*, 10 May 2012.
[1192] Prince of Wales aircraft carrier 'makes little sense' without aircraft to fly from it https://www.theguardian.com/uk-news/2015/mar/24/prince-of-wales-aircraft-carrier-makes-little-sense-report, The Guardian. Retrieved 25 October 2015.
[1193] Defence Review: Fighting old battles? https://www.bbc.co.uk/news/uk-34901846, BBC News. Retrieved 26 November 2015.
[1194] Robertson 1967, p 89
[1195] Air Ministry Orders A.666/49, 15 September 1949
[1196] https://www.raf.mod.uk/
[1197] http://www.sabre.mod.uk/
[1198] http://www.rafmuseum.org.uk/
[1199] http://www.rafbf.org/
[1200] https://uk.youtube.com/user/royalairforce
[1201] Gardner, Frank 'East of Suez': Are UK forces returning? https://www.bbc.co.uk/news/uk-22333555 BBC News 29 April 2013
[1202] http://www.raf.mod.uk/organisation/stations.cfm
[1203] https://web.archive.org/web/20040619104629/http://www.ukcoldwar.org.uk/rafbases.htm
[1204] https://www.secret-bases.co.uk
[1205] https://web.archive.org/web/20080124181456/http://www.servicepals.com/index.cfm/pcms/site.gallery.view_tag/tag/raf
[1206] https://web.archive.org/web/20080517055146/http://www.subbrit.org.uk/rsg/index.shtml
[1207] https://web.archive.org/web/20150303205841/http://www.pastscape.org.uk/default.aspx
[1208] Why do some Squadrons have letter after their number? – PPRuNe http://www.pprune.org/military-aircrew/236597-why-do-some-squadrons-have-letter-after-their-number.html
[1209] See RAF Eagle Squadrons
[1210] Axis History Forum: RAF Unit Numbers query? http://forum.axishistory.com/viewtopic.php?f=84&t=139229
[1211] No 330 – 352 Squadron Histories, Air of Authority http://www.rafweb.org/Sqn330-352.htm
[1212] Axis History Forum • View topic – RAF Unit Numbers query? http://forum.axishistory.com/viewtopic.php?f=84&t=139229
[1213] No 541 – 598 Squadron Histories, Air of Authority http://www.rafweb.org/Sqn541-598.htm

[1214] No 605 – 610 Squadron Histories, Air of Authority http://www.rafweb.org/Sqn605-610.htm
[1215] The Royal Air Force – History Section http://www.raf.mod.uk/history_old/sqn_hist601-1435.html
[1216] No 651 – 670 Squadron Histories, Air of Authority http://rafweb.org/Sqn651-670.htm
[1217] FleetAirArmArchive.net http://www.fleetairarmarchive.net/Squadrons/700index.htm
[1218] No 712 – 825 Squadron Histories, Air of Authority http://www.rafweb.org/Sqn712-825.htm
[1219] RAF Squadrons 901 – 980, Air of Authority http://www.rafweb.org/Sqn900.htm
[1220] http://www.raf.mod.uk/organisation/squadrons.cfm
[1221] 28 Tutors have been sold to the Finnish Air Force as of 2018
[1222] Empire Test Pilots' School - Our Fleet and Facilities http://www.etps.qinetiq.com/platforms/Pages/default.aspx , etps.qinetiq.com
[1223] ETPS Saab Gripen http://www.etps.qinetiq.com/school/fleet/fixedwing/Pages/Saab-Gripen.aspx
[1224] https://www.gov.uk/government/uploads/system/uploads/attachment_data/file/310189/Conventional-AF-Europe-2014-Bulletin.pdf
[1225] http://www.dasa.mod.uk/publications/equipment/CFE-vehicles-and-aircraft/2013/2013.pdf
[1226] http://www.airtanker.co.uk
[1227] Type A Operating Licence Holders http://www.caa.co.uk/default.aspx?catid=183&pageid=340
[1228] AirTanker's first flight as an airline http://www.airtanker.co.uk/news/airtanker%E2%80%99s-first-flight-as-an-airline
[1229] G-INFO - Civil Aviation Authority http://publicapps.caa.co.uk/modalapplication.aspx?catid=1&pagetype=65&appid=1&mode=summary&aocholder=airtanker retrieved 28 January 2017
[1230] http://www.airtanker.co.uk/leasing AirTanker Leasing details, accessed 27 March 2018
[1231] http://www.airtanker.co.uk/
[1232] Wall, Robert. "U.K. Cuts Aircraft Fleets in Strategic Review" http//www.aviationweek.com. *Aviation Week*, 19 October 2010.
[1233] "U.K. Makes F-35 U-Turn to Cut Costs, Narrow Carrier-Defense Gap." https://www.bloomberg.com/news/2012-05-10/u-k-makes-f-35-u-turn-to-cut-costs-narrow-carrier-defense-gap.html *Bloomberg News*, 10 May 2012.
[1234] Britain reveals combat air strategy alongside new Tempest fighter jet design https://www.defensenews.com/digital-show-dailies/farnborough/2018/07/16/introducing-tempest-the-uks-next-gen-fighter/, Beth Stevenson, DefenseNews, 2018-07-16
[1235] http://www.raf.mod.uk/organisation/24squadron.cfm
[1236] https://www.airtanker.co.uk/news-centre/news-item/2016/07/14/delivery-of-the-final-voyager
[1237] https://ukdefencejournal.org.uk/uk-takes-delivery-third-final-rc-135-rivet-joint/
[1238] https://www.gov.uk/government/news/raf-typhoons-to-get-weapons-upgrade
[1239] http://www.raf.mod.uk/newsweather/index.cfm?storyid=C68ABE90-1143-EC82-2EA56BEB107606D1
[1240] https://www.gov.uk/government/news/defence-secretary-announces-539-million-investment-in-new-missiles-systems
[1241] https://www.gov.uk/government/news/mod-orders-uk-designed-mini-missile-decoy-for-raf
[1242] //tools.wmflabs.org/geohack/geohack.php?pagename=Ministry_of_Defence_(United_Kingdom)&params=51.504_N_0.1249_W_type:landmark_region:GB
[1243] MOD civilian personnel quarterly report: 2015 https://www.gov.uk/government/statistics/mod-civilian-personnel-quarterly-report-2015, gov.uk, 1 October 2015
[1244] Budget 2015 https://www.gov.uk/government/uploads/system/uploads/attachment_data/file/416330/47881_Budget_2015_Web_Accessible.pdf HM Treasury (18 March 2015) - *see Chart 1 on page 6*
[1245] http://mod.uk
[1246] //en.wikipedia.org/w/index.php?title=Template:Politics_of_the_United_Kingdom&action=edit
[1247] The Defence Vision, Ministry of Defence website http://www.mod.uk/DefenceInternet/AboutDefence/Organisation/DefenceVision/TheDefenceVision.htm.

[1248] Strategic Defence Review 1998 http://www.mod.uk/NR/rdonlyres/65F3D7AC-4340-4119-93A2-20825848E50E/0/sdr1998_complete.pdf Ministry of Defence, accessed 8 December 2008.
[1249] "MoD orders spending clampdown", *Financial Times*, 16 November 2008, FT.com
[1250] Defence cuts 'to leave aircraft carriers without any planes', Robert Fox, 23 June 2009
[1251] Defence budget: New equipment at risk over MoD savings 'doubts' https://www.bbc.co.uk/news/uk-politics-42382002 *BBC*
[1252] Better Defence Builds Project Case Study http://www.mod.uk/NR/rdonlyres/FE7BE9AA-DD65-4971-8C00-B913E1EA84FA/0/mainbuilding.pdf
[1253] "Cuts force TA to cease training" http://news.bbc.co.uk/1/hi/uk/8300530.stm, BBC News, 10 October 2009
[1254] http://www.gov.uk/mod
[1255] http://webarchive.nationalarchives.gov.uk/20121018102851/http://www.mod.uk/DefenceInternet/Home/
[1256] http://www.sabre.mod.uk
[1257] http://www.defencemanagement.com/

Article Sources and Contributors

The sources listed for each article provide more detailed licensing information including the copyright status, the copyright owner, and the license conditions.

British Armed Forces *Source*: https://en.wikipedia.org/w/index.php?oldid=851957461 *License*: Creative Commons Attribution-Share Alike 3.0 *Contributors*: Adam Cuerden, Amerijuanican, Antiochus the Great, Athomeinkobe, AusLondonder, B.Velikov, BastionZenta, Bentogoa, BilCat, Bocaj130, Bonadea, Britishlıregts, Buckshot06, BukWeb 1, Calidum, Cantab1985, Captain Cornwall, Charles lindberg, Chase Moylan, Chris the speller, ClueBot NG, Cyberbot II, Dabbler, David Biddulph, David J Johnson, Dreddmoto, El C, Fifact, Firebrace, Gabbe, Gadget850, GeneralizationsAreBad, Good Wall of the Pyrenees, Ham II, HolyT, Huberthoff, Human., Iceonthemoon, Intellectualgoldfish, Interpuncts, Iridescent, Itititillit, Jack6771, JdannyJ2000, Jess-Pavarocks, Jim1138, Joobo, Jprg1966, KH-1, Kaloyan34-FR, Keith D, Kevin Moritz, Kkm010, Kookiethebird, Llammakey, Mandruss, Mart1234567890, Materialscientist, Mean as custard, MilborneOne, MusikAnimal, Natg 19, Necrothesp, Niceguyedc, Nick-D, Noclador, PBS, Permstrump, Quackio, Quite vivid blur, Ransewiki, Reaganomics88, Redalert2fan, Remffa, Rheinstorff, Rob984, Saturn star, Shellwood, Sietse, Skjoldbro, Slightsmile, SpyMagician, Sumorsæte, Telfordbuck, The Light Arts, TheArmchairSoldier, Thewolfchild, Tom.Reding, Twistyoak, Twobells, Wendigo5555, Whizz40, Wrestlingring, Øystein.Eide, 128 anonymous edits 1
History of the Royal Navy *Source*: https://en.wikipedia.org/w/index.php?oldid=852897613 *License*: Creative Commons Attribution-Share Alike 3.0 *Contributors*: Adicarlo, Alaney2k, Andrew Gray, Aodhdubh, Ashman1992, AtticusX, AustralianRupert, BD2412, Bender235, BilCat, CLCStudent, Chase me ladies, I'm the Cavalry, Chris the speller, ClueBot NG, Colonies Chris, Comnenus, DPdH, Dabbler, DagosNavy, Davemck, David Biddulph, Derbycountyin NZ, Derekbridges, Dewritech, Dl2000, Donner60, Dormskirk, Dreddmoto, Dudley Miles, DuncanHill, Ealdgyth, Emir of Wikipedia, Epipelagic, Euryalus, Falconflyer, Faolin42, Fishieshelper2, Fnorp, Gwillhickers, HLGallon, Hairy Dude, In ictu oculi, Indefatigable, Iridescent, Italia2006, JRPG, John of Reading, KConWiki, KTo288, Keith D, Kimdino, Limefrost Spiral, Mark Arsten, Mark Ekimov, Mdd, Mild Bill Hiccup, Modest Genius, Mogism, Moonraker, Narky Blert, Navops47, Niceguyedc, Nick Number, Nodulation, Nyttend, OberRanks, Peter Isotalo, Phleg1, Rjensen, Sadads, Seaphoto, Shanmugamp7, TAnthony, Targaryen, Tech77, The PIPE, Thom2002, TimBentley, Tobby72, Tony1hawkins, Twistyoak, UglowT, Ulric1313, Vgy7ujm, Wavelength, Xyl 54, Ylee, Zburh, ÄDA - DÄP, Uлпл $\cup$ Π, 67 anonymous edits 21
History of the British Army *Source*: https://en.wikipedia.org/w/index.php?oldid=846826458 *License*: Creative Commons Attribution-Share Alike 3.0 *Contributors*: 5 albert square, AK456, Absolutelypuremilk, Adithyak1997, Alansplodge, Albrecht, Angusmclellan, Antiquary, Antiqueight, BD2412, Berserker276, BokicaK, Buckshot06, Chris the speller, Clafomh Solais, Closedmouth, ClueBot NG, Cnwilliams, Colonies Chris, Creuzbourg, David Underdown, DevinCook, Dl2000, Dormskirk, Edmund T, Elektrik Shoos, EoGuy, EvilLair, Faceless Enemy, Flyer22 Reborn, Gaius Octavius Princeps, Gob Lofa, Greenshed, HLGallon, Hamish59, HappyCamp23, Hawkeye7, Hmains, Ionisiso, Iridescent, Italia2006, IxK85, Jayjg, Jim Sweeney, Jtle515, Kwamikagami, L293D, Lapsed Pacifist, Leithp, LilHelpa, MFIreland, MarcusBritish, Mark6597, Milesian966, Mogism, Moonraker, Nawlin Wiki, Nick-D, Opera hat, PBS, Parsley Man, Permstrump, Pmj, RA0808, Rjensen, Rjwilmsi, Robert Brukner, Rockybiggs, Rorschach, ShelfSkewed, Shorerlanger, Sideways713, Straw Cat, TMHPin, Tassedethe, Thermocycler, Timrollpickering, Tobby72, TobyJ, Totreliablesource, Tuesdaily, Turgay1985, Vgy7ujm, Vipinhari, Wally Wiglet, Westminster Watch, Whizz40, WikiTryHardDieHard, Woohookitty, Zorkohiro, ÄDA - DÄP, 74 anonymous edits 58
History of the Royal Air Force *Source*: https://en.wikipedia.org/w/index.php?oldid=850404148 *License*: Creative Commons Attribution-Share Alike 3.0 *Contributors*: Aodhdubh, Bgwhite, BotMultichill, Canglesea, Caniago, Cannolis, ChoraPete, DP7657, DVdm, Daemonic Kangaroo, Dapi89, Dawnseeker2000, Dewey101, Dewritech, Dl2000, Dormskirk, Dpm04, Elagatis, Evans1982, Excirial, FliptheCoin, Flyer22 Reborn, Flyingfacts, Gorge-CustersSabre, GraemeLeggett, Grant65, Greenshed, Ground Zero, Gwolf12321, Hohum, Hugu*, Ian Dunster, Iridescent, IxK85, JGHowes, James Dunston, Jodosma, Jprg1966, Juzhong, Khazar2, Krellis, Kriegaffe, LedgendGamer, Lestermay, LilHelpa, LtSpecter, Martinevans123, MilborneOne, Moonraker, Mr Stephen, Multipurposepaper, Narson, Neddyseagoon, Noclador, NorthernKnightNo1, Olivia Charles, Onceinawhile, Pandaplodder, Pauly04, Poliocretes, QuiteUnusual, Reedmalloy, Rich Farmbrough, Rjensen, Rjwilmsi, Rockybiggs, Sasuke Sarutobi, Sc147, Sky-surfer, Slavatrudu, Soundofmusicals, Tabletop, TexasAndroid, The PIPE, The joy of all things, TheFreeWorld, TimR, Toddy1980, Unbuttered Parsnip, Vgy7ujm, Welsh, XXzoonamiXX, 85 anonymous edits 89
Structure of the British Armed Forces in 1989 *Source*: https://en.wikipedia.org/w/index.php?oldid=832484238 *License*: Creative Commons Attribution-Share Alike 3.0 *Contributors*: Buckshot06, Jinbo4514, Mskadu, Narky Blert, Noclador 105
Nuclear weapons and the United Kingdom *Source*: https://en.wikipedia.org/w/index.php?oldid=853056697 *License*: Creative Commons Attribution-Share Alike 3.0 *Contributors*: AdamBMorgan, Alcherin, Andy Dingley, Anotherclown, Antiochus the Great, Arado, Armorbeetlecak, Arunsingh16, BHDWKEhhjswc, Banedon, Bender235, BenjaminBluesilk, Bgwhite, Brandmeister, Brigade Piron, Brunswicknic, Buckshot06, Calisthenis, Cantab1985, Chendy, ChrisGualtieri, Christiantev12, ClueBot NG, Crosbiesmith, Darkwind, Dawnseeker2000, DocWatson42, Dolphin51, Dr Gangrene, Dragonfly-Sixtyseven, Excirial, Firebrace, Freeman501, Gabbe, Gilo1969, Gobonobo, Gonzo fan2007, GraemeLeggett, Graham87, Grant65, GünniX, Hawkeye7, Heroicrelics, Ira Leviton, IronGargoyle, Jamesx12345, Jamietw, Jemcia, JJ 1982, J349, JBear-GT, JOONYYYY123, JackintheBox, kk325, Jenkin5, John of Reading, KH-1, KingUther, Kleuske, Klg luca, Kookiethebird, Lalalalandofthe, Laurel Lodged, Lightlowemon, Lkjljlkjljlkjlj, Magioladitis, Mandruss, Marchjuly, MassiveNewOrderFan, Mean as custard, Missileinfo1, Missileinfo10, Missileinfo20, Missileinfo4, Missileinfo6, Murph9000, Navops47, Necrophobia19, Neveselbert, NewEnglandYankee, Noclador, Onel5969, Orenburg1, Oshwah, Pam-javelin, Petermichaelgenner, Phinn, Quite vivid blur, Redalert2fan, Rjensen & Roger, Romanov loyalist, Samf4u, Sammartinlai, SideshowBob92, Sir-Douglas, Skjoldbro, SkyWarrior, Skyrover, Slightsmile, SpacemanSpiff, Spmilan, Spyglasses, Surtsicna, TheArmchairSoldier, Thewolfchild, Tiffywren, Tobby72, TonyBallioni, Triptropic, Twistyoak, Valenciano, Walle83, WatermillockCommon, Waterwings91, Westernpropagandadebunked1, Whhhhiteeeemaaanspropopagannndaexposed, Whiteemaaanspropogandaexposed, Whizz40, Yaris678, Zburh, 76 anonymous edits 157
List of active Royal Navy ships *Source*: https://en.wikipedia.org/w/index.php?oldid=853017272 *License*: Creative Commons Attribution-Share Alike 3.0 *Contributors*: Ajaxrocks, Antiochus the Great, Argovian, Benthefast3, BritainsRailway, Chickenhero, DJ Frame, David Biddulph, Dl2000, Dpaajones, Dulciana, Edlyons1, Elsecar, FoCuSandLeArN, Gadget850, Gtbgrhgrgdgre, Hammersfan, Hsinchonglam, Ingkb, JSD999, JackintheBox, Jakewh92, Kamrul512, Keith D, Kistara, Kookiethebird, Llammakey, Lyndaship, Mark6597, MassiveNewOrderFan, Materialscientist, Mean as custard, NavalArchitect, Phd8511, Philip Trueman, Postdlf, QuintusPetillius, Rob984, Scorponi, Scotty298, ScraplronIV, Sumorsæte, SuperNexus, TheArmchairSoldier, TheFuzzy-One, Thewolfchild, Thom2002, Twistyoak, Vulcan44, Vulcan98, Waterwings91, Whatsupwhore, Xtrememachineuk, 110 anonymous edits 210
Royal Navy Surface Fleet *Source*: https://en.wikipedia.org/w/index.php?oldid=852930896 *License*: Creative Commons Attribution-Share Alike 3.0 *Contributors*: A. B., Acalamari, Acroterion, Aldis90, AndyZ, Antiochus the Great, AsceticRose, Baycattwiakiitsreacist, Beetstra, BilCat, Boycottwikiracism, Bsadowski1, Cardi Gray, Dpaajones, Dreambroad, Euryalus, Firstconch, Floquenbeam, GraemeLeggett, Gurch, Hmainsbot1, Jamesparkin, Jim Sweeney, Klilidiplomus, Lachrie, MarbleNau, Nikai, Nkcs, Quite vivid blur, Red Jay, Rif Winfield, Sammartinlai, Sharkbait1784, ThinkingTwice, Tomalak general, Trapzor, Weaksisifullofracistsbaycattweaki, Wikiboycottforracism, Wikiisracistinnature Boycottit, 15 anonymous edits 227
Fleet Air Arm *Source*: https://en.wikipedia.org/w/index.php?oldid=851209501 *License*: Creative Commons Attribution-Share Alike 3.0 *Contributors*: Accadd, Acsian88, Alansplodge, Anonymoustofu, Antiochus the Great, Arsado, BD2412, BSc600, Bagwafu, Baycattwiakiitsreacisi, BilCat, Blackberry Sorbet, Blacksbood, Buckshot06, Cantab1985, Chase me ladies, I'm the Cavalry, ChrisGualtieri, Cjrother, Cosywafu, Cyberbot II, Dabbler, David Biddulph, Dawkeye, Dewritech, DisillusionedBitterAndKnackered, Dl2000, DogBossLayout, Dreambroad, Dreddmoto, Eagle4000, Eric Corbett, FAAAWM, FeatherPluma, Floquenbeam, Fnlayson, Fry1989, Gaia Octavia Agrippa, Garuda28, Gavbadger, Glacialfox, Gold Wiz113, GraemeLeggett, Greenshed, Hafiz-Wong, Hammersfan, Hardrightz, Haruth, Heaney554?4, Hohum, Jack6771, Jennica, Jim Sweeney, Jim1138, Kirbh-264, Klilidiplomus, Kewubo, Ldcambell, Le Deluge, Lemuellio, Letdorf, LordAnon of Essex, LostCause231, Lovetravel86, Lyndaship, Mark6597, Maturescence, MaxCon87, MilbornrOne, Mogism, Monotrono, Museli, Navops47, Nick Thorne, NicoScribe, Niki2004, Noclador, Nostalgic34, ObscureReality, Ohconfucius, Pam-javelin, Paul1776, Phd8511, Quentin X, Quite vivid blur, RayDayRN, SchreiberBike, Tbhotch, TeddyT, The Bushranger, The joy of all things, TheArmchairSoldier, Theramin, Thewolfchild, Thom2002, Tim!, Tony Mach, Twistyoak, Waterwings91, Weaksisifullofracistsbaycattweaki, Welsh, Werieth, Wustenfuchs53, Zyxw, 106 anonymous edits 237

631

Royal Marines *Source:* https://en.wikipedia.org/w/index.php?oldid=851948634 *License:* Creative Commons Attribution-Share Alike 3.0 *Contributors:* 19est66, Amerijuanican, Anotherclown, Antiochus the Great, AyodeleA1, AyodeleA2, BananaBork, BangJan1999, Barabbas1312, Barsle, Bender235, Berserker276, BilCat, Billbow9393, Blairall, Bocaj130, BubbleEngineer, C.Fred, CLCStudent, Cantab1985, Charlesdrakew, Chitt66, Chris the speller, Chrisyear, ClueBot NG, Dan100, DaveyBobBeNiceYall, David Biddulph, DerbyCountyinNZ, Dewritech, Dormskirk, Dreddmoto, Eagle4000, Eastfarthingan, Editor9217, Euryalus, FormerDirtDart, Frietjes, Fuortu, Gadget850, Garuda28, Gavbadger, Giraffedata, GoldenBoy25, Hammersfan, Hmains, Hohum, Howcheng, Hux, I dream of horses, Illegitimate Barrister, Indefatigable, JOONYYYY123, Keri, Kjerish, Lampshade Dog, Lizardmong101, Maj Harry Black, Majmjh, Mandruss, MinorProphet, Moistone1, Museaway, Nick-D, Noclador, Optakeover, Oshwah, PBS, Pablomartinez, PicturePrince, Prjherbert, Regicide1649, Rickfive, Rob984, Rodw, Royal 43 Cdo, Rubbish computer, SWF88, Sammartinlai, ScrapIronIV, Simplexity22, Sluzzelin, Sodacan, Specac, Spicemix, The Bushranger, Thewolfchild, Tktru, Tom.Reding, UnbiasedVictory, Unknown Unknowns, Vivs1234, Xypical, Yaris678, Zikking, 128 anonymous edits 257

Standing Royal Navy deployments *Source:* https://en.wikipedia.org/w/index.php?oldid=849372617 *License:* Creative Commons Attribution-Share Alike 3.0 *Contributors:* ALR, AlphaCharlieSierra12, Andrew Gray, Antiochus the Great, Aodhdubh, Apcbg, Argovian, Astrotrain, BD2412, Basisaoasis, Benandorsqueaks, BenjaminBluesilk, Bobblewik, Bornintheguz, Buckshot06, Cantab1985, Centrx, Chase me ladies, I'm the Cavalry, Cibwins2885, D6, Dewritech, Dormskirk, Foxhound66, Gavbadger, Giraffedata, Goblin086, Ground Zero, Hammersfan, Hammersfan 1, Hobohob, Iridescent, Jamesgiles86, Jdforrester, John, JonEastham, Klilidiplomus, Kosher Fan, Kotabatubara, Le Deluge, MRTWP, Magioladitis, Mandarax, Martpol, Maximus Rex, Mogism, MrGRA, Natg 19, Nathan Johnson, NavalArchitect, Nick-D, ObscureReality, Olegwiki, Phd8511, PigFlu Oink, QuiteUnusual, RWhite9629, Ryan4314, Scotty298, Sean.leicester, Textorus, TheArmchairSoldier, Thx811, Tpbradbury, Waterwings91, Whitejay251, 70 anonymous edits 290

List of Royal Navy shore establishments *Source:* https://en.wikipedia.org/w/index.php?oldid=849339044 *License:* Creative Commons Attribution-Share Alike 3.0 *Contributors:* A. Carty, ACP2011, ALR, Anthony Appleyard, Antiochus the Great, B84, Barabbas1312, Belovedfreak, Bender235, Benea, Bgwhite, BritainsRailway, BruceF1956, CS46, Cantab1985, Chase me ladies, I'm the Cavalry, Cheesy mike, Cnwilliams, Colonies Chris, Cornishpasty, Cossde, Coyets, Dana boomer, Dave1185, David Biddulph, Davidneverett, Dawkeye, Dormskirk, Dpaajones, DuncanHill, Dyvroeth, Edwardx, Eilidhmax, Emoscopes, Fionaure, Fratrep, GadgetSteve, Gavbadger, Gibmetal77, GraemeLeggett, Grafen, Hammersfan, Hethurs, Howard61313, Ibagli, Icarusgeek, Ingreatwaters, Jackyd101, Jimbolaser, Jll, Jni, John of Reading, Jrleighton, KTo288, Kane5187, Kingbird1, LUNDAVRA, Ldirwin, Lollipoplollipoplollipop, MapsMan, Mdnavman, Mervyn, Michael Hardy, Miq, Mogism, Navops47, Navsim, Neddyseagoon, Neutrality, Nitraven, Northamerica1000, Nthep, Open2universe, Petechilcott, Peterwhy, Phd8511, Pol098, Pritchard145, Pyrope, Pyrotec, R'n'B, RHaworth, Ralabaf, Rjwilmsi, Robertgreer, Rturus, Rwendland, Scanbus, Scillystuff, Shem1805, Signalhead, Snigbrook, The Bushranger, Thefrood, Timtrent, Tramp steamer1980, Travisyoung, Vclaw, W6embaLw3VOekPuVco7, WOSlinker, Waterwings91, Welsh, Whizz40, Woodwose1689, Xwejnusgozo, Yintan, 90 anonymous edits 301

Customs and traditions of the Royal Navy *Source:* https://en.wikipedia.org/w/index.php?oldid=843071577 *License:* Creative Commons Attribution-Share Alike 3.0 *Contributors:* Acsian88, Basisaoasis, BilCat, Brookesward, Buckshot06, Chase me ladies, I'm the Cavalry, CommonsDelinker, Esrever, GinoC, Hairy Dude, Hippo43, Hongooi, John of Reading, Jonkerz, Kawebb, Klilidiplomus, Lestermay, Lightmouse, Mark.murphy, Motmit, Mr. Wheely Guy, Neutrality, Newt Winkler, Parkylondon, Peter Karlsen, Pigsonthewing, Richard-of-Earth, Rjwilmsi, Saebvn, Satani, Shem1805, Streona, Tony1hawkins, Wayne Slam, Woody, Zooks527, □, 71 anonymous edits 317

British Army *Source:* https://en.wikipedia.org/w/index.php?oldid=851753091 *License:* Creative Commons Attribution-Share Alike 3.0 *Contributors:* 72, AlexWing, Amanbir IV, Anotherclown, Antiochus the Great, Aodhdubh, AvalerionV, Babymissfortune, BilCat, BobbySands67, BubbleEngineer, Buckshot06, C.Fred, CLCStudent, Chiswick Chap, Chris the speller, Clamasiatoaaa, ClueBot NG, Daranz, David Biddulph, Doc James, Dormskirk, Dthomsen8, Etothepi, Euryalus, Fahrenheit666, Favonian, Floodsmy, FriyMan, Garuda28, Gavbadger, GenQuest, Gilliam, Giraffedata, Government Man, GraemeLeggett, HJ Mitchell, Harsimaja, Hcobb, Holland85, Howardj99, Huberthoff, I dream of horses, Illegitimate Barrister, ImFluffPanda, Iridescent, J349, J947, JOONYYYY123, Jack Frost, Jakednb, Jcmcc450, Jiten D, John of Reading, Johnsoniensis, KH-1, Keith-264, Kind Tennis Fan, Lalalalandofthe, Laurel Lodged, Lkjljlkjljljlkj, Loopy30, Lucius Winslow, MORNINGSIDE, Magioladitis, Mandruss, MartinKassemJ120, MartynSGM, Materialscientist, Mattpaulmillman, Mean as custard, Mediatech492, MilborneOne, Miniapolis, Missileinfo20, Mr Stephen, Murph9000, NFLisAwesome, Nick-D, Nickel nitride, Nicnoc542, Nopphan, North Shoreman, PBS, Peacemaker67, Phuzion, Pjposullivan, Plucas58, Prometheus14, Richard-of-Earth, Rjensen, Rob984, Ronbat12, Ronyyz, Sadiedens, Samf4u, Sau226, ScrapIronIV, Serols, Sgt.price, Shellwood, Skjoldbro, Slightsmile, Stingray Trainer, The Rambling Man, TheAlphaMH, Thewolfchild, Trappist the monk, Twistyoak, TwoTwoHello, Valenciano, Wbm1058, Whhhhiteeeemaaanspropogannndaexposed, Whizz40, Wi7less, Woody, Yamaguchi先生 , Yunshui, 97 anonymous edits 321

List of equipment of the British Army *Source:* https://en.wikipedia.org/w/index.php?oldid=852504250 *License:* Creative Commons Attribution-Share Alike 3.0 *Contributors:* Absolutelypuremilk, AirWave 800S1, Aisteco, Alex Cohn, Antiochus the Great, Ashleyland1997, BanterChanelle, BilCat, Bingo Wings, Cantab1985, Chris the speller, Chrissymad, Clawdeck, Clafomh Solais, ClueBot NG, CodenameSection, CyanoTex, Darthkenobi0, Davemck, DisillusionedBitterAndKnackered, Dvaderv2, Edward, EsEinsteinium, FenixFeather, Finlay McWalter, Fnlayson, FrenchArmy, Gavbadger, Glevum, GraemeLeggett, HawkTierOne, Hawkeye7, Hibernian, Illegitimate Barrister, Iridescent, JessPavarocks, John of Reading, KinkowanWinter, KylieTastic, L293D, LordHello1, LostCause231, MORNINGSIDE, Magioladitis, MarksmanWonder, MathKnight, Melbguy05, Mr.Strat Starky, Murchison-Eye, NPDW, NeilN, Nickel nitride, Phd8511, Ppaz3, RadiculousJ, Rodw, Samf4u, Scotteaton92, ScrapIronIV, TankFanMasterUK, TankFanMasterUK2, Tankfanmasteruk3, The Quixotic Potato, TheArmchairSoldier, TheFuzzyOne, Welsh, Woggie10, 卡麥爾 073, 木の枝 , 118 anonymous edits 363

Structure of the British Army *Source:* https://en.wikipedia.org/w/index.php?oldid=852824154 *License:* Creative Commons Attribution-Share Alike 3.0 *Contributors:* 19est66, Ajaxrocks, Antiqueight, Aoi, Balin42632003, Barabbas1312, Bingo Wings, Blackshod, Brookesward, Buckshot06, Chris the speller, Cjrother, Clafomh Solais, ClueBot NG, Cyberbot II, Davix, Dormskirk, Excirial, Folks at 137, Gavbadger, Glevum, Gracefoo, Greatestrowerever, Hammersfan, Iridescent, JMRAMOS0109, Jprg1966, Khendon, Ladyman, Lampshade Dog, Lidos, LittleWink, Luke81, MTB UK, Magioladitis, MusikAnimal, Natg 19, Niceguyedc, Nick-D, Noclador, Peckingorder, Phd8511, Qixos, Rob984, Sammartinlai, Stingray Trainer, Thombodad, Tragino, Turgay1985, W. B. Wilson, WOSlinker, Wavelength, Wire723, Woohookitty, 85 anonymous edits 386

Recruitment in the British Army *Source:* https://en.wikipedia.org/w/index.php?oldid=845706670 *License:* Creative Commons Attribution-Share Alike 3.0 *Contributors:* Adam Cuerden, AddWittyNameHere, BD2412, Blaene, Buckshot06, Buistr, Choess, Chris the speller, Clafomh Solais, ClueBot NG, Cnwilliams, Cowlibob, Creuzbourg, David Underdown, Dettingen, Dewritech, Dormskirk, Dumelow, Duncan7670, Eastlaw, Excirial, Flyer22 Reborn, GMan552, Gaius Octavius Princeps, Giraffedata, Glevum, Ground Zero, Gwinva, HLGallon, Innotata, Iridescent, JoshWS, Keith D, Kind Tennis Fan, Kingbird1, Klemen Kocjancic, Lightmouse, Look2See1, Mabuska, Magioladitis, MarcusBritish, Mauls, Mild Bill Hiccup, Moonraker, Mr Taz, Murry1975, Necrothesp, Neddyseagoon, Neuteatime, Niceguyedc, Nilfanion, Oleg-ch, Omar77, R'n'B, Rafael Zink, Rcbutcher, Rjwilmsi, RobertEves92, Rockybiggs, Sassf, ShelfSkewed, Spinkzilla123, Stesmo, Tentinator, Tkynerd, Trident13, Usedtoknowthat, WOSlinker, Wbm1058, Weggie, Welsh, Widr, Wilmaw24, Woody, Woohookitty, 75 anonymous edits 404

List of British Army installations *Source:* https://en.wikipedia.org/w/index.php?oldid=846888338 *License:* Creative Commons Attribution-Share Alike 3.0 *Contributors:* BD2412, Benjamson, Bocaj130, Buckshot06, Clafomh Solais, Clpo13, Cnwilliams, Dormskirk, Frietjes, Gavbadger, GoingBatty, Hammersoft, HannanD, Hugo999, JackintheBox, JessPavarocks, Jpbowen, LasPo rocks, Libertarian12111971, Lommes, RabCr, Sworrub, Thx811, Wire723, Woodgridge, YicsHazard, 193 anonymous edits 424

Selection and Training in the British Army *Source:* https://en.wikipedia.org/w/index.php?oldid=849552160 *License:* Creative Commons Attribution-Share Alike 3.0 *Contributors:* ALR, Acsian88, Antiochus the Great, Apokrif, Bellerophon, CastawayIrvine, Clafomh Solais, Cnwilliams, Dan100, Doncram, Dormskirk, Dredwerkz, Freddie Ager, Fugitivedave, Gapino, Glevum, Hammersfan, John of Reading, Lampshade Dog, Lcawte, LilHelpa, LittleWink, McFazza, Necrothesp, NetherSarum, Niceguyedc, Obscurasky, PhoenixBlitzkrieg, Random Acts of Language, Ronz, Sct72, SmartyPants22, SoloUnEditor, The Quixotic Potato, The joy of all things, Uranium grenade, Usmarox, Wavelength, Wire723, Woohookitty, 31 anonymous edits 437

Royal Air Force *Source:* https://en.wikipedia.org/w/index.php?oldid=852832483 *License:* Creative Commons Attribution-Share Alike 3.0 *Contributors:* 72, Absolutelypuremilk, Agozer, Anotherclown, B.Velikov, BarneyHarwardIsBae, BegbertBiggs, BilCat, Bonadea, BriefAeon, BubbleEngineer, Buckshot06, C.Fred, CLCStudent, Charlesdrakew, Citizen Canine, Clamasiatoaaa, Climebear, ClueBot NG, DVdm, David Biddulph, Deeday-UK, Djsasso, Dl2000, Doc James, Dormskirk, EdmundT, FullmetalArsonist, Garuda28, Great Britains security Forces, Great Britiain Security, Greenshed, Happysailor, Hhelex, Holdoffhunger, Howcheng, Hufgh, JBear-GT, JOONYYYY123, JdannyJ2000, Joshbaumgartner, Joshuabuster1998, KH-1, Keith D, Kind Tennis Fan, Lalalalandofthe, MONGO, MRAF31, Manimony, Mart1234567890, Martinevans123, McSly, Mean as custard, MilborneOne, Mlkj, Molinaro787, Murph9000, Necrophobia19, Nick-D, Noclador, Oshwah, Pam-javelin, Quizman1967, RA0808, Raspberrypirate, Redalert2fan, RobinClay, Rwendland, SemiHypercube, Serols, ShakespeareFan00, Shellwood, Slightsmile, Soetermans, TAnthony, The joy of all things, Thewolfchild, Thx811, Tom7972, Travelbird, Waterwings91, Wire723, Woggie10, Z0, 125 anonymous edits 445

List of Royal Air Force groups *Source:* https://en.wikipedia.org/w/index.php?oldid=849930618 *License:* Creative Commons Attribution-Share Alike 3.0 *Contributors:* 489thCorsica, Astrotrain, BrownHairedGirl, Buckshot06, Chris the speller, David Newton, Dawkeye, Dl2000, Dormskirk, Gavbadger, GraemeLeggett, Grant65, Greenshed, Hugo999, John of Reading, Laoris, Letdorf, Mick Knapton, MilborneOne, NealeFamily, Nick-D, Plucas58, R'n'B, RL0919, Sammartinlai, Template namespace initialisation script, Teutonic Tamer, Timrollpickering, Waacstats, Wire723, 2 anonymous edits 482

List of Royal Air Force stations *Source:* https://en.wikipedia.org/w/index.php?oldid=851756302 *License:* Creative Commons Attribution-Share Alike 3.0 *Contributors:* 069952497a, 21stCenturyGreenstuff, 51edb, Ajaxrocks, Alifazal, Allens, Antiochus the Great, Arado, BD2412, BegbertBiggs, Ben Ben, Bgwhite, Bloovee, BrownHairedGirl, Calu2000, Climebear, ClueBot NG, Cricobr, Dave1185, David Biddulph, Dewritech, Dl2000, Domdeparis, Dormskirk, Douglas the Comeback Kid, DuncanHill, Elmeter, Exurbis67, Franknotes, Gavbadger, GiW, GraemeLeggett, Harrison49, How Shuan Shi, Hugo999, Hullwebs, Ira Leviton, Jellyfish dave, Jim Sweeney, Kingbird1, Lynbarn, Mannerheimo, MilborneOne, Mjroots, Mogism, Ng.j, Petebutt, Phd8511, Prentiz, Quizman1967, RBBrittain, Rab-k, Rob984, Rodw, Stfg, Tesscass, ThaBigCheese99, The joy of all things, Thewolfchild, Thx811, Vbruun, Vcorani, Vulcan44, WereSpielChequers, Whizz40, Winseybash, Wire723, 102 anonymous edits 494

List of Royal Air Force aircraft squadrons *Source:* https://en.wikipedia.org/w/index.php?oldid=850859152 *License:* Creative Commons Attribution-Share Alike 3.0 *Contributors:* A. Carty, Anotherclown, Barticus88, Benea, BrownHairedGirl, Buckshot06, Captain Canuck CD, Chris the speller, Colonies

Chris, Cplakidas, Crossfield Chronicler, David Underdown, Dirk P Broer, Dl2000, Doncram, FeatherPluma, FleetCommand, Gaia Octavia Agrippa, Gavbadger, Giraffedata, GraemeLeggett, Grant65, Greenshed, GünniX, Hugo999, Jagdfeld, Jim Sweeney, John of Reading, Khazar2, Klemen Kocjancic, Le Deluge, LeaveSleaves, Letdorf, LilHelpa, Magus732, MaxEspinho, McMuff, MilborneOne, Mileshawksix, Nedrutland, Oshwah, Petebutt, Plucas58, RL0919, SENIRAM, Sealman, Space 1993, Subspace1250, Tabletop, The joy of all things, Um152sqn, Waterwings91, Welsh, Yellowxander, 176 anonymous edits 509

List of Royal Air Force schools *Source:* https://en.wikipedia.org/w/index.php?oldid=851187147 *License:* Creative Commons Attribution-Share Alike 3.0 *Contributors:* Bearcat, Buckshot06, Certes, ColRad85, Dl2000, Fergus614, Gavbadger, Gbawden, Georgejdorner, Hugo999, Jonesey95, LilHelpa, Mild Bill Hiccup, Petebutt, Tabletop, The joy of all things, Topbanana, Wire723, 12 anonymous edits 543

List of active United Kingdom military aircraft *Source:* https://en.wikipedia.org/w/index.php?oldid=852144157 *License:* Creative Commons Attribution-Share Alike 3.0 *Contributors:* Ajaxrocks, Antiochus the Great, BilCat, Boreas74, Brizewatcher, Cfett75, David Biddulph, De Tourville, Funandtrvl, Gavbadger, Gipsymagpie, Gjlawrence347, Gurnotron, Gurns1995, Hammersfan, Headbomb, Iceonthemoon, Illegitimate Barrister, JRCZ97, Joshbaumgartner, Lampshade Dog, MarnetteD, Meters, MilborneOne, Molinaro787, Northamerica1000, Novarupta, Pkbwcgs, Radiostatic1, Redalert2fan, Rob984, Sammartinlai, ScrapIronIV, Steelpillow, Subspace1250, TheArmchairSoldier, TheFuzzyOne, Ton168, Twistyoak, Uli Elch, Waterwings91, Woggie10, Xose.vazquez, YSSYguy, 204 anonymous edits 560

AirTanker Services *Source:* https://en.wikipedia.org/w/index.php?oldid=845959301 *License:* Creative Commons Attribution-Share Alike 3.0 *Contributors:* AEMoreira042281, Ardfern, Arpingstone, BD2412, Beatts, CBG17, Cloudbound, Dl2000, Le Deluge, Lohchabnet, MER-C, Magioladitis, MilborneOne, Mogism, Nick, Nobody25, Plaemium, Sparkyb10123, Ssolbergj, The Original Filfi, TheAviationFan, Thryduulf, Titodutta, YSSYguy, 29 anonymous edits 566

Future of the Royal Air Force *Source:* https://en.wikipedia.org/w/index.php?oldid=850746404 *License:* Creative Commons Attribution-Share Alike 3.0 *Contributors:* 19est66, Andrewman327, Aww13, BanterChanelle, Barticus88, BilCat, Bobrayner, Brambleclawx, Canglesea, Cantab1985, Cibwins2885, Coolhawks88, Cooper 25, Dl2000, Dpnajones, Fjs95, Flosssock1, Greenshed, Hammersfan, Harrison49, Hcobb, Idaltu, J04n, JessPavarocks, Letdorf, Magioladitis, Mark6597, MatthewHaywood, Meiktila, Miker32159, Noclador, Peter Ellis, Phd8511, Quite vivid blur, SE7, Screwierdly, Sergey Tsvigun, SibelLover, Sitacuisses, Skynetworkworld, SojerPL, SomeFreakOnTheInternet, Sumors@te, Swindellspn, Tabletop, The joy of all things, TheArmchairSoldier, Thefreddy12354, Thewolfchild, Truthanado, WOSlinker, Waterwings91, Wikien2009, Wllmevans, Woggie10, 119 anonymous edits ... 569

Ministry of Defence (United Kingdom) *Source:* https://en.wikipedia.org/w/index.php?oldid=852270186 *License:* Creative Commons Attribution-Share Alike 3.0 *Contributors:* 19est66, 45ossington, Acalamari, Acsian88, AircraftZurf, Ajahewitt, AmINotCool, Antiochus the Great, Apparition11, Arado, Audiolessonover, Barabbas1312, Basisaoasis, Baycattwiakiitsreacist, Bigrossym, BilCat, Binksternet, BlueStar303, Bobrayner, Bocaj130, Bongwarrior, Boooomer124, Brianyoumans, BrownHairedGirl, C.Fred, Cameron11598, Cantab1985, Chiswick Chap, Chrisieboy, Clamasiatoaaa, Claíomh Solais, Clifton137, Clivemacd, Cloudbound, ClueBot NG, Colonies Chris, Cruckton, Cyberbot II, DVdm, Da-rb, Dbfirs, Deor, Dl2000, DocWatson42, Dormskirk, Dr Gangrene, Dual1tyx, Edwardx, EncyclopaediaNilssonia, Farleysmaster, Felamaslen, Feminist, Firstconch, Floquenbeam, Francotsangfh, Fullerraaron, Gaia Octavia Agrippa, Garyp01, Gecko177, Ghandiesque, Giraffedata, Glacialfox, Gold Wiz113, Govgovgov, Greenshed, Gulumeemee, Ham II, Harrison49, Hede2000, Hosgeorges, Huberthoff, IWJXB, Iamthemuffinman, Idaltu, Inglok, Isthmus, JaJaWa, JackofOz, James7022, Jasonlower, Jdforrester, Jeff G., JetBlast, Jim1138, Johnelwaq, Jon Kolbert, Jprg1966, Khazar2, KingUther, Kilidiplomus, Le Deluge, Lidos, Lkjljlkjljljkj, Lloydalicious, Lotje, Luckas Blade, Lynbarn, Manandro, Mark83, Materialscientist, Mattperehinec, Mayumashu, Mbryan90ROBLOX, McFlurry12, Mikhailov Kusserow, MilborneOne, Mmitchell10, Mogism, Mr Hall of England, Mrcridd, Navops47, Necrothesp, Nedrutland, NetNus, Nihiltres, Ogma the Scholar, Ohconfucius, Pam-javelin, Patrioteee, Phd8511, Picapica, PoliceChief, Proxima Centauri, Qwerty Binary, ROXETTE88, Rafael Zink, RaviC, Rcb1, Rgcarr, Rob984, Rrius, Sam11333, Schlechterwolf, Scttwind, Sdrqaz, Slightsmile, Snippy the heavily-templated snail, SonofSetanta, Spencer, Spintendo, Spiral2525, Superzohar, TaerkastUA, Tassedethe, The Anome, TheClown90, Thom2002, Thomas Courtenay, Earl of Devon, Thx811, Ticats, Tim!, Titodutta, Tpbradbury, Urshankov, Weisbrod, Welsh, West.andrew.g, WestminsterDoorkeeper, Whizz40, Wikipelli, Yunshui, 146 anonymous edits 583

Image Sources, Licenses and Contributors

The sources listed for each image provide more detailed licensing information including the copyright status, the copyright owner, and the license conditions.

Image *Source:* https://en.wikipedia.org/w/index.php?title=File:MinistryofDefence.svg *License:* Creative Commons Attribution-Sharealike 3.0,2.5,2.0,1.0 *Contributors:* User:Geord0 1

Image *Source:* https://en.wikipedia.org/w/index.php?title=File:Naval_Ensign_of_the_United_Kingdom.svg *License:* Public Domain *Contributors:* Alkari, Allforrous, AnonMoos, Avicennasis, Bender235, Benzoyl, Cathy Richards, Cycn, Dancingwombatsrule, Ec.Domnowall, Fry1989, Homo lupus, Illegitimate Barrister, Pumbaa80, SiBr4, Stunteltje, Xiengyod∼commonswiki, Yaddah, 6 anonymous edits 1

Image *Source:* https://en.wikipedia.org/w/index.php?title=File:Flag_of_the_Royal_Marines.svg *License:* Public Domain *Contributors:* Alkari, Hogweard, OgreBot 2 1

Image *Source:* https://en.wikipedia.org/w/index.php?title=File:Flag_of_the_British_Army.svg *License:* Public Domain *Contributors:* Created in Adobe Illustrator CS2, based off the above sources, by Philip Ronan 1

Image *Source:* https://en.wikipedia.org/w/index.php?title=File:Air_Force_Ensign_of_the_United_Kingdom.svg *License:* Public Domain *Contributors:* User: David Newton 1

Figure 1 *Source:* https://en.wikipedia.org/w/index.php?title=File:Battle_of_Trafalgar_Poster_1805.jpg *License:* GNU Free Documentation License *Contributors:* Akela3, BotMultichillT, Morio 3

Figure 2 *Source:* https://en.wikipedia.org/w/index.php?title=File:Royal_Irish_Rifles_ration_party_Somme_July_1916.jpg *License:* Public Domain *Contributors:* Royal Engineers No 1 Printing Company. 5

Figure 3 *Source:* https://en.wikipedia.org/w/index.php?title=File:Avro_Vulcan_Bomber_RAF.JPEG *License:* Public Domain *Contributors:* Sgt. David S. Nolan, US Air Force 6

Figure 4 *Source:* https://en.wikipedia.org/w/index.php?title=File:Ministry_of_Defence_Main_Building_MOD_45150121.jpg *Contributors:* Chase me ladies, I'm the Cavalry, Fæ, Ham II, OgreBot 2 7

Figure 5 *Source:* https://en.wikipedia.org/w/index.php?title=File:Soldiers_Trooping_the_Colour,_16th_June_2007.jpg *License:* Creative Commons Attribution 2.0 *Contributors:* Elgewen, Gryffindor, Kuerschner, Man vyi, Pegasovagante, Uaauaa 9

Figure 6 *Source:* https://en.wikipedia.org/w/index.php?title=File:Trident_II_missile_image.jpg *License:* Public Domain *Contributors:* DragonFire1024, Dual Freq, Edward, GDK, High Contrast, Martin H., Matrek, Para, Shizhao, Sumanch, Yann, 2 anonymous edits 10

Figure 7 *Source:* https://en.wikipedia.org/w/index.php?title=File:United_Kingdom_overseas_military_installations_and_operations.png *Contributors:* User:Antiochus the Great 11

Figure 8 *Source:* https//en.wikipedia.org *Contributors:* Cobatfor, Kablammo, TheArmchairSoldier, 1 anonymous edits 13

Figure 9 *Source:* https://en.wikipedia.org/w/index.php?title=File:Challenger_2_Tank_During_Amphibious_Demonstration_MOD_45152080.jpg *Contributors:* Antiochus the Great, Chase me ladies, I'm the Cavalry, Danrok, Fæ, High Contrast, Nickel nitride, Saga City 14

Figure 10 *Source:* https://en.wikipedia.org/w/index.php?title=File:Royal_Air_Force_Eurofighter_EF-2000_Typhoon_F2_Lofting-1.jpg *Contributors:* Chris Lofting 16

Figure 11 *Source:* https//en.wikipedia.org *Contributors:* Chase me ladies, I'm the Cavalry, Fæ 17

Figure 12 *Source:* https//en.wikipedia.org *License:* Public Domain *Contributors:* A. Erhardt 18

Image *Source:* https://en.wikipedia.org/w/index.php?title=File:Commons-logo.svg *License:* logo *Contributors:* Anomie, Callanecc, CambridgeBayWeather, Jo-Jo Eumerus, RHaworth 19

Image *Source:* https://en.wikipedia.org/w/index.php?title=File:Wiktionary-logo-en-v2.svg *Contributors:* User:Dan Polansky, User:Smurrayinchester 20

Image *Source:* https://en.wikipedia.org/w/index.php?title=File:Naval_ensign_of_the_United_Kingdom.svg *Contributors:* - 21

Figure 13 *Source:* https://en.wikipedia.org/w/index.php?title=File:Scottish_Red_Ensign.svg *License:* Public Domain *Contributors:* Original uploader was at 29

Figure 14 *Source:* https://en.wikipedia.org/w/index.php?title=File:Battle_of_Scheveningen_(Slag_bij_Ter_Heijde)(Jan_Abrahamsz._Beerstraten).jpg *License:* Public Domain *Contributors:* Anne97432, BotMultichill, Bukk, Ecummenic, Jarekt, Julia W, Kweniston, Shakko, Sterntreter, Stunteltje, Vincent Steenberg, 1 anonymous edits 32

Figure 15 *Source:* https://en.wikipedia.org/w/index.php?title=File:British_Battlecruiser_HMS_Hood_circa_1932.jpg *License:* Public Domain *Contributors:* Aschroet, Dcoetzee, Editor at Large, PMG, Pibwl, Reptil∼commonswiki 47

Image *Source:* https://en.wikipedia.org/w/index.php?title=File:Flag_of_the_British_Army_(1938-present).svg.png *License:* Creative Commons Zero *Contributors:* User:MartinKassemJ120 58

Figure 16 *Source:* https://en.wikipedia.org/w/index.php?title=File:Oliver_Cromwell_by_Samuel_Cooper.jpg *Contributors:* User:Dcoetzee 60

Figure 17 *Source:* https://en.wikipedia.org/w/index.php?title=File:King_Charles_II_by_John_Riley.jpg *Contributors:* User:Dcoetzee 61

Figure 18 *Source:* https://en.wikipedia.org/w/index.php?title=File:Battle_of_Blenheim_Tapestry.jpg *License:* Public Domain *Contributors:* Aschroet, Bohème, FRAYK, Judithcomm, Mmm448∼commonswiki, Rebel Redcoat∼commonswiki, Shakko 62

Figure 19 *Source:* https://en.wikipedia.org/w/index.php?title=File:Battle_of_Ramillies,_the_16th_Foot_charging_the_French_Infantry.png *License:* Public Domain *Contributors:* Cycn, Innotata, Rebel Redcoat∼commonswiki, Warburg, Иван Дулин 64

Figure 20 *Source:* https://en.wikipedia.org/w/index.php?title=File:Benjamin_West_005.jpg *License:* Public Domain *Contributors:* Adam Cuerden, Alexander Shatulin, Arctic.gnome, Aschroet, Bukk, Carlylean, Emijrp, File Upload Bot (Eloquence), Gilbertus, Hsarrazin, Jkelly, Mattes, Mutter Erde, Nonenmac, Rebel Redcoat∼commonswiki, Shakko, Skeezix1000, Slowking4, Themadchopper, 4 anonymous edits 66

Figure 21 *Source:* https://en.wikipedia.org/w/index.php?title=File:Balaklava_sick_2.jpg *License:* Public Domain *Contributors:* Simpson, William, 1823-1899, artist., Paul & Dominic Colnaghi & Co., publishers 69

Figure 22 *Source:* https://en.wikipedia.org/w/index.php?title=File:NLS_Haig_-_Troops_moving_up_at_eventide_-_men_of_a_Yorkshire_regiment_on_the_march.jpg *License:* Public Domain *Contributors:* ACrockford, Andrew Gray, GreenMeansGo, Labattblueboy, Rcbutcher, Richard Harvey, Soerfm, Steinsplitter, Taterian 71

Figure 23 *Source:* https://en.wikipedia.org/w/index.php?title=File:25-pdrs_firing_in_support_of_Guards_Armoured_Division.jpg *License:* Public Domain *Contributors:* Midgley (Sgt), No 5 Army Film & Photographic Unit 74

Figure 24 *Source:* https://en.wikipedia.org/w/index.php?title=File:Flag_of_the_United_Nations.svg *Contributors:* Wilfried Huss / Anonymous 75

Figure 25 *Source:* https://en.wikipedia.org/w/index.php?title=File:South_Belfast_1981.jpg *License:* Public Domain *Contributors:* en:User:Jeanne boleyn 79

Figure 26 *Source:* https://en.wikipedia.org/w/index.php?title=File:British_gulf_war.jpg *License:* Public Domain *Contributors:* GeorgHH, Hohum, Jarekt, Quake44, Sadads, SoLando, SuperTank17, Ultratomio, 2 anonymous edits 83

Image *Source:* https://en.wikipedia.org/w/index.php?title=File:PD-icon.svg *License:* Public Domain *Contributors:* Alex.muller, Anomie, Anonymous Dissident, CBM, Jo-Jo Eumerus, MBisanz, PBS, Quadell, Rocket000, Strangerer, Timotheus Canens, 1 anonymous edits 87

Figure 27 *Source:* https://en.wikipedia.org/w/index.php?title=File:Airco_D.H.9A_ExCC.jpg *License:* Public Domain *Contributors:* Chesipiero, FSII, Rcbutcher, Smat, Stahlkocher, Tm 90

Figure 28 *Source:* https://en.wikipedia.org/w/index.php?title=File:Z_Force_DH9_in_air_ambulance_role.jpg *License:* Public Domain *Contributors:* Chesipiero, FSII, Greenshed, JMCC1, PeterWD, 1 anonymous edits 91

Figure 29 *Source:* https://en.wikipedia.org/w/index.php?title=File:RAF_Darell's_Island.jpg *License:* Public Domain *Contributors:* Wing Commander Mo Ware, originally uploaded by Aodhdubh from English Wikipedia. 93

Figure 30 *Source:* https://en.wikipedia.org/w/index.php?title=File:Royal_Air_Force_Bomber_Command,_1942-1945._CL3400.jpg *License:* Public Domain *Contributors:* Aeroid, Ain92, AltSylt, Christoph Braun, Ducksoup, Fæ, Labattblueboy, Mogelzahn, Reykholt, Tony Mach, Túrelio, Ulf Heinsohn, UweRohwedder, 1 anonymous edits 94

Figure 31 *Source:* https://en.wikipedia.org/w/index.php?title=File:Avro_Vulcan_Bomber_RAF.JPEG *License:* Public Domain *Contributors:* Sgt. David S. Nolan, US Air Force 95

Figure 32 *Source:* https://en.wikipedia.org/w/index.php?title=File:Vulcan_bomber_18_May_1982.JPG *License:* Public Domain *Contributors:* Ken Griffiths 98

Figure 33 *Source:* https://en.wikipedia.org/w/index.php?title=File:RAF_Tornado_GR4_Iraq.JPEG *License:* Public Domain *Contributors:* SSgt. Lee O. Tucker 99

Figure 34 *Source:* https://en.wikipedia.org/w/index.php?title=File:FRBR_160716_Tornado_03.jpg *Contributors:* User:Poliocretes 101

Figure 35 *Source:* https://en.wikipedia.org/w/index.php?title=File:Ministry_of_Defence_Main_Building_MOD_45150121.jpg *Contributors:* Chase me ladies, I'm the Cavalry, Fæ, Ham II, OgreBot 2 106

Figure 36 *Source:* https://en.wikipedia.org/w/index.php?title=File:RHKAAF_Aerospatiale_Dauphin_1982.JPG *License:* Public Domain *Contributors:* SSgt. Steve McGill 110

Figure 37 *Source:* https://en.wikipedia.org/w/index.php?title=File:HMNB_Clyde.jpg *License:* Public Domain *Contributors:* http://www.nrlmry.navy.mil/ ... 134

Figure 38 *Source:* https://en.wikipedia.org/w/index.php?title=File:Radar_RAF_Fylingdales.jpg *License:* GNU Free Documentation License *Contributors:* AndreasPraefcke, File Upload Bot (Magnus Manske), Harrison49, Jakuzem, Lukasz Lukomski, MGA73bot2, OgreBot 2, PeterWD, Sitacuisses, Soerfm ... 138

Image *Source:* https://en.wikipedia.org/w/index.php?title=File:Padlock-silver.svg *Contributors:* AzaToth, BotMultichill, BotMultichillT, Gurch, Jarekt, Kallerna, Multichill, Perhelion, Rd232, Riana, Sarang, Siebrand, Steinsplitter, 4 anonymous edits ... 157

Image *Source:* https://en.wikipedia.org/w/index.php?title=File:Logo_of_the_Royal_Navy.svg *Contributors:* Kjerish ... 157

Image *Source:* https://en.wikipedia.org/w/index.php?title=File:Loudspeaker.svg *License:* Public Domain *Contributors:* User:Dbenbenn, User:Optimager, User:Tsca, User:Dbenbenn, User:Optimager, User:Tsca, User:Dbenbenn, User:Optimager, User:Tsca ... 158

Image *Source:* https://en.wikipedia.org/w/index.php?title=File:Flag_of_the_United_Kingdom.svg *License:* Public Domain *Contributors:* Anomie, Good Olfactory, Jo-Jo Eumerus, MSGJ, Mifter ... 158

Image *Source:* https://en.wikipedia.org/w/index.php?title=File:Royal_Navy_commissioning_pennant_(with_outline).svg *License:* Public Domain *Contributors:* LukeSearle ... 158

Figure 39 *Source:* https://en.wikipedia.org/w/index.php?title=File:BattleofSluys.jpeg *License:* Public Domain *Contributors:* AYE R, Alonso de Mendoza, Anne97432, Bukk, Bukvoed, Duesentrieb, Hohum, Jarekt, Kirill Lokshin, Mel22, Pufacz, Rsteen, Soerfm, Stefan Kühn, Stunteltje, Wilfridselsey, 3 anonymous edits ... 162

Figure 40 *Source:* https://en.wikipedia.org/w/index.php?title=File:Invincible_Armada.jpg *License:* Public Domain *Contributors:* Alonso de Mendoza, Hystrix, Ibn Battuta, KDS4444, Korrigan, Lmbuga, Makthorpe, Nuno Tavares, Postdlf, Rsteen, Spellcast, Themadchopper, Thib Phil, Un1c0s bot∼commonswiki, Wolfmann, 4 anonymous edits ... 164

Figure 41 *Source:* https://en.wikipedia.org/w/index.php?title=File:Battle_of_Scheveningen_(Slag_bij_Ter_Heijde)(Jan_Abrahamsz._Beerstraten).jpg *License:* Public Domain *Contributors:* Anne97432, BotMultichill, Bukk, Ecummenic, Jarekt, Julia W, Kweniston, Shakko, Sterntreter, Stunteltje, Vincent Steenberg, 1 anonymous edits ... 165

Figure 42 *Source:* https//en.wikipedia.org *License:* Public Domain *Contributors:* Aschroet, BotMultichillT, Ecummenic, Foroa, Hansmuller, Henxter, Kboht, Kweniston, Mattes, Mr.Dantes, Stunteltje, Targaryen, Vincent Steenberg, 1 anonymous edits ... 167

Figure 43 *Source:* https://en.wikipedia.org/w/index.php?title=File:An_English_Ship_in_Action_with_Barbary_Vessels_RMG_BHC0893.tiff *License:* Public Domain *Contributors:* BotMultichill, Fæ, Kresspahl ... 168

Figure 44 *Source:* https://en.wikipedia.org/w/index.php?title=File:Paton,_Battle_of_Barfleur.jpg *License:* Public Domain *Contributors:* AndreasPraefcke, Aroche, BotMultichill, Botaurus, Dormskirk, Ecummenic, File Upload Bot (Magnus Manske), Hohum, Mattes, Mike bzh, OgreBot 2, Pline, Teofilo, Verica Atrebatum ... 169

Figure 45 *Source:* https://en.wikipedia.org/w/index.php?title=File:HMS_Victory_-_bow.jpg *License:* Creative Commons Attribution 2.0 *Contributors:* Jamie Campbell from Emsworth (nr Portsmouth), U.K ... 170

Figure 46 *Source:* https://en.wikipedia.org/w/index.php?title=File:LindsayCambridge.jpg *License:* Public Domain *Contributors:* Blue Elf, BotMultichill, Botaurus, Broichmore, Bukk, Chase me ladies, I'm the Cavalry, Daderot, Hideokun, Teofilo, Ö, 1 anonymous edits ... 172

Figure 47 *Source:* https://en.wikipedia.org/w/index.php?title=File:The_battle_of_the_Saints_12_avril_1782.jpg *License:* Public Domain *Contributors:* AYE R, Broichmore, Bukk, Magicpiano, Rsteen, Thib Phil ... 173

Figure 48 *Source:* https://en.wikipedia.org/w/index.php?title=File:Bombardement_of_Algiers_1816.jpg *License:* Public Domain *Contributors:* Dzlinker, Rsteen ... 174

Figure 49 *Source:* https://en.wikipedia.org/w/index.php?title=File:Trafalgar1.jpg *License:* Public Domain *Contributors:* Bogomolov.PL, Bukk, Diwas, Erri4a, Juiced lemon, Morio, Rama, Rsteen, 1 anonymous edits ... 175

Figure 50 *Source:* https//en.wikipedia.org *License:* Creative Commons Attribution-Sharealike 2.0 *Contributors:* Andrew Thomas from Shrewsbury, UK ... 176

Figure 51 *Source:* https://en.wikipedia.org/w/index.php?title=File:British_ships_in_Canton.jpg *Contributors:* Dormskirk, Spellcast ... 177

Figure 52 *Source:* https://en.wikipedia.org/w/index.php?title=File:HMS_Dreadnought_1906_H61017.jpg *License:* Public Domain *Contributors:* U.S. Navy ... 178

Figure 53 *Source:* https://en.wikipedia.org/w/index.php?title=File:HMS_Ark_Royal_h85716.jpg *License:* Public Domain *Contributors:* United Kingdom Government ... 179

Figure 54 *Source:* https://en.wikipedia.org/w/index.php?title=File:British_Battlecruiser_HMS_Hood_circa_1932.jpg *License:* Public Domain *Contributors:* Aschroet, Dcoetzee, Editor at Large, PMG, Pibwl, Reptil∼commonswiki ... 181

Figure 55 *Source:* https://en.wikipedia.org/w/index.php?title=File:Vanguard_at_Faslane_02.jpg *Contributors:* Chase me ladies, I'm the Cavalry, Julia W, LittleWink ... 182

Figure 56 *Source:* https://en.wikipedia.org/w/index.php?title=File:HMS_Illustrious_at_Speed_MOD_45155641.jpg *Contributors:* Chase me ladies, I'm the Cavalry, Fæ, NeverDoING, OgreBot 2, Tuvalkin ... 183

Figure 57 *Source:* https://en.wikipedia.org/w/index.php?title=File:HMS_Albion_MOD_45151289.jpg *Contributors:* Andrew Gray, Chase me ladies, I'm the Cavalry, Danrok, Fæ, High Contrast, Jean11 ... 184

Figure 58 *Source:* https://en.wikipedia.org/w/index.php?title=File:BRNC-Dartmouth.jpg *License:* GNU Free Documentation License *Contributors:* Angusmclellan, File Upload Bot (Magnus Manske), Herbythyme, Jean-Frédéric, MGA73bot2, Mutter Erde, OgreBot 2, 1 anonymous edits ... 186

Figure 59 *Source:* https//en.wikipedia.org *Contributors:* Cobatfor, Kablammo, TheArmchairSoldier, 1 anonymous edits ... 187

Figure 60 *Source:* https://en.wikipedia.org/w/index.php?title=File:Duncan_(7899777334).jpg *License:* Creative Commons Attribution 2.0 *Contributors:* Mark Harkin ... 189

Figure 61 *Source:* https://en.wikipedia.org/w/index.php?title=File:HMS_Protector_Assisting_the_Antarctic_Community._MOD_45156397.jpg *Contributors:* Chase me ladies, I'm the Cavalry, Fæ, Gbawden, OgreBot 2 ... 190

Figure 62 *Source:* https://en.wikipedia.org/w/index.php?title=File:HMS_Astute_Arrives_at_Faslane_for_the_First_Time_MOD_45150806.jpg *Contributors:* Andrew Gray, Fæ, HJ Mitchell, OgreBot 2 ... 191

Figure 63 *Source:* https://en.wikipedia.org/w/index.php?title=File:UK_F-35B_Lightning_II_MOD_45157752.jpg *Contributors:* Chase me ladies, I'm the Cavalry, Fæ, Helmy oved, OgreBot 2, 1 anonymous edits ... 192

Figure 64 *Source:* https://en.wikipedia.org/w/index.php?title=File:Royal_Marines_in_Sangin_MOD_45151554.jpg *Contributors:* Chase me ladies, I'm the Cavalry, Fæ, Gbawden, OgreBot 2, Sanandros, Wieralee ... 193

Figure 65 *Source:* https://en.wikipedia.org/w/index.php?title=File:HMS_Albion_2006.jpg *License:* Public domain *Contributors:* Original uploader was Adrian Jones at en.wikipedia ... 194

Figure 66 *Source:* https://en.wikipedia.org/w/index.php?title=File:HMS_Vigilant_alongside_Faslane_Naval_Base._MOD_45147682.jpg *Contributors:* AdamBMorgan, Andrew Gray, Andy Dingley, Chase me ladies, I'm the Cavalry, Cobatfor, Fæ ... 195

Figure 67 *Source:* https://en.wikipedia.org/w/index.php?title=File:Uknavy_agustawestland_eh-101_merlin_hm1_arp.jpg *License:* Public Domain *Contributors:* User:Arpingstone ... 195

Figure 68 *Source:* https://en.wikipedia.org/w/index.php?title=File:RN_Flotilla_45154692.jpg *Contributors:* Danrok, Innotata, Le Deluge ... 197

Figure 69 *Source:* https://en.wikipedia.org/w/index.php?title=File:International_Fleet_Review._MOD_45144668.jpg *Contributors:* Blue Elf, Chase me ladies, I'm the Cavalry, Fæ, OgreBot 2 ... 200

Figure 70 *Source:* https://en.wikipedia.org/w/index.php?title=File:HMNB_Clyde.jpg *License:* Public Domain *Contributors:* http://www.nrlmry.navy.mil/ ... 200

Figure 71 *Source:* https://en.wikipedia.org/w/index.php?title=File:HMS_Richmond_MOD_45155880.jpg *Contributors:* Chase me ladies, I'm the Cavalry, Fæ, OgreBot 2 ... 201

Image *Source:* https://en.wikipedia.org/w/index.php?title=File:British_Royal_Navy_OF-10-collected.svg *Contributors:* User:Sodacan ... 203

Image *Source:* https://en.wikipedia.org/w/index.php?title=File:British_Royal_Navy_OF-9-collected.svg *Contributors:* User:Sodacan ... 203

Image *Source:* https://en.wikipedia.org/w/index.php?title=File:British_Royal_Navy_OF-8-collected.svg *Contributors:* User:Sodacan ... 203

Image *Source:* https://en.wikipedia.org/w/index.php?title=File:British_Royal_Navy_OF-7-collected.svg *Contributors:* User:Sodacan ... 203

Image *Source:* https://en.wikipedia.org/w/index.php?title=File:United_Kingdom-Navy-OF-6-collected.svg *Contributors:* User:Sodacan ... 203

Image *Source:* https://en.wikipedia.org/w/index.php?title=File:UK-Navy-OF-5-collected.svg *Contributors:* User:Sodacan ... 203

Image *Source:* https://en.wikipedia.org/w/index.php?title=File:UK-Navy-OF-4-collected.svg *Contributors:* User:Sodacan ... 203

Image *Source:* https://en.wikipedia.org/w/index.php?title=File:UK-Navy-OF-3-collected.svg *Contributors:* User:Sodacan ... 203

Image *Source:* https://en.wikipedia.org/w/index.php?title=File:UK-Navy-OF-2-collected.svg *Contributors:* User:Sodacan ... 203

Image *Source:* https://en.wikipedia.org/w/index.php?title=File:UK-Navy-OF-1b-collected.svg *Contributors:* User:Sodacan ... 203

Image *Source:* https://en.wikipedia.org/w/index.php?title=File:British_Royal_Navy_OF-1a.svg *Contributors:* User:Sodacan ... 203

Image *Source:* https://en.wikipedia.org/w/index.php?title=File:UK-Navy-OFD.svg *License:* Public Domain *Contributors:* Greentubing (talk) ... 203

Image *Source:* https://en.wikipedia.org/w/index.php?title=File:UK-Navy-OFStudent.svg *License:* Public Domain *Contributors:* Hazmat2 ... 203

Image *Source:* https://en.wikipedia.org/w/index.php?title=File:British_Royal_Marines_OF-10.svg *Contributors:* User:Skjoldbro ... 203

Image *Source:* https://en.wikipedia.org/w/index.php?title=File:British_Royal_Marines_OF-9.svg *Contributors:* User:Sodacan ... 203

Image *Source:* https://en.wikipedia.org/w/index.php?title=File:British_Royal_Marines_OF-8.svg *Contributors:* User:Sodacan ... 203

Image *Source:* https://en.wikipedia.org/w/index.php?title=File:British_Royal_Marines_OF-7.svg *Contributors:* User:Sodacan ... 203

Image *Source:* https://en.wikipedia.org/w/index.php?title=File:British_Royal_Marines_OF-6.svg *Contributors:* User:Sodacan ... 203

Image Source: https://en.wikipedia.org/w/index.php?title=File:British_Royal_Marines_OF-5.svg *Contributors:* User:Sodacan 203
Image Source: https://en.wikipedia.org/w/index.php?title=File:British_Royal_Marines_OF-4.svg *Contributors:* User:Sodacan 203
Image Source: https://en.wikipedia.org/w/index.php?title=File:British_Royal_Marines_OF-3.svg *Contributors:* User:Sodacan 203
Image Source: https://en.wikipedia.org/w/index.php?title=File:British_Royal_Marines_OF-2.svg *Contributors:* User:Sodacan 203
Image Source: https://en.wikipedia.org/w/index.php?title=File:British_Royal_Marines_OF-1b.svg *Contributors:* User:Sodacan 203
Image Source: https://en.wikipedia.org/w/index.php?title=File:British_Royal_Marines_OF-1a.svg *Contributors:* User:Sodacan 203
Image Source: https://en.wikipedia.org/w/index.php?title=File:British_Royal_Marines_OF-(D).svg *Contributors:* User:Skjoldbro 203
Image Source: https://en.wikipedia.org/w/index.php?title=File:British_Royal_Navy_OR-9.svg *Contributors:* User:Sodacan 205
Image Source: https://en.wikipedia.org/w/index.php?title=File:British_Royal_Navy_OR-7.svg *Contributors:* User:Sodacan 205
Image Source: https://en.wikipedia.org/w/index.php?title=File:British_Royal_Navy_OR-6.svg *Contributors:* User:Sodacan 205
Image Source: https://en.wikipedia.org/w/index.php?title=File:British_Royal_Navy_OR-4.svg *Contributors:* User:Sodacan 205
Image Source: https://en.wikipedia.org/w/index.php?title=File:British_Royal_Navy_OR-2.svg *Contributors:* User:Sodacan 205
Image Source: https://en.wikipedia.org/w/index.php?title=File:British_Royal_Marines_OR-9.svg *Contributors:* User:Sodacan 205
Image Source: https://en.wikipedia.org/w/index.php?title=File:British_Royal_Marines_OR-8.svg *Contributors:* User:Sodacan 205
Image Source: https://en.wikipedia.org/w/index.php?title=File:British_Royal_Marines_OR-7.svg *Contributors:* User:Sodacan 205
Image Source: https://en.wikipedia.org/w/index.php?title=File:British_Royal_Marines_OR-6.svg *Contributors:* User:Sodacan 205
Image Source: https://en.wikipedia.org/w/index.php?title=File:British_Royal_Marines_OR-4.svg *Contributors:* User:Sodacan 205
Image Source: https://en.wikipedia.org/w/index.php?title=File:British_Royal_Marines_OR-3.svg *Contributors:* User:Sodacan 205
Image Source: https://en.wikipedia.org/w/index.php?title=File:Royal_Navy_Dolphins.jpg *License:* Copyrighted free use *Contributors:* G.dallorto, Sharkbait784 205
Figure 72 *Source:* https://en.wikipedia.org/w/index.php?title=File:Elizabeth_II_v_pd.jpg *License:* Creative Commons Attribution-Sharealike 2.5 *Contributors:* CT Cooper, Desk1 207
Image Source: https://en.wikipedia.org/w/index.php?title=File:Wikisource-logo.svg *License:* Creative Commons Attribution-Sharealike 3.0 *Contributors:* ChrisiPK, Guillom, INeverCry, Jarekt, JuTa, Leyo, Lokal Profil, MichaelMaggs, NielsF, Rei-artur, Rocket000, Romaine, Steinsplitter 209
Figure 73 *Source:* https://en.wikipedia.org/w/index.php?title=File:HMS_Victory_at_dusk._MOD_45143807.jpg *Contributors:* Chase me ladies, I'm the Cavalry, Fæ, OgreBot 2 212
Figure 74 *Source:* https://en.wikipedia.org/w/index.php?title=File:Vanguard_at_Faslane_02.jpg *Contributors:* Chase me ladies, I'm the Cavalry, Julia W, LittleWink 212
Figure 75 *Source:* https://en.wikipedia.org/w/index.php?title=File:HMS_Ambush_long.jpg *License:* Copyrighted free use *Contributors:* LA(Phot) Will Haigh 213
Figure 76 *Source:* https://en.wikipedia.org/w/index.php?title=File:Royal_Navy_Trafalgar-class_submarine_HMS_Trenchant_(S91).jpg *License:* Public Domain *Contributors:* U.S. Navy photo by Mass Communication Specialist Seaman Zachary Wickline 214
Figure 77 *Source:* https://en.wikipedia.org/w/index.php?title=File:HMS_Queen_Elizabeth_in_Gibraltar_-_2018_(28386226189).jpg *License:* Creative Commons Attribution 2.0 *Contributors:* Dave Jenkins - InfoGibraltar 215
Figure 78 *Source:* https://en.wikipedia.org/w/index.php?title=File:HMS_Albion_MOD_45151289.jpg *Contributors:* Andrew Gray, Chase me ladies, I'm the Cavalry, Danrok, Fæ, High Contrast, Jean11 216
Figure 79 *Source:* https://en.wikipedia.org/w/index.php?title=File:Royal_Navy_Type_45_Destroyer_HMS_Daring_MOD_45153705.jpg *Contributors:* Chase me ladies, I'm the Cavalry, Fæ, Gbawden, OgreBot 2, Sixflashphoto, 1 anonymous edits 217
Figure 80 *Source:* https://en.wikipedia.org/w/index.php?title=File:HMS_Northumberland_MOD_45154788.jpg *Contributors:* Chase me ladies, I'm the Cavalry, Fæ, HJ Mitchell, OgreBot 2 217
Figure 81 *Source:* https://en.wikipedia.org/w/index.php?title=File:HMS_Clyde_Leaving_Portsmouth_MOD_45151373.jpg *Contributors:* Chase me ladies, I'm the Cavalry, Fæ, HJ Mitchell, Jean11, OgreBot 2 218
Figure 82 *Source:* https://en.wikipedia.org/w/index.php?title=File:HMS_Hurworth_MOD_45151313.jpg *Contributors:* Chase me ladies, I'm the Cavalry, Fæ, HJ Mitchell, OgreBot 2 219
Figure 83 *Source:* https://en.wikipedia.org/w/index.php?title=File:Sandown_Class_Mine_Hunter_HMS_Ramsey_MOD.jpg *Contributors:* Ministry of Defence 220
Figure 84 *Source:* https://en.wikipedia.org/w/index.php?title=File:P2000_Class_Royal_Navy_Patrol_Vessel_HMS_Raider_MOD_45151351.jpg *Contributors:* Chase me ladies, I'm the Cavalry, Fæ, OgreBot 2 221
Figure 85 *Source:* https://en.wikipedia.org/w/index.php?title=File:Gibraltar_Based_Patrol_Boat_HMS_Sabre_MOD_45153356.jpg *Contributors:* Chase me ladies, I'm the Cavalry, Cobatfor, Fæ, OgreBot 2 222
Figure 86 *Source:* https://en.wikipedia.org/w/index.php?title=File:HMS_Echo_(H87)_2015.jpg *Contributors:* Picture was taken by an employee of the MoD as part of their official duties 223
Figure 87 *Source:* https://en.wikipedia.org/w/index.php?title=File:HMS_Scott_at_Port_Lockroy_MOD_45151219.jpg *Contributors:* Chase me ladies, I'm the Cavalry, Fæ, HJ Mitchell, OgreBot 2 223
Figure 88 *Source:* https://en.wikipedia.org/w/index.php?title=File:Royal_Navy_Antarctic_Patrol_Ship_HMS_Protector_MOD_45153156.jpg *Contributors:* 4ing, Chase me ladies, I'm the Cavalry, Fæ, OgreBot 2, Oxyman 224
Figure 89 *Source:* https://en.wikipedia.org/w/index.php?title=File:HMS_Magpie_(H130)_sea_trials_April_2018.jpg *Contributors:* Davidshipphotos 224
Figure 90 *Source:* https://en.wikipedia.org/w/index.php?title=File:HMS_Bristol_alongside_Whale_Island-1.JPG *License:* Creative Commons Attribution-Sharealike 3.0 *Contributors:* Random Acts of Language 225
Image Source: https://en.wikipedia.org/w/index.php?title=File:Queen_Elizabeth_class_silhouette.png *Contributors:* User:Antiochus the Great .225
Image Source: https://en.wikipedia.org/w/index.php?title=File:Royal_Navy_Albion_silhouette.png *License:* GNU Free Documentation License *Contributors:* Antiochus the Great, Articseahorse, FSV, Leyo, OgreBot 2, Stunteltje 226
Image Source: https://en.wikipedia.org/w/index.php?title=File:Type45Destroyer_Silhouette.png *License:* Public Domain *Contributors:* Hlgallon 226
Image Source: https://en.wikipedia.org/w/index.php?title=File:Royal_Navy_Type_23_Frigate_silhouette.png *License:* GNU Free Documentation License *Contributors:* FSV, Kilom691, Leyo, OgreBot 2 226
Image Source: https://en.wikipedia.org/w/index.php?title=File:Vangaurd_class_SSBN_silhouette.png *Contributors:* User:Antiochus the Great .226
Image Source: https://en.wikipedia.org/w/index.php?title=File:Astute_class_SSN_silhouette.png *Contributors:* User:Antiochus the Great 226
Image Source: https://en.wikipedia.org/w/index.php?title=File:Trafalgar_class_SSN_silhouette.png *Contributors:* User:Antiochus the Great 226
Image Source: https://en.wikipedia.org/w/index.php?title=File:Fleet_Air_Arm_logo.JPG *License:* Creative Commons Attribution-Sharealike 3.0 *Contributors:* QuentinUK 237
Image Source: https://en.wikipedia.org/w/index.php?title=File:RAF_Lowris_Army_roundel.svg *License:* Public Domain *Contributors:* Aikari, Badseed, FOX 52, Fry1989, Jetijones, Joshbaumgartner, PeterWD, Pyrope, Sarang 237
Image Source: https://en.wikipedia.org/w/index.php?title=File:RAF_roundel.svg *License:* Public Domain *Contributors:* -xfi-, Benzoyl, Cathy Richards, FOX 52, Fry1989, Jetijones, Joshbaumgartner, Ketiltrout, Madmedea, Paulbe, PeterWD, Pyrope, Roomba, Sarang, Wknight94, Wst, 1 anonymous edits 237
Figure 91 *Source:* https://en.wikipedia.org/w/index.php?title=File:Wildcat_-_RIAT_2013_(12878404323).jpg *License:* Public Domain *Contributors:* 58.188user, Andrew Gray, BeatrixBelibaste, Catsmeat, Ducksoup, Fæ, Kersti Nebelsiek, Labatthlueboy, PeterWD, Rubutcher, Uli Elch, Иван Дулин 240
Figure 92 *Source:* https://en.wikipedia.org/w/index.php?title=File:SeaFury_launch.jpg *License:* Public Domain *Contributors:* Commander, Naval Forces Far East 241
Figure 93 *Source:* https://en.wikipedia.org/w/index.php?title=File:Phantom_FG1_892_Sqn_on_HMS_Ark_Royal_(R09)_1972.jpg *License:* Public Domain *Contributors:* U.S. Navy 242
Figure 94 *Source:* https://en.wikipedia.org/w/index.php?title=File:DN-SC-87-05770.JPEG *License:* Public Domain *Contributors:* USN .. 242
Figure 95 *Source:* https://en.wikipedia.org *Contributors:* Ariadacapo, Chase me ladies, I'm the Cavalry, De728631, Fæ, OgreBot 2, 1 anonymous edits 245
Figure 96 *Source:* https://en.wikipedia.org/w/index.php?title=File:Wildcat_-_RIAT_2013_(12878404323).jpg *License:* Creative Commons Attribution-Sharealike 2.0 *Contributors:* Tim Felce (Airwolfhound) 248
Figure 97 *Source:* https://en.wikipedia.org/w/index.php?title=File:ROYAL_NAVY_Merlin_and_Seaking_Helicopters_MOD_45138891.jpg *Contributors:* Ariadacapo, Chase me ladies, I'm the Cavalry, Cobatfor, Danrok, Fæ, JotaCartas, OgreBot 2 248
Figure 98 *Source:* https://en.wikipedia.org/w/index.php?title=File:RAF_F-35B_STOVL_RIAT_2016.jpg *Contributors:* GT1976, Helmy oved, TheArmchairSoldier 250
Figure 99 *Source:* https://en.wikipedia.org/w/index.php?title=File:Richard_Bell-Davies_VC_IWM_Q_69475.jpg *License:* Public Domain *Contributors:* photographer not identified 253
Image Source: https://en.wikipedia.org/w/index.php?title=File:RoyalMarineBadge.svg *License:* Public Domain *Contributors:* Unknown 257
Figure 100 *Source:* https://en.wikipedia.org/w/index.php?title=File:Major_General_John_Tupper.JPG *License:* Public Domain *Contributors:* Hohum, Profetarr 260
Figure 101 *Source:* https://en.wikipedia.org/w/index.php?title=File:Private_of_Marines.jpg *License:* Public Domain *Contributors:* S, C H (artist); Stadler, Joseph Constantine (engraver); DUPLICATE Colnaghi & Co 261

Figure 102 *Source:* https://en.wikipedia.org/w/index.php?title=File:British_Marines_in_Chania,_1897.jpg *License:* Public Domain *Contributors:* Cplakidas, DarwIn ... 262

Figure 103 *Source:* https://en.wikipedia.org/w/index.php?title=File:Commandos_archery.jpg *License:* Public Domain *Contributors:* Malindine, E G (Lt), War Office official photographer ... 264

Figure 104 *Source:* https://en.wikipedia.org/w/index.php?title=File:House_to_house_fighting_at_Riva_Bella_near_Ouistreham.jpg *License:* Public Domain *Contributors:* Laws, G (Sgt), Army Film and Photographic Unit ... 265

Figure 105 *Source:* https//en.wikipedia.org *License:* Public Domain *Contributors:* AdamBMorgan, Aloneinthewild, Fæ, Labattblueboy, Robert Weemeyer ... 266

Figure 106 *Source:* https://en.wikipedia.org/w/index.php?title=File:Raiderex.jpg *License:* Public domain *Contributors:* Hohum, Magog the Ogre, OgreBot 2, Sanandros ... 267

Figure 107 *Source:* https://en.wikipedia.org/w/index.php?title=File:Royal_Marines_in_Sangin_MOD_45151554.jpg *Contributors:* Chase me ladies, I'm the Cavalry, Fæ, Gbawden, OgreBot 2, Sanandros, Wieralee ... 269

Figure 108 *Source:* https://en.wikipedia.org/w/index.php?title=File:Royal_Marines_During_Winter_Training_in_Norway_MOD_45152252.jpg *Contributors:* AdamBMorgan, Chase me ladies, I'm the Cavalry, Duch, Fæ, OgreBot 2, Sanandros ... 270

Figure 109 *Source:* https://en.wikipedia.org/w/index.php?title=File:Viking_Training_MOD_45151364.jpg *Contributors:* Articseahorse, Chase me ladies, I'm the Cavalry, Fæ, OgreBot 2 ... 271

Figure 110 *Source:* https://en.wikipedia.org/w/index.php?title=File:Royal_Marine_Landing_Craft_MOD_45158374.jpg *Contributors:* Chase me ladies, I'm the Cavalry, Fæ ... 271

Figure 111 *Source:* https://en.wikipedia.org/w/index.php?title=File:A_Royal_Marine_LCVP_Landing_Craft_MOD_45150169.jpg *Contributors:* Chase me ladies, I'm the Cavalry, Danrok, Fæ, HantsAV, OgreBot 2 ... 272

Figure 112 *Source:* https://en.wikipedia.org/w/index.php?title=File:Royal_Marine_LCAC(LR)_Hovercraft_MOD_45154442.jpg *Contributors:* Blue Elf, Chase me ladies, I'm the Cavalry, Fæ, OgreBot 2, PeterWD, 木の枝 ... 272

Figure 113 *Source:* https://en.wikipedia.org/w/index.php?title=File:Royal_Marines_eng.png *License:* Creative Commons Attribution-ShareAlike 3.0 Unported *Contributors:* Noclador ... 274

Figure 114 *Source:* https://en.wikipedia.org/w/index.php?title=File:British_Commandos_Patch.svg *License:* Creative Commons Attribution-Sharealike 3.0 *Contributors:* Orionist ... 275

Figure 115 *Source:* https//en.wikipedia.org *License:* Public Domain *Contributors:* Benchill, BotMultichill, BotMultichillT, Chase me ladies, I'm the Cavalry, Hohum ... 276

Figure 116 *Source:* https//en.wikipedia.org *Contributors:* Arjuno3, Bulat, Chase me ladies, I'm the Cavalry, Clarice Reis, Danrok, Einstein2, Fæ, Greenshed, Jan.Kamenicek, Miya, Morio, Nilfanion, OgreBot 2, Pavlo Chemist, Thierry Caro ... 278

Figure 117 *Source:* https://en.wikipedia.org/w/index.php?title=File:Royal_marine_who_holds_gun.jpeg *License:* Public Domain *Contributors:* Photo by Lance CPL. R. L. Kugler, JR. ... 280

Figure 118 *Source:* https://en.wikipedia.org/w/index.php?title=File:Royal_Marines_snipers_displaying_their_L115A1_rifles.jpg *License:* Public domain *Contributors:* Avron, Denniss, Evers, Foroa, Francis Flinch, HantsAV, Hohum, KTo288, Man vyi, OgreBot 2, Sanandros, Túrelio, 1 anonymous edits ... 280

Figure 119 *Source:* https://en.wikipedia.org/w/index.php?title=File:Royal_Marine_Beret_Badge_MOD_45151656.jpg *Contributors:* Chase me ladies, I'm the Cavalry, Fæ, Gbawden, OgreBot 2 ... 282

Figure 120 *Source:* https://en.wikipedia.org/w/index.php?title=File:Bromsgrove_cemetery_GWGC_Barley.JPG *Contributors:* - ... 283

Figure 121 *Source:* https://en.wikipedia.org/w/index.php?title=File:Royal_Marines_on_Parade_in_the_City_of_London_MOD_45157923.jpg *Contributors:* Chase me ladies, I'm the Cavalry, Fæ, OgreBot 2, Oxyman ... 284

Figure 122 *Source:* https://en.wikipedia.org/w/index.php?title=File:HMS_Protector_Assisting_the_Antarctic_Community._MOD_45156397.jpg *Contributors:* Chase me ladies, I'm the Cavalry, Fæ, Gbawden, OgreBot 2 ... 291

Figure 123 *Source:* https://en.wikipedia.org/w/index.php?title=File:HMS-Clyde_Fox-Bay.jpg *License:* Creative Commons Attribution-Sharealike 3.0 *Contributors:* User:Guruchris ... 292

Figure 124 *Source:* https://en.wikipedia.org/w/index.php?title=File:Royal_Marines_During_Winter_Training_in_Norway_MOD_45152252.jpg *Contributors:* AdamBMorgan, Chase me ladies, I'm the Cavalry, Duch, Fæ, OgreBot 2, Sanandros ... 293

Figure 125 *Source:* https://en.wikipedia.org/w/index.php?title=File:HMS_Dragon_with_Russian_Aircraft_Carrier_'Admiral_Kuzetsov'_MOD_45157552.jpg *Contributors:* Chase me ladies, I'm the Cavalry, Fæ, Giorgi Balakhadze, JustSomePics, O484∼enwiki, Pibwl, PjotrMahh1, Retired electrician ... 294

Figure 126 *Source:* https://en.wikipedia.org/w/index.php?title=File:Trident_II_missile_image.jpg *License:* Public Domain *Contributors:* DragonFire1024, Dual Freq, Edward, GDK, High Contrast, Martin H., Matrek, Para, Shizhao, Sumanch, Yann, 2 anonymous edits ... 296

Figure 127 *Source:* https://en.wikipedia.org/w/index.php?title=File:UK's_Joint_Expeditionary_Force_(Maritime)_MOD_45162223.jpg *Contributors:* Fæ, Gbawden ... 297

Figure 128 *Source:* https://en.wikipedia.org/w/index.php?title=File:Merlin_Mk3s_prove_their_mettle_in_day-long_Gibraltar_transit_MOD_45160593.jpg *Contributors:* Akinom, De728631, Fæ, Uli Elch ... 299

Image *Source:* https://en.wikipedia.org/w/index.php?title=File:Symbol_support_vote.svg *License:* Public Domain *Contributors:* Anomie, Fastily, Jo-Jo Eumerus ... 321

Image *Source:* https://en.wikipedia.org/w/index.php?title=File:Flag_of_the_United_Kingdom_(3-5).svg *License:* Public Domain *Contributors:* Original code by Stefan-Xp with modifications to ratio by Yaddah. ... 321

Figure 129 *Source:* https://en.wikipedia.org/w/index.php?title=File:General_Thomas_Fairfax_(1612-1671)_by_Robert_Walker_and_studio.jpg *License:* Public Domain *Contributors:* FA2010, Jan Arkesteijn, Jarekt ... 323

Figure 130 *Source:* https://en.wikipedia.org/w/index.php?title=File:Oliver_Cromwell_by_Samuel_Cooper.jpg *Contributors:* User:Dcoetzee . 324

Figure 131 *Source:* https://en.wikipedia.org/w/index.php?title=File:John_Churchill_Marlborough_porträtterad_av_Adriaen_van_der_Werff_(1659-1722).jpg *Contributors:* Anathema, Auntof6, Boo-Boo Baroo, BotMultichill, DarwIn, Ecummenic, Grön, Mmm448∼commonswiki, Oursana, Rebel Redcoat∼commonswiki, Un1c0s bot∼commonswiki, Vincent Steenberg, Wolfmann, 2 anonymous edits ... 326

Figure 132 *Source:* https://en.wikipedia.org/w/index.php?title=File:Battle_of_Waterloo_1815.PNG *License:* Public Domain *Contributors:* 1970gemini, BotMultichill, DutchHoratius, Henxter, Hohum, Hsarrazin, Imnotkeller, Mathiasrex, Mykola Swarnyk, Stas1995, 3 anonymous edits ... 327

Figure 133 *Source:* https://en.wikipedia.org/w/index.php?title=File:Alphonse_de_Neuville_-_The_defence_of_Rorke's_Drift_1879_-_Google_Art_Project.jpg *License:* Public Domain *Contributors:* Alonso de Mendoza, BarretBonden, DIREKTOR, Herr Löffu, JuTa, Magnus Manske, PeterWD, Tamba52, Vincent Steenberg, 2 anonymous edits ... 328

Figure 134 *Source:* https://en.wikipedia.org/w/index.php?title=File:British_Mark_I_male_tank_Somme_25_September_1916.jpg *License:* Public Domain *Contributors:* User:NuclearWarfare ... 329

Figure 135 *Source:* https://en.wikipedia.org/w/index.php?title=File:The_Battle_of_the_Somme,_July-november_1916_Q1462.jpg *License:* Public Domain *Contributors:* Catfishmo, Fæ, HantsAV, Labattblueboy ... 330

Figure 136 *Source:* https://en.wikipedia.org/w/index.php?title=File:Scotishadvanceepsom.jpg *License:* Public Domain *Contributors:* Laing (Sgt), No 5 Army Film & Photographic Unit ... 331

Figure 137 *Source:* https://en.wikipedia.org/w/index.php?title=File:An_APC_of_the_7th_Brigade_Royal_Scots.JPEG *License:* Public Domain *Contributors:* PHC HOLMES, US Navy ... 333

Figure 138 *Source:* https://en.wikipedia.org/w/index.php?title=File:3royalanglianafghan.JPG *License:* Creative Commons Attribution-ShareAlike 3.0 Unported *Contributors:* Celticwarrior3551 ... 334

Figure 139 *Source:* https://en.wikipedia.org/w/index.php?title=File:1_RRF_engage_Iraqi_Army_positions_with_their_81mm_Mortars._Iraq._26-03-2003_MOD_45142764.jpg *Contributors:* AdamBMorgan, Ain92, Avron, Chase me ladies, I'm the Cavalry, Fæ, Hohum, Innotata, KTo288, OgreBot 2, Tm ... 335

Figure 140 *Source:* https://en.wikipedia.org/w/index.php?title=File:Cavalry_Trooping_the_Colour,_16th_June_2007.jpg *License:* Creative Commons Attribution 2.0 *Contributors:* KTo288, Kersti Nebelsiek, Man vyi, Pitke, Sandpiper, 1 anonymous edits ... 338

Image *Source:* https://en.wikipedia.org/w/index.php?title=File:Union_flag_1606_(Kings_Colors).svg *Contributors:* - ... 336

Figure 141 *Source:* https://en.wikipedia.org/w/index.php?title=File:Challenger_2-Megatron_MOD_45161542.jpg *Contributors:* Chase me ladies, I'm the Cavalry, Fæ, Nickel nitride, Wieralee ... 339

Figure 142 *Source:* https://en.wikipedia.org/w/index.php?title=File:MCV-80.jpg *License:* Public Domain *Contributors:* davric ... 340

Figure 143 *Source:* https://en.wikipedia.org/w/index.php?title=File:AS90_Self_Propelled_Gun_-_Tankfest_2009.jpg *License:* Creative Commons Attribution 2.0 *Contributors:* Simon from United Kingdom ... 340

Figure 144 *Source:* https://en.wikipedia.org/w/index.php?title=File:GUNNERS_ON_TARGET_FOR_EXERCISE_STEEL_SABRE_IN_NORTHUMBERLAND_MOD_45159595.jpg *Contributors:* Fæ, 木の枝 ... 340

Figure 145 *Source:* https://en.wikipedia.org/w/index.php?title=File:Apache_WAH64D_Helicopter_MOD_45149194.jpg *Contributors:* Andrew Gray, Chase me ladies, I'm the Cavalry, Danrok, Fæ, OgreBot 2, Tm ... 341

Figure 146 *Source:* https://en.wikipedia.org/w/index.php?title=File:An_upgraded_Laser_Light_Module_Mk_3_mounted_on_the_SA-80_Mk2._MOD_45158979.jpg *Contributors:* AdamBMorgan, Chase me ladies, I'm the Cavalry, Fæ ... 341

Figure 147 *Source:* https://en.wikipedia.org/w/index.php?title=File:The_combined_might_of_the_1_Yorkshire_Regiment_Battle_group_on_display_MOD_45158837.jpg *Contributors:* Brakeet, Chase me ladies, I'm the Cavalry, Fæ, Schlosser67, 1 anonymous edits ... 346

Figure 148 *Source*: https://en.wikipedia.org/w/index.php?title=File:Uk-sas.svg *Contributors*: British Army 348
Figure 149 *Source*: https://en.wikipedia.org/w/index.php?title=File:1939_Dominion_and_Colonial_Regiments.jpg *License*: Public Domain *Contributors*: His Majesty's Stationery Office 348
Figure 150 *Source*: https://en.wikipedia.org/w/index.php?title=File:1945_Order_of_Precedence_of_the_British_Army.jpg *License*: Public Domain *Contributors*: Her Majesty's Stationery Office 349
Figure 151 *Source*: https://en.wikipedia.org/w/index.php?title=File:Falklandsdf.jpg *License*: Creative Commons Attribution-Sharealike 3.0 *Contributors*: User:Lestalorm 350
Figure 152 *Source*: https://en.wikipedia.org/w/index.php?title=File:Detachment_of_Falkland_Islands_Defence_Force.jpg *Contributors*: User:Speeenderethal 350
Figure 153 *Source*: https://en.wikipedia.org/w/index.php?title=File:US_President_JF_Kennedy_inspects_Bermuda_Rifles_1961.jpg *License*: Public Domain *Contributors*: Robert Knudsen. White House Photographs. John F. Kennedy Presidential Library and Museum, Boston 350
Figure 154 *Source*: https://en.wikipedia.org/w/index.php?title=File:RSM_of_the_Bermuda_Regiment_1992.jpg *Contributors*: User:BermudaRegimental 351
Figure 155 *Source*: https://en.wikipedia.org/w/index.php?title=File:Bermuda_Regiment_Band.png *License*: Creative Commons Attribution-Sharealike 2.5 *Contributors*: Seán Pól Ó Creachmhaoil (Aodhdubh at en.wikipedia), modifications by Preslethe at en.wikipedia 352
Figure 156 *Source*: https://en.wikipedia.org/w/index.php?title=File:Bermuda_Regiment_PNCO_Cadre_Promotion_Parade.jpg *License*: Creative Commons Attribution-Sharealike 3.0 *Contributors*: Aloneinthewild, Auntof6, File Upload Bot (Magnus Manske), GT1976, Hohum, Innotata, OgreBot 2, Иван Дулин 352
Figure 157 *Source*: https://en.wikipedia.org/w/index.php?title=File:Changing_of_the_Guard_duo_-_Royal_Gibraltar_Regiment.jpg *License*: Creative Commons Attribution-Sharealike 2.0 *Contributors*: 5DII 352
Figure 158 *Source*: https://en.wikipedia.org/w/index.php?title=File:Royal_Gibraltar_Regiment.jpg *License*: Creative Commons Attribution-Sharealike 2.0 *Contributors*: 5DII 353
Figure 159 *Source*: https://en.wikipedia.org *License*: Public Domain *Contributors*: A. Erhardt 354
Figure 160 *Source*: https://en.wikipedia.org/w/index.php?title=File:RMAS18Je6-4685.jpg *License*: Creative Commons Attribution 3.0 *Contributors*: http://www.wyrdlight.com Author: Antony McCallum 355
Figure 161 *Source*: https://en.wikipedia.org/w/index.php?title=File:Flag_of_the_United_Kingdom_(3-5).svg *License*: Public Domain *Contributors*: Original code by Stefan-Xp with modifications to ratio by Yaddah. 356
Figure 162 *Source*: https://en.wikipedia.org/w/index.php?title=File:BritishArmyFlag2.svg *Contributors*: - 356
Figure 163 *Source*: https://en.wikipedia.org/w/index.php?title=File:British_Army_Ensign01.svg *License*: Public domain *Contributors*: Wally_Wiglet (talk) (Uploads) 357
Figure 164 *Source*: https://en.wikipedia.org/w/index.php?title=File:British_Army_Ensign00.svg *License*: Public domain *Contributors*: Wally_Wiglet (talk) (Uploads) 357
Figure 165 *Source*: https://en.wikipedia.org/w/index.php?title=File:Royal_Engineers_Ensign.png *License*: Creative Commons Zero *Contributors*: Graham Bartram 358
Image *Source*: https://en.wikipedia.org/w/index.php?title=File:British_Army_OF-10.svg *Contributors*: User:Sodacan 359
Image *Source*: https://en.wikipedia.org/w/index.php?title=File:British_Army_OF-9.svg *Contributors*: User:Sodacan 359
Image *Source*: https://en.wikipedia.org/w/index.php?title=File:British_Army_OF-8.svg *Contributors*: User:Sodacan 359
Image *Source*: https://en.wikipedia.org/w/index.php?title=File:British_Army_OF-7.svg *Contributors*: User:Sodacan 359
Image *Source*: https://en.wikipedia.org/w/index.php?title=File:British_Army_OF-6.svg *Contributors*: User:Sodacan 359
Image *Source*: https://en.wikipedia.org/w/index.php?title=File:British_Army_OF-5.svg *Contributors*: User:Sodacan 359
Image *Source*: https://en.wikipedia.org/w/index.php?title=File:British_Army_OF-3.svg *Contributors*: User:Sodacan 359
Image *Source*: https://en.wikipedia.org/w/index.php?title=File:British_Army_OF-2.svg *Contributors*: User:Sodacan 359
Image *Source*: https://en.wikipedia.org/w/index.php?title=File:British_Army_OF-1b.svg *Contributors*: User:Sodacan 359
Image *Source*: https://en.wikipedia.org/w/index.php?title=File:British_Army_OF-1a.svg *Contributors*: User:Sodacan 359
Image *Source*: https://en.wikipedia.org/w/index.php?title=File:British_Army_OF_(D).svg *Contributors*: User:Sodacan 359
Image *Source*: https://en.wikipedia.org/w/index.php?title=File:British_Army_Sergeant_Major.svg *Contributors*: User:Sodacan 360
Image *Source*: https://en.wikipedia.org/w/index.php?title=File:British_Army_OR-9b.svg *Contributors*: User:Sodacan 360
Image *Source*: https://en.wikipedia.org/w/index.php?title=File:British_Army_OR-9a.svg *Contributors*: User:Sodacan 360
Image *Source*: https://en.wikipedia.org/w/index.php?title=File:British_Army_OR-8b.svg *Contributors*: User:Sodacan 360
Image *Source*: https://en.wikipedia.org/w/index.php?title=File:British_Army_OR-8a.svg *Contributors*: User:Sodacan 360
Image *Source*: https://en.wikipedia.org/w/index.php?title=File:British_Army_OR-7.svg *Contributors*: User:Sodacan 360
Image *Source*: https://en.wikipedia.org/w/index.php?title=File:British_Army_OR-5.svg *Contributors*: User:Sodacan 360
Image *Source*: https://en.wikipedia.org/w/index.php?title=File:British_Army_OR-4.svg *Contributors*: User:Sodacan 360
Image *Source*: https://en.wikipedia.org/w/index.php?title=File:British_Army_OR-3.svg *Contributors*: User:Sodacan 360
Image *Source*: https://en.wikipedia.org/w/index.php?title=File:Flag_of_Germany.svg *License*: Public Domain *Contributors*: Anomie, Jo-Jo Eumerus 365
Image *Source*: https://en.wikipedia.org/w/index.php?title=File:Flag_of_Canada.svg *License*: Public Domain *Contributors*: Anomie, Jo-Jo Eumerus 366
Image *Source*: https://en.wikipedia.org/w/index.php?title=File:Flag_of_the_United_States.svg *License*: Public Domain *Contributors*: Anomie, Jo-Jo Eumerus, MSGJ, Mr. Stradivarius 366
Image *Source*: https://en.wikipedia.org/w/index.php?title=File:Flag_of_Italy.svg *License*: Public Domain *Contributors*: Anomie, Jo-Jo Eumerus 367
Image *Source*: https://en.wikipedia.org/w/index.php?title=File:Benelli_m4_2.jpg *License*: Public Domain *Contributors*: United States Marine Corps 367
Image *Source*: https://en.wikipedia.org/w/index.php?title=File:Accuracy_International_AW.png *License*: Creative Commons Attribution-Sharealike 3.0 *Contributors*: User:Mikesonline2011 367
Image *Source*: https://en.wikipedia.org/w/index.php?title=File:AW50.png *License*: Creative Commons Attribution-Sharealike 3.0 *Contributors*: Pjedvaj 368
Image *Source*: https://en.wikipedia.org/w/index.php?title=File:ACCURACY_INTERNATIONAL_AX-50_Rifle.jpg *License*: Creative Commons Zero *Contributors*: MORNINGSIDE, 木の枝 368
Image *Source*: https://en.wikipedia.org/w/index.php?title=File:Flag_of_Belgium_(civil).svg *License*: Public Domain *Contributors*: Allforrous, Andres gb.ldc, Bean49, Cathy Richards, David Descamps, Dbenbenn, Denelson83, Evanc0912, FreshCorp619, Fry1989, Gabriel trzy, Howcome, IvanOS, Jdx, Mimich, Ms2ger, Nightstallion, Oreo Priest, Pitke, Ricordisamoa, Rocket000, Rodejong, Sarang, SiBr4, Sir Iain, ThomasPusch, Warddr, Zscout370, 15 anonymous edits 368
Image *Source*: https://en.wikipedia.org/w/index.php?title=File:81mmMORT_L16.png *License*: Creative Commons Attribution-Sharealike 3.0,2.5,2.0,1.0 *Contributors*: Hisamikabunomura (talk)Hisamikabunomura 370
Image *Source*: https://en.wikipedia.org/w/index.php?title=File:AT-4Launcher.jpeg *License*: Creative Commons Attribution-Sharealike 3.0 *Contributors*: User:Polanksy kolbe 370
Figure 166 *Source*: https://en.wikipedia.org/w/index.php?title=File:British_Army_Sniper_with_L115A3_Rifle_Deploys_on_a_Mission_in_Afghanistan_MOD_45153555.jpg *Contributors*: Aloneinthewild, Chase me ladies, I'm the Cavalry, Danrok, Fæ, HantsAV, Hohum, OgreBot 2, Tm 372
Figure 167 *Source*: https://en.wikipedia.org/w/index.php?title=File:The_combined_might_of_the_1_Yorkshire_Regiment_Battle_group_on_display_MOD_45158837.jpg *Contributors*: Brakeet, Chase me ladies, I'm the Cavalry, Fæ, Schlosser67, 1 anonymous edits 374
Image *Source*: https://en.wikipedia.org *Contributors*: Chase me ladies, I'm the Cavalry, Fæ, Gavbadger, OgreBot 2, Tm 379
Image *Source*: https://en.wikipedia.org/w/index.php?title=File:AVLB_01.jpg *License*: Public Domain *Contributors*: davric 379
Image *Source*: https://en.wikipedia.org/w/index.php?title=File:A_Fox_NBC-detection_vehicle_is_transported_by_a_HETS_trailer.jpg *License*: Public Domain *Contributors*: Master Sgt. Jonathan Doti, U.S. Air Force 379
Figure 168 *Source*: https://en.wikipedia.org/w/index.php?title=File:Alvis_SUPACAT_ATMP_pic1.JPG *License*: Creative Commons Zero *Contributors*: Alf van Beem 382
Figure 169 *Source*: https://en.wikipedia.org/w/index.php?title=File:Apache_WAH64D_Helicopter_MOD_45149194.jpg *Contributors*: Andrew Gray, Chase me ladies, I'm the Cavalry, Danrok, Fæ, OgreBot 2, Tm 383
Image *Source*: https://en.wikipedia.org/w/index.php?title=File:AJAX,_the_Future_Armoured_Fighting_Vehicle_for_the_British_Army_MOD_45159441.jpg *Contributors*: Chase me ladies, I'm the Cavalry, Fæ, LittleWink 384
Figure 170 *Source*: https://en.wikipedia.org/w/index.php?title=File:Caricature-1780-press_gang.jpg *License*: Public Domain *Contributors*: Unspecified 406
Figure 171 *Source*: https://en.wikipedia.org/w/index.php?title=File:British_Army_Recruiting_poster_Guards.jpg *License*: Public Domain *Contributors*: National Museums Scotland - Project: 0504: National Museums Scotland Part 2 407
Figure 172 *Source*: https://en.wikipedia.org/w/index.php?title=File:Inspection-New-Colours.JPG *License*: Creative Commons Attribution 2.5 *Contributors*: Charles J Sharp 410

Figure 173 *Source:* https://en.wikipedia.org/w/index.php?title=File:British_recruits_August_1914_Q53234.jpg *License:* Public Domain *Contributors:* AnRo0002, Ardfern, Avron, Docu, Fæ, Gsl~commonswiki, IxK85, Jarry1250, Man vyi, Rcbutcher, Romary, SoLando, Thib Phil, 1 anonymous edits 411

Figure 174 *Source:* https://en.wikipedia.org/w/index.php?title=File:WWI_recruitment_poster_with_rebus.jpg *License:* Public Domain *Contributors:* Unknown. Publisher: Parliamentary Recruiting Committee, London 412

Figure 175 *Source:* https://en.wikipedia.org/w/index.php?title=File:British_Army_Recruitment_poster.JPG *License:* Creative Commons Attribution 3.0 *Contributors:* Rockybiggs (talk) 413

Figure 176 *Source:* https://en.wikipedia.org/w/index.php?title=File:AVRE-Bobbin.jpg *License:* Public Domain *Contributors:* Laing (Sgt), War Office official photographer Post-Work: User:W.wolny 414

Figure 177 *Source:* https://en.wikipedia.org/w/index.php?title=File:Army_Careers_Oxford_20051022.jpg *License:* Creative Commons Attribution-ShareAlike 3.0 Unported *Contributors:* User:Kaihsu 416

Figure 178 *Source:* https://en.wikipedia.org/w/index.php?title=File:The_Empire_Needs_Men_WWI.jpg *License:* Public Domain *Contributors:* Chuckb187, Kilom691, Lx 121, Man vyi, Rcbutcher 417

Figure 179 *Source:* https://en.wikipedia.org/w/index.php?title=File:Australian_WWI_recruiting_poster.jpg *License:* Public Domain *Contributors:* Atirador, Jarekt, Jcb, Liftarn, Matthead, OgreBot 2, Rcbutcher, Tangopaso, 1 anonymous edits 418

Figure 180 *Source:* https://en.wikipedia.org/w/index.php?title=File:Indian_Troops_in_France.jpg *License:* Public Domain *Contributors:* Photographer unknown; book more than 70 years old. 419

Figure 181 *Source:* https://en.wikipedia.org/w/index.php?title=File:Gurkhas_exercise_DM-SD-98-00170.jpg *License:* Public Domain *Contributors:* LANCE CPL. C.D. CLARK 419

Figure 182 *Source:* https://en.wikipedia.org/w/index.php?title=File:10th_(Irish)_Division_at_Basingstoke.jpg *License:* Public Domain *Contributors:* 1989, Ardfern, Gsl~commonswiki, Jarekt, Mighty Antar, Ratatosk, Rcbutcher, Slowking4, SoLando, Verica Atrebatum 420

Figure 183 *Source:* https://en.wikipedia.org/w/index.php?title=File:Johnson_Beharry,_VC.jpg *License:* Creative Commons Attribution-Sharealike 2.0 *Contributors:* RMEIKLEJ on Flickr 421

Figure 184 *Source:* https://en.wikipedia.org *License:* Public Domain *Contributors:* A. Erhardt 422

Image *Source:* https://en.wikipedia.org/w/index.php?title=File:Coldstream_Guards_WWI_poster.jpg *License:* Public Domain *Contributors:* Ernest Ibbetson 423

Image *Source:* https://en.wikipedia.org/w/index.php?title=File:RAF-Badge.svg *License:* Public Domain *Contributors:* ChevronTango, Denniss, Fry1989, Jahoe, MichaelMaggs, OgreBot 2, 1 anonymous edits 445

Image *Source:* https://en.wikipedia.org/w/index.php?title=File:Ensign_of_the_Royal_Air_Force.svg *License:* Public Domain *Contributors:* - 446

Image *Source:* https://en.wikipedia.org/w/index.php?title=File:Logo_of_the_Royal_Air_Force.svg *License:* Public Domain *Contributors:* Fry1989 446

Image *Source:* https://en.wikipedia.org/w/index.php?title=File:RAF-Finflash-Noncombat.svg *License:* Public Domain *Contributors:* User:Greentubing~commonswiki 446

Image *Source:* https://en.wikipedia.org/w/index.php?title=File:Fin_flash_of_the_United_Kingdom_Low_Visibility.svg *License:* Public Domain *Contributors:* Joshbaumgartner 446

Image *Source:* https://en.wikipedia.org/w/index.php?title=File:RAF_pilot_brevet_(Queen's_Crown).jpg *License:* Public Domain *Contributors:* Greenshed 446

Figure 185 *Source:* https://en.wikipedia.org/w/index.php?title=File:Ray_Flying_Legends_2005-1.jpg *License:* GNU Free Documentation License *Contributors:* Catsmeat, Cobatfor, Denniss, File Upload Bot (Magnus Manske), IxK85, MGA73bot2, MilborneOne, OgreBot 2, Padawane, PeterWD, Ranger Steve, Rcbutcher, Tm, 15 anonymous edits 449

Figure 186 *Source:* https://en.wikipedia.org/w/index.php?title=File:Avro_683_Lancaster_B1,_UK_-_Air_Force_AN1207411.jpg *Contributors:* Fæ, PeterWD 449

Figure 187 *Source:* https://en.wikipedia.org/w/index.php?title=File:Raf_victor_in_1961_arp.jpg *License:* Public Domain *Contributors:* User:Arpingstone 450

Figure 188 *Source:* https://en.wikipedia.org/w/index.php?title=File:Avro_Vulcan_Bomber_RAF.JPEG *License:* Public Domain *Contributors:* Sgt. David S. Nolan, US Air Force 451

Figure 189 *Source:* https://en.wikipedia.org/w/index.php?title=File:Red_Arrows_and_Typhoons_flypast_for_90th_Anniversary_of_the_RAF_MOD_45147908.jpg *Contributors:* Ariadacapo, Chase me ladies, I'm the Cavalry, De728631, Fæ, Julian Herzog, Man vyi, Morio, OgreBot 2 453

Figure 190 *Source:* https://en.wikipedia.org/w/index.php?title=File:RAF_QRA_Typhoon_Intercepting_Russian_Bear_Aircraft_MOD_45158137.jpg *Contributors:* Chase me ladies, I'm the Cavalry, De728631, Fæ, Julian Herzog, Mike1979 Russia, MilborneOne, OgreBot 2, ВоенТех 453

Image *Source:* https://en.wikipedia.org/w/index.php?title=File:Red_pog.svg *License:* Public Domain *Contributors:* Andux, Antonsusi, Bdk, Chenspec, ChrisiPK, Cuthbertwong, Davepape, Doodledoo, Er Komandante, Grolltech, Herbythyme, Körnerbrötchen, LNICOLAS, LX, Nagy, Penubag, Pieter Kuiper, Pimke, Rlevse, STyx, Saibo, Sarang, Siebrand, Steinsplitter, Trixt, TwoWings, YLSS, 46 anonymous edits 456

Image *Source:* https://en.wikipedia.org/w/index.php?title=File:Purple_pog.svg *License:* Public Domain *Contributors:* User:Andux 456

Image *Source:* https://en.wikipedia.org/w/index.php?title=File:Yellow_pog.svg *License:* Public Domain *Contributors:* Amalthea 456

Image *Source:* https://en.wikipedia.org/w/index.php?title=File:Orange_pog.svg *License:* Public Domain *Contributors:* User:Andux 456

Image *Source:* https://en.wikipedia.org/w/index.php?title=File:Steel_pog.svg *License:* Public Domain *Contributors:* derivative work: Mareklug talk Red_pog.svg: Andux 456

Image *Source:* https://en.wikipedia.org/w/index.php?title=File:Blue_0080ff_pog.svg *License:* Creative Commons Zero *Contributors:* Antonsusi, One Salient Oversight, Pierpao, Sarang, YLSS 456

Image *Source:* https://en.wikipedia.org/w/index.php?title=File:Blue_pog.svg *License:* Public Domain *Contributors:* Andux 456

Image *Source:* https://en.wikipedia.org/w/index.php?title=File:Pink_pog.svg *License:* Public Domain *Contributors:* Andux 456

Image *Source:* https://en.wikipedia.org/w/index.php?title=File:Green_pog.svg *License:* Public Domain *Contributors:* Andux, Antonsusi, Jcb, Juiced lemon, Nixón, Pd4u, Rocket000, STyx, TwoWings, Wouterhagens, YLSS, 5 anonymous edits 456

Image *Source:* https://en.wikipedia.org/w/index.php?title=File:Blue-gold_pog.svg *License:* Public Domain *Contributors:* Sarang 456

Figure 191 *Source:* https://en.wikipedia.org/w/index.php?title=File:Radar_RAF_Fylingdales.jpg *License:* GNU Free Documentation License *Contributors:* AndreasPraefcke, File Upload Bot (Magnus Manske), Harrison49, Jakuzem, Lukasz Lukomski, MGA73bot2, OgreBot 2, PeterWD, Sitacuisses, Soerfm 457

Figure 192 *Source:* https://en.wikipedia.org/w/index.php?title=File:Mount_Pleasant_Airport_-_Donald_Morrison.jpg *License:* Creative Commons Attribution 2.0 *Contributors:* Donald Morrison from Lochaish, Scotland 460

Figure 193 *Source:* https://en.wikipedia.org/w/index.php?title=File:RAF_Regiment_(8658943968)_(2).jpg *License:* Creative Commons Attribution 2.0 *Contributors:* Ronnie Macdonald from Chelmsford, United Kingdom 461

Figure 194 *Source:* https://en.wikipedia.org/w/index.php?title=File:Tornado_navigator_DN-SD-01-05054.JPEG *License:* Public Domain *Contributors:* PH1 TODD P. CICHONOWICZ, USN 463

Figure 195 *Source:* https://en.wikipedia.org/w/index.php?title=File:RAF_Regiment_Gunner.jpg *Contributors:* SAC Andy Masson 463

Image *Source:* https://en.wikipedia.org/w/index.php?title=File:Eurofighter_Typhoon_FIA_2012.jpg *License:* Creative Commons Attribution 2.0 *Contributors:* Adrian 466

Image *Source:* https://en.wikipedia.org/w/index.php?title=File:Tornado_7_(5824708543).jpg *License:* Creative Commons Attribution 2.0 *Contributors:* Tony Hisgett from Birmingham, UK 466

Image *Source:* https://en.wikipedia.org/w/index.php?title=File:Boeing.e3-d.sentry.takeoff.arp.jpg *License:* Public Domain *Contributors:* User:Arpingstone 467

Image *Source:* https://en.wikipedia.org/w/index.php?title=File:Raf-sentinel-ZJ692-071029-08-16.jpg *License:* Creative Commons Attribution-Sharealike 3.0,2.5,2.0,1.0 *Contributors:* Alan Radecki Akradecki 468

Image *Source:* https://en.wikipedia.org/w/index.php?title=File:RC-135W_Rivet_Joint_MOD_45159809.jpg *Contributors:* De728631, Fæ, LittleWink, XR728 468

Image *Source:* https://en.wikipedia.org/w/index.php?title=File:Shadow_R1_5(AC)_Sqdn_RAF_Waddington_this_morning.jpg *License:* Creative Commons Attribution 2.0 *Contributors:* Jerry Gunner 468

Image *Source:* https://en.wikipedia.org/w/index.php?title=File:MQ-9_Reaper_in_flight_(2007).jpg *License:* Public Domain *Contributors:* U.S. Air Force photo/Staff Sgt. Brian Ferguson 469

Image *Source:* https://en.wikipedia.org/w/index.php?title=File:Chinook_hc2_za682_arp.jpg *License:* Public Domain *Contributors:* User:Arpingstone 469

Image *Source:* https://en.wikipedia.org/w/index.php?title=File:RAF_Puma_Mk2_Helicopter_MOD_45156639.jpg *Contributors:* Chase me ladies, I'm the Cavalry, Fæ, Groupsixty, OgreBot 2, Rcbutcher, Russavia 469

Image *Source:* https://en.wikipedia.org/w/index.php?title=File:Bell_412EP_Griffin_HAR2,_UK_-_Air_Force_AN1560195.jpg *Contributors:* Articseahorse, Chase me ladies, I'm the Cavalry, De728631, Fæ, GT1976, LittleWink, Uli Bich 470

Image *Source:* https://en.wikipedia.org/w/index.php?title=File:C17_Transport_Aircraft_Taking_Off_from_RAF_Brize_Norton_MOD_45156519.jpg *Contributors:* Chase me ladies, I'm the Cavalry, Coldworm, De728631, Fæ, OgreBot 2, Rcbutcher, Szilas, Threecharlie 471

Image *Source:* https://en.wikipedia.org/w/index.php?title=File:RAF_A400M_Lands_at_RAF_Brize_Norton.jpg *Contributors:* Paul Crouch, © Crown copyright 471

Image *Source:* https://en.wikipedia.org/w/index.php?title=File:Hercules_C130J_,_Waddington_-_geograph.org.uk_-_1139086.jpg *License:* Creative Commons Attribution-Share Alike 2.0 Generic *Contributors:* Mick Lobb ... 471

Image *Source:* https://en.wikipedia.org/w/index.php?title=File:Royal_Air_Force_Airbus_A330MRTT_Bidini.jpg *Contributors:* Aldo Bidini ... 471

Image *Source:* https://en.wikipedia.org/w/index.php?title=File:ZE701_BAe_146_CC.2_(11329194625).jpg *License:* Creative Commons Attribution 2.0 *Contributors:* Mark Harkin ... 472

Image *Source:* https://en.wikipedia.org/w/index.php?title=File:RAF_BAE146_QC_in_Afghanistan_MOD_45156847.jpg *Contributors:* Chase me ladies, I'm the Cavalry, De728631, Fæ, Green Giant, OgreBot 2, 1 anonymous edits ... 472

Image *Source:* https://en.wikipedia.org/w/index.php?title=File:Grob_G_115E_EA-3.JPG *License:* Creative Commons Attribution-Sharealike 3.0 *Contributors:* James Humphreys - SalopianJames ... 473

Image *Source:* https://en.wikipedia.org/w/index.php?title=File:RAF_Short_Tucano.jpg *License:* Creative Commons Attribution 2.0 *Contributors:* Ariadacapo, Chesipiero, De728631, FlickreviewR, Harrison49, PeterWD, Ww2censor ... 473

Image *Source:* https://en.wikipedia.org/w/index.php?title=File:BAe_Hawk_T1_XX280_-_100_Squadron_(8680135241).jpg *License:* Creative Commons Attribution-Sharealike 2.0 *Contributors:* Trevor Hannant ... 474

Image *Source:* https://en.wikipedia.org/w/index.php?title=File:Royal_Air_Force_King_Air_B200_Training_Aircraft_MOD_45153010.jpg *Contributors:* Ariadacapo, Chase me ladies, I'm the Cavalry, Fæ, OgreBot 2, Oxyman, PeterWD, 1 anonymous edits ... 474

Image *Source:* https://en.wikipedia.org/w/index.php?title=File:GrobVikingTX1-rafhist.jpg *License:* Public Domain *Contributors:* unknown RAF photographer ... 474

Image *Source:* https://en.wikipedia.org/w/index.php?title=File:Boeing_P-8A_Poseidon_flies_over_Jacksonville_(2).jpg *License:* Public Domain *Contributors:* Cobatfor, M-MMMQ ... 475

Image *Source:* https://en.wikipedia.org/w/index.php?title=File:Pictured_is_the_first_of_the_UK's_F-35B_Lightning_II_jets_to_be_flown_to_the_UK._MOD_45160016.jpg *Contributors:* Articseahorse, Fæ, Petebutt, PeterWD ... 476

Image *Source:* https://en.wikipedia.org/w/index.php?title=File:G120_Prefect_-_RIAT_2017_(36273768463).jpg *License:* Creative Commons Attribution-Sharealike 2.0 *Contributors:* Airwolfhound from Hertfordshire, UK ... 476

Image *Source:* https://en.wikipedia.org/w/index.php?title=File:T-6A_Texan_II.jpg *License:* Public Domain *Contributors:* U.S. Air Force photo by Master Sgt. David Richards ... 477

Image *Source:* https://en.wikipedia.org/w/index.php?title=File:RAF_BAE_Systems_Hawk_T2_Lofting-1.jpg *Contributors:* Chris Lofting ... 477

Image *Source:* https://en.wikipedia.org/w/index.php?title=File:Embraer_Phenom_100_trainer_of_the_RAF_(PR-PHK)_at_RIAT_Fairford_13July2017_arp.jpg *License:* Public domain *Contributors:* Myself (Adrian Pingstone). ... 477

Figure 196 *Source:* https://en.wikipedia.org/w/index.php?title=File:Ensign_of_the_Royal_Air_Force.svg *Contributors:* - ... 478

Figure 197 *Source:* https://en.wikipedia.org/w/index.php?title=File:Royal_Banner_RAF.svg *Contributors:* User:FOX 52 ... 478

Figure 198 *Source:* https://en.wikipedia.org/w/index.php?title=File:RIAT_2016_F-35B_Typhoons_Red_Arrows.jpg *Contributors:* BotAdventures, GT1976, LittleWink, TheArmchairSoldier ... 480

Figure 199 *Source:* https://en.wikipedia.org/w/index.php?title=File:Graduates_front_of_College_Hall.jpg *License:* Creative Commons Attribution-Sharealike 3.0 *Contributors:* User:Charlesdrakew ... 495

Image *Source:* https://en.wikipedia.org/w/index.php?title=File:RAF_Voyager_at_RAF_Brize_Norton.jpg *Contributors:* Aircraft de-icing, De728631, Dyolf77 ... 494

Image *Source:* https://en.wikipedia.org/w/index.php?title=File:Squirrel_Helicopter_at_RAF_Shawbury_MOD_45151116.jpg *Contributors:* Chase me ladies, I'm the Cavalry, Fæ, OgreBot 2, Oxyman ... 494

Figure 200 *Source:* https://en.wikipedia.org/w/index.php?title=File:V-22_Osprey_(USAF)_-_RAF_Mildenhall_-_Suffolk,_England_-_17th_July_2013.jpg *License:* Creative Commons Attribution 2.0 *Contributors:* David Warrington from England ... 503

Figure 201 *Source:* https://en.wikipedia.org/w/index.php?title=File:Luis_Holden_Defence_Images_Photo_10.jpg *Contributors:* Chase me ladies, I'm the Cavalry, De728631, Kirill Borisenko, Milru, PeterWD, Tomer T, 1 anonymous edits ... 506

Image *Source:* https://en.wikipedia.org/w/index.php?title=File:Flag_of_the_United_Arab_Emirates.svg *License:* Public Domain *Contributors:* Anime Addict AA, Avala, Dbenbenn, Denniss, Duduziq, F l a n k e r, Fry1989, Fukaumi, Gryffindor, Guanaco, Homo lupus, JuTa, Kacir, Klemen Kocjancic, Krun, Ludger1961, Madden, Misisanta97, Neq00, Nightstallion, Piccadilly Circus∼commonswiki, Pmsyyz, RamzyAbueita∼commonswiki, Ricordisamoa, Schmarrnintelligenz, SiBr4, Zscout370, З.Вукобрат, 5 anonymous edits ... 506

Image *Source:* https://en.wikipedia.org/w/index.php?title=File:Flag_of_Qatar.svg *License:* Public Domain *Contributors:* (of code) ... 506

Image *Source:* https://en.wikipedia.org/w/index.php?title=File:Flag_of_the_Falkland_Islands.svg *License:* Public Domain *Contributors:* User:Nightstallion ... 507

Image *Source:* https://en.wikipedia.org/w/index.php?title=File:Flag_of_Gibraltar.svg *License:* Public Domain *Contributors:* Alkari, Bast64∼commonswiki, Benzoyl, Cycn, Dbenbenn, Denelson83, Fry1989, HJ Mitchell, Mattes, Nightstallion, Pumbaa80, SiBr4, 3 anonymous edits 507

Image *Source:* https://en.wikipedia.org/w/index.php?title=File:Flag_of_Cyprus.svg *License:* Public Domain *Contributors:* User:Vzb83 ... 507

Image *Source:* https://en.wikipedia.org/w/index.php?title=File:Location_dot_red.svg *License:* Public Domain *Contributors:* User:Droll ... 508

Image *Source:* https://en.wikipedia.org/w/index.php?title=File:Location_dot_orange.svg *License:* Public Domain *Contributors:* User:Droll ... 508

Image *Source:* https://en.wikipedia.org/w/index.php?title=File:Location_dot_green.svg *License:* Public Domain *Contributors:* User:Droll ... 508

Image *Source:* https://en.wikipedia.org/w/index.php?title=File:Location_dot_blue.svg *License:* Public Domain *Contributors:* User:Droll ... 508

Image *Source:* https://en.wikipedia.org/w/index.php?title=File:Location_dot_purple.svg *License:* Public Domain *Contributors:* User:Droll ... 508

Image *Source:* https://en.wikipedia.org/w/index.php?title=File:Location_dot_deeppink.svg *License:* Public Domain *Contributors:* User:Droll ... 508

Image *Source:* https://en.wikipedia.org/w/index.php?title=File:Location_dot_black.svg *License:* Public Domain *Contributors:* User:Droll ... 508

Figure 202 *Source:* https://en.wikipedia.org/w/index.php?title=File:Typhooon_force_in_flight_MOD_45160736.jpg *Contributors:* De728631, Fæ, Venaldavid ... 510

Figure 203 *Source:* https://en.wikipedia.org/w/index.php?title=File:MinistryofDefence.svg *License:* Creative Commons Attribution-Sharealike 3.0,2.5,2.0,1.0 *Contributors:* User:Geord0 ... 565

Image *Source:* https://en.wikipedia.org/w/index.php?title=File:AirTanker_Services_logo.svg *License:* Public Domain *Contributors:* AirTanker Services ... 566

Figure 204 *Source:* https://en.wikipedia.org/w/index.php?title=File:Airbus_Voyager_of_the_RAF_arrives_Fairford_7Jul2016_arp.jpg *License:* Public domain *Contributors:* Myself (Adrian Pingstone). ... 567

Figure 205 *Source:* https://en.wikipedia.org/w/index.php?title=File:AirbusVoyageratRIAT2011.jpg *License:* Creative Commons Attribution-Sharealike 3.0 *Contributors:* MilborneOne ... 568

Figure 206 *Source:* https://en.wikipedia.org/w/index.php?title=File:RAF_F-35B.jpg *Contributors:* LittleWink, TheArmchairSoldier ... 570

Figure 207 *Source:* https://en.wikipedia.org/w/index.php?title=File:RAF_Typhoon_inflight.jpg *Contributors:* De728631, El Grafo, Fan of Aviation, Julian Herzog, Lupo, Nick, OlEnglish, Russavia, Stoproches ... 571

Figure 208 *Source:* https://en.wikipedia.org/w/index.php?title=File:BAEMantisMockUp.JPG *License:* Public Domain *Contributors:* Mike Young 572

Figure 209 *Source:* https://en.wikipedia.org/w/index.php?title=File:TaranisModel.JPG *License:* Public Domain *Contributors:* Mike Young ... 573

Figure 210 *Source:* https://en.wikipedia.org/w/index.php?title=File:A400m_flaps_down.jpg *License:* Creative Commons Attribution-Sharealike 2.0 *Contributors:* Benurs ... 575

Figure 211 *Source:* https://en.wikipedia.org/w/index.php?title=File:RAF_Hercules_C-130J_MOD_45158035.jpg *Contributors:* Arado, Chase me ladies, I'm the Cavalry, El Grafo, Fæ, OgreBot 2, Russavia ... 575

Figure 212 *Source:* https://en.wikipedia.org/w/index.php?title=File:First_Rivet_Joint_Aircraft_Lands_at_RAF_Waddington_MOD_45156408.jpg *Contributors:* Chase me ladies, I'm the Cavalry, Chesipiero, Fæ, Ghouston, Rcbutcher, The joy of all things, Tm ... 576

Figure 213 *Source:* https://en.wikipedia.org/w/index.php?title=File:FIA2014_(15221322236).jpg *License:* Creative Commons Attribution-Sharealike 2.0 *Contributors:* tataquax from Japan ... 578

Figure 214 *Source:* https://en.wikipedia.org/w/index.php?title=File:Raf_ch-47_chinook_hc2_za707_arp.jpg *License:* Public Domain *Contributors:* User:Arpingstone ... 579

Image *Source:* https://en.wikipedia.org/w/index.php?title=File:Royal_Coat_of_Arms_of_the_United_Kingdom_(HM_Government).svg *License:* Creative Commons Attribution-Sharealike 3.0,2.5,2.0,1.0 *Contributors:* Sodacan ... 583

Figure 215 *Source:* https://en.wikipedia.org/w/index.php?title=File:Stuart_Peach_in_dress_uniform.jpg *Contributors:* Chase me ladies, I'm the Cavalry, De728631, GT1976, Greenshed, Howard61313, Innotata, N816MA ... 587

Figure 216 *Source:* https://en.wikipedia.org/w/index.php?title=File:MOD_Sign_MOD_45154855.jpg *Contributors:* Chase me ladies, I'm the Cavalry, Fæ, Ham II, OgreBot 2 ... 590

Figure 217 *Source:* https://en.wikipedia.org/w/index.php?title=File:Army_Careers_Oxford_20051022.jpg *License:* Creative Commons Attribution-ShareAlike 3.0 Unported *Contributors:* User:Kaihsu ... 591

Figure 218 *Source:* https://en.wikipedia.org/w/index.php?title=File:Ministry_of_Defence_MoD_Main_Building,_London_MOD_45152986.jpg *Contributors:* Chase me ladies, I'm the Cavalry, Fæ, Ham II, OgreBot 2 ... 594

License

Creative Commons Attribution-Share Alike 3.0
//creativecommons.org/licenses/by-sa/3.0/

Index

.338 Lapua Magnum, 367
.50 BMG, 368

AAC Middle Wallop, 397, 440, 477
Abbotsinch, 314
Aberdeen, Dundee and St. Andrews University Air Squadron, 532
Aberdeenshire, 496
Aberdeen University Air Squadron, 532
Aberdour, 315
Abeyance, 205, 360
Able Seaman (rank), 205
Accuracy International, 270, 337
Accuracy International Arctic Warfare, 337, 367
Accuracy International AW50, 368
Accuracy International AWM, 367
Accuracy International AX50, 368
Acharacle, 311
A Coruña, 28
Action of 11 November 2008, 185
Active electronically scanned array, 570
Act of Union 1707, 30
Acts of Union 1707, 3, 28, 60, 171, 322, 325
Aden, 314
Aden Communication Squadron, 537
Aden Emergency, 79, 332
Aden Protectorate Communication and Support Squadron, 537
Ad hoc, 66
Adjutant General, 63
Adjutant Generals Corps, 81, 344, 355, 356, 361, 399, 430, 437–440
Administrative Apprentice Training School, 548
Administrative structure of the field forces of the British Army, 58, 322, 363, 386, 404
Admiral, 8, 252–255, 257
Admiral-class battlecruiser, 45
Admiral of the Fleet, 255
Admiral of the Fleet (Royal Navy), 26, 203, 253
Admiral of the North, 26, 27

Admiral of the North and West, 26
Admiral of the South, 26
Admiral of the South, North and West, 26
Admiral of the West, 26, 27
Admiral (Royal Navy), 121, 198, 203, 229, 230
Admiral-superintendent Chatham, 313
Admiralty, 21, 27, 32, 45, 89, 92, 159, 210, 228, 238–240, 258, 259, 283, 290, 313, 448, 599
Admiralty Board, 8, 230
Admiralty Board (United Kingdom), 105, 160, 198
Admiralty House, Bermuda, 38
Admiralty Interview Board, 281
Admiralty Research Establishment, 105
Admiral (United Kingdom), 160, 198
Adolf Hitler, 4, 73
Adrian Johns, 255
Advanced Air Firing School, 548
Advanced Bombing and Gunnery School (Middle East), 548
Advanced Combat Optical Gunsight, 365, 366
Advanced Flying School (India), 558
Advanced Training School, 548
AEA Technology, 140
Aerial Erector School RAF, 548
Aerial Fighting and Gunnery School, 548
Aerial Fighting School, Heliopolis, 548
Aerial refueling, 109, 447
Aerial refuelling, 566
Aerial warfare, 445
Aerobatics, 479
Aerodrome, 494
Aeroplane and Armament Experimental Establishment, 105
Aérospatiale Gazelle, 108, 244, 245, 268
Aérospatiale Puma, 100, 562
Aérospatiale SA 330 Puma, 108, 270, 446, 468, 469, 481, 496, 579
Æthelred the Unready, 23, 161
Æthelstan, 23
Æthelstan of Wessex, 23

643

Æthelwulf of Wessex, 23

Afghanistan, 91, 99, 269, 327, 334, 342, 424, 467, 481
Afghan National Army, 334
Africa, 292
AG36, 366
Age of sail, 33
Agrarian society, 407
Agusta A109, 446, 470
Agusta AW109, 565
AgustaWestland Apache, 341, 383, 563
AgustaWestland AW101, 189, 192, 195, 238, 239, 249, 251, 270, 279, 562
AgustaWestland AW109, 107, 468, 564
AgustaWestland AW109S Grand, 560
AgustaWestland AW159, 192, 249
AgustaWestland AW159 Wildcat, 158, 238, 239, 248, 251, 252, 270, 279, 339, 383, 562, 563
AgustaWestland AW189, 454
AgustaWestland EH101, 100
AgustaWestland Wildcat, 158
AH-64 Apache, 339
AHQ Iraq, 491
AHQ Levant, 490
AHQ Malta, 490
Air Armament School, 548
Air assault, 15, 109, 244, 393
Air Battalion Royal Engineers, 89
Airborne Early Warning, 247
Airborne early warning and control, 101, 244, 249, 250, 447, 561
Airborne Interception School, 549
Airbridge (logistics), 506
Air burst, 138
Airbus, 566
Airbus A330, 567
Airbus A330-200, 568
Airbus A330 MRTT, 154, 447, 470, 472, 496, 507, 560, 567, 568, 576
Airbus A400M, 447
Airbus A400M Atlas, 470, 496, 560, 574
Air Cadet Central Gliding School, 559
Air charter, 566
Air Chief Marshal, 8, 124, 587
Air Command Far East and Air Headquarters Malaya Communication Squadron, 537
Air Command Southeast Asia (Internal Air Service) Squadron, 535
Air commodore, 89, 462
Air Component Field Force Communication Squadron, 537
Air Council Inspection Squadron, 535
Aircraft carrier, 22, 49, 53, 158, 183, 211, 241, 254, 569

Aircraft carriers, 187, 254
Aircraft Direction School, 549
Aircraft emergency frequency, 500
Aircrew Officers Training School, 549
Air Defence Group RAF, 493
Air Defence of Great Britain, 488
Air Defence of Great Britain Communication Squadron, 537
Air Department, 239
Air Despatch Letter Service Squadron, 535
Air Division Communication Squadron, 537
Air Electronics and Air Engineers School, 548
Air Electronics, Engineer and Loadmaster School, 548
Air Electronics School, 548
Air Experience Flight, 472, 497, 499
Airfield Construction Branch RAF, 489
Airfield Controllers School, 549
Air Fighting Development Unit, 526
Air Fighting School (Middle East), 548
Air force, 2, 89, 445, 447
Air Force Board, 8, 105, 455
Air Forces Gulf Communication Squadron, 537
Air Forces Monthly, 607, 627
Air Headquarters Burma Communication Squadron, 537
Air Headquarters East Africa, 490
Air Headquarters East Africa Communication Squadron, 537
Air Headquarters Hong Kong Communication Squadron, 537
Air Headquarters India Communication Squadron, 537
Air Headquarters Italy Communication Squadron, 537
Air Headquarters Malaya Communication Squadron, 537
Air Headquarters Malta Communication Squadron, 537
Air Headquarters Netherlands East Indies Communication Squadron, 537
Air interdiction, 101
Air Landing School, 548
Air-launched ballistic missile, 128
Airline call sign, 566
Airline hub, 566
Air Marshal, 126
Air Ministry, 89, 124, 594, 599
Air Navigation and Bombing School, 548
Air Navigation School, 548
Air Navigation School, India, 548
Air Observation Post School, 548
Air observer, 253, 255
Air Observers School, North Coates, 549
Air Officer Commanding, 255, 455

Air operators certificate, 566
Air Pilotage School, 549
Air power, 447
Air Scout, 534
Airship, 90, 239
AirTanker Services, **566**
Airth, 30, 167
Air-to-Surface Vessel School, 549
Air Training Corps, 472
Air Training Squadron, 535
Air vice-marshal, 109
Air Warfare, 551
Air Warfare Centre, 465, 501
Ajax (Scout SV), 15, 375, 384
A.J.P. Taylor, 362
Akrotiri and Dhekelia, 154, 426–428, 468, 593
Alanbrooke Barracks, 432
Alan Grose, 232
Alan Nunn May, 118
Alan West, Baron West of Spithead, 233
Albemarle Barracks, England, 432
Alberta, 343, 428
Albion-class landing platform dock, 160, 184, 185, 215
Aldershot Command, 388
Aldershot Garrison, 432–436
Alec Douglas-Home, 141
Alenia Aermacchi, 572
Alexander Backus, 233
Alexander Cochrane, 261
Alexander III of Scotland, 163
Alexander II of Scotland, 162
Alexandria, 313
Alex Burton, 234
Al Faw Peninsula, 50, 185
Alfred Thayer Mahan, 42
Alfred the Great, 23
Algiers, 312
A Life on the Ocean Wave, 257, 284
All Arms Commando Course, 276
Allegiance, 7
Allen key, 143
Allied Air Forces Central Europe Communication Squadron, 537
Allied Expeditionary Air Force, 482
Allied Expeditionary Air Force Communication Squadron, 537
Allied Forces North Norway, 268
Allied intervention in the Russian Civil War, 53, 263
Allied invasion of Italy, 75, 181
Allied invasion of Sicily, 75, 265
Allied Maritime Command, 198
Allied Rapid Reaction Corps, 12, 81, 345, 388, 390, 435
Allies of World War I, 4

Allies of World War II, 5, 75
All Terrain Mobility Platform, 381
All-terrain vehicles .28ATV.29 vehicles, 381
All-Weather Development Squadron, 535
All-Weather Fighter Combat Squadron, 535
All-Weather Fighter Leaders School, 549
Al Minhad Air Base, 506
Almondbank, 316
Alphabet, 542
Al-Qaeda, 589
Alternative words for British, 320
Al Udeid Air Base, 12, 155, 457, 480, 506
Alverstoke, 305
Alvis Stormer, 377
Alvis Unipower, 379
American-led intervention in Iraq, 100
American-led intervention in Syria, 100
American Revolutionary War, 34, 260, 327, 347, 406
American War of Independence, 67, 172
Amherstburg Royal Naval Dockyard, 308
Ammunition dump, 504
Amphibious transport dock, 158, 188, 211
Amphibious warfare, 14, 193, 257–259, 279
Amphibious warfare ship, 13, 187, 298
AMRAAM, 580
Andover, Hampshire, 14, 344, 388
Andover Training Squadron, 535
Andrew Barton (privateer), 164
Andrew Browne Cunningham, 1st Viscount Cunningham of Hyndhope, 180
Andrew Miller (Royal Navy officer), 231
Andrew Pulford, 466
Andrew Robathan, 454
Andrew Wood of Largo, 164
Anduki Airfield, 106
Aneurin Bevan, 141
Angled flight deck, 243
Anglesey, 23, 25
Anglesey Airport, 501
Anglo-Dutch Wars, 31
Anglo–Spanish War (1585), 52
Anglo-French War (1627–1629), 52, 169
Anglo-German naval arms race, 4, 177
Anglo-Irish War, 72, 329
Anglo-Japanese Alliance, 43
Anglo-Persian Oil Company, 45
Anglo-Russian Entente, 4
Anglo-Saxon, 22
Anglo-Spanish War (1625), 169
Anglo-Spanish War (1654), 52
Anglo-Spanish War (1654-1660), 166
Anglo-Zanzibar War, 177
Anglo-Zulu War, 410
Angus, Scotland, 306
Annapolis, Maryland, 54

645

Anthony Roll, 27
Anthrax, 595
Anti-Aircraft Command, 388
Anti-aircraft warfare, 188
Anti-material rifle, 368
Anti-nuclear movement, 114
Anti-nuclear protests, 140
Anti-personnel mine, 369
Anti-submarine warfare, 6, 49, 160, 243, 246
Anti-tank mine, 369
Anti-tank weapon, 370
Anti U-Boat Devices School, 549
Antler Squadron, 535
Antony Beevor, 361
Antony Preston, 56
Antwerp, 263, 266
Arabian Sea, 295
Arab League, 94
ARA General Belgrano, 49, 184, 190
Arbroath, 268, 273, 306
Archer-class patrol vessel, 221
Arctic, 293, 384
Arctic convoys, 312
Arctic convoys of World War II, 53, 181
Arctic warfare, 14, 193, 259
Ardrishaig, 314
Area bombing, 450
Argentina, 49
Argyll, 309–315
Argyll and Bute, 273
Argyll and Sutherland Highlanders, 77, 264, 287, 389
Armament and gunnery School, 549
Armament Group RAF, 493
Armed Forces Act, 2, 323
Armed-forces artificer, 311
Armed Forces Pay Review Body, 592
Armilla patrol, 53, 196, 296
Armistice of Cassibile, 75
Armoured fighting vehicle, 270, 375
Armoured infantry, 15, 393
Armoured personnel carrier, 337, 375
Armoured recovery vehicle, 375, 379
Armoured vehicle-launched bridge, 378
Armoured Vehicle Royal Engineers, 339, 378
Armoured warfare, 154
Arms race, 45, 179
Army, 321, 322
Army 2020, 345
Army Air Corps (United Kingdom), 251, 343, 344, 355, 356, 361, 390, 396, 438–440, 447, 500, 528
Army Air Corps use, 440
Army Board, 8, 105
Army Co-operation School, 549

Army Foundation College, 356, 400, 436, 438, 441
Army group, 74
Army Headquarters (United Kingdom), 58, 322, 344, 363, 386–388, 404, 592
Army Legal Services Branch, 344, 399
Army Medical Services, 344, 398
Army Reserve (United Kingdom), 12, 14, 58, 321, 322, 336, 345, 363, 386, 387, 404, 441
Army Sergeant Major, 321
Army Training Centre, Pirbright, 400, 432, 434
Army Training Regiment, 400, 436, 439, 441
Army Training Unit, 356
Arromanches Camp, 306
Arrow Squadron, 535
Arthur L. Herman, 56
Arthur Tedder, 1st Baron Tedder, 118
Arthur Travers Harris, 450
Arthur Vandenberg, 120
Arthur Wellesley, 1st Duke of Wellington, 39, 69, 327
Articles of War (Royal Navy), 32
Article XV squadrons, 448, 522, 542
Artificial satellite, 126
Artillery, 377
Artillery and Infantry Co-operation School, 549
Artillery Co-operation Squadron, 535
Artillery Observation School, 549
Artillery Observation School, Egypt, 549
Artillery sound ranging, 338
Artists Rifles, 107, 347, 401
AS-90, 338, 340, 377
Asbury Park, New Jersey, 310
Ascension Island, 3, 97, 98, 154, 481, 505
ASDIC, 180, 308
Aspect ratio, 356
ASRAAM, 465
Assault rifle, 366
Assistant Chief of the Defence Staff, 587
Assistant Chief of the Defence Staff (Reserves and Cadets), 587
Assistant Chief of the Naval Staff, 198, 230
Aster (missile family), 188
Astute class, 52
Astute-class submarine, 13, 191, 213
AT4, 364, 370
Atlantic (ocean), 184
Atlantic Ocean, 241, 291
Atlantic Seaboard, 38
Atomic bomb, 115
Atomic demolition munition, 128
Atomic Energy Act of 1946, 118
Atomic nucleus, 115

Atomic spies, 116
Atomic Weapons Establishment, 105, 114, 119
Attack aircraft, 158, 238, 446
Aubrey-Maturin series, 207
Audacious-class aircraft carrier, 48, 182
AugustaWestland EH 101, 158
AUSCANNZUKUS, 297
Australasia, 327
Australia, 144, 418
Australian Army, 349
Australian Flying Corps, 512
Austria, 365, 369, 381
Austro-Hungarian Empire, 330
AUTEC, 201
Auxiliary Air Force, 493, 539
Auxiliary Fighter Squadron (Malaya), 535
Auxiliary Fighter Squadron (Singapore), 535
Auxiliary Territorial Service, 73
Aviator, 462
Avro Lancaster, 94, 562
Avro Lancaster PA474, 449, 562
Avro Shackleton, 129
Avro Vulcan, 95, 97, 121, 128, 451
AW50F, 337
AWC (Arctic Warfare Covert), 367
Axis powers, 5
Ayios Nikolaos Station, 108, 109, 154, 343, 427
Ayr, 163
Ayrshire, 304, 311, 313, 315
Azores, 492

B28 nuclear bomb, 128, 129
B-29 Training Squadron, 535
B43 nuclear bomb, 128
B57 nuclear bomb, 129
B61 nuclear bomb, 137
Babcock International, 378, 476, 579
Babcock International, 566
Bacillus atrophaeus, 595
BAC TSR-2, 130
Badge of the Royal Air Force, 445, 479
BAe 146, 470, 472
BAE Harrier II, 192, 245, 452, 466
BAe Hawk, 158, 239, 247, 446, 472, 473, 476, 479, 580
BAE Mantis, 572
BAE Sea Harrier, 243
BAE Systems, 2, 470, 572, 574
BAE Systems Hawk, 238, 456, 476, 498, 499, 501, 561, 562, 564
BAE Systems Hawk T.1, 500
BAE Systems Nimrod MRA4, 452, 475, 577
BAE Taranis, 573
Bahrain, 3, 154, 201, 305, 312
Baker Barracks, 432

Baker rifle, 85
Balance of power in international relations, 65
Balance of power (international relations), 4
Balearic Islands, 171
Balinger, 26
Balkans, 6
Ballistic Missile Early Warning System, 137, 138, 457, 497
Ballistic missile submarine, 10, 130, 182, 190, 211
Balloch, West Dunbartonshire, 315
Baltic Air Policing, 101, 505
Baltic Sea, 33, 167, 262, 298
Baltic States, 101, 342
Bamako, 100
Band of the Royal Air Force College, 480
Band of the Royal Air Force Regiment, 480
Bandvagn 206, 378
Barbados Defence Force, 287
Barbary corsairs, 165
Barbary pirate, 32
Barbary pirates, 168
Barbary states, 176
Barcelona, 171
Bardufoss Air Station, 481
Barium, 115
Barrett M82, 368
Base Air Forces, Southeast Asia Communication Squadron, 537
Basil Liddell Hart, 73
Basingstoke, 420
Basra, 84, 335
Basrah, 491
Bath, Somerset, 486
Battalion, 265, 273, 278, 345, 347, 387
Battlecruiser, 43
Battlegroup (army), 335, 346, 347, 387, 391
Battle honour, 282
Battle honours, 282
Battle of Aclea, 23
Battle of Acre (1840), 40
Battle of Agincourt, 26, 324
Battle of Anzio, 265
Battle of Arnemuiden, 52
Battle of Bannockburn, 163
Battle of Barfleur, 169
Battle of Basra (2003), 335
Battle of Beachy Head (1690), 33, 166
Battle of Berlin (air), 94
Battle of Bladensburg, 261
Battle of Blenheim, 62
Battle of Britain, 93, 240, 447–449
Battle of Britain Bunker, 93
Battle of Britain Memorial Flight, 497, 534
Battle of Broodseinde, 71
Battle of Bunker Hill, 260

Battle of Cadiz (1656), 166
Battle of Camperdown, 174
Battle of Cape Matapan, 46, 180
Battle of Cape Passaro, 33, 171
Battle of Cape Spartel, 173
Battle of Cape St. Vincent (1797), 34
Battle of Copenhagen (1801), 35, 174
Battle of Copenhagen (1807), 175
Battle of Coronel, 44
Battle of Crete, 180, 264
Battle of Culloden, 65
Battle of Damme, 52
Battle of Dogger Bank (1915), 44
Battle of Dunbar (1650), 59
Battle of Fort Bowyer, 262
Battle of France, 74, 331
Battle of Gallipoli, 263
Battle of Hampden, 261
Battle of Heligoland (1914), 44
Battle of Java (1942), 492
Battle of Jutland, 44, 178
Battle of La Hougue, 33
Battle of Lake Erie, 37
Battle of Largs, 163
Battle of La Rochelle, 52
Battle of Les Espagnols sur Mer, 52
Battle of Lowestoft, 166
Battle of Majuba Hill, 602
Battle of Minden, 67
Battle of Naseby, 59
Battle of Navarino, 40, 52, 177
Battle of New Orleans, 262
Battle of Passchendaele, 330
Battle of Plattsburgh, 37
Battle of Portland, 166
Battle of Quiberon Bay, 172
Battle of Ramillies, 64
Battle of Rorkes Drift, 328
Battle of Saint-Mathieu, 52
Battle of Santa Cruz de Tenerife (1657), 166
Battle of Saratoga, 68
Battle of Scheveningen, 32, 165, 166
Battle of Singapore, 264, 492, 602
Battle of Sluys, 26, 52, 162
Battle of Taranto, 180, 241, 252
Battle of Tel el-Kebir, 410
Battle of the Atlantic, 47, 53, 180
Battle of the Chesapeake, 34, 173
Battle of the Dunes (1658), 59, 60
Battle of the Falkland Islands, 44
Battle of the Gabbard, 166
Battle of the Imjin River, 78
Battle of the Mediterranean, 53
Battle of the Nile, 34, 36, 174
Battle of the Plains of Abraham, 66
Battle of the River Plate, 46, 180

Battle of the Saintes, 34, 173
Battle of the Scheldt, 47, 266
Battle of the Solent, 27, 52
Battle of the Somme, 5, 70, 330
Battle of the Thames, 37
Battle of Trafalgar, 3, 4, 35, 36, 170, 175
Battle of Vigo Bay, 171
Battle of Waterloo, 327, 328
Battle of Yorktown (1781), 34, 173
Battle rifle, 366
Battlesbury Barracks, 432
Battleship, 22, 53, 241
Battles of Barfleur and La Hogue, 166
Battles of Lexington and Concord, 67
Battles of Narvik, 46, 180
Bay-class landing ship, 52, 160, 188, 197, 215, 384
Bay-class landing ship dock, 16
BBC, 208, 630
BBC News, 628
Beachley Barracks, 432
Beacon Barracks, 432
Bedfordshire, 307, 498
Bedfordshire and Hertfordshire Regiment, 64
Bedhampton Camp, 316
Beechcraft King Air, 580
Beechcraft Super King Air, 111, 238, 247, 251, 446, 467, 472, 473, 497, 501, 560, 563, 577
Beechcraft T-6A Texan II, 476
Beechcraft T-6 Texan II, 476, 564, 580
Beijing, 40
Beira Patrol, 53
Belait District, 428
Belfast, 80, 310, 333
Belfast Telegraph, 362
Belgian Training School, 549
Belgium, 263, 368
Belize, 3, 81, 97, 108, 154, 343, 424, 425
Belize City, 108
Belize District, 424, 425
Bell 212, 339, 383, 563
Bell 412, 446, 469, 472, 561
Bell Boeing V-22 Osprey, 504
Bell Griffin, 500
Benelli M4 Super 90, 367
Benito Mussolini, 45
Benjamin Bathurst (Royal Navy officer), 232
Ben Key, 158, 198
Beret, 360
Berkeley Radiation Laboratory, 117
Berkshire, 504
Berlin Airlift, 95, 450
Berlin-Dahlem, 115
Bermuda, 3, 38, 93, 155, 312, 343, 425
Bermuda Maritime Museum, 602

Bermuda Militia Artillery, 351
Bermuda sloop, 36
Bermuda Volunteer Rifle Corps, 351
Bernard Gray, 573
Berwick-upon-Tweed, 163
Beveridge Report, 414
BGM-109 Tomahawk, 50
Bibcode, 147
Bickleigh Barracks, 273, 306
Bickleigh, South Hams, 268
Big Stink (B-29), 117
Bill of Rights 1689, 2, 323, 325, 405
Biological warfare, 595
Biplane, 239
Bipod, 366, 368
Birdham, 314
Birgu, 311, 314
Birmingham, 107, 307
Birmingham Airport, 566
Birmingham University Air Squadron, 497, 532
Birnbeck Pier, 310
Bishops Palace, Kirkwall, 169
Black and Tans, 72
Blackburn Buccaneer, 130, 243
Blackburn Skua, 266
Blackwoods Magazine, 41
Blandford Camp, 433, 440
Bletchley Park, 181
Blind Approach School, 549
Blockade of Africa, 177
Blockade of Germany, 178
Bloody Sunday (1972), 80
Blue Beret Camp, 429
Blue Danube (nuclear weapon), 120
Blue Funnel Line, 318
Blue Peacock, 128
Blues and Royals, 61, 338
Blue Steel missile, 130, 451
Blue Streak missile, 130
Blue Streak (missile), 114, 123
Blue Water (missile), 129
Blue water navy, 49
Blue-water navy, 2, 160
BNFL, 140
Board of Ordnance, 63
Board of Trade, 594
Bob Ainsworth, 590
Boeing, 469, 596
Boeing B-29 Superfortress, 136
Boeing B-47 Stratojet, 136
Boeing B-50 Superfortress, 136
Boeing B-52 Stratofortress, 503
Boeing C-135 Stratolifter, 576
Boeing C-17 Globemaster III, 447, 561
Boeing CH-47 Chinook, 109

Boeing Chinook (UK variants), 270, 278, 446, 468, 469, 496, 507, 509, 561, 578
Boeing E-3 Sentry, 101, 446, 467, 501, 561
Boeing Insitu ScanEagle, 250, 251
Boeing KC-135 Stratotanker, 467, 504
Boeing OC-135B Open Skies, 504
Boeing P-8 Poseidon, 475, 577
Boeing RC-135, 446, 467, 470, 480, 501, 504, 561, 576
Bognor Regis, 314
Boko Haram, 100
Bolshevik, 72
Bomarsund, Åland, 40
Bombardment of Alexandria (1882), 40
Bombardment of Algiers (1816), 40, 174, 176
Bombardment of Kagoshima, 40
Bomber Command, 121
Bomber Command Bombing School, 549
Bomber Command Communication Squadron, 538
Bombing of Cologne in World War II, 94
Bombing of Dresden, 450
Bombing of Dresden in World War II, 94
Bombing of Hamburg in World War II, 94, 450
Bombing of Iraq (1998), 98
Bombing of Nagasaki, 117
Bombing of Pforzheim in World War II, 94
Bombings of Heilbronn in World War II, 94
Bomb ketch, 260
Boness, 315
Boosted fission weapon, 121
Bootle, Cumbria, 312
Borburata, 168
Border Campaign (IRA), 80
Border Force, 218
Bordon and Longmoor Military Camps, 435
Borneo, 79
Bosnia and Herzegovina, 83, 99
Bosnian War, 193, 259
Boston, 309
Boston Massacre, 67
Botany Bay, 260
Boulogne-sur-Mer, 27
Bourbons, 171
Bovington Camp, 432, 440
Bowman (communications system), 339, 365
Boxer Rebellion, 262, 327
Bracklesham Bay, 314
Braunton, 306
Brecon, 442
Brest, France, 34
Brian Cathcart, 147
Brian Lavery, 56
Brian Young (Royal Navy officer), 255
Brigade, 70, 269, 345–347, 387, 391

Brigade of Gurkhas, 8, 18, 76, 155, 418, 430, 441, 599, 600
Brigadier, 199, 391
Brigadier general (United States), 117
Brigadier (United Kingdom), 108, 204, 286, 347, 359
Brightlingsea, 312, 313
Brimstone missile, 570, 572, 580
Bristol, 268, 307
Bristow Helicopters, 454
Britain, Australia and the Bomb, 146
Britannia Royal Naval College, 186, 211, 303, 304, 307
BriteCloud, 580
British 16 Air Assault Brigade, 82
British 24 Airmobile Brigade, 82
British 2nd Infantry Division, 82
British 3rd Infantry Division, 82
British 4th Infantry Division, 82
British 5 Airborne Brigade, 82
British 5th Infantry Division, 82
British 63rd (Royal Naval) Division, 45
British Aerospace, 255
British Aerospace 146, 447, 561, 564
British Aerospace Harrier II, 187
British Aerospace Hawk, 251
British Aerospace Sea Harrier, 242, 244
British Air Forces of Occupation Communication Squadron, 538
British Air Forces Southeast Asia Communication Squadron, 538
British Antarctica, 190
British Antarctic Survey, 189, 223, 291
British Antarctic Territory, 291
British Armed Forces, **1**, 21, 58, 105, 153, 159, 161, 210, 211, 228, 238, 258, 273, 290, 295, 321, 322, 335, 342, 363, 374, 386, 404, 437, 454, 560, 584
British Army, 1, 2, 58, 89, 106–110, 199, 206, 259, 264, 268, 269, 273, **321**, 322, 344, 359, 360, 363, 364, 372, 386, 387, 391, 404, 405, 411, 415–417, 447, 468, 584, 586
British Army Air Corps, 15, 339
British army impressment laws, 406
British Army incremental infantry companies, 389, 394
British Army Infantry, 14, 390
British Army Jungle Warfare Training School, 154, 343, 428
British Army officer rank insignia, 2, 58, 322, 363, 386, 404
British Army of the Rhine, 5, 72, 129, 332, 388, 415
British Army other ranks rank insignia, 2, 58, 322, 363, 386, 404

British Army Training and Support Unit Belize, 12, 154, 343
British Army Training Unit Kenya, 12, 155, 343, 431
British Army Training Unit Suffield, 12, 154, 343, 428
British brigades of the Second World War, 389
British Broadcasting Corporation, 139
British Coastal Forces of World War II, 47
British Commandos, 75, 196, 264, 265, 267, 269, 270
British Commonwealth Air Communication Squadron, 538
British Commonwealth Air Training Plan, 92, 448, 522
British Crown, 355
British Dominions, 417
British East India Company, 65, 328
British Embassy in Tokyo, 314
British Empire, 4, 11, 40, 44, 59, 68–70, 74, 75, 89, 90, 96, 153, 160, 176, 181, 327, 412, 415, 417, 448, 615, 623
British expedition against Cuba, 172
British Expeditionary Force (World War I), 70, 330, 411
British Expeditionary Force (World War II), 73, 331
British expedition to Tibet, 4
British Forces Belize, 108
British Forces British Indian Ocean Territories, 11, 154
British Forces Brunei, 12, 58, 111, 154, 322, 343, 363, 386, 404, 428
British Forces Cyprus, 11, 58, 108, 154, 322, 343, 363, 386, 404, 426–429, 447, 480
British Forces Falkland Islands, 109
British Forces Germany, 12, 58, 81, 154, 322, 343, 363, 386, 404, 430
British Forces Gibraltar, 11, 58, 154, 322, 343, 363, 386, 404, 426
British Forces Hong Kong, 110
British Forces Post Office, 499
British Forces South Atlantic Islands, 343
British Government, 415
British Grand Fleet, 44, 178
British Gurkhas Nepal, 12, 155, 430
British Hong Kong, 110
British House of Commons, 93, 145
British India, 72
British Indian Army, 72, 415
British Indian Ocean Territory, 3, 153, 154, 305, 425
British infantry brigades of the First World War, 389
British Intelligence Corps, 344
British Isles, 167, 405

650

British Mandate for Palestine (legal instrument), 94
British military aircraft designation systems, 247, 465
British Military Garrison Brunei, 343
British Military Hospital, Hong Kong, 111
British military intervention in the Sierra Leone Civil War, 11, 246
British Military Mission to Poland, 72
British military rifles, 58, 84, 322, 363, 386, 404
British monarchy, 144, 462
Britishness, 422
British North America, 327
British nuclear tests at Maralinga, 135
British Overseas Territories, 2, 11, 153, 291, 349, 505, 619
British Overseas Territory, 154
British Pacific Fleet, 47, 53, 266, 492
British Raj, 4, 415
British Somaliland, 72
Brittany, 34, 260
Britten-Norman Defender, 383, 563
Britten-Norman Islander, 111, 339, 383, 563
Broadcast relay station, 503
Brock Barracks, 433
Brodie helmet, 70
Brown and Root, 140
Brown Bess, 85
Browning Hi-Power, 365
Bruce Barrymore Halpenny, 104
Bruce Richardson (Royal Navy officer), 233
Brunei, 3, 81, 106, 154, 343, 397, 428
Brunei Revolt, 343
Brunswick rifle, 85
B Squadron, 537
B Squadron, Aegean, 537
Buckingham Palace, 388
Buckinghamshire, 497, 498
Buckleigh, 311
Buckshot, 367
Budget, 592
Buffalo (mine protected vehicle), 379
Buffer state, 327
Buffs (Royal East Kent Regiment), 64
Bulford Camp, 433, 435, 437
Burma Campaign, 75, 331
Burma Campaign 1944–45, 266
Burma Communication Squadron, 537, 538
Burmese Conversion Squadron, 535
Burnham-on-Crouch, 315
Burning of Edinburgh (1544), 168
Burning of York, 39
Bushmaster Protected Mobility Vehicle, 382
Butlins Ayr, 314
Butlins Pwllheli, 312

Butlins Skegness, 314
BVRAAM, 580
BvS 10, 270, 271, 274
Byron Farwell, 423

C-130 Hercules, 470, 574
C-130J Super Hercules, 470
C-17 Globemaster III, 469, 470
C8 Carbine, 366
Cabinet of the United Kingdom, 7, 119
Cadiz, 27, 31
Cádiz Expedition (1625), 52
Caernarfonshire, 312
Cambridgeshire, 501–504
Cambridge University Air Squadron, 501, 532
Cameron Barracks, 433
Cameronians (Scottish Rifles), 410
CAMM (missile family), 385
Campaign for Nuclear Disarmament, 133, 139, 140
Camp Bastion, 334
Campbeltown, 313
Canada, 3, 93, 154, 366, 370, 428
Canadian Forces, 343
Cancun, 567
Canute the Great, 24
Cap badge, 76, 348, 360, 395, 402
Cape Finisterre, 33, 35
Cape Hatteras, 39
Capenhurst, 119
Cape of Good Hope, 174
Cape Sable Island, 39
Cape Saint Vincent, 34
Capital punishment, 36
Capital ship, 241
Captain (British Army and Royal Marines), 204, 286, 347, 359
Captain General Royal Marines, 204, 257, 273, 286
Captain (naval), 208
Captain (Royal Navy), 203, 253, 254
Capture of Belle Île, 260, 283
Capture of Gibraltar, 154, 283
Caravel, 164
Carbine, 366
Carbonite-2, 454
Card game, 320
Cardiff, 307
Cardross, Argyll and Bute, 163
Cardwell Reforms, 69, 70, 329, 409
Cargo aircraft, 159, 238, 447
Cargo transport, 574
Caribbean, 171, 172, 175, 291, 327
Carl Spaatz, 136
Carmarthenshire, 316, 505
Carrack, 27, 167

Carrier battle group, 196
Cartagena de Indias, 171
Carver Barracks, 433
Caspar John, 253
Castle-class patrol vessel, 109, 189
Castle Toward, 309, 310
Category:Naval battles involving the United Kingdom, 261
Catholic Church, 79
CATOBAR, 569
Catterick Garrison, 400, 432–435, 440, 442
Causes of World War I, 4
Causes of World War II, 4
Cavalier, 60, 325
Cavalry, 70, 387, 392
Cavalry Barracks, Hounslow, 433
Cavendish Laboratory, 115
Cawdor Barracks, 433
CBRN, 464, 501
CBRN defense, 376, 442, 498
Centaur-class aircraft carrier, 48, 182
Central Air Traffic Control School, 549
Central Asia, 4
Central Band of the Royal Air Force, 480, 499
Central Flying School, 459, 497
Central Flying School (India), 558
Central Flying School (Southern Rhodesia), 558
Central Gunnery School, 549
Central Gunnery School (Middle East), 549
Central Landing School, 549
Central Navigation and Control School, 549
Central Navigation School, 549
Central Powers, 4, 447
Central Squadron and Flight Commanders School, 549
Centurion BARV, 268
Ceredigion, 496
Ceremonial ship launching, 127
Certifiable Predator B, 572
Ceylon, 174, 309, 312, 315
CFB Goose Bay, 428
CFB Suffield, 428
Challenger 1, 379
Challenger 2, 14, 15, 154, 337, 339, 375
Chania, 262
Channel Dash, 254
Chaplain of the Fleet, 199
Charge of the Light Brigade, 68
Charles Algernon Parsons, 43
Charles de Gaulle (R 91), 318
Charles ffoulkes, 317
Charles Guthrie, Baron Guthrie of Craigiebank, 144
Charles II of England, 22, 32, 60, 166, 284, 325

Charles I of England, 31, 165
Charles Lamb (Royal Navy officer), 254
Charles Portal, 1st Viscount Portal of Hungerford, 252, 446
Charles Stickland, 199, 257, 295
Charles Style, 234
Charles Wheeler (sculptor), 594
Charter, 25
Chassepot, 84
Chatham Dockyard, 32, 166, 308
Chatham House, 589
Chatham, Kent, 259, 440
Chatham, Medway, 313, 315
Chelsea, London, 107
Chemical Defence Establishment, 105
Chemical weapons and the United Kingdom, 11
Chemical weapons in World War I, 330
Chesapeake Bay, 261
Chesapeake–Leopard Affair, 37
Cheshire, 309, 312
Cheshire Regiment, 109
Chessington, 486
Chester, 119
Chetwynd Barracks, 433
Chevaline, 132
Chibok schoolgirls kidnapping, 100
Chichester, 314
Chicksands, 307, 440
Chief of Defence Materiel, 17, 589, 591
Chief of the Air Staffs Warrant Officer, 462
Chief of the Air Staff (United Kingdom), 8, 90, 118, 445, 455, 586
Chief of the Defence Staff (United Kingdom), 1, 8, 144, 583, 586
Chief of the General Staff (United Kingdom), 8, 144, 321, 323, 344, 388, 586
Chief of the Imperial General Staff, 121
Chief Scientific Adviser to the Ministry of Defence, 106, 588
Chiefs of Staff Committee, 8, 118, 122, 584, 586
Chief technician, 462
Childers Reforms, 69, 70, 329, 409
Chilean Navy, 188
China and weapons of mass destruction, 114
China Station, 46
Chinese Air Force Cadet School, 549
Chinese Elementary Flying Training School, 558
Chinese nuclear weapon, 141
Chinook HC3, 596
Chosen man, 347
Christian, 176
Christopher Bullock, 607
Christopher Deverell, 586

Christopher Hinton, Baron Hinton of Bankside, 119
Christopher Mayhew, 48
Cinque Ports, 25
CITEREFAldrich1998, 609
CITEREFArnoldPyne2001, 609, 610, 612
CITEREFArnoldSmith2006, 612
CITEREFAsquith1981, 603
CITEREFAylen2015, 609
CITEREFBall1995, 609, 610
CITEREFBaylis1994, 609, 610
CITEREFBaylis1995, 609–611
CITEREFBaylis2008, 612
CITEREFBaylisStoddart2003, 611
CITEREFBaylisStoddart2015, 609, 611
CITEREFBernstein1976, 608
CITEREFBernstein2010, 609
CITEREFBernstein2011, 608
CITEREFBotti1987, 608, 610
CITEREFBowiePlatt1984, 610, 612
CITEREFBronk2014, 611
CITEREFBrookes1982, 609
CITEREFButlerBromley2001, 612
CITEREFCampbell1982, 612
CITEREFCathcart1995, 609
CITEREFChalmers1999, 612
CITEREFChisholm1911, 623
CITEREFChurchill1956, 603
CITEREFClark1961, 608
CITEREFCocroftNewsome2009, 612
CITEREFColburn1860, 603
CITEREFDawsonRosecrance1966, 609
CITEREFDombeyGrove1992, 610
CITEREFDumbrell2006, 611
CITEREFEpstein1966, 610, 612
CITEREFFarmelo2013, 608
CITEREFGilbert2005, 623
CITEREFGoldberg1964, 608, 609
CITEREFGott1963, 608, 610
CITEREFGowing1964, 608
CITEREFGowingArnold1974a, 608, 609
CITEREFGowingArnold1974b, 609
CITEREFGrant2011, 612
CITEREFGroom1974, 612
CITEREFGrove1987, 611
CITEREFHarrison1982, 611
CITEREFHawkings2002, 611
CITEREFHewlettAnderson1962, 608
CITEREFHewlettDuncan1969, 609
CITEREFHewlettHoll1989, 610
CITEREFHubbardSimmons2008, 610
CITEREFJones1985, 608
CITEREFJones2017, 611
CITEREFLeonard2014, 612
CITEREFLudlam2008, 611
CITEREFMacDonald2006, 611
CITEREFMacmillan1971, 610
CITEREFMallinson2009, 603
CITEREFMcIntyre2006, 610
CITEREFMcKernan2005, 623
CITEREFMiddeke2000, 611
CITEREFMoore2010, 609–611
CITEREFNailor1988, 611
CITEREFNorrisKristensen2013, 611
CITEREFOpenshawSteadmanGreene1983, 612
CITEREFPaul2000, 608, 610
CITEREFPhelps2010, 608
CITEREFRipley2008, 624
CITEREFRitchie2008, 612
CITEREFRitchie2014, 611
CITEREFRitchie2015, 610
CITEREFRitchie2016, 612
CITEREFRogers1968, 623
CITEREFRoyal Scots Greys1840, 603, 623
CITEREFScott2012, 612
CITEREFSpinardi1997, 609
CITEREFStocker2004, 612
CITEREFStoddart2012, 611
CITEREFStoddart2014a, 611, 612
CITEREFStoddart2014b, 610, 612
CITEREFSzasz1992, 608
CITEREFTaylor1976, 623
CITEREFWade2008, 612
CITEREFWheeler1985–1986, 609, 610
CITEREFWittner2003, 612
CITEREFWynn1997, 609–612
CITEREFYoung2007, 609–612
CITEREFYoung2016, 610, 611
CITEREFZimmerman1995, 608
City of Halifax, 39
City of London, 284, 389
City of Westminster, 7, 105, 106, 583
Civil Aviation Authority (United Kingdom), 566
Civil defence, 139
Civil Defence Bulletin, 139
Civil engineering, 395
Civil servant, 584
Claim of Right Act 1689, 325
Clan Donald, 167
Claro Barracks, 433
Classified information, 114
Claverton Manor, 486
Claverton, Somerset, 486
Clement Attlee, 117, 585
Clerk of the Acts, 26
Clive Barracks, 433
Close air support, 99, 466
Close combat, 281
Coalition, 323
Coastal Command, 129

Coastal Command Anti U-Boat Devices School, 549
Coastal Command Communication Squadron, 538
Coastal Command Flying Instructors School, 549
Coastal Command Gunnery School, 549
Coastal Command Instructors School, 549
Coastal Command Landplane Pilots Pool, 549
Coastal Command Tactical Development Unit, 549
Coastal Defence Development Unit, 549
Coastal Forces of the Royal Navy, 309
Cobh, 308
Cobham plc, 566
Cod Wars, 49, 53
Colchester, 593
Colchester Garrison, 432, 434, 435
Coldstream Guards, 61, 108, 389, 393, 436
Cold War, 5, 6, 49, 76, 89, 95, 96, 105, 123, 129, 138, 160, 243, 268, 323, 332, 343, 415, 429, 451, 452, 584, 589
Cold War (1985–91), 6
Colerne Communication Squadron, 538
Collapse of the Soviet Union, 142
Colombo, 309, 312
Colonel, 274
Colonel-in-Chief, 273
Colonel (UK), 204, 286, 359
Colonial war, 58
Colour sergeant, 205, 287, 360
Colours, standards and guidons, 283, 356, 402
Comacchio Group, 268
Combat Arms, 354
Combat engineering, 414
Combat engineering vehicle, 379
Combat Service Support, 15
Combat Support, 15
Combat vehicle, 364
Combat Vehicle Reconnaissance (Tracked), 337, 375
Combermere Barracks, 433
Combined Cadet Force, 206, 472
Combined Development Trust, 116
Combined Joint Expeditionary Force, 12
Combined Joint Expeditionary Force (CJEF), 297
Combined Maritime Forces, 53
Combined Policy Committee, 116
Combined Task Force 150, 295
Combined Task Force 151, 295
Comhairle nan Eilean Siar, 497
Command and control, 339
Commandant General Royal Marines, 199, 257, 268, 273
Commander, 254
Commander Field Army, 321, 345, 388
Commander-in-Chief, 7, 273
Commander in Chief Fleet, 305
Commander-in-Chief Fleet, 229, 230, 233
Commander-in-Chief, Naval Home Command (Royal Navy), 229
Commander-in-chief of the British Armed Forces, 1, 2, 197
Commander-in-Chief, South Atlantic, 46
Commander-in-Chief, The Nore, 313
Commander Land Forces, 77, 388
Commander of the Order of the British Empire, 158, 198, 199, 321, 445
Commander of the Royal Victorian Order, 199
Commander Operations (Royal Navy), 198
Commander Regional Forces (United Kingdom), 388
Commander (Royal Navy), 35, 203, 255
Commander UK Task Group, 235
Commander United Kingdom Maritime Forces, 198, 233, 235
Commander United Kingdom Task Group, 233
Command (military formation), 388, 455, 482
Commando, 265
Commando Helicopter Force, 249, 251, 270, 279, 307
Commando Logistic Regiment, 14, 274
Commando (military), 276
Commandos, 192
Commando Training Centre Royal Marines, 268, 269, 275, 281, 306, 307
Commercial off-the-shelf, 454
Commissariat, 63
Commission (document), 442
Commissioning pennant, 158
Commodore-in-Chief, 237
Commodore-in-Command, Royal Naval Barracks, Chatham, 313
Commodore (RN), 199
Commodore (Royal Navy), 203, 230
Commons:Atlas of the United Kingdom, 584
Commons:Category:Aircraft of the air force of the United Kingdom, 481
Commons:Category:British Army, 363
Commons:Category:Fleet Air Arm, 256
Commons:Category:History of the British Army, 88
Commons:Category:Military of the United Kingdom, 19
Commons:Category:Ministry of Defence (United Kingdom), 597
Commons:Category:Royal Air Force, 481
Commons:Category:Royal Marines, 289
Commons:Category:Royal Navy, 209
Commons:Category:Selection and training in the British Army, 443

Commonwealth, 416
Commonwealth of England, 31, 165
Commonwealth of Nations, 5, 18, 92, 201, 347, 354, 421, 448, 509, 542
Commonwealth realm, 201, 349
Commonwealth War Graves Commission, 593
Communications Electronics Basic Training Squadron, 535
Communication Squadron, GHQ Royal Air Force, France, 538
Communication Squadron, GHQ Royal Flying Corps, France, 538
Communication Squadron, Hendon, 538
Companion of the Order of the Bath, 198, 199
Company (military unit), 277, 345, 347, 387
Company of Scotland, 170
Composite Fighting Squadron, 535
Comprehensive Test Ban Treaty, 136
Conscript, 70
Conscription, 414
Conscription in the United Kingdom, 70, 74, 269, 330, 405
Conservative Party (UK), 142, 145, 454
Constantinople, 40, 72, 330, 361
Continental Navy, 34, 172
Continental staff system, 504
Control and Reporting Centre, 495, 496
Control and Reporting School, 549
Convair B-36 Peacemaker, 136
Convoy, 179
Copenhagen, 94
Copthorne Barracks, 433
Corfu Channel Incident, 53
Cornwall, 252, 304, 311, 500
Cornwall Airport Newquay, 500
Coronation, 253
Corporal, 205, 267, 287, 360
Corporal of Horse, 367
Corporal punishment, 408
Corps, 74, 345, 346, 390
Corps of Army Music, 344, 400, 439, 440
Corps of Colonial Marines, 39, 261
Corps of Royal Electrical and Mechanical Engineers, 439
Corps of Royal Engineers, 15, 439
Corsham, 314
Corsica, 408
Cougar (vehicle), 338, 375
Counter-battery radar, 377
Countermeasure, 132
Counter Rocket, Artillery, and Mortar, 378
County, 496, 503, 505
County Armagh, 332
County-class cruiser, 45
County-class destroyer, 48, 182, 184
County Londonderry, 314

Court martial, 63
Covey Crump, 206
Cowes, 315
Cowper Phipps Coles, 41
Coyote Reconnaissance Vehicle, 337
Craig Harrison (sniper), 367
CRARRV, 379
Creech Air Force Base, 467, 507
Cretan State, 262
Crimean War, 2, 4, 40, 41, 52, 59, 68, 70, 177, 193, 259, 262, 287, 323, 327, 409
Criminals, 406
Critical mass, 115
Croatia, 83
Cromwell tank, 267
Crown colony, 349
Crown Colony-class cruiser, 45
Crown dependencies, 2
Crown dependency, 12
Crown Estate, 390
Crown of Castile, 162
Cruise missile, 50
Cruiser, 266
C. S. Forester, 207
C. S. Forrester, 36
C Squadron, Aegean, 537
CTA International, 375
Cuban Missile Crisis, 128
Cumbria, 312, 316, 505
Cunard, 318
Curfew, 80
Curragh incident, 59
Customs and traditions of the Royal Navy, 21, 159, 210, 228, 238, 258, 290, **317**
Cuxhaven, 314
CVA-01, 48, 183, 243
Cyprus, 3, 6, 96, 108, 154, 342, 343, 428, 429, 452, 480, 505, 507

Dale Barracks, 433
Dalton Barracks, 434
Damme, 25
Danish intervention (1625–1629), 169
Danish people, 405
Dardanelles Campaign, 45, 178
Darien Scheme, 170
Daring-class destroyer (1949), 48, 182
Darrells Island, Bermuda, 93
Dartmoor, 281
Dartmouth, Devon, 25, 186, 199, 304, 310, 311
Darwin, Australia, 125
Dassault Aviation, 572
Dassault Falcon 20, 245
Dassault nEUROn, 573
Dassault Telemos, 572

655

David Benjamin Bathurst, 255
David Cameron, 145, 334, 343, 569
David Lloyd George, 584
David Luce, 48
David Snelson, 234
David Williams (Royal Navy officer), 231
David Zimmerman, 152
Day and Night Bombing Observation School, 549
Debtors, 406
Decolonisation, 332
Decolonisation and decline (1945–1997), 5
Decommissioning, 316
Defence Academy of the United Kingdom, 593
Defence and Security Media Advisory Committee, 593
Defence Business Services, 593
Defence CBRN Centre, 501
Defence College of Communications and Information Systems, 460
Defence College of Electro-Mechanical Engineering, 459
Defence College of Logistics, 434, 440
Defence College of Policing and Guarding, 440
Defence Council of the United Kingdom, 3, 8, 10, 105, 133, 160, 198, 455, 591
Defence diplomacy, 588
Defence Electronics and Components Agency, 583, 592
Defence Equipment and Support, 17, 305, 589, 592
Defence Helicopter Flying School, 192, 247, 251, 459, 497, 500, 501, 558
Defence Infrastructure Organisation, 500, 504, 592, 593
Defence Intelligence, 105, 199, 497
Defence Intelligence Fusion Centre, 502
Defence Logistics Organisation, 17
Defence Medical Services, 437
Defence Medical Services Training Centre, 440
Defence Nuclear, Biological and Chemical School, 105
Defence Procurement Agency, 17
Defence Review, 5
Defence Safety Authority, 587
Defence School of Photography, 547, 551
Defence School of Transport, 435
Defence Science and Technology Laboratory, 583, 592, 595
Defence Select Committee, 474
Defence Services Secretary, 587
Defence Test and Evaluation Organisation, 106
Defence Training Estate, 500
Defence White Paper, 415
Defense Intelligence Agency, 504
DefenseNews, 629

Defense Support Program, 137
DEFRA, 227
De Havilland Canada DHC-1 Chipmunk, 245, 562, 563
De Havilland Mosquito, 94
De Havilland Vampire, 243
Delivering Security in a Changing World, 49, 82, 188, 387, 452, 588
Demonstration Squadron, 535
Demountable Rack Offload and Pickup System, 380
Denis Healey, 145
Denison Barracks, 434
Dennis Cambell, 254
Department of Scientific and Industrial Research (United Kingdom), 118
Departments of the United Kingdom Government, 584
Deptford Dockyard, 308
Deputy Chief of the General Staff (United Kingdom), 345, 388
Deputy Chief of the Naval Staff, 199, 230
Derek Empson, 254
Derek Reffell, 232
Derry, 80, 311, 333
Des Browne, 199
Desert, 373
Desert Air Force, 490
Desert Combat Boot, 372
Designated marksman rifle, 270, 366
Destroyer, 13, 49
Destroyers, 158
Deterrence theory, 10, 115
Development Squadron, Gosport, 535
Devils Tower Camp, 426
Devon, 304, 307, 310
Devonport, Devon, 304, 311
Dhekelia Cantonment, 108, 427
Dhofar Rebellion, 6
Diego Garcia, 153, 154, 201, 305, 425
Dieppe Raid, 265
Digital object identifier, 56, 146–152
Digital radio frequency memory, 580
Director Special Forces, 107, 274
Displacement (ship), 211
Dispute with Arthur, 25
Dissolution of the Soviet Union, 160
Distinguished Flying Cross (United Kingdom), 445
Distinguished Service Order, 321
Division (military), 70, 74, 345–347, 387, 390
Diyatalawa, 315
DM Beith, 305
DM Crombie, 106, 305
DM Glen Douglas, 106
DM Gosport, 106, 305

D notice, 119
Dockyard, 199
Dominion, 327, 349
Donald Maclean (spy), 118
Dorset, 308, 310, 315
Douglas C-47 Skytrain, 562
Douglas Gracey, 78
Dounreay, 305
Dover, 312, 315
Dover Patrol, 178
Dreadnought, 4
Dreadnought (book), 55
Dreadnought-class submarine, 11, 134, 191
Dreadnoughts, 177
Dreghorn Barracks, 434
Drogheda, 328
Dry dock, 27, 162
Dry-dock, 170
D Squadron, Aegean, 537
Dubai, 201
Duke of Connaught and Strathearn, 410
Duke of Edinburghs Royal Regiment, 110
Duke of Lancasters Regiment, 393, 401, 436, 437
Duke of Wellington, 328
Dumfries and Galloway, 501
Dunbartonshire, 304, 312–314
Duncan Campbell (journalist), 147
Duncan Hamilton (racing driver), 253
Duncan Potts, 234
Duncan Sandys, 125
Dundee, 168, 309
Dunfermline, 316
Dunino, 308
Dunkirk, 169, 180
Dunkirkers, 166
Dunkirk evacuation, 53, 240, 331
Dunoon, 313
Duqm, 155
Durham University Air Squadron, 532
Dutch East Indies, 46, 77, 175
Dutch Empire, 174
Dutch Navy, 160
Dutch Republic, 165
Dwight D. Eisenhower, 124

EADS, 572
Earl Mountbatten, 284
Earl of Effingham, 28
Earl of Salisbury, 25
Earls of Bothwell, 164
Earls of Lennox, 164
East Anglia, 23
Eastchurch, 239
Eastern Association, 324
Eastern Command (United Kingdom), 76, 388

Eastern Fleet, 13, 46
Eastern Sovereign Base Area, 427
East Falkland, 292, 343, 425
East Indies Station, 46
East Lowlands University Air Squadron, 532
Eastney Barracks, 282
East of Scotland Universities Air Squadron, 498, 532
East of Suez, 154, 201, 295
East Yorkshire Regiment, 71
EC-145, 564
Ecgfrith of Northumbria, 23
Echo-class survey ship (2002), 190, 197, 223
Edgar the Peaceable, 23
Edinburgh, 268, 389, 486
Edinburgh University Air Squadron, 532
Educational and Training Services Branch, 344, 399
Edward I, 25
Edward III of England, 25, 26, 162
Edward II of England, 25, 163
Edward I of England, 163
Edward Pellew, 1st Viscount Exmouth, 40, 176
Edwards Air Force Base, 507, 570
Edward the Confessor, 24, 161
Edward Vernon, 33
Edward VI, 168
Edwin of Northumbria, 23
Effects of nuclear explosions, 113
Eglin Air Force Base, 246
Eglinton, Northern Ireland, 314
EGLM, 366
Egon Bretscher, 122
Egypt, 313
Electrical and Wireless School, 549
Electric Boat Company, 43
Electromagnetic separation, 117
Electromagnetic spectrum, 576
Electronic surveillance, 574
Elementary and Reserve Flying Training School, Kenya, 558
Elementary Flying Training Squadron, 535
Eleven Years Tyranny, 61
Elizabeth II, 1, 2, 144, 237, 322, 355, 445
Elizabeth II of the United Kingdom, 7
Elizabeth I of England, 28, 164
Embraer Phenom 100, 476, 564, 580
Empire Air Armament School, 549
Empire Air Navigation School, 549
Empire Central Flying School, 549
Empire Flying School, 558
Empire Radio School, 549
Empire Test Pilots School, 496, 549
Emu Field, 134
Encyclopædia Britannica Eleventh Edition, 361
Endnote a, 337

Endnote b, 336
End of British Raj, 415
Enemy alien, 115
Engineer and Logistic Staff Corps, 402
Engineering Officer, 464
England, 157, 227, 229, 257, 405, 496–502, 505, 567
English Armada, 28
English Army, 259, 322, 327
English Channel, 23, 28, 31, 46, 178, 294
English Civil War, 31, 165, 323, 328
English Electric Canberra, 127, 244, 245
English Empire, 347
English overseas possessions, 615, 623
English Restoration, 22, 31, 32
Ensign, 357
Entente Cordiale, 43, 329
EOKA, 78, 332
Episkopi Cantonment, 108, 426
Eric Geddes, 71
Eric Grove, 148
Eric Winkle Brown, 254
Ernest Bevin, 119
Ernest Brooks (photographer), 71, 329
Ernest King, 47
Ernest Titterton, 117
Ernest Walton, 115
Ernle Chatfield, 1st Baron Chatfield, 584
Escherichia coli, 595
Escort carriers, 181
Esher Report, 70
Esprit de corps, 477
Esquimalt Royal Navy Dockyard, 308
Essex, 315
Ethnic groups in Europe, 176
Euchre, 320
Eugene Esmonde, 253
EU Navfor Med, 185
Eurocopter AS350, 446, 472
Eurocopter AS350 Écureuil, 500, 564
Eurocopter Dauphin, 111, 159, 339, 383, 562, 563
Eurocopter EC135, 251, 477, 564
Eurocopter EC145, 477
Eurofighter Typhoon, 16, 98, 100, 101, 154, 446, 452, 453, 456, 466, 507, 561, 565, 574, 580
Eurofighter Typhoon FGR4, 465, 497, 499
Eurofighter Typhoon variants, 472
Europe, 168, 373
European Economic Community, 131
European Infrastructure Consolidation, 502
European Maritime Force, 297
European migration crisis, 185
European Theatre of World War II, 46, 116, 180

European Union, 197, 295
Excellency, 255
Exclusive Economic Zone, 196, 294
Exercise Joint Warrior, 295
Exercise RIMPAC, 297
Expeditionary Air Wing, 458, 505
Expeditionary warfare, 6, 12, 153, 160, 193, 257, 259, 323, 505
Experimental Armament Squadron, 535
Experimental Group RAF, 493
Experimental Mechanized Force, 72
Explosive lens, 120
External neutron initiator, 122

F-15E, 504
F-15E Strike Eagle, 137
F-35B, 245
F-35 Lightning II, 188, 192, 474, 475, 569
F-35 Lightning II, 466
F-4 Phantom II, 243
F-86 Sabres, 96
Failed state, 584
Fairbairn-Sykes Fighting Knife, 270
Fairey IIID, 240
Fairey Swordfish, 92, 239, 253, 254, 563
Falkland Islands, 3, 53, 81, 109, 154, 155, 189, 201, 292, 305, 332, 343, 377, 425, 460, 481, 505, 507, 567, 619
Falkland Islands Defence Force, 12, 109, 155, 350
Falklands Islands, 425
Falklands War, 6, 11, 49, 53, 81, 97, 131, 153, 154, 183, 184, 190, 193, 237, 243, 255, 259, 267, 332, 338, 410, 452, 507
Fall of Singapore, 287
Fallout shelter, 139
Falls Curfew, 80
Falls Road (Belfast), 80
Falmouth, Cornwall, 311
Far East, 5, 295, 314
Far East Air Force Examining Squadron, 535
Far East Air Force Training Squadron, 535
Far East Combined Bureau, 309
Far East Communication Squadron, 538
Far East Fleet, 229
Fareham, 304
Farnborough Airshow, 101, 475, 574
Fascism, 7
Faslane, 131, 134, 200, 304
Faslane Naval Base, 199
Fearn, Highland, 313
Felixstowe, 310
Fenham Barracks, 434
Fenian, 328
Fenian raids, 327, 329
Ferry Squadron RAF, 535

FGM-148 Javelin, 270, 370
Field army, 74
Fieldcraft, 281
Field hospital, 276
Field Marshal (UK), 359
Field marshal (United Kingdom), 75
Field Marshal von Blücher, 327, 328
Field officers, 259
Fife, 305, 307, 308, 310, 312, 316, 498
Fifth rate, 170
Fighter aircraft, 158, 446, 447, 479
Fighter Command Communication Squadron, 538
Fighter Command Control and Reporting School, 549
Fighter Leaders School, 550
Fighter Weapons School (United Kingdom), 550
Figurehead (object), 317
Fiji, 421
Fiji Infantry Regiment, 417
File:Bahrain adm location map.svg, 303
File:Falkland Islands location map.svg, 304
File:FleetAirArm wings.jpg, 205
File:Heart of Oak.ogg, 158
File:Japan Air Self-Defense Force roundel.svg, 479
File:RAF Far East Command roundel.svg, 479
File:Royal Marine and Albanian Commando.jpg, 277
File:Union flag 1606 (Kings Colors).svg, 623
File:United Kingdom adm location map.svg, 508
File:United Kingdom relief location map.jpg, 303, 306, 456
Financial Times, 589
Fire-and-forget, 370
Firebombing, 94
Fireteam, 278, 347, 368
First Anglo-Afghan War, 4
First Anglo-Dutch War, 166
First Anglo–Dutch War, 52
First Barons War, 25
First Battle of Ushant, 34
First Boer War, 327
First English Civil War, 60
First Fleet, 260
First French Empire, 327, 407
First Gulf War, 53
First Indochina War, 78
First Lord of the Admiralty, 585
First Opium War, 40, 177, 262, 327
First-rate, 211
First Sea Lord, 8, 43, 121, 158, 160, 177, 188, 198, 253, 255, 257, 279, 586, 590
First strike, 130

First Thatcher ministry, 132
First World War, 178, 263, 405, 413, 448, 509
Firth of Clyde, 131
Firth of Forth Group RAF, 493
Fiscal year, 2, 583
Fishery Protection Squadron, 227, 294
Fishing, 294
Fissile material, 114
Fission (biology), 115
Five nuclear-weapon states under the NPT, 114
Five Power Defence Arrangements, 3, 12, 155, 297
Five Powers Defence Arrangements, 197
Flag, 458
Flag officer, 107–109
Flag Officer 1st Flotilla, 231
Flag Officer, Carriers and Amphibious Ships, 230
Flag Officer, First Flotilla, 231
Flag Officer, Flotillas, Home Fleet, 229
Flag Officer, Flotillas, Mediterranean Fleet, 229
Flag Officer Naval Air Command, 243
Flag Officer Scotland and Northern Ireland, 199
Flag Officer Sea Training, 199, 207, 252, 294
Flag Officer, Second Flotilla, 231, 232
Flag Officer, Surface Flotilla, 233
Flag Officer, Third Flotilla, 230–232
Flag rank, 252, 253, 255
Flagship, 170
Flanders, 24, 25
Fleet Air Arm, 21, 91, 130, 157, 159, 180, 185, 196, 210, 227, 228, **237**, 238, 258, 266, 270, 279, 290, 306, 312, 447, 448, 452, 509, 529
Fleet Air Arm Memorial, 594
Fleet Air Arm Museum, 246, 593
Fleet Commander, 13, 158, 198, 230, 233, 269, 273
Fleet Protection Group Royal Marines, 259
Fleet Requirements Air Direction Unit, 251
Fleet Requirements and Aircraft Direction Unit, 244
Fleet Review, 253
Fleet review (Commonwealth realms), 207
Fleet Review, Royal Navy, 206, 318
Fleet School of Aerial Fighting and Gunnery, 550
Fleet submarine, 160, 211
Flight deck, 254
Flight Lieutenant, 19, 89, 460, 462
Flight (military unit), 15, 460
Flight officer, 462
Flight simulator, 472
Flight training, 17

Floatplane Training Squadron, 535
Flogging, 177, 405
Floreana Island, 169
Florence Nightingale, 68
Florida, 34
Flotilla, 227
Flying ace, 241
Flying boat, 96, 451
Flying Boat Instructors School, El Khanka, 558
Flying Instructors School (India), 558
Flying Instructors School, The Curragh, 558
Flying Instructors School, Upavon, 558
Flying Instructors Training School, 558
Flying Refresher School, 558
Flying Selection Squadron, 535
Flying Training Command Communication Squadron, 538
Fly-past, 253
FN FAL, 85
FN Minimi, 270, 337, 364, 368
Focus city, 566
Foden Trucks, 380
Folkestone, 309, 310
Folland Gnat, 479
Foot Guards, 360, 389
Force Troops Command, 14, 388
Foreign and Commonwealth Office, 201
Foreign Military Sales, 572
Formation and early history (1918–1939), 412
Formation Recconnaisance, 15
Formation reconnaissance regiment, 392
Former Soviet Republics, 114
Fort George, Scotland, 434
Fort Halstead, 105, 119
Forthside Barracks, 434
Fort St Angelo, 311, 314
Fort William, Highland, 314
Fort Worth, Texas, 569
Forward operating base, 503
Foulness, 139
Four Days Battle, 32, 166
Fragmentation grenade, 369
France, 4, 12, 172
France and weapons of mass destruction, 114
Francis Drake, 27, 28
Francis Pym, 132
Franco-Belgium Air Training School, 550
Franklin Roosevelt, 116
Frederick Curzon, 7th Earl Howe, 585
Frederick L. Hovde, 116
Frederick Sykes, 479
Freetown, 431
Fremington, Devon, 309
French and Indian War, 66, 327
French Army, 70, 263
French campaign in Egypt and Syria, 35

French Huguenots, 405
French Indochina, 77
French ironclad Gloire, 41
French navy, 27, 160, 172
French Revolution, 34
French Revolutionary Wars, 4, 34, 52, 68, 173
French ship Ville de Paris (1764), 173
French West Indies, 174
Fresnel Lens Optical Landing System (FLOLS), 243
Friendly fire, 100
Frigate, 13, 19, 49, 120, 172, 185, 211, 246, 292
Frigates, 158, 188
Frisch–Peierls memorandum, 115
Fritz Strassmann, 115
Froissarts Chronicles, 162
Front Line First, 387
Fuel tanker, 380
Fulwood Barracks, 434
Fusilier, 262
Future Combat Air System Technology Initiative, 574
Future Integrated Soldier Technology, 384
Future of the British Army (Army 2020 Refine), 15, 336
Future of the Royal Air Force, **569**
Future of the Royal Navy, 21, 159, 210, 228, 238, 258, 290
Future Rapid Effect System, 384
Future Soldier, 384
Future Strategic Tanker Aircraft, 566, 568
FV101 Scorpion, 109
FV103 Spartan, 109
FV430 series, 337, 370, 375
FV432, 337

G3-class battlecruiser, 45
Galleass, 27
Galley, 25, 27, 29
Gallipoli Campaign, 330
Gallipoli Lines, 110
GAM-87 Skybolt, 128, 183
Gamal Abdel Nasser, 79
Gamecock Barracks, 434
Garrison, 74
Gascony, 25
Gaseous diffusion, 117
Gateshead, 307
Gatow Airport, 450
Gavin Williamson, 1, 574, 583, 585
Gay Pride, 19
GCHQ, 427
GCSE, 354, 416
Geddes Axe, 71
Gen 75 Committee, 118

General, 8
General Atomics, 475
General Atomics Aeronautical Systems, 572
General Atomics MQ-9 Reaper, 446, 467, 501, 505, 507, 561, 572
General Dynamics, 385
General Dynamics F-111, 136
General Officer Commanding Scotland, 389
General-purpose machine gun, 368
General Reconnaissance and Air Navigation School (India), 550
General Reconnaissance School, 550
General Service Corps, 344, 414
General Service Respirator, 371
General (United Kingdom), 121, 204, 286, 359
General (United States), 136
Gentlemen at Arms, 603
Gentlemen Pensioners, 603
Geoffrey Hornby, 40
Geographic coordinate system, 583
Geolocate, 576
George Anson, 1st Baron Anson, 33
George Bertram Cockburn, 239
George Cockburn, 39
George H. W. Bush, 135
George III of the United Kingdom, 260, 282
George IV of the United Kingdom, 282
George Martin, 255
George Mills (RAF officer), 126
George Monck, 61
George Paget Thomson, 115
George Prevost, 39
George Prévost, 37
George Zambellas, 234
Gerald Templer, 121
German Air Force, 461
German Army (German Empire), 70
German Army (Wehrmacht), 73, 75, 331
German battleship Bismarck, 46, 180, 241, 254
German battleship Scharnhorst, 46, 180
German battleship Tirpitz, 241
German cruiser Königsberg, 266
German Empire, 4, 177, 329
German-occupied Europe, 93
German People, 408
Germany, 3, 92, 154, 365–367, 369, 376, 379, 380
Gerry Grimstone, 588
Gestapo, 94
G for George, 542
Ghana, 421
Gibraltar, 3, 33, 81, 154, 155, 171, 283, 298, 305, 314, 343, 394, 426, 480, 490, 505, 507, 619
Gibraltar Barracks, Bury St Edmunds, 434
Gibraltar International Airport, 507

Gibraltar Squadron, 201, 298, 619
Gilbert Blane, 173
Girls Venture Corps Air Cadets, 534
G. I. Taylor, 117
GIUK gap, 48, 160
Glasgow, 307, 314, 567
Glasgow Airport, 532, 534
Glasgow University Air Squadron, 532
Glenbranter, 313
Glen Caladh, 312
Glencorse Barracks, 434
Glenfinnart, 310
Glenn Haughton, 321
Glider Exercise Squadron, 536
Glider Training Squadron, 536
Global Combat Ship, 188
Glorious First of June, 34, 174
Glorious Revolution, 33, 166
Gloster Gladiator, 241
Gloster Hill, 78
Gloster Meteor, 96
Gloucestershire, 499, 503
God in Abrahamic religions, 355
Godwin, Earl of Wessex, 23
Golden share, 140
Good Friday Agreement, 81, 333
Gordon Barracks, 434
Gordon Foxley, 595
Gordon Messenger, 586
Gosport, 304, 308, 310–312, 314
Government of Canada, 343
Government of Gibraltar, 507
Government of the United Kingdom, 584
Governor of Gibraltar, 255
Grace Dieu (ship), 26
Graham Farmelo, 148
Grand Fleet, 485, 486
Grand Fleet School of Aerial Fighting and Gunnery, 550
Gravity bomb, 451
Great Britain in the Seven Years War, 52
Great Depression, 45, 412
Great Famine (Ireland), 420
Great Harry, 27
Great Lakes, 37
Great Michael, 30
Great Northern War, 33
Great power, 2, 4, 33, 323
Great Rift Valley, 155
Great ship, 26
Great Sound, Bermuda, 38
Great Victoria Desert, 134
Great Yarmouth, 313, 316
Greco-Turkish War (1897), 262
Greece, 200
Greeks, 408

Greek War of Independence, 40, 176
Green Bamboo, 122
Green beret, 284
Green Grass (nuclear warhead), 123
Green Howards, 64, 109
Greenock, 311, 313
Greenwich, 107
Grenada, 421
Grenade launcher, 369
Grenadier Guards, 61, 389, 393
Griffin HAR2, 506
Grimsby, 310
Grippen, 574
Grob G103a Twin II, 446, 472, 473, 498, 500, 561, 580
Grob G109, 472
Grob G 109, 499, 501
Grob G 115, 238, 251, 446, 472, 496, 501, 561, 563, 580
Grob G 120TP, 476, 496, 512, 564, 580
Grob Tutor, 158, 247, 472, 473
Ground burst, 138
Ground Controlled Approach Squadron, 536
Ground Defence Gunners School, 550
Ground Launched Cruise Missile, 137
Ground warfare, 321
Group (air force), 15, 482
Group captain, 89, 117, 457, 462
Group (military aviation unit), 456
Growth of the dockyard, 49
Gruffydd ap Llywelyn, 24
Guangzhou, 40, 177
Guards Armoured Division, 74
Guards Division, 344, 390, 393, 441
Guatemala, 343
Guided missile destroyer, 188, 189, 211
Guided-missile destroyer, 292
Guided Weapons Development Squadron, 536
Gulf of Aden, 295
Gulf Railway, 155
Gulf War, 49, 83, 89, 98, 185, 193, 237, 246, 249, 259, 332, 367, 452
Gunner (rank), 264
Gurkha, 594
Gurkhas, 59, 421
Gurkha Transport Regiment, 106, 111
Guy F. Liardet, 232
Gwynedd, 24

Habsburg, 171
Hai He, 262
Hakon Hakonsson, 163
Haldane Reforms, 70, 329
Hamble-le-Rice, 315
Hamburg, 94
Hampshire, 304, 305, 307, 309–316, 500

Hamworthy, 306
Hand grenade, 364
Handley-Page Halifax, 94
Handley Page Jetstream, 244, 245
Handley Page Victor, 121, 128, 450
Harfleur, 26
Harley Davidson, 381
Harold F. Williamson, 603
Harold Godwinson, 24
Harold Macmillan, 125, 150
Harold Wilson, 141, 145
Harrier GR9, 506
Harrogate, 311, 400
Harry Truman, 117
Harthacnut, 24
Harwich, 310
Haslemere, 310
Havana, 34, 172
Hawker Beechcraft, 470
Hawker Hunter, 244, 245, 565
Hawker Hurricane, 562
Hawker Sea Fury, 243, 563
Hawker Sea Hawk, 255, 563
Hawker Siddeley Harrier, 97, 108, 243
Hawker Siddeley Nimrod, 129
Hayling Island, 313
Headgear, 360
Head of state, 7
Headquarters, 494
Headquarters Air Command Southeast Asia (Communication) Squadron, 538
Headquarters British Forces Aden Communication Squadron, 538
Headquarters Communication Squadron, Royal Air Force, 538
Headquarters Communication Squadron, Royal Flying Corps, 538
Headquarters House, Hong Kong, 110
Headquarters Middle East Air Force Communication Squadron, 538
Headquarters Middle East Communication Squadron, 538
Headquarters Royal Air Force Burma Communication Squadron, 538
Headquarters Royal Air Force Northern Ireland Communication Squadron, 538
Heart of Oak, 158, 320
Heavy conversion units, 483
Heavy cruisers, 46, 180
Heavy Equipment Transport System, 379
Heavy machine gun, 368, 369
Heckler & Koch AG36, 364
Heckler & Koch GMG, 369
Heckler & Koch HK417, 366
Heckler & Koch MP5, 367
Hectare, 593

Heinz Guderian, 73
Helensburgh, 273
Helicopter, 239, 246, 270, 279
Helicopter training, 500
Helmand Province, 334
Hendon Air Show, 91
Henry Allingham, 90, 461
Henry Fancourt, 253
Henry Grace à Dieu, 27
Henry III of England, 25
Henry III of Germany, 24
Henry II of England, 25
Henry Tizard, 115
Henry VIII of England, 27, 164, 168, 594
Henry VII of England, 27, 162
Henry V of England, 26, 162, 324
Heraldry, 479
Herbert Kitchener, 1st Earl Kitchener, 18, 354, 411
Hereford, 107, 347
Her Majestys Government, 192
Her Majestys Naval Service, 1, 13, 21, 157, 159, 160, 210, 211, 228, 237, 238, 258, 290, 615
Her Majestys Ship, 202
Hermes, 183
Hessian (soldiers), 67, 405
H. G. Wells, 115
HH-60G Pave Hawk, 504
Hide (unit), 161
High Explosive Anti Tank, 370
Highland (council area), 505
Highlanders (Seaforth, Gordons and Camerons), 433
Highly enriched uranium, 119
High Seas Fleet, 178
Highway of Death, 333
His Majestys Ship, 202
History of nuclear weapons, 113
History of the British Army, 58, **58**, 322, 364, 386, 404
History of the Royal Air Force, **89**, 447, 455
History of the Royal Marines, 21, 159, 210, 228, 238, 258, 290
History of the Royal Navy, 21, **21**, 159, 210, 228, 238, 258, 290
Hitler, 448
HMNB Clyde, 115, 161, 199, 200, 211, 221, 227, 255, 268, 273, 293, 303, 304, 306, 307
HMNB Devonport, 161, 199, 211, 227, 232, 303, 304, 306, 307
HMNB Portsmouth, 25, 27, 161, 162, 199, 211, 227, 231, 232, 252, 303, 304, 306, 307
HMS Abastor, 309

HMS Abatos, 309
HMS Afrikander, 309
HMS Agamemnon (1852), 41
HMS Aggressive (shore establishment), 309, 312
HMS Albion (L14), 184, 187, 194, 215, 276
HMS Albion (R07), 183
HMS Alecto (1839), 41
HMS Allenby, 309
HMS Ambrose, 309
HMS Ambush (S120), 213
HMS Amethyst (F116), 53
HMS Anderson, 309
HMS Appledore, 309
HMS Ararat, 309, 310
HMS Arbella, 309
HMS Archer (P264), 221
HMS Argus (I49), 53
HMS Argyll (F231), 216
HMS Ariel, 309
HMS Ark Royal (91), 45, 46, 179, 180
HMS Ark Royal (R09), 182, 183, 208, 242, 243
HMS Artful, 52
HMS Artful (S121), 191, 213
HMS Astute (S119), 191, 213
HMS Attack (shore establishment), 310
HMS Badger (shore establishment), 310
HMS Bangor (M109), 219
HMS Barfleur (1768), 173
HMS Barham (04), 46, 180
HMS Beagle, 202
HMS Bee, 310
HMS Beehive, 310
HMS Bellerophon, 310
HMS Benbow, 310
HMS Biter (P270), 221
HMS Blazer (P279), 221
HMS Blyth (M111), 220
HMS Boscawen (shore establishment), 310
HMS Brecon (M29), 211, 304
HMS Bristol (D23), 211, 225, 304
HMS Brocklesby (M33), 219
HMS Brontosaurus, 309, 310
HMS Bulwark (L15), 187, 215, 276
HMS Bulwark (R08), 183
HMS Caledonia, 305, 307, 310
HMS Calliope (shore establishment), 307
HMS Cambria (shore establishment), 307
HMS Cambridge (1956), 310
HMS Captain (1869), 41
HMS Caroline (1914), 310
HMS Cattistock (M31), 219
HMS Centaur (R06), 183
HMS Centurion (shore establishment), 310
HMS Ceres (shore establishment 1946), 310

HMS Ceres (shore establishment 1984), 310
HMS Ceres (shore establishment 2015), 307
HMS Charger (P292), 221
HMS Chatham (F87), 295
HMS Chiddingfold (M37), 219
HMS Cicala, 310
HMS Claverhouse (shore establishment), 310
HMS Clyde (P257), 154, 189, 196, 218, 292
HMS Cochrane, 310
HMS Collingwood, 307
HMS Collingwood (establishment), 304
HMS Comet (1821), 40
HMS Conqueror (S48), 49, 184, 190
HMS Cornwall (56), 46, 180
HMS Cornwall (F99), 50
HMS Courageous (50), 45, 46, 180
HMS Cricket (shore establishment), 311
HMS Cromer (M103), 211, 304
HMS Dalriada (shore establishment), 307, 311
HMS Daring (D32), 202, 216
HMS Dartmouth, 304
HMS Dasher (P280), 221
HMS Dauntless (D33), 216
HMS Defender (D36), 216
HMS Defiance (shore establishment 1884), 311
HMS Defiance (shore establishment 1970), 311
HMS Demetrius, 310
HMS Devastation (1871), 42
HMS Diamond (D34), 216, 298
HMS Dinosaur, 311
HMS Dolphin, 311
HMS Dorsetshire (40), 46, 180
HMS Dragon (D35), 216, 294, 300
HMS Drake, 304
HMS Dreadnought (1906), 43, 53, 177, 178
HMS Dreadnought (S101), 48, 53, 126, 182
HMS Dryad (establishment), 311
HMS Duke (shore establishment), 311
HMS Dumbarton Castle, 30
HMS Duncan (D37), 188, 189, 216, 298
HMS Dundonald, 311
HMS Eagle (R05), 183
HMS Eaglet (shore establishment), 307
HMS Echo (H87), 223, 295
HMS Edinburgh, 30
HMS Egmont, 311
HMS Enterprise (H88), 223
HMS Example (P165), 221
HMS Excellent (shore establishment), 198, 304, 619
HMS Exeter (68), 46, 180
HMS Exploit (P167), 221
HMS Explorer (P164), 221
HMS Express (P163), 221

HMS Fearless (L10), 268
HMS Ferret (shore establishment 1940), 311, 314
HMS Ferret (shore establishment 1982), 307
HMS Fervent, 311
HMS Fisgard (1946), 311
HMS Flycatcher, 311
HMS Flying Fox (shore establishment), 307
HMS Forest Moor, 311
HMS Forth (P222), 189, 218
HMS Forward (shore establishment 1939), 311
HMS Forward (shore establishment 1984), 307
HMS Fox (shore establishment), 312
HMS Furious (47), 45
HMS Ganges (shore establishment), 312
HMS GANNET, 304
HMS Gannet SAR Flight, 243
HMS Glasgow, 30
HMS Glendower, 312
HMS Glorious, 45, 46, 180
HMS Glory (R62), 241
HMS Grimsby (M108), 219
HMS Gunner, 312
HMS Haig, 312
HMS Hannibal, 312
HMS Helder, 312
HMS Helicon, 312
HMS Hermes (95), 46, 180, 240
HMS Hermes (R12), 97, 183, 452
HMS Heron, 304
HMS Hibernia (shore establishment), 307
HMS Highflyer, 312
HMS Holland 1, 53
HMS Hood (51), 46, 180, 181
HMS Hornet, 312
HMS Hurworth (M39), 219
HMS Illustrious (R06), 183, 185, 187, 300
HMS Indefatigable (R10), 266
HMS Inskip, 312
HMS Intrepid (L11), 268
HMS Invincible (R05), 318
HMS Iron Duke (F234), 217
HMS Jackdaw, 312
HMS Jackdaw II, 308
HMS James Cook, 312
HMS Jufair, 12, 154, 305, 312
HMS Kent (F78), 217
HMS Kestrel, 309, 312
HMS Kestrel (shore establishment), 308
HMS King Alfred (shore establishment 1939), 312
HMS King Alfred (shore establishment 1994), 307
HMS Lancaster (F229), 216, 300
HMS Lanka, 312
HMS Ledbury (M30), 219

HMS Leeds Castle (P258), 109
HMS Leopard (1790), 37
HMS Lightning (1823), 40
HMS Lizard (shore establishment), 312
HMS Lochailort, 312
HMS Lochinvar (shore establishment), 312
HMS Louisburg, 312
HMS Macaw, 312
HMS Magpie (H130), 223
HMS Malabar (shore establishment), 312
HMS Manatee, 312
HMS Mastodon, 312
HMS Mauritius (shore establishment), 312
HMS Medina (shore establishment), 313
HMS Mentor, 313
HMS Mercury (shore establishment), 313
HMS Merlin, 310
HMS Mersey (P283), 218, 294
HMS Middleton (M34), 219
HMS Midge, 313
HMS Monarch (1868), 41
HMS Monck, 313
HMS Monmouth (F235), 217
HMS Montrose (F236), 217
HMS Nelson, 304, 307
HMS Neptune, 304
HMS Newt (shore establishment), 313
HMS Nile, 313
HMS Nimrod (1940), 313
HMS Northney, 313
HMS Northumberland (F238), 217
HMS Nuthatch, 308
HMS Ocean (L12), 185, 279, 298
HMS Owl, 313
HMS Pasco, 313
HMS Peacock (P239), 111
HMS Pembroke (establishment), 313
HMS Pembroke (M107), 219
HMS Penzance (M106), 219
HMS Phoenix (shore establishment, Portsmouth), 313
HMS Pickle (1800), 36
HMS Plover (240), 111
HMS Plym (K271), 120
HMS Portland, 19
HMS Portland (F79), 217
HMS President (shore establishment), 307, 313
HMS Prince of Wales (53), 46, 180, 287
HMS Prince of Wales (R09), 188
HMS Prince Royal, 31
HMS Prosperine, 313
HMS Protector (A173), 189, 190, 211, 223, 291
HMS Puncher (P291), 221
HMS Pursuer (P273), 221
HMS Pyramus, 313

HMS Quebec (shore establishment), 314
HMS Queen Elizabeth (R08), 13, 160, 187, 188, 215
HMS Raider (P275), 221, 293
HMS Raleigh, 303
HMS Raleigh (shore establishment), 186, 199, 211, 252, 304, 307
HMS Ramsey (M110), 220
HMS Ranger (P293), 221
HMS Rattler (1843), 52
HMS Repulse (1916), 46, 180, 287
HMS Resolution (S22), 48, 131
HMS Richmond (F239), 217
HMS Robertson, 314
HMS Robin, 308
HMS Rooke (1946 shore establishment), 314
HMS Roseneath, 314
HMS Royal Albert, 314
HMS Royal Arthur (shore establishment), 314
HMS Royal Charlotte, 314
HMS Royal Oak (08), 46, 180
HMS Royal Oak (1809), 39
HMS Sabre (P285), 221, 298
HMS Saker, 305
HMS Salford, 314
HMS Sanderling, 314
HMS Scimitar (P284), 221, 298, 299
HMS Scotia, 314
HMS Scotia (shore establishment), 307
HMS Scott (H131), 190, 223
HMS Sea Eagle, 314
HMS Seahawk, 304
HMS Sea Serpent, 314
HMS Sembawang, 314
HMS Shah, 42
HMS Sheba, 314
HMS Sherwood (shore establishment), 307
HMS Shoreham (M112), 220
HMS Simbang, 314
HMS Siskin, 308
HMS Smiter (P272), 221
HMS Somerset (F82), 217
HMS Sovereign of the Seas, 31
HMS Spartiate, 314
HMS Splendid (S106), 50
HMS Squid, 314
HMS St Albans (F83), 188, 217
HMS Standard (1942), 315
HMS St Angelo, 314
HMS Starling (P241), 111
HMS St Barbara, 314
HMS St Christopher (shore establishment), 314
HMS Stopford, 315
HMS St Vincent (Gosport shore establishment), 314

HMS St Vincent (London shore establishment), 314
HMS Sultan, 307
HMS Sultan (establishment), 304, 308
HMS Sutherland (F81), 217
HMS Talent (S92), 213
HMS Tamar (shore station), 111, 315
HMS Tarlair, 315
HMS Temeraire, 304
HMS Tern, 308
HMS Terror, 314
HMS Thunderer, 315
HMS Tireless, 52
HMS Tireless (S88), 295
HMS Tormentor, 315
HMS Tracker (P274), 221, 293
HMS Trenchant (S91), 213
HMS Triumph (S93), 213
HMS Trumpeter (P294), 221
HMS Turbulent (S87), 50
HMS Turtle, 315
HMS Tyne (P281), 218
HMS Uva, 315
HMS Vanguard (23), 53
HMS Vanguard (S28), 132, 182, 212
HMS Varbel, 315
HMS Varbell II, 315
HMS Vectis (shore establishment), 315
HMS Vengeance (S31), 133, 212
HMS Vernon (shore establishment), 315
HMS Victorious (R38), 183, 266
HMS Victorious (S29), 132, 212
HMS Victory, 4, 158, 170, 211
HMS Vigilant (S30), 132, 212
HMS Vivid (shore establishment 1957), 307
HMS Vulcan, 303
HMS Wagtail, 315
HMS Warren, 315
HMS Warrior, 305
HMS Warrior (1860), 41, 53, 176
HMS Wasp, 315
HMS Westcliffe, 315
HMS Westminster (F237), 217
HMS Wildfire (shore establishment 1964), 315
HMS Wildfire (shore establishment 2000), 307
HMS Woolvestone, 315
HMY Britannia, 255
Ho Chi Minh, 77
Hochseeflotte, 44
Holland No. 1, 43
Holyhead, 310
Holy Loch, 130
Home Command (British Army), 345, 387, 388
Home Command Communication Squadron, 538
Home Defence Squadron, 536
Home Fleet, 46, 229
Honest John missile, 129
Hong Kong, 315
Hong Kong Auxiliary Squadron, 536
Hong Kong Fighter Squadron, 536
Hong Kong Military Service Corps, 111
Hong Kong Patrol Squadron, 111
Hong Kong Volunteer Defence Corps, 417
Honorary Chaplain to the Queen, 199
Honourable Artillery Company, 259, 360, 389, 395, 402, 441
Horatio Hornblower, 36, 207
Horatio Nelson, 35, 170
Horatio Nelson, 1st Viscount Nelson, 4, 35, 174
Hornblower (TV series), 208
Horn of Africa, 295
Horse Guards Avenue, 594
Horse Guards (building), 389
Hospital ship, 17
Hotel Cecil (London), 448
Household Cavalry, 15, 73, 438, 440
Household Cavalry Mounted Regiment, 389, 435
Household Cavalry Regiment, 392, 433
Household Division, 15
House of Commons, 119
House of Commons of the United Kingdom, 11, 134, 415
House of Hanover, 329
House of Lords, 585
House of Stewart, 65
Hove, 312
Howe Barracks, 434
Howitzer, 270, 377
Hoy, 313
Huff-Duff, 180
Hugh F. Durrant-Whyte, 588
Hugh Gaitskell, 141
Hugh Trenchard, 90, 607
Hugh Trenchard, 1st Viscount Trenchard, 446
Hugo White, 232
Humanitarian aid, 2, 187
Hundred Years War, 26, 159, 162
Hunt-class mine countermeasures vessel, 190, 219
Hunting Engineering, 140
Hurricane, 291
Hurricane Irma, 291
Hyde Park Barracks, London, 435
Hydrography, 196
Hydrophone, 315
Hydrophones, 180
Hythe, Hampshire, 315

Iain Henderson (Royal Navy officer), 255
Ian Forbes, 233
Ian Wheatley, 199
IATA airline designator, 566
ICAO airline designator, 566
Icebreaker, 158, 211, 291
Iceland, 48
Icelandic Coast Guard, 48
I Corps (United Kingdom), 76, 107, 332, 390
IFOR, 83
IISS2010, 620
IISS2012, 628
Ilfracombe, 309
Illegal drug trade, 291
Illustrious-class aircraft carrier, 45
Image intensifier, 365
Imjin Barracks, 435
Immingham, 310
Imperial Chemical Industries, 116
Imperial College London, 115
Imperial German Navy, 43, 177
Imperialism, 58
Imperial Japanese Army, 75
Imperial Japanese Naval Air Service, 92
Imperial War Cabinet, 89
Imphal Barracks, 435
Implementation Force, 332
Impressment, 35, 175, 206, 318, 405, 406
Inchgarvie, 30, 167
Independent Air Force, 485
Independent Highland Companies, 64
India, 4, 172
India and weapons of mass destruction, 114
India Detachment, Chinese Air Force Cadet School, 550
Indian independence movement, 332
Indian Mutiny, 287
Indian Ocean, 53, 172, 295
Indian Rebellion of 1857, 68, 327
Indigenous peoples of the Americas, 67, 327
Indigo Hammer, 128
Indonesia, 77, 96
Indonesia–Malaysia confrontation, 53, 79, 332
Industrial Revolution, 68, 176, 407
Infantry, 70, 259, 387, 464
Infantry Battle School, 356, 434, 441, 442
Infantry mobility vehicle, 375
Infantry of the British Army, 344
Infantry Training Centre (British Army), 356, 400, 439, 440, 442
Inflatable Raiding Craft, 270
Information Systems & Services, 498
Information technology, 590
Inner London, 138
In ordinary, 35
Inskip, Lancashire, 312

Instructors School, 558
Intelligence Corps (United Kingdom), 345, 355, 356, 361, 397, 439, 440
Intelligence, surveillance, target acquisition, and reconnaissance, 339, 456, 501, 560
Intercontinental ballistic missile, 137
Intermediate Range Ballistic Missile, 128
Intermediate-Range Nuclear Forces Treaty, 137
International Fleet Review 2005, 200
International Institute for Strategic Studies, 9, 256, 461, 481
International MXT-MV, 376
International Standard Book Number, 54–57, 85–88, 104, 146–152, 208, 209, 236, 255, 256, 288, 289, 316, 361–363, 422, 423, 481, 508, 509, 542, 560
International Standard Serial Number, 146–151
International terrorism, 584
Internment, 80
Interregnum (England), 60, 325
Interserve, 504
Interwar period, 336
Invasion of Poland, 4, 331
Inverailort House, 312
Inverary, 314
Inverclyde, 311
Invergordon, 311
Invergordon Mutiny, 46, 53, 179
Inverkip, 311
Inverness-shire, 312, 314
Invicta Park Barracks, 435
Invincible class aircraft carrier, 243
Invincible-class aircraft carrier, 50, 183, 187, 202
In Which We Serve, 207
Ipswich, 312, 315
Iranian Embassy Siege, 81
Iraq, 49, 50, 83, 332, 342, 431, 467
Iraqi Armed Forces, 342
Iraqi Navy, 49, 197
Iraqi no-fly zones, 19, 98
Iraq War, 6, 12, 50, 89, 193, 237, 259, 452
Ireland Island, Bermuda, 38
Irgun, 78
Irish Army (Kingdom of Ireland), 325
Irish Free State, 72
Irish Guards, 393, 421
Irish nationalist, 80
Irish Rebellion of 1798, 328
Irish Republican Army, 72, 329
Irish Republican Army (1922–1969), 80
Irish Republicanism, 80
Irish War of Independence, 327
Iron, 41

Ironclad, 41
Iron Cross, 479
Iron sights, 337
Irvine, North Ayrshire, 311
Islamic State of Iraq and the Levant, 7, 335, 458, 466
Islamist groups, 589
Island-class patrol vessel, 189
Island-class patrol vessel (2013), 221
Isle of Anglesey, 499, 501
Isle of Bute, 315
Isle of Man, 12, 23, 163, 315
Isle of Portland, 308, 310
Isle of Sheppey, 239
Isle of Wight, 27, 312, 313, 315
Israel, 94, 370
ISTAR, 447, 467
Isthmus of Darien, 170
Italian Campaign (World War II), 267, 331
Italian War of 1551–59, 168
Italy, 185, 367, 376
Iveco LMV, 338, 375, 376
Ivy Mike, 121

Jackal (vehicle), 270, 376
Jackstaff, 206, 317
Jack Tar, 206, 320
Jacobite rising of 1745, 33
Jacobite risings, 64
Jacobitism, 59
Jacobs Engineering Group, 140
Jamaica, 166, 421
James Bond, 207
James Burnell-Nugent, 234
James Chadwick, 115, 117
James F. Byrnes, 119
James Hope (Royal Navy officer), 262
James III of Scotland, 30, 164
James II of England, 32, 33, 325
James II of Scotland, 30, 164
James I of England, 31
James I of Scotland, 29, 163
James IV of Scotland, 30, 164
James L. Tuck, 117
James VI of Scotland, 29
James Wolfe, 66
Janes Defence Weekly, 607, 621
Janes Information Group, 299
Jankel, 382
Jan Smuts, 89, 448
Japan, 314
Japan Air Self-Defense Force, 102
Java, 175
Java (island), 77
Javelin Instrument Rating Squadron, 536
Javelin (surface-to-air missile), 109

JCB HMEE, 379
Jeffery Amherst, 1st Baron Amherst, 67
Jeffrey Quill, 254
Jeremy Bernstein, 147
Jeremy Black (Royal Navy officer), 232
Jeremy Corbyn, 134
Jet2.com, 568
Jet aircraft, 241
J. F. C. Fuller, 73
JHFS Aldergrove, 532
Joe 1, 120
Joe 4, 121
John Anderson, 1st Viscount Waverley, 116
John Brigstocke, 232, 233
John Byng, 34
John Churchill, 1st Duke of Marlborough, 326
John Clere (c. 1511–57), 169
John Cockcroft, 115
John Cox (Royal Navy officer), 231, 232
John de Beauchamp, 1st Baron Beauchamp de Warwick, 25, 26
John F. Coward, 232
John Fieldhouse, Baron Fieldhouse, 231
John Fisher, 1st Baron Fisher, 43, 177
John Fitzgerald Kennedy, 351
John F. Kennedy, 131
John Gordon, 1st Viscount of Kenmure, 169
John Hawkins (naval commander), 28
John Kerr (Royal Navy officer), 232
John Laird Sons and Company, 41
John Mills, 208
John Moffat (pilot), 254
John Moore (British Army officer), 408
John Nott, 184
John of England, 25
John Pitcairn, 260
John Riley (painter), 61
John Russells Regiment of Guards, 61
John Slessor, 124
Johnson Beharry, 421
John Treacher, 254
John Weale (Royal Navy officer), 199
Joint Aircraft Recovery and Transportation Squadron, 496
Joint Air Transport Establishment, 107
Joint Arms Control Implementation Group, 498
Joint Combat Aircraft, 474, 569
Joint Committee on Atomic Energy, 120
Joint Elementary Flying Training School, 559
Joint Expeditionary Force (Maritime), 12, 297
Joint Force Air Component Headquarters, 455
Joint Force Harrier, 192, 245, 249, 252, 452, 482
Joint Forces Command, 502, 505, 586, 592
Joint Forces Intelligence Group, 502

Joint Forward Air Controller Training and Standards Unit, 107, 498
Joint Helicopter Command, 82, 196, 279, 447, 468, 494, 496, 500
Joint Intelligence Operations Center Europe Analytic Center, 504
Joint Intelligence Training Group, 440
Joint Rapid Reaction Force, 12
Joint Rapid Reaction Force (United Kingdom), 82
Joint Service Defence College, 107
Joint Services Command and Staff College, 465
Joint Special Forces Aviation Wing, 500
Joint Trials and Training Squadron, 536
Joint Warfare Centre, 503
Jonathon Band, 188
Jordan, 410
Jo Salter, 19
Joule, 113
Józef Piłsudski, 519
Józef Poniatowski, 519
JSTOR, 146–149, 151
Judge Advocate General of the Armed Forces, 105
Julian Oswald, 232
Julin Bristol, 135
Junior officer, 460
Junior technician, 462

Kabul, 334, 424
Kaiserliche Marine, 44
Kai Tak Airport, 111, 311
Kamchatka peninsula, 50, 185
Kandahar Airfield, 99
Kate Pyne, 146
Kathmandu, 430
Keith Blount, 247
Kendrew Barracks, 435
Kennedy administration, 131
Kenneth Bloomfield, 623
Kenneth Hubbard, 122, 149
Kenneth More, 254
Kent, 308, 313–315
Kenya, 3, 96, 155, 343, 431, 432, 452
Kevin ODonoghue, 17, 589
Keyham, Devon, 315
Kielder, Northumberland, 315
Kilt, 64
Kim Jong-un, 102
King Abdullah II, 410
King and Country, 411
Kingdom of England, 22, 28, 161, 620
Kingdom of France, 159
Kingdom of Great Britain, 2, 3, 22, 33, 171, 336, 405, 620
Kingdom of Hanover, 65, 405

Kingdom of Scotland, 28, 615, 623
Kingdom of the Isles, 163
Kingdom of the Two Sicilies, 171
King Edward I, 25
King George III, 409
King George V-class battleship (1939), 45, 179
King Richard III, 26
Kings African Rifles, 349
Kingsbarns, 308
Kings Commissioned Indian Officer, 418
Kings Division, 344, 390, 393, 440
Kingsfield Airfield, 108
Kings Royal Hussars, 360, 392, 432
Kings shilling, 406
Kingston Royal Naval Dockyard, 308
Kings Troop, Royal Horse Artillery, 389, 395
Kinloss Barracks, 435, 498
Kiritimati, 135
Kirkwall, 308, 313
Kirkwall Castle, 169
Kitcheners Army, 45, 70, 330, 411
Klaus Fuchs, 117
Kneller Hall, 440
Knight Commander of the Order of the Bath, 158, 198, 445
Konfrontasi, 96, 452
Korean War, 53, 78, 96, 237, 243, 451
Kosovo, 84, 332, 588
Kosovo conflict, 185
Kosovo War, 89, 99, 193, 259, 452
Kuala Lumpur Fighter Squadron, 536
Kuala Lumpur Squadron, 536
Kuwait, 98, 332

L109, 369
L115A3, 270, 337
L118 Light Gun, 109, 268, 270, 338, 377
L128A1, 337
L129A1, 366
L16 81mm Mortar, 270, 337, 370
L17A2 UGL, 337
L7 (machine gun), 270, 337, 368
L85 Rifle, 270
L86 LSW, 337, 364
L9 Bar Mine, 369
Labour Party Conference, 141
Labour Party (UK), 82, 142, 183
Ladyville, 108
Laikipia County, 431
Lancashire, 119
Lance corporal, 205, 287, 360
Landing craft, 265, 267, 276
Landing craft tank, 314
Landing platform dock, 187
Landing Platform Helicopter, 185
Landing ship dock, 16

Land Rover Defender, 338, 381
Land Rover Wolf, 270, 338, 381
Land warfare, 2
Largs, 311, 313, 315
Larkhill, 440
La Rochelle, 31
Latin, 479
Latin language, 158, 257, 445
Laurence Olivier, 253
Lawrence Radiation Laboratory, 130
Lawrence S. Wittner, 151
LCAC (United Kingdom), 270
LCVP Mk5, 270, 272
LCVP (United Kingdom), 268
Leader of the Opposition (United Kingdom), 134
Leading rating, 205
League of Nations, 4
Leeds, 307
Lee–Enfield, 85
Lee–Metford, 85
Lee-on-the-Solent, 308
Lee shore, 172
Legitimists, 408
Leinster, 328
Leith, 29, 30, 163, 310
Leonard Cheshire, 117
Leonardo, 574
Leonardo-Finmeccanica, 580
Leonardo S.p.A., 475
Leonard Owen, 120
Lerwick, 312
Les Espagnols sur Mer, 26
Leslie Hore-Belisha, 1st Baron Hore-Belisha, 413
Leslie R. Groves, 117
Letter of marque, 169
Letters of last resort, 144
Letters of marque, 164
Letters patent, 25, 462
Leuchars Station, 498, 533
Levitated pit, 120
Lewis gun, 330
Lewis Machine and Tool Company, 337, 364, 367
Lewis machine gun, 70
Lewis Strauss, 120
Lews Castle, 313
Leyland 4-tonne truck, 380
Liberal Party (UK), 141
Libya, 185
Libyan no-fly zone, 6
Licensed production, 339
Lieutenant, 347, 442
Lieutenant (British Army and Royal Marines), 204, 286

Lieutenant-Colonel (UK), 204, 286, 359
Lieutenant Colonel (United Kingdom), 275, 347
Lieutenant Commander, 253, 254
Lieutenant-Commander, 254
Lieutenant commander (Royal Navy), 203
Lieutenant-General (United Kingdom), 204, 286, 359, 388
Lieutenant (navy), 203
Life Guards (British Army), 61
Light Aircraft School, 550
Light Cavalry, 15, 392
Light Dragoons, 392
Light infantry, 15, 192, 258, 393, 408
Light machine gun, 368
Limassol, 428, 429
Lincolnshire, 121, 309, 496, 497, 500, 501, 505
Lindsay of Pitscottie, 30
Line of battle, 32
Liquid drop model, 115
Lisbon, 25, 165
Lisburn, 307
Lise Meitner, 115
List of active Royal Marines military watercraft, 270
List of active Royal Navy ships, 13, 21, 157–160, 210, **210**, 228, 238, 258, 290
List of active United Kingdom military aircraft, 15, 447, **560**
List of aircraft carriers of the Royal Navy, 227, 301
List of aircraft of the RAF, 455
List of aircraft wings of the Royal Navy, 302
List of air stations of the Royal Navy, 302
List of amphibious warfare ships of the Royal Navy, 301
List of battlecruisers of the Royal Navy, 301
List of bomb vessels of the Royal Navy, 301
List of breastwork monitors of the Royal Navy, 301
List of British armies in World War I, 389
List of British armies in World War II, 389
List of British Army installations, **424**
List of British Army regiments, 58, 322, 363, 386, 390, 404
List of British Army regiments (1881), 389
List of British Army regiments (1962), 77, 387, 389
List of British Army regiments (1994), 82, 387, 389
List of British Army regiments (2008), 387, 389
List of British Army Yeomanry Regiments converted to Royal Artillery, 389

List of British Commands and Army groups, 389
List of British corps in World War I, 389
List of British corps in World War II, 389
List of British divisions in World War I, 389
List of British divisions in World War II, 389
List of conflicts in Europe, 58
List of conflicts involving the United Kingdom, 2
List of corvette and sloop classes of the Royal Navy, 301
List of countries by military expenditures, 9
List of cruiser classes of the Royal Navy, 301
List of destroyer classes of the Royal Navy, 301
List of destroyers of the Royal Navy, 227
List of dreadnought battleships of the Royal Navy, 301
List of early warships of the English Navy, 302
List of equipment of the British Army, 58, 322, 363, **363**, 386, 404
List of escort aircraft carriers of the Royal Navy, 301
List of estimated death tolls from nuclear attacks on cities, 113
List of fast patrol boats of the Royal Navy, 227
List of fireships of the Royal Navy, 301
List of Fleet Air Arm aircraft squadrons, 530
List of fleets and major commands of the Royal Navy, 302
List of French possessions and colonies, 172
List of frigate classes of the Royal Navy, 301
List of frigates of the Royal Navy, 227
List of gunboats and gunvessels of the Royal Navy, 301
List of gun-brigs of the Royal Navy, 301
List of hospitals and hospital ships of the Royal Navy, 302
List of ironclads of the Royal Navy, 301
List of Lord High Admirals of Scotland, 171
List of Lords High Admiral, 171
List of mine countermeasure vessels of the Royal Navy, 301
List of minesweepers of the Royal Navy, 227
List of monitors of the Royal Navy, 301
List of nicknames of British Army regiments, 390
List of nuclear weapons, 114
List of patrol boats of the Royal Navy, 301
List of pre-dreadnought battleships of the Royal Navy, 301
List of Regiments of Foot, 389
List of Royal Air Force aircraft independent flights, 534
List of Royal Air Force aircraft squadrons, **509**
List of Royal Air Force groups, **482**
List of Royal Air Force schools, **543**

List of Royal Air Force stations, 455, **494**
List of Royal Armoured Corps Regiments in World War Two, 389
List of Royal Artillery Batteries, 389
List of Royal Navy losses in World War II, 46, 180
List of Royal Navy shore establishments, 211, **301**, 302
List of Royal Yachts of the United Kingdom, 301
List of seaplane carriers of the Royal Navy, 301
List of senior officers of the British Army, 58, 322, 363, 386, 404
List of senior officers of the Royal Navy, 21, 159, 210, 228, 238, 258, 290
List of ship names of the Royal Navy, 21, 159, 210, 228, 238, 258, 290, 301
List of ship names of the Royal Navy (A), 301
List of ship names of the Royal Navy (B), 301
List of ship names of the Royal Navy (C), 301
List of ship names of the Royal Navy (D–F), 301
List of ship names of the Royal Navy (G–H), 301
List of ship names of the Royal Navy (I–L), 301
List of ship names of the Royal Navy (M–N), 301
List of ship names of the Royal Navy (O–Q), 301
List of ship names of the Royal Navy (R–T), 301
List of ship names of the Royal Navy (U–Z), 301
List of ships of the line of the Royal Navy, 301
List of squadrons and flotillas of the Royal Navy, 302
List of states with nuclear weapons, 114
List of submarine classes of the Royal Navy, 302
List of Sultans of Brunei, 343
List of support ships of the Royal Navy, 302
List of survey vessels of the Royal Navy, 302
List of Territorial Army units (2012), 389
List of torpedo boat classes of the Royal Navy, 301
List of units of the British Army Territorial Force 1908, 389
List of warships of the Scots Navy, 302
Lithium, 115
Lithium-6, 123
Lithium-7, 123
Lithium deuteride, 123
Littoral, 184
Liverpool, 268, 307
Liverpool University Air Squadron, 502, 532
Llangennech, 316

671

Lloyd Quinan, 142
Lochailort, 312
Loch Ewe, 312
Loch Striven, 315
Lockheed C-130 Hercules, 109, 154, 507
Lockheed Martin, 13, 140, 476, 579
Lockheed Martin C-130J Super Hercules, 447, 496
Lockheed Martin Desert Hawk III, 339
Lockheed Martin F-35 Lightning II, 13, 158, 192, 245, 249, 251, 446, 499, 504–507, 561, 563, 565, 580
Lockheed Martin Super Hercules, 561
Lockheed Martin UK, 375
Lockheed MC-130, 504
Lockheed TriStar (RAF), 101
Logistics Officer, 186, 464
London, 1, 7, 105, 106, 157, 257, 268, 315, 481, 499, 583
London Area Control Centre, 500
London Blitz, 139
London City Airport, 101, 452
London District, 388, 390
London District (British Army), 14, 388
London Evening Standard, 590
London Eye, 101, 452
London Naval Treaty, 45, 179
London Regiment, 401
London Stansted Airport, 567
London University Air Squadron, 532
Longest recorded sniper kills, 367
Long Parliament, 59, 324
Long Range Reconnaissance Patrol, 107
Long ton, 30
Long underwear, 360
Lord Callaghan, 145
Lord Cherwell, 116
Lord High Admiral of Scotland, 163
Lord High Admiral (United Kingdom), 26, 158, 197
Lord Mayor of the City of London, 284
Lord of the Isles, 29, 167
Lord Portal, 119
Lord President of the Council, 116
Lord Protector, 324
Lordship of Ireland, 328
Lords of the Isles, 29
Lord Wentworths Regiment, 61
Lorient, 283
Lorna Arnold, 146, 148
Los Alamos Laboratory, 117
Lossiemouth, 308
Loughgall Ambush, 80
Louisbourg Grenadiers, 66
Louis Mountbatten, 1st Earl Mountbatten of Burma, 48, 80, 121

Louis XIV of France, 33, 166
Lowestoft, 313
Low Flying Operations Squadron, 536
Low Level and Air Defence Training Squadron, 536
Lowton, 310
Loyalist (American Revolution), 67
Loyal toast, 319
Ludham, 311
Ludo (board game), 206, 320
Luftwaffe, 93, 448
Luke de Tany, 25
Lumley Lyster, 252, 254
Lympstone, 268, 281, 306

M110 howitzer, 129
M113 armored personnel carrier, 378
M115 howitzer, 129
M16A2, 367
M18 Claymore mine, 369
M203, 367
M270 Multiple Launch Rocket System, 341, 376
M2 Browning, 368
M2 Browning machine gun, 270, 368
M3 Amphibious Rig, 379
M6-640, 369
M67 grenade, 369
M6 motorway, 140
M72 LAW, 364
Machine Gun Corps, 71
Machine Gun School, 550
Mackenzie King, 117
Madagascar, 264
Mahón, 33
Main battle tank, 14, 337, 339, 375
Maindy Barracks, 435
Maintenance Command Communication and Ferry Squadron, 538
Maintenance Command Communication Squadron, 538
Majesty, 273
Major, 408
Major-general, 273
Major General, 390
Major-general (United Kingdom), 108–110, 204, 286, 347, 359
Major (UK), 359
Major (United Kingdom), 204, 286, 347
Malaya Communication Squadron, 538
Malayan Campaign, 264
Malayan Emergency, 78, 96, 332, 451
Malaysia Airlines Flight 370, 295
Malcolm Rifkind, 132
Malden Island, 122, 135
Mali, 100

Malta, 46, 96, 175, 311, 313–315, 452
Malta Communication and Target Towing Squadron, 538
Malta convoys, 181
Malta Dockyard, 308
Malvern, Worcestershire, 105
Manadon, 315
Manchester, 567
Manchester Guardian, 141
Manhattan Project, 116
Manila, 34, 172
Manoel Island, 313, 315
Man-of-war, 163
Man-portable air-defense systems, 370
Māori people, 328
Maralinga, 122
Maralinga, South Australia, 135
March, 284
March (music), 320
March of the Preobrazhensky Regiment, 257
Mare Harbour, 154, 292, 304, 305
Margaret Beckett, 145
Margaret Gowing, 148
Marie-Galante, 261
Marine Corps Air Station Beaufort, 506
Marine Observers School, Aldeburgh, 550
Marine Observers School, Leysdown, 550
Marines, 205, 257, 287
Maritime patrol aircraft, 577
Maritime Reserve (United Kingdom), 186, 615
Mark 15 nuclear bomb, 127
Mark 39 nuclear bomb, 127
Mark 5 nuclear bomb, 127
Mark 7 nuclear bomb, 127
Mark Carleton-Smith, 321, 586, 587
Mark (designation), 465
Mark I tank, 70, 329
Mark Lancaster, 585
Mark Oliphant, 115
Mark Poffley, 587
Mark Stanhope, 590
Maroon beret, 361
Marshal of the Royal Air Force, 118, 252
Martin Frobisher, 28
Martini–Enfield, 85
Martini–Henry, 85
Martin La T. Wemyss, 231
Mary II of England, 325
Mary I of England, 27
Mary, Queen of Scots, 168
Mary Rose, 27
Master and Commander: The Far Side of the World, 207
MATADOR, 370
MAUD Committee, 115
Mau Mau, 96, 452

Mau Mau uprising, 78, 332
Mauritius, 175, 312
Maxim machine gun, 70
MBDA, 475, 572, 574
MBT LAW, 370
McDonnell Douglas F-15 Eagle, 504
McDonnell Douglas F-4 Phantom II, 109
MDPGA Wethersfield, 533
Mechanised infantry, 15
Mechanised Infantry Vehicle, 385
Mechanized infantry, 393
Media:Heart of Oak.ogg, 158
Medical evacuation, 574
Mediterranean and Middle East Communication Squadron, 538
Mediterranean and Middle East theatre of World War II, 74
Mediterranean Expeditionary Force, 330
Mediterranean Fleet, 46
Mediterranean Sea, 185, 298
Medium-altitude long-endurance unmanned aerial vehicle, 572
Medium Atomic Demolition Munition, 129
Medium-range ballistic missile, 123
Medium Tactical Vehicle Replacement, 380
Medway Division, 307
Megatons, 138
Meindl (company), 373
Members, 417
Memorandum of Understanding, 127
Menorca, 171
Mercenaries, 422
Merchant Navy (United Kingdom), 160, 291
Mercian Regiment, 393, 401, 601
Merseyside, 502
Mesopotamia, 70
Mesopotamian campaign, 486
Mess dress, 263, 284
Meteor (missile), 580
Meteorological, 196
Metropolitan Communication Squadron, 538
MGM-52 Lance, 129
MGM-5 Corporal, 129
Miami, 39
Michael Boyce, Baron Boyce, 233
Michael Fallon, 143
Michael Hordern, 254
Michael Perrin, 119
Michael P. Gretton, 233
Michael (ship), 167
Microbiological Research Establishment, 105
Middle Ages, 22
Middle East Command, 388
Middle East Communication Squadron, 538
Middlesex, 305, 307
Middlesex, England, 229

Middlesex Regiment, 330
Middle Wallop, 311
Midland Area Flying instructors School, 559
Midland Area School of Special Flying, 559
Mikoyan-Gurevich MiG-15, 243
Military, 2
Military Aid to the Civil Authorities, 468
Military Aid to the Civil Community, 388
Military air base, 494
Military aircraft, 560
Military awards and decorations of the United Kingdom, 7
Military branch, 107
Military Corrective Training Centre, 432
Military Corrective Training Centre (MCTC), 432, 593
Military history of the United Kingdom, 2, 330, 447
Military intelligence, 464
Military intervention against ISIL, 6, 342, 480
Military intervention against the Islamic State of Iraq and the Levant, 53, 100
Military of the Falkland Islands, 11, 58, 154, 292, 322, 363, 386, 404, 481
Military police, 464
Military Provost Guard Service, 344, 400, 599, 600
Military Provost Staff, 344
Military Provost Staff Corps, 399
Military Secretary (United Kingdom), 63
Military Service Act (United Kingdom), 412
Military strategy, 115
Military Training Act 1939, 414
Military use, 505
Militia (United Kingdom), 70, 329, 407
MIM-104 Patriot, 100
Mina Salman, 154, 305
Mine countermeasures vessel, 154, 158, 190, 211
Mine-countermeasure vessel, 160
Minehunter, 190, 196
Miner, 73
Minesweeper, 13
Minesweeper (ship), 190
Minié rifle, 85
Minimi 7.62, 368
Minister for Co-ordination of Defence, 240, 584
Minister for Defence Equipment, Support and Technology, 17
Minister for Defence Procurement, 105, 586
Minister of State for the Armed Forces, 8, 454, 585
Ministry of Agriculture, Fisheries and Food (United Kingdom), 48
Ministry of Aviation Supply, 585

Ministry of Defence (1947–64), 585
Ministry of Defence Main Building (United Kingdom), 583, 594
Ministry of Defence Police, 17, 105
Ministry of Defence (United Kingdom), 1, 3, 7, 8, 17, 101, 105, 106, 157, 198, 228, 323, 372, 421, 447, 452, 495, 565, 566, **583**
Minorca, 33, 34
Mirror.co.uk, 615
Mk 101 Lulu, 129
Mk 6 helmet, 371
MLRS, 338
Mobile Artillery Monitoring Battlefield Radar, 338
Mobile Naval Air Bases, 311
MoD Boscombe Down, 465, 470, 495, 496, 533
MoD Lyneham, 440
MoD Procurement Executive, 105
MOD St Athan, 306, 307, 457, 495, 500, 533, 534
Modus Vivendi, 119
Mohammed Abdullah Hassan, 72
Moluccas, 175
Monarch, 7, 587
Monarchy of the United Kingdom, 2, 166, 197, 211
Monmouth Rebellion, 325
Monte Bello Islands, Western Australia, 120
Montreal Laboratory, 117
Montserrat, 3, 155
Moors, 25
Moray, 498, 499
Mortar (weapon), 369
Mosquito Squadron, 528
MOTAT, 246
Motor Gun Boat, 310
Motor Launch, 309
Motor Torpedo Boat, 310
Mountain warfare, 14, 193, 259
Mounted infantry, 373
Mowag Duro, 381
MPGS, 400
MQ-9 Reaper, 467, 475
MT350E, 381
Mulberry harbour, 47
Multicam, 372
Multi-Engine Training Squadron, 536
Multilateral Force, 131
Multi-National Division (South-East) (Iraq), 84
Multiple independently targetable reentry vehicle, 115
Multiple rocket launcher, 346
Multirole combat aircraft, 16
Multi Role Vehicle-Protected, 385

Multi-Terrain Pattern, 360
Munich Crisis, 73
Mutiny Act, 62
Mutiny on the Bounty, 207
Mutiny on the Bounty (novel), 207
MWMIK, 337

N3-class battleship, 45
Nairobi, 431
Nairobi County, 432
Nakajima B5N, 92
Namsos Campaign, 264
Naples, 172
Napoleon, 36, 175
Napoleon Bonaparte, 174, 327
Napoléon Eugène, Prince Imperial, 410
Napoleonic Wars, 2, 4, 22, 33, 34, 59, 63, 68, 173, 259, 261, 323, 326, 327, 407, 420
Napoleon III, 41
Napoléon III, 410
Napoleon I of France, 327
Narrow Water, 80
NASA, 506
Nassau Agreement, 131
National Army Museum, 592
National Audit Office (United Kingdom), 596
National interest, 584
Nationalist Chinese, 78
National Missile Defense, 137
National Museum of the Royal Navy, 592
National Security Agency, 504
National Service, 76, 103, 332
National Service Act 1948, 415
National Volunteers, 420
Native Americans in the United States, 66
NATO, 3, 5, 12, 96, 268, 295, 297, 381, 461, 502, 569
NATO Double-Track Decision, 137, 140
NATO Response Force, 197, 293, 342
Nature (journal), 115
Naval aircraft, 239
Naval Air Squadron, 254, 255
Naval Air Station, 254, 255
Naval artillery, 50
Naval artillery in the Age of Sail, 167
Naval base, 292
Naval battle of Gravelines, 28
Naval Careers Service, 21, 159, 210, 228, 238, 258, 290
Naval Crown, 317
Naval Defence Act 1889, 42, 176
Naval Ensign, 237
Naval fleet, 227
Naval Gunfire Support, 185
Naval Institute Press, 617
Naval Jack, 158

Naval operations in the American Revolutionary War, 52
Naval Party (Royal Navy), 155, 305
Naval rating, 199, 254
Naval Secretary, 199
Naval Service (United Kingdom), 237, 283
Naval Shipyards, York (Upper Canada), 308
Naval Strike Wing, 245
Naval Submarine Base Kings Bay, 132
Naval Support Facility Diego Garcia, 154
Naval warfare, 157
Naval warfare of World War I, 53
Navigation Act 1651, 31
Navigation Acts, 165
Navigational, 17
Navigation School, 550
Navigation Training School, 550
Navy, 28, 157, 159, 166
Navy Board, 198
Navy Board (1964-present), 230
Navy Command Headquarters, 198, 273
Navy Command (Royal Navy), 229, 230, 592
Nazi Germany, 4, 178, 331, 412, 414
Nazi Party, 73
NCO Training School, 550
Neil Kinnock, 142
Neil Morisetti, 234
Nelson-class battleship, 45
Neoclassical architecture, 594
Nepal, 3, 155, 430, 431
Netheravon Flying School, 559
Netherlands, 3, 65, 172, 200, 266
Netherlands Marine Corps, 184, 193, 259, 282, 288
Network enabled capability, 569
Network-enabled capability, 374
Neutron, 115
Nevada Test Site, 135
Never was so much owed by so many to so few, 93, 448
Neville Chamberlain, 414, 584
New Amsterdam, 32
Newcastle upon Tyne, 268
New Forest, 595
Newfoundland (island), 33, 171
New France, 67, 172, 327
Newhaven, East Sussex, 309, 311–313
Newhaven, Edinburgh, 30, 167
New Model Army, 59, 324, 325
New South Wales, 260
New Statesman, 139, 141
New Zealand, 522
New Zealand Wars, 327
Nicholas Goodhart, 254
Nicholas Hill-Norton, 232, 233
Nicholas Hine, 198

Nicholas Hunt, 231
Nicholas Rodger, 56
Nick Carter (British Army officer), 1, 583, 586
Nickname, 318
Nicosia, 429
Nicosia Airport, 108
Nidderdale, 311
Niels Bohr, 115, 117
Nigeria, 100, 200
Night vision device, 365, 371
Nimrod Line Squadron, 536
Nimrod MR2, 97
Nimrod R1, 101
Nine Years War, 52, 170
NL Landing Force, 288
No. 100 Group RAF, 489
No. 100 Squadron RAF, 473, 498, 513
No. 101 Flying Refresher School RAF, 556
No. 101 Squadron RAF, 513, 576
No. 102 Flying Refresher School RAF, 556
No. 102 Squadron RAF, 513
No. 103 Flying Refresher School RAF, 556
No. 103 Squadron RAF, 513
No. 104 Flying Refresher School RAF, 556
No. 104 Squadron RAF, 513
No. 105 Squadron RAF, 513
No. 106 Group RAF, 489
No. 106 Squadron RAF, 513
No. 107 Squadron RAF, 513
No. 108 Squadron RAF, 513
No. 109 Squadron RAF, 513
No. 10 (Advanced) Flying Training School RAF, 553
No. 10 Air Experience Flight RAF, 502, 535
No. 10 Air Gunnery School RAF, 543
No. 10 Air Navigation School RAF, 543
No. 10 Air Observers Navigation School RAF, 544
No. 10 Air Observers School RAF, 544
No. 10 Bombing and Gunnery School RAF, 544
No. 10 Civil Air Navigation School RAF, 545
No. 10 Elementary and Reserve Flying Training School RAF, 553
No. 10 Elementary Flying Training School RAF, 554
No. 10 Flying Instructors School (Elementary) RAF, 556
No. 10 Flying Training School RAF, 556
No. 10 Group RAF, 483
No. 10 Radio School RAF, 545
No. 10 Reserve Flying School RAF, 557
No. 10 School of Recruit Training RAF, 546
No. 10 Service Flying Training School RAF, 558
No. 10 Squadron RAF, 510, 576

No. 10 Training Depot Station, 530
No. 110 Squadron RAF, 514
No. 111 Squadron RAF, 514
No. 112 Squadron RAF, 514
No. 113 Squadron RAF, 514
No. 114 Squadron RAF, 514
No. 115 Squadron RAF, 514
No. 116 Squadron RAF, 514
No. 117 Squadron RAF, 514
No. 118 Squadron RAF, 514
No. 119 Squadron RAF, 514
No. 11 Air Experience Flight RAF, 498, 535
No. 11 Air Gunnery School RAF, 543
No. 11 Air Observers Navigation School RAF, 544
No. 11 Elementary and Reserve Flying Training School RAF, 553
No. 11 Elementary Flying Training School RAF, 554
No. 11 Flying Instructors School RAF, 556
No. 11 Flying Training School RAF, 556
No. 11 Group RAF, 457, 483
No. 11 Radio School RAF, 545
No. 11 Reserve Flying School RAF, 557
No. 11 School of Recruit Training RAF, 547
No. 11 School of Technical Training RAF, 546
No. 11 Service Flying Training School RAF, 558
No. 11 Squadron RAF, 465, 497, 510, 571
No. 11 Training Depot Station, 530
No. 120 Squadron RAF, 514, 578
No. 121 Squadron RAF, 514, 519
No. 122 Squadron RAF, 514
No. 123 Squadron RAF, 514
No. 124 Squadron RAF, 514
No. 125 Squadron RAF, 514
No. 126 Squadron RAF, 514
No. 127 Squadron RAF, 514
No. 128 Squadron RAF, 514
No. 129 Squadron RAF, 514
No. 12 Air Experience Flight RAF, 498, 535
No. 12 Air Gunners School RAF, 543
No. 12 Elementary and Reserve Flying Training School RAF, 553
No. 12 Elementary Flying Training School RAF, 554
No. 12 Flying Instructors School (Operational) RAF, 556
No. 12 Flying Training School RAF, 556
No. 12 Group RAF, 483
No. 12 Radio School RAF, 545
No. 12 Reserve Flying School RAF, 557
No. 12 School of Recruit Training RAF, 547
No. 12 Service Flying Training School RAF, 558
No. 12 Squadron RAF, 463, 499, 510, 571

No. 12 Training Depot Station, 530
No. 130 Squadron RAF, 514
No. 1310 Flight RAF, 534
No. 1312 Flight RAF, 109, 154, 534
No. 131 Squadron RAF, 514
No. 132 Squadron RAF, 514
No. 133 Squadron RAF, 514, 519
No. 134 Squadron RAF, 514
No. 135 Squadron RAF, 514
No. 136 Squadron RAF, 514
No. 137 Squadron RAF, 514
No. 138 Squadron RAF, 514
No. 139 Squadron RAF, 514
No. 13 Air Gunners School RAF, 543
No. 13 Elementary and Reserve Flying Training School RAF, 553
No. 13 Elementary Flying Training School RAF, 555
No. 13 Flying Training School RAF, 556
No. 13 Group RAF, 484
No. 13 Reserve Flying School RAF, 557
No. 13 School of Recruit Training RAF, 547
No. 13 Service Flying Training School RAF, 558
No. 13 Signals Unit, 109
No. 13 Squadron RAF, 467, 501, 510
No. 13 Training Depot Station, 530
No. 140 Squadron RAF, 514
No. 1417 Flight RAF, 108
No. 141 Squadron RAF, 514
No. 142 Squadron RAF, 514
No. 1435 Flight RAF, 109, 154, 460, 534, 537
No. 143 Squadron RAF, 514
No. 144 Squadron RAF, 514
No. 145 Squadron RAF, 514
No. 146 Squadron RAF, 514
No. 147 Squadron RAF, 514
No. 148 Squadron RAF, 514
No. 149 Squadron RAF, 514
No. 14 (Advanced) Flying Training School RAF, 553
No. 14 Elementary and Reserve Flying Training School RAF, 553
No. 14 Elementary Flying Training School RAF, 555
No. 14 Flying Training School RAF, 556
No. 14 Group RAF, 484
No. 14 Radio School RAF, 545
No. 14 Reserve Flying School RAF, 557
No. 14 Service Flying Training School RAF, 558
No. 14 Squadron RAF, 501, 511, 577
No. 14 Training Depot Station, 530
No. 150 Squadron RAF, 514
No. 151 Squadron RAF, 515
No. 152 Squadron RAF, 515

No. 153 Squadron RAF, 515
No. 154 Squadron RAF, 515
No. 155 Squadron RAF, 515
No. 1563 Flight RAF, 108
No. 156 Squadron RAF, 515
No. 157 Squadron RAF, 515
No. 158 Squadron RAF, 515
No. 159 Squadron RAF, 515
No. 15 Elementary and Reserve Flying Training School RAF, 553
No. 15 Elementary Flying Training School RAF, 555
No. 15 Flying Training School RAF, 556
No. 15 Group RAF, 484
No. 15 Reserve Flying School RAF, 557
No. 15 School of Recruit Training RAF, 547
No. 15 Service Flying Training School RAF, 558
No. 15 Squadron RAF, 466, 511
No. 15 Training Depot Station, 530
No. 160 Squadron RAF, 515
No. 161 Squadron RAF, 515
No. 162 Squadron RAF, 515
No. 163 Squadron RAF, 515
No. 164 Squadron RAF, 515
No. 165 Squadron RAF, 515
No. 166 Squadron RAF, 515
No 1674 Heavy Conversion Unit RAF, 484
No. 167 Squadron RAF, 515
No. 168 Squadron RAF, 515
No. 169 Squadron RAF, 515
No. 16 Elementary and Reserve Flying Training School RAF, 553
No. 16 Elementary Flying Training School RAF, 555
No. 16 Flight AAC, 108
No. 16 Group RAF, 484
No. 16 (Polish) School of Technical Training RAF, 546
No. 16 (Polish) Service Flying Training School RAF, 558
No. 16 Reserve Flying School RAF, 557
No. 16 Squadron RAF, 501, 511
No. 16 Training Depot Station, 530
No. 170 Squadron RAF, 515
No. 171 Squadron RAF, 515
No. 172 Squadron RAF, 515
No. 173 Squadron RAF, 515
No. 174 Squadron RAF, 515
No. 175 Squadron RAF, 515
No. 176 Squadron RAF, 515
No. 177 Squadron RAF, 515
No. 178 Squadron RAF, 515
No. 179 Squadron RAF, 515
No. 17 Elementary and Reserve Flying Training School RAF, 553

No. 17 Elementary Flying Training School RAF, 555
No. 17 Group RAF, 484
No. 17 Reserve Flying School RAF, 557
No. 17 Service Flying Training School RAF, 558
No. 17 Squadron RAF, 507, 511, 570
No. 17 Training Depot Station, 530
No. 180 Squadron RAF, 515
No. 181 Squadron RAF, 515
No. 182 Squadron RAF, 515
No. 183 Squadron RAF, 515
No. 184 Squadron RAF, 515
No. 185 Squadron RAF, 515
No. 186 Squadron RAF, 515
No. 187 Squadron RAF, 515
No. 188 Squadron RAF, 515
No. 189 Squadron RAF, 515
No. 18 Elementary and Reserve Flying Training School RAF, 553
No. 18 Elementary Flying Training School RAF, 555
No. 18 Group RAF, 484
No. 18 Reserve Flying School RAF, 557
No. 18 Squadron RAF, 500, 509, 511, 578
No. 18 Training Depot Station, 530
No. 190 (Depot) Squadron, 531
No. 190 Squadron RAF, 515
No. 191 (Depot) Squadron, 531
No. 191 Squadron RAF, 515
No. 192 (Depot) Squadron, 531
No. 192 Squadron RAF, 516
No. 193 Squadron RAF, 516
No. 194 Squadron RAF, 516
No. 195 Squadron RAF, 516
No. 196 Squadron RAF, 516
No. 197 Squadron RAF, 516
No. 198 (Depot) Squadron, 531
No. 198 Squadron RAF, 516
No. 199 (Depot) Squadron, 531
No. 199 Squadron RAF, 516
No. 19 Elementary and Reserve Flying Training School RAF, 553
No. 19 Elementary Flying Training School RAF, 555
No. 19 Flying Training School RAF, 556
No. 19 Group RAF, 484
No. 19 Reserve Flying School RAF, 557
No. 19 Squadron RAF, 511
No. 19 Training Depot Station, 530
No. 1 Air Armament School RAF, 547
No. 1 Air Electronics School RAF, 547
No. 1 Air Experience Flight RAF, 534
No. 1 Air Gunners School RAF, 543
No. 1 Air Gunnery School (India) RAF, 547
No. 1 Air Gunnery School RAF, 547

No. 1 Air Navigation School RAF, 543
No. 1 Air Observers Navigation School RAF, 544
No. 1 Air Observers School RAF, 544
No. 1 Air Signallers School RAF, 547
No. 1 (Auxiliary) School of Aerial Gunnery RAF, 547
No. 1 Basic Air Navigation School RAF, 547
No. 1 Basic Flying Training School RAF, 552
No. 1 Beam Approach School RAF, 547
No. 1 Blind Approach School RAF, 547
No. 1 Bombing and Gunnery School RAF, 544
No. 1 British Flying Training School RAF, 552
No. 1 Civil Air Navigation School RAF, 545
No. 1 Coastal Defence Training Unit RAF, 547
No. 1 (Coastal) Engine Control Demonstration Unit RAF, 547
No. 1 (Coastal) Operational Training Unit RAF, 549
No. 1 (Communication) Squadron, 539
No. 1 Electrical and Wireless School RAF, 547
No. 1 Elementary and Reserve Flying Training School RAF, 553
No. 1 Elementary Flying Training School (India), 554
No. 1 Elementary Flying Training School RAF, 554
No. 1 Elementary Gliding Training School RAF, 559
No. 1 Fighting School RAF, 545
No. 1 Flying Instructors School (Advanced) RAF, 555
No. 1 Flying Instructors School RAF, 555
No. 1 Flying Training School RAF, 459, 499, 556
No. 1 General Service Training School RAF, 547
No. 1 Grading School RAF, 547
No. 1 Ground Defense Gunners School RAF, 547
No. 1 Group RAF, 15, 455, 456, 482, 498
No.1 Guided Weapons Trials Squadron, 536
No. 1 (Indian) Flying Training School, 556
No. 1 (Indian) Group RAF, 493
No. 1 (Indian) Service Flying Training School, 557
No. 1 Initial Training School RAF, 547
No. 1 Lancaster Finishing School RAF, 545
No. 1 Marine Observers School RAF, 547
No. 1 (Middle East) Central Gunnery School RAF, 547
No. 1 Middle East Training School RAF, 545
No. 1 (Observers) School of Aerial Gunnery RAF, 547
No. 1 Observers School RAF, 547

No. 1 Officers Advanced Training School RAF, 547
No. 1 Parachute and Glider Training School RAF, 547
No. 1 Parachute School RAF, 547
No. 1 Parachute Training School RAF, 501, 547
No. 1 PRU, 489
No. 1 Radio School RAF, 460, 497, 545
No. 1 Refresher Flying Training School RAF, 557
No. 1 Refresher School RAF, 557
No. 1 Reserve Flying School RAF, 557
No. 1 School of Aerial Fighting and Gunnery RAF, 546
No. 1 School of Aerial Fighting RAF, 547
No. 1 School of Aerial Navigation and Bomb Dropping RAF, 546
No. 1 School of Air Navigation RAF, 547
No. 1 School of Army Co-operation RAF, 547
No. 1 School of General Reconnaissance RAF, 547
No. 1 School of Navigation and Bomb Dropping RAF, 546
No. 1 School of Recruit Training RAF, 546
No. 1 School of Special Flying RAF, 557
No. 1 School of Technical Training RAF, 459, 497, 546
No. 1 Service Flying Training School RAF, 557
No. 1 Signals School RAF, 546
No. 1 Squadron RAAF, 512
No. 1 Squadron RAF, 97, 499, 510, 570
No. 1 Torpedo Refresher School RAF, 547
No. 1 Torpedo Training Squadron, 536
No. 1 Training Depot Station, 530
No. 1 (Training) Wireless School RAF, 547
No. 200 Group RAF, 490
No. 200 Squadron RAF, 516
No. 201 Advanced Flying School RAF, 552
No. 201 Group RAF, 490
No. 201 Squadron RAF, 516, 578
No. 201 Training Depot Station, 531
No. 202 Advanced Flying School RAF, 552
No. 202 Group RAF, 490
No. 202 Squadron RAF, 516
No. 202 Training Depot Station, 531
No. 203 Advanced Flying School RAF, 552
No. 203 Group RAF, 490
No. 203 Squadron RAF, 516
No. 203 Training Depot Station, 531
No. 204 Advanced Flying School RAF, 552
No. 204 Group RAF, 490
No. 204 Squadron RAF, 516
No. 204 Training Depot Station, 531
No. 205 Advanced Flying School RAF, 552
No. 205 Group RAF, 490
No. 205 Squadron RAF, 516
No. 205 Training Depot Station, 532
No. 206 Advanced Flying School RAF, 552
No. 206 Group RAF, 490
No. 206 Squadron RAF, 516
No. 206 Training Depot Station, 532
No. 207 Advanced Flying School RAF, 552
No. 207 Flying Training School RAF, 556
No. 207 Group RAF, 490
No. 207 Squadron RAF, 516, 570
No. 207 Training Depot Station, 532
No. 208 Advanced Flying School RAF, 552
No. 208 Squadron RAF, 95, 516
No. 208 (Temporary) Training Depot Station, 532
No. 209 Advanced Flying School RAF, 552
No. 209 Group RAF, 490
No. 209 (Seaplane) Training Depot Station, 532
No. 209 Squadron RAF, 516
No. 20 Elementary and Reserve Flying Training School RAF, 553
No. 20 Elementary Flying Training School RAF, 555
No. 20 Flying Training School RAF, 556
No. 20 Group RAF, 484, 485
No. 20 Reserve Flying School RAF, 557
No. 20 Service Flying Training School RAF, 558
No. 20 Squadron RAF, 511
No. 20 Training Depot Station, 530
No. 210 Advanced Flying School RAF, 552
No. 210 Group RAF, 490
No. 210 Squadron RAF, 516
No. 210 Training Depot Station, 532
No. 211 Advanced Flying School RAF, 552
No. 211 Flying Training School RAF, 556
No. 211 Group RAF, 490
No. 211 Squadron RAF, 516
No. 211 Training Depot Station, 532
No. 212 Group RAF, 490
No. 212 Squadron RAF, 516
No. 212 Training Depot Station, 532
No. 213 Group RAF, 490
No. 213 Squadron RAF, 516
No. 213 Training Depot Station, 532
No. 214 Group RAF, 491
No. 214 Squadron RAF, 516
No. 215 Advanced Flying School RAF, 552
No. 215 Group RAF, 491
No. 215 Squadron RAF, 516
No. 216 Group RAF, 491
No. 216 Squadron RAF, 516
No. 217 Group RAF, 491
No. 217 Squadron RAF, 516

No. 218 Group RAF, 491
No. 218 Squadron RAF, 516
No. 219 Group RAF, 491
No. 219 Squadron RAF, 516
No. 21 Elementary and Reserve Flying Training School RAF, 553
No. 21 Elementary Flying Training School RAF, 555
No. 21 Flying Training School RAF, 556
No. 21 Group RAF, 485
No. 21 Reserve Flying School RAF, 557
No. 21 Service Flying Training School RAF, 558
No. 21 Squadron RAF, 511
No. 21 Training Depot Station, 530
No. 220 Squadron RAF, 516
No. 221 Group Communication Squadron, 538
No. 221 Group RAF, 491
No. 221 Squadron RAF, 516
No. 222 Group RAF, 491
No. 222 Squadron RAF, 516
No. 223 Group RAF, 491
No. 223 Squadron RAF, 516
No. 224 Group RAF, 491
No. 224 Squadron RAF, 516
No. 225 Group RAF, 491
No. 225 Squadron RAF, 516
No. 226 Group RAF, 492
No. 226 Squadron RAF, 516
No. 227 Group RAF, 492
No. 227 Squadron RAF, 517
No. 228 Group RAF, 492
No. 228 Squadron RAF, 517
No. 229 Group RAF, 492
No. 229 Squadron RAF, 517
No. 22 Elementary and Reserve Flying Training School RAF, 553
No. 22 Elementary Flying Training School RAF, 555
No. 22 Flying Training School RAF, 556
No. 22 Group, 15
No. 22 Group RAF, 455, 457, 482, 485, 498
No. 22 Reserve Flying School RAF, 557
No. 22 Service Flying Training School RAF, 558
No. 22 Squadron RAF, 511
No. 22 Training Depot Station, 530
No. 230 Group RAF, 492
No. 230 Squadron RAF, 496, 517, 579
No. 231 Group RAF, 492
No. 231 Squadron RAF, 517
No. 232 Group Communication Squadron, 538
No. 232 Group RAF, 492
No. 232 Squadron RAF, 517
No. 233 Group RAF, 492
No. 233 Squadron RAF, 517
No. 234 Squadron RAF, 517
No. 235 Squadron RAF, 517
No. 236 Squadron RAF, 517
No. 237 Squadron RAF, 517
No. 238 Group Communication Squadron, 538
No. 238 Group RAF, 492
No. 238 Squadron RAF, 517
No. 239 Squadron RAF, 517
No. 23 Elementary and Reserve Flying Training School RAF, 553
No. 23 Elementary Flying Training School RAF, 555
No. 23 Group RAF, 485
No. 23 Reserve Flying School RAF, 557
No. 23 Service Flying Training School RAF, 558
No. 23 Squadron RAF, 511
No. 23 Training Depot Station, 530
No. 240 Squadron RAF, 517
No. 241 Group RAF, 492
No. 241 Squadron RAF, 517
No. 242 Group RAF, 492
No. 242 Squadron RAF, 517
No. 243 Squadron RAF, 517
No. 244 Squadron RAF, 517
No. 245 Squadron RAF, 517
No. 246 Group RAF, 492
No. 246 Squadron RAF, 517
No. 247 Group RAF, 492
No. 247 Squadron RAF, 517
No. 248 Squadron RAF, 517
No. 249 Squadron RAF, 517
No. 24 Bombing and Gunnery School RAF, 544
No. 24 Bombing, Gunnery and Air Navigation School RAF, 548
No. 24 Combined Air Observers School RAF, 544
No. 24 Elementary and Reserve Flying Training School RAF, 553
No. 24 Elementary Flying Training School RAF, 555
No. 24 Group RAF, 485
No. 24 Reserve Flying School RAF, 557
No. 24 Squadron RAF, 511, 574, 576
No. 24 Training Depot Station, 530
No. 2503 Squadron RAF Regiment, 501
No. 250 Squadron RAF, 517
No. 251 Squadron RAF, 517
No. 252 Squadron RAF, 517
No. 253 Squadron RAF, 517
No. 254 Squadron RAF, 517
No. 255 Squadron RAF, 517
No. 256 Squadron RAF, 517
No. 257 Squadron RAF, 517
No. 258 Squadron RAF, 517

No. 259 Squadron RAF, 517
No. 25 Elementary and Reserve Flying Training School RAF, 553
No. 25 Elementary Flying Training School RAF, 555
No. 25 Elementary Flying Training School (Southern Rhodesia) RAF, 555
No. 25 Flight AAC, 108, 397
No. 25 Group RAF, 485
No. 25 Reserve Flying School RAF, 557
No. 25 Squadron RAF, 511
No. 25 Training Depot Station, 530
No. 260 Squadron RAF, 517
No. 261 Squadron RAF, 517
No. 2620 Squadron RAF Regiment, 499
No. 2622 Squadron RAF Regiment, 499
No. 262 Squadron RAF, 517
No. 263 Squadron RAF, 517
No. 264 Squadron RAF, 517
No. 265 Squadron RAF, 517
No. 266 Squadron RAF, 518
No. 267 Squadron RAF, 518
No. 268 Squadron RAF, 518
No. 269 Squadron RAF, 518
No. 26 Elementary and Reserve Flying Training School RAF, 553
No. 26 Elementary Flying Training School RAF, 555
No. 26 Elementary Flying Training School (Southern Rhodesia) RAF, 555
No. 26 Group RAF, 485
No. 26 Squadron RAF, 511
No. 26 Training Depot Station, 530
No. 270 Squadron RAF, 518
No. 271 Squadron RAF, 518
No. 272 Squadron RAF, 518
No. 273 Squadron RAF, 518
No. 274 Squadron RAF, 518
No. 275 Squadron RAF, 518
No. 276 Squadron RAF, 518
No. 277 Squadron RAF, 518
No. 278 Squadron RAF, 518
No. 279 Squadron RAF, 518
No. 27 Elementary and Reserve Flying Training School RAF, 553
No. 27 Elementary Flying Training School RAF, 555
No. 27 Elementary Flying Training School (Southern Rhodesia) RAF, 555
No. 27 Group RAF, 485
No. 27 Squadron RAF, 500, 511, 578
No. 27 Training Depot Station, 530
No. 280 Signals Unit, 109
No. 280 Squadron RAF, 518
No. 281 Squadron RAF, 518
No. 282 Squadron RAF, 518
No. 283 Squadron RAF, 518
No. 284 Squadron RAF, 518
No. 285 Squadron RAF, 518
No. 286 Squadron RAF, 518
No. 287 Squadron RAF, 518
No. 288 Squadron RAF, 518
No. 289 Squadron RAF, 518
No. 28 Elementary and Reserve Flying Training School RAF, 553
No. 28 Elementary Flying Training School RAF, 555
No. 28 Elementary Flying Training School (Southern Rhodesia) RAF, 555
No. 28 Group RAF, 485
No. 28 Squadron RAF, 111, 496, 511
No. 28 Training Depot Station, 530
No. 290 Squadron RAF, 518
No. 291 Squadron RAF, 518
No. 292 Squadron RAF, 518
No. 293 Squadron RAF, 518
No. 294 Squadron RAF, 518
No. 295 Squadron RAF, 518
No. 296 Squadron RAF, 518
No. 297 Squadron RAF, 518
No. 298 Squadron RAF, 518
No. 299 Squadron RAF, 518
No. 29 Elementary and Reserve Flying Training School RAF, 553
No. 29 Elementary Flying Training School RAF, 555
No. 29 Elementary Navigation and Air Gunnery School (Southern Rhodesia) RAF, 548
No. 29 Group RAF, 486
No. 29 Squadron RAF, 465, 497, 511, 571
No. 29 Training Depot Station, 530
No. 2 Air Armament School RAF, 547
No. 2 Aircrew Grading School RAF, 547
No. 2 Air Experience Flight RAF, 534
No. 2 Air Gunners School RAF, 543
No. 2 Air Navigation School RAF, 543
No. 2 Air Observers Navigation School RAF, 544
No. 2 Air Observers School RAF, 544
No. 2 Air Signallers School RAF, 547
No. 2 (Auxiliary) School of Aerial Gunnery RAF, 547
No. 2 Basic Air Navigation School RAF, 547
No. 2 (Basic) Flying Training School RAF, 552
No. 2 Basic Flying Training School RAF, 552
No. 2 Bombing and Gunnery School RAF, 544
No. 2 British Flying Training School RAF, 552
No. 2 Central Flying School RAF, 552
No. 2 Civil Air Navigation School RAF, 545
No. 2 (Communication) Squadron, 539
No. 2 Electrical and Wireless School RAF, 548

No. 2 Elementary and Reserve Flying Training School RAF, 553
No. 2 Elementary Flying Training School RAF, 554
No. 2 Elementary Gliding Training School RAF, 559
No. 2 Fighting School RAF, 545
No. 2 Flying Instructors School (Advanced) RAF, 555
No. 2 Flying Instructors School RAF, 555
No. 2 Flying Training School RAF, 459, 500, 534, 556
No. 2 Grading School RAF, 548
No. 2 Group Communication Squadron, 538
No. 2 Group RAF, 15, 455, 456, 482, 498
No. 2 (Indian) Group RAF, 493
No. 2 Marine Observers School RAF, 548
No. 2 Middle East Training School RAF, 545
No. 2 Observers School RAF, 548
No. 2 Officers Advanced Training School RAF, 548
No. 2 Radio School RAF, 545
No. 2 Reserve Flying School RAF, 557
No. 2 School of Administration Training, 548
No. 2 School of Aerial Fighting and Gunnery RAF, 546
No. 2 School of Aerial Fighting RAF, 548
No. 2 School of Aerial Navigation and Bomb Dropping RAF, 546
No. 2 School of Air Navigation RAF, 548
No. 2 School of Army Co-operation RAF, 548
No. 2 School of General Reconnaissance RAF, 548
No. 2 School of Navigation and Bomb Dropping RAF, 546
No. 2 School of Recruit Training RAF, 546
No. 2 School of Special Flying RAF, 557
No. 2 School of Technical Training RAF, 546
No. 2 Service Flying Training School RAF, 557
No. 2 Signals School RAF, 546
No. 2 Squadron RAAF, 512
No. 2 Squadron RAF, 465, 499, 510, 571
No. 2 Torpedo Refresher School RAF, 548
No. 2 Training Depot Station, 530
No. 2 Wireless School RAF, 548
No. 300 Group RAF, 492
No. 300 Land of Masovia Polish Bomber Squadron, 519
No. 301 Polish Bomber Squadron, 519
No. 302 Polish Fighter Squadron, 519
No. 303 Kosciuszko Polish Fighter Squadron, 519
No. 303 Signals Unit, 109
No. 304 Polish Bomber Squadron, 519
No. 305 Polish Bomber Squadron, 519
No. 306 Polish Fighter Squadron, 519
No. 307 City of Lwów Polish Fighter Squadron, 519
No. 308 City of Kraków Polish Fighter Squadron, 519
No. 309 Land of Czerwien Polish Fighter-Reconnaissance Squadron, 519
No. 30 Elementary and Reserve Flying Training School RAF, 553
No. 30 Elementary Flying Training School (Kenya) RAF, 555
No. 30 Elementary Flying Training School RAF, 555
No. 30 Group RAF, 486
No. 30 Squadron RAF, 511, 574, 576
No. 30 Training Depot Station, 530
No. 310 Squadron RAF, 519
No. 311 Squadron RAF, 519
No. 312 Squadron RAF, 519
No. 313 Squadron RAF, 519
No. 314 Technical Services Unit, 519
No. 315 City of Deblin Polish Fighter Squadron, 520
No. 316 City of Warsaw Polish Fighter Squadron, 520
No. 317 Polish Fighter Squadron, 520
No. 318 Polish Fighter Squadron, 520
No. 31 Air Navigation School RAF, 543
No. 31 Bombing and Gunnery School RAF, 544
No. 31 Elementary and Reserve Flying Training School RAF, 553
No. 31 Elementary Flying Training School RAF, 555
No. 31 Group RAF, 486
No. 31 Service Flying Training School RAF, 558
No. 31 Squadron RAF, 466, 475, 499, 511
No. 31 Training Depot Station, 531
No. 320 Squadron RAF, 520
No. 321 Squadron RAF, 520
No. 322 Squadron RAF, 520
No. 326 Squadron RAF, 520
No. 327 Squadron RAF, 520
No. 328 Squadron RAF, 520
No. 329 Squadron RAF, 520
No. 32 Air Navigation School RAF, 543
No. 32 Elementary and Reserve Flying Training School RAF, 553
No. 32 Elementary Flying Training School RAF, 555
No. 32 Group RAF, 486
No. 32 Service Flying Training School RAF, 558
No. 32 Squadron RAF, 95, 469, 470, 511
No. 32 (The Royal) Squadron RAF, 499

No. 32 Training Depot Station, 531
No. 330 Squadron RAF, 520
No. 331 Squadron RAF, 520
No. 332 Squadron RAF, 520
No. 333 Group RAF, 492
No. 333 Squadron RAF, 520
No. 334 Squadron RAF, 520
No. 335 Squadron RAF, 521
No. 336 Squadron RAF, 521
No. 33 Air Navigation School RAF, 543
No. 33 Elementary and Reserve Flying Training School RAF, 554
No. 33 Elementary Flying Training School RAF, 555
No. 33 Flying Instructors School, Southern Rhodesia RAF, 556
No. 33 Group RAF, 486
No. 33 Service Flying Training School RAF, 558
No. 33 Signals Unit, 109
No. 33 Squadron RAF, 496, 511, 579
No. 33 Training Depot Station, 531
No. 340 Squadron RAF, 521
No. 341 Squadron RAF, 521
No. 342 Squadron RAF, 521
No. 343 Squadron RAF, 521
No. 344 Squadron RAF, 521
No. 345 Squadron RAF, 521
No. 346 Squadron RAF, 521
No. 347 Squadron RAF, 521
No. 34 Elementary and Reserve Flying Training School RAF, 554
No. 34 Elementary Flying Training School (Canada) RAF, 555
No. 34 Group RAF, 486
No. 34 Service Flying Training School RAF, 558
No. 34 Squadron RAF, 511
No. 34 Squadron RAF Regiment, 109, 498
No. 34 Training Depot Station, 531
No. 351 Squadron RAF, 521
No. 352 Squadron RAF, 521
No. 353 Squadron RAF, 521
No. 354 Squadron RAF, 521
No. 355 Squadron RAF, 521
No. 356 Squadron RAF, 521
No. 357 Squadron RAF, 521
No. 358 Squadron RAF, 521
No. 35 Elementary and Reserve Flying Training School RAF, 554
No. 35 Elementary Flying Training School (Canada) RAF, 555
No. 35 Service Flying Training School RAF, 558
No. 35 Squadron RAF, 511
No. 35 Training Depot Station, 531

No. 360 Squadron RAF, 521
No. 361 Squadron RAF, 521
No. 36 Elementary and Reserve Flying Training School RAF, 554
No. 36 Elementary Flying Training School (Canada) RAF, 555
No. 36 Service Flying Training School RAF, 558
No. 36 Squadron RAF, 511
No. 36 Training Depot Station, 531
No. 37 Elementary and Reserve Flying Training School RAF, 554
No. 37 Service Flying Training School RAF, 558
No. 37 Squadron RAF, 511
No. 37 Training Depot Station, 531
No. 38 Elementary and Reserve Flying Training School RAF, 554
No. 38 Group RAF, 15, 455, 457, 482, 486, 498
No. 38 Service Flying Training School RAF, 558
No. 38 Squadron RAF, 511
No. 38 Training Depot Station, 531
No. 39 Elementary and Reserve Flying Training School RAF, 554
No. 39 Service Flying Training School RAF, 558
No. 39 Squadron RAF, 467, 507, 511
No. 39 Training Depot Station, 531
No. 3 Air Experience Flight RAF, 534
No. 3 Air Gunners School RAF, 543
No. 3 Air Navigation School RAF, 543
No. 3 Air Observers Navigation School RAF, 544
No. 3 Air Observers School RAF, 544
No. 3 (Auxiliary) School of Aerial Gunnery RAF, 548
No. 3 (Basic) Flying Training School RAF, 552
No. 3 Basic Flying Training School RAF, 552
No. 3 Bombing and Gunnery School RAF, 544
No. 3 British Flying Training School RAF, 552
No. 3 Civil Air Navigation School RAF, 545
No. 3 (Communication) Squadron, 539
No. 3 Electrical and Wireless School RAF, 548
No. 3 Elementary and Reserve Flying Training School RAF, 553
No. 3 Elementary Flying Training School RAF, 554
No. 3 Elementary Gliding Training School RAF, 559
No. 3 Fighting School RAF, 545
No. 3 Flying Instructors School (Advanced) RAF, 555
No. 3 Flying Training School RAF, 459, 496, 497, 501, 556

683

No. 3 Force Protection Wing RAF, 499
No. 3 Group RAF, 482
No. 3 (Indian) Group RAF, 493
No. 3 Lancaster Finishing School RAF, 545
No. 3 Middle East Training School RAF, 545
No. 3 Parachute Training School RAF, 548
No. 3 Radio Direction Finding School RAF, 548
No. 3 Radio School RAF, 545
No. 3 Reserve Flying School RAF, 557
No. 3 School of Aerial Fighting and Gunnery RAF, 546
No. 3 School of Aerial Navigation and Bomb Dropping RAF, 546
No. 3 School of General Reconnaissance RAF, 548
No. 3 School of Navigation and Bomb Dropping RAF, 546
No. 3 School of Recruit Training RAF, 546
No. 3 School of Technical Training RAF, 546
No. 3 Service Flying Training School RAF, 557
No. 3 Signals School (India) RAF, 546
No. 3 Signals School RAF, 546
No. 3 Squadron RAAF, 512
No. 3 Squadron RAF, 465, 497, 510, 571
No. 3 Training Depot Station, 530
No. 400 Squadron RCAF, 522
No. 401 Squadron RCAF, 522
No. 402 Squadron RCAF, 522
No. 403 Squadron RCAF, 522
No. 404 Squadron RCAF, 522
No. 405 Squadron RCAF, 522
No. 406 Squadron RCAF, 522
No. 407 Squadron RCAF, 522
No. 408 Squadron RCAF, 522
No. 409 Squadron RCAF, 522
No. 40 Elementary and Reserve Flying Training School RAF, 554
No. 40 Group RAF, 486
No. 40 Squadron RAF, 511
No. 40 Training Depot Station, 531
No. 410 Squadron RCAF, 522
No. 411 Squadron RCAF, 522
No. 412 Squadron RCAF, 522
No. 413 Squadron RCAF, 522
No. 414 Squadron RCAF, 522
No. 415 Squadron RCAF, 522
No. 416 Squadron RCAF, 522
No. 417 Squadron RCAF, 522
No. 418 Squadron RCAF, 522
No. 419 Squadron RCAF, 522
No. 41 Elementary and Reserve Flying Training School RAF, 554
No. 41 Group RAF, 486

No. 41 Service Flying Training School RAF, 558
No. 41 Squadron RAF, 497, 511
No. 41 Training Depot Station, 531
No. 420 Squadron RCAF, 522
No. 421 Squadron RCAF, 522
No. 422 Squadron RCAF, 522
No. 423 Squadron RCAF, 522
No. 424 Squadron RCAF, 522
No. 425 Squadron RCAF, 522
No. 426 Squadron RCAF, 522
No. 427 Squadron RCAF, 522
No. 428 Squadron RCAF, 522
No. 429 Squadron RCAF, 522
No. 42 Elementary and Reserve Flying Training School RAF, 554
No. 42 (Expeditionary Support) Wing RAF, 501
No. 42 Group RAF, 486
No. 42 Squadron RAF, 511
No. 42 Training Depot Station, 531
No. 430 Squadron RCAF, 522
No. 431 Squadron RCAF, 523
No. 432 Squadron RCAF, 523
No. 433 Squadron RCAF, 523
No. 434 Squadron RCAF, 523
No. 435 Squadron RCAF, 523
No. 436 Squadron RCAF, 523
No. 437 Squadron RCAF, 523
No. 438 Squadron RCAF, 523
No. 439 Squadron RCAF, 523
No. 43 Elementary and Reserve Flying Training School RAF, 554
No. 43 Group RAF, 486
No. 43 Squadron RAF, 511
No. 43 Training Depot Station, 531
No. 440 Squadron RCAF, 523
No. 441 Squadron RCAF, 523
No. 442 Squadron RCAF, 523
No. 443 Squadron RCAF, 523
No. 44 Elementary and Reserve Flying Training School RAF, 554
No. 44 Group RAF, 487
No. 44 (Royal Marine) Commando, 265
No. 44 Squadron RAF, 511
No. 44 Training Depot Station, 531
No. 44 Training School RAF, 548
No. 450 Squadron RAAF, 523
No. 451 Squadron RAAF, 523
No. 452 Squadron RAAF, 523
No. 453 Squadron RAAF, 523
No. 454 Squadron RAAF, 523
No. 455 Squadron RAAF, 523
No. 456 Squadron RAAF, 523
No. 457 Squadron RAAF, 523
No. 458 Squadron RAAF, 523

No. 459 Squadron RAAF, 523
No. 45 Elementary and Reserve Flying Training School RAF, 554
No. 45 Group RAF, 487
No. 45 Squadron RAF, 511
No. 45 Training Depot Station, 531
No. 460 Squadron RAAF, 523
No. 461 Squadron RAAF, 523
No. 462 Squadron RAAF, 523
No. 463 Squadron RAAF, 523
No. 464 Squadron RAAF, 523
No. 466 Squadron RAAF, 523
No. 467 Squadron RAAF, 523
No. 46 Elementary and Reserve Flying Training School RAF, 554
No. 46 (Royal Marine) Commando, 265
No. 46 Squadron RAF, 511
No. 46 Training Depot Station, 531
No. 47 Elementary and Reserve Flying Training School RAF, 554
No. 47 Group RAF, 487
No. 47 (Royal Marine) Commando, 265
No. 47 Squadron RAF, 511
No. 47 Training Depot Station, 531
No. 485 Squadron RNZAF, 524
No. 486 Squadron RNZAF, 524
No. 487 Squadron RNZAF, 524
No. 488 Squadron RNZAF, 524
No. 489 Squadron RNZAF, 524
No. 48 Elementary and Reserve Flying Training School RAF, 554
No. 48 Group RAF, 487
No. 48 (Royal Marine) Commando, 265
No. 48 Squadron RAF, 511
No. 48 Training Depot Station, 531
No. 490 Squadron RNZAF, 524
No. 49 Elementary and Reserve Flying Training School RAF, 554
No. 49 Squadron RAF, 511
No. 49 Training Depot Station, 531
No. 4 (Advanced) Flying Training School RAF, 553
No. 4 Air Experience Flight RAF, 534
No. 4 Air Gunners School RAF, 543
No. 4 Air Navigation School RAF, 543
No. 4 Air Observers Navigation School RAF, 544
No. 4 Air Observers School RAF, 544
No. 4 (Auxiliary) School of Aerial Gunnery RAF, 548
No. 4 Basic Flying Training School RAF, 552
No. 4 Bombing and Gunnery School RAF, 544
No. 4 British Flying Training School RAF, 552
No. 4 Civil Air Navigation School RAF, 545
No. 4 Commando, 265
No. 4 (Communication) Squadron, 539

No. 4 Elementary and Reserve Flying Training School RAF, 553
No. 4 Elementary Flying Training School RAF, 554
No. 4 Fighting School RAF, 545
No. 4 Flying Instructors School (Elementary) RAF, 555
No. 4 Flying Instructors School RAF, 555
No. 4 Flying Instructors School (Supplementary) RAF, 555
No. 4 Flying Training School RAF, 459, 501, 537, 556
No. 4 Group RAF, 482
No. 4 Middle East Training School RAF, 545
No. 4 Parachute Training School RAF, 548
No. 4 Radio School RAF, 545
No. 4 Reserve Flying School RAF, 557
No. 4 School of Aerial Fighting and Gunnery RAF, 546
No. 4 School of Aerial Navigation and Bomb Dropping RAF, 546
No. 4 School of Navigation and Bomb Dropping RAF, 546
No. 4 School of Recruit Training RAF, 546
No. 4 School of Technical Training RAF, 546
No. 4 Service Flying Training School RAF, 557
No. 4 Signals School RAF, 546
No. 4 Squadron RAAF, 512
No. 4 Squadron RAF, 501, 510
No. 4 Training Depot Station, 530
No. 500 Squadron RAF, 524
No. 501 Squadron RAF, 524
No. 502 Squadron RAF, 524
No. 503 Squadron RAF, 524
No. 504 Squadron RAF, 524
No. 505 Squadron RAF, 524
No. 50 Elementary and Reserve Flying Training School RAF, 554
No. 50 Group RAF, 487
No. 50 Initial Training School RAF, 548
No. 50 Squadron RAF, 511
No. 50 Training Depot Station, 531
No. 510 Squadron RAF, 524
No. 511 Squadron RAF, 524
No. 512 Squadron RAF, 524
No. 513 Squadron RAF, 524
No. 514 Squadron RAF, 524
No. 515 Squadron RAF, 524
No. 516 Squadron RAF, 524
No. 517 Squadron RAF, 524
No. 518 Squadron RAF, 524
No. 519 Squadron RAF, 524
No. 51 Elementary and Reserve Flying Training School RAF, 554
No. 51 Group RAF, 487

No. 51 OTU, 526
No. 51 Squadron RAF, 501, 512, 577
No. 51 Squadron RAF Regiment, 499
No. 51 Training Depot Station, 531
No. 520 Squadron RAF, 524
No. 521 Squadron RAF, 524
No. 524 Squadron RAF, 524
No. 525 Squadron RAF, 525
No. 526 Squadron RAF, 525
No. 527 Squadron RAF, 525
No. 528 Squadron RAF, 525
No. 529 Squadron RAF, 525
No. 52 Elementary and Reserve Flying Training School RAF, 554
No. 52 Group RAF, 487
No. 52 Squadron RAF, 512
No. 52 Training Depot Station, 531
No. 530 Squadron RAF, 525
No. 531 Squadron RAF, 525
No. 532 Squadron RAF, 525
No. 533 Squadron RAF, 525
No. 534 Squadron RAF, 525
No. 535 Squadron RAF, 525
No. 536 Squadron RAF, 525
No. 537 Squadron RAF, 525
No. 538 Squadron RAF, 525
No. 539 Squadron RAF, 525
No. 53 Elementary and Reserve Flying Training School RAF, 554
No. 53 Group RAF, 487
No. 53 OTU, 526
No. 53 Squadron RAF, 512
No. 53 Training Depot Station, 531
No. 540 Squadron RAF, 489, 525
No. 541 Squadron RAF, 489, 525
No. 542 Squadron RAF, 489, 525
No. 543 Squadron RAF, 525
No. 544 Squadron RAF, 489, 525
No. 547 Squadron RAF, 525
No. 548 Squadron RAF, 525
No. 549 Squadron RAF, 525
No. 54 Elementary and Reserve Flying Training School RAF, 554
No. 54 Group RAF, 485, 487
No. 54 Squadron RAF, 501, 512
No. 54 Training Depot Station, 531
No. 550 Squadron RAF, 525, 526
No. 551 Squadron RAF, 526
No. 552 Squadron RAF, 526
No. 553 Squadron RAF, 526
No. 554 Squadron RAF, 526
No. 555 Squadron RAF, 526
No. 556 Squadron RAF, 526
No. 557 Squadron RAF, 526
No. 558 Squadron RAF, 526
No. 559 Squadron RAF, 526

No. 55 Elementary and Reserve Flying Training School RAF, 554
No. 55 OTU, 526
No. 55 Squadron RAF, 512
No. 55 Training Depot Station, 531
No. 560 Squadron RAF, 526
No. 561 Squadron RAF, 526
No. 562 Squadron RAF, 526
No. 563 Squadron RAF, 526
No. 564 Squadron RAF, 526
No. 565 Squadron RAF, 526
No. 567 Squadron RAF, 525
No. 569 Squadron RAF, 525
No. 56 Elementary and Reserve Flying Training School RAF, 554
No. 56 OTU, 526
No. 56 Squadron RAF, 501, 512
No. 56 Training Depot Station, 531
No. 570 Squadron RAF, 525
No. 571 Squadron RAF, 525
No. 575 Squadron RAF, 525
No. 576 Squadron RAF, 525
No. 577 Squadron RAF, 525
No. 578 Squadron RAF, 525
No. 57 Elementary and Reserve Flying Training School RAF, 554
No. 57 OTU, 526
No. 57 Squadron RAF, 512
No. 57 Training Depot Station, 531
No. 582 Squadron RAF, 525
No. 586 Squadron RAF, 525
No. 587 Squadron RAF, 525
No. 58 Elementary and Reserve Flying Training School RAF, 554
No. 58 OTU, 526
No. 58 Squadron RAF, 512
No. 58 Training Depot Station, 531
No. 595 Squadron RAF, 525
No. 597 Squadron RAF, 525
No. 598 Squadron RAF, 525
No. 59 Elementary and Reserve Flying Training School RAF, 554
No. 59 OTU, 526
No. 59 Squadron RAF, 512
No. 59 Training Depot Station, 531
No. 5 (Advanced) Flying Training School RAF, 553
No. 5 Air Experience Flight RAF, 501, 534
No. 5 Air Gunners School RAF, 543
No. 5 Air Navigation School RAF, 543
No. 5 Air Observers Navigation School RAF, 544
No. 5 Air Observers School RAF, 544
No. 5 Basic Flying Training School RAF, 552
No. 5 Bombing and Gunnery School RAF, 544
No. 5 British Flying Training School RAF, 552

No. 5 Civil Air Navigation School RAF, 545
No. 5 (Communication) Squadron, 539
No. 5 Elementary and Reserve Flying Training School RAF, 553
No. 5 Elementary Flying Training School RAF, 554
No. 5 Fighting School RAF, 545
No. 5 Flying Instructors School (Elementary) RAF, 555
No. 5 Flying Instructors School RAF, 555
No. 5 Flying Instructors School (Supplementary) RAF, 556
No. 5 Flying Training School RAF, 556
No. 5 Force Protection Wing RAF, 499
No. 5 Group RAF, 482
No. 5 Lancaster Finishing School RAF, 545
No. 5 Middle East Training School RAF, 545
No. 5 Reserve Flying School RAF, 557
No. 5 School of Recruit Training RAF, 546
No. 5 School of Technical Training RAF, 546
No. 5 Service Flying Training School RAF, 557
No. 5 Squadron RAF, 501, 510, 577
No. 5 Training Depot Station, 530
No. 600 Squadron RAF, 499, 527
No. 601 Squadron RAF, 527, 581
No. 602 Squadron RAF, 527
No. 603 Squadron RAF, 527
No. 604 Squadron RAF, 527
No. 605 Squadron RAF, 527
No. 606 Squadron RAF, 527
No. 607 Squadron RAF, 527
No. 608 Squadron RAF, 527
No. 609 Squadron RAF, 498, 527
No. 60 Group RAF, 487
No. 60 Squadron RAF, 251, 500, 512
No. 60 Training Depot Station, 531
No. 610 Squadron RAF, 527
No. 611 Squadron RAF, 502, 527
No. 611 Volunteer Gliding Squadron RAF, 533
No. 612 (County of Aberdeen) Squadron RAF, 498
No. 612 Squadron RAF, 527
No. 612 Volunteer Gliding Squadron RAF, 533
No. 613 Squadron RAF, 527
No. 613 Volunteer Gliding Squadron RAF, 497, 533
No. 614A Squadron RAF, 527
No. 614 Squadron RAF, 527
No. 614 Volunteer Gliding Squadron RAF, 533
No. 615 Squadron RAF, 527
No. 615 Volunteer Gliding Squadron RAF, 533
No. 616 Squadron RAF, 527
No. 616 Volunteer Gliding Squadron RAF, 498, 533
No. 617 Squadron RAF, 450, 499, 506, 527, 570
No. 617 Volunteer Gliding Squadron RAF, 533
No. 618 Squadron RAF, 527
No. 618 Volunteer Gliding Squadron RAF, 533
No. 619 Squadron RAF, 527
No. 61 Group RAF, 488
No. 61 OTU, 526
No. 61 Squadron RAF, 512
No. 61 Training Depot Station, 531
No. 620 Squadron RAF, 527
No. 621 Squadron RAF, 527
No. 621 Volunteer Gliding Squadron RAF, 533
No. 622 Squadron RAF, 527
No. 622 Volunteer Gliding Squadron RAF, 533
No. 623 Squadron RAF, 527
No. 624 Squadron RAF, 527
No. 624 Volunteer Gliding Squadron RAF, 533
No. 625 Squadron RAF, 527
No. 625 Volunteer Gliding Squadron RAF, 533
No. 626 Squadron RAF, 527
No. 626 Volunteer Gliding Squadron RAF, 533
No. 627 Squadron RAF, 527
No. 628 Squadron RAF, 527
No. 62 Group RAF, 488
No. 62 Squadron RAF, 512
No. 630 Squadron RAF, 527
No. 631 Squadron RAF, 527
No. 631 Volunteer Gliding Squadron RAF, 533
No. 632 Volunteer Gliding Squadron RAF, 533
No. 633 Volunteer Gliding Squadron RAF, 533
No. 634 Volunteer Gliding Squadron RAF, 533
No. 635 Squadron RAF, 527
No. 635 Volunteer Gliding Squadron RAF, 534
No. 636 Volunteer Gliding Squadron RAF, 534
No. 637 Volunteer Gliding Squadron RAF, 499, 534
No. 639 Squadron RAF, 527
No. 63 Group RAF, 488
No. 63 Squadron RAF, 512

No. 640 Squadron RAF, 528
No. 642 Volunteer Gliding Squadron RAF, 534
No. 643 Volunteer Gliding Squadron RAF, 534
No. 644 Squadron RAF, 528
No. 644 Volunteer Gliding Squadron RAF, 534
No. 645 Volunteer Gliding Squadron RAF, 534
No. 64 Group RAF, 488
No. 64 Squadron RAF, 512
No. 650 Squadron RAF, 528
No. 651 Squadron RAF, 528
No. 652 (AOP) Squadron RAF, 528
No. 653 Squadron RAF, 528
No. 654 (AOP) Squadron RAF, 528
No. 655 (AOP) Squadron RAF, 528
No. 656 (AOP) Squadron RAF, 528
No. 657 (AOP) Squadron RAF, 528
No. 657 Squadron AAC, 396, 500
No. 658 (AOP) Squadron RAF, 528
No. 658 Squadron AAC, 397
No. 659 (AOP) Squadron RAF, 528
No. 65 Group RAF, 488
No. 65 Squadron RAF, 512
No. 660 (AOP) Squadron RAF, 528
No. 660 Squadron AAC, 106, 111, 251
No. 661 (AOP) Squadron RAF, 528
No. 661 Volunteer Gliding Squadron RAF, 534
No. 662 (AOP) Squadron RAF, 528
No. 662 Volunteer Gliding Squadron RAF, 534
No. 663 (AOP) Squadron RAF, 528
No. 663 Volunteer Gliding Squadron RAF, 534
No. 664 Squadron RAF, 528
No. 664 Squadron RCAF, 528
No. 664 Volunteer Gliding Squadron RAF, 534
No. 665 Squadron RCAF, 528
No. 666 Squadron RAF, 528
No. 666 Squadron RCAF, 528
No. 667 Squadron RAF, 529
No. 668 Squadron RAF, 529
No. 669 Squadron RAF, 529
No. 66 Group RAF, 488
No. 66 Squadron RAF, 512
No. 670 Squadron RAF, 529
No. 671 Squadron RAF, 529
No. 672 Squadron RAF, 529
No. 673 Squadron RAF, 529
No. 679 Squadron RAF, 529
No. 67 Group RAF, 488
No. 67 Squadron RAF, 512
No. 680 Squadron RAF, 529
No. 681 Squadron RAF, 529
No. 682 Squadron RAF, 529
No. 683 Squadron RAF, 529
No. 684 Squadron RAF, 529
No. 68 Squadron RAF, 512
No. 691 Squadron RAF, 529
No. 692 Squadron RAF, 529
No. 695 Squadron RAF, 529
No. 69 Squadron RAF, 512
No. 6 (Advanced) Flying Training School RAF, 553
No. 6 Air Experience Flight RAF, 535
No. 6 Air Gunners School RAF, 543
No. 6 Air Navigation School RAF, 543
No. 6 Air Observers Navigation School RAF, 544
No. 6 Air Observers School RAF, 544
No. 6 Bombing and Gunnery School RAF, 544
No. 6 British Flying Training School RAF, 552
No. 6 Civil Air Navigation School RAF, 545
No. 6 (Communication) Squadron, 539
No. 6 Elementary and Reserve Flying Training School RAF, 553
No. 6 Elementary Flying Training School RAF, 554
No. 6 Flying Instructors School (Elementary) RAF, 556
No. 6 Flying Instructors School RAF, 556
No. 6 Flying Instructors School (Supplementary) RAF, 556
No. 6 Flying Training School RAF, 459, 497, 501, 536, 556
No. 6 Group RCAF, 483
No. 6 Lancaster Finishing School RAF, 545
No. 6 Radio School RAF, 545
No. 6 Reserve Flying School RAF, 557
No. 6 School of Recruit Training RAF, 546
No. 6 Service Flying Training School RAF, 558
No. 6 Squadron RAF, 465, 499, 510, 571
No. 6 Training Depot Station, 530
No. 70 Group RAF, 488
No. 70 Squadron RAF, 512, 574
No. 71 Group RAF, 488
No. 71 Squadron RAF, 512, 519
No. 72 Group RAF, 488
No. 72 Squadron RAF, 499, 513
No. 73 Squadron RAF, 513
No. 74 Squadron RAF, 513
No. 751 Signals Unit, 109
No. 75 Squadron RAF, 513
No. 76 Squadron RAF, 513
No. 77 Squadron RAF, 513
No. 78 Squadron RAF, 109, 513
No. 79 Squadron RAF, 513

No. 7 Air Experience Flight RAF, 535
No. 7 Air Gunners School RAF, 543
No. 7 Air Navigation School RAF, 543
No. 7 Air Observers Navigation School RAF, 544
No. 7 Air Observers School RAF, 544
No. 7 Bombing and Gunnery School RAF, 544
No. 7 British Flying Training School RAF, 552
No. 7 Civil Air Navigation School RAF, 545
No. 7 (Communication) Squadron, 539
No. 7 Elementary and Reserve Flying Training School RAF, 553
No. 7 Elementary Flying Training School RAF, 554
No. 7 Flight AAC, 154, 397
No. 7 Flying Instructors School (Advanced) RAF, 556
No. 7 Flying Instructors School RAF, 556
No. 7 Flying Training School RAF, 556
No. 7 Group RAF, 483
No. 7 Reserve Flying School RAF, 557
No. 7 School of Recruit Training RAF, 546
No. 7 Service Flying Training School RAF, 558
No. 7 Signals Unit, 109
No. 7 Squadron RAF, 500, 510, 578
No. 7 Training Depot Station, 530
No. 80 Squadron RAF, 513
No. 81 Group RAF, 488
No. 81 Squadron RAF, 513
No. 82 Group RAF, 488
No. 82 Squadron RAF, 513
No. 83 Expeditionary Air Group (United Kingdom), 12, 15, 155, 457, 482, 489, 506
No. 83 Group Communication Squadron, 538
No. 83 Squadron RAF, 513
No. 84 Group RAF, 489
No. 84 Squadron RAF, 108, 506, 513
No. 85 (Expeditionary Logistics) Wing RAF, 501
No. 85 Group Communication Squadron, 538
No. 85 Group RAF, 489
No. 85 Squadron RAF, 513
No. 85 Wing Communication Squadron, 539
No. 86 Squadron RAF, 513
No. 87 Group RAF, 489
No. 87 Squadron RAF, 513
No. 88 Group Communication Squadron, 538
No. 88 Group RAF, 489
No. 88 Squadron RAF, 513
No. 89 Squadron RAF, 513
No. 8 (Advanced) Flying Training School RAF, 553
No. 8 Air Experience Flight RAF, 535
No. 8 Air Gunners School RAF, 543
No. 8 Air Observers Navigation School RAF, 544
No. 8 Air Observers School RAF, 544
No. 8 Bombing and Gunnery School RAF, 544
No. 8 Civil Air Navigation School RAF, 545
No. 8 (Communication) Squadron, 539
No. 8 Elementary and Reserve Flying Training School RAF, 553
No. 8 Elementary Flying Training School RAF, 554
No. 8 Flight AAC, 107
No. 8 Flying Training School RAF, 556
No. 8 Group RAF, 483
No. 8 Reserve Flying School RAF, 557
No. 8 School of Recruit Training RAF, 546
No. 8 Service Flying Training School RAF, 558
No. 8 Squadron RAF, 501, 510
No. 8 Training Depot Station, 530
No. 901 (County of London) Balloon Squadron AAF, 539
No. 902 (County of London) Balloon Squadron AAF, 539
No. 903 (County of London) Balloon Squadron AAF, 539
No. 903 Expeditionary Air Wing (United Kingdom), 506
No. 904 (County of Surrey) Balloon Squadron AAF, 539
No. 905 (County of Surrey) Balloon Squadron AAF, 539
No. 905 Expeditionary Air Wing (United Kingdom), 507
No. 906 (County of Middlesex) Balloon Squadron AAF, 539
No. 906 Expeditionary Air Wing (United Kingdom), 506
No. 907 (County of Middlesex) Balloon Squadron AAF, 539
No. 908 (County of Essex) Balloon Squadron AAF, 539
No. 909 (County of Essex) Balloon Squadron AAF, 539
No. 90 Group RAF, 489
No. 90 Signals Unit RAF, 498
No. 90 Squadron RAF, 513
No. 910 (County of Essex) Balloon Squadron AAF, 539
No. 911 (County of Warwick) Balloon Squadron AAF, 539
No. 912 (County of Warwick) Balloon Squadron AAF, 539
No. 913 (County of Warwick) Balloon Squadron AAF, 539
No. 914 (County of Warwick) Balloon Squadron AAF, 540

No. 915 (County of Warwick) Balloon Squadron AAF, 540
No. 916 (County of Warwick) Balloon Squadron AAF, 540
No. 917 (County of Warwick) Balloon Squadron AAF, 540
No. 918 (County of Derby) Balloon Squadron AAF, 540
No. 919 (West Lancashire) Balloon Squadron AAF, 540
No. 91 Group RAF, 485, 489
No. 91 Squadron RAF, 513
No. 920 Balloon Squadron AAF, 540
No. 921 (West Lancashire) Balloon Squadron AAF, 540
No. 922 (West Lancashire) Balloon Squadron AAF, 540
No. 923 (West Lancashire) Balloon Squadron AAF, 540
No. 924 Balloon Squadron AAF, 540
No. 925 (East Lancashire) Balloon Squadron AAF, 540
No. 926 (East Lancashire) Balloon Squadron AAF, 540
No. 927 (County of Gloucester) Balloon Squadron AAF, 540
No. 928 Balloon Squadron AAF, 540
No. 929 Balloon Squadron AAF, 540
No. 92 Group RAF, 489
No. 92 Squadron RAF, 513
No. 930 (Hampshire) Balloon Squadron AAF, 540
No. 931 (Hampshire) Balloon Squadron AAF, 540
No. 932 (Hampshire) Balloon Squadron AAF, 540
No. 933 (Hampshire) Balloon Squadron AAF, 540
No. 934 (County of Devon) Balloon Squadron AAF, 540
No. 935 (County of Glamorgan) Balloon Squadron AAF, 540
No. 936 (County of Northumberland) Balloon Squadron AAF, 540
No. 937 (County of Northumberland) Balloon Squadron AAF, 540
No. 938 (County of Northumberland) Balloon Squadron AAF, 540
No. 939 (West Riding) Balloon Squadron AAF, 540
No. 93 Group RAF, 489
No. 93 Group Screened Pilots School RAF, 548
No. 93 Squadron RAF, 513
No. 940 (West Riding) Balloon Squadron AAF, 540
No. 941 (West Riding) Balloon Squadron AAF, 540
No. 942 (East Riding) Balloon Squadron AAF, 540
No. 943 (East Riding) Balloon Squadron AAF, 540
No. 944 (East Riding) Balloon Squadron AAF, 540
No. 945 (City of Glasgow) Balloon Squadron AAF, 540
No. 946 (City of Glasgow) Balloon Squadron AAF, 540
No. 947 (City of Glasgow) Balloon Squadron AAF, 540
No. 948 Balloon Squadron AAF, 540
No. 949 Balloon Squadron AAF, 540
No. 94 Squadron RAF, 513
No. 950 Balloon Squadron AAF, 540
No. 951 Balloon Squadron AAF, 540
No. 952 Balloon Squadron AAF, 540
No. 953 Balloon Squadron AAF, 540
No. 954 Balloon Squadron AAF, 541
No. 955 Balloon Squadron AAF, 541
No. 956 Balloon Squadron AAF, 541
No. 957 Balloon Squadron AAF, 541
No. 958 Balloon Squadron AAF, 541
No. 959 Balloon Squadron AAF, 541
No. 95 Squadron RAF, 513
No. 960 Balloon Squadron AAF, 541
No. 961 Balloon Squadron AAF, 541
No. 962 Balloon Squadron AAF, 541
No. 963 Balloon Squadron AAF, 541
No. 964 Balloon Squadron AAF, 541
No. 965 Balloon Squadron AAF, 541
No. 966 Balloon Squadron AAF, 541
No. 967 Balloon Squadron AAF, 541
No. 968 Balloon Squadron AAF, 541
No. 969 Balloon Squadron AAF, 541
No. 96 Squadron RAF, 513
No. 970 Balloon Squadron AAF, 541
No. 971 Balloon Squadron AAF, 541
No. 972 Balloon Squadron AAF, 541
No. 973 Balloon Squadron AAF, 541
No. 974 Balloon Squadron AAF, 541
No. 975 Balloon Squadron AAF, 541
No. 976 Balloon Squadron AAF, 541
No. 977 Balloon Squadron AAF, 541
No. 978 Balloon Squadron AAF, 541
No. 979 Balloon Squadron AAF, 541
No. 97 Squadron RAF, 513
No. 980 Balloon Squadron AAF, 541
No. 981 Balloon Squadron AAF, 541
No. 982 Balloon Squadron AAF, 541
No. 983 Balloon Squadron AAF, 541
No. 984 Balloon Squadron AAF, 541
No. 985 Balloon Squadron AAF, 541

No. 986 Balloon Squadron AAF, 541
No. 987 Balloon Squadron AAF, 541
No. 988 Balloon Squadron AAF, 541
No. 989 Balloon Squadron AAF, 541
No. 98 Depot Squadron, 531
No. 98 Squadron RAF, 513
No. 990 Balloon Squadron AAF, 541
No. 991 Balloon Squadron AAF, 541
No. 992 (Barrage Balloon) Squadron RAF, 541
No. 993 (Mobile) Balloon Squadron AAF, 541
No. 994 (Mobile) Balloon Squadron AAF, 541
No. 995 (Mobile) Balloon Squadron AAF, 541
No. 996 Balloon Squadron AAF, 542
No. 997 Balloon Squadron AAF, 542
No. 998 Balloon Squadron AAF, 542
No. 999 Balloon Squadron AAF, 542
No. 99 Depot Squadron, 531
No. 99 Squadron RAF, 513
No. 9 (Advanced) Flying Training School RAF, 553
No. 9 Air Experience Flight RAF, 535
No. 9 Air Gunners School RAF, 543
No. 9 Air Observers Navigation School RAF, 544
No. 9 Air Observers School RAF, 544
No. 9 Bombing and Gunnery School RAF, 544
No. 9 Civil Air Navigation School RAF, 545
No. 9 Elementary and Reserve Flying Training School RAF, 553
No. 9 Elementary Flying Training School RAF, 554
No. 9 Flying Training School RAF, 556
No. 9 Group RAF, 483
No. 9 Reserve Flying School RAF, 557
No. 9 School of Recruit Training RAF, 546
No. 9 Service Flying Training School RAF, 558
No. 9 Squadron RAF, 466, 499, 510, 571
No. 9 Training Depot Station, 530
Noël Coward, 207
Non-commissioned officer, 276
Nore, 36
Norfolk, 316, 499, 501, 504
Normandy Landings, 53, 265, 267, 331
Normans, 25
North African Campaign, 331
North America, 417
North America and West Indies Squadron, 38
North America and West Indies Station, 46
North American F-100 Super Sabre, 136
Northamptonshire, 501, 503
North Atlantic, 49
North Atlantic Treaty Organisation, 76, 131, 364, 390
North Carolina, 39

Northeastern Area Flying Instructors School, 559
Northern Area Flying Instructors School, 559
Northern Command (United Kingdom), 76, 388
Northern Communication Squadron, 538
Northern Cyprus, 429
Northern Germany, 329
Northern Ireland, 79, 307, 311, 314, 332
Northern Patrol, 178
North Korea and weapons of mass destruction, 114
Northrop Grumman B-2 Spirit, 503
North Sea, 6, 23, 31, 46, 178, 294
Northumberland, 315, 496
Northumberland Hussars, 434
Northumbria, 23
Northumbrian Universities Air Squadron, 498, 532
Northwest African Air Forces, 490
Northwestern Area Flying Instructors School, 559
North-West Frontier (military history), 72
Northwood Headquarters, 143, 197, 198, 229, 295, 303, 305, 307
Northwood, London, 198, 305, 307
North Yorkshire, 137, 138, 497–501, 504
Norton Manor Camp, 273
Norway, 211, 481
Norwegian Campaign, 53, 74
Notable products, 270
Nottingham, 307
Nottinghamshire, 500
Nova Scotia, 33, 39, 171
November 11, 2008 incident off Somalia, 50
Nuclear arms race, 114
Nuclear bombs, 450
Nuclear depth bomb, 129
Nuclear deterrence, 5
Nuclear deterrent, 133
Nuclear disarmament, 114
Nuclear espionage, 114
Nuclear ethics, 114
Nuclear explosion, 113
Nuclear Explosions (Prohibition and Inspections) Act 1998, 136
Nuclear fallout, 135
Nuclear fission, 115
Nuclear labor issues, 114
Nuclear marine propulsion, 190
Nuclear Non-Proliferation Treaty, 3, 113
Nuclear power, 140
Nuclear proliferation, 114
Nuclear reactor, 118
Nuclear reactor core, 127
Nuclear submarine, 53, 126, 191, 211, 619

691

Nuclear terrorism, 114
Nuclear Test Ban Treaty, 141
Nuclear warfare, 113
Nuclear weapon, 76, 96, 113, 451
Nuclear weapon design, 113
Nuclear weapons, 114, 140
Nuclear weapons and Israel, 114
Nuclear weapons and the United Kingdom, 13, 48, 89, 95, **113**, 114, 160, 183, 190, 451
Nuclear weapons and Ukraine, 114
Nuclear weapons delivery, 113
Nuclear weapons testing, 113
Nuclear weapon yield, 113
Nuclear winter, 113

Observation Post, 107
Observers School of Reconnaissance and Aerial Photography, 550
Occupied Europe, 448, 518
Ocelot (vehicle), 338, 376
OCLC, 104, 146–152, 208
Offensive Support Role Support Squadron, 536
Office of Scientific Research and Development, 116
Officer and Aircrew Selection Centre, 497
Officer (armed forces), 276
Officer Cadet, 204, 286
Officer candidate, 203, 204, 286, 359
Officer of the Order of the British Empire, 198, 199, 321
Officers Advanced Training School, 550
Offshore Raiding Craft, 270
Oil and Pipelines Agency, 593
Olaf I of Norway, 23
Oliver Cromwell, 324, 328
Oman, 155, 410
Omar Ali Saifuddin III, 343
Operation Agreement, 265
Operational Conversion Unit, 465, 472, 476
Operation Allied Force, 53
Operational Requirement, 123
Operational Training Unit, 488, 525
Operation Archery, 264
Operation Atalanta, 197, 295
Operation Banner, 79, 332, 333
Operation Banquet, 526
Operation Barras, 84
Operation Black Buck, 97
Operation Buffalo, 122
Operation Carthage, 94
Operation Chastise, 94, 450
Operation Demetrius, 80
Operation Deny Flight, 99
Operation Doomsday, 489
Operation Dracula, 492
Operation Dragoon, 490

Operation Dynamo, 180
Operation Ellamy, 11, 53, 100
Operation Enduring Freedom, 334
Operation Enduring Freedom – Horn of Africa, 11
Operation Epsom, 331
Operation Flavius, 80
Operation Frankton, 267
Operation Granby, 83, 338
Operation Grapple, 122, 135
Operation Herrick, 11, 53, 99, 237, 334
Operation Hurricane, 120
Operation Husky, 181
Operation Jericho, 450
Operation Journeyman, 53
Operation Kipion, 296, 457, 506
Operation Market Garden, 74
Operation Meridian, 241
Operation Mosaic, 134
Operation Motorman, 80
Operation Musketeer (1956), 96, 452
Operation Musketeer (Suez Crisis), 237
Operation Overlord, 47, 75, 181, 266
Operation Palliser, 6, 53, 84, 342
Operation Paraquet, 255
Operation Pedestal, 46
Operation Plunder, 265
Operation Redwing, 122
Operation Roast, 265
Operation Saracen, 526
Operation Sea Lion, 93, 448
Operation Serval, 100
Operation Shader, 11, 53, 100, 335, 342, 447, 457, 467, 480, 506
Operation Telic, 11, 53, 84, 99, 100
Operation Temperer, 335
Operation Toral, 334, 342, 424, 481
Operation Torch, 47, 181, 492
Operation Totem, 134
Operation Tungsten, 241
Operation Veritas, 99
Opium, 40
Opium War, 52
Optical landing system, 254
Options for Change, 81, 387, 452
Orange Herald, 122
Order in Council, 62
Order of precedence, 64
Order of the British Empire, 509
Orfordness, 32
Orford Ness, 139
Orkney, 169, 308, 313
Ormesby St Margaret with Scratby, 169
Osborne House, 318
Other, 519, 520
Otto Frisch, 115

Otto Hahn, 115
Ottoman Empire, 4, 45, 70, 176, 178, 329, 330
Ouistreham, 265
Outer Hebrides, 496
Outer space, 504
Overseas military bases of the United Kingdom, **153**
Oxford, 591
Oxfordshire, 496, 501, 503
Oxford University Air Squadron, 532

P1000 Class Picket Boat, 211
P229, 270, 365
PAAMS, 188
Pacific Ocean, 135, 300
Paddle steamer, 52
Paddlewheel, 40
Paid off, 188
Paiforce, 491
Pakistan, 200
Pakistan and weapons of mass destruction, 114
Palace Barracks, Holywood, 435
Palace of Whitehall, 594
Pall Mall Gazette, 42
Pals battalion, 411
Panama, 33
Panavia Tornado, 101, 446, 456, 465, 466, 561, 565
Panavia Tornado ADV, 465
Panavia Tornado GR4, 100, 497
Parachute Exercise Squadron, 536
Parachute Regiment (United Kingdom), 75, 344, 361, 366, 393, 441
Parachute Training Centre, 550
Parachute Training School (India), 550
Paramilitary, 80
ParcAberporth, 496
Parent company, 566
Parkhead Hall, 486
Parliament of England, 31, 325
Parliament of Ireland, 325
Parliament of Scotland, 325
Parliament of the United Kingdom, 2, 323
Partial Test Ban Treaty, 135
Partition of India, 332
Pashtun people, 72
Pathfinder Force, 483
Pathfinder Group, 366
Patrick OBrian, 207
Patrick Sanders (British Army officer), 321
Patrol aircraft, 158, 238
Patrol boat, 13, 160, 211
Patrol ship, 190
Pattern 1853 Enfield, 85
Paul Bennett (Royal Navy officer), 198, 227, 234

Paul Brickhill, 627
Paul Halton, 198
Paul Harris Nicolas, 289
Paul Kennedy, 48, 182
Paul Kennedy (historian), 56
Paul Skinner, 588
Pax Britannica, 4
Peacekeeping, 2, 6
Peace of Amiens, 35, 175
Peace of Utrecht, 33
Peacock-class corvette, 111
Pegasus Bridge, 267
Pembroke Dockyard, 308
Pembrokeshire, 316
Penang Fighter Squadron, 536
Penang Squadron, 536
Penetanguishene Naval Yard, 308
Peninsular War, 39, 327
Pennant number, 202
People of Nepal, 418
Peoples Republic of China, 82
Per Ardua ad Astra, 445, 479
Permanent Joint Headquarters, 198, 275, 345, 387
Permanent Secretary, 474, 588, 591
Permanent Under Secretary, 583
Permanent Under-Secretary of State, 588
Permissive Action Link, 143
Persian Gulf, 53, 155, 196, 295, 589
Personal Role Radio, 365
Perth University Air Squadron, 533
Peter Abbott, 232
Peter Compston, 254
Peter Franklyn, 233
Peter Herbert (Royal Navy officer), 231
Peter Hudson (Royal Navy officer), 234
Peterloo Massacre, 59
Peter Pomegranate, 27
Petersfield, Hampshire, 313
Peter Stanford (Royal Navy officer), 231
Peter Watkins (civil servant), 588
Peter Whiteley (Royal Marines officer), 255
Peter Woodhead, 232, 233
PGM-17 Thor, 128, 482
Phased array, 138, 457
Philip Augustus of France, 25
Philip Hammond, 474
Philip II of Spain, 27, 165
Philip Jackson (sculptor), 594
Philip Jones (Royal Navy officer), 158, 198, 234, 257, 586
Philip Joubert de la Ferté, 104
Philippines, 300
Philip S. W. Goldson International Airport, 108
Phineas Pett, 31

693

Picatinny rail, 337
Pilatus PC-21, 564
Pilots and Observers Aerial Gunnery and Aerial Fighting School, 550
Pinks War, 91
Pinnace (ships boat), 27
Pinzgauer High Mobility All-Terrain Vehicle, 270
Pinzgauer High-Mobility All-Terrain Vehicle, 381
Piracy, 177, 197
Pirates of the Caribbean, 207
Pith helmet, 284
Pit (nuclear weapon), 121
Planned French invasion of Britain (1744), 172
Planned French invasion of Britain (1759), 172
Platoon, 277, 347
Platoon leader, 442
Platoons, 345, 387
Plutonium, 114, 118
Plymouth, 199, 259, 268, 273, 306, 307, 311, 315
Pokhara, 431
Polaris missile, 48, 96, 183, 451
Polaris Sales Agreement, 131
Police Service of Northern Ireland, 332, 333
Polish Army, 72
Polish Fighting Team, 519, 520
Polish–Soviet War, 72
Political union, 30
Politics by region, 584
Politics of the United Kingdom, 584
Pontiacs War, 67, 327
Poole, 107, 268, 315
Poole, Dorset, 306
Portal:British Army, 58, 322, 364, 387, 405
Portal:United Kingdom, 584
Port Bannatyne, 315
Port Edgar, 312
Port Glasgow, 313
Portland Bill, 106
Portland Harbour, 308
Port of Gibraltar, 154, 305
Porton Down, 105, 595
Portsdown, 105
Portsmouth, 200, 227, 230, 259, 304, 307, 310, 313, 315
Portsmouth Historic Dockyard, 282
Portugal, 165
Poseidon missile, 132
Post-Soviet, 415
Pounds sterling, 412
Pound sterling, 188
Power projection, 6, 447
Precision-guided munition, 98
Predannack Airfield, 304

Pre-emptive nuclear strike, 143
Preobrazhensky Regiment, 284
President of the United States, 116
Pressurised water reactor, 126
Preston, Lancashire, 312
Prestwick, 304
Price Barracks, 108, 424
Prime Minister, 93, 144
Prime Minister of Canada, 117
Prime Minister of the United Kingdom, 7, 116, 586
Prince Andrew, Duke of York, 237, 255, 410
Prince Frederick, Duke of York and Albany, 408, 409
Prince Harry, 410
Prince Harry, Duke of Sussex, 257, 273
Prince of Wales Building, 110
Prince of Wales Division, 440
Prince Philip, Duke of Edinburgh, 158, 197
Princess Marys Royal Air Force Nursing Service, 455
Princess of Waless Royal Regiment, 287, 332, 360, 393, 401
Princess Royal Barracks, Deepcut, 434
Prince William, 410
Prince William of Gloucester Barracks, 435
Privateer, 27, 36, 38, 165
Private finance initiative, 160, 380, 454, 579, 594
Private (rank), 263, 360
Prize rules, 179
Project Alberta, 117
Project E, 96, 127, 451
Project Emily, 128
Propeller, 52
Property portfolio, 198
Protect and Survive, 139
Protectorate, 327, 349
Protestant, 79
Proton, 115
Provisional IRA campaign 1969–1997, 80
Provisional Irish Republican Army, 80, 332, 333
Prussia, 67, 330
Public Accounts Committee (United Kingdom), 596
Public domain, 87
Public duties, 390, 393
Public information film, 139
Public Record Office of Northern Ireland, 623
Pubs, 320
Puckpool, 313
Pump-action shotgun, 367
Punitive expedition, 39
Punta Cana, 567
PWR1, 127

Pyongyang, 96
Python Minefield Breaching System, 339, 378

Qaboos bin Said al Said, 410
Qatar, 3, 155, 480, 505, 506
QinetiQ, 311, 495–497, 501, 504, 596
Qinetiq Zephyr, 560, 574
Qing dynasty, 177
Quartermaster General, 63
Quebec, 170
Quebec Agreement, 116
Quebec Conference, 1943, 116
Queen Alexandras Royal Army Nursing Corps, 344, 360, 398
Queen Alexandras Royal Naval Nursing Service, 21, 159, 210, 228, 238, 258, 290
Queen Elizabeth Barracks, Strensall, 436
Queen Elizabeth class aircraft carrier, 245, 569
Queen Elizabeth-class aircraft carrier, 13, 50, 155, 185, 187, 188, 192, 201, 215, 249
Queen Elizabeth II, 207, 273, 594
Queens Colour, 478
Queens Colour Squadron, 499
Queens Division, 344, 390, 393, 440
Queens Gate Terrace, 313
Queens Guard, 388
Queens Gurkha Engineers, 110
Queens Gurkha Signals, 106, 110, 394
Queens Own Yeomanry, 401
Queens Royal Hussars, 392, 430
Queens Royal Lancers, 433
Quiberon Bay, 34
Quick Reaction Alert, 465, 495, 497, 499
Quota System (Royal Navy), 35

Radar, 115, 138
Radar Research Squadron, 536
Radio direction finder, 487
RAE Bedford, 105
RAE Farnborough, 105
RAF, 372, 567
RAF Air Command, 15, 455, 498, 501, 592
RAF Air Defence Radar Museum, 499
RAF Air Support Command, 487
RAF Akrotiri, 96, 109, 154, 452, 458, 468, 480, 506, 566
RAF Alconbury, 502, 503
RAF Aldergrove, 107
RAF Aldermaston, 105, 139
RAF Al Udeid, 12, 155
RAF Army Cooperation Command, 485, 488
RAF Ascension, 154
RAF Ascension Island, 11, 97, 153, 447, 452, 481, 506
RAF Balloon Command, 486
RAF Barford St John, 503

RAF Barkston Heath, 251, 459, 496
RAF Barnham, 121, 496
RAF battle honours, 458
RAF Belize, 343
RAF Benbecula, 496
RAF Benson, 456, 468, 494, 496, 532, 535
RAF Bircham Newton, 485
RAF Bomber Command, 91, 450, 482, 483, 485, 489
RAF Boscombe Down, 105, 534
RAF Boulmer, 456, 495, 496, 499, 500
RAF Brize Norton, 107, 137, 456, 458, 470, 494, 496, 501, 566, 574, 575
RAF Buchan, 496
RAF Butterworth, 96, 451
RAF Catterick, 435
RAF Centre of Aviation Medicine, 498
RAF Coastal Command, 91, 241, 484, 487, 490, 492
RAF Colerne, 532, 534
RAF College Cranwell, 462, 497
RAF Coningsby, 456, 458, 465, 494, 497, 534, 571
RAF Cosford, 457, 495, 497, 533, 535
RAF Cranwell, 456, 457, 459, 465, 494–497, 535, 580
RAF Croughton, 502, 503
RAF Digby, 497
RAF Donna Nook, 505
RAF Eagle Squadrons, 519, 628
RAF Eastern Air Command, 492
RAF Eastleigh, 96, 452
RAF Episkopi, 109
RAF Fairford, 503, 504
RAF Faldingworth, 121
RAF Far East Air Force, 96, 451
RAF Feltwell, 504
RAF Ferry Command, 487
RAF Fighter Command, 91, 241, 482, 483, 486–488
RAF Flowerdown, 311
RAF Flying Training Command, 485–487
RAF Force Protection Force Headquarters, 494, 498
RAF Fylingdales, 137, 456, 457, 497
RAF Germany, 5, 96, 127, 451
RAF Gibraltar, 154, 447, 480, 507
RAF Greenham Common, 137
RAF Hal Far, 96, 452
RAF Halton, 457, 462, 465, 497
RAF Harrier II, 99
RAF Henlow, 498
RAF High Wycombe, 455, 457, 498
RAF Holbeach, 505
RAF Home Command, 488
RAF Honington, 494, 496, 498

RAF Hullavington, 533
RAF Intelligence, 464
RAF Iraq Command, 91, 448
RAF Keevil, 498
RAF Kenley, 533
RAF Kinloss, 498
RAF Kirknewton, 498, 534
RAF Lakenheath, 137, 504
RAF Leeming, 107, 456, 458, 494, 498, 532, 535
RAF Legal Branch, 465
RAF Leuchars, 535
RAF Linton-on-Ouse, 456, 457, 459, 499, 501, 533, 535, 580
RAF Little Rissington, 499, 534
RAF Lossiemouth, 456, 458, 465, 466, 494, 499, 571, 577
RAF Luqa, 96, 452
RAF Machrihanish, 129
RAF Maintenance Command, 486, 489
RAF Marham, 128, 246, 251, 456, 458, 465, 466, 494, 499, 506, 570
RAF Medical Branch, 464
RAF Medical Services, 455
RAF Memorial, 101, 452
RAF Menwith Hill, 504
RAF Merryfield, 487
RAF Mildenhall, 502, 504
RAF Molesworth, 137, 502–504
RAF Mona, 499
RAF Mount Batten, 484
RAF Mount Pleasant, 98, 109, 154, 201, 304, 343, 447, 452, 460, 481, 507, 534, 567
RAF munitions storage during World War II, 486
RAF Neatishead, 499, 501
RAF Nicosia, 96, 452
RAF Northolt, 456, 470, 480, 499, 500
RAF Oakington, 487
RAF Odiham, 396, 456, 468, 494, 500
RAF officer ranks, 2, 455
RAF other ranks, 2, 455
RAF Pembrey, 505
RAF Police, 15, 498
RAF Ramat David, 94
RAF Regiment, 19, 98, 100, 108, 109, 394, 455, 461, 463, 464, 496, 498
RAF Reserve Command, 485, 487, 488
RAF roundel, 542
RAF Saxa Vord, 500
RAF Scampton, 456, 479, 500
RAF Search and Rescue, 454
RAF Sek Kong, 111
RAF Shawbury, 251, 456, 457, 459, 477, 497, 500, 501
RAF Signals Command, 489

RAF Spadeadam, 456, 505
RAF St Mawgan, 129, 457, 500
RAF Strike Command, 482, 484, 486, 487, 489
RAF Support Command, 489
RAF Syerston, 459, 500, 534, 580
RAF Tain, 505
RAF Technical Training Command, 484, 485
RAF Tengah, 96, 451
RAF Ternhill, 501, 533
RAF Topcliffe, 432, 501, 534
RAF Tornado GR1, 96, 99, 451
RAF Training Command, 484, 485, 493
RAF Transport Command, 482, 486, 487, 489, 492
RAF Trimingham, 501
RAF Troodos, 109, 154, 428, 507
RAF Uxbridge, 93
RAF Valley, 456, 457, 459, 473, 477, 494, 499, 501, 580
RAF Volunteer Reserve, 455
RAF Waddington, 456, 458, 467, 479, 494, 501
RAF Welford, 504
RAF West Freugh, 501
RAF Weston-on-the-Green, 501
RAF Wethersfield, 136
RAF Wittering, 456, 457, 459, 486, 494, 501, 532–534, 580
RAF Woodbridge, 436
RAF Woodvale, 502, 532, 533, 535
RAF Worthy Down, 312
RAF Wroughton, 316
RAF Wyton, 502
Raid on the Medway, 32, 166, 167
Raincoat, 360
Ralph Richardson, 253
Ramsgate, 311
Ranks and insignia of NATO, 586
Ranks and insignia of NATO navies officers, 202
Rapid Reaction Force, 193, 259
Rapier (missile), 108, 109, 338, 377
Raymond Lygo, 255
Raytheon Sentinel, 101, 446, 467, 501, 561, 577
Reach for the Sky, 254
Reactive armour, 370
Reading, 139
Rear admiral, 198
Rear-Admiral, 255
Rear admiral (Royal Navy), 108, 109, 203, 234, 243
Rear Admiral Submarines, 199, 229, 230
Recognized Air Picture, 495
Reconnaissance vehicle, 375

Recruiting Act 1778, 406
Recruiting Act 1779, 406
Recruitment in the British Army, 58, 322, 364, 386, 404, **404**
Recruit training, 437
Red Arrows, 101, 452, 453, 500
Red Beard, 128, 130
Red Beard (nuclear weapon), 121, 127
Red coat (British army), 65
Red Duster (missile), 128
Red Ensign, 29
Redford Barracks, 436
Red Sea, 295
Red Snow, 129
Ref a, 337
Ref b, 337
Refresher Flying Squadron, 536
Refresher Flying Training School, 559
Regency of Algiers, 176
Regents Park Barracks, 436
Regiment, 345, 387
Regimental system, 329
Regional Command (British Army), 388
Regional Training Centre, 441
Regular Reserve (United Kingdom), 2, 8, 187, 336, 461, 599, 600, 615, 627
Remington 870, 367
Republic F-84F Thunderstreak, 136
Republic F-84 Thunderjet, 96
Republic of Genoa, 162
Republic of Ireland, 18, 420, 421
Republic of Korea, 102
Republic of Korea Air Force, 101
Reserve Command Communication Squadron, 538
Reserved occupation, 73
Reserve Flying School, Brough, 559
Reserve Flying School, Coventry, 559
Reserve Flying School, Filton, 559
Reserve Flying School, Hamble, 559
Reserve Flying School, Renfrew, 559
Reserve Flying School, Stag Lane, 559
Reserve Forces and Cadets Association, 593
Reserve Training Squadron, 536
Resolute Support Mission, 342, 481
Resolution-class submarine, 182
Response Force Task Group, 196
Restoration, 325
Restoration (1660), 325
Restoration (England), 59, 322, 325
Retail Price Index, 603
Reuters, 615
RFA Argus (A135), 17
RFA Diligence (A132), 295
RFA Mounts Bay (L3008), 291, 299
RFA Tidespring (A136), 294

Rheinmetall MAN Military Vehicles (RMMV) HX range of tactical trucks, 380
Rhineland, 265
Rhode Island, 34
Rhodesia, 53
Rhodesian Central Flying School, 550
Rhuddlan, 24
RIAT, 195, 567
Richard Attenborough, 208
Richard Bell Davies, 252, 253
Richard Dannatt, Baron Dannatt, 589
Richard Fitch, 232
Richard FitzAlan, 10th Earl of Arundel, 26
Richard Garwood, 587
Richard G. Hewlett, 149
Richard Holmes (military historian), 362
Richard II of England, 26
Richard Nugee, 587
Richard Thomas (Royal Navy officer), 232
Richborough, 314
Rifle green, 361
Rigid-hulled inflatable boat, 278
Rigid Raider, 270
Risley, Warrington, 312
River-class patrol vessel, 189, 218
River Clyde, 163
River Forth, 164
River Hamble, 26, 311
River Tay, 164
RMB Chivenor, 306
RM Chivenor, 274
RM Condor, 273, 306
RM Poole, 274, 306
RMS Lancastria, 46, 180
RM Tamar, 274
RNAD Broughton Moor, 316
RNAD Coulport, 131, 268, 305
RNAD Crombie, 316
RNAD Dean Hill, 316
RNAD Gosport, 316
RNAD Trecwn, 316
RNAS Culdrose, 303
RNAS Culdrose (HMS Seahawk), 244, 251, 304, 307, 465
RNAS Donibristle, 308, 310
RNAS Lee-on-Solent (HMS Daedalus), 308, 316
RNAS Lossiemouth (HMS Fulmar), 308
RNAS Merryfield, 304
RNAS Portland (HMS Osprey), 244, 308
RNAS Predannack, 533
RNAS Prestwick, 243
RNAS Worthy Down, 309
RNAS Yeovilton, 243, 268, 274, 303, 306, 307
RNAS Yeovilton (HMS Heron), 245, 246, 251, 252, 304, 307

RNH Bighi, 309
RNH Mtarfa, 309
RNH Simons Town, South Africa, 309
RNSD Almondbank, 316
RNSD Copenacre, 316
RNSD Coventry, 316
RNSD Eaglescliffe, 316
RNSD Lathalmond, 316
RNSD Llangennech, 316
RNSD Woolston, 316
RNVR, 312
Robert Barton of Over Barnton, 164
Robert Blake (admiral), 31
Robert Gerken, 232
Robert I of Scotland, 163
Robert K. Massie, 55, 602
Robert Magowan, 198
Robert McNamara, 131
Robert Ross (general), 39
Robert Ross (Royal Marines officer), 260
Robertson Barracks, Norfolk, 436
Robert Tarrant, 234
Robert the Bruce, 29, 163
Robert Woodard, 255
Robin Trower Hogg, 232
Rocket artillery, 376
Rockwell B-1 Lancer, 503
ROF Burghfield, 105, 139
ROF Cardiff, 105, 139
ROF Risley, 119
Rogers Rangers, 66
Rolls-Royce, 574
Rolls-Royce Holdings, 2, 566
Rolls-Royce Limited, 127
Roman numeral, 509
Ronald Cuthbert Hay, 241
Ronald W. Clark, 147
Rosneath, 312–314
Ross-shire, 313
Rosyth, 305, 307, 310
Rosyth Dockyard, 199, 303, 305, 308
Rotary Wing Test Squadron, 496
Roundel, 237
Roundhead, 60
Routledge, 256, 481
Rowland Hill, 1st Viscount Hill, 408
Royal Aero Club, 239
Royal Aircraft Establishment, 105
Royal Air Force, 1, 2, 59, 89, 107–109, 111, 180, 192, 199, 239, 240, 245, 249, 252, 270, 339, 344, 371, 387, **445**, 454, 455, 494, 496, 509, 542, 543, 566, 569, 580, 584, 586, 607
Royal Air Force Air Cadets, 497, 534
Royal Air Force and Army Co-operation School, 550

Royal Air Force and Navy Co-operation School, 550
Royal Air Force (Belgian) Training School, 550
Royal Air Force Centre for Air Power Studies, 465
Royal Air Force Chaplains Branch, 465
Royal Air Force College Air Squadron, 536
Royal Air Force College Service Flying Training School, 559
Royal Air Force Ensign, 446, 478
Royal Air Force Germany, 482
Royal Air Force Germany Communication Squadron, 538
Royal Air Force March Past, 445
Royal Air Force Memorial, 90, 594
Royal Air Force (Middle East) Central Gunnery School, 550
Royal Air Force (Middle East) Gunnery School, 550
Royal Air Force Museum, 592
Royal Air Force Museum Cosford, 497
Royal Air Force Police, 455, 498
Royal Air Force Regiment, 15, 19
Royal Air Force School, India, 550
Royal Air Force School of Army Co-operation, 550
Royal Air Force School of Aviation Medicine, 550
Royal Air Force School of Catering, 550
Royal Air Force station, 456
Royal Anglian Regiment, 77, 334, 360, 393, 401, 434
Royal Armament Research and Development Establishment, 105
Royal Armoured Corps, 15, 73, 344, 356, 375, 390, 438–440
Royal Army Chaplains Department, 344, 400
Royal Army Dental Corps, 344, 398
Royal Army Educational Corps, 399
Royal Army Medical Corps, 15, 155, 344, 355, 356, 398, 434, 438–440
Royal Army Ordnance Corps, 399
Royal Army Pay Corps, 399
Royal Army Physical Training Corps, 344, 400, 434
Royal Army Veterinary Corps, 111, 344, 398
Royal Artillery, 14, 16, 63, 98, 260, 268, 299, 344, 345, 355, 356, 375, 395, 410, 438, 440
Royal Artillery Barracks, 436
Royal Australian Air Force, 93, 96, 448, 523
Royal Australian Navy, 44, 188, 202
Royal Auxiliary Air Force, 16, 455, 461, 524, 581
Royal Bermuda Regiment, 343, 350, 425
Royal Canadian Air Force, 92, 448, 483, 522

Royal Canadian Navy, 44
Royal Corps of Signals, 339, 344, 355, 356, 390, 396, 433, 439, 440
Royal Dragoon Guards, 392, 432
Royal Egyptian Air Force, 94
Royal Electrical and Mechanical Engineers, 111, 344, 355, 356, 375, 398, 435, 436, 438, 440
Royal Engineers, 14, 63, 71, 89, 155, 268, 343, 344, 355, 356, 358, 395, 433, 435, 438, 440
Royal Family, 410
Royal Fleet Auxiliary, 16, 22, 49, 52, 159, 160, 184, 188, 210, 211, 215, 228, 238, 250, 258, 290, 371, 384
Royal Fleet Reserve, 187
Royal Flying Corps, 59, 89, 180, 192, 239, 330, 448, 479, 509
Royal Flying Corps Squadron, 535
Royal Gibraltar Regiment, 12, 155, 343, 350, 393, 394, 426
Royal Gurkha Rifles, 82, 154, 343, 344, 361, 394, 427
Royal Hellenic Air Force, 521
Royal Highland Fusiliers, 434
Royal Highness, 237
Royal Hong Kong Auxiliary Air Force, 110, 111
Royal Hong Kong Regiment, 111
Royal Horse Artillery, 391, 395
Royal Hospital Chelsea, 593
Royal Hospital Haslar, 309
Royal Household, 587
Royal International Air Tattoo, 480, 503
Royal Irish Rangers, 77
Royal Irish Regiment (1992), 18, 84, 393, 401, 433, 435, 440
Royal Irish Rifles, 5
Royalist, 174
Royal Italian Army during World War II, 75
Royal Lancers, 392
Royal Logistic Corps, 81, 299, 344, 345, 355–357, 384, 397, 434–436, 438–441
Royal Marine Commando, 246
Royal Marines, 1, 2, 21, 81, 107, 154, 159, 160, 185, 186, 193, 198, 199, 203, 205, 210, 211, 221, 228, 238, 241, 247, 249, 255, **257**, 258, 285–287, 290, 293, 332, 338, 343, 468
Royal Marines Armoured Support Group, 274
Royal Marines Band Service, 276
Royal Marines Base Chivenor, 306
Royal Marines Museum, 282, 593
Royal Marines other ranks, 285
Royal Marines Police, 268

Royal Marines Reserve, 21, 159, 186, 210, 228, 238, 257, 258, 268, 269, 290
Royal Military Academy Sandhurst, 355, 400, 424, 438, 442
Royal Military Academy, Woolwich, 408
Royal Military Police, 111, 344, 361, 366, 367, 399, 433, 434, 440
Royal Military School of Music, 440
Royal Monmouthshire Royal Engineers, 402
Royal Montserrat Defence Force, 12, 155, 350
Royal Naval Air Service, 89, 180, 237, 239, 448, 509
Royal Naval Air Service Gunnery School, 550
Royal Naval Armaments Depot, 305
Royal Naval College, Greenwich, 314
Royal Naval Commandos, 310
Royal Naval Division, 263
Royal Naval Dockyard, Bermuda, 38
Royal Naval Engineering College, 315
Royal Naval Engineers, 186
Royal Naval Fighter Squadron, 536
Royal Naval Hospital Gibraltar, 309
Royal Naval Hospital (Hong Kong), 309
Royal Naval Patrol Service, 47
Royal Naval Reserve, 21, 159, 186, 210, 228, 238, 247, 258, 290, 302, 307
Royal Navy, 1, 2, 21, 22, 28, 30, 58, 66, 108, 109, 111, **157**, 159, 203, 205, 210, 211, 227, 228, 237–239, 254, 255, 257, 258, 262, 276, 279, 290, 299, 302, 306, 317, 327, 344, 371, 372, 387, 405, 447, 468, 509, 530, 569, 584, 586
Royal Navy Chaplaincy Service, 21, 159, 210, 228, 238, 258, 290
Royal Navy Dockyards, 199
Royal Navy Elementary Flying Training School, 559
Royal Navy Fleet Flagship, 619
Royal Navy Historic Flight, 252
Royal Navy Medical Service, 21, 159, 210, 228, 238, 258, 290
Royal Navy officer rank insignia, 2, 21, 159, 202, 210, 228, 238, 258, 290
Royal Navy of Oman, 298
Royal Navy Police, 21, 159, 210, 228, 238, 258, 290
Royal Navy ratings rank insignia, 2, 21, 159, 205, 210, 228, 238, 258, 290
Royal Navy Submarine Museum, 593
Royal Navy Submarine Service, 10, 13, 21, 159, 210, 227, 228, 238, 258, 290
Royal Navy Surface Fleet, 21, 159, 210, **227**, 228, 238, 258, 290
Royal Navy uniform, 186
Royal Netherlands Air Force, 520
Royal Netherlands Navy, 202

Royal New Zealand Air Force, 524
Royal New Zealand Navy, 44
Royal Norwegian Navy, 293
Royal Ordnance Factory, 119, 139
Royal Prerogative in the United Kingdom, 7
Royal Radar Establishment, 311
Royal Regiment of Artillery, 439
Royal Regiment of Foot, 325
Royal Regiment of Fusiliers, 335, 393, 401
Royal Regiment of Scotland, 389, 393, 401, 440
Royal Research Ship, 223, 291
Royal Rhodesian Air Force, 517
Royal School of Artillery, 355, 436, 440
Royal School of Military Engineering, 355, 395, 433, 434, 440
Royal School of Signals, 440, 460
Royal Scots, 61
Royal Scots Army, 325
Royal Scots Borderers, 434
Royal Scots Dragoon Guards, 360, 392
Royal Scots Greys, 73
Royal Scots Navy, 22, 167
Royal Signals, 71, 432, 434, 438
Royal Signals and Radar Establishment, 105, 311
Royal Swedish Navy, 202
Royal Tank Regiment, 71, 73, 330, 360, 376, 392
Royal Ulster Constabulary, 79, 80, 332, 333
Royal United Services Institute, 9
Royal Victorian Order, 255
Royal Welsh, 393, 401, 435
Royal Wessex Yeomanry, 375, 401
Royal West African Frontier Force, 418
Royal Yeomanry, 401
RRH Benbecula, 496, 497
RRH Buchan, 496
RRH Portreath, 500
RRH Staxton Wold, 500
RRS Ernest Shackleton, 291
RRS James Clark Ross, 291
Rudolf Peierls, 115
Rudyard Kipling, 421
Rule, Britannia, 320
Rule of the Major-Generals, 61
Rules of engagement, 179
Russia, 176, 466
Russia and weapons of mass destruction, 114
Russian aircraft carrier Admiral Kuznetsov, 294
Russian Air Force, 452
Russian Civil War, 72
Russian Empire, 4, 327, 330
Russo-Turkish War (1877–1878), 40
Ruttonjee Hospital, 309
Ryde, 313
Rye, East Sussex, 312

S10 NBC Respirator, 371
S1850M, 188
S5W, 126
SA80, 85, 337, 342, 364, 366, 373, 374
Saab JAS 39 Gripen, 564
SACEUR, 127
Saddam Hussein, 83
Sailor, 320
Sailor (TV series), 208
Saint Helena, Ascension and Tristan da Cunha, 506
Sale of commissions, 409
Salerno landings, 265
Salford, Greater Manchester, 314
Salisbury, 316
Salisbury Journal, 628
Salonika, 486
Salute, 318
SAM Laboratories, 117
SAMPSON, 188
Samuel Pepys, 32
San Carlos, Falkland Islands, 81
Sandown-class minehunter, 190, 219
Sandwich, Kent, 23
Sandy Woodward, 232
Sardinia, 171
Saudi Arabia, 98
Savoy, 171
Scandinavia, 167
ScanEagle, 158
Scapa Flow, 308, 312
SC Group, 382
Schneider Trophy, 91
School for Anti-Submarine Inshore Patrol Observers, 550
School for Marine Operational Pilots, 550
School for Wireless Operators, 550
School of Aerial Co-operation with Coastal Artillery, 550
School of Aerial Fighting and Bomb Dropping, 550
School of Aerial Fighting (Canada), 550
School of Aerial Fighting, Heliopolis, 550
School of Aerial Gunnery, Aboukir, 551
School of Aerial Gunnery and Bombing, 550
School of Aerial Gunnery, (Canada), 550
School of Aerial Gunnery, Hythe, 551
School of Aerial Gunnery, Loch Doon, 551
School of Aerial Gunnery, Marske, 551
School of Aerial Gunnery, New Romney, 551
School of Aerial Gunnery, Turnberry, 551
School of Aerial Navigation, 551
School of Aerospace Battle Management, 496

School of Air Navigation, 551
School of Air Pilotage, 551
School of Air Sea Rescue, 551
School of Air Support, 551
School of Air Traffic Control, 551
School of Air Transport, 551
School of Army Co-operation, 551
School of Artillery Co-operation (Canada), 551
School of Aviation Medicine, 551
School of Control and Reporting, 551
School of Fighter Control, 551
School of General Reconnaissance, 551
School of Naval Co-operation, 551
School of Naval Co-operation and Aerial Navigation, 551
School of Photography, Maps and Reconnaissance, 551
School of Refresher Flying, 559
School of Special Flying (Canada), 559
School of Special Flying, Gosport, 559
Scientific Advisory Committee on the Medical Implications of Less-Lethal Weapons, 592
Scimitar-class patrol vessel, 221
Scorpio 45, 50, 185
Scotland, 22, 227, 267, 307, 405, 496–501, 505
Scots Greys, 63, 326
Scots Guards, 389, 393
Scottish and North Irish Yeomanry, 401
Scottish Command, 76, 388
Scottish Green Party, 142
Scottish Highlands, 64
Scottish National Party, 142
Scottish Reformation, 30
Scottish Socialist Party, 142
Scottish warship Margaret, 167
Scottish, Welsh and Irish Division, 344, 390, 393
Scramble (magazine), 601
Scrambling (military), 452
Screw propeller, 40
Scurvy, 320
Sea Cadets, 206
Sea Dogs, 28
Seaforth Highlanders, 331
Sea Harrier, 97, 245, 452, 569
Sea Harriers, 183, 184
SEAL Delivery Vehicle, 270
Seaplane Squadron, Alexandria, 536
Seaplane Squadron, Port Said, 536
Seaplane Training Squadron, 536
Sea power, 59
Search and Rescue, 109, 243, 246, 249
Sea Skua, 49, 249
Seaslug (missile), 128

Seaview, Isle of Wight, 315
Second Anglo-Afghan War, 4
Second Anglo-Dutch War, 32, 52, 166
Second Battle of El Alamein, 331
Second Boer War, 327, 420
Second English Civil War, 60
Second Italo-Abyssinian War, 45
Second Lieutenant, 442
Second London Naval Treaty, 45, 179
Second Opium War, 40, 53, 177, 262, 327
Second Sea Lord, 13, 158, 198, 199
Second Wilson ministry (United Kingdom), 132
Second World War, 89, 160, 241, 264, 405, 415, 448, 542
Secretarial Branch Training School, 551
Secretary of State for Air, 585
Secretary of State for Defence, 1, 3, 7, 8, 125, 145, 160, 198, 574, 583, 585, 586, 590
Secretary of State for Foreign and Commonwealth Affairs, 119, 145
Secretary of State for War, 413, 585
Secretary of State for War and the Colonies, 63
Secretary of State of the United States, 119
Section (military unit), 347
Selection and Training in the British Army, **437**
Self-denying Ordinance, 324
Self-governing colony, 349
Self-propelled artillery, 377
Sembawang, 12, 155, 305
Semi-automatic pistol, 365
Semi-automatic shotgun, 367
Sentry Training Squadron, 536
September 11, 2001 attacks, 84
September 11 attacks, 6
Serco, 140
Serco Marine Services, 22, 159, 210, 211, 228, 238, 258, 290
Sergeant, 205, 287, 360
Seria, 106, 427
Service Ferry Squadron, 536
Service Ferry Training Squadron, 536
Service Prosecuting Authority, 593
Seven Years War, 2, 4, 34, 65, 172, 259, 323, 327, 347, 420
Sexual orientation and the military of the United Kingdom, 19
SFOR, 84
Sharkey Ward, 255
Shatt al-Arab, 50
Sheerness, 315
Sheerness Dockyard, 308
Sheffield, 486
Shetland, 312, 500
Ship commissioning, 127, 170
Ship money, 29

Ship of the line, 36, 211
Ship prefix, 211
Ships Names and Badges Committee, 317
Shoreham-by-Sea, 312
Shorncliffe Army Camp, 436
Shorncliffe System, 408
Short Brothers, 253
Shorts Tucano, 580
Shorts Tucano T.1, 499
Short Tucano, 446, 456, 472, 473, 501, 562
Short Tucano T1, 564
Shotley, Suffolk, 312
Shrapnel shell, 70
Shropshire, 497, 500, 501
Sicily, 33, 171
Sick and Hurt Board, 173
Siege of Saint-Martin-de-Ré (1627), 169
Siege of Sevastopol (1854–1855), 40
Siege of Tsingtao, 70
Siege of Yorktown, 68
Sierra Leone, 53, 84, 279, 342, 431
Sierra Leone Civil War, 193, 259
SIGINT, 314
Signals Command Development Squadron, 536
Signals intelligence, 11, 108, 109, 154, 447, 467, 470, 503, 504, 507, 561, 576
Signals Squadron, 536
SIG Sauer P226, 365
Sikorsky S-92, 454
Silverplate, 136
Simon & Schuster, 362
Simons Town, 309
Simons Town Dockyard, South Africa, 308
Simon Williams (Royal Navy officer), 199
Singapore, 3, 155, 305
Singapore Squadron, 535
Single-ship action, 37
Single Source Regulations Office, 592
Sinking of Prince of Wales and Repulse, 287
Sink the Bismarck, 254
Sir John Moore Barracks, 436
Sir Kenneth Mackenzie Douglas, 1st Baronet, 408
Sir Thomas Inskip, 92, 240
Si vis pacem, para bellum, 158
Skanska, 594
Skipjack-class submarine, 126
Skybolt missile, 130
Slang, 320
Slavery, 165
Slave trade, 177
Slingsby T67 Firefly, 111
Slobodan Milošević, 84
Small arms, 364
Small Arms School Corps, 344, 400
Snape, Suffolk, 22

Snatch Land Rover, 376
Snider–Enfield, 85
Sniper rifle, 367
Solent, 23
Solidarity (Scotland), 142
Somalia, 295
Somaliland campaign (1920), 91
Somerset, 17, 304
Somme Barracks, 436
South Africa, 309, 410
South Africa and weapons of mass destruction, 114
Southampton, 312, 314, 315
Southampton University Air Squadron, 533
South Atlantic, 81, 97, 452
South Australia, 134, 135
South Ayrshire, 314
South China Sea, 177
Southeast Asia Communication Squadron, 539
Southeast Asia (Internal Air Service) Squadron, 536
South-East Asian theatre of World War II, 53, 74, 331
Southeastern Area Flying Instructors School, 559
Southend, 315
Southern Command (United Kingdom), 76, 388
Southern Communication Squadron, 539
South Georgia Island, 292
South Queensferry, 312
Southwestern Area Flying Instructors School, 559
Southwick, Hampshire, 311
Southwick House, 440
Sovereign Base Areas, 343
Sovereign Base Areas of Akrotiri and Dhekelia, 506
Soviet Navy, 49
Soviet Union, 6, 96, 116, 160, 451, 452, 584
Spain, 3
Spanish Armada, 28, 164, 165
Spanish Empire, 27
Spanish Netherlands, 28, 165
SPEAR 3, 580
Spearfish torpedo, 190
Special Air Service, 7, 75, 81, 107, 344, 347, 361, 367, 383, 394, 563
Special Boat Service, 21, 82, 107, 159, 193, 210, 228, 238, 258, 267, 268, 274, 276, 281, 290, 394
Special Communication Squadron, 539
Special Forces, 80, 276, 347, 394
Special Forces Support Group, 82, 193, 259, 347, 394
Special Installation Squadron, 536

Specialised Low Attack Instructors School, 551
Specialised Low Attack Instructors School (India), 551
Special operations, 339
Special Reconnaissance Regiment, 82, 344, 347, 394
Special Reconnaissance Unit, 107
Special Relationship, 114, 117
Special Service Brigade, 265
Special Transport Squadron, 536
Spithead, 36
Spithead and Nore mutinies, 174
Spithead and Nore mutinies (1797), 36
Sponsored Reserves, 2, 599, 600
Springfields, 119
Sputnik 1, 126
Sputnik crisis, 126
Squad automatic weapon, 366
Squadron, 536
Squadron (aviation), 15, 509
Squadron (cavalry), 347
Squadron Leader, 19, 460
Square Leg, 138
SS Great Britain, 41
SSN (hull classification symbol), 182, 190, 295
S Squadron, 537
Stabilisation Force in Bosnia and Herzegovina, 332
Stable belt, 360
Staff Navigators School (Middle East), 551
Staff Sergeant, 360
Standing army, 59, 67, 323, 330
Standing NATO Maritime Group 1, 293
Standing NATO Maritime Group 2, 298
Standing NATO Mine Countermeasures Group 1, 298
Standing NATO Mine Countermeasures Group 2, 298
Standing Royal Navy deployments, 21, 159, 160, 188, 196, 210, 227, 228, 238, 258, 290, **290**
St. Andrews and Dundee Universities Air Squadron, 533
St. Andrews University Air Squadron, 533
Stanley Baldwin, 584
Stanley, Falkland Islands, 81, 109, 304
Stanley Fort, 110
Stanley Orr, 241
Stan Openshaw, 150
Starstreak, 370
Starstreak (missile), 338, 377
State of Israel, 78
Status of forces agreement, 502
Stavanger, 503
Stay-behind, 107
Steam catapult, 243

Steam Gun Boat, 309
Steam power, 40
Steam ship, 317
Steam turbine, 43, 53
St Enochs Hotel, 314
Stephen Hillier, 445, 586
Stephen Lovegrove, 583, 588
Stephen R. Meyer (Royal Navy officer), 233
Stern Gang, 78
Stevedore, 73
St George Barracks, Gosport, 314
St Georges Barracks, North Luffenham, 436
St. Georges, Bermuda, 38
Stirling Lines, 397
St Magnus Cathedral, 169
Stockholm International Peace Research Institute, 9
Stone frigate, 302
Stonehouse Barracks, 274, 275
Stonehouse, Plymouth, 306
Storm Shadow, 465, 570, 580
Stornoway, 313
STOVL, 245, 569
Strachur, 313
Strategic Air Command, 119, 121, 136
Strategic airlift, 447
Strategic bomber, 95, 128, 450, 451
Strategic bombing, 92, 448, 450
Strategic Defence and Security Review 2010, 154, 188, 245, 297, 336, 343, 387, 452, 466, 588
Strategic Defence and Security Review 2015, 9, 245, 336, 385, 387, 392, 466, 475, 569, 570, 574, 575, 577, 580, 589
Strategic Defence Review, 49, 82, 142, 387, 452, 588
Strike aircraft, 447
Strike Command Bombing School, 551
Strike Command Communication Squadron, 539
Structure of the British Armed Forces in 1989, **105**
Structure of the British Army, 58, 322, 363, 386, **386**, 404
Stuart Andrew, 586
Stuart Peach, 587
Subaltern, 442
Subcritical testing, 135
Sub-Lieutenant, 203
Submachine gun, 367
Submarine, 4, 22, 43, 49, 53, 114, 190
Submarine Command Course, 208
Submarine-launched ballistic missile, 10
Submarine-launched ballistic missiles, 131
Submarines, 158, 184, 615
Suez Canal, 40, 79

Suez Canal Zone, 79
Suez Crisis, 5, 53, 96, 125, 246, 267, 332, 452
Suez War, 79
Suffolk, 121, 310, 312, 496, 498, 504
Sumatra, 241
Supercarrier, 13, 187
Supermarine, 309
Supermarine Seafire, 254
Supermarine Spitfire, 94, 449, 562
Supermarine Spitfire (Griffon powered variants), 95
Supermarine Spitfire (late Merlin powered variants), 94
Supermarine Walrus, 240
Superpower, 76, 160
Supply Officer, 186, 255
Support Command (United Kingdom), 388, 392
Suppressor, 367
Supreme Commanders Headquarters (Air) Communication Squadron, 539
Supreme Headquarters Allied Expeditionary Force (RAF) Communication Squadron, 539
Surbiton, 486
Surface combatant, 227
Surface-to-air missile, 128, 377
Surrey, 310, 486
Surveillance aircraft, 158, 238, 446
Survey ships, 158
Survey vessel, 211
SUSAT, 337, 365, 366
Sussex, 23, 312, 314
Sutton Hoo, 22
Sveaborg, 40
Sweden, 370
Swein Forkbeard, 24
Swimmer Delivery Vehicle, 270
Swindon, 316
Switzerland, 365, 369, 381
Syria, 7, 467

Tactical Air Force (Burma) Communication Squadron, 539
Tactical airlift, 447
Tactical Imagery-Intelligence Wing, 499
Tactical nuclear weapon, 115
Tactical recognition flash, 360
Tadeusz Kościuszko, 519
Taliban, 84, 99, 334
Tangier Regiment, 61
Tank, 330
Taunton, 17, 268, 273, 306
Tawe Division, 307
Tay Division, 307
Technical Group RAF, 493

Teesside, 316
Telecommunications Research Establishment, 311
Teller-Ulam, 126
Temperate, 373
Tempest (experimental fighter), 574
Template:British Army, 58, 322, 364, 387, 405
Template:British Army Arms, 344
Template:Nuclear weapons, 114
Template:Politics of the United Kingdom, 584
Template:RAF, 455
Template:Royal Navy, 22, 159, 210, 228, 239, 258, 290
Template:Royal Navy ship types, 302
Template talk:British Army, 58, 322, 364, 387, 405
Template talk:British Army Arms, 344
Template talk:Nuclear weapons, 114
Template talk:Politics of the United Kingdom, 584
Template talk:RAF, 455
Template talk:Royal Navy, 22, 159, 210, 228, 239, 258, 290
Template talk:Royal Navy ship types, 302
Temporary Air Observers School, 551
Ten Year Rule, 71
Terrier Armoured Digger, 339, 379
Territorial Army (United Kingdom), 411, 596
Territorial Force, 70, 329, 336
Terrorism, 589
Test pilot, 254
Test pilots, 255
Test Pilots School, 551
Thales, 572
Thales Group, 566
Thales Watchkeeper WK450, 339, 383, 564
Thames, 101, 452
The 1850s Naval Arms Race, 41
The Allied attack, 265
Theater (warfare), 74
The Barracks, Brecon, 436
The Beatles, 255
The Cameronians (Scottish Rifles), 77
The Canadas, 327
The Cenotaph, Whitehall, 356
The Crown, 323
The Daily Telegraph, 617
The Economist, 141
The Gloucestershire Regiment, 77
The Great Game, 4
The Great Rapprochement, 43
The Guardian, 361, 362, 595, 606
The Lancaster House Treaties (2010), 12, 588
The Light Infantry, 77
The Maritimes, 327
The Navy Lark, 208

The Nigeria Regiment, 418
Theobald Wolfe Tone, 328
The Officers Advanced Training School, 551
The Parachute Regiment (United Kingdom), 15
The Protectorate, 325
The Queens Regiment, 77
The Recruiting Officer, 405
Theresa May, 145
The Rifles, 344, 361, 394, 401, 430, 440
Thermal Imaging System, 365
Thermonuclear weapon, 10, 121
The Royal Bermuda Regiment, 12, 155
The Royal Green Jackets, 77
The Royal Hampshire Regiment, 77
The Royal Irish Regiment (27th (Inniskilling) 83rd and 87th and Ulster Defence Regiment), 332
The Royal Regiment of Fusiliers, 77
The Senior Service, 318
The Ships Badges Committee, 317
The Somerset Light Infantry (Prince Alberts), 78
The Spy Who Loved Me (film), 207
The Staffordshire Regiment, 83
The Sunday Times, 466
The Troubles, 6, 332
The Troubles in Bessbrook, 332
The United Kingdom in the Napoleonic Wars, 52
The Venerable, 199
The World Set Free, 115
The York and Lancaster Regiment, 77
Thiepval Barracks, 436
Third Air Force, 136
Third Anglo-Dutch War, 52, 166
Third Churchill ministry, 122
Third Crusade, 25
Third Reich, 329
Thirteen Colonies, 173, 327
Thomas Cook Airlines, 567, 568
Thomas Fairfax, 324
Thomas Gage, 66
Thomas Gordon (Royal Scots Navy officer), 30
Thomas Sydney Beckwith, 408
Thomas Wolsey, 594
Thorkell the Tall, 24
Thorney Island (London), 107
Three-decker, 31
Tidworth Camp, 432–436
Tiger-class cruiser, 48, 182
Tighnabruaich, 312
Timeline of the British Army, 58, 322, 364, 386, 404
Timeline of the Royal Air Force, 455
Tinian, 117
Tipner, 313

Titan, 378
Tizard Committee, 115
Tizard Mission, 116
TNT Airways, 470
TNT equivalent, 113
Toast (honor), 319
Tobias Ellwood, 586
Tokyo, 314
Tomahawk (missile), 191
Tomcar, 381
Tom Hunter (VC), 267
Tommy Sheridan, 142
Tomorrow Never Dies, 207
Tonne, 211
Tonnes, 160
Tony Blair, 133, 146
Tony Radakin, 158, 199, 234
Top Trumps, 320
Torpedo, 4, 43
Torpedo Aeroplane School, 551
Torpedo bomber, 254
Torpedo Bombing School, 551
Torpedo Maintenance School, 551
Torpedo Training School, 551
Torpoint, 199, 304, 311
Torpoint, Cornwall, 186
Torquay, 595
To Shatter the Sky, 104
Tostig Godwinson, 24
Total war, 187, 461
Toulon, 33, 171
Toward, 309, 310
Tower Bridge, 307
Tower of London, 390
Town class cruiser (1936), 48, 181
Town-class cruiser (1936), 45
Toyota Hilux, 382
TPz Fuchs, 376
Trading fund, 592
Trafalgar 200, 200
Trafalgar class submarine, 52
Trafalgar-class submarine, 191, 194, 213
Traffic congestion, 140
Trainer (aircraft), 158, 238, 446
Trainer helicopter, 446
Training, 440
Training Commands Communication Squadron, 539
Training Group, 485
Training Group RAF, 493
Training Squadron, Sylt, 536
Transport Command Communication Squadron, 539
Transport helicopters, 246
Treasury, 263
Treaty of Paris (1763), 34

Treaty of Ryswick, 405
Treaty of Union, 28
Treaty of Utrecht, 154
Treaty of Versailles, 4, 178
Treaty on the Non-Proliferation of Nuclear Weapons, 10, 114
Trecwn, 316
Trenchard Lines, 437, 533
Trench warfare, 70, 330
Tribal-class destroyer (1936), 45
Trident missile, 115, 190
Trident (missile), 297
Trident nuclear programme, 10, 295
Trident (UK nuclear programme), 114
Trincomalee, 312
Trincomalee Dockyard, 308
Trinidad, 175, 310
Tripoli, 168
Tristan da Cunha, 310
Tritium, 124
Trojan Armoured Vehicle Royal Engineers, 339, 378
Troodos Mountains, 507
Troon, 311
Troop, 277, 347
Trooping the Colour, 9, 338
Troopship, 46, 180
Troop transport, 246, 574
Tropics, 384
T Squadron, Egypt, 537
Tube Alloys, 116
Tubular pin tumbler lock, 143
TUI Group, 568
Tullichewan, 315
Tunisia Campaign, 75, 265
Tunnels of Gibraltar, 426
Tupolev Tu-95, 453
Turbinia, 43
Turkish War of Independence, 72
Turnhouse Communication Squadron, 539
Turret, 41
Tutong District, 428
Twatt, Orkney, 308
Twelfth Siege of Gibraltar, 283
Two-man rule, 144
Tyne & Wear, 307
Type 21 frigate, 185
Type 22 frigate, 185
Type 23 frigate, 154, 160, 185, 188, 194, 197, 201, 202, 216, 227
Type 26 frigate, 185
Type 42 destroyer, 185, 188
Type 45 destroyer, 13, 154, 160, 185, 188, 189, 201, 216, 227
Type 82 destroyer, 225
Typhoon FGR4, 466

Typhoon Haiyan, 300

U-boat Campaign (World War I), 44
U-boats, 179
Uckers, 206, 317, 320
UGM-133 Trident II, 10, 13, 113, 132
UGM-27 Polaris, 130
UK£, 574
UK government, 17
UK Hydrographic Office, 17
UK Joint Expeditionary Force, 12
UK Joint Logistics Support Base, 155
UK Maritime Component Command, 154
UK Military Flying Training System, 456, 477, 494, 496, 564, 579
UK Mobile Air Movements Squadron, 536
UK MOD, 571
UK Polaris programme, 10
UKSF, 281
UK Special Forces, 276
Ulster, 328
Ulster Defence Regiment, 80, 332
Ulsterisation, 80
Ulster loyalism, 79, 80
Ulster-Scots, 328
UNFICYP Flight AAC, 108
Uniforms, 202
Uniforms of the Royal Canadian Navy, 202
Uniforms of the Royal Marines, 284
Uniforms of the Royal Navy, 21, 159, 210, 228, 238, 258, 290
Uniforms of the United States Navy, 202
Unilateral nuclear disarmament, 141
Union Flag, 477
Unionism in Ireland, 333
Union Jack, 119, 356
Union of Crowns, 169
Union of the Crowns, 22, 29, 30
United Arab Emirates, 505, 506
United Irishmen, 328
United Kingdom, 2, 89, 93, 96, 105, 159, 201–203, 205, 211, 227, 257, 268, 270, 290, 317, 321, 322, 347, 359, 360, 364, 366–370, 375–381, 417, 445, 560, 566, 583, 587
United Kingdom Admiralty, 585
United Kingdom Air Ministry, 585
United Kingdom and Commonwealth, 204, 286, 347, 359
United Kingdom and weapons of mass destruction, 11
United Kingdom Atomic Energy Authority, 140
United Kingdom cabinet committee, 118
United Kingdom general election, 1964, 141
United Kingdom general election, 1987, 142

United Kingdom Hydrographic Office, 583, 592
United Kingdom Ministry of Aviation, 585
United Kingdom of Great Britain and Ireland, 37, 336, 407
United Kingdom of Great Britain and Northern Ireland, 336, 584
United Kingdom (RM), 203, 205, 286, 287
United Kingdom Special Forces, 107, 193, 268, 299, 347, 366, 367
United Nations, 5, 75, 83, 364
United Nations General Assembly, 146
United Nations peacekeeping, 323
United Nations Peacekeeping Force in Cyprus, 108, 342, 429
United Nations Protection Force, 332
United Nations Security Council, 3
United States, 3, 144, 305, 366–370, 375, 376, 379, 380, 506, 507
United States Africa Command, 504
United States Air Force, 96, 467, 470
United States Air Forces in Europe, 136
United States and weapons of mass destruction, 114
United States Armed Forces, 497
United States Atomic Energy Commission, 120
United States Capitol, 39
United States Department of Defense, 502
United States dollar, 2
United States European Command, 502
United States Intelligence Community, 503
United States invasion of Afghanistan, 99
United States Marine Corps, 193, 259, 264, 282, 506
United States national missile defense, 137
United States Navy, 37, 160
United States Secretary of Defense, 131
United States Space Surveillance Network, 497
Universities of Glasgow and Strathclyde Air Squadron, 533
University Air Squadron, 459, 472, 499
University of Birmingham, 115
University of Birmingham Air Squadron, 533
University of Cambridge, 115
University of London Air Squadron, 501, 533
University Royal Naval Unit, 211
University Service Units, 599, 600
Unmanned aerial vehicle, 250, 251, 339
Unmanned combat aerial vehicle, 573
UNPROFOR, 83
UN Security Council, 75
Upgraded Early Warning Radar, 137
Upward Spiral, 48, 182
Uranium, 115
Uranium-235, 114, 115, 127
Uranium enrichment, 119

Urgent Operational Requirement, 364, 365
US$, 574
U.S. Air Force, 246
U.S. Army Rangers, 82
Users, 270
U.S. Marine Corps, 246
US Marines, 129
USMC, 369
U.S. Navy, 242
US Navy, 243
USS Chesapeake (1799), 37
USS Dwight D. Eisenhower, 242
USS OBannon (DD-987), 276
Utility helicopter, 446

Vagabond (person), 405
Vagrants, 405
Vale of Glamorgan, 500
Vanguard-class, 160
Vanguard class submarine, 196
Vanguard-class submarine, 10, 13, 114, 132, 134, 182, 190, 200, 212, 296
Vauxhall Barracks, 436
V bomber, 96, 183, 450, 451, 482
V bombers, 121
Vessels, 218
Vice-Admiral, 252–254
Vice admiral (Royal Navy), 198, 203, 230
Vice-Chief of the Defence Staff (United Kingdom), 586
Vickers, 43
Vickers machine gun, 70
Vickers Valiant, 121
Vickers VC10, 101
Victoria Barracks, Windsor, 436
Victoria Cross, 252, 253, 262, 267, 328
Victoria of the United Kingdom, 318
Viking, 163
Vikings, 23
Vincent Harris, 594
Violet Club, 123
Violet Mist, 128
Violet Vision, 129
Visiting Forces Act 1952, 502
VLRA, 382
VMFAT-501, 246, 506
Voltaire, 34
Volunteer Cadet Corps, 206
Volunteer Force (Great Britain), 329
Volunteer Gliding Squadron, 459, 472, 497, 499, 528
Volunteer Reserves (United Kingdom), 2, 8, 59, 599, 600
VT Group, 189
VTOL, 243
Vulcan Bomber, 6

Vulcan Naval Reactor Test Establishment, 305

W31, 129
W33 (nuclear warhead), 129
W34 (nuclear warhead), 129
W44, 128
W45, 129
W47, 130
W49, 130
W76, 132
Walcheren, 47, 266
Walcheren Barracks, 437
Wales, 24, 307, 496, 499–501, 505
Wallace Akers, 116
Walter Couchman, 253
Wandsworth, 268
War flag, 321
War in Afghanistan (2001–14), 6
War in Afghanistan (2001–present), 89, 99, 185, 193, 259, 452
Warminster, 442
War of 1812, 37, 52, 175, 261, 327, 347
War Office, 63, 585, 599
War of Jenkins Ear, 33, 171
War of Spanish Succession, 59
War of the Austrian Succession, 33, 52, 172
War of the Grand Alliance, 33, 166, 325
War of the Quadruple Alliance, 52, 171
War of the Spanish Succession, 33, 52, 171, 325, 405
War on Terror, 6, 153
War on Terrorism, 84
Warrington, 309, 310
Warrior IFV, 340
Warrior Infantry Fighting Vehicle, 337
Warrior tracked armoured vehicle, 154, 375
Warsaw Pact, 76
Warship, 291
Warship (TV series), 208
Wars of Scottish Independence, 29
Warwick Camp (Bermuda), 425
Washington Naval Treaty, 45, 179
Waterloo Lines, 441
Water tank, 380
WE.177, 10, 96, 114, 451
Weapons engineering, 144
Weapons Mount Installation Kit, 376
Weapons of mass destruction, 584
Weeton Barracks, 437
Wehrmacht, 73, 75
Welbeck College, 106
Wellington Barracks, 437
Welsh Guards, 9, 108, 393
Wembury, 310
West Africa, 172, 418

West Africa Command Communication Squadron, 539
West Africa Communication Squadron, 539
West African Ebola virus epidemic, 342
West Africa Transport and Communication Squadron, 539
Western Allied invasion of Germany, 75
Western Approaches Command, 314
Western Command (United Kingdom), 76, 388
Western Communication Squadron, 539
Western Desert Air Force, 490
Western Desert Campaign, 74
Western Europe, 96, 451
Western Fleet (United Kingdom), 13, 229
Western Front (World War I), 70, 263, 330
Western Isles, 29, 313
Western Pacific Naval Symposium, 300
Western Sovereign Base Area, 426
Western Union Examining Squadron, 536
Westfalen Garrison, 430
West Germany, 76
West India Regiment, 349, 417
West Indies, 33, 34, 168, 327, 417
West Indies Guard Ship, 108
Westland Affair, 255
Westland Gazelle, 339, 383, 564
Westland Lynx, 239, 244, 246, 248, 249, 268, 295
Westland Puma, 97
Westland Scout, 106, 111
Westland Sea King, 109, 158, 192, 239, 243, 244, 246, 247, 249, 252, 454, 562, 565
Westland WAH-64 Apache, 82, 339
Westland Wasp, 239, 246
Westland Wessex, 108, 111, 246
West Lothian, 498
Weston-super-Mare, 310
West Wales, 316
West Yorkshire, 307
Wetherby, 310
Wexford, 328
Weymouth, Dorset, 310
Whale Island, Hampshire, 304, 307
What information to include, 319
Whitby, 168
White Army, 72
White Ensign, 158, 206, 317
Whitehall, 7, 106, 138, 157, 257, 356, 445, 583, 594
White House, 39
White paper, 145
White phosphorus (weapon), 364
Whittington Barracks, 437, 440
Wikipedia:Citation needed, 108, 153, 227, 239, 250, 252, 318, 580, 595
Wikipedia:Media help, 158

Wikipedia:Please clarify, 596
Wikisource, 209
Wikisource:Portal:Royal Navy, 209
Wiktionary:Appendix:Glossary of British military slang and expressions, 20
Wilhelm II of Germany, 411
William Coventry, 32
William de Leybourne, 25
William de Wrotham, 25
William Ewart Gladstone, 42
William George Penney, 117
William III of England, 33, 61, 325
William I of England, 25
William IV of England, 603
William Staveley (Royal Navy officer), 231
William the Lion, 162
William Warrender, 199
Wiltshire, 314, 496, 498, 501
Winchelsea, 26
Winchester, 309, 400
Windscale, 119
Windsor Castle, 388
Wing (air force unit), 15
Wing Commander (rank), 89, 122, 457, 462
Winston Churchill, 93, 116, 448, 585
Winterbourne Gunner, 105
Wireless and Observers School, 551
Wireless School, 551
Wireless School, Brooklands, 551
Wireless School, Egypt, 551
Wireless Telephony School, 551
Women, 19
Womens Royal Air Force, 89
Womens Royal Army Corps, 399
Womens Royal Naval Service, 49, 186, 310
Woodbury Common, Devon, 281
Woolston, Hampshire, 309
Woolston, Southampton, 316
Woolwich, 261
Woolwich Dockyard, 308
Worksop, 106
World Trade Center (1973–2001), 84
World war, 75
World War I, 2, 4, 18, 44, 89, 90, 160, 259, 317, 323, 354, 412, 415, 420, 447, 584
World War II, 2, 4, 93, 139, 160, 180, 237, 259, 323, 331, 447, 594
World War Two, 228
Worthy Down Barracks, 440
WRAF Clerical Trades Training School, 551
Wroughton, 316
Wyvern Barracks, 437

X (Canadian) Reserve Squadron, 537
X class submarine, 315
X Squadron, 537

X Squadron, Egypt, 537

Yangtze River, 53
Yarmouth, Isle of Wight, 312
Yarmouth Roads, 316
Y (Canadian) Reserve Squadron, 537
Yeadon, West Yorkshire, 310
Yellow Anvil, 129
Yellowjacks, 479
Yellow Sun (nuclear weapon), 128, 130
Yeomanry, 15, 329, 442
Yeomen of the Guard, 603
York-class cruiser, 45
Yorkshire, 310, 486
Yorkshire Regiment, 346, 374, 393, 401, 432
Yorkshire Universities Air Squadron, 533
YouTube, 210
Y Squadron, Egypt, 537
Y Squadron, Iraq, 537
Y-stations, 311
Yugoslavia, 83, 332

Zeebrugge, 45
Zeebrugge Raid, 263
Zionist, 78
Z Squadron, Aegean, 537
Z Squadron, Egypt, 537
Zwyn, 26
Zygi, 429

www.ingramcontent.com/pod-product-compliance
Lightning Source LLC
Chambersburg PA
CBHW030512230426
43665CB00010B/596